Teaching Reading to Students Who Are at Risk or Have Disabilities

A Multi-Tier Approach

SECOND EDITION

William D. Bursuck
University of North Carolina-Greensboro

Mary Damer
The Ohio State University

Boston   Columbus   Indianapolis   New York   San Francisco   Upper Saddle River
Amsterdam   Cape Town   Dubai   London   Madrid   Milan   Munich   Paris   Montreal   Toronto
Delhi   Mexico City   Sao Paulo   Sydney   Hong Kong   Seoul   Singapore   Taipei   Tokyo

Vice President and Editor in Chief:
Jeffery W. Johnston
Acquisitions Editor: Ann Castel Davis
Editorial Assistant: Penny Burleson
Vice President, Director of Marketing: Quinn Perkson
Marketing Manager: Erica DeLuca
Senior Managing Editor: Pamela D. Bennett
Senior Project Manager: Mary M. Irvin
Senior Operations Supervisor: Matt Ottenweller

Senior Art Director: Diane Lorenzo
Cover Designer: Ali Mohrman
Cover Art: Mia Song/Star Ledger/Corbis
Full-Service Project Management: Ravi Bhatt, Aptara®, Inc.
Composition: Aptara®, Inc.
Printer/Binder: Edwards Brothers
Cover Printer: Lehigh-Phoenix Color Corp.
Text Font: ITC Century

Credits and acknowledgments borrowed from other sources and reproduced, with permission, in this textbook appear on appropriate page within text.

Every effort has been made to provide accurate and current Internet information in this book. However, the Internet and information posted on it are constantly changing, so it is inevitable that some of the Internet addresses listed in this textbook will change.

Library of Congress Cataloging-in-Publication Data

Bursuck, William D.
    Teaching reading to students who are at risk or have disabilities/William D. Bursuck, Mary Damer.—2nd ed.
      p. cm.
    Rev. ed. of: Reading instruction for students who are at risk or have disabilities : Pearson/Allyn and Bacon, c2007.
    Includes index.
    ISBN-13: 978-0-13-705781-8
    ISBN-10: 0-13-705781-4
      1. Reading—Remedial teaching.   I. Damer, Mary.   II. Title.

LB1050.5.B87 2011
372.43—dc22

2009053920

10 9 8 7 6 5 4

www.pearsonhighered.com

ISBN 10:   0-13-705781-4
ISBN 13: 978-0-13-705781-8

To Beth and Stephen for allowing us the immense professional space required to bring this project to fruition. Without your patience, love, and support, this book would not have been possible.

Preface

New To This Edition

Reflecting increased accountability in general education and the impact of the Individuals with Disabilities Education Act (IDEA), this second edition expands coverage of how effective research-based assessment and teaching strategies in the field of reading can be used in both RTI and multi-tier models of instruction. Each chapter goes into greater depth on assessment, giving teachers multiple options for screening, diagnosing, and monitoring student progress by using a greater variety of assessment measures. Although the National Reading Panel Report does not include spelling, research shows that spelling and reading need to be integrated for beginning as well as advanced readers, and this new edition reflects that emphasis. The theoretical foundations for integrating the three stages of spelling instruction into reading lessons is discussed, and practical ideas and resources in spelling are integrated into Chapters 2–6.

This edition offers more direction for teaching older readers with a more in-depth scope and sequence for teaching structural analysis to advanced readers as well as sample formats to teach those skills. While the first edition provided much information about how to systematically and explicitly teach phonemic awareness, phonics, reading fluency, and vocabulary, in this second edition, we wanted to illustrate more of that approach for reading comprehension instruction. The reorganization of Chapter 7 shows teachers how to use explicit research-based strategies such as questioning and think-alouds for teaching a wider range of comprehension skills to struggling readers.

Vignettes at the beginning of each chapter help the reader relate text content to actual classroom settings. Because one of the greatest challenges for teachers is "putting all the pieces together," in this edition, sample lesson plans for working with beginning and more advanced readers have been included. To facilitate translating research into practice, we have added a new feature called "In Your Classroom" that provides practical suggestions for implementing evidence-based reading practices in real-life classroom settings. Changes to the new edition are summarized below.

- Greater emphasis on providing differentiated instruction
- Increased coverage of RTI
- Expanded assessment coverage
- Expanded spelling coverage
- Teaching vignettes at the beginning of each chapter
- Added support for teachers on how to teach comprehension systematically and explicitly
- New "In Your Classroom" feature stressing research to practice
- Updated sections on older and English language learners
- Updated technology features

Between 2000 and 2004 we implemented Project PRIDE, a four-year federal model demonstration project that employed evidence-based practices to prevent reading problems in children who were at risk in three diverse, high-poverty urban schools. The principals of these schools opted to reverse their course from a more naturalistic reading program and make the commitment to retraining their staff because of a history of chronic reading problems and a teaching environment permeated by failure. Failure rates on the Illinois State Achievement Test (ISAT) for PRIDE schools had ranged from 50% to 78%. Over the course of the project, through ongoing progress monitoring of student achievement and a close working relationship with the teachers, we had the opportunity to fine-tune instructional strategies to a degree that would not have been possible without that collaboration.

During the four years of Project PRIDE, we gained an even greater appreciation for Louisa Moats's expression, "Teaching reading is rocket science." On a daily basis we observed that as the human mind acquires the intellectual muscle to learn to read, the teacher must not only know how to carefully teach the sequence of small steps needed for reading at grade level but also to recognize the missteps that can thwart those efforts. Whether students came to school from high-poverty backgrounds, with no parental support, with learning disabilities or behavior disorders, with medical conditions, from backgrounds of abuse, or without English-speaking skills, most of them were able to learn to read. The research in reading, summarized by the report of the National Reading Panel (2000), the invaluable research in reading, multi-tier and response to intervention (RTI) approaches that have occurred since, and our own extensive work in public schools after Project PRIDE, provide a clear guide for the use of systematic and explicit instruction to teach the largest number of students to read. In this book we have translated that guide into a detailed blueprint based on 1) explicit, systematic instruction, 2) a multi-tier or RTI model, 3) data-based decision making, and 4) professional development.

Professional development and coaching for PRIDE teachers and staff who carried out instruction in Tier 1, Tier 2, and Tier 3 was provided by the two authors of this text. All teachers attended after-school workshops and a series of summer institutes and received on-site coaching. The after-school workshops and summer institutes were used to introduce various teaching and assessment strategies, allow teachers to observe taped or live models of the strategies, and provide practice for the teachers in small groups using simulated experiences. During on-site coaching visits, data on tier implementation were gathered directly in the classroom; teachers were given feedback on their instruction until they demonstrated competence.

The impetus for writing and now revising this text came from the results attained during our four years of PRIDE implementation as well as work with other urban school districts that followed. Our results have shown that all children can make progress toward learning to read when a system of assessments guides staff to identify children who are not responding to instruction, allowing them to meet their individual needs using evidence-based instructional options of varying intensities. The assessment and teaching strategies that have been successful are those that occupy the pages of this text.

The data shown in Table 1 from one project school and a control school reflect the percentage of children meeting or exceeding standards on the ISAT. Note the significant increases from 1999–2000 to 2003–2004, the latter being scores for our first PRIDE cohort. It is interesting that the ISAT scores for our PRIDE school began improving for the 2002–2003 school year, despite the fact that these were students who were not officially part of the project. We believe that at least part of that increase resulted because the school, seeing that PRIDE was working so well in the early grades, began to implement some of the same practices in the later grades that were not part of the PRIDE project.

It is clear from these results that more children met state standards in reading as a result of Project PRIDE. It is also true that about 30% of the students did not meet state standards.

TABLE 1   Percentage of Children Meeting or Exceeding Standard on the Illinois State Achievement Test

Third Grade Reading	1999–2000	2000–2001	2001–2002	2002–2003	2003–2004
School 1	31	22	15.2	55.2	68.2
Control	39	40	36.4	28.6	39

These were largely students who were receiving support in either Tier 2 or Tier 3. Nonetheless, our results showed that even though many Tier 2 and Tier 3 students did not meet standards, they did make significant gains on all of the DIBELS measures. Nonetheless, challenges remain. Key among them is finding ways to implement multi-tier or RTI models more successfully with those students who continue to struggle. We know that more instructional time is needed, and that scientifically based reading practices need to be implemented with greater fidelity. The improved delivery of multi-tiered instruction will take enlightened and courageous leadership on the part of principals, more effective professional development for teachers, and a can-do attitude in the face of chronic shortages of resources.

A common drawback of having different instructional options for children is that racial minorities tend to be overrepresented in the groups of children who are not responding to instruction. In PRIDE, children were assessed five to six times per year using highly efficient assessments directly tied to curricular goals and objectives. These assessments allowed us to make decisions in the best interest of individual children without being influenced by potentially biasing factors such as race. Our results showed that the proportion of African American children served in Tier 2 and Tier 3 was no greater than could be expected given their proportion in our school population at large.

Whatever disagreements exist in the field about how to teach reading, few would argue with the overarching goal of a nation of lifelong learners who enjoy reading for information as well as for pleasure. We are troubled when educational strategies such as skill-based grouping, pull-out, and drill-practice-and-review are viewed as antithetical to the enjoyment of reading. Our results showed that child success is what truly matters when it comes to students' attitudes toward reading. Clearly, drill is one ingredient of an effective reading program for students who are at risk and, if done effectively, can *thrill*—not *kill.*

We know that however positive the results, it is often teacher acceptance of an instructional approach that determines the likelihood that it will continue to be used over time. At the end of each year of the project, we surveyed our teachers to find out their feedback on all aspects of the PRIDE model. Satisfaction was of particular interest to us because of our emphasis on teacher accountability for the reading achievement of each and every student. Our teacher satisfaction results, shown in Figure 1, were very encouraging, with acceptance ratings after the first year for all parts of the model being consistently rated over 3 on a 4-point scale, with 4 representing the highest satisfaction. In the words of one of our principals, "It is interesting to watch the teachers' perceptions of Project PRIDE transition from

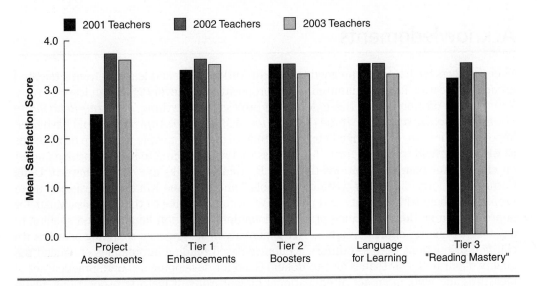

FIGURE 1 Teacher Satisfaction

fear and distrust to such high levels of satisfaction now that they are held directly accountable for student growth. I've watched them quickly develop their capacities to serve all of the learning needs within their classrooms after systematic professional development."

At the conclusion of the project, we asked teachers whether they thought their school should continue to implement Project PRIDE the following year. Twenty-nine, or 85%, of our project teachers responded to the question. Of the 29 teachers who responded, 28 (97%) wanted the project to continue.

Project PRIDE, with its emphasis on regular progress monitoring of all students and the provision of a range of instructional supports based on need, is consistent with recent trends in teacher accountability and implementation of RTI models as a way of identifying students with learning disabilities. The results for children in all three of our tiers showed that 95% of the children made reading progress, and that their attitudes toward reading were positive. Our Title I, general education, and special education teachers found the model acceptable. Recently one of our schools invited us to come back to do what they referred to as a "refresher" session. Teachers were concerned about the quality of model implementation when they saw their test scores in reading begin to decrease and they wanted us to "put them back on the right track." All of these results have encouraged us to revise this book in hopes that it will empower even more teachers to teach children to read who have been chronically unsuccessful.

Video of Teaching Formats

In our work with teachers, the following concern was repeatedly raised: "Everyone talks and writes about how I should teach reading, but it would be such a help to actually see these skills being taught to children." That concern provided the impetus for producing a companion DVD that was included with copies of the first edition, but that now can be accessed at the Companion Website at http://www.pearsonhighered.com/bursuck2e. The video footage shows a teacher using the reading formats from the book to teach critical reading skills to students in a small-group classroom situation. Viewers can refer to the text as they watch phonemic awareness, letter–sound correspondence, word reading, vocabulary, and passage reading with comprehension being taught.

Acknowledgments

Over the years we have had the good fortune of working with and learning from a talented group of educators firmly committed to the proposition that every child can learn to read. Without the contributions of these dedicated professionals, writing *Teaching Reading to Students Who Are at Risk or Have Disabilities: A Multi-Tier Approach* would have been impossible. First, we owe a huge debt of gratitude to all of the people who have provided us as well as our field with a blueprint for success that will continue to have a positive impact on children for many generations to come. Particular thanks are offered here to Doug Carnine and Jerry Silbert for writing our "bible," and to Diane Kinder for inspiring us to prepare teachers with integrity and passion. We would also like to thank Louisa Moats for impressing on us the importance of foundational information in language and spelling to any teacher-change effort in reading. Her generosity in serving as a sounding board as we clarified distinctions between different phonics-based reading approaches enhanced the quality of our text. Our thanks also to Roland Good for developing a sound, practical set of measures and who, in an act of educational philanthropy of historic proportions, made them available free on the Internet so that the data-based decision making so essential to a multi-tier model could be accomplished. Many thanks to Sonia Martin for her invaluable assistance with the preparation of the manuscript.

We also wish to thank the many colleagues who were instrumental in helping with the development and refinement of the many aspects of the multi-tier model, but especially Shirley Dickson, from whom we have learned so much. Thanks also to Val Bresnahan and Sue Grisco for their help with the Tier 3 tables.

We are indebted to the federal government for funding Project PRIDE through a Model-Demonstration grant (CFDA 84.324.T; H324T990024). We also owe a great debt of gratitude to Kishwaukee School, whose conscientious effort to implement multi-tier instruction long past the funding period showed that we could have a positive impact on children who had previously fallen through the cracks. A particular note of thanks goes to Paula Larson and Nancy Dornbush, whose belief in the model and commitment to children sustained us.

Special thanks go to the reviewers of the book whose careful, constructive attention to the manuscript gave us the confidence to proceed while at the same time improving the final product: Claudia Cornett, Wittenberg University, and Christina M. Curran, Central Washington University.

A final thanks to teachers everywhere who are willing to do whatever it takes to deliver effective, evidence-based reading instruction to their students. Your efforts will always teach and inspire us as we continue to pursue the vision of helping every child learn to read.

Companion Website Acknowledgments

Portraying the teaching formats discussed throughout the book would not have been possible without the skill of our master teacher Kelly Bolas, the children of Bluford Communications Magnet School in Greensboro, North Carolina (Brianna Lorrick, Christina Brown, Kamari Purvis, Jaquin Miller, and Paul Gaurdin), and their former principal, LaToy Kennedy. Tom Lipscomb and Associates grasped the goals of the video immediately and captured on video everything we wanted and more.

Contents

Chapter 6   Vocabulary Instruction   229

Chapter 7   Comprehension   272

List of Teaching Formats

Chapter 6   **229**

1 An Introduction to Systematic, Explicit Reading Instruction

Objectives

After reading this chapter, you will be able to:

1. State the prevalence and characteristics of students who are at risk for reading problems and which students are likely to struggle while learning to read.

2. Identify and describe five key skill areas that should comprise a reading curriculum for students who are at risk.

3. Describe the rationale for using a prevention-based multi-tier or Response to Intervention (RTI) model of reading.

4. Describe the role of assessments in a multi-tier or RTI model of reading.

5. Identify and describe ways to enhance reading instruction for students who are at risk by making it more explicit and systematic.

Companion Website

To check your comprehension of the content covered in this chapter, go to the Companion Website (www.pearsonhighered.com/bursuck2e) and complete the Chapter Quiz for Chapter 1. Here you will be able to answer practice questions, receive feedback on your answers, and then access resources that will enhance your understanding of chapter content.

Sitting in the teachers' lounge, the reading coach, Mrs. Gowdy, listened to the staff discuss the new kindergartener, Bryan. *"Why didn't they just start him out in the special education program? He's going to be there by second grade anyway." "Our test scores are low enough anyway, and I can't imagine Bryan ever reading."* The discouraged, pessimistic teachers sitting around the table, worked in a high-poverty school tagged by the state as "failing" because so many children could not read. Over the years, the teachers had without success implemented the latest fads in reading and felt that many of the students in their school were incapable of working at grade level. Past experience led them to believe that they would be unsuccessful with a student like Bryan who took medication for attention deficit disorder resulting from Tourette's syndrome, whose lead levels were "off the charts" when he was a toddler, and whose drug-addicted mother was so negligent she lost custody. Mrs. Gowdy barely listened to the teachers' conversation because she was busy preparing the beginning-of-the-year screening tests that signaled the start of the school's new multi-tier reading program for which staff had trained that summer.

That fall, when Bryan's kindergarten teacher gave him the universal screening tests in reading, he was unable to say the sounds of any letters, blend spoken sounds into words, or name letters of the alphabet. The tests indicated that Bryan needed intensive help. By midyear kindergarten, he was working with a small group of students in a Tier 3 intensive research-based reading curriculum taught by one of the Title 1 teachers. Of all the kindergarten Tier 3 groups, his was progressing the slowest; the weekly testing that his teacher did to monitor progress showed only small gains. Bryan's teacher referred him for special education services, but his parents did not want him tested. Mrs. Gowdy observed his instruction and was reassured that the intensive Tier 3 reading instruction was meeting his needs. Bryan's end-of-the-year benchmark testing showed that he had learned the sounds of only eight letters but could blend them into words.

The pessimistic lunchtime conversations in the teachers' lounge didn't end when Bryan started first grade, since his September testing confirmed the teachers' beliefs and showed that the same Tier 3 group was still appropriate for him. His first-grade Tier 3 teacher was a skilled paraprofessional supervised by the special education teacher. Using a scripted reading program, the paraprofessional was highly motivating; she taught energetically and enthusiastically and helped the students master the reading material by providing repeated practice on new skills. By midyear first grade, Mrs. Gowdy was elated to learn that Bryan was racing ahead of the other students and should be moved up to a faster-moving Tier 3 group. With the multi-tier reading model, group placement decisions like this had to be supported with testing data, so Mrs. Gowdy checked Bryan's weekly progress-monitoring tests and noted this same growth. By the end of first grade, Bryan was reading short three-letter words and could do all of the activities requiring him to manipulate sounds. During a team meeting, Mrs. Gowdy and other teachers remarked that without the ongoing testing, they probably would not have thought to move Bryan to the higher group.

That summer, Bryan went to summer school and continued in the intensive Tier 3 scripted-reading curriculum. This year the "buzz" in the teachers' lounge was about the growth Bryan had made. His tests showed that he was still behind, but if he continued to make these gains, he would finish second grade at grade level. Sure enough, Bryan continued to respond to instruction and, to the staff's surprise, by the middle of the year he tested at grade level. The slower pace and extra practice in the intensive curriculum had finally made a significant difference. Because the multi-tier reading model was still relatively new to the staff, they were worried that moving Bryan up to Tier 2 might set him back. Mrs. Gowdy reassured the team that when test scores indicate a child needs less support, he should be successful in grade-level reading curriculum. Besides, now that he was in Tier 2, Bryan would still get 30 minutes of tutoring support each day, reviewing what he had learned in the larger second-grade class.

At the end of second grade, when the students had been tested in reading, Mrs. Gowdy was pleased to announce to the team that Bryan had finished at the top of his class, scoring higher than any other second grader. He no longer needed the 30 minutes of Tier 2 tutoring and would start third grade in Tier 1 with no extra reading support. That day in the teachers' lounge, one of the staff said, "You know, I've learned that if Bryan could reach grade level, any student entering this school can." Another teacher remarked, "We have to stop making these assumptions about students and make sure that we teach reading to all of them as if they can come as far as Bryan." Mrs. Gowdy reflected on how staff conversations about students were more optimistic these days. Teachers felt empowered with the tools and structure needed to increase reading achievement. The staff anticipated that state test scores would increase as they had the previous year and that Bryan's response to instruction was an example of why the number of students identified with learning disabilities was decreasing in their school.

Why do you think many of the teachers initially thought Bryan should be in special education? What factors do you think were responsible for his progress?

"Some people there are who, being grown, forget the horrible task of learning to read. It is perhaps the greatest single effort that the human undertakes, and he must do it as a child."

John Steinbeck (1976)

No other skill learned by children is more important than reading, described as the gateway to all other achievement by the American Federation of Teachers (2007). Yet, despite its critical importance for success in our society, millions of children in the United States are failing to learn to read; in fact, many of them attend schools like the one in the chapter-opening vignette. The 2007 National Assessment of Educational Progress (NAEP) report indicated that 33% of fourth graders and 26% of eighth graders were below the basic level in reading, unable to demonstrate even partial mastery of fundamental knowledge and skills. Only 31% of eighth-grade students in the United States scored at or above the proficient level, which represents grade-level expectations. Rates of failure in urban areas and among Black and Hispanic children are even higher (Lee, Grigg, & Donahue, 2007). Reading problems do not just reside among schoolchildren but pervade our entire society. Experts estimate that more than 90 million adults lack a foundation of basic literacy skills necessary to function in society, losing over 200 billion dollars a year in income (Whitehurst, 2003). Given these statistics, it is not surprising to hear the current spate of literacy problems referred to as a national health problem (Lyon, 1998).

In response to public concerns about unacceptably high rates of illiteracy and demands for increased accountability, the U.S. Congress passed the No Child Left Behind (NCLB) Act in 2001. A central provision of this act was the mandate that all of our nation's children be reading at grade level by the school year 2013–2014. While the goals of NCLB are laudable, this bold legislation has rightfully raised many questions among teachers trying to meet those goals. For example, which children have more trouble learning to read and why? How can we identify them? Are there effective methods available to teach these children to read? When is the most opportune time to teach children to read? Do all children learn to read the same way? Can we really teach all children to read? Teachers need practical answers to these and other questions if they are to make a legitimate attempt to teach all children to read.

Explanations about why large percentages of students do not attain minimum literacy levels echo the reasons that students are at risk in the first place:

- These students were raised in poverty.
- Their parents never read to them as children.
- These students have learning disabilities.
- English is not their first language.
- These students were premature babies.

Although educators agree that students who come to school with some or all of these factors present greater challenges, effective reading teachers believe that there are no excuses. These teachers can and will teach every student to read. Yes, John's mother took cocaine before he was born, but he will learn to read. Yes, Marissa has an exceptionally difficult time hearing the individual sounds in words, but she will learn to read. Yes, Shyron's mother has been married three times and amid a blended family of eight kids, he's lost in the shuffle. But he will learn to read. This tenacious attitude is necessary for teachers who get all or most of their students who are at risk to read at grade level.

A tenacious attitude alone isn't sufficient for success. Because of the greater challenges in teaching students who are at risk to read, teachers need effective teaching techniques and curriculum that have a proven track record of success with these students. Students who are at risk for reading failure require more carefully coordinated curriculum and skill instruction than do other students. Fortunately for today's teachers, the reports of the National Reading Panel (NRP, 2000) and the National Early Literacy Panel (NELP, 2008) help translate research into practice. Both panels included leading reading researchers, college professors, teachers, administrators, and parents. The panels spent considerable time identifying those studies that met the highest empirical standards of scientific investigation. Those high-quality studies were used to determine the most effective ways of teaching reading to the greatest number of students and included students who were at risk, had learning disabilities, or were underachieving.

Between 2000 and 2004, we implemented Project PRIDE, a 4-year federal model demonstration project that employed evidence-based practices to prevent reading problems in children who are at risk in three diverse, high-poverty urban schools. Bryan, the subject of the vignette at the beginning of this chapter, was a student in one of our Project PRIDE schools. As the story of Bryan shows, given the right tools and a guiding and sustaining belief in evidence-based reading practices, all children can make progress toward learning to read. The assessment and teaching strategies that were successful in PRIDE are those that occupy the pages of this text.

Who Are the Students at Risk for Reading Problems?

The strategies for teaching early literacy described in this text are based on the idea that when it comes to reading instruction, "one size does not fit all." Figure 1.1 shows how many children in a typical first-grade classroom are likely to struggle while learning to read. These figures are based on research sponsored by the National Institute of Child and Health and Development (NICHD; Lyon, 1998). Looking at the chart, you can see these trends:

- About 5% of students come to school already able to read. These children learn to read naturally without any formal instruction.
- Another 20% to 30% of students learn to read with ease, regardless of the approach to reading instruction used.
- For 20% to 30% of students, learning to read will take hard work, with some extra support needed. If parents work with these students every night, reviewing books read in class and serving as tutors, the students may learn to break the code. Extra practice with a volunteer tutor may be enough to help them break the code.
- An additional 30% of students will only learn to read if they are given intensive support. These students require explicit systematic phonics instruction and extensive practice reading the new words they are learning until they are at least able to read second-grade text accurately and fluently. If they do not receive appropriate support before second grade, many of these students will have a reading level significantly

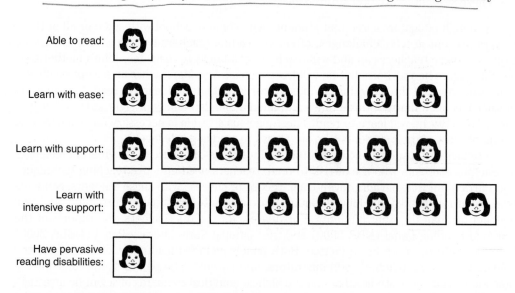

FIGURE 1.1 Typical First-Grade Classroom

behind their peers and never catch up. Some may be incorrectly diagnosed as having learning disabilities.

- The remaining 5% of students have serious, pervasive reading disabilities and are served in special education.

In high-poverty schools, the number of children who need extra or intensive support may be even higher (Bursuck and Damer, 2005). This book refers to any students who require extra support to learn as **at risk**. Regardless of the cause, these students will learn to read if a systematic, supportive approach is in place.

When Is the Best Time to Begin Reading Instruction for Children Who Are at Risk?

Years ago, educators believed that reading skills developed naturally and that as long as children were immersed in a literature-rich environment, they would eventually learn to read when they were "ready." In a system based on this belief, struggling readers were often not given extra support until second or even third grade. Since then, educators have been confronted by a large body of research that has emphasized the importance of early identification. Educators now recognize that many children who are at risk will never develop reading skills naturally. Even more disturbing is evidence that once they are behind in reading, most students do not catch up. For example, Juel (1988) found that only one in eight readers who were behind at the end of first grade would catch up by fourth grade. Francis and colleagues (1996) followed 407 children who were classified as poor readers in third grade and found that 74% of these students still remained poor readers when they reached ninth grade. Edward Kame'enui (2007) explained:

> There's a myth, and probably a popular myth, that if kids start off slow they'll eventually catch up, and what we know from the research is that that's simply not the case. Kids who start off slow, their trajectory of learning and reading continues to flatten out. In fact, their performance decreases over time. So, what we know is that we need to intervene early and we need to intervene because we don't have any time to waste. Time is precious. Kids face the tyranny of time. And in order to catch up, we have to be very strategic in what we do in the early years.

Why is later reading intervention so ineffective for students who are at risk? One key reason is that once students get behind, it takes a significant expenditure of time and resources to catch them up, resources that budget-strapped schools may not have available. For example, getting older students who have not attained reading fluency by the end of third grade to grade level costs seven to eight times as much in time and money (Wendorf, 2003). Not only do older students have to relearn ineffective habits they have acquired, they also must overcome pervasive feelings of failure and stress related to reading. Clearly, the best method is to identify children as early as possible and provide them with the supports they need to prevent reading problems in the first place. Although the teaching strategies described in this text are effective for students of all ages, they are most effective when used early.

What Essential Skills Do Students Need to Become Mature Readers?

The NRP (2000) and NELP (2009) identified five key skill areas that should comprise the reading curriculum for students who are at risk. These areas include phonemic awareness, phonics, reading fluency, vocabulary, and reading comprehension. The key skills comprising each of these areas are shown in Figure 1.2 and described in this section. The time

	Kinder Fall	Kinder Spring	First Fall	First Spring	Second All Year	Third All Year
Phonemic Awareness						
Segmenting	X	X	X			
Blending	X	X	X			
Alphabetic Principle						
LS Correspondence	X	X	X	X	X	X
Regular Word Reading		X	X	X	X	X
Irregular Words		X	X	X	X	X
Spelling	X	X	X	X	X	X
Reading Fluency				X	X	X
Vocabulary	*	X	X	X	X	X
Reading Comprehension	*	X	X	X	X	X
*Orally taught						

FIGURE 1.2   Scientifically Based Reading Curriculum

frame information in Figure 1.2 is intended to represent when each skill area is emphasized as part of a core developmental reading program. These skills are also essential for remedial readers. The only difference is that remedial readers will learn them later than their peers. Chapters in this text will provide a clear description of what is and what is not systematic and explicit reading instruction in each of the five skill areas.

Publications from the NRP and reports from NELP are free and available for downloading at **http://www.nationalreadingpanel.org/Publications/publications.htm** and **http://www.nifl.gov/nifl/NELP/NELP09.html.**

Increasingly, reading researchers are questioning why the National Reading Panel did not include spelling as the sixth key skill area to investigate. The old-fashioned notion of spelling as a visual task or task of memorization does not incorporate current research indicating that effective spelling instruction enhances word reading, fluency, vocabulary, and comprehension. Because of the reciprocal relationship between spelling and reading, each chapter will also include information on how effective spelling instruction can enhance instruction in the highlighted skill area.

Phonemic Awareness

Phonemic awareness is the ability to hear and manipulate the smallest units of sound in spoken language (Ball & Blachman, 1991). Students who are at risk are less likely to develop this important foundational skill naturally. Word play activities and language games often do not provide enough support. A considerable body of research shows that teaching phonemic awareness skills to students who are at risk within a language-rich environment makes it easier for them to learn to read (Armbruster, Lehr, & Osborn, 2001). Although there are many different phonemic awareness skills, this book stresses the two that researchers have concluded have the most value in a beginning reading program: segmenting and blending (Ball & Blachman). **Segmenting** is the ability to break apart words into their individual phonemes or sounds. A student who can segment says /f/-/i/-/sh/ when asked to say the sounds in *fish*. The ability to segment helps students strategically attack words they will be reading in text and break words into phonemes when spelling. **Blending**, the opposite of segmenting, is the ability to say a spoken word when its individual phonemes are said slowly. A student who can blend can say the word *fish* after the teacher slowly says the individual sounds /f/-/i/-/sh/. Blending enables students to read unfamiliar text by combining single sounds into new words. You will learn more about phonemic awareness and how to teach it to students who are at risk in Chapter 2.

Phonics

Although a small percentage of students naturally become fluent readers, many will only develop these skills through activities stressing the connection between written letters and their most common sounds. **Phonics** is the teaching strategy described in this text to teach the relationships between written letters, or graphemes, and the speech sounds, or phonemes. Programs that emphasize phonics will often refer to teaching **sound–spelling relationships** or **graphophonemic knowledge**. Both terms refer to the connection between speech sounds (**phonemes**) and letters of the alphabet (**graphemes**). Although some would argue otherwise, the English language has more than enough regularity to merit the teaching of phonics. The Research Note at the end of this section on page 9 covers this issue more in depth.

The utility of teaching phonics has been clearly established, but not all phonics approaches are equally effective. After identifying thousands of research studies and submitting them to rigorous review, the NRP (2000) and NELP (2009) concluded that systematic and explicit phonics programs are most effective for teaching students to read, particularly students who are at risk. Armbruster, Lehr, and Osborn (2001) summarized the key differences between systematic and nonsystematic phonics programs. These differences are shown in Figure 1.3. The phonics strategies described in this book are designed to be both systematic and explicit to ensure the success of students who are at risk.

Examples
Systematic programs that teach phonics effectively . . .

- help teachers explicitly and systematically instruct students in how to relate letters and sounds, how to break spoken words into sounds, and how to blend sounds to form words.

- help students understand why they are learning the relationships between letters and sounds.

- help students apply their knowledge of phonics as they read words, sentences, and text.

- can be adapted to the needs of individual students, based on assessment.

- include alphabetic knowledge, phonemic awareness, vocabulary development, and the reading of text, as well as systematic phonics instruction.

Nonexamples
Nonsystematic programs that do not teach phonics effectively include ...

- **Literature-based programs** that emphasize reading and writing activities. Phonics instruction is embedded in these activities, but letter–sound relationships are taught incidentally, usually based on key letters that appear in student reading materials.

- **Basal reading programs** that focus on whole-word or meaning-based activities. These programs pay only limited attention to letter–sound relationships and provide little or no instruction in how to blend letters to pronounce words.

- **Sight-word programs** that begin by teaching children a sight-word reading vocabulary of from 50 to 100 words. After children learn to read these words, they receive instruction in the alphabetic principle.

FIGURE 1.3   Evaluating Programs of Phonics Instruction

Source: Armbruster, B., Lehr, F., & Osborn, J. (2001). *Put Reading First: The Research Building Blocks for Teaching Children to Read* (pp. 16–17). Washington, DC: Partnership for Reading.

Ehri (2005) developed a five-phase model that describes the development of word reading skills. As readers learn spelling–sound relationships fluently, they eventually are able to unconsciously and automatically recall the pronunciation and meaning of known words. This seemingly effortless process is called sight-word reading.

Phase 1.   **Pre-alphabetic phase:** Students do not yet have an understanding of the alphabetic principle and read words as memorized visual forms. A student might remember the word *school* because of the two "eyes" in the middle of the word, or the word *ladder* because of the tall letters that remind him of a ladder. Students in this phase who learn words by their visual characteristics will become easily confused when encountering words that look alike, such as *school* and *shoot*.

Phase 2.   **Partial-alphabetic phase:** The development of alphabetic principle allows students to begin to associate some letters with their associated sounds and use that insight to recognize words. Students at this phase might remember the word *sail* by associating the beginning *s* and the final *l* with their respective sounds. These letter–sound connections help students remember words more efficiently than in the previous phase where they had to rely on visual cues. Words that look alike and words where letters have no relationship to their common sound will still be confusing.

Phase 3.   **Full-alphabetic phase:** Students have learned the most common letter–sound associations and use this knowledge to **decode** unfamiliar words. Students reading the word *pan* for the first time would scan the word from left to right, making the letter–sound connection for *p*, the vowel sound /ă/ for *a*, and the sound associated with *n* in order to read the word *pan* as a whole word. Associating the letters with the sounds that represent them helps students at this phase commit new words to long-term memory as sight words. Readers now start to learn words more quickly by sight than in previous phases.

Phase 4.   **Consolidated-alphabetic phase:** Students consolidate phase 3 knowledge of grapheme–phoneme blends into larger units that recur in different words. Instead of processing individual letter sounds, they recognize multiletter sequences called chunks, such as syllables and parts of words like *ime* and *ing*, which leads them to learn longer words more easily. Instead of having to process the ten sounds in a new word like *concentrate*, a reader would probably read three chunks /con/ /cen/ /trate/. By this phase, the reader can process and read a chunk as fast as a single letter.

Phase 5.   **Automatic phase:** Students recognize words as whole words quickly by sight, unconsciously associating letters with their associated sounds. Their accurate, fluent word reading in connected text allows them to focus on comprehending the meaning of the text.

If the reader has developed alphabetic principle and has adequate knowledge of letter–sound associations, when he reads a new word he forms a connection between the letters he sees in the spelling of a word and the sounds in their pronunciation. These connections secure the word in long-term memory. After several encounters reading a new word, a typical reader can then recall it by sight. Knowing how to recognize the phase at which a student is reading helps a teacher plan effective instruction for a struggling reader. For example, a teacher working with a beginning reader (Phases 1–3 in Ehri's model) would design lessons to develop alphabetic principle and letter–sound associations rather than have a student spend time arduously memorizing lists of words relying on visual memory. Sebastian Wren argues that "teaching children in the first and second grades to memorize words only detracts from one of the primary goals of reading instruction—as early as

Research Note

Does Teaching Phonics Make Sense?

1. We must *polish* the *Polish* furniture.

2. "Tom, go around the corner and come to me now."

Judging from these examples, teaching students to read would be much easier if there were only one symbol for each phoneme or sound in our speech. In that case, the letter *o* would have the same sound regardless of context or what letter it happened to be positioned next to in a word. Unfortunately, as these examples show, that sound (as in *polish*), depends on the meaning of the words surrounding it. In the second sentence, seven of the words contain the letter *o*, and *o* makes a different sound in each word, depending in large part on the adjacent letters. The question is, given all of this irregularity, does teaching phonics still make sense? The truth is only about 13% of English words are exceptions with highly unpredictable letter–sound relations, whereas 87% of English language words are either very predictable or consist of more complex spelling patterns that can be explicitly taught (Venezky, 1970; Wijk, 1966). In addition, many of the exceptions, such as *said* and *where*, are easier to remember when some of their sounds are taken into account. Research also shows that context clues may only be helpful 10% to 20% of the time (Gough, 1983). Add to this over 30 years of research evidence in support of teaching phonics, and the inescapable conclusion is that the teaching of phonics is definitely justified.

possible, children need to learn to attend to the letters within the words, and to decode the words, and children need to become so proficient at this skill that words are decoded rapidly and effortlessly" (Wren, 2000).

Phonics instruction helps students acquire skills in the following areas: identifying letter–sound correspondences, sounding out words containing letter sounds previously taught, reading text containing those words and new words with letter–sound correspondences that have previously been taught, and identifying words by sight. As noted earlier, spelling instruction should be integrated into all aspects of phonics instruction because of the benefits of having students spell words they are also learning to read. Chapters 3 to 5 will explain how learning these skills will help your students become fluent readers. Teaching students decoding skills involves some of the most difficult and precise teaching you will do. The aim of Chapter 3 is to provide information and guides for teachers so all students become automatic phase readers, whose attention and memory resources are available to focus on comprehending the meaning of the text they are reading.

Reading Fluency

Reading fluency is the ability to read text accurately, quickly, and with expression. Students who are able to read fluently can focus their energy on finding out what the text means. Conversely, students who read in a choppy, word-by-word fashion are so focused on getting the words right that they have little energy left for deciphering their meaning. Reading fluency is an important part of the reading curriculum for students who are at risk because they may not develop it naturally, even if they have attained the alphabetic principle (Speece & Ritchey, 2005). Unfortunately, teachers often omit teaching and assessing this skill, which prevents many students who are at risk from transitioning into fluid,

TABLE 1.1 Vocabulary in Oral and Written Communication

	Oral Communication	Written Communication
Receptive Vocabulary	*listening comprehension* Example: The student knows the meaning of a vocabulary word in a story that the teacher reads aloud.	*reading comprehension* Example: The student knows the meaning of a vocabulary word in a story that she reads.
Expressive Vocabulary	*meaningful speech* Example: Correctly using the vocabulary from a story, the student describes the sequence of events in the story that he read or that was read aloud.	*meaningful writing* Example: Correctly using the vocabulary from a story, the student writes a description of the events that took place in a story that she read or that was read aloud.

expressive readers. Fortunately, there is a large body of research showing that fluency can be assessed and effectively taught (Fuchs, Fuchs, Hosp, & Jenkins, 2001; Wolf & Katzir-Cohen, 2001), particularly for students reading at grade levels 1 to 6 (Edmonds et al., 2009). In Chapter 5, you will learn to do both.

Vocabulary

Vocabulary is the fourth key component of effective early literacy programs for students who are at risk. As shown in Table 1.1, vocabulary can be either receptive or expressive and oral or written. Oral **receptive vocabulary** involves understanding the meaning of words when people speak; written receptive vocabulary concerns understanding the meaning of words that are read. Oral **expressive vocabulary** means using words in speaking so that other people understand you; written expressive vocabulary is communicating meaningfully through writing.

Knowledge of the meaning of a wide variety of words enables students to identify words more easily. A student who knows the meaning of the word *skeptic* from hearing it in conversations, but who has never read the word before, will more fluently apply his decoding knowledge when reading a sentence containing that word. He will also be more apt to understand the meaning of the sentence. In turn, knowledge of letter–sound associations provides a valuable memory cue and helps students remember vocabulary words more easily (Ehri, 2005). Students who are at risk, including those in poverty, those having disabilities, or those who speak a second language, are likely to lag behind their peers in vocabulary development (Hart & Risley, 1995). Equally disturbing is that vocabulary differences grow larger over time, due to a lack of exposure at home and failure to teach vocabulary extensively at school (Beck, McKeown, & Kucan, 2002; Biemiller, 2001). Hart and Risley (1995) estimate the gap in words learned per year between students who are at risk and their peers who are not at risk amounts to more than 2,000 words per year.

The extent of students' vocabulary knowledge can have a significant impact on their early reading achievement. For one thing, reading is infinitely more meaningful and rewarding when students understand the meaning of the words they are decoding. Imagine what reading would be like if you were reading only nonsense words! A knowledge of vocabulary is also essential for reading connected text for meaning, the ultimate goal of reading instruction.

It is widely believed that most vocabulary is learned indirectly—either through speaking with others, being read to, or reading independently. However, many students who are at risk come to school with significantly less exposure to these naturalistic experiences.

Clearly, for students who are at risk, vocabulary instruction is an essential part of teaching them to speak, read, and write adequately. Vocabulary instruction should have two key emphases: direct teaching of the meanings of important, useful, and difficult words; and strategies for figuring out the meaning of words independently using context, meanings of word parts, and the dictionary (Stahl & Nagy, 2006). In Chapter 6, you will learn how to teach vocabulary so that students have the opportunity to extensively use new words in their oral language, reading, and writing.

Reading Comprehension

One area on which reading experts agree is that reading comprehension is the ultimate goal of reading instruction. Students who understand what they read are able to decode connected text accurately and fluently and know the meanings of a variety of vocabulary words. Good comprehenders also read purposefully and actively engage with and think about what they are reading (RAND Reading Study Group, 2002). Reading comprehension is a complex process because it is influenced by factors such as the person who is reading, the text being read, the task the reader is trying to accomplish, and the context in which the reading is being done (RAND Reading Study Group, 2002). Despite its complexity, the NRP (2000) and NELP (2009) identified a number of strategies that help students derive meaning from text. These strategies are as follows:

- Activate background knowledge and use it to make meaning out of text.
- Generate and ask questions while reading.
- Evaluate or draw conclusions from information in a text.
- Get meaning by making informed predictions.
- Summarize information by explaining in their own words what the text is about.
- Monitor comprehension, including knowing when they understand and do not understand, and using additional strategies to improve when understanding is blocked.
- Derive meaning of narrative and expository text by being able to identify relevant text structures.

Chapter 7 explains teaching techniques that help students who are at risk to consistently use these strategies while engaged with the content of the text.

Which Students Are Likely to Struggle When Learning to Read?

To explain the interconnection between various systems that help the reader decode and comprehend, Marilyn Adams (1990) described a processing model that she developed from a comprehensive review of the reading research literature in education, cognitive science, and psychology. Her model describes the process that occurs as fluent readers simultaneously and successfully engage the following four processors as they read text: **orthographic processor, phonological processor, meaning processor,** and **context processor.** The more fluent the reader, the more unaware he is of how his brain is coordinating information on the sounds, letter shapes, meaning of words, and context as his eyes rapidly move across the text from left to right (Adams, 1990). The work of each processor and its connections with the others was described by Adams: "As the parts of the system are refined and developed in proper relation to one another, each guides and reinforces the growth of the other" (p. 6).

When the reader sees text on a page, the orthographic processor recognizes the visual image of words as interconnected sets of letters. For example, when the reader sees the word *cat,* the orthographic processor sees the letters clustered into a spelling pattern *cat.*

The phonological processor is the system that processes the speech sounds of language. When the reader sees the word *cat*, the "inner voice," called the phonological processor, identifies and orders the sounds of the word /c/ /a/ /t/ rather than the letters *c-a-t*. In order to develop the automatic word reading described by Ehri, the phonological and orthographic processors must work together efficiently and fluently to make the graphophonemic connections that activate associations of past experiences with "cats." The meaning processor focuses on definitions rather than the letters or sounds and the reader thinks "furry four-legged pet that meows" when reading *cat*. This meaning processor works quickly for words the reader knows, but slower for unknown words as it connects parts of the word to meaning. Coordinating with the meaning processor, the context processor brings prior knowledge to bear on understanding the meaning of the word. When the reader sees *cat*, the context processor might think about his friend's cat.

Struggling readers have problems in one or more of these four processing domains, and effective interventions need to address their specific area of difficulty. Students with deficits primarily in phonological and orthographic processing have the vocabulary and conceptual knowledge to bring meaning to text read to them but cannot decode printed words accurately and fluently enough to extract meaning on their own (Foorman & Torgesen, 2001). These students require careful instruction in word reading and fluency. A second group of struggling readers includes children living in poverty who enter school with delayed development in all areas of language that prevent the efficient functioning of all four processors. These children require intensive instruction in vocabulary and language concepts as well as word reading and fluency. A third group of children have deficits in vocabulary and concept knowledge but adequate phonological and orthographic skills. This group of struggling readers, often referred to as "word callers," comprises at most 10% of struggling readers, and includes English language learners. Students in this group need carefully targeted comprehension instruction, including both vocabulary and language concepts. These three groups of struggling readers share two common characteristics: the inability to comprehend written text and the need for early identification and reading support.

Recent studies using computerized imaging show that serious reading problems may be brain-based, with the brain activity of the most deficit readers differing from those of students who are skilled readers (Shaywitz & Shaywitz, 2007). Many deficit readers show a pattern of underactivation in a region in the back of the brain that enables first accurate and then automatic reading. These brain scans, which differ from those of skilled readers, provide insight about why these students have problems learning to decode accurately and fluently (Shaywitz, 2003). Fortunately, research also shows that effective language instruction, including systematic instruction in phonemic awareness and phonics, generates repair in underactivated sections of the brain (Shaywitz, 2003; Simos et al., 2007), reinforcing the importance of early identification and remediation.

What Is the Most Effective Way to Teach Essential Reading Skills to Children Who Are at Risk?

The evidence is clear that students who are at risk benefit from reading instruction that is explicit and systematic. **Explicit instruction** is the clear, direct teaching of reading skills and strategies and includes these:

- Clear instructional outcomes (what you want the student to do with the information you've taught)
- Clear purpose for learning

- Clear and understandable directions and explanations
- Adequate modeling/demonstration, guided practice, and independent practice as part of the teaching process
- Clear, consistent corrective feedback on student success and student errors

The second-grade teachers at Fourth Avenue School use an explicit reading curriculum to teach reading. They expect their students to read at least 90 words per minute by the end of the year and to apply that skill when reading books of different genres for school assignments and for enjoyment. If the students are taking turns reading a play, the teachers explain the directions beforehand and tell students the procedure for rotating turns and for correcting errors. Because the teachers are so clear, the students, after misreading a word, have formed the habit of immediately starting again at the beginning of the sentence and rereading. The teachers always introduce new concepts by first showing the students how to do them and then supporting their learning until independence. Because the two- and three-syllable words introduced last week were difficult for many of the students, the teachers spent an extra day reviewing them so students had more practice. Whenever students make mistakes, the teachers follow the systematic error correction procedures that you will read about later in this chapter. By correcting errors using these procedures, teachers make sure that students know how to perform the skill correctly the next time they are called on.

Systematic instruction is teaching that clearly identifies a carefully selected and useful set of skills and then organizes those skills into a logical sequence of instruction. For example, Mr. Prince decides to teach his students to sound out regular words because there is not enough time for them to memorize all the words with which they come in contact. Before he works on sounding out words, Mr. Prince teaches his students to say the sounds in words they hear and to blend sounds into whole words. Gradually, he begins teaching his students letter sounds. By the time his students begin sounding out words, they will have all the skills they need to be successful.

Students vary in the amount of explicit, systematic instruction they need for learning to read. Reflect back on the typical first-grade class (Figure 1.1) with its wide range of learners. In a typical class, some students learn new material as fast as the teacher can teach it; other students need extra practice before they learn it; and a third group needs very deliberate teaching that slowly moves from easier skills to more difficult concepts. Because of these differences, schools need a range of instructional options to meet the diverse needs of their students. Teaching that provides this broader range of options is known as differentiated instruction (Friend & Bursuck, 2009).

Throughout this book, we will show you how to provide differentiated instruction through two schoolwide approaches, the **multi-tier** model and the **Response to Intervention** (RTI) model, both designed to provide support for struggling readers at the first sign of difficulty (Gersten et al., 2009). In a multi-tier model, which was the prevention-based system of delivering reading instruction in Project PRIDE, students who needed additional support in reading were identified through regularly scheduled research-based assessments of essential reading skills. Students who needed more support received additional research-based interventions of varying intensity. Varying levels of intensities are called "tiers," and in a typical multi-tier model, Tier 1 is the general classroom curriculum, Tier 2 provides additional small-group tutoring support, and Tier 3 is a more intensive alternative reading program (Hoover & Patton, 2008). The tiers depicted in Figure 1.4 are described in more detail later in this chapter. Assessments given on a weekly or monthly basis provide information about whether students are responding to the amount of support they receive, and adjustments are made as needed.

In RTI, a multi-tier system of instruction provides the foundation, but in addition, a process is included to determine whether a student is eligible for learning disability services. In RTI, a student's lack of response (i.e., lack of improvement) to several high-quality research-based Tier 2 and Tier 3 interventions can be viewed as evidence of an underlying

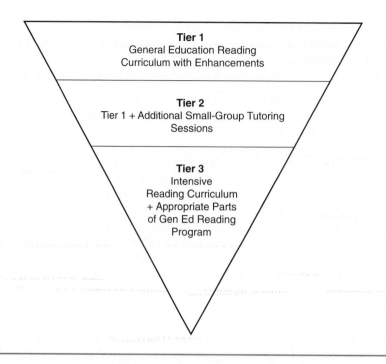

FIGURE 1.4   Multi-Tiered Model of Differentiated Instruction

---

Learn more about RTI at the National Center on Response to Intervention at **http://www.rti4success.org/.**

learning disability if other testing or data support that diagnosis (Brown-Chidsey & Steege, 2005). Both RTI and multi-tier models include these components:

- Research-based instruction in the general education classroom
- Ongoing student assessment—frequently monitored student progress to examine student achievement and gauge the effectiveness of the interventions
- Tiered instruction—specific research-based interventions of varying intensities matched to student need

Tier 1 Instruction

Tier 1 in a multi-tier or RTI model is the least intensive, first level of instruction and consists of the core reading program used in the classroom, whether it is basal, strictly literature-based, or a combination of the two. In Project PRIDE we added a number of research-based teaching enhancements to the core reading program that helped our students who were at risk learn more efficiently and effectively (Bursuck et al., 2004; Kame'enui, Good, Simmons, & Chard, 2002). Throughout the text we will teach you ways to use these same enhancements to maximize the effectiveness of your Tier 1 core reading program so that you can meet the needs of as many of your students as possible. Of course, more students who are at risk will learn to read successfully with the additional Tier 1 enhancements if the core reading program already reflects effective reading practices described in the NRP (2000) and NELP (2009) reports and is implemented as designed for at least 90 minutes per day (Arndt & Crawford, 2006). An effective Tier 1 program should be able to serve 80% of the students, though in schools with large numbers of students who are at risk, that number may be smaller, even with the use of enhancements (Bursuck & Damer, 2005). While instruction using small homogeneous groups of 3 to 4 students has been shown to be the most effective grouping procedure in general (Elbaum, Vaughn, Hughes, & Moody, 2000), extensive use of small groups in Tier 1 can reduce instructional time with the teacher, a key predictor of student success (Rosenshine, 1986). Also, behavior problems proliferate in classes where students work independently for more than 15 or 20 minutes, waiting for the teacher to work with their small group. In Project PRIDE, the instructional enhancements were designed to make large-group instruction more effective. Small-group instruction was then provided for those students needing additional support in Tier 2 and Tier 3, a practice recommended by Gersten et al. (2009). Regardless of the approach, the quality of the core reading program and the amount of time students receive systematic, explicit instruction with feedback from the teacher are critical features of effective Tier 1 instruction.

Tier 2 Instruction

Tier 2 in a multi-tier or RTI model consists of Tier 1 instruction plus additional daily small-group intervention sessions that provide extra practice on key skills covered in Tier 1. Students enter Tier 2 when their performance dips below benchmark scores or a set percentile on universal screening or progress-monitoring measures described later in this chapter. In Project PRIDE, Tier 2 sessions usually lasted 10 minutes in kindergarten and 30 to 40 minutes in the later grades—practices consistent with research-based guidelines recommended by the Institute for Education Sciences (Gersten et al., 2009). While the institute recommends group sizes of three to four, in Project PRIDE we were often able to accommodate slightly larger group sizes by using the same enhancements employed in Tier 1, such as unison responding. Tier 2 instruction ensures that students become fluent, accurate readers by providing extra practice on essential foundational word reading skills in the primary grades with more of an emphasis on vocabulary and comprehension skills after third grade. Word reading skills are emphasized in the primary grades because a high percentage of students who are at risk fail to comprehend what they are reading because they cannot read connected text accurately and fluently (Adams & Bruck, 1993). Their comprehension will not mature until their word reading improves, enabling them to focus more attention on the meaning of the text. Tier 2 sessions are carried out by a variety of staff, including general education teachers, Title I teachers, special education teachers, and paraprofessionals, all carefully prepared to ensure quality implementation. Having effective Tier 1 and Tier 2 programs in place should enable you to meet the needs of all but 5% of your students, although high-poverty schools usually have more students who require Tier 3 support (Bursuck & Damer, 2005).

Tier 3 Instruction

Tier 3 in a multi-tier or RTI model includes all of the enhancements that are in Tiers 1 and 2 plus a more systematically designed and explicitly taught reading curriculum. Students placed in Tier 3 have failed to make substantial progress despite a Tier 1 enhanced general education reading program and extra help in Tier 2 intervention groups. In Project PRIDE, Tier 3 sessions were conducted in small groups daily for 60 to 90 minutes. Research indicates that Tier 3 interventions that focus on key foundational skills and are conducted in small groups of one to four students are highly systematic and explicit and are longer in duration, resulting in increased reading achievement results (Gersten et al., 2009).

Fewer than 5% of students make little progress even in the presence of otherwise effective instruction (Torgesen, 2000). Students in this group have serious, pervasive reading disabilities and in an RTI model are more appropriately served in special education (Wanzek & Vaughn, 2008), which, depending on the specific multi-tier model, can be included as a part of Tier 3 or a separate Tier 4. These students may benefit from doubling their reading time using a practice called "double dosing." However, double dosing only works when what you are doubling is well-designed, systematic, and explicit instruction (Wanzek & Vaughn, 2008).

Some Title 1 or special education teachers work with older students on a remedial basis, but by the time their students begin instruction, typically after third grade, they are significantly behind their classmates. Although this later start to intervention poses difficult challenges, upper-grade teachers are responsible for catching up these students so they are reading at grade level. Catching up students is difficult due to limits in district time and resources, but even so, older students reading below a fourth-grade reading level should be taught for at least 2 hours per day using a well-designed Tier 3 program (Archer, Gleason, & Vachon, 2003).

Although the focus of this text is on making sure that you can teach most children using Tiers 1 and 2, experience shows that, depending on where you are teaching, at least a third of your children may need Tier 3 instruction (Damer, Bursuck, & Harris, 2008). The intensity of Tier 3 programs differs from district to district in terms of time, size of group, and curriculum. Ideally, students who do not respond to interventions in Tier 3 should receive increased intensity of services such as double dosing, the implementation of a formal motivational behavior program, reduced group size, or a change in curriculum. Districts in high-poverty areas that implement multi-tier or RTI models and identify up to 60% of second-grade or older students as so far behind that only a Tier 3 intervention will provide "catch-up," face an ethical dilemma when, because of cost, they only provide those services to the lowest performing 10% of students. Meeting the needs of a large group of older students requiring Tier 3 instruction forces schools to be creative, using new strategies such as training general education teachers to teach Tier 3 groups or enlisting everyone in the building from the principal to the music teacher to teach reading to at least a small Tier 2 reading group. When enhanced Tier 1 and Tier 2 instruction begins in preschool or kindergarten, the percentage of older students who need Tier 3 should decrease significantly.

The ultimate purpose of Tier 3 is to catch students up to their peers, which means that students need instruction that is well designed and efficiently and competently taught. Otherwise, Tier 3 groups can become a dumping ground with an irrelevant, watered-down curriculum in which students fall further behind and become at high risk for dropping out of school. Too often in the past, remedial programs have become such dead-end options. Because of potential risks associated with remedial pull-out programs, we suggest using a prepackaged, commercially produced reading program that is evidence based, has teacher-friendly formats that are relatively easy to implement, and provides scaffolding to teachers without a lot of prior experience teaching explicit reading.

How can you determine which alternative reading program will have the most success with the largest number of your students? How do you know whether the alternative program has an adequate phonemic awareness emphasis? How can you tell if the alternative program is a systematic phonics program? These questions are confusing for many educators who are faced with testimonials defending reading curricula as having research support. To assist you or your school in deciding on a Tier 3 program, toward the end of each chapter we have listed key characteristics to look for in alternative reading programs. These characteristics include the skill focus, design, and instructional approach as they relate to students who are at risk or who have disabilities. In addition, we have analyzed some commonly used alternative reading programs to determine which ones include these characteristics.

We also suggest that whenever feasible, Tier 3 groups take place in the classroom. In-class groups are preferred because they provide a valuable instructional model for general education teachers and can lead to shared responsibility for the reading outcomes of all students (Friend & Cook, 2007). Many of the intensive reading programs do not include adequate vocabulary and comprehension instruction, so students in Tier 3 need to develop those skills in the larger classroom group. As long as the teacher conducting the large group doesn't humiliate Tier 3 students by expecting them to orally read frustration-level text in front of their peers and differentiates instruction by having them listen to the text before the large group takes place, all students can participate in vocabulary and comprehension development activities. A sample schedule for a classroom using a three-tier approach is shown in Figure 1.5.

Large-Group Instruction: Tiers 1, 2, 3 students **(20 minutes)**

Who Teaches: Mrs. James
Prereading, vocabulary, carryover comprehension activities from last story/article.

Large-Group Instruction: (30 minutes)
Tier 1 and Tier 2 students work with Mrs. James on parts of core curriculum that would be at frustration level for students in Tier 3.

- Letter–sound identification
- Word reading, spelling, first read-through of the story/article in the corereading curriculum.

Small-Group Instruction: (60 minutes)
One or two small Tier 3* groups, conducted by Title 1 teacher, special education teacher, classroom aide trained to conduct scripted reading lessons, or another assigned general education teacher, work on intensive reading lessons at small tables in the room.

Small-Group Instruction and Centers: (30 minutes)

- Tier 2 support group meets to review new sounds and words taught in class and/or read decodable text. These students work with Mrs. James.
- Tier 1 students independently work on challenging center activities.

Large-Group Instruction: Tiers 1, 2, 3 students **(25 minutes)**

Who Teaches: Mrs. James
All students work on comprehension and vocabulary activities related to the story that students read earlier. Although students in Tier 3 do not orally read frustration-level text, they fully participate in all of the comprehension and vocabulary activities related to the story. Tier 1 and Tier 2 students have another opportunity to read the text with comprehension integrated at the sentence level.

Extra Small-Group Instruction: Tiers 1, 2, 3 students **(15 minutes)**

Who Teaches: Mrs. James
Other times during the day when reading instruction takes place:

- After lunch, Mrs. James reads to the students (50% of the time reads nonfiction) using graphic organizers and frequent questions to develop listening comprehension.
- During math, Mrs. James challenges advanced readers by teaching them to read the names of difficult shapes.
- During the social studies and science block, Mrs. James uses a combination of large group and centers, integrating vocabulary, reading, writing, and comprehension into her volcanoes activity.
- During "sponge times" (waiting outside the lunch room, lining up in the room), Mrs. James provides extra practice and asks students to segment words, spell words, identify vocabulary words on the word wall, etc.

FIGURE 1.5 120-Minute Core Reading Block Conducted in Mrs. James's First Grade Classroom

* For these Tier 3 students to catch up to their peers, it is recommended that in the afternoon they have another 30 minutes of intensive instruction in the same curriculum, incorporating spelling instruction.

How Do I Identify Struggling Readers, Monitor Student Progress, and Diagnose Instructional Needs in a Multi-Tier or RTI Model?

Assessments in multi-tier or RTI models serve three purposes: universal screening, progress monitoring, and diagnosis. Regardless of the purpose, the assessments used must accurately measure essential early reading skills, be easy to give, take up little classroom time, predict later classroom problems, and enable teachers to readily monitor student progress (Jenkins, 2009). In multi-tier or RTI models, criterion-referenced tests are most often used. Criterion-referenced tests compare student performance to a specific level of performance or benchmark. One particularly useful type of criterion-referenced assessment is curriculum-based measurement (CBM; Deno, 2003). CBM is an assessment method that directly measures basic academic skills. CBM is characterized by an extensive research base establishing its technical adequacy as well as tasks and scoring procedures that are brief, grounded in the classroom curriculum, standardized, and fluency based. Fluency, or how quickly a student can perform a skill or recall academic content, adds an important dimension to assessment that level of accuracy alone can't provide. Students who are fluent in a skill are more likely to retain it and master more advanced skills based on its foundation (Friend & Bursuck, 2009).

Universal screening involves identifying students who, despite a strong reading program in Tier 1, are not making adequate progress and require extra support in Tier 2 or Tier 3. Quality screening measures accurately identify students who are at risk for future reading failure, are efficient, and result in students' reading needs being met (Jenkins & Johnson, 2007). These screening measures, sometimes called "benchmark assessments," are typically administered at the beginning, middle, and end of the year to ensure that students who require increased or decreased support get it. The assessments should address skills related to both word reading and comprehension (Catts, Fey, Zhang, & Tomblin, 1999) and reflect grade-level differences. In the early grades, letter knowledge, phonemic awareness, and phonics should be stressed, while vocabulary and comprehension take on increased importance in the later grades (Jenkins & Johnson, 2007). Screening measures are best given by general education classroom teachers because they afford teachers the opportunity to learn about the attention, verbal skills, and attitudes of students not in their reading groups.

Some schools identify students who are at risk by defining deficit reading as a score corresponding to a percentile such as performing below the 50th percentile or in the bottom 10% of their school or district. Other screening assessments define deficit reading as falling below a predetermined standard, which is often a cutoff point either on a state high-stakes test or on a curriculum-based measure that is predictive of future reading problems. Universal screening identifies accurately students who are truly in need and avoids either identifying children for extra tier help who don't need it (**false positives**) or not identifying children for extra tier help who need it (**false negatives**). While too many false positives can drain resources in times of reduced funding, having too many false negatives can have more dire consequences for students whose reading needs are neglected. That is why we recommend caution when using cutoffs such as identifying only the bottom 10% or 20% of a given school or district as being eligible to receive extra Tier 3 support, particularly when engaged in screening activities in urban districts where a much higher percentage of children are likely to be at risk when a multi-tier program is first implemented.

Throughout this book, universal-screening subtests that assess the skills highlighted in each chapter will be discussed. These subtests have been selected from four larger assessment batteries because they are most frequently discussed in the RTI literature as being credible assessments, have established reliability and validity, and take a relatively short amount of time to administer. Appendix A shows how the Dynamic Indicators of Basic

Literacy Skills (DIBELS), AIMSweb, Phonological Awareness Literacy Screening (PALS), and Texas Primary Reading Inventory (TPRI) can be used as universal screeners within multi-tier or RTI models.

As much as we know about evidence-based practices in reading, we still cannot predict how each student will respond to a given instructional intervention. That is why measuring student growth is such an important part of multi-tier and RTI models. **Progress monitoring** enables teachers to make important decisions such as whether a student should remain in a tier, enter a more intensive tier, or exit into a less-intensive tier. Progress-monitoring assessments are given repeatedly over time and must be of approximately equal difficulty, a feature of CBM that makes them ideal for measuring student progress. Generally, students in Tier 1 are assessed at a minimum of three times per year, while Tier 2 and Tier 3 students can be assessed every 3 to 4 weeks (Jenkins, 2009), or more often if desired. Jenkins describes a four-step process of progress monitoring: setting growth goals, selecting progress monitoring assessments of approximately equal difficulty, measuring performance every 3 to 4 weeks to determine growth rates, and adjusting instruction when growth is inadequate. Jenkins also recommends obtaining multiple measures (at least two, ideally three) of each skill on each progress monitoring occasion to ensure the accuracy of the growth rates.

At the heart of the "one size doesn't fit all" reading model is the need to provide differentiated instruction, including materials and tasks at varied levels of difficulty and with varying levels of support through the use of multiple grouping arrangements (Friend & Bursuck, 2009). Differentiation is achieved by diagnosing the needs of students shown to be at risk on universal screening measures. **Diagnostic assessments** can be used to determine these needs:

- What skills students need to practice in Tier 2
- The reading level at which a student should be instructed
- Which letter–sound correspondences or phonemic awareness skills are in need of instruction
- Whether there is a need for fluency building in passage reading or for modeling and guided practice when students are sounding out multisyllable words
- Which students can be grouped together to work on comprehension skills, such as finding the main idea

For Tier 2 students, classroom teachers can give simple diagnostic tests or identify error patterns based on student performance on universal screeners. Two of the larger assessment batteries described in Appendix A include diagnostic tests to help plan smaller instructional groups. In an RTI model, Tier 3 students who are not responding to interventions at an acceptable rate and whose eligibility for special education services is being considered receive further diagnostic assessment by a reading teacher, special education teacher, speech and language pathologist, or school psychologist.

> To learn more about RTI, go to the IRIS Center Web site and complete the RTI (Part 1) Overview Module at **http://iris.peabody.vanderbilt.edu/rti01_overview/chalcycle.htm.**

What Are the Instructional Enhancements for Students Who Are at Risk?

The instructional enhancements for students who are at risk described in this section are evidence based and can provide the consistency, predictability, and structure students who are at risk need to be successful (Stichter, Stormont, & Lewis, 2009) because they are based on the principle of **universal design** of instruction (Pisha & Stahl, 2005). The idea behind universal design is that instructional materials and methods designed with built-in supports minimize the need for differentiated instruction later on (Friend & Bursuck, 2009). The enhancements include advance organizers, unison responses through the use of effective signals, perky pace, efficient use of teacher talk, increased practice, support for new learning using a My Turn–Together–Your Turn format, systematic error correction, cumulative review, teaching to success, and motivational strategies. Each of these enhancements is described in this section, and throughout this book, we provide ways for you to maximize the learning of all students by integrating them into your teaching.

Advance Organizers

When students are easily distracted or come from chaotic home environments, they want and need structure and predictability in their environment. Disorganized students often do not automatically draw connections from one part of a learning task to another. Unless the teacher has told students that the words they are reading on the board will be in that day's story, some of the students who are more disorganized will not make the connection to those words when they open their books to the new story and begin to read. Teachers establish a comfortable level of predictability when they use advance organizers at the start of each lesson by telling students what they are learning, why they are learning it, and what the behavioral expectations are during the lesson (Marzano, 2003). When these advance organizers provide the beginning organization for each day's lesson, students learn to anticipate connections between what they are learning and how they will apply the new learning to other situations. By briefly describing the sequence of activities covered during the reading lesson and checking each one off after it is completed, teachers also motivate students who are likely to tune out or act out in a part of the lesson that they find difficult. For example, reading the new long-vowel words might be difficult for Debra, but if she knows that word practice is followed by an interesting story about a lizard that bakes cakes, she will pay closer attention and work harder. Advance organizers should include a graphic depiction along with a brief verbal description, especially for younger students. A sample visually presented advance organizer for a kindergarten lesson is shown in Figure 1.6. It includes the comments the teacher makes to prepare the students to learn.

Unison Responding

Students who are at risk need more practice of the key skills they are learning than their peers who are not at risk. They need to be actively engaged with many opportunities to orally practice the new sounds, read the new words, read the longer stories, and use new vocabulary words in increasingly longer sentences (Lemoine, Levy, & Hutchinson, 1993). For example, to learn to automatically recognize a written word as a sight word, the average student requires between 4 and 14 exposures, while struggling readers need 20 or more exposures (Lyon, 1998). Students with disabilities may require 50 to 100 exposures to automatize the recognition of a new word in context (Honig, 2001). In a class of 20 or 30 students, teachers can only provide that amount of practice by having all of the students answer in unison. Rather than ask one student to say the sound of the new letter l, the teacher increases academic learning time for everyone by asking all of the students to answer at the same time.

As an added benefit, students who are actively participating are more likely to pay attention to instruction and follow classroom rules. Students who are constantly answering and reading have little time to be off task, staring out the window, or disrupting the class.

1. Segmenting Lesson—"Let's pull some words apart!"

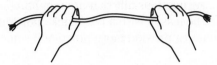

2. Blending—"Next we'll put some sounds together to make words."

3. Letter Sounds—"Then we'll work with the letter **d** and its buddies."

Working with the letter. . . **d** and its buddies.

4. Reading Words—"Then we'll read some words."

5. Spelling—"Then we'll spell some words."

During the lesson today I would like you to. . .
- Sit up nice and tall in your seats.
- Listen very closely.
- And answer on my signal.

FIGURE 1.6   Advance Organizer—Letter and Sounds Lesson

Source: Hicks, A. (2006). Model advance organizer. Unpublished manuscript, University of North Carolina at Greensboro.

Since students who are at risk also need to have their answers carefully monitored to make sure that they are acquiring the skills that are taught, teachers are more effective if they follow each section of the lesson with a few quick, individual questions. These quick checkouts enable the teacher to provide more practice if some students still are making errors.

Effective Signals

Effective signals help a teacher get all the students to answer together, speaking in one voice as if in a choir. If students answer too early or too late, reading instruction will not be as effective. One or two students who immediately grasp the concept may answer ahead of everyone else, creating the illusion that the class does not need any more practice. Students who are at risk may answer after everyone else, relying on other students' answers and not sounding out the words by themselves. The parts of an effectively delivered signal that will get all students to answer together are described in Table 1.2.

Note that the teacher first focuses the students' attention on the question. Questions that teachers ask in beginning reading instruction include the following:

- Asking students to name letter sounds
- Asking students to sound out words
- Asking students to say all of the sounds in the words they hear
- Asking students to read simple sentences

TABLE 1.2 Effective Signals

Component	Description
1. FOCUS students' attention, and then ask your question.	The teacher gains students' attention by having them focus on the word they will read or on an oral question.
	■ When asking an oral question, hold up a hand to gain students' attention and tell students what they will do. Example: Hold up a hand and say, "You are going to take some words apart. First word is *mat.*"
	■ If asking students to read, tell students what they will do and point a finger to the left of the first word. Example: Tell students, "Get ready to read the word when I touch it," and point to the left of the word.
2. THINK Time	A brief pause of no more than three seconds provides students with time to formulate an answer. If the questions are easy or review, the teacher gives a very short thinking pause. If the questions are difficult or new, the teacher gives a longer thinking pause.
3. SIGNAL	The teacher gives the signal that indicates everyone should answer at that very instant. The signal always comes **after** the directions, never at the same time. Thus a teacher never talks and signals at the same time. Chapters 2 and 3 describe specific signals including: ■ Hand-drop ■ Hand-clap ■ Finger-raise ■ Loop signal

Next the teacher provides think time, waiting for a few seconds after asking the question and calling on the students. The amount of think time will vary depending on the question. For new or more difficult questions, the think time is longer than for easier or review ones. Following the thinking pause, the teacher asks the question, pauses one second, and then gives the signal. The type of signal used depends on the nature of the question that students are asked. For example, when students are asked to sound out words listed on the board, the teacher points to the letters in the word signaling for students to sound them out. When asking students to orally take apart words ("What are the sounds in *fish:* /f/ /i/ /s/ /h/?"), the teacher either snaps two fingers, claps hands together, or drops a hand as the signal. Specific strategies for using signals are covered in the chapters that follow. Some teachers develop their own signals, such as moving their arms as if directing an orchestra, using a clicker in the shape of a bug, moving fingers in the air, or tapping fingers on a surface.

Efficient Use of Teacher Talk

The clarity with which teachers present information to students at risk has a strong influence on their learning. Students in classrooms where teachers present material in concise statements, using language the students understand, are more likely to be on task than students whose teachers provide lengthy explanations and present information unrelated to the task at hand. Teaching in a clear and concise manner is easier said than done. We have included scripted teaching formats for all of the key skills covered in the text as a scaffold for teachers as they develop their abilities to teach more clearly.

Perky Pace

Teachers can also increase student attention and learning by employing a perky pace throughout every lesson (Englert, Tarrant, & Mariage, 1992). Teachers who use a perky pace start with a brief advance organizer and minimize the transition time between activities, as well as between each student answer and the teacher's next question. Students give more of their attention to a teacher who uses an animated teaching style, conveying her enthusiasm for what they are learning. They are less likely to waste time, be uncooperative, or tune out when a theatrical teacher uses exaggerated affect, enthusiastic voice tones, and dramatic gestures

My Turn–Together–Your Turn Format

All students require support or scaffolding when they are learning new skills or content. Think about the frustration you felt when a math or physics teacher introduced a new concept and then, without adequately giving you practice using the new concept, expected you to apply it to that night's homework problems. As you tried to solve problems that depended on your knowledge of the new concept, your frustration and tension level increased as you stared at the work. Unless you could find a better teacher in the form of a friend, a tutor, or a detailed book, your learning was at a standstill. Students who are at risk require even more support when they are learning to read and write. An effective way to scaffold their new learning is to use the My Turn–Together–Your Turn strategy used in explicit instruction (Archer, 1995). The components of this approach are as follows:

- **My Turn:** The teacher first demonstrates how to do the new skill so that students have no difficulty understanding exactly what the new skill looks like.
- **Together:** The teacher practices the skill with his students until they are able to do it without him. Students experience a higher level of success and less frustration if

they first have the opportunity to practice with the teacher. In this way, students are prevented from practicing the errors and acquiring habits that, once learned, are difficult to break.

- **Your Turn:**   The teacher monitors students as they do the skill independently. By closely monitoring his students, the teacher can correct any errors and prevent them from acquiring habits that, once learned, are difficult to break.

Teachers who use a My Turn–Together–Your Turn format for teaching new critical skills are explicitly teaching so that students are successful from the start. These teachers know that when students inadvertently learn errors such as saying /sh/ for the /th/ sound, valuable time will be wasted reteaching. Jerry Ameis (2003) cautions, "Reteaching is a significant waste of time for students and teachers. It is far better to spend the needed time on trying *'to get it right'* the first time than to bore and/or frustrate students (and yourself) by reteaching and reteaching . . ." (Ameis, 2003). Eventually teachers move to using "Your Turns" as students' accuracy shows they have learned the new skill. Moving to "Your Turns" represents an important transition because providing more support than is needed can thwart student independence and prevent accurate progress monitoring. Indeed, when the building is complete, the scaffolds come down.

Cumulative Review

Teachers who work with students who are at risk often observe that these students have difficulty retaining new information or skills. Just when it seems that they have learned something new, the very next day they have already forgotten it. In addition to problems with retention, students who are at risk also have trouble discriminating between new information and information previously learned. For example, Delarnes learned the sound /b/ several weeks ago, but since learning other sounds has practiced it only once or twice. This week, he learned the new /d/ sound on Thursday. On Friday, he read all of the *b* words in his decodable book as if they contained the letter *d*. If Delarnes's teacher had continued to practice the /b/ sound every day after he learned it, he would have been less likely to confuse it with /d/. **Cumulative review** is a method of selecting teaching examples where the teacher adds previously learned material to examples of newly learned material. Cumulative review increases student retention and helps students discriminate between new and old learning. To use cumulative review, simply add examples of previously learned material to examples of newly learned material.

Systematic Error Correction

No matter how systematic and explicit the reading instruction, students will always make some errors. Research shows that in an effective lesson, students answer at least eight out of every ten answers correctly (McEwan & Damer, 2000). This minimum level of success instills confidence and reduces frustration for at-risk students. The way that teachers correct student errors is critical. If errors are not corrected appropriately, students continue to make the same errors and develop habits that can seriously undermine the goal of fluent, accurate reading with comprehension.

In making a **systematic error correction**, the teacher corrects the students immediately after they make the error by modeling the correct answer/skill ("My Turn"), guiding the students to correct the error as needed ("Together"), and then re-asking the same question so students have the opportunity to independently answer the question correctly ("Your Turn"). Later in the lesson, the teacher provides even more practice by asking students to answer the same question again. If students answer correctly, the teacher knows that she can move ahead in the lesson.

Teachers who use systematic error corrections provide high levels of feedback to their students, an important component of explicit instruction. According to Fisher and colleagues (1980), academic feedback should be provided as often as possible to students. When more frequent feedback is given, students pay closer attention and learn more. In their research, academic feedback was more strongly and consistently related to learning than any of the other teaching behaviors.

Teaching to Success

Children who are at risk or have disabilities often require more time to learn to read. When teaching reading to students who are at risk, teachers often need to spend more time on a given skill, continuing instruction and not moving on to the next skill until students have clearly learned the one currently being taught. Research shows that if instruction is evidence based, most children can learn, given the right amount of time (Ornstein & Lasley, 2004). For example, Mr. Lazaro's class was struggling to correctly identify the short sound for the letter a. While he had originally planned to introduce the sound for the letter p on the following day, Mr. Lazaro decided he would continue working on the sound of a, not introducing a new sound until his students could correctly identify the first one. Mr. Lazaro knew that if his students could not automatically identify the sound for the letter a, they would struggle with the many words they would subsequently be reading that contained it. Another teacher using this strategy was Ms. Gentry. Her class was orally reading the latest story in their reader. Ms. Gentry, who was keeping track of the number of words her students missed, found that they were missing more than two words per page and that their accuracy was below 90%. Before Ms. Gentry moved to the next story, she had her students practice reading the words they misread and had them reread the current story until they could read it with 97% accuracy. In the past, when Ms. Gentry had moved her students to the next story regardless of their accuracy, she found that they made more errors. Sometimes our Project PRIDE teachers repeated lessons for several extra days, even an entire week. For example, when students first learned blends such as st, sk, and br, their teacher spent an extra week having them read words with those sound patterns before moving on. During social studies, one of our teachers took two or three additional days teaching comprehension, moving through the text paragraph by paragraph using graphic organizers. Time is of the essence when students are behind in reading, and teachers cannot afford to spend the long hours that are needed to reteach a skill that a child has learned incorrectly. Zig Engelmann (2007) explains that if by fourth grade a child has learned to misread words, it will take about 400 teaching trials to reteach those words. The older the student becomes, the more difficult the task of reteaching errors, and by high school, reteaching those errors can take almost three times the effort, or more than 1,000 trials.

Student Motivational System

Students who are at risk often enter school with a more limited repertoire of appropriate social and academic behaviors. As a result, learning can initially be quite difficult for them, even when the instruction provided by the teacher is systematic and explicit. Once students experience the success that results from well-designed instruction, success alone may be enough to keep them motivated and working hard. Until then, teachers often need to use a student motivational system to maintain a positive classroom atmosphere and to strengthen key academic and social behaviors that students who are at risk often lack. When Pressley and colleagues (2001) investigated what types of teachers were most effective in teaching primary-level literacy, they found that the most effective teachers had classrooms that were positive learning environments. The authors found

In Your Classroom

Using the Teacher–Class Game

Getting a classroom of students to pay attention to the reading lesson, follow the classroom rules and procedures, and answer in unison can be challenging, especially when some students come to school without these basic behavior skills needed for learning:

- Wait for a turn to speak or act.
- Understand and follow directions.
- Actively listen.
- Work independently.
- Accept consequences of behavior.

When students are not answering in unison or when misbehavior is interfering with learning time, the Teacher–Class game teaches students these skills while enabling the teacher to maintain a positive classroom environment. To organize the game before class starts, the teacher writes a T-grid on the board so he can easily award points to the class or to himself. A sample completed grid at the end of class looks like Figure 1.7.

During the lesson introduction, the teacher informs students that they will be playing the Teacher–Class game and reminds them how they can earn points. Periodically throughout the lesson when students are following the rules, the teacher awards the class points. Whenever a student does not follow the rules, the teacher gives himself a point. The more frequently the teacher gives the class a point and compliments students on their behavior, the more motivating the lesson becomes. As students work hard to get more points than the teacher, they learn successful school behaviors in the process. On Friday during the advance organizers for reading class, Mr. Setinz introduced the game to his class sitting on the rug by saying:

"Remember to pay attention to my signals, to keep your hands and feet to yourself, and to do your

best work. We are going to play the Teacher–Class game again today. Every day this week you have earned more points than I have (exaggerated sigh of exasperation). If you beat me today, that is five days in a row, and so everyone earns an extra recess at the end of the day. You'll need to pay close attention because I am going to try my hardest to win today. I would like to win at least one day, but this class is hard to beat."

Without interrupting the flow of his teaching during the lesson, Mr. Setinz juggled paying attention to students' answers along with closely monitoring their behavior. He provided some of the following feedback as he gave or took away respective points:

"Everyone followed my signal and read those first six words, so the class gets a point."

"That's my point. Tanya and Robert, I need you to answer with everyone."

"You took out your books so quickly that I just have to give you a point."

Whether a behavior strategy succeeds or fails depends on how effectively the teacher uses it. To teach positive behaviors with this game, the following guidelines are recommended:

- **Do not give warnings about potential points lost.** If your rules are that no one gets out of his seat or talks out of turn, you need to immediately give yourself a point when a student does either of those behaviors. If you warn students by saying, *"Next time, I'm going to give myself a point,"* you are actually encouraging higher rates of misbehavior because students recognize that sometimes they get away with breaking the rules.
- **Remember to notice positive student behaviors and give points for them.** *"Row 3 has been working so hard and listening to my instructions that they've earned a point for the class."* The game helps teachers maintain a positive classroom by frequently giving feedback on the positive actions of their students.
- **Put thought into selecting rewards.** Students should want the reward they will earn so they will be motivated to do their best work. Avoid using the same award every week because it will lose its impact as students become bored with it. Some

Teacher	Class
~~HHH~~ ‖‖	~~HHH~~ ~~HHH~~
	~~HHH~~ ~~HHH~~
7	20

FIGURE 1.7 The Teacher–Class Game

rewards that Project PRIDE teachers used included these:

- The opportunity for a drawing period using the white boards
- The opportunity to go to the music room and play some instruments
- A special cartoon sticker choice
- The opportunity to have extra computer lab time
- A small box of crayons to bring home
- The opportunity to use stamping markers or to earn one to bring home
- The opportunity to fly paper airplanes
- The opportunity to earn books that the teacher had purchased at garage sales the summer before

Note: This game is as successful with older students as it is with younger ones, as long as the rewards are adjusted for that age level.

- **Give students frequent points in the beginning** so they experience success and win the game the majority of the time. Otherwise, the game will not be effective.
- **Always give feedback with the points,** describing the reason why students earned or didn't earn points. Younger students require more enthusiastic, animated feedback than older ones when they earn a point. Your positive feedback will be effective if accompanied by a change in

voice or facial expression that indicates you are genuinely pleased with their success. Feedback for teacher points should be explained in a matter-of-fact, no-nonsense voice tone: *"Some students forgot to follow with their finger so I get a point. Remember to use your reading finger."*

The Teacher–Class game has many variations. Some teachers will call the game Ms. Garvey vs. the Raptors, or Mr. Wood = St. Louis Cardinals vs. Class = Chicago Cubs. Teachers can give students several points when they see more effort than usual, *"We worked so hard that we finished the lesson by 10:00 and can move on to another one. This class deserves five points."* As student behaviors improve, the game should become more challenging. The teacher can tell the class that in order to win they cannot let him win more than 5 points during the entire class; or that they must earn twice as many points as he has earned to win. Another variation that is more complicated but commonly used is dividing the class into rows or teams. The teacher draws a grid for each team and for himself. Feedback might sound like this: *"Teams 1, 3, and 4 were listening and have earned points."* *"I've earned a point on Teams 2 and 4's grid because some people did not remember to follow with their fingers."* In the beginning, the teacher needs to give frequent feedback, awarding points after every one or two answers. Later, when students are accustomed to answering together and rarely cause disruptions that interfere with work, the teacher can award points after an entire section of the lesson.

that these teachers frequently praised students' work and their behavior, in contrast to criticizing them.

In classrooms that are positive learning environments, teachers make three or four positive comments about students' work or behavior to every one criticism or correction (McEwan & Damer, 2000). When this ratio is reversed, the teacher is caught in a criticism trap, and students learn less and actually increase their misbehavior. If students come to school uncooperative and without school readiness skills, a teacher needs to consistently praise social behaviors such as staying in a seat, answering on the teacher's signal, and keeping hands to oneself in addition to correct answers or effort put into schoolwork. If that praise alone is not enough to maintain the necessary 3:1 ratio of positive-to-negative teacher comments, the teacher needs to develop a student motivational system. If only one or two students need the additional motivation to be successful, the teacher can plan a motivational system just for them. Otherwise, the teacher can plan a class or group strategy for injecting positive motivation. Some teachers will find that extra motivation is only necessary to diminish frustration when students are first learning new skills or when they are practicing difficult ones. Strategies for motivating students who are at risk are described throughout this book. Table 1.3 shows what to do and what not to do when using all of the teaching enhancements just described. The *In Your Classroom* feature tells how to motivate your students using the Teacher–Class Game.

TABLE 1.3   Instructional Enhancements—What to Do and Not Do

	Examples What to do	Nonexamples What not to do
Advance Organizers	The teacher starts the lesson by saying, "Today we are going to learn a new letter sound and read words the fast way. This will help you learn how to read so you can decide what kind of ice cream you want when you read the Dairy Queen menu." The teacher places symbols for activities on the board as she describes them. "First we will practice a new tiger-roaring letter sound; then you will read some words that will be in our story. Today's story is about a red rabbit that gets mixed up about everything! Remember to sit up tall, keep your hands and feet to yourself, and answer when I signal."	The teacher begins the lesson by saying, "I'll sound out a word very slowly; then you read the whole word fast, like we've done before." When the teacher says "/m/-/a/-/n/," one student shouts, "man." The teacher tells the students to start over and wait for her to clap her hands before they answer.
Unison Responding	The teacher asks all of the students in the group to sound out a word by saying the sound of each letter in the word when she touches under it.	Individual students take turns coming to the board to sound out regular words.
	The teacher asks all of the students in the group to say the first sound in the spelling word *ran* when she drops her hand.	The teacher doesn't use a visual signal when students in unison read words that are on the word wall. Some hesitant students in the group consistently answer late, reading the words a second after the more fluent readers.
Efficient Use of Teacher Talk	Wanting students to read a row of words written on the board, the teacher points to the first word and says, "Sound it out. Get ready." The teacher then signals by touching under each letter as students sound out the word.	Wanting students to read a row of words, the teacher points to the first word and says, "Let's sound out this word. It's one we've worked on before. See if you can remember it. Careful now. Don't forget. This word is a weird one."
	The teacher points to the letter combination *sh* and asks, "What sound?"	The teacher points to the letter combination *sh* and says, "Let's read the sound of these two letters. Remember the rhyme we always say every morning about them. Tanya, that is always your favorite rhyme! What is the sound these two letters make when they come together in a word?"
Perky Pace	The teacher points to the first sight word on the list and asks, "What word?" and then when students read it correctly moves immediately to the next word.	The teacher points to the first sight word on the list and asks, "What word?" The students answer correctly. The teacher pauses at least 5 seconds between the student answer and the next sight word. The delay could be due to the teacher's excessive talking, a slow reaction time, or the time required to put the next word on the board.
	The teacher writes the letters for the letter–sounds activity on the board before the daily reading lesson begins.	The teacher writes the *ch* combination on the board and asks students what sound it makes. The teacher then says, "Let's try another one," and writes the next letter–sound combination on the board. The teacher continues this pattern of asking a question and writing the next letter–sound combination for the rest of the lesson.

TABLE 1.3 Continued

	Examples What to do	Nonexamples What not to do
My Turn—Together—Your Turn Format	The teacher says, "Today we are going to sound out some words for the first time," and models sounding out /m/-/a/-/n/ = *man*. Then the teacher has students sound out the word twice with him before having them sound it out on their own. The teacher provides this support for the first four new words on the list and then asks students to read the rest of the new words on their own.	The teacher says, "Today we are going to sound out some words for the first time." Then the teacher asks students to sound out /m/-/a/-/n/ = *man* one time. About 60% of the students loudly answer, and the teacher moves on to the next word.
	The teacher points to a new letter combination, *ar,* which is written on the board and says, "These letters say /ar/. Listen again: /ar/." The students then say /ar/. The teacher continues, "When I touch, you say the sound." The teacher points then touches under /ar/. "What sound?" Note that this task does not require a Together step unless students have trouble articulating the /ar/ sound.	The teacher points to a new letter combination *ar* on the board and says, "This is the sound you hear in *park*. What sound do these letters make?" The teacher then moves on to another letter sound.
Cumulative Review	The teacher just introduced regular words that begin with *s* blends such as *stop* and *slow*. When the students are able to correctly read the *s* blend words, the teacher has the students read a list of words containing *s* blends plus other previously learned words beginning with *sh* and *th*.	The teacher just introduced regular words that begin with *s* blends, such as *stop* and *slow*. When the students are able to read a list of words beginning with *s* blends, the teacher introduces words with *p* blends.
	The teacher included two more difficult words from last week's spelling list on the spelling list for this week.	The teacher's spelling list this week has fifteen new words and no review words from previous lessons.
Systematic Error Correction	During a letter–sound teaching activity, the teacher touches the letter combination *ch* and asks, "What sound?" The student says /sh/. The teacher responds, "These letters say /ch/. What sound?" The teacher then provides extra practice by alternately asking the student to say the sound for *sh* and six other sounds previously learned. Later in the lesson, she asks the student one more time to tell the sound for *sh*.	During a letter–sound teaching activity, the student says /sh/ when the teacher points to *ch*. The teacher says, "No, think about something good to eat." After the student names foods, the teacher says, "Chocolate is good to eat. What letters does chocolate begin with? Do you see those letters on the board? What sound do they make?" When the student says /ch/, the teacher moves on to the next word.
	During a sight word reading, the teacher points to the word *ghost* and says, "What word?" Several students pronounce the word incorrectly. The teacher says, "The word is *ghost*. What is this word?" When students answer correctly, the teacher returns to the top of the list of five words and has the students read all five words again, including the word *ghost*.	During a sight word reading activity, the students say *gets* when they see the word *ghost*. The teacher says, "The word is *ghost*. Let's try the next word."

Continued

TABLE 1.3 Continued

	Examples What to do	**Nonexamples** What not to do
Teaching to Success	The teacher introduced the *ou* sound to her students for the first time. The next day she tested her students to see if they could identify the *ou* sound when it was mixed in with the previously learned combinations of *sh, ea, ow,* and *th.* Her students made repeated errors on the *ou* sound and missed *th* and *sh* as well. The following day, the teacher decided to provide more practice on all of the sounds from the day before. She would only introduce *ar* when the students were able to identify these other sounds correctly.	The teacher introduced the *ou* sound to her students for the first time. The next day she tested her students to see if they could identify the *ou* sound when it was mixed in with the previously learned letter combinations of *sh, ea, ow,* and *th.* Her students made repeated errors on the *ou* sound and missed *th* and *sh* as well. The following day the teacher introduced a new letter combination: *ar.*
	The teacher had her students read today's story orally. The group made 20 errors, reading the story with about 88% accuracy. The following day the teacher provided a drill for the students on the words missed the previous day. She also had the students reread the story until they read it with 97% accuracy.	The teacher had her students read today's story orally. The group made 20 errors, reading the story with about 88% accuracy. The following day the teacher moved to the next story in the book.
Student Motivational System	During small-group instruction, Billy often leaves his seat. The teacher frequently praises Billy for staying in his seat and working so hard. She also praises other students for staying in their seats. The teacher seldom has to tell Billy to come back to his seat.	During small-group instruction, Billy often leaves his seat. Often when Billy leaves his seat, the teacher says, "Billy, if you can't pay attention, I'll have to call your mom." The teacher does not praise Billy when he is in his seat.
	While sight-reading a list of words, students continue to miss a number of them. Before reading through the list again, the teacher tells the students that their goal is reading every word correctly. This time, she praises the students immediately after each of the sight words is read correctly. When the list is finished, she smiles and exclaims, "I knew you could do it. Every one right! Give yourself a pat on the back!"	While sight-reading a list of words, students continue to miss a number of them. Each time they miss a word, the teacher makes a comment like, "This sure is a bad day," or "I don't know what you are all thinking about." When students continue to make mistakes, the teacher ends the lesson saying, "Maybe tomorrow you will all be awake."

APPLIED ACTIVITIES

1. Explain what is wrong about each nonexample in Table 1.3. Be sure to focus your answer on the particular enhancement in question.
2. Think of the most difficult class you had this past year. If the teacher used a My Turn–Together–Your Turn strategy to support your success in learning the material, describe how that teaching strategy was used. If the teacher did not use a My Turn–Together–Your Turn strategy, describe how that strategy could have been used to help you more successfully learn the course material.

3. Have you worked for a boss who maintained a 3:1 ratio of positive comments to critical comments? Have you worked for a boss who had a ratio of 3:1 critical comments to positive comments? How did you feel about each of these individuals for whom you worked? Who was more motivating and why? How did you behave differently for each of these individuals?
4. Describe your experience as a student with a teacher who used unison responses as part of his or her teaching technique. How did the teacher get everyone to answer and how well did you learn the material?

Companion Website

Now go to Chapter 1 in the Companion Website (www.pearsonhighered.com/bursuck2e) where you can do the following activities:

- Complete Activities that can help you more deeply understand the chapter content.
- Check your comprehension on the content covered in the chapter by going to the Chapter Quiz. Here you will be able to an-

swer practice questions, receive feedback on your answers, and then access resources that will enhance your understanding of chapter content.

- Find Web Links that will extend your understanding of the content and strategies.

REFERENCES

Adams, M. (1990). *Beginning to read: Thinking and learning about print.* Cambridge, MA: MIT Press.

Adams, M. S., & Bruck, M. (1993). Word recognition: The interface of educational policies and scientific research. *Reading and Writing: An Interdisciplinary Journal, 5,* 113–139.

Ameis, J. (2003). *Early years e-text book: Three stages of teaching* [Electronic version]. Retrieved June 7, 2009, from University of Winnipeg Department of Education: http://web.archive.org/web/20070807070201/http://io.uwinnipeg.ca/~jameis/New+Pages/EYR5.html

American Federation of Teachers (2007). Where we stand: K–12 literacy. [Electronic version]. Retrieved June 7, 2009, from http://www.aft.org/pubs-reports/downloads/teachers/WWS-K12literacy.pdf

Archer, A. (Speaker). (1995). *The time is now* [Cassette recording]. Eugene, OR: World Association of Direct Instruction 21st Annual Conference.

Archer, A., Gleason, M. M., & Vachon, V. (2003). Decoding and fluency: Foundation skills for struggling older readers. *Learning Disability Quarterly, 26,* 89–101.

Armbruster, B., Lehr, F., & Osborn, J. (2001). *Put reading first: The research building blocks for teaching children to read.* Washington, DC: Partnership for Reading.

Arndt, E., & Crawford, E. (2006). Effective reading interventions: Characteristics, resources and implications for SLPs [Electronic version]. Retrieved July 27, 2009, from http://www.fcrr.org/science/powerpoint/crawford/ASHA2006presentation.ppt

Ball, E. W., & Blachman, B. A. (1991). Does phoneme awareness training in kindergarten make a difference in early word recognition and developmental spelling? *Reading Research Quarterly, 24,* 49–66.

Beck, I., McKeown, M., & Kucan, L. (2002). *Bringing words to life: Robust vocabulary instruction.* New York: The Guilford Press.

Biemiller, A. (2001). Teaching vocabulary: Early, direct, and sequential. *The American Educator, 25*(1), 24–28.

Brown-Chidsey, R., & Steege, M. (2005). *Response to Intervention: Principles and strategies for effective practice.* New York: The Guilford Press.

Bursuck, W., & Damer, M. (2005). *Project PRIDE* (CFDA 84.334T August 2005 Final Report). Unpublished manuscript.

Bursuck, B., Smith, T., Munk, D., Damer, M., Mehlig, L., & Perry, J. (2004). Evaluating the impact of a prevention-based model of reading on children who are at risk. *Remedial and Special Education, 25,* 303–313.

Catts, H. W., Fey, M. E., Zhang, X., & Tomblin, J. B. (1999). Language basis of reading and reading disabilities: Evidence from a longitudinal investigation. *Scientific Studies of Reading, 3,* 331–361.

Damer, M., Bursuck, W., & Harris, R. (2008, Spring). A year later: Performance of students who exit Tier 3 direct instruction within a multi-tier reading model. *Direct Instruction News.*

Deno, S. L. (2003). Developments in curriculum-based measurement. *Journal of Special Education, 37,* 184–192.

Edmonds, M. S., Vaughn, S., Wexler, J., Reutebuch, C., Cable, A., Klingner, J., & Tackett, K. (2009). A synthesis of reading interventions and effects on reading comprehension outcomes for older struggling readers. *Review of Educational Research, 79,* 262–300.

Ehri, L. C. (2005). Learning to read words: Theory, findings, and issues. *Scientific Studies of Reading, 9,* 167–188.

Elbaum, B., Vaughn, S., Hughes, M. T., & Moody, S. W. (2000). Grouping practices and reading outcome for students with disabilities. *Exceptional Children, 65,* 399–415.

Englert, C., Tarrant, K., & Mariage, T. (1992). Defining and redefining instructional practice in special education: Perspectives on good teaching. *Teacher Education and Special Education, 15*(2), 62–86.

Engelmann, Z. (2007). *Teaching needy kids in our backward system.* Eugene, OR: ADI Press.

Fisher, C., Berliner, D., Filby, N., Marliave, R., Cahen, L., & Dishaw, M. (1980). Teaching behaviors, academic learning time, and student achievement: An overview. In C. Denham & A. Lieberman (Eds.), *Time to learn: A review of the Beginning Teacher Evaluation Study* (pp. 7–32). Washington, DC: Department of Health, Education, and Welfare.

Foorman, B., & Torgesen, J. (2001). Critical elements of classroom and small-group instruction promote reading success in all children. *Learning Disabilities Research & Practice, 16,* 203–212.

Francis, D. J., Shaywitz, S. E., Stuebing, K. K., Fletcher, J. M., & Shaywitz, B. A. (1996). Developmental lag vs. deficit models of reading disability: A longitudinal individual growth curves analysis. *Journal of Educational Psychology, 1,* 3–17.

Friend, M., & Bursuck, W. D. (2009). *Including students with special needs: A practical guide for classroom teachers* (4th ed.) Boston: Pearson/Allyn & Bacon.

Friend, M., & Cook, L. (2007). *Interactions: Collaborative skills for school professionals* (5th ed.). Boston: Allyn & Bacon.

Fuchs, L., Fuchs, D., Hosp, M., & Jenkins, J. (2001). Oral reading fluency as an indicator of reading competence: A theoretical, empirical, and historical analysis. *Scientific Studies of Reading, 5,* 239–256.

Gersten, R., Compton, D., Connor, C. M., Dimino, J., Santoro, L., Linan-Thompson, S., & Tilly, W. D. (2009). Assisting students struggling with reading: Response to Intervention and multi-tier intervention for reading in the primary grades. A practice guide (NCEE 2009-4045) [Electronic version]. Washington, DC: National Center for Education Evaluation and Regional Assistance, Institute of Education Sciences, U.S. Department of Education. Retrieved May 28, 2009, from http://ies.ed.gov/ncee/wwc/publications/practiceguides/

Gough, P. (1983). Context, form, and interaction. In K. Rayner (Ed.), *Eye movements in reading* (pp. 331–358). Cambridge, MA: MIT Press.

Hall, S., & Moats, L. (1999). *Straight talk about reading.* Chicago: Contemporary Books.

Hart, B., & Risley, T. (1995). *Meaningful differences.* Baltimore: Paul H. Brookes Publishing.

Honig, B. (2001). *Teaching our children to read: The components of an effective, comprehensive reading program.* Thousand Oaks, CA: Corwin Press.

Hoover, J. J., & Patton, J. R. (2008). The role of special educators in a multitiered instructional system. *Remedial and Special Education, 43,* 195–202.

Jenkins, J. (2009). Measuring reading growth: New findings on progress monitoring. *New Times for DLD, 27,* pp. 1–2.

Jenkins, J., & Johnson, E. (2007). Universal screening for reading problems: Why and how should we do this? Retrieved June 11, 2009, from RTI Action Network: http://www.rtinetwork.org/Essential/Assessment/Universal/ar/ReadingProblems

Juel, C. (1988). Retention and nonretention of at-risk readers in first grade and their subsequent reading achievement. *Journal of Learning Disabilities, 21,* 571–580.

Kame'enui, E., Good, R., Simmons, D., & Chard, D. (2002). Project CIRCUITS: Toward a primary, secondary, and tertiary prevention system in schools. Paper presented at the Annual Convention of the Council for Exceptional Children, New York.

Kame'enui, E. (2007) An Interview with Edward Kame'enui [Electronic version]. Retrieved from http://www.pbs.org/launchingreaders/soundsandsymbols/meettheexperts_2.html

Lee, J., Grigg, W., & Donahue, P. (2007). *The nation's report card: Reading 2007* (NCES 2007-496). National Center for Education Statistics, Institute of Education Sciences, U.S. Department of Education, Washington, DC.

Lemoine, H. E., Levy, B. A., & Hutchinson, A. (1993). Increasing the naming speed of poor readers: Representations formed across repetitions. *Journal of Experimental Child Psychology, 55,* 297–328.

Lyon, R. (1998). Why reading is not a natural activity. *Educational Leadership, 3,* 14–18.

Lyon, R. (1998, April 28). *Overview of reading and literacy initiatives.* Statement to Committee on Labor and Human Resources, Bethesda, MD [Electronic version]. Retrieved from http://www.dys-add.com/ReidLyonJeffords.pdf

Marzano, R. J. (2003). *What works in schools: Translating research into action.* Alexandria, VA: Association for Supervision and Curriculum Development.

McEwan, E., & Damer, M. (2000). *Managing unmanageable students.* Thousand Oaks, CA: Corwin Press.

National Reading Panel. (2000). *Teaching children to read: An evidence-based assessment of the scientific research literature on reading and its implications for reading instruction.* Washington, DC: National Institute of Child Health and Human Development.

National Early Literacy Panel. (2008). *Developing early literacy: Report of the National Early Literacy Panel.* Washington, DC: National Institute for Literacy.

Ornstein, A. C., & Lasley, T. J. II (2004). *Strategies for effective teaching* (4th ed.). New York: McGraw-Hill.

Pisha, B., & Stahl, S. (2005). The promise of new learning environments for students with disabilities. *Intervention in School and Clinic, 41,* 67–75.

Pressley, M., Wharton-McDonald, R., Allington, R., Block, C., Morrow, L., Tracey, D., et al. (2001). A study of effective first-grade literacy instruction. *Scientific Studies of Reading, 5*(1), 35–58.

RAND Reading Study Group. (2002). Reading for understanding: Toward an R&D program in reading comprehension [Electronic version]. Retrieved May 17, 2009, from http://www.rand.org/pubs/monograph_reports/MR1465/

Rosenshine, B. (1986). Synthesis of research on explicit teaching. *Educational Leadership, 43*(7), 60–69.

Shaywitz, S. (2003). *Overcoming dyslexia: A new and complete science-based program for reading problems at any level.* New York: Knopf.

Shaywitz, S. E., & Shaywitz, B. E. (2007). What neuroscience really tells us about reading instruction. *Educational Leadership, 64,* 74–76.

Simos, P. G., Fletcher, J. M., Sarkari, S., Billingsley-Marshall, R. L., Denton, C. A., & Papanicolaou, A. C. (2007). Intensive instruction affects brain magnetic activity associated with oral word reading in children with persistent reading disabilities. *Journal of Learning Disabilities, 40,* 37–48.

Speece, D. L., & Ritchey, K. D. (2005). A longitudinal study of the development of oral reading fluency in young children at risk for reading failure. *Journal of Learning Disabilities, 38,* 387–399.

Stahl, S., & Nagy, W. (2006). *Teaching word meanings.* Mahwah, NJ: Lawrence Erlbaum Associates.

Steinbeck, J. (1976). The acts of King Arthur and his noble knights: Introduction to his translation of *Le Morte d'Arthur.* In *The Winchester Manuscripts of Thomas Malory & Other Sources* (pp. 3–4). Portsmouth, NH: Heinemann Publishing Company.

Stichter, J., Stormont, M., & Lewis, T. (2009). Instructional practices and behavior during reading: A descriptive summary and comparison of practices in title one and non-title elementary schools. *Psychology in the Schools, 46,* 172–183.

Torgesen, J. K. (2000). Individual differences in response to early interventions in reading: The lingering problem of treatment resisters. *Learning Disabilities Research and Practice, 15,* 55–64.

Vellutino, F. R., Scanlon, D. M., Sipay, E. R., Small, S. G., Pratt, A., Chen, R., et al. (1996). Cognitive profiles of difficult-to-remediate and readily remediated poor readers: Early intervention as a vehicle for distinguishing between cognitive and experiential deficits as basic causes of specific reading disability. *Journal of Educational Psychology, 88,* 601–638.

Venezky, R. L. (1970). *The structure of English orthography.* The Hague: Mouton.

Wanzek, J., & Vaughn, S. (2008). Response to varying amounts of time in reading intervention for students with low response to intervention. *Journal of Learning Disabilities, 41,* 126–142.

Wendorf, J. (2003, September 10). Interview: *Children of the code* [Electronic version]. Interviewer: David Boulton. Retrieved March 24, 2009, from http://www.childrenofthecode.org/interviews/wendorf.htm#TheCostsofTeachingReading

Whitehurst, G. (2003, September 10). Interview: *Evidence-based education science and the challenge of learning to read* [Electronic version]. Interviewer: David Boulton. Retrieved May 12, 2009, from http://www.childrenofthecode.org/interviews/whitehurst.htm

Wijk, A. (1966). *Rules of pronunciation for the English language.* Oxford: Oxford University Press.

Wolf, M., & Katzir-Cohen, T. (2001). Reading fluency and its intervention. *Scientific Studies of Reading, 5,* 211–238.

Wren, S. (2000). *Reading by sight* [Electronic version]. Retrieved June 6, 2009, from the Southwest Educational Development Laboratory Web site: http://www.sedl.org/reading/topics/sightwords.pdf

CHAPTER

2 Phonemic Awareness

Objectives

After reading this chapter, you will be able to:

1. Identify and pronounce sounds needed to teach phonemic awareness and beginning word reading skills to students who are at risk.

2. Identify and describe the sequence of the essential phonemic awareness skills of segmenting and blending and implement teaching strategies to enhance phonemic awareness instruction.

3. Identify and describe key assessments for measuring segmenting and blending skills and use assessment data to identify students who are at risk, diagnose skill deficits, and monitor instructional progress in a multi-tier or RTI model.

4. Implement teaching strategies to provide Tier 2 support and identify and describe the phonemic awareness component of five commonly used intensive Tier 3 reading programs.

5. Explain how instruction in phonemic awareness can be carried out with English language learners and older students.

6. Describe ways games and activities can be used to provide more practice with phonemic awareness skills.

Companion Website

To check your comprehension of the content covered in this chapter, go to the Companion Website (www.pearsonhighered.com/bursuck2e) and complete the Chapter Quiz for Chapter 2. Here you will be able to answer practice questions, receive feedback on your answers, and then access resources that will enhance your understanding of chapter content.

Most of the parents in Ms. Mabin's school couldn't afford to get a babysitter on parent-conference night, so it wasn't unusual to see them arrive for their conference with three or four children in tow. Thus, when Ms. Mabin walked out into the hall to get Lydell Jackson's parents, she expected the usual hubbub of tired children who would rather be at home. Instead, she noticed that two of her first graders were sitting with their younger brothers and sisters playing teacher. Imitating Ms. Mabin's tone of voice and gestures, Lydell reminded his younger siblings to look at him as he thrust out a finger for each sound "/b//a//t/. What word?" The two preschool-aged twins smugly replied, "bat."

Across the hall, Syraiah's brother was struggling to say the first sound in each word that Syraiah said and so, just like Ms. Mabin, Syraiah corrected him with the phrase, *"My Turn,"* before saying the sound and asking him to repeat it. During recess, Ms. Mabin had noticed the children playing "teacher" on the playground, doing the same phonemic awareness activities she'd done that morning with them in large group. Some of the students in her class were so adept with their signals, that she gave them a turn teaching as a special reward. Seeing herself imitated so well, even the way she praised the children for their hard work, was a bit unnerving. Ms. Mabin reflected that if her students were going home and practicing phonemic awareness skills with their younger siblings, her job would be much easier in the next year or two when those children came to her as first graders. Many of her students had never been read to as children and struggled blending simple sounds into words. By playing "teacher," her students were engaging their siblings in valuable word play that would ultimately make the task of learning to read much easier.

Why do you think Ms. Mabin's class liked to play teacher?

Why is student practice such an important feature of effective reading instruction?

What Letter Sounds Do Teachers Need to Know for Teaching Phonemic Awareness and Phonics Skills to Students Who Are at Risk?

Before teaching phonemic awareness or beginning word reading (Chapter 3), you need to know how to clearly pronounce the basic letter sounds as well as teach them to your students. Too often teachers mispronounce or incorrectly articulate the individual letter sounds with an extra /uh/ at the end. This extra phoneme, called a schwa, sometimes prevents students who are at risk from learning to blend, segment, or sound out words. If the teacher adds schwas to the end of letter sounds, even though she intends to ask students to blend the three sounds /p/-/a/-/t/ into the word *pat*, she is instead asking them to blend /puh/-/a/-/tuh/. Rather then simply blending these three sounds into a word, now the students must first take off the two /uh/ endings before saying the word *pat*.

Using the Chart of Letter Sounds

The letter-sounds chart in Table 2.1 lists information about phonemes that will help you say and teach them. You should study this chart and become fully familiar with it. Exercises at the end of this chapter will help you get started. Here are some pointers to orient you:

1. The Phonetic Pronunciation column lists a word or words that contain the letter sound.
2. Sounds that are produced when the vocal cords are vibrating are called **voiced sounds**. Sounds that are produced when the vocal cords do not vibrate are called **unvoiced sounds**. If you put your fingertips on your throat, you can feel the vibration for voiced sounds. Often, when students cannot hear the difference between two sounds, the sounds are identical with the exception that one is voiced and the other unvoiced. Say the sounds for /b/ and /p/. Notice that when you say each one, both of your lips pop open and the sound pops out of your mouth with a burst of air. But when you put your hand to your throat while saying /b/, you feel the vocal chord vibration,

TABLE 2.1 Using the Correct Sounds in Effective Phonics Instruction

Letter Sound	Phonetic Pronunciation	Voiced or Unvoiced	Articulation	Stop or Continuous Sound? ⚠ = don't add a schwa	When Students Have Difficulty Saying the New Letter Sound:
/ă/	as in *sat*	voiced	Widely spread smiling mouth position; tongue low in mouth.	continuous	Ask students to cry like a baby as they say the sound. If students have difficulty distinguishing /ă/ from /ĕ/, ask them to put their hand on their jaw as they say *bed* and *bat*. They will feel their jaw lower when they say /ă/.
/ā/	as in *bake*	voiced	More open smiling mouth position; tongue in middle of mouth; increased mouth tension.	continuous	Ask students to make a big smile as they say the sound, /ā ā ā/.
/b/	as in *bell, baby,* and *tab*	voiced	Both lips pop open; sound pops out of mouth with a burst of air.	stop ⚠	Show students how their lips pop open when they say the sound. Have students a hold a piece of paper close to their mouths as they say the sound.
/k/	as in *cat, maker,* and *tack*	unvoiced	Back part of tongue in contact with the soft palate toward the back of the mouth; tongue drops and a burst of air is expelled.	stop ⚠	Ask students to touch the back of the roof of their mouth the first time they say /k/. Have them hold their hand in front of their mouth and feel the pop of air.
/d/	as in *dog, sudden,* and *bad*	voiced	Tongue taps behind upper teeth, drops, and a sound pops out of mouth with a burst of air.	stop ⚠	Model how the tip of your tongue goes up and down as you say the sound. Ask them to make the hard popping sound of /d/, overemphasizing the sound to clearly differentiate it from /t/.
/ĕ/	as in *pen*	voiced	Smiling mouth position; tongue centered in the mid front.	continuous	Recognize that this is often the most difficult vowel to pronounce. See the last tip for /ă/. Ask students first to say easy words with /ĕ/, before saying just the sound: (*Ed*, /ĕ/; *egg*, /ĕ/).

TABLE 2.1 Continued

Letter Sound	Phonetic Pronunciation	Voiced or Unvoiced	Articulation	Stop or Continuous Sound? ⚠ = don't add a schwa	When Students Have Difficulty Saying the New Letter Sound:
/ē/	as in *feet*	voiced	Smiling mouth position with lips open wide; tongue high in mouth near front; increased mouth tension.	continuous	Ask students to smile as if for a picture and say /ē ē ē ē/. Exaggerate the tense spread of lips.
/f/	as in *fish, safer,* and *calf*	unvoiced	Upper front teeth on lower lip: air gust expelled between the teeth and lip.	continuous	Ask students to bite on their lower lip and blow.
/g/	as in *go, hugging,* and *tag.*	voiced	Back part of the tongue in contact with the soft palate toward the back of the mouth; tongue drops and sound pops out of mouth with a burst of air.	stop ⚠	Ask students to grab the top part of their neck as they say the sound, feeling the vibration.
/h/	as in *hat* and *enhance*	unvoiced	Air gust quickly expelled; tongue and mouth assume position of vowel following /h/.	stop ⚠	Have students silently blow air on their upraised hand or on a feather.
/ĭ/	as in *pin*	voiced	Lips are parted and spread; tongue is high.	continuous	Have students make the icky sound they would say after seeing something disgusting.
/ī/	as in *like*	voiced	Smiley face; tongue and jaw raise to a high position.	continuous	Ask students to first say words with /ī/, then to say /ī/ (ice, /ī/; mice, /ī/.)
/j/	as in *jet* and *enjoy*	voiced	Tip of tongue briefly contacts the roof of mouth; a burst of air is expelled with sound.	stop ⚠	Ask students to make the sound a large train engine makes: /j/ /j/ /j/.
/l/	as in *lip, mailing,* and *fill*	voiced	Tongue tip lifts behind upper teeth; air passes over sides of tongue.	continuous	Practice saying "la-la" to watch the tongue move. Raise and lower the tongue to create awareness.

Continued

TABLE 2.1 Continued

Letter Sound	Phonetic Pronunciation	Voiced or Unvoiced	Articulation	Stop or Continuous Sound? ⚠ = don't add a schwa	When Students Have Difficulty Saying the New Letter Sound:
/m/	as in *man, summer,* and *same*	voiced	Lips pressed together; air expelled through nose.	nasal: continuous	Have students imagine that they smell a pizza and ask them to press their lips together saying /mmmm/.
/n/	as in *nap, sunny,* and *in*	voiced	Front of tongue behind upper teeth; sides of tongue touch side teeth; air expelled through nose.	nasal: continuous	Have students pinch their nostrils as they say the sound of a mosquito.
/ŏ/	as in *pop*	voiced	Lips are tightly rounded; back part of tongue is low in mouth; jaw is open wide.	continuous	Ask students to pretend they are at the doctor's office and must open their mouths to say /ŏŏŏ/
/ō/	as in *rope*	voiced	Rounded mouth that shuts like a camera shutter; tongue in middle; increased mouth tension.	continuous	Have students form their mouth into a circle just like the letter *o*.
/p/	as in *pet, hippo,* and *lip*	unvoiced	Both lips pop open and air blows out.	stop ⚠	Have students blow a feather to experience the airflow.
/q/ = /kw/	as in *queen*	unvoiced	/qu/ sounds like /kw/ and is comprised of two phonemes. Refer to the description of those letter sounds and say this sound, quickly blending them together into one sound. Immediately pronounce the next vowel sound after the *u*.	continuous	Ask students to make the sound of a cuckoo clock: "kwoo-kwoo."
/r/	as in *rip, marry,* and *stare*	voiced	Tongue tip slightly bunches towards the center of the mouth; sides of tongue touch upper back gums and teeth; mouth puckers.	continuous	Ask students to make the sound of a lion roaring.

TABLE 2.1 Continued

Letter Sound	Phonetic Pronunciation	Voiced or Unvoiced	Articulation	Stop or Continuous Sound? ⚠ = don't add a schwa	When Students Have Difficulty Saying the New Letter Sound:
/s/	as in *sad, missing,* and *fuss.*	unvoiced	Top of tongue behind upper teeth toward front of mouth; air blowing out.	continuous	Ask students to put their fingers in front of their mouths to feel the air as they say the sound. Ask students to make a long hissing snake sound /sssss/ or the sound of air coming out of a balloon.
/t/	as in *tub, bottom,* and *hat*	unvoiced	Tongue taps behind upper teeth.	stop ⚠	Ask students to make the sound of a ticking watch. Have them look at or feel the tip of their tongues going up and down. Ask them to feel the pop of air on their hand.
/ŭ/	as in *mud*	voiced	Lips slightly parted; tongue at rest in center of mouth.	continuous	Ask students to make the sound they would make if punched in the stomach or the sound they make when they don't know an answer.
/ū/	as in *use*	voiced	Sounds like /y/ + /oo/; refer to those letter sounds.	continuous	Have students point an index finger at other students and in a scolding voice say, "you, you, you."
/v/	as in *vest, heavy,* and *save.*	voiced	Upper front teeth on lower lip. Air gust expelled between teeth and lip.	continuous	Ask students to make the sound of a big flying insect.
/w/	as in *well* and *sandwich*	voiced	Round your lips as if you are going to pronounce /ū/; vibrate your vocal cords for a very short /woo/ sound; then open your lips to pronounce the next sound in the word.	continuous	Ask students to pucker their lips as if about to kiss and then push the sound out. Ask students to hoot like owls in the forest at night. Be sure to keep your lips in a circle and don't overpronounce the /oo/.
/x/	as in *fox* and *mixer*	unvoiced	/x/ sounds like /ks/; refer to the description of those letter sounds.		Say the word *box,* exaggerating the /ks/ sound. Then ask the students to repeat the /ks/ sound. Repeat several familiar words ending in /x/, repeating the /ks/ letter sound after each word (*box,* /x/; *fix,* /x/).

Continued

TABLE 2.1 Continued

Letter Sound	Phonetic Pronunciation	Voiced or Unvoiced	Articulation	Stop or Continuous Sound? ⚠ = don't add a schwa	When Students Have Difficulty Saying the New Letter Sound:
/y/	as in *yes* and *yo-yo*.	voiced	Blade of tongue in middle of mouth; sounds like /yee/. Immediately pronounce the next vowel sound in the word.	continuous	Tell your students to make their lips smile as they say this sound. Be sure that you and they are not saying /ē/ for this sound.
/z/	as in *zoo, gazing,* and *fuzz*	voiced	Tongue behind upper teeth toward front of mouth; air blowing out.	continuous	Tell your students to feel the tickle when they make the buzzing bee sound: /zzzz/.

Source: Avery, P., & Ehrlich, S. (1992); Celce-Murcia, M., Brinton, D., & Goodwin, J. (1996); Ladefoged, P. (1975); Lott, D. (2007); McCormick, C., Throneburg, R., & Smitley, J. (2002); Singh, S., & Singh, K. (1976).

whereas you do not feel it when you say /p/. Other pairs include: /k/ and /g/; /t/ and /d/; /f/ and /v/; th and th; /ch/ and /j/; and /s/ and /z/. When students have difficulty hearing the difference between a similar voiced and unvoiced sound, an effective teaching technique is to have them feel the vibration or lack of it for themselves.

3. The Articulation column provides information about how the sound is produced. Knowing how each sound is articulated will help you work with students who are not able to reproduce the sound after you introduce it. If Treena cannot reproduce /n/, using a small hand mirror you can show her how the front of your tongue rests behind your upper teeth toward the front of your mouth while the air is expelled through your nose. Treena can then hold the mirror and practice as you help her reproduce the sound.

4. Knowing whether a sound is a stop or a continuous sound will also help you correctly articulate the sound. With **stop sounds**, the air is completely blocked before it is expelled either because the lips come together as with /p/ or because the tongue touches the upper mouth as when saying /d/. This air blockage accounts for the higher level of difficulty in learning to read words that begin with stop sounds. Avoiding schwa endings is also more difficult with stop sounds. With **continuous sounds**, also known as continuants, the airflow does not stop as the sound is pronounced, so the sound can be held as long as some air remains in the lungs. When first teaching a continuous letter sound, the teacher holds the sound for several seconds.

5. The last column in Table 2.1 is a list of tips that teachers use to help students who have difficulty reproducing the sound when it is first introduced.

We recommend that you use the phonetic pronunciation for each letter sound that reflects how the phoneme sounds when it is blended into words. The three letter sounds that may surprise you are /qu/, /w/, and /y/, but if you take apart words that contain those sounds, you can clearly hear the phonetic pronunciation. Try this test with /qu/, which Table 2.1 indicates is pronounced like /kwoo/. First say the word *quick*. Then say each sound slowly (/kwoo/ +/i/ +/ck/). Now blend those sounds together faster; and finally as fast as you can say them as you once again hear the word *quick*. Do this same exercise for /w/ = /woo/ and the word *will*; repeat the exercise a final time for /y/ = /yee/ and the word *yak*.

What Phonemic Awareness Skills Do I Need to Teach?

Words in the English language are made up of approximately 41 to 44 individual sounds called **phonemes** that are conventionally represented between slash marks. Phonemic awareness is the ability to hear these smallest units of sounds in spoken language and to manipulate them. The word *cat* has three phonemes (/c/ /a/ /t/), as does the word *shut* (/sh/ /u/ /t/), and the word *hope* (/h/ /ō/ /p/). Word-play activities, such as changing the first sound to make a new rhyming word to fit into a song or changing the last sound in a word to create another word, involve hearing and manipulating phonemes. Phonemic awareness falls under the broader category of **phonological awareness,** which involves perceiving and manipulating the sounds of language at the larger word and syllable levels as well as at the phoneme level. The phonemic awareness word-play activity described above and instruction that requires students to count words in a sentence or clap syllables in a word are activities that develop phonological awareness. Those activities that develop broader phonological awareness skills, such as rhyming games and word-play books requiring students to manipulate language, do not necessarily develop a child's phonemic awareness skills and are not directly related to later word reading (Rathvon, 2004).

Phonemic awareness is one of the critical foundational skills for learning to read, but children who are at risk are much less likely to develop phonemic awareness skills naturally. Fortunately, phonemic awareness skills can be taught. The National Reading Panel (2000) reported that phonemic awareness training not only developed phonemic awareness skills but also improved the reading and spelling performance of students who are at risk. A teacher's first important decision involves determining which phonemic awareness skills to teach. Figure 2.1 shows all of the possible choices. Notice that all of these skills rely on students hearing individual phonemes, not seeing them. As one of our teachers told us recently, "You can do phonemic awareness activities in the dark."

As stressed in Chapter 1, teachers can ill afford to spend time on skills that may be only marginally related to reading. Researchers have concluded that two skills have the most value when teaching children to read and that instruction directly teaching these phonemic awareness skills is more effective than instruction covering three or more. These two critical skills are segmenting and blending (National Reading Panel, 2000). Segmenting is the ability to break apart spoken words into their individual phonemes. A student who can segment says /f/ /i/ /sh/ when asked to say the sounds in *fish*. The ability to segment helps

---

Rhyming: What word rhymes with *can*?

Phoneme deletion: What word would be left if the /k/ sound were taken away from *cat*?

Word to word matching: Do *pen* and *pipe* begin with the same sound?

Blending: What word would we have if you put these sounds together: /s/-/ă/-/t/?

Sound isolation: What is the first sound in *rose*?

Phoneme segmentation: What sounds do you hear in the word *hot*?

Phoneme counting: How many sounds do you hear in the word *cake*?

Deleting phonemes: What sound do you hear in meat that is missing in *eat*?

Odd word out: What word starts with a different sound: *bag, nine, beach, bike*?

Sound to word matching: Is there a /k/ in *bike*?

FIGURE 2.1 Examples of Phonemic Awareness Tasks

Source: Stanovich, K. (1994). Romance and reality. *The Reading Teacher, 47*(4), 280–291.

students strategically attack words they will be reading in text and break words into phonemes when spelling. Blending, the opposite of segmenting, is the ability to say a spoken word when its individual phonemes are said slowly. A student who can blend says the word *fish* after the teacher slowly says the individual sounds, /f/-/ĭ/-/sh/. Blending enables students to read unfamiliar text by combining single sounds into any new word.

Effective instruction for students who are at risk is careful and deliberate, and a successful teacher needs to break down larger skills into their more basic components. The following list of blending and segmenting skills will help you guide students from the earliest, most basic segmenting and blending skills through more difficult ones.

Segmenting and Blending Sequence

1. **Segmenting: First Sound**

   Description: After hearing the teacher say a whole word, students identify the first sound in a word.

   Example skills: teacher: "What's the first sound in *cat*?"
   students: "/k/"

   teacher: "What's the first sound in *end*?"
   students: "/ĕ/"

2. **Blending: Onset-Rime**

   Description: After hearing the teacher slowly say the **onset** [the beginning sound(s) that precedes the vowel in a syllable] and the **rime** [the rest of the syllable that contains the vowel and all that follows it], students say the whole word.

   Example skills: teacher: "/s/-/ĕll/. What word?"
   students: "sell"

   teacher: teacher: "/m/-/āke/. What word?"
   students: "make"

3. **Segmenting: Onset-Rime**

   Description: After hearing the teacher say the whole word, students say the onset and the rime.

   Example skills: teacher: "Say the sounds in /pit/."
   students: "/p/-/ĭt/"

   teacher: "Take apart /home/."
   students: "/h/-/ōme/"

4. **Blending: Individual Sounds**

   Description: After hearing the teacher slowly say the individual sounds in the word, students say the whole word.

   Example skills: teacher: "/n/-/ă/-/p/. What word?"
   students: "nap"

   teacher: "/ă/ -/s/-/k/. What word?"
   students: "ask"

5. **Segmenting: Individual Sounds**

   Description: After hearing the teacher say the whole word, students say the individual sounds in the word.

   Example skills: teacher: "Say the sounds in /leg/."
   students: "/l/-/ĕ/-/g/"

   teacher: "Say the sounds in /stop/."
   students: "/s/-/t/-/ŏ/-/p/"

Phonemic awareness instruction for children in preschool or just beginning kindergarten should start at segmenting first sound. Once the majority of students have learned to segment first sound for each of the sounds you have taught in your classroom, begin teaching blending onset-rime. Gradually move through the skill sequence until students in your classroom are able to segment individual sounds. For first-grade students and older beginning readers, simply start blending and segmenting instruction at the individual sound level.

> Reading research conducted during the past decade highlights how a well-designed kindergarten curriculum can provide necessary prereading skills so that kindergarteners who are at risk are on track for reading in first grade. *What Kids Should Know Before Entering First Grade* describes key skills kindergarteners should have by the end of the year. **www.readingrockets.org/articles/381.**

How Do I Assess Phonemic Awareness Skills in a Multi-Tier or RTI Model?

Because segmenting and blending are important foundational skills for reading, teachers must first assess these skills to determine which skills students already know and which skills students still need to learn. Fall screening assessments for preschool, kindergarten, or first-grade students should minimally include at least one phonemic awareness measure. Assessing either blending or segmenting skills or both allows the teacher to determine from the beginning of the year which students need additional Tier 2 or Tier 3 support learning how to read. Some of the children who are identified as needing support from the beginning of kindergarten may need more intensive Tier 3 reading instruction until the end of second grade or longer, but for others the intensive support enables them to move to Tier 2 or Tier 1 by midyear kindergarten. By receiving early support in phonemic awareness skills, some students will stay on track to become grade-level readers. Because of factors that can influence a student's development in reading, screening assessments typically occur three times a year—beginning, middle, and end.

Screening Assessments for Phonemic Awareness

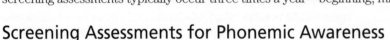

Throughout this book, subtests assessing skills highlighted in each chapter are described. These subtests have been selected from the four larger assessment batteries described in Appendix A, which are most frequently discussed in the RTI literature as being credible screening assessments that have established reliability and validity and are relatively quick and easy to administer. The Dynamic Indicators of Early Learning Skills (DIBELS) (Good & Kaminski, 2002) and AIMSweb (NCS Pearson, 2010) assess segmenting as the key phonemic awareness skill. DIBELS and AIMSweb timed assessments are almost identical in tasks, directions, and scoring procedures. PALS (Invernizzi & Meier, 2002) assesses both blending and segmenting tasks, whereas the Texas Primary Reading Inventory (TPRI) (Texas Education Agency and University of Texas System, 2006) assesses blending. The following section provides more specific information on how these tests are used to screen students in phonemic awareness.

Skill 1. Identification of Initial Sound in Words   Students who are at risk often begin school unable to identify the first sound in words. Even when teachers teach individual letter–sound correspondences, many students, unless provided with direct and explicit instruction, will not be able to identify first sounds in orally presented words. When giving the DIBELS or AIMSweb Initial Sound Fluency (ISF) assessment, the teacher presents four pictures to the student, names each picture, and then, for three of the pictures, asks the student to identify by pointing to or saying the picture that begins with the sound said orally by the teacher. For example, the teacher says, "This is *sink, cat, gloves*, and *hat*. Which picture begins with /s/?" In response, the student points to the correct picture. For the fourth picture, students are required to produce the first sound. For example, the teacher says, "What sound does *hat* begin with?" The student continues working until the last question is answered. Caution is advised when interpreting the initial sound fluency scores of English language learners or students with limited vocabularies. Because students sometimes do not remember the names for all four pictures, their low test score may reflect those limited language skills rather than segmenting ability. The untimed PALS-K Beginning Sound Awareness task avoids this picture identification problem by reducing the memory requirements. On the PALS-K subtest, students place a named card under one of four pictures that starts with the same sound immediately after the teacher says its name. The student repeats this action for ten picture cards.

When is it given?

- DIBELS and AIMSweb Initial Sound Segmentation Fluency or ISF: Fall and midyear of kindergarten
- PALS Individual Beginning Sound Awareness task: Fall and spring of kindergarten

At the official DIBELS website at **https://dibels.uoregon.edu/measures/psf.php** you can watch a teacher giving the phonemic segmentation fluency assessment to a student. Teachers whose school districts do not use established screening tests to determine which students need more support in critical phonemic awareness areas can download the phonemic segmentation fluency screening and progress-monitoring assessments at the same website. Directions to administer and score the test and copies of the tests can be downloaded at no charge.

Skill 2: Segmenting Individual Phonemes In the DIBELS and AIMSweb Phonemic Segmentation Fluency (PSF) subtests, students are presented with a series of spoken words and asked to say the phonemes or sounds in each word. The teacher says words for one minute and records the number of correct phonemes the student identifies in that time. Samples of completed DIBELS scoresheets are in Figures 2.2 and 2.3.

Benchmark scores indicate that a student has a high probability of meeting the next benchmark without the support of Tier 2 or Tier 3. Note that the DIBELS PSF end-of-kindergarten benchmark in Appendix B is reported as a range from 35 to 45 segments correct per minute. Teachers should set high expectations and aim to get as many students as possible to this benchmark by the end of the year. The higher figure of 45 should be used in situations where children have received systematic, explicit instruction in phonemic segmentation. Because of the practice students have had, higher benchmark cutoffs may be more predictive of future reading performance. The PSF assessment is difficult to score when students are rapidly saying phonemes and requires more teacher training

Name: Darrell

Date: May 21

bad	/b/ /a/ /d/	lock	/l/ /o/ /k/	6 / 6
that	/th/ /a/ /t/	pick	/p/ /i/ /ck/	6 / 6
mine	/m/ /ie/ /n/	noise	/n/ /oi/ /z/	5 / 6
coat	/c/ /oa/ /t/	spin	/s/ /p/ /i/ /n/	7 / 7
meet	/m/ /ea/ /t/	ran	/r/ /a/ /n/	6 / 6
wild	/w/ /ie/ /l/ /d/	dawn	/d/ /o/ /n/	6 / 7
woke	/w/ /oa/ /k/	sign	/s/ /ie/ /n/	6 / 6
fat	/f/ /a/ /t/	wait	/w/] /ai/ /t/	4 / 6
side	/s/ /ie/ /d/	yell	/y/ /e/ /l/	_ / 6
jet	/j/ /e/ /t/	of	/o/ /v/	_ / 5
land	/l/ /a/ /n/ /d/	wheel	/w/ /ea/ /l/	_ / 7
beach	/b/ /ea/ /ch/	globe	/g/ /l/ /oa/ /b/	_ / 7

Total 46 segments per minute

FIGURE 2.2 Darrell's DIBELS Phonemic Segmentation Fluency Score Sheet

Source: Good, R. H., & Kaminski, R. A. (Eds.). (2002). *Dynamic indicators of basic early literacy skills* (6th ed.). Eugene, OR: Institute for the Development of Educational Achievement. Available at http://dibels.uoregon.edu/.

Name: <u>Mose</u>

Date: <u>May 21</u>

bad	/b̲/ /a̶/ /d̶/	lock	/l̶/ /o̶/ /k̶/	<u>1</u>	6
that	/t̶h̶/ /a̶/ /t̶/	pick	/p̲/ /i̶/ /k̶/	<u>1</u>	6
mine	/m̲/ /i̶/ /n̶/	noise	/n̲/ /o̶i̶/ /z̶/	<u>2</u>	6
coat	/c̲/ /o̶a̶/ /t̶/	spin	/s̲/ /p̶/ /i̶/ /n̶/	<u>1</u>	7
meet	/m̲/ /e̶a̶/ /t̶/	ran	/r̲/ /a̶/ /n̶/]	<u>2</u>	6
wild	/w/ /ie/ / l/ /d/	dawn	/d/ /o/ /n/	_	7
woke	/w/ /oa/ /k/	sign	/s/ /ie/ /n/	_	6
fat	/f/ /a/ /t/	wait	/w/ /ai/ /t/	_	6
side	/s/ /ie/ /d/	yell	/y/ /e/ /l/	_	6
jet	/j/ /e/ /t/	of	/o/ /v/	_	5
land	/l/ /a/ /n/ /d/	wheel	/w/ /ea/ /l/	_	7
beach	/b/ /ea/ /ch/	globe	/g/ /l/ /oa/ /b/	_	7

Total   <u>7 segments per minute</u>

FIGURE 2.3 Mose's DIBELS Phonemic Segmentation Fluency Score Sheet

Source: Good, R. H., & Kaminski, R. A. (Eds.). (2002). *Dynamic indicators of basic early literacy skills* (6th ed.). Eugene, OR: Institute for the Development of Educational Achievement. Available at http://dibels.uoregon.edu/.

than any of the other phonemic awareness screening tests. Researchers have found that it is a less powerful predictor of a student's future reading achievement than other DIBELS or AIMSweb assessments (Catts, Petscher, Schatschneider, Bridges, & Mendoza, 2009)

In the untimed PALS Sound to Letter Task, students are asked to name the letter that corresponds to either the beginning, final, or middle sound of 40 designated words said by the teacher. Students are expected to gain this skill by the end of first grade

When is it given?

- DIBELS and AIMSweb Phonemic Segmentation Fluency (PSF): After the first semester of kindergarten through the beginning of second grade
- PALS Sound to Letter: Fall and spring of first grade or whenever a student in second or third grade fails the more difficult screening tests

Skill 3: Blending The beginning and end of kindergarten TPRI screening requires students to blend onset-rimes and phonemes into words (for onset-rime: teacher says "/c/" + "/at/" and the child says "cat"). By first grade, only individual phonemes are orally presented to students in this screening test. Blending is assessed in the first-grade PALS subtest by having students say a word after hearing a teacher slowly say the sounds in that word. The main differences between the TPRI and PALS blending tasks include the grade level at which administration begins, the benchmark criterion levels, and the length of words, with the TPRI presenting longer words with more phonemes.

When is it given?

- TPRI Blending: Beginning and end of kindergarten; beginning and end of first grade
- PALS Blending: Fall and spring of first grade unless a student in second or third grade fails the more difficult screening tests

Screening decisions to determine the support a student needs at the beginning of the year for kindergarten or for new students are more difficult to make since so often these students have not had research-based reading instruction. Thus, we recommend waiting

In Your Classroom

Identifying Students for Tier 3 in Kindergarten

Some districts wait until the middle or end of October to screen kindergartners so that students who come to school with few preliteracy skills but who respond quickly to instruction remain in Tier 1 or Tier 2. The decision about which students need Tier 3 instruction in a multi-tier or RTI program can be made based on their progress during the first two months of school. By October, the teacher will have introduced between three and five letter sounds, and the decision about how much support to provide is easier. Children whose initial screening indicates that they need Tier 3 support at the start of the school year, but whose progress monitoring shows that they are gaining phonemic awareness skills and at mastery learning the new letter sounds receive Tier 2 support. The other students whose screening indicates that they need Tier 3 support, but whose progress monitoring indicates that they did **not** gain phonemic awareness skills or learn the new letter sounds to mastery, move into the more intensive Tier 3. The combination of screening data plus individual student response to intervention results in more students remaining in Tier 1 and Tier 2 than the beginning-of-year tests would have projected. Figure 2.4 describes the steps involved in screening students at the beginning of kindergarten

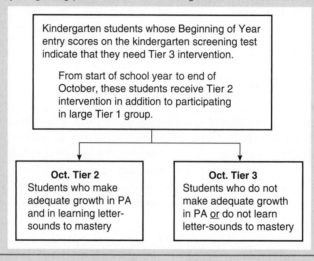

FIGURE 2.4 Screening Kindergarten Students

for at least two months to establish a dual discrepancy: a low assessment score coupled with inadequate progress when given evidence-based instruction (Fuchs et al., 2003). The *In Your Classroom* feature provides ideas for beginning-of-the-year decision making that we developed when coaching kindergarten teachers in the schools.

Progress-Monitoring Assessments for Phonemic Awareness

After teachers begin teaching phonemic awareness, **progress-monitoring assessments** help them determine which students are making adequate progress learning how to segment and blend.

Segmenting: Assessments for Progress Monitoring   In addition to the three-times-a-year benchmark DIBELS and AIMSweb phonemic segmentation fluency assessments that teachers use for screening students, progress-monitoring forms of these same assessments are available so that teachers can monitor and chart students' progress from week to week and month to month. As learned in Chapter 1, the process of progress monitoring involves these steps: set student goals, select progress-monitoring assessments of equal difficulty, measure regularly (every 3 to 4 weeks) to determine growth rates, and adjust instruction when growth is unsatisfactory (Jenkins, 2009). Mr. Glenn is a kindergarten teacher who uses monthly assessments to help guide his Tier 1 teaching. The October progress-monitoring assessments that he gave his students showed that almost everyone in the class had learned to segment first sounds and blend at the onset-rime level. Mr. Glenn was delighted that his instruction was so effective because he had been teaching these skills every day. While he continued to provide some extra help to monitor the progress of two students not performing as well, during November, Mr. Glenn moved to the next skill and taught his students to segment onset-rimes. If the assessment Mr. Glenn gives his students at the end of November shows that students have learned that skill, he will begin teaching blending individual sounds.

As just described, Mr. Glenn assessed his class more often than the required three benchmark periods; he monitored his class monthly to be sure students were acquiring essential phonemic awareness skills as planned. To do this, he compared the level of performance of his students to criterion levels on that particular skill. When most or all of his students were at criterion or above, he moved on to the next skill in the sequence. This approach of monitoring student progress once per month is practical for Tier 1 because of the number of students involved and the fact that most Tier 1 students are by definition not experiencing learning problems.

Teachers need to monitor progress more frequently for students in Tier 2 and Tier 3. These students already have an established history of learning difficulties and are likely to require more changes in intervention. Teachers may not want to wait a month before making instructional changes. In addition, more frequent testing provides a more accurate indicator of student progress.

Tessa, a student in Ms. Lilly's kindergarten class whose performance on the DIBELS PSF assessment is shown in Figure 2.5, provides an example of progress monitoring for a student in Tier 2. Tessa started receiving Tier 2 support in January when her Benchmark DIBELS Phonemic Segmenting Fluency score of 10 segments per minute supported Ms. Lilly's daily classroom observations that she was at "some risk." (See Appendix B.) Ms. Lilly set a goal of 35 segments per year by the end of the year, which is the benchmark level, and drew an aimline from Tessa's current performance of 10 to her goal in June of 35 segments correct per minute.

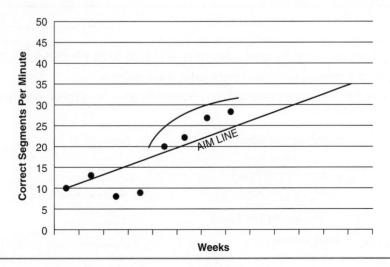

FIGURE 2.5 Progress Monitory PSF

Ms. Lilly decided to monitor Tessa's progress in PSF weekly for 8 weeks. At the end of that period, she would determine whether the Tier 2 support was working or whether Tessa needed Tier 3 support. Ms. Lilly used the recommended "4 above and below" rule to make her decisions:

- If the last 4 data points are above the aimline, keep the current program and consider raising the goal if appropriate.
- If the last 4 data points are below the line, make a change in intervention, tier, or both.
- If some data points are above the line and some below, keep the current program and goal in place (Fuchs, Fuchs, Hintze, & Lembke, 2007).

Tessa's performance for the 8-week period is shown in Figure 2.5. Note that the last four data points are above the line, meaning that if Tessa continued at this level of progress, she would meet or exceed the benchmark goal of 35 correct segments per minute by the end of the year. Based on the progress monitoring data, Mrs. Lilly kept Tessa in Tier 2.

The PALS assessment battery includes untimed Quick Checks to monitor the progress of students who have not met the PALS task benchmark. These Quick Checks are brief assessment probes designed to measure progress in essential literacy skills every two weeks. Teachers monitor whether students are correctly answering more questions until finally reaching the benchmark established for that task. Note that for phonemic awareness, the Beginning Sound Quick Check is more difficult than the task used on the screening assessment. The teacher says a key word that corresponds to a picture before asking the student to say the beginning sound of that word. She keeps a record of how many of the 10 sounds the student says correctly. Over time, the words become more difficult.

Blending: Informal Assessments for Screening or Progress Monitoring   Teachers can develop brief informal assessments to gauge their students' skill level for blending individual phonemes into words. By selecting five words similar to words practiced every day during blending instruction, a teacher can write a test similar to the one shown in Figure 2.6. As blending lessons begin to include more difficult words, such as those containing short /e/ or those beginning with the /h/ sound, words used for this assessment should reflect that level of difficulty.

Date: _____   Student Name: _____

Directions–Teacher says, "First I am going to say a word slowly, and then I'm going to say the word fast. If I say /m/-/ă/-/n/, the word is *man*. Let's try one: /k/-/ă/-/t/. What's the word?"

After the student answers, continue with the rest of the assessment.

Scoring: Score 1 for each correct word said and 0 for an incorrect or no response. Add the numbers and record the total score.

Blending Individual Phonemes	Score (0, 1)
1. /b/ - /a / - /t/ [bat]	_____
2. /m/ - /u/ - /d/ [mud]	_____
3. /p/ - /a/ - /n/ [pan]	_____
4. /s/ - /i/ - /k/ [sick]	_____
5. /h/ - /a/ - /n/ - /d/ [hand]	_____
Total Correct	_____

FIGURE 2.6   Blending Individual Phonemes: Informal Assessment

When giving students this informal blending assessment, the teacher follows this procedure:

1. Say the individual phonemes of the word.
2. Ask the student to say the whole word.
3. Record whether the student said the correct word.

This informal assessment is not timed. When the majority of students are blending four of the five words said by the teacher, blending activities become integrated with instruction in word reading. Students who do not show that success level require extra practice. If student performance in this and other areas such as letter sounds and segmenting does not improve, even with extra daily practice, a more intensive reading curriculum such as those described at the end of this chapter may be required.

Diagnostic Assessments for Phonemic Awareness

Diagnostic assessments for phonemic awareness are given to provide information that teachers can use to plan more effective instruction. They may also be required when a student is being evaluated for special education eligibility. Although Fletcher, Lyon, Fuchs, and Barnes (2007) stress that responsiveness to intervention should be the critical component when identifying learning disabilities, they concede that it cannot be the only condition for identification decisions. Because the presence of evidence-based instruction in all tiers is not guaranteed (Bursuck & Smallwood, 2009), diagnostic tests can provide an important layer of accountability and information to guide eligibility and instructional decisions.

Both the PALS and TPRI were designed to provide teachers with information they could use for planning differentiated instruction for students whose screening or progress monitoring scores indicate that they need more support. Students whose scores on the TPRI screening measure indicate their skills are "not developed" are given a more extensive inventory that provides information to help teachers plan instruction. Teachers select activities for children from a TPRI Intervention Manual. These activities correspond to "not developed" scores for specific skills. In one such phonemic awareness activity designed for a small group of students whose scores indicated that they needed this practice, the teacher threw a beanbag to one student before asking "*Say the word* **same**. *Now say* **same** *without the* /**s**/." If the student answered correctly, then he tossed the beanbag to another student and the teacher repeated the task with a different word.

The Comprehensive Test of Phonological Processing (CTOPP) (Wagner, Torgesen, & Rashotte, 2008), an individually administered normative assessment designed for students between 5 and 24 years of age, assesses phonological awareness, phonological memory, and rapid naming. Separate quotient scores and norms are provided for each area. Administering the core test takes between 20 to 30 minutes with one version available for children ages 5 to 6 years and another for students ages 7 to 24. Information about the specific subtests are in the Reading Assessment database at http://www.sedl.org/cgi-bin/mysql/rad.cgi?searchid=222. Because relatively few items are used for each skill tested, the CTOPP has more usefulness in predicting future reading problems than for planning specific instruction (Rathvon, 2004).

The Yopp-Singer Test of Phoneme Segmentation (YST) is another relatively easy-to-administer diagnostic assessment that takes between 5 to 10 minutes to give. As with the DIBELS and AIMSweb Phonemic Segmentation Fluency Assessment, a student says the individual sounds in words said by the tester. Unlike the first two tests, this one is not timed. To learn more about this test, go to the www.sedl.org website listed for the CTOPP and put this test's name in the search engine. As shown in the *In Your Classroom* feature, some diagnostic information can also be gleaned by detecting error patterns on the screening measures already described.

In Your Classroom

Diagnosing Student Error Patterns

The following account demonstrates how student scores from DIBELS Phonemic Segmentation Fluency can help guide teachers' phonemic awareness instruction.

At the end of kindergarten, in addition to assessing individual sound blending and letter sounds, Ms. Lee gave the one-minute DIBELS Phonemic Segmentation Fluency assessment to every student in her class. Ms. Lee knew that, based on segmenting benchmarks for this assessment, children who score 35 phonemes per minute or more at the end of kindergarten are more likely to have success with beginning word reading in first grade; children scoring between 10 and 34 are emerging and at some risk for having difficulty with word reading in first grade; and children scoring below 10 are deficit and at risk for having problems learning to read in first grade. Ms. Lee also knew that her students' scores in blending and letter sounds would help her identify children at risk for future reading problems.

Later, when Ms. Lee examined the assessment results, she reflected on the different needs of two students in her class and the recommendations she was making to the first-grade teachers based on the test results. Darrell, who segmented the words said by his teacher into 46 phonemes correct per minute, attained a score above benchmark levels. Darrell's assessment was shown in Figure 2.2 on page 44. Notice that the teacher scored correct segments by underlining the corresponding phonemes. In the word *bad*, Darrell correctly said all three phonemes. Therefore, all three phonemes were underlined. In the word *spin*, Darrell identified only three out of the four phonemes, failing to separate the /s/ and /p/. As a result, Ms. Lee underlined the /s/ and /p/ together. This assessment showed that Darrell was able to quickly break most of the spoken words into individual sounds. He also knew how to blend and could identify the sounds of individual letters in isolation without error. With effective instruction, Darrell should be able to apply his skills to reading written words. Ms. Lee knew that he was on track to read in first grade.

Mose, on the other hand, earned a score of seven phonemes correct per minute. Only first sounds of the words were underlined on the scoresheet in Figure 2.3 on page 45 because Mose still identified only the first sound in words. Also, Mose only knew 50% of his individual letter sounds in isolation and had yet to reach mastery level in blending individual sounds. Ms. Lee knew that Mose needed extensive help in first grade if he was to be able to meet benchmark levels and move out of the deficit category. She found it helpful to discuss the assessment with Mose's parents when they met to talk about the intensive reading program he would participate in during first grade.

Companion Website

Go to the Video Activities section of Chapter 2 in the Companion Website (www.pearson-highered.com/bursuck2e) and complete the activity entitled *DIBELS: Progress Monitoring.*

How Do I Teach Students to Segment and Blend?

In Chapter 1, the diagram of a typical first-grade classroom showed that some children learn to read with relative ease while children who are at risk or have learning disabilities require a more explicit, systematic approach. The multi-tier and RTI approaches described in this text allow teachers to accommodate a range of students when teaching students to segment and blend. Enhancements to large-group Tier 1 instruction are elaborated in this section.

Enhancements to Large-Group Tier 1 Instruction

The needs of many children are met when large-group instruction in early reading is carried out effectively. Sample scripts for presenting blending and segmenting to students are shown in Tables 2.2, 2.3, and 2.4.

In this next section, you will learn how to use the scripts to enhance your students' success in learning phonemic awareness skills. The strategies introduced in Chapter 1 and expanded here enable teachers to increase student responding and attention, provide support for new learning, correct errors consistently, increase skill retention through cumulative review, increase student motivation, and teach to success. Depending

TABLE 2.2 Segmenting 1: Format for Segmenting First Sound

Objective	After hearing a three-phoneme word (*cat*), students will say the first sound (/k/).
Materials Needed	List of three-phoneme words starting with letter sounds that the students have already learned in class. At least 25% of the words should begin with the new letter sound of the week.
Signaling	Extend your index finger; finger snap or hand drop as you say the first sound.
Time	3–5 minutes for 10 words

Instructions	Teacher	Students
	1. Advance Organizer	
	2. My Turn **"It's time to play the *first-sound* game. I'm going to say a word, and you'll say the first sound in the word. My turn. First sound in *sat* is "/s/."**	/s/
	3. Together: The teacher answers with students this time: **"Together, First sound in *sat*?"** (signal) **"/s/. Yes, /s/."** Teach three to eight more words.	/s/
	4. Your Turn **"Your turn. First sound in *sat*?"** (answer) **"Yes, /s/."**	/s/
	5. Individual Student Checkout **"Individual turns. First sound in *sat*? Jontrell."** (signal) (answer) **"Yes, /s/."** **"First sound in *mop*? Corinne."** (signal) (answer) **"Yes, /m/."** Call on several individual students to check accuracy.	/s/ /m/
Scaffolding Reduction	6. When presenting words containing a new letter sound, use steps 2–5 for the first three or four words. Then if students are accurately segmenting first sound, just use Steps 4 and 5 (Your Turn and Individual Student Checkout) for the remaining words. For review sessions, use only Steps 4 and 5 for all the words.	
Error Correction	If students make an error, immediately return to a My Turn–Together–Your Turn pattern. Later present the word that was missed two more times during the lesson.	
Perk Up Your Drill	▪ Hold up pictures matching the words on the day's list. Use an animal puppet to say the words and signal.	
Adaptations	▪ Inattentive students should sit next to you so their attention can be refocused on your mouth. For extra emphasis during the first week, overemphasize the first sound as you say each word. ▪ When students reach criteria, begin segmenting first sound of classmate's names, funny animals, or favorite holidays. ▪ Hold continuous sounds for two seconds as you say them so students clearly hear the sound.	

TABLE 2.3   Blending: Format for Blending Individual Phonemes

Objective	After hearing a three-phoneme word broken into individual phonemes (/n/-/a/-/p/), students will say the word at a normal speed *(nap)*.
Materials Needed	List of three-phoneme words starting with letter sounds that the students have already learned in class. At least 25% of the words should begin with the new letter sound of the week.
Signaling	Choose one signal:
	Signal 1: Extend your index finger as you say the first sound, extend your middle finger as you say the second sound, extend your ring finger as you say the third sound, and signal that students should say the entire word by arching your other hand in a rainbow motion over all three fingers. Be careful how you position your hand when showing students how to do this. You want them to read your fingers left to right, just as they would read text. (See Figure 2.8.)
	Signal 2: Use a fingersnap/handclap for the entire word.
Time	3–5 minutes for 10 words

Instructions	**Teacher**	**Students**
	1. Advance Organizer	
	2. My Turn **"Today we're going to play *Say It Fast.* I'm going to say a word slowly, and then fast. My turn. /n/-/a/-/p/. The word is *nap.*"**	
	3. Together: The teacher answers with students this time: **"Together."** (extend fingers) **"/n/-/a/-/p/. What word?"** (arch palm) **"nap. Yes, *nap.*"**	nap
	4. Your Turn **"Your turn."** (extend fingers) **"/n/-/a/-/p/. What word?"** (arch palm) (answer) **"Yes, nap."** Teach three to eight more words.	nap
	5. Individual Student Checkout **"Individual turns."** (extend fingers) **"/m/-/o/-/p/. What word? Mary."** (arch palm) (answer) **"Yes, mop."** (extend fingers) **"/r/-/u/-/n/. What word? Telly."** (arch palm) (answer) **"Yes, *run.*"** Call on several individual students to check accuracy.	mop run

Scaffolding Reduction	When presenting words containing a new letter sound, use Steps 2–5 for the first three or four words. Then if students are accurately blending the words, use Steps 4–5 (Your Turn and Individual Student Checkout) for the remaining words. For review sessions, only use Steps 3 and 5.
Error Correction	If students make an error, immediately return to a My Turn–Together–Your Turn pattern. Later present the word that was missed two more times during the lesson.
Perk Up Your Drill	▪ Say the sounds using "robot talk" and get your class to answer in the same monotone.
Adaptations	▪ Use manipulatives to help make this task more concrete. You can use blocks, magnetic letters, cardboard letters, letter blocks, etc. Since manipulatives add extra challenges in a large group, work in a small group with a few students whose test results indicate that they are not blending. ▪ When students can easily blend three phonemes, provide practice blending more difficult four-phoneme words and words containing long vowels. Students are now ready to move into reading words and sentences containing three-phoneme words. ▪ If students have trouble holding words in their short-term memory, avoid using the oral cue "What word" and just go straight to the arch signal.

Source: This script is based on one originally developed and field-tested by Carnine, D. W., Silbert, J., Kame'enui, E. J., & Tarver S. (2010). *Direct Instruction Reading* (5th ed.). Boston: Merrill Prentice Hall.

TABLE 2.4   Segmenting 2: Format for Segmenting Individual Phonemes

Objective	After hearing a three-phoneme word spoken at a normal rate (*rap*), students will say the individual sounds in the word (/r/-/a/-/p/).
Materials Needed	List of three-phoneme words starting with letter sounds that the students have already learned in class. At least 25% of the words should begin with the new letter sound of the week.
Signaling	Choose one signal:
	Signal 1: Extend your index finger as you say the first sound, extend your middle finger as you say the second sound, extend your ring finger as you say the third sound. Be careful how you position your hand when showing students how to do this. You want them to read your fingers left to right, just as they would read text. (See Figure 2.7.)
	Signal 2: Use a fingersnap/handclap for each sound.
Time	3–5 minutes for 10 words

Instructions	**Teacher**	**Students**
	1. Advance Organizer	
	2. My Turn: **"I'm going to say a word and all the sounds in the word. My turn. Say the sounds in *leg*. /l/-/e/-/g/. The sounds are /l/-/e/-/g/."**	
	3. Together: The teacher answers with students this time: **"Together. Say the sounds in *leg*."** (extend finger) **"/l/"** (extend finger) **"/e/"** (extend finger) **"/g/. Yes, the sounds in *leg* are /l/-/e/-/g/."**	/l/-/e/-/g/
	4. Your Turn: **"Your turn. Say the sounds in *leg*."** (extend finger) (answer) (extend finger) (answer) (extend finger) (answer) **"Yes, the sounds in *leg* are /l/-/e/-/g/."** Teach three to eight additional words.	/l/-/e/-/g/
	5. Individual Student Checkout **"Individual turns. Say the sounds in *men*. Sharnicca."** (extend finger) (answer) (extend finger) (answer) (extend finger) (answer) **"Yes, the sounds in *men* are /m/-/e/-/n/."**	/m/-/e/-/n/
	"Say the sounds in *win*. Bryan." (extend finger) (answer) (extend finger) (answer) (extend finger) (answer) **"Yes, the sounds in win are /w/-/i/-/n/."** Call on several individual students to check accuracy.	/w/-/i/-/n/

Scaffolding Reduction	When presenting words containing a new letter sound, use Steps 2–5 for the first three or four words. Then if students are accurately segmenting all of the phonemes, use only Steps 4–5 (Your Turn and Individual Student Checkout) for the remaining words.
Error Correction	If students make an error, immediately return to a My Turn–Together–Your Turn pattern. Later present the word that was missed two more times during the lesson.
Perk Up Your Drill	■ Tell your students they are cheerleaders and have them cheer the segments, using right arm out, both arms up, left arm out motions. ■ Ask parents to come in with younger sisters and brothers and watch students successfully segment. ■ Have students do imaginary karate chops for every phoneme.
Adaptations	■ As long as you remember My Turn–Together–Your Turn, the more students practice sound/word spelling (see Chapter 3), the better they will become at segmenting. Everyone should do daily sound/word spelling. ■ Once the students can easily segment three phonemes, provide practice segmenting words with more phonemes and difficult letter sound patterns.

Source: This script is based on one originally developed and field-tested by Carnine, D. W., Silbert, J., Kame'enui, E. J., & Tarver S. (2010). *Direct Instruction Reading* (5th ed.). Boston: Merrill Prentice Hall.

The *Tampa Reads* website, which contains a number of phonemic awareness worksheets, explains: "the most difficult sounds to learn are—h - l - m - n - q - r - w and y (at the beginning of words). It will take 3–5 times more practice for a child to memorize these sounds in comparison to other consonant sounds, so please give special attention to their mastery." **www. tampareads.com/phonics/whereis/ index.htm.**

on the percentage of students who are at risk in the community where you teach, the effective use of these strategies can ensure that the needs of 50% to 90% of students are met. As your students learn to blend and segment, draw their attention to your mouth and how it looks as it makes the sounds. Research also supports the effectiveness of providing students with the visual support of seeing how the tongue and mouth look as students segment and blend more difficult sounds (O'Connor, 2007).

Signaling for Segmenting   You'll notice the teacher in the video clip using the segmenting signals from the formats to get unison responses from all her students. Before trying out the formats yourself, you will want to practice these signals. Use the following steps to establish effective signaling for segmenting instruction.

1. Focus students' attention by holding up the palm of your hand toward the class, making sure that everyone is looking directly at you.
2. Begin segmenting instruction by turning the hand, holding up a closed fist with fingers toward your face.
3. Say the word and ask students to segment the word.
4. Signal by raising one finger at a time for each sound that is said. Extend the index finger as you say the first sound, extend the middle finger as you say the second sound, and extend the ring finger as you say the third sound.
5. When introducing segmenting for the first time, practice with students and model the signals as well as the expected answers.

Signaling for Blending   Figure 2.7 shows a teacher's view as she signals her students to say the sounds in *sat*. Although other signals such as finger-snapping, arm patting, or clapping can be used, an advantage of the fingers-up format is that children raise their own fingers when saying the sounds in words, providing them with a multisensory cue. Fingers-up signals are also helpful when students say the sounds in words before spelling them.

Use these steps to establish effective signals for blending instruction.

1. Focus students' attention by holding up the palm of your hand toward the class, making sure that everyone is looking directly at you.
2. Begin blending instruction by turning your hand so that students will see the letters from left to right just as they would read text. Say the sounds slowly: extend your index finger as you say the first sound, extend your middle finger as you say the second

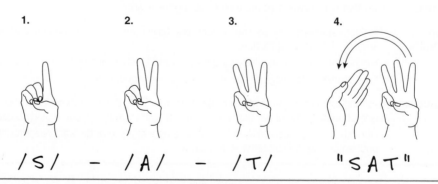

FIGURE 2.7   Hand Signals for Blending Sounds

sound, and extend your ring finger as you say the third sound. Students may want to respond when they see you extend your fingers. Be sure to tell them to wait until you give them the signal to say the word the fast way.

3. Ask students to say the word the fast way and signal by arching your palm in a rainbow motion over all three fingers as you and/or your students say the entire word.

4. Model the signals and expected responses when introducing blending for the first time.

Increase Student Responding and Attention   Providing an advance organizer is the first thing teachers can do to increase student responding and attention. As discussed in Chapter 1, advance organizers make clear to students what is being covered, why it is being taught, and what behavioral expectations are in place during instruction. Such clarity helps students focus on the task at hand and sets the occasion for active student answering and attentive behavior. For example, before she starts her phonemic awareness lesson, Ms. Grenaldi tells her students, *"Today we will say the sounds in 10 words. Learning how to say the sounds in words will help you learn to spell so that you can write a story about your favorite TV show. Remember to answer on signal, keep your hands and feet to yourself, and look at me."*

Increasing student responding and attention also involves the judicious use of teacher talk. Keeping teacher talk to a minimum helps attain a lively teaching pace that, in turn, increases student attention. Students learning to identify first sounds or to blend sounds into words need to maintain all of their attention on the word or sounds in the words. A teacher who provides unnecessary details about a word risks losing the focus of students with short attention spans. If, after asking students to tell her the sounds in *mop*, Ms. Grenaldi talks about how she hates to mop floors, Tan may be unable to say /m/-/ŏ/-/p/ because he is thinking about how funny she would look mopping the classroom floor.

Require Answering in Unison   Requiring students to answer in unison also helps keep the attention of students who are at risk. When students are required to respond frequently, they are so busy answering questions that they do not have time for distractions. Unison responses also guarantee that children who are at risk receive the practice manipulating sounds that they need to reach mastery on all essential phonemic awareness skills by the end of kindergarten. For example, students who do not hear the first sound in words beginning with /h/ or /a/ need to practice saying the first sound in many words that begin with those phonemes. A teacher's quandary is how to provide that practice yet keep the phonemic awareness section of the lesson from taking more than 10 minutes of class time and running the risk of boring the students. When every student gets practice segmenting all 10 words beginning with /h/ or /a/, the lesson moves faster and more students experience success with a difficult skill. The key to getting unison responses from students during phonemic awareness instruction is using a clear and consistent system of signaling for answers.

Maintain a Perky Pace   Another way to gain student attention and provide the most practice is to maintain a perky pace by minimizing the transition time between questions or activities. Mr. Williams always conducted a lively, fast-paced class. His students sat crisscross on the rug during his animated segmenting instruction. When he taught students to segment the following four words—*run, mat, sit,* and *fun*—he thrust out his fingers with a staccato rhythm which students copied as they segmented the words. After the students had segmented *run* correctly, Mr. Williams immediately presented the word *mat*. He knew that an effective teacher is also an actor and that quick transitions were essential to keeping the attention of his audience. After his students had segmented all of the words, Mr. Williams moved quickly to the next part of the lesson: letter sounds.

Increase Support for New Learning   Segmenting and blending spoken words are often difficult skills for students to learn. You can increase support for children as they learn these skills by first carefully demonstrating the new skill, then performing the skill with the students, and finally having students perform the skill on their own. Scaffolding refers to the level of support that a teacher needs to provide to a student so that he can successfully do an activity. When a teacher is instructing new skills, My Turns and Togethers provide increased support so that the student can do the task successfully. Gradually the teacher reduces the amount of scaffolding until she can introduce new words at the Your Turn level. The students' accuracy lets the teacher know if she made the correct decision in reducing scaffolding. Let's take a look at how Ms. Ortez ensured her students' success on the first day she taught blending consonant–vowel–consonant words beginning with continuous sounds such as /m/ and /r/.

Step 1: My Turn   Ms. Ortez introduced the first new word by saying the three sounds (/m/ /a/ /n/) before quickly blending them into the new word *man*. **"All eyes up here. Today we're going to play *Say It Fast*. I'm going to say a word slowly, and you'll say the word fast. My turn. /m/-/ă/-/n/. man."**

Step 2: Together   Ms. Ortez then repeated the same learning activity with her students saying, **"Together. /m/-/ă/-/n/. What word?"** (signal) ***"man*. Yes, the word is 'man.'"** If students blended the correct word with her, she moved on to the next step.

Step 3: Your Turn   Finally, Ms. Ortez asked the students to blend the word on their own. **"Your turn. /m/-/ă/-/n/. What word?"** (signal). **"Yes, the word is 'man.'"** When students blended all seven words correctly, Ms. Ortez called on two or three students individually to blend the word. She usually called on students whose test results showed that they were having more difficulty blending so that she could provide extra help on the spot. Since students still had difficulty blending some of the words, Ms. Ortez introduced the next word with a My Turn.

The number of Togethers that a teacher uses during a lesson depends on the difficulty of the skill. Students usually catch on to blending more quickly and require fewer questions asking them to answer with the teacher. During the blending part of the lesson, after teaching the first two words, Ms. Ortez would probably reduce scaffolding and begin to skip Step 2 in her instruction. As long as the students are correctly answering, that step would not be necessary. In contrast, segmenting sounds is more difficult than blending, often requiring that a teacher say the sounds with the students for most of or all the lesson. Students have more difficulty articulating /ĕ/ in *pen* or splitting the word *hat* into /h/-/ă/-/t/. Learning to hear and say the sound of the vowel when segmenting onset-rime or individual phonemes will be the most difficult step for your students, and you will need to increase your scaffolding at that point. For several days or weeks, a teacher may do five or six My Turn–Togethers, overarticulating the vowel sound as she says it with her students until all the children are able to hear the sound. How do you know precisely the right time to move from Togethers to Your Turns? Student accuracy is the only way to make this determination. Move on when students respond firmly and seem to anticipate your response before you make it.

The end goal of instruction is getting students to answer independently. Teachers know their students have acquired a new skill when instruction begins with Step 3, Your Turn, and the class correctly answers every question. Our teacher, Ms. Ortez, knew that her students were ready to move on to a new skill when she could ask them Your Turn questions for blending consonant–vowel–consonant words beginning with continuous sounds, and they would rapidly blend the words without help. The next day Ms. Ortez began asking her students to blend more difficult words, beginning with stop sounds. Because she was teaching a new skill, Ms. Ortez again started her instruction with My Turn examples for the new words.

Project PRIDE teachers discovered that students who were unable to learn how to blend onset-rimes needed to have that blending activity broken into even smaller steps. Many students only learned how to blend onset-rimes after the teacher went back a half-step and asked them to blend compound words for several days or weeks. The teacher slowly said the two parts of compound words, requiring students to say the whole word fast: *cow + boy = cowboy, tooth + brush = toothbrush, snow + man = snowman, cough + drop = coughdrop, play + ground = playground, cheese + burgers = cheeseburgers.*

Once the students were blending compound words, the teacher next practiced onset-rimes with students' names. Students easily blended their classmates' names such as /v/-/ictoria/, /l/-/atoya/, or /s/-/kyler/.

In the approach for teaching segmenting described thus far, children are taught to pause between each of the segmented sounds. This approach is the most common one used in beginning reading programs and works well for a majority of students (Bursuck et al., 2004). However, pausing between the sounds may make blending the sounds into spoken words more difficult for students who are at risk (Burns, 2006; O'Connor, 2007; Weisberg, Savard, & Christopher, 1993). For example, while Mr. Halpern's students were able to say each of the individual sounds in *mat,* when asked to blend the sounds together, many students said *at,* leaving out the first letter. Chard and Osborne (1999) suggest that many children who are at risk benefit from teachers modifying the segmenting task by stretching out and connecting the sounds, such as saying the sounds in *Sam* as /sssăăămmm/. By not pausing or stopping between the sounds, children are less likely to make blending errors. As all children who are at risk do not need this stretch approach, teachers might want to use it as extra support as part of Tier 2 or Tier 3 instruction. On the other hand, making stretch blending/segmenting a part of your Tier 1 instruction may allow you to meet the needs of more of your students within the larger instructional group.

Provide Ongoing Review   Phonemic awareness skills build on themselves, so ongoing review is automatic as long as students move through the skills according to the sequence described in the text. For example, segmenting at the onset-rime level (*mat* = /m/-/ăt/) automatically incorporates first sound segmenting, so a student who is segmenting onset-rime does not need to also practice that earlier skill.

Since phonemic awareness skills are sequential, teachers who teach to success, checking out whether students are at mastery before moving on to more difficult skills, have more students in their class meet DIBELS benchmarks. When Mr. Halpern's students were struggling with blending individual sounds, he did not move on to the more difficult format of segmenting individual sounds. Instead, he provided more support for blending, conducting blending activities at the My Turn level, increasing the time students spent in Tier 2 sessions, and using opportunities throughout the day to provide short practice sessions. He knew that if he moved on too quickly to individual sound segmenting, some of his students would be so confused that they would not learn either blending or segmenting. Imagine how difficult it would be for a student who could not yet identify first sound to have the teacher ask him to identify final sounds the next day. Some phonemic awareness curricula make it more difficult for struggling students by switching from skill to skill every few days, introducing an unnecessary element of confusion. Even though a few other teachers at his grade level were several lessons ahead of his class, Mr. Halpern knew that the extra time taken to teach this important skill to his students would pay off.

Increase the Motivation   When students first move to the next phonemic awareness skill or when the words used for that skill are more difficult, teachers who recognize the increased difficulty level and integrate more motivation into the lesson keep students working their hardest. Teachers can raise the motivation level by increasing their animated teaching level, by increasing the number of times they praise students for their hard work, and by telling students that if they work their hardest during the phonemic awareness activity, they will be able to play a favorite sound game after the lesson. Students may need increased motivation during these more difficult phonemic awareness activities:

- Blending or segmenting words that contain more sounds
- Blending or segmenting words that begin with stop sounds
- Blending or segmenting words that begin with or contain consonant blends such as /tr/ or /st/
- Blending or segmenting words that contain the /ĕ/ sound
- Manipulating the medial vowel sound

On a long Monday, some teachers vary their inflection as they blend sounds to create novelty. Using "turtle talk" or "whisper talk," teachers and students slowly and quietly enunciate the sounds for the day's words. On school picture day, when students are excitable and increased motivation helps maintain a perky pace, these teachers tell their students that it is "robot talk" day and everyone will segment and blend in a robotic monotone.

During her planning period, Ms. Orton decided that the next day when she asked her students to blend several words starting with the /l/ sound, she would teach to success by telling her class that if they did their best work and put together all of their new words correctly, Toby the Tiger would come out of his box and sing a song about his favorite roaring sounds. Teachers like Ms. Maben at the beginning of the chapter energize students by picking a child who has learned the formats and corrections to be the "teacher" for two or three of the words.

Companion Website

Go to the Video Activities section of Chapter 2 in the Companion Website (www.pearson-highered.com/bursuck2e) and complete the activities entitled *Blending Individual Sounds and Segmenting Individual Sounds*. Watch the teacher instructing students in phonemic awareness using the scripts shown in Tables 2.3 and 2.4.

Applying the Enhancements to a Commercial Reading Program

Often the teaching activities suggested in commercial reading programs are not systematic and explicit enough for your students who are at risk. Shown below is a phonemic awareness activity similar to ones that often appear in commercial general education reading programs. The objective for the activity is to segment the three-phoneme words *bat*, *tap*, and *rat*.

> Using a puppet, have the puppet show the children a picture of a man. After the children say the picture name out loud, have the puppet ask the children to say the word *man* slowly— that is, to segment the sounds. If necessary, have the puppet say /m/-/ă/-/n/. Once the children grasp the idea, have them segment other words such as *bat*, *tap*, and *rat*.

As written, this lesson may not provide the level of support needed for most of your students to learn to segment. The impact of this lesson on student learning can be maximized and the need for more labor-intensive differentiated instruction minimized by using the Tier 1 enhancements described in the text.

To increase student responding and attention, use the puppet's clapping as a signal for the students' unison answers. Each time the puppet's hands come together, the children should say the next sound in the word. To set a perky pace, keep your talk to a minimum as you emphatically tell students: *"Today Mr. Puppet will teach you to say words the slow way. Every time Mr. Puppet claps, say a sound."* To further increase the number of answers students make per minute, have the list of words accessible so you can move quickly from one word to the next.

If segmenting represents new learning for the children, do a My Turn–Together–Your Turn as follows:

"Listen to Mr. Puppet say the sounds in *man*. /m/ /ă/ /n/."

"Together with Mr. Puppet. Say the sounds in *man*." (extend finger) "/m/" (extend finger) "/ă/" (extend finger) "/n/. Yes. The sounds in man are /m/ /ă/ /n/."

"Your turn. Say the sounds in *man*." (extend finger) "/m/" (extend finger) "/ă/" (extend finger) "/n/. Yes. The sounds in man are /m/ /ă/ /n/."

If students are struggling with segmenting, teach to success by continuing with the Together step until students are able to segment accurately on their own. When students have learned to segment sounds and are applying that new learning, have Mr. Puppet provide the signal for a series of Your Turn questions. When students make an error while segmenting with Mr. Puppet, consistently correct by having the puppet demonstrate and say the word slowly. Next, ask students to say the word slowly with the puppet before asking them to say the word slowly by themselves. Remember to ask students to segment a missed word at least two more times during the lesson as well as later in the day. Try first teaching students to segment two phoneme vowel–consonant words such as *it* that are easier than consonant–vowel words like *my* or consonant–vowel–consonant words like *tap* (Uhry & Ehri, 1999).

If the students do not respond on signal or start making a number of errors, integrate increased motivation into the activity. Tell your students that they will have a contest with Mr. Puppet to see who can get more points. The puppet will get a point every time students do not answer to the signal or when they make an error segmenting a word. Students get points for answering to the puppet's claps and for saying the correct sounds in a word.

Because segmenting individual sounds incorporates all the earlier segmenting skills, you do not have to add segmenting review. Blending individual sounds is not included in this lesson, so you need to provide review by having Mr. Puppet ask the students to say some words the fast way. Be aware that phonemic awareness tasks such as "tell me the sounds in *pan* /p/ /a/ /n/" require less working memory than when asking students to reverse sounds in words (e.g., "Say *pan*. Now say it backwards: *nap*"). Adding pictures or letter tiles to the activity will help students who struggle to remember the initial three phonemes while manipulating them for the reversal task. Teaching strategies to provide review of phonemic awareness skills throughout the school day are described in the *In Your Classroom* feature.

In Your Classroom

Teaching Phonemic Awareness All Day

Teaching phonemic awareness takes place all day—not just during reading block. When you are discussing the afternoon assembly that was about birds of prey, ask students to tell you the first sound they hear in the word *falcon*. If some students do not answer, use a My Turn–Together–Your Turn pattern and immediately teach on the spot. Ask them to take apart the word *eagle*.

After a fire drill, ask students to tell you what sound they hear at the beginning of *fire*. You will probably get giggles when you ask for the sound at the start of the word *bathroom,* just before you walk down to that room. After morning announcements ask the students to tell you the first sound in *morning*. Do not forget to ask about the word *music* before your students trot down to music class. Try to catch important words that start with the sounds your students are learning.

What Can I Do for Students Who Are Not Learning to Segment and Blend Even with Enhancements?

Depending on where you teach, as many as one to two thirds of your students may need extra practice learning to segment and blend despite enhanced instruction carried out in the large group. Tier 2 interventions conducted in small groups or one-to-one provide extra practice before or after your large-group phonemic awareness instruction.

Tier 2 Intervention Groups

Tier 2 intervention groups typically involve more practice with the skills covered that same day in Tier 1 and can be taught by the classroom teacher or by paraprofessionals or even peer or cross-age tutors, provided they are appropriately trained. Reduce background noise for this oral task by working in a relatively quiet corner in the classroom, hallway, or a corner of the library. Teachers who conduct Tier 2 sessions often pull students during quiet time or work with a small group in the hallway during computer lab. Given the time and personnel constraints involved, the key to having an effective system of Tier 2 intervention groups is efficiency. You want to teach as effectively as possible in the smallest amount of time. If you use unison responses during the sessions, the formats shown in Tables 2.2 to 2.4 can be delivered in approximately 10 minutes.

Student scores on screening and progress-monitoring assessments provide information about which students need Tier 2 support. Your Tier 2 group will be comprised of the following categories of students:

- Students whose benchmark screening assessment indicates the need for Tier 2 support
- Students who were in Tier 1 but whose progress monitoring scores indicate that their scores have leveled off or even decreased and they have been under the aimline for four consecutive weeks
- Students who exited Tier 3 and need support during the transition to the general education reading curriculum

To determine what phonemic awareness skills to teach during small-group Tier 2 instruction, look at the blending and segmenting sequence of instruction on page 42 and select the format(s) that represent(s) the earliest sequential skill that the student hasn't mastered. Form a small group of students who need to work on that skill. For example, Tina and Javon, students whose benchmark assessment indicated that they should receive Tier 2 support, are in Ms. Glendell's large-group class, which is now working on segmenting onset-rime. Because Tina and Javon still cannot segment first sounds, Ms. Glendell practices segmenting first sound during their Tier 2 group time. If Tina's and Javon's assessments show that blending onset-rime is the lowest skill in the blending and segmenting sequence that they have not mastered, Ms. Glendell will practice those formats with them during the Tier 2 intervention group. Later in the month, if Tina and Javon master blending onset-rime, Ms. Glendell will work on the next step in the sequence, segmenting onset-rime, during Tier 2 intervention. When next month's assessment is given, Tina and Javon, having caught up to the group, may no longer need Tier 2 interventions, but two or three other students may now need to start. These extra Tier 2 practice sessions ensure that students immediately get the extra support they need when screening shows that they are slightly behind established benchmarks or when their level of progress is limited.

Kindergarten teachers and school staff working in Project PRIDE conducted daily 5- to 10-minute Tier 2 intervention groups for students whose monthly phonemic awareness test scores indicated that they were not successful with that skill.

The staff learned to incorporate these procedures:

- Form groups containing between one and three students.
- Place students having the most difficulty in the smallest groups.
- Conduct instruction in a relatively quiet location so students could clearly hear the sounds.
- Keep focusing distractible students' attention on their mouths.
- Stretch out difficult sounds that students had difficulty hearing.
- Use manipulatives to jump-start blending and segmenting for students who were not progressing.
- Use mirrors to help provide visual feedback for students who had difficulty saying a new sound.
- Carefully train anyone teaching Tier 2 groups so that they consistently taught the phonemic awareness formats and articulated the sounds just as the classroom teacher did.
- Analyze why students who did not make adequate progress with the support of Tier 2 adaptations were unsuccessful and learn to adapt instruction to prevent some students from needing the more intensive alternative Tier 3 reading curriculum.

Read about when to use manipulatives for teaching phonemic awareness in small Tier 2 intervention groups in this *Research Note*.

Research Note

Using Manipulatives to Teach Phonemic Awareness

Many beginning reading programs recommend the use of manipulatives to teach phonemic awareness. The purpose of the manipulatives is to make the abstract concept of sounds within spoken words more concrete. The type of manipulatives used varies. Some programs use interlocking plastic blocks. Students say a sound for each block and then lock all the blocks together to make a word. Other programs have students place plastic counters on a row of empty boxes appearing on a page as they say the sounds in a word and then blend the sounds together.

Unfortunately, only three studies have looked directly at the relationship between manipulatives and student learning of phonemic awareness skills (Elkonin, 1973; Lewkowicz & Low, 1979; Miller-Young, 1999). The results of these studies are mixed. Elkonin and Lewkowicz and Low found that students who were taught to segment using manipulatives performed better than children who were not. Elkonin also found that the various types of manipulatives were equally effective. Miller-Young, on the other hand, found that direct instruction formats with and without manipulatives were equally effective.

Given the mixed results of the research, as well as our own classroom experience, the following approach to the use of manipulatives is recommended.

- Use manipulatives only after less-intrusive strategies such as the ones recommended in this chapter (see Tables 2.2 to 2.4) have been attempted first.
- Use manipulatives when working with students in small groups or one-to-one. Using manipulatives in larger groups can be difficult to manage and monitor.
- Once students are able to segment or blend using manipulatives, gradually fade them out.

What Can I Do for Students Who Are Not Learning to Segment and Blend Even with Tier 2 Support?

The decision to place a student into an alternative, more intensive reading program is an important, yet difficult, one. On the one hand, you want all students to succeed in the general education reading program. On the other hand, given the poor catch-up rate for students who get behind, you don't want to prolong their placement in a more intensive program. Because of the importance of the Tier 3 placement decision, it is recommended that performance in multiple areas be considered, including phonemic awareness as well as letter–sound identification, word and passage reading, and vocabulary and listening comprehension, assessments for which are covered in subsequent chapters. The results of additional assessments can help strengthen the case for Tier 3 instruction, particularly in borderline cases. You learned about how to place students into Tier 3 in the *In Your Classroom* feature on page 46.

Tier 3 Placement Rules in a Multi-Tiered RTI Model

In order to avoid discrimination or arbitrary placement decisions based on subjective judgment, school teams should predetermine decision rules to indicate when students scoring below a certain level should begin Tier 3 instruction and when they are ready to exit Tier 3. Currently RTI models have no agreed-upon standards as to when students should exit and enter Tier 3. Some districts make Tier 3 placement decisions based on which students place below a set score criterion, while others use a set percentile criterion. Others base Tier 3 decisions on student rate of progress toward meeting end-of-year goals. When using cutoff scores, the staffing team needs to discuss at length all students who fall one or two points above or below a score to allow for measurement error. For example, if Troy is one point below the cutoff for Tier 3 but has been reading higher-level books with understanding, the team might decide to keep him in Tier 2 and monitor his progress more frequently. If Anton has the same score but is highly distractible and has no support at home, the team might decide that he will increase his rate of learning only with a Tier 3 intervention.

Exiting students so that they don't "bounce back" into Tier 3 several months later is another difficult determination, especially with younger students. Although we found that more than 85% of students exiting Tier 3 remained in Tier 1 or Tier 2 one year later, this was not the case for students who had exited in kindergarten (Damer & Bursuck, 2008). Because a larger percentage of students who exit Tier 3 in kindergarten bounce back to Tier 3 within a year, we recommend caution in exiting kindergarten students from Tier 3 at this younger age. It may be more prudent to determine exit criteria using scores based on tasks more directly approximating reading, such as letter sounds, nonsense words, sight words, or oral reading fluency.

In districts that have a larger proportion of students who are at risk, more students will need the support of a Tier 3 intervention, and to help with the larger numbers some general education teachers may need training in teaching Tier 3 curricula. If the Tier 3 program is effective, progress-monitoring data should show that the majority of students are responding to the increased scaffolding provided by an alternative program. Students whose progress-monitoring information shows that they are not responding to the intensive Tier 3 instruction at a predicted level of growth from month to month should be discussed by the team to determine whether a referral for special education services and further testing is appropriate. If more than 10% of students are not responding to Tier 3 interventions, the district team needs to increase scaffolding and determine whether increased time, smaller groups, more teacher training and coaching, or another Tier 3 program is warranted.

Intensive, Alternative Reading Programs for Tier 3

Table 2.5 lists and compares five reading programs (*Direct Instruction: Reading Mastery, Lindamood®: LiPS, Reading Recovery, Wilson Reading System,* and *Language!*) that are frequently used by school districts in different parts of the country for students requiring an intensive intervention. These programs represent different approaches to beginning reading, differing substantially in their emphases on phonemic awareness and phonics, how those skills are taught, and how they are connected to word and story reading. Subsequent chapters will include an analysis of how these and sometimes other reading programs teach the critical reading skill addressed in that chapter. Additional curricula with an emphasis on phonemic awareness that could be considered for Tier 3 instruction but weren't included because of space constraints are *Earobics, Ladders for Literacy, Waterford Early Reading Program,* and *Headsprout Early Reading.*

How Can I Teach Phonemic Awareness to English Language Learners?

More than 5 million students in the United States, or about 10% of the school-age population, are English language learners (National Clearinghouse for English Language Acquisition and Language Instruction Education Program, 2006). Adding to the challenges posed by language differences, between 60% and 68% of these students come from high-poverty households (Capps et al., 2005). Language and poverty provide a double challenge for reading educators, and far too often these students are identified as needing special education services. Equally problematic is the high proportion of secondary-level English language learners whose frustration with school and the reading demands of the higher grades leads them to drop out before the 12th grade.

The connection between phonemic awareness and reading has been demonstrated in both alphabetic and nonalphabetic languages. Research studies with Spanish-speaking students who comprise 77% of English language learners have shown that phonemic awareness in Spanish skills predicts later word recognition in English (Garcia, Jensen, & Scribner, 2009). More than IQ or language ability, phonemic awareness assessment provides a way for schools to identify who will need additional early, intensive support in reading (Quiroga, Lemos-Britton, Mostafapour, Abbott, & Berninger, 2002).

As with native English speakers, phonemic awareness training improves later reading performance in English language learners, even when the student receiving the phonemic awareness training is not proficient in English (Roberts & Corbett, 1997). High- and middle-performing students in a kindergarten class of English language learners who received 300 minutes of systematic and explicit phonological awareness training in rhyming, blending, and segmenting made significant growth in word reading when compared with a comparable group of students not receiving the intervention. The researchers hypothesized that the gains for the lowest-performing students were not significantly different from the control group because they needed a higher level of intensity than 10 weeks of twice-a-week instruction for 15-minute sessions (Leafstedt, Richards, & Gerber, 2004). When phonemic awareness training is paired with sound spelling and decoding instruction, word reading shows significant growth (Durgunoğlu & Öney, 1999).

TABLE 2.5 Comparison of Commonly Used Tier 3 Approaches

	Direct Instruction: Reading Mastery	Lindamood®: LiPS	Reading Recovery	Wilson Reading System	Language!
What phonemic awareness skills are explicitly taught?	Blending Segmenting Rhyming	Blending Segmenting Phoneme deletion Counting phonemes Phoneme manipulation	Segmenting and blending	Segmenting and blending are not taught as separate skills, but in context of phonics.	Blending Segmenting Rhyming Phoneme deletion Phoneme substitution Phoneme reversals
How much time is spent on phonemic awareness instruction?	Beginning 30- to 60-minute lessons are split between phonemic awareness and letter–sound identification and writing.	Beginning 45- to 60-minute lessons are split between phonemic awareness, letter–sound identification, and writing.	Segmenting and blending instruction comprises a small part of the 30-minute lessons that cover seven activities each day.	Students finger-tap sounds (segmentation) when decoding words (approximately 30% of lesson)	5 to 10 minutes of the lesson
What is the instructional setting?	One-to-one instruction, small group, or large classroom	One-to-one instruction, small group, or large classroom	One-to-one instruction	One-to-one, unless with a Wilson certified teacher, who works with small groups of 3 to 5 students. Wilson group certification enables teacher to work with 10 to 12 students.	One-to-one instruction, small group, or large classroom
What determines students' placement in curriculum?	Current achievement level placement test	Current achievement level All students start at beginning of program. Some students will move more quickly through curriculum.	No grouping	All students must begin in Step 1. Some students will move more quickly through curriculum.	Current achievement level, based on placement test.
Are students required to know letter sounds of words they are orally blending or segmenting?	No	Yes	No	Yes	Yes

TABLE 2.5 Continued

	Direct Instruction: Reading Mastery	Lindamood®: LiPS	Reading Recovery	Wilson Reading System	Language!
Are words taught during phonemic awareness specifically coordinated with first words read in isolation and later in stories?	Yes	Yes	No	Coordination of first sounds, first words read in isolation, and later in stories.	Yes
Do lessons move from simpler phonemic awareness skills to ones that are more difficult?	Yes	Yes	No	No. Phonemic awareness (blending and segmenting) is taught in context of reading.	Yes
What multi-sensory activities are included as part of beginning phonemic awareness/letter–sound recognition instruction?	Lessons include student action requiring students to hold up fingers for sounds that they segment, and move fingers as they blend sounds into words. Visual feedback (pictures) is provided after some blending activities.	Lessons include moving lip pictures, moving blocks, moving counters, moving letter tiles, use of mirrors to provide feedback on phoneme production, and the manipulation of syllable cards.	Lessons include placing counters or letters into sound boxes.	Finger tapping (each finger is tapped to the thumb) while the student says the separate sounds of the word, moving magnetic letters to form words, repeating sounds and locating appropriate graphemes, moving graphemes to form words.	Fingers are raised for each separate sound in a word. Various activities in which students move markers or letters. Sound and letter cards are manipulated.
Are continuous sounds stretched longer for emphasis in phonemic awareness instruction?	Stretched sounds are used throughout the curriculum, both in phonemic awareness activities and later in decoding words.	Stretched sounds are sometimes used when the student has difficulty with phonemic awareness tasks.	No	No	No
What other intensive supports are used to teach phonemic awareness?	Scripted lessons follow a carefully designed sequence of instruction. Students move from teacher-guided instruction to independent	Use of Socratic questioning throughout lessons develops the student's ability to evaluate his own thinking and to self-monitor.	Teacher–student conversations are emphasized as a technique to assist student in problem solving.	None	An extensive resource binder includes numerous activities for developing phonemic awareness. There is a separate book titled *Sounds and Letters*

Continued

TABLE 2.5 Continued

	Direct Instruction: Reading Mastery	Lindamood®: LiPS	Reading Recovery	Wilson Reading System	Language!
	student-guided instruction through careful implementation of the My Turn–Together–Your Turn strategy. Coordinated correction procedures are used for student errors.	Choice and contrast questioning is used as correction procedure for student errors, allowing student to discover errors and correct them.	Students move from teacher-guided instruction to independent student-guided instruction through modeling and questioning.		for Readers and Spellers: Phonemic Awareness Drills for Teachers and Speech-Language Pathologists. The book contains a variety of sequenced phonemic awareness drills to be used with each lesson. Use of counters, stickies and other manipulatives is encouraged. Various templates aid listening to sounds in words.
What assessments are conducted?	Brief placement test assesses how much teacher support a student will need for success. Students begin the curriculum at the lesson designated by the assessment. Short mastery tests given to students approximately every five lessons determine whether students are ready to move to the next lesson or should move to a faster- or slower-paced group.	The Lindamood Auditory Conceptualization (LAC) Test, which contains a variety of phonemic awareness measures paralleling skills taught in the program, is given to determine appropriate groups for instruction. Although some groups may move through lessons more quickly, all students start at the beginning of the program. Ongoing observation of the student's daily performance on phonemic awareness tasks during lessons provides the foundation for decisions on how quickly to move the student through the program.	The phonemic awareness section of the initial battery of observational assessments requires students to write a sentence or two dictated by the teacher, who then analyzes the number of written phonemes. Ongoing observation of writing helps the teacher determine words to use for segmenting.	No separate assessment for phonemic awareness. Sound segmentation through finger tapping is a basic part of each lesson. Students must be able to correctly tap (segment) each word before moving to the next substep.	Mastery tests at the end of each unit include a section on phoneme segmentation. However, this is tied in with decoding. There is no separate purely auditory phonemic-awareness assessment.

When teaching phonemic awareness in English to second language learners, you can increase your effectiveness by increasing the cross-connections you make to the first language culture (Gersten, Baker, & Marks, 1998).

1. Once students have mastered a blending or segmenting stage, ask them to blend or segment words in their first language.
2. During story time, ask students to segment key words from a book you've selected about their culture.
3. Find a speaker of the student's first language and train him to teach short phonemic awareness drills. Supplement English phonemic awareness training with training in the native language.
4. Since modeling is critical for English language learners, stay longer at the My Turn phase of instruction.
5. Maintain consistent language and avoid metaphors and idioms that might be confusing.
6. Speak at a slower pace, teaching from a script such as the ones shown in Tables 2.2 to 2.4.
7. Hold up pictures of the words you are segmenting or blending to increase students' vocabularies.

Additional field-tested strategies for teaching phonemic awareness to English language learners are described below in *The Reflective Teacher*.

The Reflective Teacher

Intercultural "Blending"

Three months before Project PRIDE started, our staff assessed the phonemic awareness skills of the Laotian and Vietnamese children in the bilingual kindergarten class at one of our three schools. Although these students recognized common sight words and could identify letter sounds in isolation, only 17% could blend simple consonant–vowel–consonant words. The K–5th grade Laotian, Thai, and Vietnamese teachers taught in English for the majority of the day, but students learned to read in both languages, with an emphasis on English. Some teachers described their frustration teaching reading to students who came from Laotian hill tribes without established written languages.

During the teacher training sessions, we wondered if it was realistic to expect the Laotian teachers to use the precise sound articulation for blending and segmenting, a skill the other teachers learned in the first two sessions. Lao and Vietnamese are monosyllabic and tonal languages in which five or six tones determine the meaning of single syllables. When we visited the Laotian classes, we observed that students and teachers had these language issues:

- Pronounced /f/ as /th/
- Omitted the final /d/ in words or pronounced it as /t/
- Did not use plurals
- Often pronounced /s/ and /j/ as /sh/
- Pronounced /ā/ as /ē/; pronounced /ĭ/ as /ē/

Our decision about whether to conduct phonemic awareness training in Lao or English was resolved by the bilingual teachers who wanted to use the same Midwestern pronunciation as their peers. Using audiotapes to practice at home and practicing with the teaching coach at school, the teachers learned to articulate the precise Midwestern phonemes for their blending and segmenting instruction with the exception of /ĭ/. Because even with extended practice, teachers and students continued to pronounce /ĭ/ as /ē/, everyone agreed to accept that substitution.

Another issue that arose during the initial training sessions was more quickly resolved. During the first practice session of the training, a distraught Thai teacher approached us and said that

Continued

she could not snap her fingers as a signal for unison answers, a signal we were modeling during training. She explained that in her culture snapping fingers indicated that a woman was a prostitute. Assuring us that she was not offended when Westerners snapped our fingers, she said, "We understand that Americans do not understand this. Anything you do is okay. We just cannot do." The Thai teacher was visibly relieved when we told her that alternative signals such as clapping were just as effective as finger snapping.

Student success in learning to blend and segment in the bilingual classes was accelerated through the teaching style of the Asian teachers. Accustomed to integrating more drill and memorization activities into daily lesson plans than their American counterparts, the teachers often extended the recommended 10-minute time period for phonemic awareness skills so that their students had more time to practice articulating the precise phonemes. Maintaining the expectation that every student in their class would honor them by doing well on the assessment, teachers gave more turns to students having the most difficulty.

The teachers honored their students by praising their good work at least once every minute. Correct answers for difficult words were often followed by praise in the form of group applause. Routinely, the teachers praised their students 10 or 11 times for each time they corrected their work or their behavior.

After being taught phonemic awareness skills since the beginning of the school year, the new group of kindergarten bilingual students was tested in March to see if teaching phonemic awareness had made a difference. This time, 80% of the students blended words successfully. Explicit practice ensured that almost everyone had learned the key phonemic awareness skills needed to successfully meet the challenges of first grade.

How Important Is Phonemic Awareness Instruction for Older Learners?

Although the National Reading Panel showed that phonemic awareness training improved reading skills in students from second to sixth grade, the relatively few studies with older students leave more questions than answers. Phonemic awareness instruction for older students does not lead to the same improvement in spelling that is observed in younger students (National Reading Panel, 2000). Meanwhile, debate continues about whether valuable classroom time spent in actual decoding instruction with written text, when students are blending letters into words, will more efficiently accelerate older learners' progress than by teaching phonemic awareness skills such as blending and segmenting in isolation.

When assessment shows that older students are still not fluently blending or segmenting and you believe they would benefit from 5 minutes of practice each day, use the individual sound formats: *"Say the sounds in shake. /sh/-/ā/-/k/."* Be sure that students also verbally segment words before they write them. When students make mistakes segmenting, use the explicit teaching strategies My Turn–Together–Your Turn by immediately modeling the correct phonemes and then asking students to repeat them. A few minutes later, ask the students to segment the same troublesome word. Using a rap rhythm to segment motivates some older students, as does holding a microphone. Add a karaoke machine for additional motivation.

 Although the phonemic awareness screening assessments can be used with older students the benchmarks may not be applicable. For a norm-referenced measure of phonological processing that can be used with older students either as a screening or a diagnostic test, use the CTOPP, a test described earlier in the chapter. Teaching basic skills using computers can be an effective option for students of all ages. Criteria for selecting software to teach phonemic awareness is described in the *Technology* feature.

Technology

Phonemic Awareness

Although research has demonstrated that computer-assisted instruction can lead to student growth in phonemic awareness, teacher instruction is still more effective. Educators hope that as increasingly sophisticated computer programs are developed, the gap between instruction presented by a teacher versus a computer will be reduced. To date, the inability of computers to recognize phonemes and words pronounced by students remains the greatest drawback of computer-assisted instruction in teaching phonemic awareness. A teacher hears that a student said /n/ instead of /m/ and provides immediate feedback, first pronouncing the correct phoneme and then saying it with the student. Computer-assisted instruction is still unable to incorporate this type of feedback.

Despite this major drawback, computer-assisted instruction teaching phonemic awareness has improved substantially over the past decade. High-quality graphics and improved digitized speech accompany programs using game formats. These instructional games will predictably lead to growth for students who can quickly learn phonemic awareness through a My Turn instructional format. Students receiving computer instruction have increased their phonemic awareness,

and this increase has led to improvement in reading. Some teachers attempt to lessen the disadvantages of computer-assisted instruction by training paraprofessionals or volunteers to provide feedback and immediate corrections as they sit with students working at the computer. Here are some questions to ask when selecting a computer-assisted training program.

1. Does the pronunciation of the phonemes match what I teach during classroom phonemic awareness instruction? Are the stop sounds articulated without schwas?
2. Does the program allow the teacher to determine a sequence of sounds? If I have taught the following sounds, /a/, /i/, /b/, /m/, /s/, /t/, /f/, can I adjust the program to have students segment words that contain only those phonemes?
3. Is the game format distracting to the instruction? Will students continue their adventure quest even though they make errors?
4. Does the program keep a record that I can later use to identify the accuracy rate for an individual student's work?

What Games and Activities Will Reinforce Students' Phonemic Awareness Skills?

During the **acquisition stage of learning**, when students are first learning to accurately blend or segment, teachers should avoid games and minimize the number of errors that students who are at risk make in order to avoid spending unnecessary time reteaching. After students acquire the new skill and move into the second stage of learning, the **fluency stage**, they will continue to need practice with the new skill in order to become more fluent. Once students are accurate and fluent with the new skill, instruction can then focus on assisting them to **generalize** the skill to new situations. A student who has just learned to segment individual sounds with a high level of accuracy will still score below 35 phonemes per minute on the DIBELS Phonemic Segmentation Fluency Assessment because she has not yet developed the speed needed to effortlessly apply this skill at a rapid rate. Gradually increasing the pace of teaching during the Your Turn phase of your instruction develops students' fluency through expanded opportunities for practice. A teacher conducting challenging drill sessions using the segmenting individual sounds format uses rapid-fire questions as she asks the students, *"Say the sounds in bat,"* *"Say the sounds in bun,"* *"Say the sounds in cake."*

In addition to more challenging drills, structured games also provide opportunities to extend learning after students

> At the *Phonemic Awareness in Young Children* website, reading experts discuss phonemic awareness and provide ideas for related phonemic awareness game activities. **www.readingrockets.org/articles/408.**

have accurately acquired a skill. After Mr. Jeffries' class was successful segmenting first sound, his class went outside and played *Spiderweb*. When everyone was sitting in a circle, Mr. Jeffries asked one of the students to name the first sound in *cat*. As soon as the student answered, Mr. Jeffries held on to one end of a yarn ball and tossed it to her. Once again he quickly called out another word, and a spider web began taking form after the second correct answer and another throw of the yarn ball. For the next few weeks, Mr. Jeffries would play a number of different games requiring students to segment first sounds. In another month, when the class was successful with blending onset-rime, he would start playing the *I Have a Secret* game, asking students to blend the secret words he was making with the onset-rimes he said (/g/-/ōld/).

Games can help or hinder your goal to develop fluency with a newly learned skill depending on how well you structure the game. Games can trigger increased behavior problems if they require long waiting times, have infrequent student turns, last too long, involve rules the students do not fully understand, are perceived by the students as being unfair, or involve manipulatives that the teacher cannot monitor. You can avoid these problems by incorporating these suggestions:

- Preteach the rules to the game and ask students to practice them before actually playing the game.
- Avoid unnecessary manipulatives.
- Use team games where ⅓ to ½ of the students respond together.
- Keep the game time limited to no longer than 10 or 15 minutes.

The selection of games you use will depend on the maturity level and behavioral skills your students have. This year, Mr. Jeffries' class is able to play the *Spiderweb* game without students yanking the string out of another student's hand and having the ball roll into the middle of the circle. His class last year was less mature, with more children who were behaviorally challenging. Last year, this *Spiderweb* game would have collapsed into chaos within 4 or 5 minutes. The extended time it would take to walk outside was not worth the lost learning time. Thus last year, Mr. Jeffries adapted the game into an indoor *Frog Hopping* game, to include more turns and structure. He divided his class into four teams and had each team sit on a line that was part of a larger square. Then Mr. Jeffries called out, *"Team 1, what's the first sound in cat?"* If Team 1 answered by yelling out "/c/," he gave a thumbs up and called out a number. All the students on team one then had the opportunity to jump up and down like frogs the specified number of times. Anyone who did not follow the rules and started pushing over the other frogs in his line had to leave the game and sit by Mr. Jeffries' side. Since individual students had turns at least once every 1 or 2 minutes, students rarely were called out to the sidelines. After 5 minutes of much-needed exercise, the class was ready to listen to a story.

What Activities Help Students Apply their New Phonemic Awareness Skills to Reading Words?

Despite its importance to early reading, student acquisition of phonemic awareness skills alone does not guarantee reading achievement. The report of the National Reading Panel (2000) indicates that the effectiveness of phonemic awareness instruction is significantly enhanced if, at some point during the instruction, children are helped to apply their newly acquired phonological awareness skills directly to simple reading and spelling tasks. As you have probably already noticed, the chapters in this text are organized around key clusters of skills needed to become a mature reader, such as phonemic awareness, phonics, reading fluency, and so forth. While this organizational framework makes conceptual sense, it is not intended to imply that skills within each area are taught in isolation from each other and/or at different times. Therefore, it is critical to integrate letter sounds and beginning word reading and spelling as soon as possible into your phonemic awareness instruction.

By midyear, kindergarten students are ready to apply their phonemic awareness skills and blend the letter sounds they have learned into words. Wanting to avoid errors during this acquisition stage of learning, the teacher writes large consonant–vowel–consonant words on the board and asks the class to say each letter sound in unison before blending the sounds into a word. Some teachers use large magnetic letters for this early word reading; others have large magnetic word cards they put on the board. Large flip books with three columns of letters that flip over, with vowels in the middle column, allow a teacher to change letters easily so students can read the next word. Early word reading when the class is sounding out novel words without the teacher's assistance should be celebrated by the teacher and communicated to students and parents. Young children have no greater thrill than reading a word on their own for the first time. Teachers who help their at-risk students make the connections between these words and interesting books that they will soon be reading increase motivation for learning to read with enthusiastic feedback, *"Wow! You read the words, **cat**, **Sam**, and **hat**. The library has some funny books about cats, and you are learning to read some of the words that will be in those books."* Once students are easily reading three-letter words, the teacher can move on to simple sentences. The use of large sentence strips connected with a ring enables the teacher to have the entire class read the sentence in unison. After students read a sentence, the teacher asks comprehension questions to connect meaning to the sentences. Even a simple sentence such as *"Sam has a hat,"* allows a teacher to ask, *"Who has a hat?" "What is Sam wearing?" "What kind of animal do you think Sam is?" "Why do you think Sam is wearing a hat?"* By learning individual letter sounds and blending skills, students rapidly move into independent reading and comprehension connected to that reading. Formats for doing these early reading activities are described in Chapter 3.

The effectiveness of segmenting instruction is also enhanced by connecting segmenting and letter–sound recognition to spelling. From the day when they learn their first letter sound, students should learn to write the letter when their teacher says the sound, *"Write /t/." "Write /s/."* If you have taught students to write the sounds they have learned each week, students can write readable words as soon as they learn to segment. When students first begin to apply their segmenting to spelling, use large magnetic letters on the board, asking individual students to spell a word that the class has just segmented. The other students are then instructed to give a "thumbs up" if the word is spelled correctly, a task which requires everyone's active thinking. Before Ms. Jones asks her class to write *jam,* she first asks them to segment the sounds, /j/-/ă/-/m/. After they have orally segmented the sounds, she asks her students to write the word on the small chalkboards they are holding. To immediately correct any mistakes, Ms. Jones has the students hold up their chalkboards facing her as soon as they have written the word. During center times, in addition to writing practice, many teachers use magnetic letters with small groups of students who are segmenting and spelling. Some teachers use more structured sound boxes, requiring students to put sounds of the specified word into each box. Once students are using interchangeable magnets to spell words after segmenting them, the teacher can introduce phoneme manipulation. *"You read the word **jam** on the board. Now turn **jam** into **Pam**."* Chapters 3 and 4 will provide more ideas on how to move your students into reading and spelling.

In this chapter, research-based strategies for teaching phonemic awareness have been described. These strategies are summarized in Table 2.6 and compared to strategies often used in classrooms that are not using research-based practices. The *In Your Classroom* feature tells how to increase the time you have for reading instruction and reduce student behavior problems by teaching classroom routines and procedures to students starting the first day of school.

TABLE 2.6 Is Your Phonemic Awareness Instruction Research-Based?

Components of Instruction	Research-based	Nonresearch-based
Phonological and phoneme awareness	Explicit teaching of the speech sounds, distinct from the letters that represent those sounds; attention called to sound and word pronunciation; emphasis on blending and separating sounds in spoken words.	Minimal or incidental instruction about speech sounds, their features or contrasts; insufficient instruction in separating and blending the sounds in a whole word; confusion of phonemic awareness with phonics; little or no practice breaking words into parts; emphasis on rhyming rather than on segmenting and blending.

Source: Adapted from Moats (2007). *Whole-language high jinks: How to tell when "scientifically based reading instruction" isn't.* Washington, DC: Fordham Foundation.

Table 2.7 lists other classroom procedures teachers need to establish before they start teaching their first reading class. Only by actively monitoring are teachers aware of students who are and who are not following the rules and procedures. Whether directly teaching, supervising independent work, or coordinating a transition to another room, a teacher can minimize behavior problems by establishing a feeling of "with-itness" in the classroom (Gunter, Shores, Jack, Rasmussen, & Flowers, 1995). Teachers who are effectively monitoring move around to all corners of the classroom, use their eyes to scan other sections of the classroom than the one they are in, expect eye contact from students in their group, and give feedback on positive as well as off-task behavior.

In Your Classroom

Teaching Classroom Routines and Procedures

Structure and routines provide the predictability so many students who are at risk need to learn. Teachers who preplan rules and procedures, teach them, consistently follow them, and in turn praise students for following them are able to spend more time teaching because their students have fewer disruptive behaviors. These teachers can focus the majority of their attention toward acknowledging student success.

"Everyone in Team 4 is listening to Corisha talk about the dragonfly she saw. Good listening, Team 4."

"Class, give yourselves a pat on the back. We were so quiet walking down the hallway today that no other class was interrupted."

"Two days in a row where everyone remembered to turn in their homework. Way to go."

Transition times between one activity and the next will take less time when students are accustomed to following the classroom procedures and they know what materials are needed and where to go. When young students move between classes for "walk to read," teachers don't want to waste any precious instructional time correcting behavior. During the first week of class, a teacher of a more challenging class can teach students to go to their individual work groups by following this procedure:

- Tell students the procedure for breaking into their groups. For example, students should walk quickly and quietly to the designated area when their name or row is called, sit down, and start working on the assigned task.
- Explain that you will always tell the students what materials they need to bring to their groups so they will need to listen carefully.
- Explain that you will set the timer for 3 minutes, which is how long they will have to move into their groups and start working.
- Give the students an easy task so they can practice the transition. Set the timer and monitor the students by walking around and providing redirection if necessary.
- When the timer rings, praise students and give team points for making a smooth transition. If students don't meet the time limit, explain the rules and practice again.
- Once students are following the procedures, discontinue using the timer.

TABLE 2.7 Classroom Procedures for Reading Classes

Question	Elaboration
1. How do students participate during class discussions?	Are students supposed to silently raise their hands until called upon? How is this behavior taught? What happens when it is not followed?
2. How do students learn to answer in unison?	How are students taught to follow a signal? What happens when everyone does not answer?
3. What are the procedures for completing assignments?	Do students have a special folder or book for assignments? Is there a designated place in the classroom for them? Are students reminded at the end of the day about materials they need to bring home? How are parents involved in homework completion? What are the consequences for homework that is not completed?
4. What are individual seatwork procedures?	Is quiet talk allowed or are students expected to work silently? Is there a cue such as a raised hand to indicate when the noise level is too high? What is the procedure for interrupting? How do students indicate that they need help when the teacher is walking around and monitoring the class? How do students indicate that they need help when the teacher is working with another group?
5. How are books and materials passed out?	How are students selected to help with these tasks? Have students learned what behaviors are expected while they wait for their materials? Are materials organized so that waiting time is minimized?
6. What are the procedures for students turning in work?	Are there shelves or folders where students turn in completed assignments? What do students do when they have completed their assignments before the allotted time?
7. What are the out of seat policies?	When do students need permission to be out of their seats? What do they do if their pencil breaks? What do they do if they need a drink of water or have to go to the bathroom?

APPLIED ACTIVITIES

1. Two fact or fiction questions about teaching phonemic awareness to students who are at risk are included below. Pair up with a partner and take turns defending your position for one of these questions using references from research sources cited in the chapter or from information on the website resources listed in the sidebars.
   a. Teaching skills in phonemic awareness is not sufficient for helping students who are at risk become successful readers. Is this fact or fiction? Why?
   b. Teaching children using scripted lessons is boring for both the teacher and students. Is this fact or fiction? Why?

2. Listed below are key blending and segmenting skills. Number each skill in the list in the order in which you would teach it.
   a. Blending–Individual Sounds _____
   b. Segmenting–Onset-Rime _____
   c. Blending–Onset-Rime _____
   d. Segmenting–First Sound _____
   e. Segmenting–Individual Sounds _____

3. Using a handheld mirror, say each letter sound and observe how the sound is reproduced. Compare what you see to the description in the Articulation column of Table 2.1.

4. Ms. Garcia is a new kindergarten teacher. In unison as a group, tell her how to say these letter sounds without adding schwas: q, w, b, h, o, e, i, p, and y.

5. Use Table 2.1, which lists the basic letter sounds, to complete the following tasks:
   a. Circle each of the phonemes that are stop sounds and explain why they are called stop sounds.
   b. Circle each voiced phoneme in the following pairs; explain what differentiates a voiced phoneme from an unvoiced one.

f	v
b	p
k	g
t	d
h	u

   c. Which letter sounds are nasal (air expelled through nose)?
   d. Which letter sounds are formed by the tongue tapping behind the front teeth?
   e. Show how you would help a child who was unable to say /h/ learn to articulate that phoneme.

6. By November, most students in Ms. Gregg's kindergarten class can tell her the first sound in words that begin with any of the seven sounds taught during the first two months of school. The children can also blend words if she says the word's onset and rime. Describe what skills Ms. Gregg should teach next and in what order she should teach them.

7. During the third week of May, Ms. Harvey gave her kindergarten class the DIBELS test of phonemic segmentation fluency, and curriculum-based assessments in blending and identifying letter sounds in isolation. Ms. Harvey wanted to identify the students who were at risk for not reading at grade level so that the first-grade teacher could provide them with intensive support from the first day of school. Her students' scores on these three assessments are shown in Table 2.8. Using the DIBELS benchmark guide in Appendix B, place each child into one of the following categories based on his or her performance in phonemic segmentation fluency: *benchmark, emerging, deficit.* How did children in each of these categories perform in blending and letter sounds?

8. Figure 2.8 shows a DIBELS phonemic segmentation fluency score sheet for Damien. Is Damien at benchmark, emerging, or deficit in phonemic segmentation fluency? Based on his answers, identify Damien's current skill level in segmenting (What is he currently able to do?), and describe what skills you will now teach him (What skill do I teach him next?).

9. Orally segment the following four phoneme words into their smallest phonemes without adding any schwas. Count the number of letters in each word. For each word, determine whether the number of letters equals the number of phonemes. Explain.

   Fred   dump   black   stop   gags   help   spray

10. Blend each group of phonemes into a word and write your answer in the blank:
    a. /k/ /r/ /ă/ /k/ /s/ _____
    b. /b/ /r/ /ē/ /d/ _____
    c. /t/ /ē/ /m/ _____
    d. /l/ / ŭ/ /v/ /d/ _____

11. Identify the first and final letter sounds in each of the following words.

	First letter–sound	Final letter–sound
a. try	_____	_____
b. bride	_____	_____
c. fudge	_____	_____
d. camp	_____	_____

12. Every day, Ms. Hextel asks her class to segment the first sound of words. Demonstrate how you would instruct Ms. Hextel's class using the format in Table 2.2 to teach segmenting first sounds using the following words as examples:

    sat   man   bell   fit   sip

13. By January, the kindergartners at Davis Elementary School are ready to begin blending individual phonemes. You are working in one of the classrooms as a substitute teacher. Use the format in Table 2.3 to teach blending individual phonemes using the words listed below as examples. Remember to articulate the phonemes without adding schwas.

    cat   mill   big   win   yes

14. Map the phonemes in each of the following words. The first two have been completed for you.

close	k	l	/ō/	z		
greet	g	r	/ē/	t		
grand						
drain						
sell						
famed						
handed						
mass						
fanned						
sprig						
spill						

15. The following blending activity resembles activities included in commercial general education reading programs. Read the activity and then tell how you would enhance it to increase student responding and attention, provide support for new learning, correct errors consistently, include continual review and practice, add motivation, and teach to success.

    "Tell students they are going to play a guessing game with some words. Ask them to listen as you say the word *cat* slowly, separating the three sounds: /k/ /ă/ /t/. Segment the word several times, each time blending the sounds a little more. Then say the word *cat* in a normal way."

    Now ask the students to say other words that you will say in the same way. Encourage them to blend the sounds to say the words.

/k/-/ă/-/p/	cap	/k/-/ŏ/-/p/	cop
/k/-/ō/-/ch/	coach	/k/-/ŭ/-/p/	cup
/k/-/a/-/r/	car	/k/-/ŭ /-/t/	cut

16. Mr. Mixay is teaching his bilingual class how to segment words into individual sounds. On Tuesday, he segmented 10 words with his class, and students made errors on 4 of the 10 words presented. Acquisition of this skill has been difficult for the class, and Mr. Mixay noticed that the interest level of a number of students was waning. To get the

```
Name: Damien
Date: May 25
bad     /b/ /a/ /d/          lock    /l/ /o/ /k/        3 / 6
that    /th/ /a/ /t/         pick    /p/ /i/ /ck/       3 / 6
mine    /m/ /ie/ /n/         noise   /n/ /oi/ /z/       4 / 6
coat    /c/ /oa/ /t/         spin    /s/ /p/ /i/ /n/    4 / 7
meet    /m/ /ea/ /t/         ran     /r/ /a/ /n/        4 / 6
wild    /w/ /ie/ /l/ /d/     dawn    /d/ /o/ /n/        5 / 7
woke    /w/ /oa/ /k/ ]       sign    /s/ /ie/ /n/       1 / 6
fat     /f/ /a/ /t/          wait    /w/ /ai/ /t/       _ / 6
side    /s/ /ie/ /d/         yell    /y/ /e/ /l/        _ / 6
jet     /j/ /e/ /t/          of      /o/ /v/            _ / 5
land    /l/ /a/ /n/ /d/      wheel   /w/ /ea/ /l/       _ / 7
beach   /b/ /ea/ /ch/        globe   /g/ /l/ /oa/ /b/   _ / 7
                            Total   24 segments per minute
```

FIGURE 2.8 Damien's DIBELS Phonemic Segmentation Fluency Score Sheet

Source: Good, R. H., & Kaminski, R. A. (Eds.). (2002). *Dynamic indicators of basic early literacy skills* (6th ed.). Eugene, OR: Institute for the Development of Educational Achievement. Available at http://dibels.uoregon.edu/.

TABLE 2.8 Classroom Score Sheet for May

Names	May Blending Score Percent Correct	May DIBELS Segmenting Score	May Letter Sounds Percent Correct
Allison Cooke	100%	57	88%
Ben Bradley	100%	61	92%
Benito Valancia	80%	16	38%
Carla Gartyn	80%	39	100%
Dayrone Carton	60%	24	96%
Garret Crane	100%	37	73%
Jordan Morris	100%	16	100%
Juan Menesia	100%	40	100%
Kendra Thomas	100%	36	100%
Kent Gray	100%	48	77%
Kent Schrock	100%	37	96%
Kissick Bailey	100%	47	92%
Maria Gomez	100%	51	100%
Mia Mantos	100%	43	100%
Monikee Green	100%	48	96%
Shayleen Sanders	60%	5	85%
Shireel Brown	80%	57	100%
Simone Ashton	100%	56	96%
Tan Lee	100%	41	92%
Tan Souveythong	80%	49	92%
Tricia Wilson	100%	14	100%
Tyrell Jordan	100%	46	96%

students motivated, he decided to have them play a board game on Wednesday. In small groups, students moved around the board by segmenting words into individual sounds. What do you think of Mr. Mixay's decision to introduce the board game on Wednesday? What else could he have done in this situation to help his students meet the challenge of segmenting words in to individual sounds?

17. Carmen is an English language learner in Mr. Bartez's class. When segmenting the word *tape*, she said /d/-/ā/-/p. What should Mr. Bartez do?

18. If you are currently involved in the schools, examine the literacy curriculum used for struggling readers in kindergarten and first grade. Select six of the areas listed in the left-hand column of Table 2.5 and describe how that curriculum addresses each one.

Companion Website

Now go to Chapter 2 in the Companion Website (www.pearsonhighered.com/bursuck2e) where you can do the following activities:

- Complete Activities that can help you more deeply understand the chapter content.
- Check your comprehension on the content covered in the chapter by going to the Chapter Quiz. Here you will be able to an-

swer practice questions, receive feedback on your answers, and then access resources that will enhance your understanding of chapter content.
- Find Web Links that will extend your understanding of the content and strategies.

REFERENCES

Avery, P., & Ehrlich, S. (1992). *Teaching American English pronunciation.* New York: Oxford Press.

Burns, B. (2006). *How to teach balanced reading and writing* (2nd ed., p. 44). Thousand Oaks, CA: Corwin Press.

Bursuck, B., Smith, T., Munk, D., Damer, M., Mehlig, L., & Perry, J. (2004). Evaluating the impact of a prevention-based model of reading on children who are at-risk. *Remedial and Special Education, 25,* 303–313.

Bursuck, W. D., & Smallwood, G. (2009, April). *The reality of RTI: A study of two first year projects.* Presented at CEC Convention and Expo, Seattle, WA.

Capps, R., Fix, M., Murray, J., Ost, J., Passel, J., & Herwantoro, S. (2005). The new demography of America's schools: Immigration and the No Child Left Behind Act. Washington, DC: Urban Institute.

Carnine, D. W., Silbert, J., Kame'enui, E. J., & Tarver, S. (2010). *Direct instruction reading* (5th ed.). New Jersey: Merrill Prentice Hall.

Carnine, D. W., Silbert, J., Kame'enui, E. J., & Tarver, S. (2010). *Direct instruction reading* (5th ed.). Boston: Merrill Prentice Hall.

Catts, H., Petscher, Y., Schatschneider, C., Bridges, M., & Mendoza, K. (2009). Floor effects associated with universal screening and their impact on the early identification of reading disabilities. *Journal of Learning Disabilities, 42*(2), 163–176.

Celce-Murcia, M., Brinton, D., & Goodwin, J. (1996). *Teaching pronunciation: A reference for teach-*

ers of English to speakers of other languages. New York: Cambridge University Press.

Chard, D. J., & Osborn, J. (1999). Phonics and word recognition instruction in early reading programs: Guidelines for accessibility. *Learning Disabilities Research & Practice, 14*(2), 107–117.

Clay, M. (1993). *Reading recovery: A guidebook for teachers in training.* Portsmouth, NH: Heinemann.

Damer, M., & Bursuck, W. (2008). A year later: Performance of students who exit tier 3 direct instruction within a multi-tier reading model. *Direct Instruction News: ADI Effective School Practices, 8*(1), 12–16.

Durgunoğlu, A., & Öney, B. (1999). A cross-linguistic comparison of phonological awareness and word recognition. *Reading and Writing: An Interdisciplinary Journal, 11,* 281–299.

Elkonin, D. B. (1973). U.S.S.R.: Methods of teaching reading. In J. Downing (Ed.), *Comparative reading: Cross-national studies of behavior processes in reading and writing* (pp. 551–580). New York: Macmillan.

Engelmann, S., & Bruner, E. C. (2003). *Reading mastery classic.* Columbus, OH: SRA/McGraw-Hill.

Fletcher, J., Lyon, G., Fuchs, L., & Barnes, M. (2007). *Learning disabilities: From identification to intervention.* New York: The Guilford Press.

Fuchs, D., Mock, D., Morgan, P. L., & Young, C. L. (2003). Responsiveness to intervention: Definitions, evidence, and implications for the learning disabilities construct. *Learning Disabilities Research & Practice, 18*(3), 151–171.

Fuchs, L. S., Fuchs, D., Hintze, J., & Lembke, E. (2007). *Progress monitoring in the context of response to intervention.* Presentation at the National Center on Student progress Monitoring Summer Institute: Nashville.

Garcia, E., Jensen, B., & Scribner, K. (2009). The demographic imperative. *Educational Leadership, 66*(7), 8–13.

Gersten, R., Baker, S. K., & Marks, S. U. (1998). Strategies for teaching English-language learners. In K. R. Harris, S. Graham, & D. Deshler (Eds.), *Teaching every child every day: Learning in diverse schools and classrooms* (pp. 208–249). Cambridge, MA: Brookline Books.

Good, R. H., & Kaminski, R. A. (Eds.). (2002). *Dynamic indicators of basic early literacy skills* (6th ed.). Eugene, OR: Institute for the Development of Education Achievement.

Greene, J. (2009). *Language! The comprehensive literacy curriculum.* Longmont, CO: Sopris West Educational Services.

Gunter, P., Shores, R., Jack, S., Rasmussen, S., & Flowers, J. (1995). On the move: Using teacher/student proximity to improve students' behavior. *Teaching Exceptional Children, 28,* 12–16.

Invernizzi, M., & Meier, J. (2002). *PALS 1-3: Phonological Awareness Literacy Screening,* 2002–2003. Charlottesville: Curry School of Education, University of Virginia Press.

Jenkins, J. (2009). Measuring reading growth: New findings on progress monitoring. *New Times for DLD, 27,* pp. 1–2.

Ladefoged, P. (1975). *A course in phonetics* (pp. 1–57). New York: Harcourt Brace Jovanovich.

Leafstedt, J., Richards, C., & Gerber, M. (2004). Effectiveness of explicit phonological-awareness instruction for at-risk English learners. *Learning Disabilities: Research and Practice, 19*(4), 252–261.

Lewkowicz, N. K., & Low, L. Y. (1979). Effects of visual aids and word structure on phonemic segmentation. *Contemporary Educational Psychology, 4,* 238–252.

Lindamood, P., & Lindamood, P. (1998). *The Lindamood® phoneme sequencing program for reading, spelling, and speech: LiPS® teacher's manual for the classroom and clinic* (3rd ed.). Austin, TX: PRO-ED.

Lott, D. (2007). *Super star speech: Speech therapy made simple.* Huntsville, AL: Super Star DML Publishing.

McCormick, C., Throneburg, R., & Smitley, J. (2002). *A sound start: Phonemic awareness lessons for reading success.* New York: The Guilford Press.

Miller-Young, R. (1999). *The impact of concrete phonemic representations on phonological awareness acquisition of at-risk kindergartners.*

Unpublished dissertation, Northern Illinois University, DeKalb.

Moats, L. (2007). *Whole-language high jinks: How to tell when "scientifically based reading instruction" isn't.* Washington, DC: Fordham Foundation.

National Clearinghouse for English Language Acquisition and Language Instruction Educational Program. (2006). *What are the most common language groups for LEP students?* (NCELA FAQ). Retrieved July 29, 2009, from www.ncela. gwu.edu/expert/faq105oplangs.html

National Reading Panel. (2000). *Teaching children to read: An evidence-based assessment of the scientific research literature on reading and its implications for reading instruction.* Washington, DC: National Institute of Child Health and Human Development.

NCS Pearson Inc. (2010) AIMSweb.

O'Connor, R. (2007). *Teaching word recognition: Effective strategies for students with learning difficulties.* New York: The Guilford Press.

Quiroga, T., Lemos-Britton, Z., Mostafapour, E., Abbott, R. D., & Berninger V. W. (2002). Phonological awareness and beginning reading in Spanish-speaking ESL first graders: Research into practice. *Journal of School Psychology, 40,* 85–111.

Rathvon, N. (2004). *Early reading assessment: A practitioner's handbook.* New York: The Guilford Press.

Roberts, T., & Corbett, C. (1997). *Efficacy of explicit English instruction in phonemic awareness and the alphabetic principle for English learners and English proficient kindergarten children in relationship to oral language proficiency, primary language and verbal memory.* (ERIC Document Reproduction Service No. ED 417 403.)

Singh, S., & Singh, K. (1976). *Phonetics principles and practices.* Baltimore: University Park Press.

Stanovich, K. (1994). Romance and reality. *The Reading Teacher, 47*(4), 280–291.

Texas Education Agency and University of Texas System (2006). *The Texas Primary Reading Inventory (TPRI).* Austin, TX: Author.

Uhry, J. K., & Ehri, L. C. (1999). Ease of segmenting two- or three-phoneme words in kindergarten: Rime cohesion and vowel salience. *Journal of Educational Psychology, 91*(4), 594–603.

Wagner, R., Torgesen, J., & Rashotte, C. (2008). *Comprehensive test of phonological processing (CTOPP).* Austin, TX: PRO-ED.

Weisberg, P., Savard, P., & Christopher, F. (1993). Teaching preschoolers to read: Don't stop between the sounds when segmenting words. *Education and Treatment of Children, 16*(1), 1–18.

Yopp, H. (1995). A test for assessing phonemic awareness in young children. *The Reading Teacher, 49*(1), 20–29.

3 Beginning Reading/Early Decoding

Objectives

After reading this chapter you will be able to:

1. Identify and describe the sequence of skills needed for students to become full alphabetic phase readers.

2. Use assessment data to identify students who need more support, diagnose specific letter–sound and word-reading difficulties, and monitor student progress in beginning word reading in a multi-tier or RTI program.

3. Implement strategies for teaching letter–sound correspondences and beginning word reading that maximize the probability of students becoming full alphabetic phase readers.

4. Implement Tier 2 strategies to provide extra support for students, and identify and describe the beginning word and passage reading instruction of five commonly used Tier 3 reading programs.

5. Identify and describe ways to help older students and English language learners become full alphabetic phase readers.

6. Describe games and activities that can be used to reinforce students' decoding skills.

Companion Website

To check your comprehension of the content covered in this chapter, go to the Companion Website (www.pearsonhighered.com/bursuck2e) and complete the Chapter Quiz for Chapter 3. Here you will be able to answer practice questions, receive feedback on your answers, and then access resources that will enhance your understanding of chapter content.

Mr. Lange stared at the large rocket ship on the back wall of the classroom. "Teaching reading is rocket science; teaching reading is rocket science." The refrain echoed in his head and helped him maintain his perky teaching style while he led his students through reading that day's word list for the third time. With the energy of a football coach, he told his small group of seven students, *"If you read every word in this row correctly, it will be a 'firecracker row,' and we'll take a minute and pretend we are firecrackers going up in the air and coming down."*

Teaching kindergarten was so much easier ten years ago. Students were expected to learn through play, so much of his day was spent working in the different centers around the classroom. Mr. Lange had always been a kid at heart, and wielding a sword in the dress-up area or pretending to make bacon in the kitchen area came naturally to him. All of the students spent some time each day at the learning center, and by the end of the year most of the students could print all of the letters, knew their names, and were able to read some familiar books that the class had read together many times.

But when a multi-tier system was introduced into the school two years ago, and the literacy coach told the kindergarten teachers that the goal was to get 80% of the kindergarten students reading 15 nonsense words in a minute so that they would go into first grade with grade-level decoding skills, Mr. Lange hoped that what he regarded as one more teaching fad would disappear soon. He worked in a high-poverty neighborhood, and keeping his wiggly five-year-olds sitting and reading letter sounds and sounding out words as they followed his signals seemed impossible at first. However, when Mr. Lange listened to kindergarten teachers from similar schools talk about students' progress after beginning a multi-tiered reading program, he knew he had to try to replicate their results. His kids deserved the best, and if those teachers at Gary Elementary were saying the best was possible, maybe it was.

After attending summer training, Mr. Lange worked closely with a reading coach who came to his room every other week. After his students had learned several sounds, getting them to sound out words containing those sounds seemed to take forever. But the literacy coach wasn't satisfied with him having his students read the words only one time during the lesson. *"Your students need to practice reading these words several times if the sound-spellings are going to be stored in their long-term memory,"* the coach explained. *"As your students learn more words, they'll start learning new sounds and words more quickly."* All Mr. Lange could do was trust the coach and try to do his best with this new method.

In June, all the effort paid off when, after final benchmark testing, data showed that 85% of Mr. Lange's students had met the goal. He was as amazed as anyone, because secretly he hadn't thought it possible. He had doubted if more than three or four of his students last year would have read any of the nonsense words. When the principal asked Mr. Lange why his students were more successful than the rest of the kindergartners in the school, Mr. Lange looked at the rocket ship that he used as a reminder to teach to mastery and said, *"I just tried to follow the recommendations exactly. It was the hardest teaching I've ever done, but I've never had so many of my students pick up books that they've never seen before and read them. I thought that doing all this practice would turn them off from reading, but it's had the opposite effect. I'm so proud of them."*

What do you think was the biggest change for Mr. Lange and his students?

Why do you think more of Mr. Lange's students were able to read books they had never seen before?

What Beginning Reading Skills Do I Need to Teach?

Chapter 2 emphasized the importance of assessing and systematically teaching phonemic awareness to students who are at risk and explaining how an understanding of the sound system of spoken language relates to reading. Although this knowledge of our system of spoken language is essential, phonemic awareness is only one component needed for developing accurate and fluent reading. An effective reading program for students who are at risk must also help them attain alphabetic principle, which is "the recognition that there are systematic and predictable relationships between written letters and spoken sounds" (Armbruster, Lehr, & Osborn, 2001, p. 12). Gaining alphabetic principle through learning letter–sound relationships is the first step that indicates students have moved out of the first prealphabetic phase of reading where they view words as memorized visual forms. This understanding of alphabetic principle provides the foundation for students to then learn how to sound out individual phonemes before blending them into a word (/k/ + /a/ + /t/ = *cat*). Eventually, they will learn to read words automatically as whole words (*cat*). As readers mature, they learn to decipher new and familiar regular words accurately and automatically. Most importantly, the fluent decoding that characterizes students who read fluently enables them to focus more thought on the meaning of the text they are reading. In this chapter the term "beginning readers" will refer to students who are still reading at the first three phases described in Ehri's phase model of word reading in Chapter 1.

> Learn more about alphabetic principle and the role it plays in decoding: **http://www.readingrockets.org/ article/3408/.**

The purpose of phonics instruction is to teach students the relationship between written letters, or **graphemes,** and the 41 to 44 sounds of spoken language, or phonemes. Educators who minimize the role of phonics in teaching reading argue that the English language does not incorporate a one-to-one relationship between the 41 to 44 sounds and 26 letter symbols. For example, sometimes the sound of /ĕ/, as in *red,* also appears as *ea,* as in *bread.* The sound /ā/ can be written *ay* as in *may, a_e* as in *made,* or *ai* as in *maid.* These critics ignore the large proportion of regularity in English that justifies the teaching of phonics, which is supported by extensive research validating its effectiveness, particularly with children who are at risk or who have disabilities.

The foundation of our approach to teaching decoding is based on a systematic and explicit phonics approach called **synthetic phonics,** in which student success and independence are emphasized through the use of carefully supported teaching strategies and curricula. A teacher using a synthetic phonics approach first teaches the most common letter–sound associations in isolation using a logical, success-oriented sequence. With carefully supported teacher instruction, students learn to apply their phonemic awareness skills and knowledge of letter–sound correspondences to sounding out words in lists and sentences as well as spelling from dictation. The teacher provides substantial practice so that students can apply their decoding skills to reading and writing. Beginning reading books and written assignments are carefully coordinated with those skills.

Synthetic phonics is not the only explicit and systematic way of teaching phonics. Other systematic and explicit phonics programs include analytic phonics, analogy phonics, and phonics through spelling. **Analytic phonics** emphasizes first teaching the whole word before analyzing letter–sound relationships. In this approach, students learn letter–sound relationships using words they already know. Letter sounds are not introduced in isolation. **Analogy-based** phonics emphasizes using known word family patterns to identify unknown words. **Phonics through spelling** emphasizes phonetic spelling as the foundation for word reading. In this approach, students learn to break apart words into phonemes and to spell words by translating the phonemes into letters. Although the many varied systematic and explicit phonics programs are based primarily on one of these categories, realistically, most of the programs incorporate strategies from some or all of these approaches. In this book, when we describe how to effectively teach synthetic phonics, we also include recommendations from spelling, analytic, and analogy phonics approaches.

The systematic and explicit phonics approach described in this text follows a logical sequence of skills needed to read **regular words** accurately and fluently. The first words taught contain the most common sounds of individual letters. Once the student can decode some basic consonant–vowel–consonant (CVC) words, a relatively small number of irregular or exception words are introduced. A list of skills in a typical systematic phonics program is shown in Figure 3.1. Three skills specifically related to beginning reading are described in the following section. Note that the first group of words is likely to appear in beginning phonics programs when students are still unable to visualize the multiletter sequences needed to perceive larger word parts. Instruction for students who are still learning beginning reading skills at the individual letter–sound level should focus on the most common letter–sound correspondences, including the short vowels. The second group of more

Words for a Beginning Reader

1. CVC words beginning with a continuous sound:
   mad, mop, red, rig, sun
2. CVC words beginning with a stop sound:
   bad, did, gun, hot, jet
3. CVCC words ending with a consonant blend or double consonants:
   band, pond, jump, miss, kept
4. CCVC words ending with a consonant blend:
   clam, frog, glad, skin, step
5. CCVCC, CCCVC, and CCCVCC words beginning and/or ending with a consonant blend:
   Blink, glass, slump, split, struck
6. Compound words composed of CVC words or CVC variants such as "catnip" or "sandbox."

Words for an Advanced Reader

1. Digraphs
   *ma**sh**, **ch**op, **th**is, **ch**imp*
2. VCe (silent e) pattern words in which the vowel is long (VCV rule)
   - Words beginning with a single consonant (CVCe):
     hope, cute, Pete, mile, tape
   - Words beginning with a consonant blend (CCVCe):
     skate, spoke, froze, bride, stripe
   - Multisyllable words with a VCe syllable:
     Hopeless, excuse, likely, stampede, grateful
3. Letter combinations:
   *r**ai**n, h**ar**m, gr**ee**n, cl**ou**d, **sh**ed*
4. CVCe derivative words:
   - Words with *s* endings:
     *bite**s**, cube**s**, mope**s**, plane**s**, time**s***
   - Words with *er* endings:
     *lat**er**, smok**er**, us**er**, brav**er**, tim**er***
   - Words with *ed* endings:
     *hop**ed**, nam**ed**, smil**ed**, smok**ed**, glid**ed***
   - Words with *ing* endings:
     *nam**ing**, rid**ing**, clos**ing**, shad**ing**, bit**ing***
   - Words with *y* endings:
     *grav**y**, spic**y**, bon**y**, shin**y**, wav**y***
   - Words with *est* endings:
     *cut**est**, lat**est**, wis**est**, saf**est**, wid**est***
5. Y-derivative words:
   *fogg**iest** (foggy), funn**ier** (funny), part**ies** (party), bab**ied** (baby)*
6. Suffixes
   *cheer**ful**, ac**tion**, argument, trace**able***
7. Prefixes:
   ***a**mount, **con**duct, **mis**lead, **pro**test, **trans**late, **under**go*

FIGURE 3.1 Phonics Word Types for Beginning and Advanced Readers

advanced words mainly appears after students are reading at the consolidated alphabetic phase, when they begin to decode clusters as opposed to individual letter sounds.

Sequence for Teaching Beginning Reading

Identify the Most Common Sounds of Individual Letters in Isolation   All systematic phonics programs identify a planned sequence for teaching letter–sound correspondences. The most common letter–sound correspondences are stressed because they lend more predictability to the beginning reading process and also lead to the eventual

identification of more words. A beginning reader who first learns both sounds of *a* does not yet have the skills to scan the whole word *plane* and automatically make the decision between reading /ă/ or /ā/. Without those skills, she is still unable to differentiate consistently between two visually similar words such as *plan* and *plane*. Unable to make the decision logically between two sounds needed for more advanced reading, she may start guessing whenever she has to determine which sound to associate with a specific letter. Learning first to associate the grapheme *a* with /ă/ and then learning to read words in which *a* is associated with its most common sound /ă/ prevents the development of guessing strategies that lead to reduced word reading accuracy in text. A list of the most common letter sounds was shown in Table 2.1. Note that teaching the sounds of letters is recommended before teaching letter names. Students who are at risk are more likely to come to school unable to identify the letters of the alphabet by name. Since these students may have difficulty learning the letter names and sounds at the same time, letter–sound correspondences should be taught first because they lead more directly to reading words.

An often neglected key to teaching phonics effectively is the careful pronunciation of letter sounds. As you learned in Chapter 2, in the approach to sounds recommended here, great care is taken when teaching students to pronounce consonants without adding an *uh* or schwa sound to each. Guidelines for pronouncing letter sounds correctly were shown in Table 2.1 on pages 36–40.

Each systematic phonics program presents its own rationale for the sequence of letter–sound correspondences that are introduced. Although the National Reading Panel report (2000) didn't address the issue, the order in which the letter sounds are taught can influence how quickly students acquire them during instruction (Carnine, Silbert, Kame'enui, & Tarver, 2010). Letter–sound correspondences are most easily learned when the sound of the letter is in the onset of the letter's name, such as *k* (*kā*) *or v* (*vē*). More difficult to learn are letter–sound correspondences where the sound of the letter is in the final position of the letter's name, such as *l* (*el*) or *f* (*ef*). Letter sounds that have no connection with their name, such as the sound for *h*, are the most difficult for students to remember (McBride-Chang, 1999). *The Reflective Teacher* summarizes the rationale behind the order in which letter–sound correspondences are taught in two systematic phonics programs.

Read CVC Words   Orally **sound out** lists of single-syllable words that contain letter–sound correspondences previously taught. As they decode a word, students say each sound in succession from left to right. Students then blend the sounds together to quickly say a word. The first words students read are often referred to as short vowel words or consonant–vowel–consonant (CVC) words, such as *mat* or *sit*. Words beginning with stop sounds (*t, d, b*) are more difficult to read than those beginning with continuous sounds (*m, s, f*). CVC words are **regular words,** meaning that they can be sounded out.

Read CVC-Variant Words   Orally sound out and read lists of single-syllable **CVC-variant** words that contain blends composed of letter sounds previously taught. Single-syllable words that begin or end with consonant blends are more difficult to read than regular CVC words. **Consonant blends,** also called **consonant clusters,** are two or three successive consonant sounds said in sequence without losing their identity. Examples of consonant blends include *st* as in *stop, nd* as in *sand,* and *st* and *nd* as in *stand.* Since each consonant in a blend retains its individual sound, the blend *st,* which has two graphemes, is a two-phoneme blend since both /s/ and /t/ have distinct sounds. Thus, the word *stop* has four phonemes, /s/ /t/ /ŏ/ /p/, while the word *stand* has five phonemes, /s/ /t/ /ă/ /n/ /d/. A three-letter consonant blend such as *str* is composed of the three phonemes /s/ /t/ /r/. Because the phonemes are blurred to make a smooth sequence, students have a more difficult time hearing and spelling these individual sounds. Shut your eyes as you say these words slowly and feel your mouth change position as you say each phoneme. Appendix D lists initial and final blends with examples for each.

The Reflective Teacher

Sequencing the Teaching of Letter–Sound Correspondences

The order in which letter–sound correspondences are introduced can have a big impact on how easily they are learned. Described below are two different strategies for sequencing letter–sound correspondences used in reading programs shown to be successful with students who have great difficulty learning to read: *Reading Mastery* and *Lindamood®: LiPS*. Even if you don't use these programs, the rules they use for sequencing letters can be applied to adapt other programs, or, at least, give you clues to where your students might experience difficulty. As you read the descriptions of the way that letter–sound correspondences are introduced in the two programs, determine the strengths and weaknesses of each.

Rationale 1: Direct Instruction

Reduce confusion when learning letters with similar sounds or appearance.
Letters that have a similar sound or are similar in apperance should not be introduced to students at the same time. At least six letters should be introduced between them. Letters that have both a similar sound and a similar appearance should be separated by at least six letters. Carnine and colleagues (2010) further suggest that when introducing vowels, teachers should separate them by at least three letters, and that /ĭ/ and /ĕ/ be separated by six letters. Table 3.1 lists specific letters that students are likely to confuse and that are in need of separating when teaching.

TABLE 3.1 Letter Characteristics

Letters with Similar Sound	Letters with Similar Appearance	Letters with Similar Sound and Appearance
b and *d*	*b* and *d*	*b* and *d*
b and *p*	*b* and *p*	*m* and *n*
m and *n*	*m* and *n*	*b* and *p*
ĭ and ĕ	*q* and *p*	
k and *g*	*h* and *n*	
t and *d*	*v* and *w*	
ŏ and ŭ	*n* and *r*	
f and *v*		

Move into story reading earlier by teaching high-frequency letter sounds
Introduce more-useful letter sounds (consonant sounds such as /m/, /n/, /s/, /t/; all of the vowel sounds) before less-useful letter sounds (/x/, /z/, /q/).

Teach lowercase letters before uppercase letters
Most uppercase letters are not identical to their lowercase counterparts, and learning both at the same time can place an undue burden on a student who is at risk. Since beginning reading passages contain mostly lowercase letters, these are the letters that should be taught first.

Rationale 2: *Lindamood: LiPS*

Choose Your Approach
Depending on the needs of the students, teachers can opt for Path 1 or Path 2. In Path 1, all of the consonant sounds are taught before the vowel sounds. These sounds are then applied to manipulating phonemes, spelling, and reading. Path 1 is typically used for older students. In Path

Continued

2, three consonant pairs (a total of six sounds) and three vowel sounds are taught and then used in manipulating phonemes, spelling, and reading. When students have success applying those letter sounds to reading and spelling, the other consonants and vowels are taught. Path 2 is more appropriate for younger children and remedial students who have experienced consistent failure (Lindamood & Lindamood, 1998).

Teach the Brothers

Teach consonant pairs called *brothers*. Each consonant pair consists of a voiced and an unvoiced consonant formed with the same mouth movements. Examples of consonant pairs are:

/p/ and /b/
/t/ and /d/
/k/ and /g/

Teach the Cousins

After students know the brothers, teach the groups of consonants called the *cousins*. Nose sounds (/m/, /n/, /ng/), wind sounds (/w/, /wh/, /h/), and lifters (/l/, /r/) fall in this category.

Teach the Borrowers

Next teach the last group of consonants, called the *borrowers* because they borrow the sounds of other letters (/c/, /x/, /qu/, /y/).

Teach the Vowel Circle

Fifteen long and short vowels are categorized into four distinct groups according to the way they are formed by the mouth and tongue. Students discover where the vowel sounds are articulated, using sensory information to organize them into the following categories: round, smile, sliders, and open. Students learn to organize the vowels into a linguistic vowel circle depicted in Figure 3.2, organized by tongue placement and shape of the mouth for each vowel.

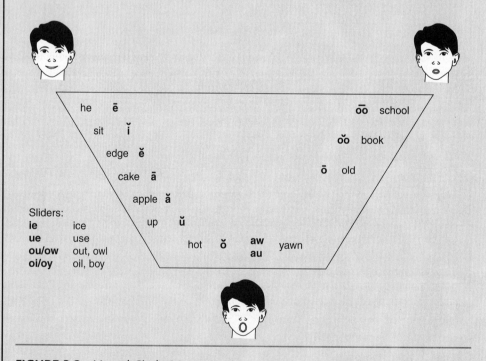

FIGURE 3.2 Vowel Circle Map

Source: Gildroy, P. G., & Francis, S. (1999). Learning about phonemes (Module I, Lesson 2). In B. K. Lenz & P. G. Gildroy (Eds), *Beginning word reading* [Online]. Lawrence. KS: University of Kansas, Center for Research on Learning. Available online at www.academy.org.

Either just before or after consonant blends are taught, students learn to read words ending in double consonants represented by one phoneme. Students learn to say the one sound that is represented by *ll, ss, ff,* or *zz* at the end of words. The knowledge that a word like *still,* which begins with a blend and ends with a double consonant, has four phonemes, /s/ /t/ /i/ /l/, helps you teach your students to decode similar words.

CVC words containing blends are described by their consonant–vowel pattern and are termed **CVC Variants.** *Stop* is a CCVC word, *sand* is a CVCC word, and *stand* is a CCVCC word. In a multisensory reading program, these CVC and CVC-variant words are referred to as *closed syllables* because each word has only one short vowel sound. Teachers explain that the vowel says its short sound because the word is *closed* at the end by one or more consonants.

> Teach blends in isolation, just as you would teach letter sounds. Predrawn initial consonant blend flashcards can be downloaded at the following website: **http://www.firstschoolyears.com/ literacy/word/phonics/clusters/ worksheets/initial%20cluster% 20letters.doc.**

Read a Small Number of High-Frequency Exception Words Needed to Read Passages

By teaching students a limited number of high-frequency or common exception words required for reading beginning text (for example, *the* and *have*), teachers can focus student attention on critical sounding-out strategies. **Exception** words, sometimes called irregular words, are words that cannot be conventionally sounded out and so must be learned as whole words. *From* is an exception word, because if the reader decoded it relying on the conventional letter–sound relationships, he would read the word as /frŏm/ since the short vowel /ŏ/ typically corresponds to the letter *o* in a CVC-variant word. *Said, where,* and *could* are other commonly used exception words in early reading books. If regular words have letter–sound correspondences that students have not yet learned in isolation, these words also must be learned as whole words and are considered exception words until the student has learned those letter–sound correspondences. The word *stop* is an exception word for a student who has not yet learned the sound associated with *p*. During the first two reading phases identified by Ehri (2005), before students have consolidated their letter–sound knowledge, learning to read exception words takes many exposures to the word until the word can be easily retrieved from a child's long-term memory (Reitsma, 1983). Teachers who wait to introduce most exception words until students are past the beginning reading phases save time because their students then learn these words much more quickly.

Sound Out Previously Taught One-Syllable Words in Sentences and Passages

Decodable books are those in which at least 70% of the text is composed of words that can be sounded out interspersed with a relatively small proportion of previously taught high-frequency exception words. Passage reading differs from reading lists of individual words in that students are reading connected text, scanning each word from left to right, moving from word to word, learning how punctuation marks affect meaning, and answering comprehension questions. In early passage reading, students are required to sound out words by independently moving their fingers from letter to letter as they orally sound out the words. Requiring students to move from letter to letter while pointing to each letter reinforces left-to-right reading and keeps the reader focused on each letter in the words, strengthening letter–sound associations. Because students who are at risk need more practice reading a word until its sound–spelling pattern is remembered, instruction should focus on decodable books containing mainly words that can be sounded out, with key words repeated at least several times during the passages.

Read One-Syllable Words and Passages by Sight

When students have ample opportunities to read word lists and text coordinated with letter–sound correspondences they have learned, they begin *subvocal sounding out* by silently moving their lips or silently reading the sounds before blending. Since some students will not make this leap on their own, teachers of students who are at risk will be more effective if they explicitly teach subvocal sounding out and provide practice for their students to use the new strategy. In the beginning have your students read words, first sounding them out loud orally, then subvocally, without making an audible sound, and finally by sight if their accuracy is high. Students then learn to read words by sight in lists followed by passages or connected text. Students who begin to use subvocal sounding-out are starting to become full alphabetic phase readers. Gradually, with more practice they will move to automatic word recognition.

Spelling and Writing What Is Read   Once students start reading CVC and CVC-variant words by sight, a more advanced sequence of letter combinations, rule-based reading, and structural analysis skills is taught to prepare students to read multisyllable words. Chapter 4 describes strategies to teach these more complex words.

Systematic phonics programs should also incorporate spelling and writing as soon as the students learn their first letter–sound correspondence. As students spell words, their knowledge of sound–spelling relationships improves and reading becomes more fluent (Joshi, Treiman, Carreker, & Moats, 2008). After learning to say letter sounds, students learn to write those same sounds. As students learn to read words, they are taught to spell those same words and incorporate them into their writing.

Following a skill sequence such as the letter–sound and word-reading ones described in the text does not mean that each skill is taught by itself and then dropped when the next skill in the sequence is introduced. In a systematic phonics program, newly introduced skills remain in play even as other, newer skills are introduced. For example, once students have learned a few common letter sounds, carefully planned instruction moves between applying these new sounds to reading words in lists and passages and applying them to spelling and written expression.

How Do I Assess Beginning Reading Skills in a Multi-Tier or RTI Model?

Screening Assessments

Teachers need to assess two key skills as their students develop beginning reading skills: individual letter–sound correspondences and sounding out of words. Careful assessment of individual letter–sound correspondences informs a teacher when to introduce regular sounding out of words. For example, when Ms. Remick assessed her students to determine whether they knew the six letter–sound correspondences she had taught during the first three weeks of school, almost every student in her class correctly identified the /a/, /m/, /t/, /r/, /s/, and /l/ sounds. Because previous assessments in phonemic awareness showed that her students could also segment and blend at the individual sound level, Ms. Remick knew that her students were ready to learn how to sound out CVC words beginning with continuous sounds. After giving the letter–sound assessment, Ms. Remick selected a decodable book that had only regular words containing the /a/, /m/, /r/, /s/, and /l/ sounds in addition to three exception words her students knew.

While not a skill that is initially useful in sounding out words, the ability to name letters of the alphabet or numbers rapidly is useful in identifying students who are at risk for future reading problems. These assessments of rapid automatized naming (or RAN) appear to measure **lexical retrieval,** or the efficiency with which a reader can locate and apply to reading previously learned information about letters and words stored in long-term memory. Lexical retrieval is an early indicator of fluency and is highly predictive of later reading ability (Jones, Branigan, & Kelly, 2009). In order to decode, students must retrieve sounds quickly so that they can blend them into words, and RAN assessments allow you to quickly identify students with weak lexical retrieval. Research indicates that RAN assessments requiring students to name letters or numbers are more predictive than those requiring students to name colors or objects. Among younger struggling readers, those who have stronger rapid-naming speed typically respond more quickly to intervention (Rathvon, 2004). Low scores on RAN assessments are characteristic of younger readers who need intensive intervention and of adults with reading disabilities, which is why these assessments are described in this section and should always be used to screen younger students or as part of a diagnostic testing battery for older ones.

Because RAN tests of rapid letter naming are included in many early screening assessments, sometimes teachers teach students to say letter names at a faster pace even though this instruction does not increase reading achievement and therefore wastes precious classroom instructional time. Although students can be taught to say letter names more quickly, teaching this isolated skill does not appear to translate into developing faster lexical retrieval with other naming tasks that haven't been practiced (Fugate, 1997). Such training risks invalidating student scores for any RAN test normed on a population of students who did not receive specific training in this isolated skill. In these situations, a student who has poor lexical retrieval but has had weeks of practice saying the letter names quickly might score higher on the rapid-naming test and might not appear to need support in reading because his score has been artificially inflated by the teaching.

Teachers also need to directly assess word reading to determine whether students are making progress toward reading at the consolidated phase. Although a regular word-reading assessment provides helpful information before second or third grade, a teacher doesn't know whether a child is reading these relatively easy words by applying decoding strategies or is reading them at the prealphabetic phase as visual images. A beginning prealphabetic phase reader who has memorized a large number of words in combination with guessing could do well on a regular word-reading assessment in first grade but still not have developed decoding skills. For that reason, in addition to regular word reading, students should be tested in reading nonsense words, also called pseudowords. The advantage of using nonsense words is that nonsense words can only be decoded by accurate sounding out. Nonsense words control for context as well as sight word memorization and are therefore a relatively pristine measure of a student's ability to sound out. Because nonsense words such as *vug, phlaim,* or *seeply* follow regular spelling rules, the results of a test of nonsense word reading enable the teacher to assess students' knowledge of letter–sound correspondences as well as the ability to blend letters to form words. Specific screening assessments for letter–sound correspondence, rapid automatized naming, and word sounding-out for beginning readers are described in the next section.

Letter–Sound Correspondence   The tasks for assessing letter–sound correspondence can differ greatly, as descriptions of these screening assessment subtests demonstrate. In the untimed PALS Letter–Sound subtest, students are shown 26 capital letters and asked to point to each one and say its sound. In the untimed TPRI Letter–Sound subtest, students are shown 10 upper- and lowercase letters and asked to say each letter's name and sound. Students receive a point only for correctly saying the letter sounds. The third subtest, the AIMSweb Letter–Sound Fluency subtest, is a one-minute test. Students are given a sheet of lowercase letters in rows and asked to identify as many sounds as possible in one minute. Incorrect answers are subtracted from the total. Because students need to retrieve letter sounds quickly, one would expect a letter–sound fluency test such as the AIMSweb subtest to be more predictive of reading problems than the letter-naming test described in the previous section. However, Rathvon (2004) writes that to-date research indicates that the letter-naming task is more predictive.

When Is It Routinely Given?

- The **PALS** and **TPRI Letter–Sound** subtests and the **AIMSweb Letter–Sound Fluency** subtest are routinely given in kindergarten and at the beginning of first grade.

Rapid Automatized Naming (RAN)   Because the ability to name letters of the alphabet is not needed to read beginning words, we recommend that this screening subtest, which tests a student's ability to say letter names rapidly, be used strictly as a screening measure and/or diagnostic measure and not as an outcome- or progress-monitoring measure. The validity of RAN assessments depends on some initial exposure to or knowledge of the alphabet; therefore, when students enter kindergarten without this exposure or knowledge, the measure should be given in winter of kindergarten at the earliest. The AIMSweb and DIBELS tests are almost identical. Students are given a minute to name as many of the upper- and lowercase letters of the alphabet as they can. For the DIBELS LNF assessment, students receive credit for every letter identified correctly. Desmon, the student in Figure 3.3, identified 28 letters correctly per minute in May of his kindergarten year. Locate the score in the DIBELS tables in Appendix B and note that a score of 28 letter names correctly read on the Letter Naming Fluency assessment indicates Desmon is at risk for future reading difficulties and thus has only a 20% chance of meeting the next benchmark without intervention. Depending on Desmon's scores in other areas such as letter–sound correspondence, DIBELS Phonemic Segmentation Fluency, and Nonsense Word Fluency, Desmon's teachers might decide to place him in a Tier 3 intensive reading program. Both the TPRI and PALS screening assessment batteries have subtests requiring students to say letter names, but because these are not timed tests, they do not assess rapid automatized naming.

When Is It Given?

- **DIBELS and AIMSweb Letter Naming Fluency:**   Beginning/end of kindergarten and beginning of first grade

Benchmark 1
DIBELS™ Letter Naming Fluency

Name: Desmon   Date: May 10

V	I	h	g	S	y	Z	W	L	N
I	K	T	D	K	T	q	d	Z	w
h	w	Z	m	U	r	j	G	X	u
g	R	B	Q	I	f	I	Z	s	r
S	n	C	B	p	Y	F	c	a	E
y	s	Q	P	M	v	O	t	n	P
Z	A	e	x	f	F	h	u	A	t
W	G	H	b	S	I	g	m	i	i
L	L	o	o	X	N	E	Y	p	x
N	k	c	D	d	y	b	j	R	v
V	M	W	q	V	I	h	g	S	y

Total: 28

Figure 3.3   Sample DIBELS LNF Score Sheet (for Desmon)

Source: Official DIBELS home page: https://dibels.uoregon.edu/measures/lnf.php

Reading Pseudowords   The DIBELS and AIMSweb Nonsense Word Fluency (NWF) assessments are also almost identical. As the name suggests, in the NWF assessment students are given one minute to read a series of make-believe words, all having the most common sounds of letters arranged according to a VC or CVC word pattern. The wording and scoring for the Nonsense Word Fluency test can be a problem, because if a student reads all of the words as individual sounds rather than as words, he receives the same number of points as if he read whole words. On the DIBELS NWF assessment, students receive credit for every letter–sound correspondence identified correctly, regardless of whether the sounds are identified individually or as a part of a whole word. For example, when Jamarius came to the nonsense word *bif,* he read it as three separate sounds, /b/-/i/-/f/. He received a score of 3 for three letter sounds identified correctly. When Matoria came to the same word, she read *bif* accurately as a whole word and also received 3 points, one for each letter sound in the word. Matoria's final score of 52 sounds correct per minute, with 18 words read accurately, indicates that she decodes words so fluently that she is starting to read chunks of letters and is ready for more advanced word reading. Jamal's final score of 52 sounds correct per minute and 0 words read indicates that he is unable to decode words phonetically and needs explicit instruction in learning to sound out. In the event students score 50–60 by reading single letter sounds only, Good and colleagues have added the following criterion for meeting benchmark: Students must also read at least 15 words as whole words (Good, Kaminski, & Howe, 2005).

The standardized directions for both the DIBELS and AIMSweb Nonsense Words Fluency assessments can be misleading for students who are told that they can read either letter sounds or words. We found that teachers could get students to read whole words rather then the letter sounds by doing the following:

- Talking to students before the assessment about how they would have a chance to read those silly **words**
- Stressing *"Read as whole **words** if you can"* when they say the directions
- Giving informative feedback after the assessment about how many **words** a student read

In our work with thousands of students, we found that more students met benchmarks in first grade if we set the bar higher for nonsense word reading. Students who left kindergarten reading fewer than four words typically started to fall behind in first grade as shown by their mid- or end-year benchmark scores indicating they needed Tier 3 support. When a higher benchmark was set, these students received the support they needed earlier. Appendix C, showing RTI/multi-tier decision rules set by one district, reflects those revised higher benchmark scores.

Some schools use PDAs, also called personal digital assistants, which are small handheld digital devices that store information, analyze data, and chart progress for progress monitoring. When teachers input NWF scores into PDAs, only the total scores of sounds read is recorded in the charts. Because this score can be misleading, in order to analyze NWF scores for screening, the number of words read should always be included in the analysis. Under the progress-monitoring section, Table 3.2 depicts an easy record teachers used in some of our project schools to track the number of nonsense words students read.

When Is It Routinely Given? DIBELS and AIMSweb Nonsense Word Fluency   Middle of kindergarten through the beginning of second grade

Reading High-Frequency Regular and Exception Words   Struggling readers have deficits in word reading; therefore, some beginning reading screening inventories

At the official DIBELS website **(https://dibels.uoregon.edu/measures/nwf.php)**, you can watch a teacher giving the Nonsense Word Fluency assessment to a student. Directions to administer and score the test are available at the same website, as are copies that can be downloaded at no charge.

TABLE 3.2 Nonsense Word Record Form

Student Name	Feb	Feb	March	March	April	April
		number of letter sounds/number of whole words read accurately				
Paula	44/10	55/10	58/12			
Pete	32/8	44/11	55/10			
Roberta	10/0	18/4	20/6			
Ted	36/8	44/10	44/11			
Steve	44/2	45/6	48/8			
Peyton	59/7	59/12	62/13			

include word reading as a subtest, either timed or untimed. The assumption is that when students read a combination of regular and exception real words, both phonemic decoding ability and automatic sight word reading are assessed. Since many students can retain up to 400 words in visual memory (Hempenstall, 2001), it is possible to do well on a real word-reading test in the early grades either by relying on phonemic decoding or by using visual memory. Not until fourth grade, when the visual memory demand increases to 4,000 words, are some students who have been relying on a strong visual memory identified as needing support when their visual memory is no longer adequate for more advanced reading (Hempenstall, 2001).

A typical word-reading test is the PALS Word Recognition in Isolation subtest. Students read high-frequency words from a list of 60 words. The TPRI Word Reading test is similar to the PALS with the exception that there are only 10 high-frequency words to read.

The Test of Word Reading Efficiency (TOWRE) has two subtests that can be used for screening. In the first 45-second subtest, Sight Word Efficiency, students read real words that range from one to four syllables. In the second 45-second subtest, Phonemic Decoding Efficiency, students read nonsense words that range from two phonemes to four syllables. For more information go to http://www.sedl.org/cgi-bin/mysql/rad.cgi?searchid=225.

When Is It Given?

- **PALS Word Recognition in Isolation:**   Optional for kindergarten; fall and spring of first through third grade
- **TPRI Inventory Word Reading:**   Fall and spring of first grade; fall of second and third grade
- **Test of Word-Reading Efficiency (TOWRE):**   Since the norming group for this fluency-based assessment includes adolescents, this test is appropriate for a wide range of students at any time during the school year.

Progress Monitoring for Beginning Word-Reading Skills

Letter–Sound Correspondence   When students are first learning letter–sound correspondences, teachers can informally monitor their progress by asking them to identify the letter sounds that they have learned after every four or five letter sounds taught in the reading program. This assessment should always include all the letter sounds taught from the beginning of the year until the time of the current assessment. Accuracy of 100% is required. By the end of October, Ms. Bolas had taught her class letter sounds for the following letters: *a, h, m, d,* and *s.* Then, in order to determine whether her instruction was effective, for two days during center time she worked with students one at a time, giving them a brief letter–sound assessment. The student test sheet, score sheet, and directions for the letter–sound correspondence assessment she gave are shown in Figures 3.4 and 3.5.

Note that in the measure, only the letters Ms. Bolas taught until the end of October were assessed. Note also that Ms. Bolas taught her students the sounds for both upper- and lowercase letters. If you are teaching your students the sounds for lowercase letters first, then your assessment should only include lowercase letters. Although some teachers add a column for letter names, the score for this assessment is based only on students' accurate identification of letter sounds necessary for word reading.

When giving the letter–sounds assessment, Ms. Bolas put a student test sheet in front of the student. Letters on the test sheet were typed in a large font matching the font used

H	h
T	t
A	a
M	m
D	d
O	o
S	s

FIGURE 3.4 Letter–Sound Assessment: Student Test Sheet

Student Name: <u>Caryn</u>   Date: <u>Oct. 31</u>

Directions: Place the Test Sheet in front of the student and hold the Record Sheet on a clipboard so that the student cannot see the scores you record. Point to the letters and say, "Look at these upper- and lowercase alphabet letters. I want you to tell me the sound that each letter makes." Cover all the letters except the first one with a sheet of paper, point to that first letter, and say, "What sound does this letter make?" If the student says the correct letter sound, write the score, slide the paper down one row, point to the next letter, and ask the same question. If the student says the letter name, say, "___ is the name of this letter. Now tell me what sound this letter makes." Uncover one letter at a time, until you have asked for the sound of every letter on the sheet. If the student says the long vowel sound, say, "That's one sound this letter makes. What is another sound this letter makes?"

Scoring: Score 1 point for every correct letter sound. Score 0 for every incorrect letter sound.

Testing Tips: The child either knows a letter sound or does not know a letter sound. Do not prompt any answers by giving hints. If a child cannot say just the letter sound, but has to say a keyword jingle that matches it ("/ă/ - apple - /ă/") or has to say the letter sound three or four times in succession (/h/, /h/, /h/), count the answer as incorrect. In order to accurately decode words, a student must be able to say the letter sound once and continue decoding.

Letter	Letter Sound
1. H h	1
2. T t	1
3. A a	0
4. M m	1
5. D d	1
6. O o	1
7. S s	1
Total Correct	6
Percent	86%

FIGURE 3.5 Letter–Sound Assessment: Teacher's Directions and Score Sheet

in classroom instruction. While the example above uses manuscript letters, if you are teaching D'Nealian, fonts in that script are available for your classroom computer.

Reading Pseudowords   Because teachers need to regularly monitor student progress in decoding, ideally a nonsense word–reading fluency assessment such as AIMSweb or DIBELS NWF should be given at least every two to four weeks for beginning readers in Tiers 2 and 3 starting in the winter of kindergarten until the student has met benchmark and the skill is scored as "established." Once students meet the benchmark score, they do not need to be monitored with this assessment any longer because their phonological decoding of CVC words now enables them to read new CVC and CVC-variant words by sight. Reading 15 words and 50 sounds on a Nonsense Words Reading Fluency subtest lets a teacher know when to start teaching the advanced word-reading skills presented in Chapter 4. A sample score sheet for the DIBELS NWF subtest is shown in Figure 3.6.

When one or two students in a class do not make adequate progress in developing decoding skills, that lack of progress reflects their individual need for more support. When the majority of students in a class do not make adequate progress on NWF assessments, the reading curriculum, the quality of teaching, and the amount of practice for everyone needs to be investigated. Teachers often ask if they should have their students practice reading nonsense words. Although some phonics programs use a few nonsense words for occasional practice, having students decode real words is more productive. Through additional practice decoding real words, the students are more likely to eventually learn to read them by sight. As students gain skills in phonological decoding, the NWF test scores will reflect that growth.

The 25 PALS Quick Checks allow teachers to monitor progress in pseudoword decoding. These untimed assessments begin by assessing CVC words, but by Quick Check #6 include words with blends and digraphs; by #21 they emphasize words with long vowel patterns. Because the nonsense words progressively get more difficult on the later tests, these Quick Checks can be used to monitor progress for both beginning word reading and some of the

Name: _____			Date: _____		
f a p	b o s	f i c	d i f	v i m	___/15
l o m	o v	v e f	h i z	b e j	___/14
r i z	m a g	v e g	f e v	u b	___/14
y u f	h o z	w u c	m i d	m e z	___/15
n a k	y i p	w u l	f e c	k a l	___/15
k u d	z u t	j u b	s u p	a d	___/14
t o f	n e z	l a l	d o c	b u j	___/15
r u d	p e s	s i g	n u d	z u r	___/15
a c	r i s	w o v	b o l	t a j	___/14
m o d	r o g	m o z	w u c	r o m	___/15

Total: ___

Error Pattern:

FIGURE 3.6   DIBELS NWF Assessment and Score Sheet (Blank)

Source: Official DIBELS home page: https://dibels.uoregon.edu/measures/nwf.php

earlier advanced word-reading skills. For older students, the TOWRE Phonemic Decoding Efficiency Subtest can be used for progress-monitoring nonsense word reading at "relatively short intervals" if only one alternative form A or B is given at a time (Torgesen, Wagner, & Rashotte, 1999).

Reading High-Frequency Regular and Exception Words Another set of PALS Quick Checks allows teachers to monitor progress in reading high-frequency regular and exception words. In this untimed assessment the words range from preprimer to third grade. For older students, the TOWRE Sight Word Efficiency Subtest can be used for monitoring progress in high-frequency regular word reading at "relatively short intervals" if only one alternative form A or B is given at a time (Torgesen et al., 1999).

Diagnostic Assessments for Beginning Word-Reading Skills

By looking at individual student answer patterns as well as the cumulative score on Nonsense Word Fluency subtests, you can tell how to adapt your instruction to move the student into the next decoding phase. Student scores on Nonsense Word Fluency assessments indicate four definite patterns as students develop beginning reading skills. These patterns are shown in Figure 3.7. Note that student 1, Jervon, is still reading at the individual sound level as indicated by the scoring of his nonsense word reading. Every letter is marked because he said only the individual letter sounds as he read words on the test. Student 2, Tori, is beginning to sound out by saying the individual letter–sound correspondence in each word and then blending those letter sounds together into whole words. The third student, Yolanda, is sounding out many words as onset rime before reading them as whole words. She is beginning to read many two-letter words automatically as one word without needing to sound out. At this stage, students' scores begin to increase substantially as they develop the skills of a full alphabetic phase reader. Finally, the fourth student, Katina, represents a student who is moving into the consolidated alphabetic reading phase. Of the four students, only Katina will score at benchmark levels. She is ready to sound out more complex words like those discussed in Chapter 4 and work on fluency in grade-level text. Jervon needs more practice sounding out and blending basic CVC words. Tori needs to transition to subvocal sounding out, so she begins to read words the fast way or more automatically. Yolanda is almost there. Continued daily practice with word and passage reading will help Yolanda go that extra step and move into the advanced word reading stage that characterizes someone at the consolidated alphabetic phase.

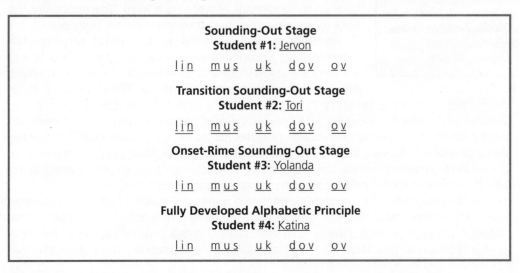

FIGURE 3.7 Sample DIBELS Scoring Patterns

The Woodcock Reading Mastery Test Revised (WRMT-R) contains two word-reading subtests that are normed for individuals from 5 to 75+ years. The untimed Word Identification subtest includes high-frequency regular and exception words. The Word Attack subtest requires students to sound out a series of nonsense words of increasing complexity. While this measure lacks the fluency component of the DIBELS Nonsense Word Fluency subtest, the use of multisyllable nonsense words provides teachers with more in-depth diagnostic information for older students. For more information on the Woodcock Reading Mastery Tests, go to http://www.pearsonassessments.com/wrmtrnu.aspx. To assess word-reading fluency, the TOWRE can also be used for diagnostic assessment for a wide age range of students.

Rathvon (2004) cautions that different regular word-reading subtests used for diagnostic testing can yield significantly different scores. Therefore, corroborating your findings with other formal and informal word-reading measures is recommended, particularly when making decisions such as the identification of a learning disability. When diagnostic tests are used to determine eligibility for a learning disability in reading, tests of RAN should be included. One alternative for assessing older students is the CTOPP mentioned in Chapter 2, which has four rapid-naming assessments and is normed for students from 5 to 24 years of age. Another option for older students is the test of Rapid Picture Naming on the Woodcock-Johnson III Test of Cognitive Abilities, which has norms for examinees from 2 through 90 years of age.

Appendix E includes an informal phonics diagnostic assessment to provide information for teachers whose students are beginning readers. The measure tells you which beginning letter–sound correspondences students have learned and which CVC variants students are able to decode. This information can then be used to identify letter sounds and word types for instruction. For example, if on this assessment Grace misreads only the letter sound for x, but then misreads all CCVC words with beginning blends and the more difficult words, Mr. Farley knows to teach her the sound of x and to begin teaching her to read blends in isolation, in words, and in text.

Spelling Assessment

Three of the four assessment screening batteries have spelling tests that can be used for either screening, progress monitoring, or diagnostic purposes. AIMSweb has first- through eighth-grade spelling tests that can be used for screening or progress monitoring. The 12 words on each test represent high-frequency words, some regular and some irregular. Students have up to 10 seconds to write each word. Teachers score the tests by counting the number of correct letter sequences.

More information on curriculum-based measurement spelling probes and how to compute correct letter sequences can be found at **http://www.jimwrightonline.com/pdfdocs/cbmresources/cbmdirections/cbmspell.pdf.**

Spelling is also assessed in the PALS Kindergarten Letter–Sound Knowledge section on an untimed test where students are asked to spell five CVC words, receiving one point for each letter sound correctly written. The Grades 1–3 PALS also includes a spelling inventory as part of the Word Knowledge screening section. Because all of the words are regular with specific types of phonics patterns (e.g., blends, digraphs, nasals, long vowels), this subtest provides diagnostic information to help a teacher plan instruction. Points are awarded for specific phonics features that are spelled correctly. Quick Checks requiring students to spell regular words that get progressively more difficult over the course of the school year allow for progress monitoring.

On the first-grade TPRI, students complete a number of spelling tasks with magnetic boards and letters. After students spell an orally dictated CVC word, they manipulate the magnetic letters to make requested final consonant substitutions, middle vowel substitutions, and initial and final blending substitutions. Both the second- and third-grade inventories include regular word-spelling tests.

How Do I Teach Beginning Reading Skills to My Students?

As emphasized in Chapters 1 and 2, the multi-tier and RTI approaches described in this text allow teachers to accommodate a range of learners. The teaching enhancements described in those chapters also apply for each of the key skill areas in beginning reading instruction. The general education reading program for children who are at risk is enhanced through the use of advance organizers, unison responding, perky pace, support for new learning using My Turn–Together–Your Turn, systematic error corrections, cumulative review, integrated motivational strategies, and teaching to success. The following formats for teaching letter–sound correspondences, word reading, and text reading are used for large-group Tier 1 instruction and also small-group Tier 2 interventions. In addition, descriptions of more intensive programs appropriate for Tier 3 are provided along with special strategies for English language learners and older students.

Identifying Letter–Sound Correspondences

Even when students can segment and blend, before learning to sound out words they must be able to automatically identify some letter–sound correspondences in isolation. For example, Carnine and colleagues (2010) recommend that at least six to eight letter–sound correspondences, including one or two vowels, be taught prior to the introduction of sounding out words. Failure to work on letter–sound correspondences in isolation prior to sounding out words can result in the problem shown in the following example:

> Keionda's teacher showed her how to sound out the word *man,* but Keionda had not learned /ă/, the most common sound of the letter *a.* Keionda's teacher had to stop the decoding instruction temporarily in order to practice the /ă/ letter–sound correspondence. Stopping to work on a letter sound that should have been learned previously slowed the pace of the lesson and diverted Keionda's attention from learning the decoding strategy. This spur-of-the-moment instruction on /ă/ did not provide enough practice for Keionda to predictably remember that letter sound the next day.

Many programs teach sounds using an indirect approach. Instead of introducing letter sounds in isolation, teachers write a list of words that begin with a new letter on the board. After asking the students what letter sound is the same in all of these words, the teacher asks the students to say the sound of the new letter. For students with disabilities or who are at risk, this approach is clearly not explicit enough. Such an approach does not provide enough practice of the new letter–sound correspondence or review of previously introduced sounds. The format in Table 3.3 directly teaches letter–sound correspondences and provides extensive student practice and review. The first part of this format introduces the new letter–sound correspondence using the My Turn–Together–Your Turn strategy shown in steps 2–5 in Table 3.3. In Part B of this format, the teacher provides practice of the new letter–sound correspondence in combination with six or seven other previously introduced sounds. In Part B, the teacher reduces scaffolding by first testing the group (Your Turn) on the new and review letter sounds before checking student mastery by calling on individual students to read the letter sounds.

Figure 3.8 shows the LOOP signal used by the teacher to elicit unison answers from the group. As shown, the teacher first points to the left of the letter, provides a thinking pause, asks "what sound?" and then loops his finger to touch underneath the letter. He pauses under the letter two to three seconds for continuous sounds and immediately bounces out for stop sounds. When he bounces off to return to the starting point or loops

FIGURE 3.8 LOOP Signal

TABLE 3.3 Format for Teaching New Letter Sounds in the General Curriculum

Objective	After seeing a new letter, students will say its sound with 100% accuracy
Materials Needed	Board, chart paper, or overhead transparency and writing implement
Signaling	Before starting letter–sound drill, students should practice responding to your loop signal, so they learn to say the sound of the letter as long as your finger stays on the letter. Place your finger to the left of the letter. **"What sound?"** initiates the signal for unison answers.
	Signal for continuous sounds: After looping to the letter, hold your finger under it for 2 seconds as students say the sound, before looping your finger back to the starting point.
	Signal for stop sounds: After looping to the letter, immediately bounce your finger out as students say the sound, and return to the starting point.
Time	3–5 minutes

Teaching New Letter Sounds: Part A

Instructions	Teacher	Students
	1. Advance Organizer	
	2. My Turn (examples given for continuous and stop sounds). During the beginning reading phases typically only one sound would be introduced.	
	Write a lowercase letter *s* on the board and point to the letter:	
	Signal for *continuous sounds:* (finger to the left of letter) **"Here's our new sound for today."** (loop signal) **"/s/."** (loop back to starting point) **"This letter says"** (loop signal) **"/s/"** (end signal).	
	Write a lowercase letter *t* on the board and point to the letter:	
	Signal for *stop sounds:* (finger to the left of letter) **"Here's our new sound for today."** (loop signal and bounce out) **"/t/."** (back to starting point) **"This letter says"** (loop signal and bounce out) **"/t/."** (end signal).	
	3. Together	
	The teacher answers with students this time.	
	Signal for *continuous sounds:* (finger to the left of letter) **"Together. What sound?"** (loop signal) **"/s/."** (loop back to starting point) **"Yes, /s/."**	/s/
	Signal for *stop sounds:* (finger to the left of letter) **"Together. What sound?"** (loop signal and bounce out) **"/t/."** (back to starting point) **"Yes, /t/."**	/t/
	Repeat this sequence several times.	
	4. Your Turn	
	Signal for *continuous sounds:* (finger to the left of letter) **"Your turn. What sound?"** (loop signal) (answer) (loop back to starting point) **"Yes, /s/."**	/s/
	Signal for *stop sounds:* (finger to the left of letter) **"Your turn. What sound?"** (loop signal and bounce out) (answer) (back to starting point) **"Yes, /t/."**	/t/
	Repeat several times.	
	5. Individual Student Checkout	
	Signal for *continuous sounds:* (finger to the left of letter) **"Individual turns. What sound? Marissa."** (loop signal) (answer) (loop back to starting point) **"Yes, /s/."**	/s/
	Signal for *stop sounds:* (finger to the left of letter) **"Individual turns. What sound? Tonia."** (loop signal and bounce out) (answer) (back to starting point) **"Yes, /t/."**	/t/
	Call on several individual students and check accuracy.	
Error Correction	If students make an error, immediately return to a My Turn–Together–Your Turn pattern. You may need to refocus students to your mouth position as you say the letter.	

TABLE 3.3   Continued

Teaching New Letter Sounds with Review Sounds: Part B		
Instructions	**Teacher**	**Students**
Scaffolding Reduction	1. Advance Organizer	
	2. Your Turn	
	The teacher uses an alternating pattern to teach the new letter sound by writing the new lowercase letter on the board followed by one previously taught letter, followed by the new letter, followed by two previously taught letters. This pattern is continued until five letters separate the last two new letters (for example, **s** t s a t **s** m t a **s** h m t a **s** a t h m f **s**). The teacher provides more practice identifying the more difficult previously taught letters and vowels by including them in the list every day.	
	Signal for *continuous sounds:* (finger to the left of letter) **"Your turn. What sound?"** (loop signal) (answer) (loop back to starting point) **"Yes, /s/."**	/s/, /t/, /s/, /a/, /t/,
	Signal for *stop sounds:* (finger to the left of letter) **"Your turn. What sound?"** (loop signal and bounce out) (answer) (back to starting point) **"Yes, /t/."**	/s/, /m/, /t/ /s/
	3. Individual Student Checkout	
	Signal for *continuous sounds:* (finger to the left of letter) **"Individual turns. What sound? Kyle."** (loop signal) (answer) (loop back to starting point) **"Yes, /s/."**	/s/
	Signal for *stop sounds:* (finger to the left of letter) **"Individual turns. What sound?** **Lynnette."** (loop signal and bounce out) (answer) (back to starting point) **"Yes, /ă/."** Call on several individual students to check accuracy.	/ă/
Error Correction	If students make an error, immediately return to a My Turn–Together–Your Turn pattern. Then alternate between the missed letter and familiar letters until students identify the missed letter correctly three times.	
	For example, if you are working on *a, m, r, s,* and *i,* and the students missed *s,* say, (finger to the left of letter) **"This sound is /s/."** before asking, **"What sound?"** (loop signal and end) **"Yes, /s/."**	
	Then ask the students to identify letter sounds using the following alternating pattern: **a s** m **i s** r **i** m **s**.	
Perk Up Your Drill	▪ Vary the color of the letters.	
	▪ Hold your pointer finger on a continuous sound letter for an extra second or two and praise everyone who had enough air to hold it the entire time.	
	▪ Occasionally tell students that they will say the sounds in booming lion voices, in squeaky mouse voices, or in robot voices.	
	▪ Occasionally signal using an unusual pointer such as a puppet's hand, a wand, or a baton. Decorate a pointer to fit the occasion; dress it up with ribbons and glitter or an appropriate theme for the time of year.	
	▪ Some teachers teach their students to finger-spell the new letter as they say it. Other teachers add easier hand signals for the more difficult letters. For example, when students say /p/, the teacher has them point their finger down; when students say /i/, the teacher holds up a pretend antenna to represent an *insect.* Signals can provide extra motivation as long as teachers eventually fade them out. Signals should not interfere with the pace of instruction.	
Adaptations	▪ When students have reached 100% accuracy on Part B, you can begin to use a combination of upper-case and lowercase letters.	
	▪ Before teaching the new letter sound, see if students in the class can repeat the new sound after they hear you say it. Some students may need articulation practice. For example, if students have difficulty saying /p/, put your fingers to your lips and show the students how your lips pop when you say the /p/ sound. Next ask the students to put their fingers on their lips and make the same lip-popping sound. If some of the students are vocalizing the /b/ sound instead of the /p/ sound, ask students to put their hands on their necks in order to feel the difference between a voiced sound and an unvoiced sound.	

Source: This script is based on one originally developed and field-tested by Carnine, D. W., Silbert, J., Kame'enui, E. J., & Tarver, S. (2010). *Direct Instruction Reading* (5th ed.). Boston: Merrill.

back to the starting point, students stop saying the letter sound. In this way, the teacher can calibrate the length of time students say the sound.

Two Best Practices for Teaching Letter–Sound Correspondences   Let's look at how Mrs. Nguyen taught letter sounds to her class, using the following effective teaching strategies.

Use Classroom Time Efficiently   Since many of Mrs. Nguyen's students came to school with limited language skills, she started teaching letter–sound correspondences by the second week of school. Although the general education curriculum was designed to teach one letter–sound correspondence a week, she knew that she could not waste any time because many of her kindergartners would need two weeks on each vowel sound and the more difficult consonant sounds. Every morning after calendar time, she immediately started her language arts instruction by following the letter–sound format in Table 3.3 for three to five minutes. When teaching a new letter–sound correspondence, Mrs. Nguyen used the format in Table 3.3 Part A: Steps 1–5 for the first two or three days. Every day after teaching the new letter sound of the week, Mrs. Nguyen reviewed the previous letter sounds. Immediately after practicing the new /b/ sound, Mrs. Nguyen used the format in Table 3.3: Part B, reviewing the /f/, /s/, /a/, and /m/ letter sounds that she had taught during the first month and a half of school.

Give More Individual Turns to Students Who Have the Most Difficulty   Shoshana, Greg, and Tracy's scores on last month's letter–sound assessment showed that they had learned the fewest sounds, so Mrs. Nguyen asked them more questions during individual student checkouts.

Companion Website

Go to the Video Activities section of Chapter 3 in the Companion Website (www.pearson-highered.com/bursuck2e) and complete the activities entitled *Letter Sounds in Isolation: Introducing New Sounds and New Sounds Review.* Watch a teacher using the script found in Table 3.3.

Writing Letter–Sound Correspondences

Students' learning of letter–sound correspondences is enhanced when they are required to spell the sounds and words they are reading. Therefore, when you are teaching letter sounds in isolation, students should also write as well as say the sounds. For example, Ms. Chapelle's students can identify the most common sounds for the following letters: *s, r, m, t, a,* and *d.* After her students practice saying the letter sounds, Ms. Chapelle has her students take out their whiteboards and write the same letter sounds from dictation using the format shown in Figure 3.9.

Louisa Moats describes why spelling (encoding) instruction helps students' ability to read (decoding) and the complementary relationship between the two:

> Ehri and Snowling (2004) found the ability to read words "by sight" (i.e., automatically) rests on the ability to map letters and letter combinations to sounds. Because words are not very visually distinctive (for example, *car, can, cane*), it is impossible for children to memorize more than a few dozen words unless they have developed insights into how letters and sounds correspond. Learning to spell requires instruction and gradual integration of information about print, speech sounds, and meaning—these, in turn, support memory for whole words, which is used in both spelling and sight reading. (Moats, 2005, p. 12)

Sound Spelling Activity: Children write /t/ and /r/.

Teacher: **"You're going to write some letter sounds."**
  "First sound /t/. What sound?" (signal) (answer) **"Yes, /t/."**
  "Write /t/." Check children's answers and give feedback.
  "Next sound /r/. What sound?" (signal) (answer) **"Yes, /r/."**
  "Write /r/." Check children's answers and give feedback.

FIGURE 3.9   Sound Writing Format

Source: This script was adapted from Engelmann, S., & Bruner, E. (1995).
Reading Mastery I: Teacher's guide. Columbus, OH: SRA Macmillan/McGraw-Hill.

Make sure that your teaching objectives integrate teaching students to say and to write the letter–sound associations you teach. The kindergarten teacher, Ms. Krill, would be teaching ten letter sounds in the next ten weeks. Thus, when she wrote her teaching objectives for that quarter, in addition to expecting students to look at a letter and say the most common sound associated with it, she wrote the following spelling objective: "When orally presented with the sounds /s/, /f/, /m/, /t/, /a/, /p/, /b/, /i/, /c/, and /d/, the students will write the correct letter for 10 out of the 10 sounds." Because many of Ms. Krill's students came to school unable to write their letters, she made handwriting instruction a part of sound instruction until students could reproduce the letters. For students requiring more support, she integrated handwriting into some of her Tier 2 groups.

Although none of the four assessment batteries tests spelling at the sound–symbol level, be sure that beginning readers can spell the new letter–sound correspondences you are teaching. The informal letter–sound assessment described earlier in the diagnostic section can be used to assess students' encoding of letter sounds. Give each student a sheet of paper with blank lines and ask them to write the letter that represents a sound you say.

> Read about the 12 components of research-based reading programs at the Reading Rockets website: **http://www.readingrockets.org/articles/242.**

Applying the Enhancements to a Commercial Reading Program

The following lesson introducing the most common sound for the letter *u* is a typical lesson from a commercial reading program:

> Say *us* and *under* slowly, focusing on the /u/ sound. Ask the students what sound they hear at the beginning of both words. Write a large uppercase *U* and lowercase *u* on the blackboard and say, "This is uppercase *U* and this is lowercase *u.*" Tell the students that a vowel can stand for several sounds. Call on volunteers to identify words in a rhyme printed on a chart that begin with the letter *u.*

> Write *us* and *under* on the chart and have the students tell you other words that begin with the /u/ sound. Add these words to the chart and read them all together with the students.

This activity is likely to create several problems for children who are at risk. First, and most importantly, the lesson doesn't provide adequate practice and support by introducing the letter sound using a My Turn–Together–Your Turn strategy. Students never directly hear the sound that the letter *u* represents, nor are they given any direct practice on saying the letter sound while the teacher points to the letter. Pointing to words with *u* in the rime and volunteering words that begin with the letter *u* can all be done without making the association between the sound and the written letter *u*. If the teacher has called on individual students to answer these questions, adequate practice for everyone is not provided. Students who are at risk will be unlikely to be able to identify the short sound for the letter *u* when they come to a word that has its most common sound.

Another problem with this lesson is that the words on the chart that students read are not in any way coordinated with the letter sounds and skills they have already learned. During the previous week students may have learned the difficult letter sound /j/, which still needs daily practice. When words on the chart do not incorporate cumulative review, prior learning is frequently forgotten. Students are encouraged to memorize the words, thus promoting the idea that reading words involves memorization, not sounding out.

Enhancing this lesson for students who are at risk includes adding more My Turn–Together–Your Turn opportunities so everyone gets enough practice. The format for introducing new letter sounds in the general curriculum, which was shown in Table 3.3 (pages 96–97), can be used by teachers to instruct any new letter–sound correspondence. Once students receive more directed instruction and practice with the new letter–sound association by itself, teachers have students practice the new letter sound along with previously introduced sounds using Part B of the same format. Any teacher using a reading curriculum containing lessons similar to the example /u/ lesson can modify letter–sound activities by starting lessons using the formats included in Table 3.3. Although it is important that students directly see how the letter sounds and phonemic awareness skills they are learning relate to word reading, having students read these words as sight words can undermine their acquisition of the alphabetic principle. Instead of having students read the words, ask them to say the first letter sound when you point to and read the words on the chart. Additional ways you can help your students learn letter–sound correspondences are described in the *In Your Classroom* feature.

In Your Classroom

Helping Your Students Articulate and Differentiate Letter Sounds

The *b* vs. *d* Conundrum

When your daily teaching shows that some of the first graders are still mixing lowercase *b*'s with *d*'s, they will benefit from practicing reading words with these letter sounds. The key to this practice is focusing on accuracy. The more /b/-/d/ errors your students make, the more reteaching you have to do. Show students how the lowercase *b* looks like a bat and ball. Ask them what letter sound *bat* starts with, and then ask what letter sound *ball* starts with. Then ask, "If the letter looks like a bat and ball, what is its sound?" Make a list of six CVC words containing *d*'s or *b*'s, and before asking the students to read the word, tell them to say the first sound in the word. Each time, point out the "bat and ball" letter. Tell students they will earn a point for every word read correctly and that 6 points wins the game.

Getting Students to Hear *j*

These tips about the production of /j/ should make your task easier if students are saying a different sound for this letter. According to the Lindamood: LiPS Program, /j/ is a "Noisy Fat-Pushed Air" sound (Lindamood & Lindamood, 1998).

Why Is /j/ Noisy????

If you put your hand on your throat as you say /j/, you can feel the vibration. With quiet sounds such as /s/ and /p/, you will not feel this vibration. Help your children feel their necks vibrate as they say /j/.

What Is "Fat-Pushed Air?"

As you say /j/, hold the back of your hand in front of your mouth and feel the air push out. Unlike /s/ or

/sh/, where one's air comes out in a smooth flow, /j/ requires a fat-push of air that sprays all over.

What Else Can I Do to Help My Students Hear This Sound?

Practice the "segmenting first-sound" phonemic awareness drill exercises from Chapter 2. Compose a list of /j/ words that are familiar to your students with words like *jet, jump, jelly,* and *jellybean.* Following the script, say, "My turn, *jet.* First sound? /j/." Follow this with a Together and a Your Turn until the children begin to produce a clear /j/ sound. Remember to loudly and clearly say the /j/ sound, overaccentuating it. You will have to work at saying /j/ loudly and clearly so that your children distinctly hear it.

The Elusive /ĕ/

Frequently, some first graders and kindergartners confuse the sounds of /ĕ/ and /ă/. For example, when asked to blend /p/-/ĕ/-/n/, students confusing these two phonemes reply *pan.* They are likely to make the same mistake when reading the word *pan.* When asked what the new word means, they proudly explain that it is something to write with. Slipping the follow-ing activities into your day for five to ten minutes will help end the confusion:

- Play a short game where the children hold up one "man" if you say *man,* and two "men" if you say *men.*
- Ask students to say *cook* if you say *pan,* and *write* if you say *pen.*
- Make sure that students can write *e* when you say that letter sound. Expect students to sound-write all the vowels.
- Write the vowel letters in a circle on the board and have the students "say the vowel circle" as you point to the letters. Listen to be certain students are accurately saying each letter sound. Be sure that your voice and jaw go down when you say /ă/, overaccentuating the dip.
- Line up with a vowel focus: As you call students to line up, instead of saying, "Table 1 line up," ask Table 1 to first say the letter sound for *e* before lining up. Locate your students at Table 1 who still have vowel confusion and ask them to individually tell you the difficult letter sound. Example: "Table 1, tell me the sound of *e* before you line up." (signal) "Good. Jessie and Dustin, let me hear you say the sound for *a* one more time." (signal) "Table 2. . . ."

Reading Regular Words: A Three-Part Process

There are three parts to the format for reading regular words. In Part 1, students sound out each word orally before reading it as a whole word, receiving added support from the teacher using My Turn–Together–Your Turn as needed. In Part 2, students continue to sound out the words, but do so subvocally, in their heads. In Part 3 student sounding out is at an automatic level where students read each regular word by sight, without any conscious sounding out. In this section a description of each of these parts, including when to use them based on students' DIBELS and AIMSweb NWF scores, is provided.

Part 1: Sounding Out Orally   Sounding out regular words should begin as soon as possible, because phonemic awareness and knowledge of letter sounds are not sufficient for students who are at risk to learn to read. Systematic, explicit instruction in sounding out words is a key component for learning to read. Students who are at risk require extensive practice in sounding out words before they are ready for advanced word reading. Accurate, fluent sounding out and blending of regular words is a key prerequisite to the automatic sight–word reading necessary for fluent reading. When students sound out loud, the teacher can closely monitor their accuracy, providing corrections and additional teaching when needed.

You can begin teaching students to sound out words as soon as they have learned between six and eight letter sounds, including one or two common vowel sounds. Beginning sounding out is most effectively taught when word selection is first confined to the VC, CVC, and CVC-variant words. As described earlier, these are one-syllable words formed using the most common sounds of all single consonants and vowels. Some teachers may want to follow the easy-to-hard sequence of CVC words shown in Figure 3.1 (p. 81), starting with CVC words that begin with continuous sounds, because these are the words that are easiest to blend.

In Part 1 of regular word reading, students orally sound out regular words. This teaching procedure, which is shown in Table 3.4, is most helpful for students reading at the

TABLE 3.4 Format for Reading Regular Words—Part 1: Oral Sounding Out

Objective	After seeing a regular word, students will orally sound out the letter sounds before saying the word.
Materials Needed	Board, chart paper, or overhead transparency and writing implement. Write the regular words that students will read in rows on the board. For example, if students are reading eight words, write two rows of four words.
Signaling	Three-part signal: Finger is in starting position to the left of the word. **"Sound out,"** or **"What word?"** initiates the signal for unison answers.
	1. Use loop signal for orally sounding out the letter sounds in the words.
	2. As students are saying the final letter sound, immediately loop finger back to the starting point.
	3. Pause for a moment of think time before asking students **"What word?"** and side-slash to the end of the word.
Time	Depends on number of new words and difficulty level. Kindergarten students often work on this skill for between 5 and 15 minutes each day. First-grade students may need to work on this skill for up to 20 minutes if the curriculum has introduced many new words or a new letter–sound pattern.

Instructions	**Teacher**	**Students**
	1. Advance Organizer	
	2. My Turn (Note: See Ms. Elizondo's fourth tip on page 104 in the text to determine whether to start at Step 2, 3, or 4.)	
	(finger to the left of the first letter) **"My turn sounding out this word."** (loop from letter to letter) **"/f/-/ă/-/n/"** (loop back to starting point) **"What word?"** (side-slash signal) **"fan."**	
	3. Together	
	The teacher answers with students this time:	
	(finger to the left of the first letter) **"Together, sound out this word."** (loop from letter to letter) **"/f/-/ă/-/n/."** (loop back to starting point) **"What word?"** (side-slash signal) **"fan."** (loop to starting point) **"Yes, fan."**	/f/-/ă/-/n/ fan
	4. Your Turn	
	(finger to the left of the first letter) **"Your turn to sound out this word."** (loop from letter to letter) (answer) (loop back to starting point) **"What word?"** (side-slash signal) (answer) (loop to starting point) **"Yes, fan."** Repeat step 4 for every word in the row.	/f/-/ă/-/n/ fan
	5. Individual Student Checkout:	
	Point to the first regular word written on the board (fan) and place your finger slightly to the left of the word.	
	"Individual turns. Sound out this word. Grant." (loop from letter to letter) (answer) (loop back to starting point) **"What word?"** (side-slash signal) (answer) (loop to starting point) **"Yes, fan."**	/f/-/ă/-/n/ fan
	"Sound out this word. Leila." (loop from letter to letter) (answer) (loop back to starting point) **"What word?"** (side-slash signal) (answer) (loop to starting point) **"Yes, sip."**	/s/-/ĭ/-/p/ sip
	Call on several students to check for accuracy. When students' correct answers show you that they know all of the words in the row, move to the second row of words.	

TABLE 3.4   Continued

Scaffolding Reduction	6. Be sure to move to using mainly Your Turns as soon as possible.
Error Correction	If students make an error, immediately return to a My Turn–Together–Your Turn pattern, always requiring them to sound out the word. Then return to the beginning of the row and have students reread words the fast way.
Perk Up Your Drill	Do not assume that students are connecting word reading to story reading, even when you do both activities each day. In addition to providing the rationale for word reading at the beginning of the lesson, at least once or twice during the lesson explain to your students how learning to read words will enable them to read books about interesting topics: "You just read the word *sip* all by yourself. When you read books about birthday parties, you might see the word *sip* used when everyone in the story sips some pop before eating the cake." Telling students that the words they are reading on the board will later appear in the story motivates them to do their best.
	When students are beginning readers and need to slowly sound out before blending words, you may find following this format tedious and slow going. Be assured that this is the most important drill that you can do and if you carefully follow the scripts allowing students to practice their sounding out, your class will soon acquire alphabetic principle and move on to faster word reading.
Adaptations	Although you may have readers in your class, you cannot assume that they have learned alphabetic principle, since they may have originally memorized the beginning regular words rather than learned to decode them. Thus, they will benefit from practice with decoding these words. If any readers in your class appear to be reading one or two grade levels above your other students, work with your school team to determine whether it is appropriate for them to participate in a higher grade-level reading group. Use a higher grade-level DIBELS Oral Reading Fluency assessment (Chapter 5) to determine whether the student(s) in question should move up to another reading group or a reading class in a higher grade.
	Some students can automatically read new words after one or two times of sounding them out and blending the letter sounds. Before the end of the lesson, ask these students to read the words the fast way.

Source: This script is based on one originally developed and field-tested by Carnine, D. W., Silbert, J., Kame'enui, E. J., and Tarver, S. (2010). *Direct Instruction Reading* (5th ed.). Boston: Merrill.

prealphabetic or partial alphabetic phase as represented by a score of less than 30 sounds per minute on the DIBELS or AIMSweb NWF assessment, with few if any nonsense words read as whole words. Part 1 stresses several critical skills required to sound out words: sounding out words from left to right and attending to every letter in the word before reading the whole word. Note that students are first taught to sound out words in lists so that they avoid the use of picture and context clues. Picture and context clues can undermine student acquisition of the alphabetic principle by encouraging guessing and are not recommended when teaching beginning students who are at risk to read. Reading clues will be discussed at length later in this chapter and in Chapter 4. Students should remain at Part 1 of regular word reading until they are able to sound out lists of CVC words with 100% accuracy, and without the teacher having to provide support in the form of My Turn–Together–Your Turn.

The signaling procedure for Part 1 of reading regular words is shown in Figure 3.10. First the teacher points to the left of the word to show that sounding always begins on the left side of a word and that sounding is about to begin. The teacher then uses a looping motion as she moves from letter to letter in the word.

Students say the letter sound as the teacher's finger rests underneath the letter for one or two seconds. As students are saying the final letter sound, the teacher immediately loops

FIGURE 3.10   Signal for Sounding Out Regular Words

her finger back to the first letter sound. After a pause, the teacher asks students, "What word?" and side-slashes to the end of the word.

Five Best Practices for Teaching Oral Sounding Out   Let's look at how Ms. Elizondo used Part 1 of regular word reading with her students at the early sounding-out stage using the following five best practices:

Provide More Time as Needed for Teaching Difficult Skills to Mastery   Most of Ms. Elizondo's students came to first grade knowing their letter sounds. Many of them still needed more practice blending because they slowly and often inaccurately sounded out words. In order to make sure that her students were ready for advanced word reading by January, when digraphs and long vowels were introduced, she spent more time than the general education reading curriculum recommended on word reading. Every day before class, she wrote the new words presented in the regular curriculum and the new passage reading on the board and started by using the Part 1 format listed in Table 3.4 to teach them. Although the curriculum recommended a lesson a day, when the words were especially difficult, she spent two or even three days on the problematic lesson until students could sound them out quickly on their own when she pointed to them out of order. At that point, unless she was correcting an error or using a My Turn for a particularly difficult word, Ms. Elizondo never read the words with the students, because she wanted them to do their own thinking, and some of them might simply chime in after hearing her voice. Because the principal had decided that all assemblies or other activities would always be scheduled in the afternoon, she was more confident moving through the curriculum at a slower pace. With nothing interfering in the morning, she had gained more teaching days.

Avoid Adding Schwas to Stop Sounds   Ms. Elizondo was careful to avoid adding schwas to her letter sounds when using the My Turn strategy the first time through the word list. Although she had learned the correct pronunciation of letter sounds, the teaching coach had pointed out that when Ms. Elizondo was blending words, she sometimes added those cumbersome schwas. While the coach was observing her, she had actually blended *pal* as /puh/+/a/+/luh/. Sometimes bad habits pop up at the most embarrassing times. Ms. Elizondo was careful to make sure that situation never happened again.

Calibrate Think Time to Difficulty of the Task   Once Ms. Elizondo moved from the My Turn to the Your Turn step, she was careful to calibrate the amount of think time that she provided students before asking, "What word?" If she didn't pause between the time when students said the letter sounds and when they said the entire word, only her best students would answer. Ms. Elizondo knew that when those three or four louder readers answered at lightning speed, she could easily be fooled into believing that the entire class knew the new words taught that day. The first time she had students read the words on a new list, she gave more think time than the second or third time, because her goal was having students read the words faster.

When Students Are Successful in Sounding Out New Words, Reduce Scaffolding and Start Teaching at Step 4   During the first and sometimes the second time students were reading through the word list, Ms. Elizondo carefully progressed through all of the steps in Table 3.4. When her students were more proficient and orally sounding out the words independently, she phased out the My Turn and Together steps and started teaching at Step 4 (Your Turn). As soon as Ms. Elizondo noticed that her students were reading new CVC words accurately and more rapidly the first time they saw them, she began encouraging independence by also starting at Step 4 for the new word lists. After all, Ms. Elizondo knew that readers must develop confidence when sounding out new words they are seeing for the first time. When the new list had a more difficult word that she anticipated her students would miss, she continued to use the entire My Turn–Together–Your Turn sequence for that word.

Use Assessment Information to Determine Individual Turns   Every day Ms. Elizondo gave more turns during individual checkouts to her students who received the lowest scores on the DIBELS Nonsense Word Assessment. When her students were able to sound out words accurately without her help, Ms. Elizondo added Part 2 of regular word reading to her daily instruction in reading regular words.

Companion Website

Go to the Video Activities section of Chapter 3 in the Companion Website (www.pearson-highered.com/bursuck2e) and complete the activity entitled *Beginning Reading Part 1*. Watch a teacher using the Table 3.4 format.

Applying the Enhancements to a Commercial Reading Program

A typical reading curriculum details an early word-reading lesson in which the purpose of the activity is blending sounds into words using the new letter sound /n/ and several other letter sounds previously introduced. The teacher is instructed to give each student the letter cards n, i, a, p, and t and tell everyone to place each letter in their mini pocket chart. As each letter is placed in the chart, the students are to say the sound associated with it.

Next the teacher is advised to place the letters a and n in her large pocket chart and direct the students to do the same in their small ones. Instructions in the curriculum guide indicate that the teacher should demonstrate blending the word *an* by sliding her hand under the letters as she slowly stretches the sounds /ăăănnn/. She is supposed to say the word *an* naturally before asking her students to do the same.

Finally, the teacher is instructed to give the following directions before students blend letter sounds to read new words:

"Put p at the beginning. What word did you make?" (*pan*)

"Change the a in *pan* to i. What word did you make?" (*pin*)

"Make the p and n change places. What word did you make?" (*nip*)

The major problem with this activity is that it doesn't provide enough support for blending sounds into words. Evidently, the lesson assumes that with no guided practice, after one example students will learn to sound out these new words automatically and independently. Unless modified, this activity does not provide the support and practice that many students who are at risk need to learn to sound out words. A final problem with this activity is that students are asked to respond individually with their own letters. Managing students' behavior and monitoring their work under these conditions present additional challenges in many classrooms.

This activity could be enhanced in a number of ways. First, to avoid the behavior management and monitoring problems that can occur when using manipulatives in a large group, the teacher could have students respond in unison as she manipulates the letters on her large pocket chart. The teacher could also use the format in Table 3.4, injecting My Turn–Together–Your Turn for each of the words the first time the students blend them. The second time through the list, the teacher could switch to Your Turn for these same words, first asking students to sound out each word before reading it by sight. The teacher could also use individual turns with some of her lowest performers to make sure that all of the students acquire the emphasized word-reading skill.

Sometimes students are unable to blend past stop sounds. They can blend the sounds and read words that start with continuous sounds like *man* and *fit*, but they get stuck on words like *can* and *bit*. Teaching students to blend past all stop sounds so they learn to sound out *can* as /că/ /n/ or *bit* as /bĭ/ /t/ solves this problem. A reading program online has activities for "stopping at the vowel" where students blend all words to the vowel, as in the examples *can* or *bit*. For a student whose progress has been stalled because he can't blend past stop sounds, this approach sometimes is effective. Go to http://www.readingkey.com/demo/Files/CD-1/strategy/strategy.doc to learn more.

As we have shown, repeated practice or drill is an indispensable part of teaching students who are at risk to read, particularly when reading material for the first time (Engelmann & Bruner, 1995). Nonetheless, the use of repeated practice and drill is often criticized on the grounds that it decreases student motivation. The impact of systematic, explicit instruction on students' attitude toward reading is explained in the *Research Note*.

Research Note

Attitudes of Students Who Are At Risk

Effective teaching for children who are at risk involves providing them with frequent opportunities to practice the skills they are learning. Practice activities are most successful when a teacher is animated, teaches at a perky pace, and challenges her students without frustrating them. Still, much controversy surrounds the issue of student practice, with repeated practice activities often being referred to as "drill and kill."

Particularly challenging for teachers and students alike was having to sound out words in both lists and passages before reading them the fast way. While our students seemed to enjoy the lively pace and the reading success brought by the practice, given the controversy in the field over the use of practice, we wanted to be certain that the daily drill and decodable reading were not dampening student interest in reading.

In order to investigate exactly how our students felt about reading, we assessed our first cohort of students at the end of grades 1 and 2 using the "Elementary Reading Attitude Survey" (McKenna & Kear, 1990). In this survey, student attitudes toward both academic and recreational reading are assessed. Students are asked to circle a picture of Garfield the cat that best depicts how they feel in response to items that are read aloud by the teacher. Ten of the items assess academic reading, while another 10 assess recreational reading or reading for fun. To answer each question, students select either the "very happy" Garfield standing with a big smile, the "little bit happy" Garfield, the "little bit upset" Garfield, or the "very upset" Garfield who has a distinctive scowl. Questions such as "How do you feel about reading instead of playing?" assess students' attitudes toward recreational reading. Questions such as "How do you feel about the stories you read in reading class?" assess academic reading.

Scores for all of the instructional tiers for both grades 1 and 2 were uniformly high; students enjoyed both academic and recreational reading, scoring an average of 3 out of 4 on both types of items. Despite the frequent presence of drill in the reading instruction, students in all of the tiers liked to read, confirming our strong belief that when practice is lively and geared to student needs on skills leading to important outcomes, practice will thrill, *not* kill.

Part 2: Sounding Out Words Subvocally   A key goal of reading instruction is the accurate, fluent reading of connected text. Once students can orally decode words sound by sound independently and with a high degree of accuracy, teachers need to prepare them for the next phase of reading by adding Part 2 to their daily regular word-reading instruction: sounding out words in their heads, or **subvocal sounding out.** It was once thought that fluent adult readers relied mainly on context and background knowledge to figure out words, engaging in what was often called a guessing game as they made their way through connected text. More recent research shows just the opposite; while mature readers are fluent, they still attend to the letters in words, but at an automatic level. Pausing to look at pictures or using word attack strategies that focus on the middle or the end of the word interrupts the reading process. Consider this description by Shaywitz (2003) of a consolidated alphabetic phase reader chunking when encountering a new word.

> She sees a word and scans all the letters. Do any of the letters fall into a familiar pattern? Do they resemble letter groups—parts of words—that she has stored? If so, she is able to take these letter patterns and connect them to a known pronunciation. For example, if she sees the unfamiliar printed word *architect,* meaning a designer of buildings, she may know that the letters t-e-c-t go together and how they are pronounced. She may also know from experience that the letters a-r-c-h are often grouped together and that arch sounds either like arch of your foot or Noah's ark. She tries to pronounce the unknown word both ways, arch-itect or ar-ki-tect, and uses the surrounding text to judge which pronunciation fits. From the context, she realizes that the word is *architect,* meaning a designer of buildings, and is pronounced like ark (ar-ki-tect). Once she has successfully decoded this word, it joins the other words stored in her lexicon. (p. 104)

Note that in this example, the reader first scans the word from left to right, looking for graphophonemic clues. Only after the reader looks at the letters does she use context clues to make her final decoding decision. This example of a process happening in milliseconds demonstrates the importance of automatic decoding and why it needs to be established first before other decoding clues such as using the context are introduced.

Teachers cannot assume that most students who are at risk will make a successful transition from oral sounding out to silently reading words by sight without adding a transition step that provides subvocal sounding-out practice. Once students no longer need to say each sound aloud, their speed with word reading will increase. Part 2 of regular word reading shown in Table 3.5 is a format for helping students make the transition from sounding out loud to sounding out words in their heads. This teaching procedure is especially effective for students scoring below 30 on the DIBELS or AIMSweb NWF who are also orally sounding out each word before blending them, like the pattern shown for Student 2 in Figure 3.7 (p. 93).

The signals used for subvocal sounding out are the same as those used for sounding out words aloud. The only difference is that when the teacher engages in the looping motion from letter to letter, students are mouthing the sounds without saying them out loud. The only time the students answer out loud is when the teacher asks them to read the word.

Three Best Practices for Teaching Subvocal Sounding Out   Ms. Elizondo was delighted when she was able to add Part 2, subvocal sounding out, to her daily instruction in regular word reading. She used Part 2 when her students were able to sound out the words for the day with 100% accuracy using Part 1. She then moved to Part 2 while using these three best practices to help her students transition to subvocal sounding out:

Carefully Watch Students' Eye Movements   Ms. Elizondo carefully watched eye movement to check if students' eyes were moving from left to right as they directly looked at the words on the board. When she saw students' eyes staring into the distance, she tapped their shoulder or called their name to redirect them to the reading work. Because Ms. Elizondo wanted to maintain a motivating classroom, she gave students points for paying attention to the words.

TABLE 3.5   Format for Reading Regular Words—Part 2: Subvocal Sounding Out

Objective	After seeing a regular word, students will subvocally sound out the letter sounds before saying the word.
Materials Needed	Board, chart paper, or overhead transparency and writing implement. Write the regular words that students will read in rows on the board. For example, if students are reading eight words, write two rows of four words.
Signaling	Three-part signal: Finger is in starting position to the left of the word. **"Ready," "Sound out in your heads,"** or **"What word?"** initiates the signal for unison answers.
	1. Use loop signal for orally sounding out the letter sounds in the words.
	2. As students are saying the final letter sound, immediately loop finger back to the starting point.
	3. Pause for a moment of think time before asking students **"What word?"** and side-slash to the end of the word.
Time	Depends on number of new words and difficulty level. Kindergarten students often work on this skill for 5 minutes each day. First-grade students may need to work on this skill for up to 20 minutes if the curriculum has introduced many new words or a new letter–sound pattern.

Instructions	**Teacher**	**Student**
	1. Advance Organizer	
	2. My Turn (Use several times until students know what to do; then eliminate and start with step 3.)	
	(finger to the left of the first letter) **"My turn sounding out this word in my head."** (loop from letter to letter and silently mouth letter sounds /f/-/ă/-/n/) (loop back to starting point) **"What word?"** (side-slash signal) **"fan."**	fan
Scaffolding Reduction	3. Your Turn	
	(finger to the left of the first letter) **"Your turn. Sound out this word in your heads."** (loop from letter to letter) (students mouth sounds) (loop back to starting point) **"What word?"** (side-slash signal) **"Yes, fan."**	fan
	4. Individual Student Checkout	
	(finger to the left of the first letter) **"Individual turns. Sound out this word in your head. Maria."** (loop from letter to letter) (student mouths sounds) (loop back to starting point) **"What word?"** (side-slash signal) (answer) (loop to starting point) **"Yes, fan."** Call on several individual students to check for accuracy.	fan
	5. Read the Row: Reading the row of words by sight	
	Note: If you provide three seconds of think time before signaling for an answer, students should be ready to read the row of words the fast way. Use the Part 3 format for this section:	
	"Let's read all four words the fast way this time."	
	(think time) **"What word?"** (side-slash signal) (answer) (loop to starting point) **"Yes, fan."**	fan
	(think time) **"What word?"** (side-slash signal) (answer) (loop to starting point) **"Yes, sip."**	sip
	(think time) **"What word?"** (side-slash signal) (answer) (loop to starting point) **"Yes, let."**	let
	(think time) **"What word?"** (side-slash signal) (answer) (loop to starting point) **"Yes, cat."**	cat
Scaffolding Reduction	Be sure to move to using mainly Your Turns as soon as possible or you are just telling students the word rather than having them independently use their subvocal decoding.	
Error Correction	If students make an error, immediately return to a My Turn–Together–Your Turn pattern requiring them to sound the word out loud. Then return to the beginning of the row and have students reread words the fast way.	

TABLE 3.5 Continued

Perk Up Your Drill	■ Students love to reach a predetermined goal. Before reading all the words in a row, tell students that their goal is reading every single word in that row. If they read the words correctly, quickly draw a star next to the row and tell them that they just earned their first "starred" row. ■ When students are reading with 100% accuracy, perk up the pace by giving less think time. As long as the accuracy remains high, you can comfortably move at this quicker pace.
Adaptations	■ As your students transition to Part 3, begin to switch between the Part 2 and Part 3 scripts depending on the difficulty of the word. If your students are solid on CVC words containing any vowel but /ĕ/, start asking them to read those easier CVC words by sight from the beginning. When you come to a CVC word containing an /ĕ/, have the students subvocally sound out the word. If you anticipate that students will almost certainly make an error on a difficult word the first time they read the word, ask them to sound it out loud.

Source: This script is based on one originally developed and field-tested by Carnine, D. W., Silbert, J., Kame'enui, E. J., & Tarver, S. (2010). *Direct Instruction Reading* (5th ed.). Boston: Merrill.

When Students Are Subvocally Sounding Out New Words Accurately With Teacher Support, Reduce Scaffolding and Start Teaching at Step 4   When her students became more proficient at subvocal sounding out, Ms. Elizondo again faded out the My Turn and Together steps and started teaching at Step 4, Your Turn. She continued to use the entire My Turn–Together–Your Turn sequence for difficult new words.

Once Students Can Subvocally Sound Out Words Without Help, Add Part 3, Reading Words the Fast Way, to Your Daily Regular Word Reading   As her students moved through Part 2 reading and were able to subvocally sound out words accurately without added teacher support, Ms. Elizondo added Part 3, reading words by sight, to her daily instruction in reading regular words. It was at this point that Ms. Elizondo noticed that her students' DIBELS NWF scores were beginning to approach 30 sounds per minute, reading at least eight whole words, the point at which they would start reading CVC word lists by sight, using oral or subvocal sounding out only for more difficult words or for making error corrections.

Companion Website
Go to the Video Activities Activities section of Chapter 3 in the Companion Website (www.pearsonhighered.com/bursuck2e) and complete the activity entitled *Beginning Reading Part 2*.
Watch a teacher using this subvocal sounding-out format described in Table 3.5.

Part 3: Reading Words by Sight   Once students are able to sound out words in their heads accurately, add Part 3 to your daily teaching. In this part, students read words by sight, sounding out at an automatic level. While interpretations of the meaning of sight reading vary, a common implication drawn from the term is that the words have been memorized first rather than sounded out. For the purposes of this text, reading by sight is preceded by sounding out, not visual memorization. When reading regular words by sight is introduced into your daily word-reading exercises, students are beginning to say the words without pausing to sound out the individual letter sounds because the process is becoming automatic. Table 3.6 describes Part 3, the format for teaching students to read words by sight. When your students' DIBELS NWF scores reach 30 sounds per minute or higher reading whole words, they are beginning to see words in chunks, rather than as individual sounds. You can detect this when you notice that your students are reading at the onset-rime stage on their DIBELS NWF (starting to read *dov* as /d//ov/ rather than as /d//o//v/). They may also be reading the nonsense

TABLE 3.6   Format for Reading Regular Words—Part 3: By Sight

Objective	After seeing a regular word, students will orally read the word the fast way.
Materials Needed	Board, chart paper, or overhead transparency and writing implement. Write the regular words that students will read in rows on the board. For example, if students are reading eight words, write two rows of four words.
Signaling	Finger is in starting position to the left of the word. **"What word?"** initiates the side-slash signal for unison answers.
Time	Depends on number of new words and difficulty level. First-grade students may need to work on this skill for up to 20 minutes if the curriculum has introduced many new words or a new letter–sound pattern. Older students with alphabetic principle may only have a few new one-syllable words that are appropriate for this format.

Instructions	Teacher	Student
	1. Advance Organizer	
	2. My Turn (use for first word only, and only for the first day or two using this format) (finger to the left of the first letter) **"My turn to read this word the fast way."** (side-slash signal) ***"fan."***	
	3. Your Turn	
	Note: For new words that you anticipate your students misreading, use the Part 1 sounding-out format the first time the word is introduced in the list.	
	"Your turn to read the rest of the words by yourself."	
	(point and pause) **"What word?"** (side-slash answer) (loop back to starting point) **"Yes, *fan.*"**	fan
	(point and pause) **"What word?"** (side-slash answer) (loop back to starting point) **"Yes, *hat.*"**	hat
	(point and pause) **"What word?"** (side-slash answer) (loop back to starting point) **"Yes, *sit.*"**	sit
	(point and pause) **"What word?"** (side-slash answer) (loop back to starting point) **"Yes, *Pam.*"**	Pam
	4. Individual Student Checkout	
	(point and pause) **"Individual turns. What word? Ali."** (side-slash answer) (loop back to starting point) **"Yes, *fan.*"**	fan
	(point and pause) **"What word? Toni."** (side-slash answer) (loop back to starting point) **"Yes, *sit.*"**	sit
	Call on several individual students to check for accuracy.	

Error Correction	If students make an error, immediately return to Part 1 sounding out aloud using a My Turn–Together–Your Turn pattern. Then return to the beginning of the row and have students reread words the fast way.
Perk Up Your Drill	■ Tell students that words they read correctly will go in their weekly dictionaries taken home to parents. Create a sense of drama about the large number of words that are going into the dictionary. ■ Ask a student to lead the drill, signaling just as you do.
Adaptations	■ Many students who are at risk will not automatically know the meaning of common vocabulary such as *snap, pal,* or *tap.* Connecting words to their usage or meaning will help students remember them while expanding their vocabulary. After students read a word for which they don't know the meaning, some teachers will connect the word to its meaning and use the word in a brief sentence, saying the key word louder for emphasis. **"A *pal* is a friend. In our story yesterday, Big Bear's *pal* was mouse."**

Source: This script is based on one originally developed and field-tested by Carnine, D. W., Silbert, J., Kame'enui, E. J., & Tarver, S. (2010). *Direct Instruction Reading* (5th ed.). Boston: Merrill.

words slowly, but as whole words. When students reach this point, use Part 3 exclusively for their daily regular word reading, except for particularly difficult words, the first day when new letter sounds are introduced, or when correcting student errors.

Teachers who expect their students to read regular words by sight before they are ready risk having their students memorize the visual form of the word rather than reading it through an automatic decoding process. Students who are not ready for this format will make far more errors if expected to read new words by sight. Deciding to use this format too early can be a temptation because the instruction is far less demanding than that during earlier formats where every letter sound is articulated orally. When teachers begin to use this format they will also still be using Part I: Oral Sounding Out for new words that contain new and difficult letter–sound combinations. Mr. McCoy was able to use the Part 3 format Reading by Sight with his students for any new CVC word, but when blends such as *br, cl,* and *sm* were introduced, he knew his students would misread many of these words if they read them by sight. He adapted his teaching and went back to using the Part 1 format until his students were more accurate reading CVC-variant words with blends.

The signaling procedure for reading words by sight consists of touching to the left of the word, providing a thinking pause, saying, "What word?" and then giving the side-slash signal. Tips for teaching students to read words by sight are as follows.

Three Best Practices for Teaching Part 3: Reading Words by Sight   Note how Ms. Elizondo used the following four best practices when she used Part 3 in teaching her students to read words by sight.

Use Assessment Information to Guide Teaching   Every morning, Ms. Elizondo wrote the new words from the daily lesson on the board and presented a brief advance organizer, telling her students that first they would read words that would later appear in the new elephant story. Since almost everyone in her class had scored 50 or higher on the DIBELS NWF assessment, and was reading whole words, she used Part 3 only for her regular word reading unless the story had a particularly difficult word that needed to be sounded out, when her students made errors, or when a new letter–sound correspondence was introduced.

Gradually Decrease Your Think Time   Ms. Elizondo knew that think time was critical during this stage of reading. The first time students read through the word list, Mrs. Elizondo paused for three seconds before asking, "What word," and then giving the signal to read the word. This longer think time increased her students' success in reading the words the first time. The second time she went through the list, she paused for only one or two seconds of think time.

Preplan by Using the Optional Step for Difficult Words   To prevent errors when a difficult new word was on the list, Ms. Elizondo used the "optional step" and asked students first to orally sound out the difficult word. For example, when /str/ was introduced in the new lesson, she returned to a My Turn–Together–Your Turn Part 1 sounding-out pattern to show students how to apply the new letter sounds to *strum, strap,* and *strict.* She knew that whenever students make errors reading a word, it takes much longer for them to unlearn the error and then learn the correct word.

Companion Website

Go to the Video Activities section of Chapter 3 in the Companion Website (www.pearson-highered.com/bursuck2e) and complete the activity entitled *Beginning Reading Part 3.* Watch a teacher using the sight-reading format described in Table 3.6.

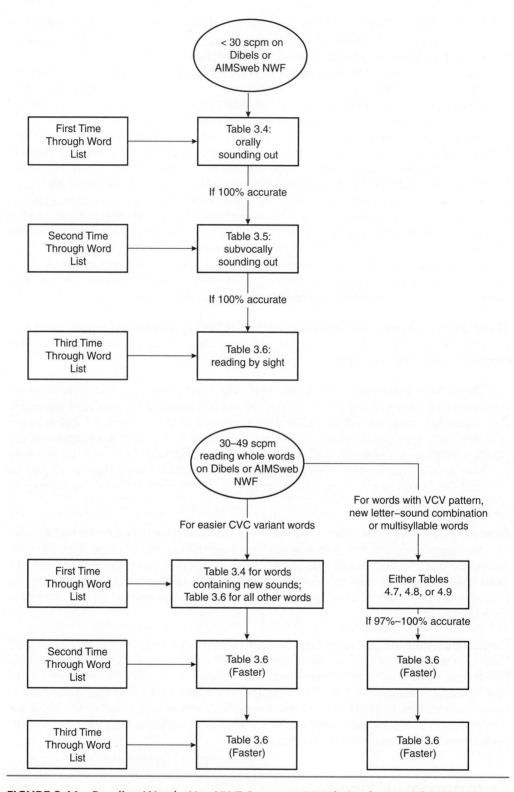

FIGURE 3.11 Reading Words: Use NWF Scores to Match Students with Formats

---

Spelling activity: Students write *in, pin, pat.*

Teacher: "You're going to write the word *in*. Listen. *In*. Say the sounds in *in*."
Signal for each sound by using a finger snap, clap, or extended finger as the children say /ĭĭĭ/ (pause) /nnn/. Repeat until firm.

Teacher: "Everybody, write the word (pause) ***in*."**
Check children's answers so you can give feedback.

Repeat for ***pin*** and ***pat*.**

FIGURE 3.12   Regular Word Spelling Format

Source: Adapted from Engelmann, S., & Bruner, E. (1995). *Reading Mastery I: Teacher's Guide.* Columbus, OH: SRA Macmillan/McGraw-Hill.

The process of helping students become readers at the consolidated alphabetic phase so they are ready for advanced word reading is critical, but important decisions about when to use which of the three word-reading formats, and with which students, can be complicated. A chart of how to match your students with the appropriate formats based on their scores on the DIBELS or AIMSweb NWF measure is shown in Figure 3.11.

Spelling and Writing Regular Words

Students benefit when they are writing or spelling the same regular words that they are learning to sound out and read. For example, Mr. Drake's students sounded out the following words in their daily lesson: *man, rap, top, pat, stop,* and *grab.* He then asked his students to spell each of these words using the format shown in Figure 3.12.

Students benefit when teachers ask them to substitute, add, and delete letter sounds in words that they spell. Hardware supply stores will cut large white boards used for showers into smaller boards your students can use for spelling instruction. Mrs. Kilroy asked her students to spell *tan.* Then she asked them to turn *tan* into *an,* and after checking their work, asked them to turn *an* into *pan.* Students were just learning how to read words that started with blends, and so before moving on to vowel substitutions, Mrs. Kilroy asked her students to turn pan into *span.*

Grapheme–phoneme mapping with small letter tiles works well as a small-group activity. Students construct the VC and CVC words dictated by the teacher. Later, students map the letter sounds on phoneme–grapheme mapping paper. You can make your own phoneme–grapheme mapping paper by printing out a table with four or five columns and one row for each word students will spell. Each letter sound representing a phoneme in the word is "mapped" in an individual square. The words *stop* and *sit* are mapped in Table 3.7. Representing the vowel with a different-colored tile than the consonant tiles helps students conceptualize the vowel decisions they will be making when they move to advanced word reading. When students map using grid paper, they can shade the vowel square(s) (Grace, 2007).

Teachers often wonder whether they should start instruction by teaching students to blend individual letter sounds into words, or start with larger units or word families and have students use them to read words. *The Reflective Teacher* helps answer this question.

TABLE 3.7   Phoneme–Grapheme Mapping for Beginning Readers

s	t	o	p
s	i	t	

The Reflective Teacher

Which Is the Best Way to Teach Beginning Readers?

Two of the most common beginning phonics approaches are letter–sound blending and word-family instruction (Wanzek & Hagger, 2003). In letter–sound blending, students are first taught the most common sounds of letters in isolation and are then taught to blend them into words. The approach that is used in this text is referred to as synthetic phonics. For example, Mr. Ellis taught his students to identify the letter sounds /m/, /s/, /t/, and /a/ in isolation. Once these letter sounds were learned, and his students could orally segment and blend, Mr. Ellis taught them to read words such as *Sam, sat,* and *mast.* Another beginning phonics approach starts by using larger units of sounds such as word families. In this approach, called analogizing, students are typically taught a rime pattern and then taught to use that known word part to form new words. This instruction forces the student to chunk the beginning letter(s) of the word and rime. For example, Ms. Calhoun taught her students to read the rime /am/. She then had her students read by sight related words such as *Sam, ham,* and *jam* that they had decoded and read in previous lessons.

If introduced after decoding is first taught, word-family instruction can help students read faster and remember spellings of words more easily (Durrell, 1963). If introduced too early, students can overgeneralize rhyming as a strategy for reading, which can lead to students reading the first sound and guessing at the rest of the word (Nation, Allen, & Hulme, 2001). The National Reading Panel (2000) found that both letter–sound blending and analogizing were effective in teaching beginning word reading to students. Which of these approaches should teachers use with their students who are at risk? Wanzek and Hagger (2003) suggest that both be used with letter–sound blending coming first because it is a necessary preskill for word reading, and word-family instruction next because it helps students better generalize their decoding skills to more complex words. Follow these guidelines for teaching analogizing to beginning readers.

- Select rimes that consist of previously taught letter–sound correspondences or letter combinations. If you have taught students to sound out and read a number of CVC words ending in the rime *an* (e.g., *can, Dan, man, pan*) using Part 1 and Part 2 of the Format for Reading Regular Words, begin your lesson by writing *an, Dan, can, man, pan* on the board. Ask students to read *an* and then show them that all the words end in *an.* Finally, ask them to read the words by sight. In order to read the words accurately, they have to read the sound of the onset letter, chunking it together with the rime. Their accuracy with word-family sight reading will tell you if they are ready for this strategy.
- Coordinate with the scope and sequence in your curriculum and select words that progress from simple onsets (*man*) to blends (*Stan*).
- Have students spell words based on the word families they are learning and have them substitute beginning, final, and middle sounds. Teacher: *"Everyone write **tap, sap,** and **map** on your whiteboards."* (Students write.) Teacher: *"Now change **tap** to **lap.**"*
- At this beginning word-reading stage, teach only the following rimes for closed syllables: *ad, am, an, *ap, *at, ax, ed, eg, en, ep, et, ib, id, ig, im, *in, *ip, it, ix, od, *op, ot, ox, uf, ud, *ug, un, up, us, ut.* The rimes with stars in front of them are the most frequently used ones.

Reading Exception Words

Reading connected text, even when most of the words can be sounded out, requires recognition of the most frequently used exception words. Students who are at risk or who have disabilities need extra practice learning exception words, especially when they are beginning readers. When a new exception word is introduced, students are first told what the word is and are asked to repeat it. The students then spell the word as the teacher points to each individual letter. Finally, the students say the word again. Spelling the word reinforces the important idea that even for words that can't be sounded out, it is still important to look at all the letters of words in a left-to-right sequence.

The importance of viewing the words from left to right rather than as a picture makes sense if you think of Adams' processor model described in Chapter 1. Irregular and regular words are both stored in lexical memory in the same way (Gough & Walsh, 1991). Most letters in irregular words correspond to their associated sounds, which helps the reader connect the word's orthography to its pronunciation, just as with a regular word. Although there is some variation for this number depending upon the phonics rules taught in a curriculum, of the 150 most frequent words in printed school English according to the *American Heritage Word Frequency Book* (Carroll, 1971), only 44 are exception words, and of those words 39 have only one letter–sound association that makes the word irregular. For example, in the word *what,* only the grapheme *a* deviates from its conventional letter–sound association. The *wh* as well as the *t* are associated with their most common sounds and thus will bond in the reader's memory more easily. Ehri (2005) described this letter–sound association as the glue that binds the word to memory. Teaching students to spell the exception words that they learn creates an even stronger bond, reducing the time until students read the exception word by sight. Students reading at the final consolidated alphabetic phase learn exception words like *what* much faster than students who are reading at earlier levels because they can chunk past the irregular letter sounds. For that reason, we advise teachers to prioritize decoding for young or struggling readers and only teach exception words that are necessary for reading.

Once exception words are introduced, they are thereafter read by sight as whole words. If the student misreads one, the teacher returns to a My Turn, supplying the word and asking students to spell it just as if the word was being introduced for the first time. The format for introducing exception words is shown in Table 3.8.

Three Tips for Teaching Exception Words
Try these strategies to enhance your teaching of exception words:

Avoid Teaching Similar Exception Words Together, Such as Where and Were   Include similar exception words together only after students can automatically read each individual word when it is presented by itself.

Attach Meaning by Saying a Clear Sentence After Abstract Exception Words   Some exception words reflect abstract concepts and can be meaningless, especially to English language learners. Definitions for these words can be even more confusing. Using a clear, short sentence after introducing a vague exception word will attach meaning and make it more likely that students will remember the word. When you say the sentence to students, place more emphasis on the word in the sentence. For example, when introducing the word *would,* Mrs. Amonette pointed to the word and said, *"**Would.** (pause) I know that Shantell **would** like to have some chocolate ice cream right now. **Would.**"* Mrs. Amonette then continued with the format.

Provide Multiple Opportunities to Practice Exception Words   When you are teaching students a list of words, they often forget the words at the top of the list by the time you get to the end of the list. To prevent this from happening, we suggest that you "firm the list " to avoid memory slippage and the loss of time it takes to reteach those first words. You "firm a list" when, after teaching students to read the second word on the list, you have them go back and read the first word and then the second one. After students read the third word on the list, you have them go back and read the first two words before reading the third one. Repeated practice like this makes it more likely that information is stored in **long-term memory** where, because it is readily available to the person, it can be activated automatically (Marzano, 2004). The following practice strategies will also help your

TABLE 3.8   Format for Reading Exception Words

Objective	After seeing an exception word, students will orally read the word by sight.
Materials	Board, chart paper, or overhead transparency and writing implement. Teacher writes the new exception words in a column. The review exception words are written in another column.
Signaling	Two-part signal: **"What word?"** or **"Spell _____"** initiates the signal for unison answers.
	1. After asking **"What word?"** or **"Spell _____,"** use a side-slash signal, and after students answer, loop back to the starting point before affirming the answer.
	2. After saying **"Spell _____,"** point under each letter as students spell the word.
Time	3–5 minutes

Instructions	**Teacher**	**Student**
	1. Advance Organizer	
	Part 1: Introduction of new words.	
	2. Write the new exception words from the daily story in a column on the left side of the board: for example, *today, father, strange.* Write four review exception words in a column on the right side of the board: for example, *was, isn't, should, great.* Teach the first exception sight word written on the board (*today*).	
	a. (finger to the left of the first letter) **"This word is"** (side-slash while saying **"today."**) (loop back to starting point)	
	b. **"What word?"** (side-slash-answer) (loop back to starting point) **"Yes, *today.*"**	today
	c. **"Spell *today.*"** (point to each letter as students answer) (loop back to starting point)	t-o-d-a-y
	d. **"What word?"** (side-slash-answer) (loop back to starting point) **"Yes, *today.*"**	today
	e. (finger to the left of the first letter) **"This word is"** (side-slash while saying **"father."**) (loop back to starting point)	
	f. **"What word?"** (side-slash-answer) (loop back to the starting point) **"Yes, *father.*"**	father
	g. **"Spell *father.*"** (point to each letter as students answer) (loop back to starting point)	f-a-t-h-e-r
	h. **"What word?"** (side-slash-answer) (loop back to starting point) **"Yes, *father.*"**	father
	i. Return to the top of the list and point to the left of the first word. Pause and ask, **"What word?"** (side-slash-answer) (loop back to starting point) **"Yes, *today.*"**	today
	Quickly point to the left of the second word. Pause and ask, **"What word?"** (side-slash-answer) (loop back to starting point) **"Yes, *father.*"**	father
	j. Repeat steps e–i with the remaining words until students can quickly read all of the words in the column without errors.	
	k. Individual Student Checkout: Call on between one and three students to check for accuracy.	
	Part 2: Students sight read new words and review words.	
Scaffold Reduction	3. Point to words randomly.	
	a. **"When I signal, read the word."**	
	(finger to the left of the first letter) **"What word?"** (side-slash-answer) (loop back to starting point) **"Yes, *father.*"**	father
	(finger to the left of the first letter) **"What word?"** (side-slash-answer) (loop back to starting point) **"Yes, was."**	was
	(finger to the left of the first letter) **"What word?"** (side-slash-answer) (loop back to starting point) **"Yes, should."**	should
	b. Individual Student Checkout: Call on between one and three students to check for accuracy.	
Error Correction	If students make an error, immediately return to a My Turn. Tell students the word, ask them to spell the exception word, to read the word (Part 2: steps a-d), and then return to the top of the list asking them to read all of the words again.	

TABLE 3.8 Continued

Perk Up Your Drill	■ On the last section of the exception word script (Part 2), tell students that you will erase every word they read correctly. The goal is to have all words erased on the first read-through.
	■ If you are working with a smaller group, you can write each exception word on a large card to hold up. Construct a "we know that" box, and on the last section of the exception word script (Part 2), dramatically throw each word that students read correctly into the box.
Adaptations	■ Many students who are at risk will not automatically put exception words such as *was, where, should,* and *couldn't* into context unless you briefly add that component at the start. Connecting words to their usage or meaning will help students remember them while expanding their vocabulary. The first time they introduce a new exception word, some teachers will use the word in a brief sentence, saying the word louder for emphasis: **"This word is *should*. Your mom says, 'It's late and you *should* go to bed.'"** Later in the lesson, if students make an error, the teacher will use another sentence to connect the word to its meaning.

Source: This script is based on one originally developed and field-tested by Carnine, D. W., Silbert, J., Kame'enui, E. J., & Tarver, S. (2010). *Direct Instruction Reading* (5th ed.). Boston: Merrill.

students acquire the ability to read exception words by sight whenever they encounter them in text.

■ Reading a new exception word several times
■ Spelling the word so letter–sound associations are used to strengthen the word in memory
■ Connecting the word with meaning when first learning it
■ Connecting the new word with meaning when accurately reading it in a text shortly after the word-reading lesson

Additional strategies for helping students remember exception words are in the *In Your Classroom* feature.

Companion Website

Go to the Video Activities section of Chapter 3 in the Companion Website (www.pearson-highered.com/bursuck2e) and complete the activity entitled *Exception Words*. Watch a teacher using the format for reading exception words described in Table 3.8.

You can learn ways to find more time for your students to practice word reading in *In Your Classroom*. Strategies for making Word Walls a part of your systematic explicit reading program are discussed in *The Reflective Teacher* feature.

Reading Decodable Sentences

After students can sound out a number of regular words and know a few exception words, they can begin reading sentences. Sentence reading provides a good opportunity to explicitly teach students to read connected text. Using this format, students quickly learn to follow a line of print, recognize that spaces mark boundaries between words, automatically move from left to right, read word by word, recognize that sentences are composed of words, and recognize final punctuation marks. If your students' DIBELS or AIMSweb NWF scores are under 30 and they are still learning new words by orally or subvocally sounding them out before reading the whole word (Tables 3.4–3.5), use those same formats during

In Your Classroom

Finding More Time for Practice

Killer Word Boost

If your class has a "killer word" for the week, wear a scarf one day and tape the difficult word on the scarf or pin the word to your lapel. Students' eyes will alight on the word every time they look at you. Tell students you will try to trick them throughout the day by asking them to read the word at moments when they least expect that question.

Beat the Clock

If you routinely write all new exception words on large cards, you can pull these cards out when your class is waiting to get their pictures taken or you go to an assembly and have 5 minutes to fill. Each new word should be written on three cards to play this game. Select a set of exception words that students have already learned to correctly identify for the game (for example, *through, beautiful, where, enough, though*). Your goal is getting students to recognize these words more fluently.

- Include multiple cards of each word in the card deck.

- Set a goal such as 25 words correct per minute. Tell the students that you will play a game with them and that their goal is to correctly read at least 25 word cards in 1 minute.
- Start the timer or have an appointed student start it.
- Hold up the first word card so that all students can answer in unison.
- Provide quick corrective feedback whenever students make errors ("This word is *because.*").
- Continue presenting words until the timer rings.
- Put correctly identified words in the throwaway box.
- Put incorrectly read words in a pile next to you.
- At the end of 1 minute, count the number of words correct and let the class know whether they met the goal.
- Pick up the cards in the pile and review errors with the students before repeating the activity for another minute.

The Reflective Teacher

Can I Still Use My Word Wall?

A Word Wall is a group of high-frequency written words displayed in alphabetical order on a bulletin board or a section of a classroom wall. The purpose of the wall is to make the words accessible so that students can find them when reading and writing and teachers can readily focus on them when providing practice in class (Cunningham, 2000). The Word Wall gives children extra practice reading, writing, and understanding the meaning of high-frequency regular words and exception words. This purpose is consistent with the objectives of the phonics approach described in this text. In addition, the "chanting" often used when reading from the Word Wall is very similar to the unison response formats used here. Problems with the Word Wall can occur when the words on the wall are not decodable; that is, they include regular words containing untaught sounds, untaught words, or too many exception words. Here are four keys to using the Word Wall effectively with students who are at risk.

1. Select only regular words that contain sounds that have already been taught.

2. Select only exception words that have already been taught.

3. For every five regular words, select one exception word.

4. When asking your students to read the words, use teaching strategies that discourage student guessing. For example, have students sound out the regular words while they are chanting, rather than having them sight read the words if they are not yet at that phase. Try putting regular and exception words in separate colors. Use signals so everyone answers together. Calibrate your think time for students' reading ability.

sentence reading starting with the First Reading described in Table 3.9 for story reading. When students come to an exception word, have them read it as a whole word. When students' NWF scores are still below 30 sounds per minute reading whole words, you still need to use the First, Second, and Third Readings in Table 3.9, moving from step to step on each subsequent read as long as student accuracy is high. Your students are still at the prealphabetic or partial alphabetic phase of reading and need to sound out words a number of times until they finally learn them automatically as sight words.

Once your students' NWF scores are higher than 30 sounds per minute reading whole words, you can start reducing the scaffolding and gradually phase out First Readings, eventually having students read whole words in text the first time through it. Your students will quickly start reading the sentences in unison, but expect that the first few times your pace will slow as you teach students to follow the signals when reading an entire sentence. If you maintain high expectations for students to read together, they will quickly adopt the habit during this part of instruction. If you do not start with a clear signal for each word (*"What word?"*), your best readers who do not need as much think time will jump ahead with the word, and students who need an extra second or two will soon stop trying and coast by echoing the faster readers. You will be fooled into thinking that students are fluently reading when, in reality, three or four of the best readers are doing all the work for the rest of the class.

From the time your students begin to read sentences, connect meaning to what they are reading by asking questions. Chapters 6 and 7 discuss vocabulary and comprehension, but students need to develop the habit of actively thinking about what they are reading as soon as they begin reading connected text. If students still have difficulty answering concrete lower-level questions (*who, what, where* questions) where the answers are given in the sentence, ask that type of direct question. As soon as those questions become too easy, start asking inferential ones as described in Chapter 7 in the section on teaching comprehension at the sentence level (pp. 289–293). In the most basic decodable sentence, *"Matt ran and got the ham,"* you can ask students whether Matt was moving very slowly and what word in the sentence gave the clue for the answer. Or you could ask whether Matt went and got a vegetable. Inferential questions like these can be difficult for younger students who are at risk.

Tips for Teaching Decodable Sentence Reading   The curriculum that Ms. Elizondo was using in her class introduced sentence reading by the middle of September, so she wrote two or three sentences on the board each day. When her students were still sounding out words (DIBELS NWF < 30), she had them sound out each word before reading it in the sentence: *"Sound out." "What word?" "Sound out." "What word?" "Sound out." "What word?"* If she didn't have students sound out the words on the first read, some students were unable to apply their decoding skills. Although she sometimes felt like a broken record signaling across the sentence, she knew that with enough practice, students would soon develop the automaticity necessary to move into reading words by sight, reading their sentences without sounding out each word. By the third time students read each sentence, Ms. Elizondo had students read the sentences by sight, using normal intonation. At that point, she asked at least one inferential question for every sentence. She wanted her students to think of themselves as detectives, finding the clue word that let them know the answer and ultimately the meaning of the text.

Reading Decodable Passages in Beginning Reading

"The average child needs between four and fourteen exposures to automatize the recognition of a new word. Therefore, in learning to read it is vital that children read a large amount of text at their independent reading level (95% accuracy) and that the text format provides specific practice in the skills being learned" (Lyon, 1998; p. 6). Students who are at risk often need even more opportunities to practice reading books that contain the words they have learned in class. The texts used in classes today often provide fewer opportunities than many students need to read new words and map letter–sound associations until those new words become sight words. Supplementary decodable books can provide that practice. Decodable books contain a high percentage of regular words composed of sounds the students have learned plus a few high-frequency exception words. For example, Ms. Rodriguez's students had learned the most common sounds for *s, c, n, a, r, t, l, b,* and *i*. They also learned the exception words *the, a, said, were, to,* and *is*. The following sentence represents decodable text for her students:

Nat ran to the bin.

The students would be able to sound out the regular words *Nat, ran,* and *bin* and read the exception words *to* and *the.* The following sentence, while including high-frequency words, would not be decodable for the same group of students:

Come here, Bob.

In this sentence the sight words *come* and *here* haven't been learned yet. Students have also not learned the most common sound of the letter *o* and would not be able to sound out the word *Bob.* This sentence is not decodable. For information on how to select decodable books for your students, see the feature on decodable books later in this chapter.

During the first half of first grade, before students typically score 50 on the DIBELS or AIMSweb NWF assessment reading whole words, the teacher has students read in unison so they get the most practice possible on sounding out and reading regular words, developing the necessary connections between Orthographic and Phonological processors. When students are explicitly taught to read connected text, they quickly learn to follow a line of print and recognize that spaces mark boundaries between words. They automatically move from left to right, read word by word, recognize that sentences are composed of words, and identify final punctuation marks.

The actual steps of the passage reading format are described in Table 3.9. For students whose scores on the DIBELS or AIMSweb NWF are less than 30 scpm, the teacher uses all three readings described in the format, as follows. On the first reading, the students sound out all words in unison except for exception words, which are read by the group as whole words. If students read with 97% accuracy or higher, the teacher moves to the second reading. If students read below 97% accuracy, they sound out the story again, orally. During the second reading, the students subvocally sound out each word in the decodable text before saying it. For the third reading, students read each word in unison by sight. If the teacher has selected a book that matches the students' word-reading skills, this third reading is usually done accurately the first time through. As was done with the first reading, the second and third readings are repeated if student accuracy is less than 97%. The same recommendations for integrating comprehension with sentence reading apply to passage reading. Typically, we recommend that teachers ask questions after each sentence or paragraph when students are reading text, but asking comprehension questions of beginning readers whose cognitive resources are focused on decoding words diverts their attention away from the text. Beginning readers slowly decoding will misread more words and will not be able to answer the comprehension questions. Thus, at this beginning reading stage, we recommend that comprehension questions follow an accurate whole-word reading.

You learned earlier that students whose scores on the DIBELS or AIMSweb NWF assessment are between 30 and 49 scpm reading whole words are now beginning to read whole words in their list reading. Therefore, their passage reading begins with the third reading on Table 3.9, reading words by sight in unison. Students read the story through two

TABLE 3.9 Format for Reading Stories in the Curriculum and Decodable Books: Beginning Readers

Objective	Students who have scored less than 30 letter sounds per minute on the DIBELS or AIMSweb NWF assessment will read a book containing words or word patterns taught in class, sounding out the words before reading them with 100% accuracy. Students who score between 30 and 49 on DIBELS or AIMSweb NWF reading whole words will read words by sight using the procedures described in the third reading.
Materials Needed	Use decodable text or text containing regular and exception words that the students are capable of reading with at least 90% accuracy.
Signaling	Finger-snap or hand-clap. **"Sound it out."** or **"What word?"** initiates the signal for unison answer.
Time	Between 15 and 30 minutes

Instructions	Teacher	Students
	Advance Organizer	
	Steps to reading stories and books (Prealphabetic Principle):	
	First Reading(s)	
	1. Suggested wording for focusing students to follow along: **"We are first going to sound out each word and then we will read it the fast way. When I clap, say the sound of the first letter. When I clap again, move your finger and say the next sound. When you are at the end of the word, move your finger back to the beginning of the word so you can read it the fast way. Watch me do it first."** (You will need to use a finger snap with your nondominant hand as you show students how you follow along to the signal, sounding out and reading the words.) **"Everybody, put your finger under the first letter of the very first word."**	Students touch under the first letter of the first word.
	2. Focus students on accurate reading and tell them the goal you've set: **"Our goal is to miss no more than one word today."**	
	3. Pause 1 second and then say, **"Sound it out"** and clap for the first sound. After 1 to 1½ seconds, clap for the next sound. One to 1½ seconds later, clap for the last sound. When students have said the last sound correctly, make sure that they move their finger back to the left of the word. Ask, **"What word?"** and clap. Students side-slash their finger as they read the word the fast way. Then they immediately move their finger to the left of the next word.	Students say sounds, pointing under the letters as they say them; they move their finger back to the beginning of the word before orally reading the word at a normal rate.
	4. Pause 1 second and then say, **"Sound it out"** and clap for the first sound. After 1 to 1½ seconds, clap for the next sound. One to 1½ seconds later, clap for the last sound. When students have said the last sound correctly, make sure that they move their finger back to the left of the word. Ask, **"What word?"** and clap. Students side-slash their finger as they read the word the fast way. Then they immediately move their finger to the left of the next word.	
	5. For exception words, avoid sounding out. When students move their fingers to the left of an exception word, say, **"What word?"** and clap to signal students to say the word.	Students read the whole word without sounding it out.
	6. Continue using this format to the end of the story or to the end of the page.	
	7. Wrap Up: Have students reread the story, sounding out each word until the error limit is met. When the error limit is met, give individual turns. Do not move on to the second reading format until the error limit is met.	

Continued

TABLE 3.9   Continued

	Second Reading(s) 1. Repeat Steps 1–5, but have students subvocally sound out the words as in Stage 2 regular word reading (Table 3.6). At the end of the story have students practice reading any missed words. Do not move on to the third reading format until the error limit is met.	Students subvocally sound out before saying the word at a normal rate.
	Third Reading(s) 1. Repeat Steps 1–5, but have students read words the fast way as in Stage 3 (Table 3.7) word reading. 2. Use individual checkouts to determine whether students are solid on reading the story. Have each student read one sentence.	Students read the words in the story the fast way.
Error Correction	When students make a sounding-out error, immediately say, **"My Turn,"** and sound out the word correctly. Move into a **"Your Turn"** and ask students to sound out the word before always going back to the beginning of the sentence. Any error (missed word, plural ending left off, etc.) is treated as an error.	
Perk Up Your Drill	■ Approach each story with a high degree of enthusiasm. If you convey your interest in the characters and plot, no matter how simple the story, the students' interest level and motivation will be heightened. During the second or third reading of the story, you will need to model voice inflection to match punctuation and emphasis in the story. Then ask students to reread the same text using an appropriate tone of voice. ■ If students grumble about reading a story one more time, reminding them that their accuracy will determine when they move to the next story empowers them and motivates them to do their best. ■ The day that students take home the story they have learned to read, ask them to whom they will read it. Encourage them to think about reading to a younger sibling, a parent, a grandparent, or a cousin. At the start of the next day's lesson, be sure to ask students about their story reading at home.	
Adaptations	■ Kindergartners and first graders who are still scoring under 30 on the DIBELS NWF assessment may need to repeat the first reading steps several times until they are ready to subvocally sound out the same words. ■ If your students are at Part 2, subvocal regular word reading, begin the story with the second reading format. When your students come to a difficult word, move back into first reading sounding out for that word. ■ If your students are nearing alphabetic principle (DIBELS NWF scores in the 30–49 range and nonsense words read as whole words) and they read most CVC-variant words as whole words, read new stories starting at the third reading procedure.	

Source: This script is based on one originally developed and field-tested by Carnine, D. W., Silbert, J., Kame'enui, E. J., & Tarver, S. (2010). *Direct Instruction Reading* (5th ed.). Boston: Merrill Prentice Hall.

times in unison as a group, reading each word by sight with the teacher and building fluency by gradually decreasing the thinking time required over the course of the two readings. If students perform fluently with 97% accuracy the second time through, the teacher gives individual turns, with each student reading one sentence. Check comprehension during this third reading. Once students reach benchmark levels on the NWF assessment, they are ready to read stories in a more traditional fashion by taking individual turns as described in the SAFER oral-passage-reading format in Chapter 5 (see Table 5.3, p. 203).

We found that one of the most difficult decisions for teachers was determining when to reduce scaffolding. Some teachers provide too little support and move into whole-word sight reading too quickly. When this happens, students make many errors and do not comprehend the text. Other teachers provide too much support and always start with First Readings, even when the DIBELS scores indicate that students no longer need that much support. To help the teachers determine when to reduce scaffolding when students are

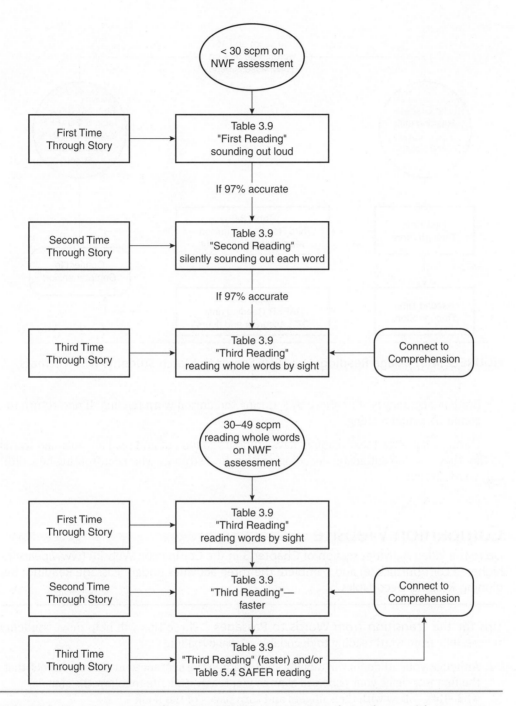

FIGURE 3.13 Passage Reading: Use NWF Scores to Match Students with Formats

reading text, we developed these guidelines reflected in Figures 3.13 and 3.14. Reduce scaffolding and start with the Third Reading if the following apply:

- Students are scoring above 30 sounds per minute reading whole words on the DIBELS or AIMSweb NWF assessment.
- You pretaught letter sounds and words in the story that contain those sounds to mastery by having students sound out the words in lists before whole-word reading. Students should then be able to read those same words in the story by sight.

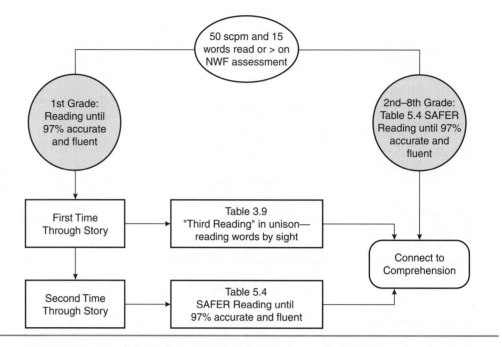

FIGURE 3.14   Passage Reading: Use NWF Scores to Match Students with Formats

- Student accuracy is at or above 97% during the unison word reading. If not, return to sound-by-sound reading.

During whole-word text reading, have students sound out and read any misread words so that they develop automatic decoding as their first strategy when confronting new difficult words in text.

Companion Website

Go to the Video Activities section of Chapter 3 in the Companion Website (www.pearson-highered.com/bursuck2e) and complete the three activities under "Passage Reading: Beginning Reading Decodables."

Tips for the Transition from Words to Passages   These tips will help move students successfully from word reading to decodable passage reading.

1. Although your students will quickly start reading the sentences in unison, expect that the first few times your pace will slow as you teach students to follow the signals while they follow with their fingers and turn pages of the book.
2. Take time to teach students how to follow the text with the pointer finger of their dominant hand. When students are following along with their fingers, whether reading in unison or when another child is reading, you know they are paying attention. Since consistently following the text will be difficult for your most inattentive students, provide an incentive with the Teacher-Student game in the beginning for consistent finger pointing: *"The class just earned another point because everyone remembered to follow with their fingers."* Teachers in one of our schools reminded students before they began reading to use their "smooth reading finger." Teachers in classrooms with older students frequently complained about students whose previous teachers had not encouraged a smooth reading finger. These students followed text with a finger that

bounced on every word, that was turned in an awkward position following on the tops of words, or that covered the text as they read. Breaking this ingrained habit of older students was difficult.

3. Some teachers clarify key vocabulary when students first read words they do not know during the first read-through. Other teachers focus exclusively on sounding out words or reading during a first read and wait until the second reading to ask comprehension questions and discuss vocabulary. Other teachers preteach the meaning of vocabulary words that they anticipate the children will not know. Chapter 6 discusses strategies to teach vocabulary explicitly.

An additional consideration when moving from words to passages is whether the passage should include pictures. The role that pictures play in beginning passage reading is discussed in the *Research Note*.

Research Note

Should I Use Pictures with My Beginning Readers?

Teachers are often confused about how to use pictures in their beginning reading programs. Some experts say that pictures are an important motivator for students and that they also help students with comprehension. Other experts warn that pictures can impede progress toward attaining the alphabetic principle by sending students the message that the text is not the primary source for decoding words. Current optical brain research about how skilled readers approach text provides the rationale for directing the beginning reader's attention to the text rather than interrupting that focus by having students move their eyes back and forth between pictures and text. A skilled reader's eyes move from left to right, word by word, only occasionally skipping function words such as *in* or *to,* visually processing each individual letter, recognizing each word within milliseconds as the brain translates speech to print. Rather than flow smoothly across the page, the eyes rapidly dart about seven to nine letters before stopping for approximately 200–250 msec (Larson, 2007; Rayner, Chace, Slattery, & Ashby, 2006). Figure 3.15 shows the course of typical eye movements called saccades, represented by arcs, and the stopping points called fixations, where two arcs intersect.

About 10% to 20% of the time, when the reader approaches a difficult word or has difficulty comprehending text, his eyes move in a backward saccade to reread the text, as happened in the second section in Figure 3.15. During the fixations when the eyes pause, readers process text and comprehension occurs. The brain first takes in the orthographic information, but within about five or ten milliseconds converts it to a phonological pattern (Larson, 2007; Rayner et al., 2006). As could be expected, beginning readers and students with reading disabilities have longer fixations and shorter saccades. Their saccades move backward more frequently as they relook at words or text to comprehend (Rayner et al., 2006; Rayner, Foorman, Perfetti, Pesetsky, & Seidenberg, 2001).

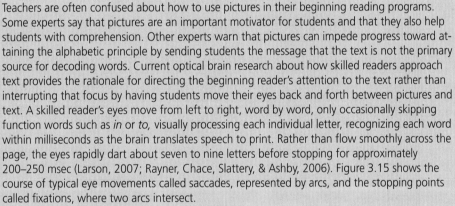

Current optical and brain research about how skilled readers approach

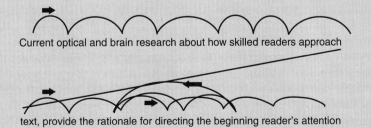

text, provide the rationale for directing the beginning reader's attention

FIGURE 3.15 Saccades

Continued

When teachers ask beginning readers to move their eyes between the text they are reading and pictures, to routinely skip words, or to skip ahead to the end of the sentence, this normal reading pattern is interrupted.

Can teachers resolve this dilemma with beginning readers, using pictures to motivate and clarify meaning, yet without the side effect of interfering with the teaching of systematic sounding out? Yes—simply by having pictures follow text rather than having them occur on the same page. Pictures that are shown after text is read can function as a reward for accurate reading as well as a stimulus for discussing the meaning of the text. Teachers further discourage guessing for early readers when they expect students to point to each word with their fingers and continually remind them to look at the letters in the word.

Selecting Decodable Books

The role of decodable books in beginning reading instruction remains a contentious topic (see *The Reflective Teacher* on pp. 127–128). Unfortunately, the National Reading Panel report provides no direct guidance and instead recommends that more research is needed to investigate this question (National Reading Panel, 2000). Meanwhile, since most explicit and systematic phonics curricula use decodable texts as a key part of beginning reading instruction, teachers of students who are at risk need to familiarize themselves with decodable materials and investigate the issues for themselves.

Moats (2000) explained that decodable books serve as "a bridge between phonics instruction and the reading of trade books" (p. 148). Why are decodable books so important for beginning readers? Decodable books provide more practice opportunities for students who are learning to decode letter–sound patterns. As noted earlier in this chapter, the average child needs between 4 and 14 exposures to a new pattern before it is identified automatically. Students who are at risk are likely to need even more exposure.

After Mr. Jerry's class successfully read the list of words starting with *st*, *tr*, and *d* consonant blends, he wanted to give his students more practice reading these same words in connected text. He knew that if the next story his students read contained only one or two words beginning with these new consonant blends, many students would not get enough practice and would be unable to identify the pattern successfully when it appeared in the next week's story.

Leveled texts, an option for passage reading used in many classrooms, provide much less support than decodables for struggling readers' word recognition and no support for developing decoding skills. For example, when the books in a typical kindergarten curriculum were recently analyzed, 51% of the words appeared fewer than three times, with 25% of the words appearing only once (Hiebert, 2008). Struggling readers need more practice reading words than that.

Because decodable books incorporate words or sounds that students have already learned in class, students typically are highly successful reading decodable books, even for the first time. By providing students with the opportunity to read successfully on their own, decodable books can help students develop confidence and a more positive attitude toward reading (Bursuck et al., 2004; Stanovich, 1993/1994).

While most comprehension instruction for students at the beginning reading stage is done through listening and discussing different genres of children's literature, if used correctly, decodable books can also provide opportunities for comprehension development. A creative teacher can draw out several questions even from a short decodable story. For example, after reading the decodable book *Frank the Fish Gets His Wish*, Mr. Jerry had his students identify main characters, explain why Frank was lonely, sequence events in the story, visualize how they would feel if they were the fish, and talk about the fantasy aspects of the book. When students reread the story the second time, they used fish voices and tried to express fear when knocked out of their fishbowl.

TABLE 3.10 Selecting Decodable Books Based on Word Difficulty

Skill	Examples
VC and CVC words that begin with continuous sounds	*it, fan*
VCC and CVCC words that begin with a continuous sound	*lamp, ask*
CVC words that begin with a stop sound	*cup, tin*
CVCC words that begin with a stop sound	*dust, hand*
CCVC words	*crib, blend, snap, flat*
CCVCC, CCCVC, and CCCVCC words	*damp, spent, scrap, scrimp*
Long vowels and short vowel combinations	*late, stand, stay, Pam*

Teachers selecting supplementary decodable books need to systematically match the sequence of letter sounds and word patterns taught in their classroom with text in decodable books. Because some books selling as decodables include a relatively high percentage of exception words, teachers cannot assume that a book labeled as such is decodable. Put simply, many books advertised as decodables frequently are not. Table 3.10 lists a common scope and sequence listing increasingly difficult words that you can use as a guide for selecting decodable books.

> For specific information about how to teach decoding and use decodable readers, visit the *Teaching Decoding* website: **http://www.aft.org/pubs-reports/american_educator/spring_sum98/moats.pdf.**

When selecting additional books, consider these questions:

- Are the students beginning readers and able to follow only one or two lines of text on a page?
- Do flashy pictures interrupt the students' concentration when sounding out the words?
- Are the students older readers who need a decodable chapter book with a more mature look to it?
- Are full pages of text needed because the students are ready to transition to chapter books?
- What letter–sound correspondences and types of words have the students learned to decode? What exception words do students know? Does this book match their skills?

Some reading experts advocate the use of predictable books with beginning readers (Yopp, 1995). Predictable books (also called pattern books) are texts that contain repeated phrases and language patterns (Maring, Boxie, & Wiseman, 2000). These patterns allow students to read the books successfully by guessing based on the context and/or pictures. The purpose of the predictable books is to provide a successful early reading experience for students. The issue of whether to use predictable or decodable books with beginning readers is discussed in *The Reflective Teacher*.

The Reflective Teacher

Should I Use Predictable Books?

Struggling readers often overuse the context to recognize unknown words. For example, students with reading problems tend to guess when they come to a word they don't know by using the context (*"What word makes sense?"*) or by looking at the first letter of a word (*"This word*

Continued

begins with sss,"). Research shows that content words, those that are most important for text comprehension, can be predicted from the surrounding text only 10% to 20% of the time (Gough, Alford, & Holley-Wilcox, 1981). Predictable books are designed to make guessing pay off, giving students the idea that they don't have to look at all parts of words when figuring them out. Students who are at risk need to develop a consistent sounding strategy before they are taught to use the context. This means that their early reading experiences should involve as little guessing as possible. If students are required to sound out words in one setting and guess in another, they are likely to be confused and may not learn a systematic sounding strategy at all. Therefore, the use of predictable books with students who have yet to attain the alphabetic principle is not recommended. Decodable text based on the letter–sound correspondences the students are learning is much more likely to result in a strategic reader as opposed to a guesser.
If you must use predictable texts:

1. Avoid having students reread the texts if they are beginning to memorize the story.
2. Prior to having them read the story, circle words that students can decode (either a regular word for which they know the sounds or an exception word). As you read the story, students can be responsible for reading the decodable words. If decodable words are missed, make sure you use sounding out as part of your correction procedure.
3. Occasionally model sounding out when reading predictable texts. Through your example, students see that reading is not all memorization.

Divide your class into two groups. Use predictable books with the higher groups and decodable books with your students who are below the DIBELS benchmarks.

What Can I Do for Students Who Are Not Learning Beginning Reading Skills Even with Enhancements?

Students' scores on the informal letter–sound correspondence assessment let you know who needs extra Tier 2 practice reviewing letter sounds. Student scores on the DIBELS or AIMSweb NWF assessment as well as the PALS or TPRI word reading lists inform you who needs extra Tier 2 practice with decoding skills. Tier 2 intervention sessions vary, depending on whether students are just working on letter sounds or are also learning to decode.

For students just learning letter–sound correspondence in kindergarten, small-group Tier 2 sessions last between 5 and 10 minutes. Students whose letter–sound assessment indicates that they know fewer than 90% of the letter sounds taught by the teacher should receive Tier 2 intervention immediately, so that they don't fall too far behind the class. Because many kindergarten students who need letter–sound practice also need phonemic awareness practice, you can combine the two skills into one short tutoring session. During the Tier 2 tutoring group session, practice with the same letter–sound format (Table 3.3) that was used during large-group Tier 1 instruction. Each day students practice one letter, continuing to practice that same letter each day until mastery. The class may have learned sounds for the letters *s, t, a, m, f, b, i,* and *l,* but if Keivon does not know the sounds for *f, b,* and *l,* the teacher has him identify the sound of *f* every day until he knows it. Each day she also reviews the sounds he knows. After Keivon learns the sound for *f,* she begins working on the sound for *b.* Teaching more than one letter sound at a time to students who are not keeping up with the pace of the class is not effective because it is likely to be confusing, particularly for students in the primary grades.

Students learning to blend letter sounds into words need longer daily 30-minute Tier 2 tutoring sessions in which they can practice new letter sounds, regular and exception words, and passage reading. Some teachers like to schedule small Tier 2 groups before reading class so that the students who just practiced the material can participate more fully with the class. Other teachers prefer to schedule Tier 2 groups just after lunch. These teachers like to have the students' practice spaced so that there are morning and afternoon practice sessions. Since beginning decoding tutoring sessions last longer, some schools elect to have another teacher or trained paraprofessional work with each small group, taking them to a relatively quiet location. Although small groups of three to four students are ideal (Gersten et al., 2009), some schools with many students who are at risk do not have enough personnel for such small groups. In our project schools we found that having six or fewer students in each Tier 2 intervention group worked well. Tier 2 groups at our three schools were taught by a music teacher, a French teacher, a Spanish teacher, a former *Reading Recovery* teacher, a librarian, a special education teacher, a Title 1 teacher, or a paraprofessional. Each of these individuals first learned to teach the same scripts used by the classroom teacher so that they used the same signals, said the same letter sounds, and followed the same formats. These are the scripts included in this text.

Some Tier 2 groups are able to keep up with the pace of the classroom and practice the same skills and words that were taught in class that day. Other tutoring groups fall behind when difficult new patterns such as *ch* are introduced. These groups continue to practice the earlier lessons until they have success. Because Tier 2 teachers can fit only letter–sound practice, regular word reading, exception word reading, and sentence reading into the 30-minute sessions, often there isn't enough time for reading decodable books. Some school teams used tutors or paraprofessionals to provide additional time for Tier 2 students to read more decodable text.

What Can I Do for Students Who Are Not Learning Beginning Reading Skills Even with Tier 2 Support?

In Chapter 2, the need for more intensive Tier 3 instruction for some students in kindergarten who are particularly at risk was discussed, and decision rules were provided to help you identify those students. However, not all students who need Tier 3 enter it in kindergarten. Some enter in first grade, as well. Later placements into Tier 3 can occur for a number of reasons. Some students manage to acquire enough segmenting, blending, and letter–sound correspondence skills to remain in Tier 2 in kindergarten, but exhibit much difficulty moving past the partial alphabetic phase in grade 1. Other students may move into your school from a school that did not stress phonemic awareness and letter–sound skills in kindergarten.

Appendix C lists the decision rules one district developed for students in the districtwide K–3 multi-tier reading program. Compare the NWF guidelines on that chart with recommendations listed below for placement into Tier 3 developed by Good, Simmons, Kame'enui, and Wallin (2002):

- In September of Grade 1, the student scores below 13 letter sounds per minute on DIBELS NWF, or less than 25 letters correct per minute on the DIBELS Letter Naming Fluency, or less than 10 segments correct per minute in DIBELS Phonemic Segmentation Fluency.
- In January of Grade 1, the student scores below 30 letter sounds correct per minute on the DIBELS NWF, or less than 20 words correct per minute on DIBELS Oral Reading Fluency (ORF is discussed in Chapter 5).
- In May of Grade 1, the student scores less than 30 letter sounds correct per minute on the DIBELS NWF, or less than 20 words correct per minute on DIBELS Oral Reading

Fluency. The DIBELS recommendation at less than 20 is based on an end-of-first-grade benchmark of 40. Chapter 5 provides discussion about why a year-end benchmark of 60 may be more desirable.

While the decision rules described are research-based and generally accurate, experience dictates that teacher judgment be part of the decision-making equation as well. For example, in some cases teachers have requested that the assessments be given again because the scores did not reflect students' performance in class. In other cases, students who had borderline scores and who also presented behavior problems in class were placed into Tier 3 because their behavior and attention were improved in a small-group setting. Table 3.11 describes how beginning reading skills are taught in each of the five alternative programs described in Chapter 2.

Companion Website

Go to the Video Activities section of Chapter 3 in the Companion Website (www.pearsonhighered.com/bursuck2e) and complete the activity entitled *Reading: Direct Instruction.*

How Can I Teach Beginning Reading Skills to English Language Learners?

Systematic and explicit phonics benefits English language learners whether they are first taught to read in English or in their native language. Numerous research studies in the United States and England demonstrate that when young English language learners receive explicit teaching of the alphabetic principle, they outperform their peers in word recognition and comprehension (Francis, Rivera, Lesaux, & Rivera, 2006; Gunn, Biglan, Smolkowski, & Ary, 2000.) Even when students are not yet fluent in English, explicit practice in sounding out words develops both English reading skills and English speaking skills, if explicit vocabulary instruction accompanies the phonics. Teachers who show pictures or use gestures to depict the meaning of unfamiliar words after students decode those words are teaching both alphabetic principle and comprehension. English language learners also require extra practice learning to articulate letter sounds that have no equivalent in their native language. The length of time learning explicit phonics may be crucial for grade-level reading, with many English language learners requiring two years to catch up to their English-speaking peers.

Companion Website

Go to the Assignments and Activities section of Chapter 3 in the Companion Website (www.pearsonhighered.com/bursuck2e) and complete the activity entitled *An ELL Vocabulary Lesson.*

Fortunately, "cracking the code" in one language often expedites learning to read in a second language. If students first read at the full alphabetic phase in their native language, their ability to decode can transfer to later English reading (Durgunoğlu, 2002). This transference will be more difficult for students who have had trouble learning to read in their native language, and these same students will be at high risk for reading failure in English unless they get intensive support (Gersten, 1996). English language learners who need additional support learning to read can be identified as early as kindergarten through phonemic awareness, graphophonemic knowledge, and rapid naming screening assessments.

TABLE 3.11 Comparison of Five Common Tier 3 Approaches

	Direct Instruction: Reading Mastery	Lindamood: LiPS Program	Reading Recovery	Wilson Reading System	Language!
Do lessons introduce a predesigned sequence of letter sounds?	Yes	Yes	No	Yes. However, several sounds are introduced within one substep.	Yes
Does curriculum specifically coordinate letter sounds taught in isolation with first words read in isolation and later in passages?	Yes	Yes	No	Yes	Yes
Do students practice letter sounds and word reading, only moving to the next lesson after they are successful?	Yes	Yes	No	Yes	Yes
Are phonics clues encouraged as the primary method for reading unfamiliar words?	Yes	Yes	No	Yes; pictures are never used in this program.	Yes
Do lessons introduce a sequence of regular words that are increasingly difficult to decode? (Example: VC or CVC followed by CVC variants)	Yes	Yes	No	Yes	Yes
Are students discouraged from guessing at words as one strategy for word reading?	Yes	Yes	No	Yes	Yes
Is decodable reading used to help students apply the letter–sound knowledge they have learned?	Yes. Program includes decodable reading books that are coordinated with letter sounds and words taught to students.	Yes. Teachers select decodable reading that is coordinated with letter sounds and words taught to students.	No. Program discourages decodable reading.	Yes. Decodable reading in sentences and passages is coordinated with letter sounds and words taught to students.	Yes. Program includes decodable reading books that are coordinated with letter sounds and words taught to students.

Continued

TABLE 3.11 Continued

	Direct Instruction: Reading Mastery	Lindamood: LiPS Program	Reading Recovery	Wilson Reading System	Language!
What is the amount of time spent on development of learning letter sounds, sounding out words, writing them, and sounding out words in passages?	After first 30 lessons, almost the entire daily lesson is spent on learning these skills. Comprehension development is also included in lessons.	Beginning lessons are split between phonemic awareness and development of alphabetic principle.	The use of magnetic letters and word boxes to analyze words comprises a small proportion of the 30-minute lessons, which cover seven activities each day.	Between 66% and 90% of lesson is devoted to learning these skills. Some lessons also include listening comprehension development.	Each literacy lesson is divided into 10 sections and is designed to take between 90 to 180 minutes. Of those 10 sections, four are devoted to these skills.
Are sight words pretaught before they appear in reading passages?	Yes	Yes	No	Teachers are encouraged to preteach.	Yes
Are the first sight words taught limited to high-frequency words necessary for story reading?	Yes	Yes	No	No. Both real and nonsense words are taught.	Yes
Is left-to-right blending stressed throughout all word- and passage-reading activities?	Yes	Yes	No	Yes	Yes
Do students write words that they are learning to read?	Yes	Yes	Yes	Yes	Yes
How are students assessed?	Short mastery tests of word or passage reading given to students approximately every five lessons determine whether students are ready to move to the next lesson or move to a faster- or slower-paced group.	Ongoing observation of the students' daily performance on reading tasks during lessons provides the foundation for decision making about how quickly to move through the program.	Teachers keep daily running records, notating errors that students read in predictable books.	Specific criteria are set for reading and spelling per lesson/per substep. Students are post-tested at the end of every step. Assessment determines how quickly student moves through curriculum.	Each unit of 10 lessons contains mastery tasks for the skills presented in that unit. Students are expected to achieve 80% on all tasks in order to proceed to the next unit.

The four test batteries identified in this book either have or are developing equivalent versions in Spanish. Unfortunately, at this point in time, we simply don't know under what circumstance, if any, reading instruction for English language learners should begin in the student's primary language (Goldenberg, 2008). Too often, an ELL student's reading intervention is delayed because the assumption is that the root cause of the reading difficulty is that English is not the student's primary language. Developing English skills is prioritized and reading is deemphasized while waiting for the oral skills to develop. Meanwhile, valuable time is lost because English language learners who struggle with reading, whether they are from nonalphabetic or alphabetic backgrounds, need explicit, systematic, and intensive instruction in reading, and they need that intervention sooner rather than later. Becoming more proficient in English will not help a student who has poor phonological skills associate sounds with the letters they represent. In Chapter 1 you learned that students in a typical first-grade classroom needed a range of supports in order to learn to read. English language learners need that same support (Francis et al., 2006). Fortunately, research has shown that students can develop oral language and reading skills simultaneously, and that the more students read, the more language they learn (Goldenberg, 2008).

When you listen to an English language learner read, you may have difficulty determining whether a misread word is an actual error or just an articulation difference. Becoming aware of articulation patterns in students' native languages will help your analysis in these situations. Table 3.12 details pronunciation difficulties that native Spanish speakers may have when reading English text.

> For many practical ideas on teaching reading to English language learners, go to **http://www.colorincolorado. org.**

TABLE 3.12 Potential English Pronunciation Problems for Native Speakers of Spanish

Consonants	Vowels
/v/ is often pronounced as /b/ or a sound close to /w/; *vase* becomes *base*.	/ă/ is often confused with /ĕ/; *mat* becomes *met*.
At the beginning of a word, /p/ is often pronounced as /b/; *pet* becomes *bet*.	/ē/ is often pronounced as /ē/; *meet* becomes *mit*.
At the beginning of a word, /t/ is often pronounced as /d/; *tap* becomes *dap*.	/ā/ is often pronounced as /ā/; *make* becomes *mek*.
At the beginning of a word, /k/ is often pronounced as /g/; *kit* becomes *git*.	/oo/ is often pronounced as /o͞o/; *book* becomes *bo͞ok*.
/sh/ is usually pronounced as /ch/; *ship* becomes *chip*.	
/y/ is often pronounced as /j/; *yell* becomes *jell*.	
/z/ is often pronounced as /s/; *zig* becomes *sig*.	
/m/, /n/, and /ng/ may be substituted for each other; *ping* becomes *pin*.	
When words begin with consonant clusters (*pr, cl, pl, sl*), an extra vowel is often inserted at the beginning of the word; *speak* becomes *espeak*.	
When words end with consonant clusters, the final consonant sound is often omitted; *fast* becomes *fas*.	
When a voiced /th/ occurs in the middle or the end of a word, /d/ is often substituted; *mother* becomes *moder*.	

Source: Adapted from Avery, P., & Ehrlich, S. (1992). *Teaching American English Pronunciation*. New York: Oxford Press, pp.149–153.

How Important Are Beginning Reading Skills for Older Learners?

While systematic phonics instruction produces the biggest impact on growth in reading when it begins in kindergarten or Grade 1 (National Reading Panel, 2000), teachers are responsible for bringing significant numbers of struggling older readers to proficient levels of reading. The National Assessment of Educational Progress 2007 Report indicated that 33% of fourth graders and 26% of eighth graders fell below the basic level in reading, unable to demonstrate even partial mastery of reading (Lee, Gregg, & Donahue, 2007). These students do not have the skills to acquire new knowledge from text (Lee et al., 2007).

It is often difficult to determine whether a struggling older reader has learning disabilities or has not been effectively taught. According to Roberts, Torgesen, Boardman, and Scammacca (2008), "Many older struggling readers are victims of poor early reading instruction. They were not taught or were insufficiently taught the basic skills necessary for fluent reading and deep processing of text. Some of these students are able to catch up in critical reading skills if provided with additional, sustained instruction in small, focused instructional groups" (p. 63). The authors go on to explain that a second group of older readers struggle despite having received research-based reading instruction taught well. Typically, diagnostic testing or intervention in an RTI model reveals that students in this second group have learning disabilities. If they are fortunate enough to get research-based intervention of sufficient intensity, they will respond more slowly to that instruction than many of the students in the first group.

Studies investigating older students and adults who have reading problems reveal that most have basic deficits in decoding skills. Of those older students with decoding deficits, there appear to be two groups (Archer, Gleason, & Vachon, 2003). Older students in one group, the smaller of the two groups, read at the first- and second-grade level. These students are still beginning readers without adequate skills for fluent sight reading. The second group are those reading between the third- and fifth-grade levels. While these students read single-syllable words and some high-frequency words by sight, they struggle to decode multisyllable words and have considerable difficulty reading connected text fluently. The needs of the smaller group of students who have yet to attain the alphabetic principle are addressed in this chapter. The needs of the larger group of older students with decoding problems are discussed in Chapters 4 and 5.

Share & Stanovich (1995) have aptly pointed out that it is tempting to focus reading instruction for older students on whole-word recognition because beginning phonics strategies appear to be babyish. In addition, progress in developing systematic word-attack skills can be slow at first, as guessing habits acquired during many years of previous instruction are difficult to unlearn. Slow progress combined with student reluctance can act to weaken teachers' resolve to stay the alphabetic principle course. Nonetheless, teachers are urged to use with these older readers curricula that systematically and explicitly provide practice reading words to link their spellings to their pronunciations, while adding meaning through having students read the words in connected text. Otherwise these students will remain stuck in the word-guessing mode for the rest of their lives. Interventions stressing word study can increase reading achievement both in word reading and comprehension, though less so in comprehension (Roberts et al., 2008; Wexler, Edmonds, & Vaughn, 2007). Providing systematic explicit instruction in vocabulary and comprehension is recommended as well.

The teacher's only productive option when teaching decoding to older learners is to step back and teach phonemic awareness, letter–sound skills, regular word-reading skills, and coordinated passage-reading skills previously described in Chapters 2 and 3. However, doing so presents two challenges. The first is to find a text that is not only explicit and systematic but also has age-appropriate stories and doesn't look "babyish." Three evidence-based programs that have these features are *Corrective Reading* (Engelmann, Carnine, Johnson, Meyer, Becker, & Eisele, 2008), *Language!* (Greene, 2009), and *Wilson Reading System* (Wilson, 2004). The second challenge is to find enough instructional time during the school day. Programs such as the three identified here are designed for a minimum of an hour and a half to two hours of intensive teaching each day.

Computer-assisted instruction is a potentially powerful way to teach word identification skills to students of all ages. The effectiveness of computer-assisted instruction in teaching beginning word identification is discussed in *Technology*.

> This article by Louisa C. Moats, "When Older Students Can't Read," explains some of the benefits that result from teaching phonics to older struggling readers: **http://www.cdl.org/ resource-library/articles/older_read. php.**

Technology

Beginning Word Reading

Because there is so little published research investigating the effectiveness of computer-assisted phonics instruction, the National Reading Panel could only conclude that computer technology appears to hold promise for reading instruction (National Reading Panel, 2000). To date, computer software designed to improve reading instruction is still in its infancy and is most appropriately used in classrooms to supplement or reinforce a systematic, explicit phonics program. A 2007 study commissioned by the federal government testing the effectiveness of reading software programs on reading achievement over a two-year period of time showed almost no improvement in classrooms with computer-assisted instruction over classrooms where the software programs weren't used (Dynarski et al., 2007). Complaints were lodged about factors that weren't controlled for, such as the amount of time students used the software and how well the teacher integrated it into their classroom. The lesson to be learned is that simply purchasing a reading software program, even if it is of high quality, and putting students in front of a computer without feedback from an adult or monitoring of mastery is not sufficient to predictably increase reading achievement.

Teaching students who are at risk to move from letter sounds to the consolidated alphabetic stage requires extremely careful, coordinated instruction. *More* instruction is not always *better* instruction, especially when poorly designed activities contribute to mistakes that the student will later have to unlearn. Teachers who are evaluating software to supplement their instruction in letter sounds, word reading, or passage reading should consider the following factors:

- How closely coordinated is the teaching of letter sounds with the students' daily reading curriculum? Check the order in which the letter sounds are introduced. If the order is different, reorder the sequence presented in the computer program. If the computer software program includes digitized speech, the letter sounds should match your articulation. For example, letter sounds should be articulated without schwas. Finally, check the intelligibility of the synthesized speech. Although the quality of synthesized speech continues to improve, the longer sentences are sometimes unintelligible.

- How well do the games and activities involving regular word reading reflect skills that students have learned? For example, if students have not yet learned to decode consonant blends, they should not be expected to read consonant blend words while playing a computer game. If the skills stressed in the games and activities do not match your reading curriculum, find out whether the design allows you to modify types of words and text that are read.

- Does the program introduce regular words composed of letter sounds that the students can identify? Are those same words practiced later in sentences, paragraphs, or stories? If not, the activities are likely to be of little benefit in strengthening skills covered in the daily reading curriculum.

Continued

- Is the phonics program systematic and explicit? Computer-assisted instructional phonics programs may include nonsystematic phonics activities reminiscent of those in the most tedious workbooks of years past. Computer phonics programs may also undermine your systematic phonics program by encouraging students to guess at words and memorize too many whole words. Finally, since students aren't using their fingers while reading, monitoring left-to-right reading is difficult, if not impossible.
- Does the software program include performance checks to ensure that students reach mastery before moving on to a more difficult skill?
- Does the program have a built-in monitoring system that allows you to evaluate how the student is progressing?

What Games and Activities Reinforce Students' Beginning Reading Skills?

Once your students are decoding CVC and CVC-variant words, use every opportunity to take advantage of the school environment for more practice. Using the words your students can decode, make posters with short poems or captions describing a funny picture, and display these posters in areas where your students routinely wait—outside the bathroom, in the lunchroom waiting line, near the library. Draw your students' attention to the posters, asking them questions about content. You will help your students feel like readers, actively applying their reading to the outside world.

> For a closer look at well-designed computer software in teaching beginning reading skills, download free samples at Headsprout, **http://www.headsprout.com/school/**; Funnix, **http://www.funnix.com/**; and Waterford Early Learning, **http://www.waterfordearlylearning.org/**.

After students have successfully read a decodable book, play "Landing on Mars" with them. Ask them to turn to a page in their book and hold up their index finger as the rocket. When you call out a word that is on the page, they are to launch their rocket into the air and land it on the word you named. Say, for example, "Find *shut.*" (pause) "Find *"pigpen."* (pause) "Find *rack.*" (pause) "Yes! This class landed on Mars all three times!" Students will work their hardest to find the words quickly, speeding up the rate at which they are decoding.

By midyear of first grade, students on track to read at grade level should be starting to move into the consolidated alphabetic phase, indicating that they are ready to read more difficult words containing long vowels, more advanced sound clusters such as *tch,* and multisyllable words. Students will advance more quickly if they have the opportunity to receive feedback and help when needed by reading aloud to the teacher, tutors, parents, or older siblings. Some classrooms have successfully used First-Grade Peer-Assisted Literacy Strategies (PALS) (Grade 1–Grade 2) to provide more oral reading practice of connected text. In these classrooms, a stronger reader is paired with a weaker reader to coach him or her. Students are taught to cooperate with their partners, praise their partners, and work steadily at reading. Student coaches learn to teach and practice letter–sound identification, word reading, and connected text reading. By the time they begin working independently with their partners, these students have even learned to give a My Turn–Your Turn response any time the weaker student makes an error. The positive feedback and effective error correction are critical elements in this process (Mathes & Babyak, 2001). A similar PALS strategy has also been effective with weaker high school readers (Fuchs, Fuchs, & Kazdan, 1999).

Connecting reading to spelling and, ultimately, students' writing further develops reading skills. Not only should students be able to read CVC and CVC variants by sight no later than December of first grade, but they should also accurately spell regular CVC words, where the letters match the sounds. Once students can read words that contain *blends,* they should also write words that contain those same patterns. Rather than having to memorize words such as *plot, clam, send,* and *stand,* students should learn to automatically

FIGURE 3.16   Grid

spell them by sound once they have learned to read similar words containing blends. The teacher who then tells her students to write a story about a big fat red bug extends her students' new learning even further. Shortly after the beginning of first grade is also the time to begin teaching the spelling of a few of the most common exception words that students are reading in their stories. The more students read, formally spell, and use these words in their writing, the more automatically they will recognize them in text.

The Word Box Game

The Word Box Game is a fun way to connect reading and spelling for your students. Put several clear word-building boxes on an accessible shelf so that students can play Word Box when they have completed other work.

Prepare the Game   Put the following inside each box:

- Lowercase letters of only the letter sound correspondences you have taught your students. All the vowels should be a distinctive color or marked with a distinctive tape.
- A laminated grid that students use to make words, placing a letter on each square (Figure 3.16)
- A pencil
- A "rocket" sheet that students can use for writing their words (see Figure 3.17)

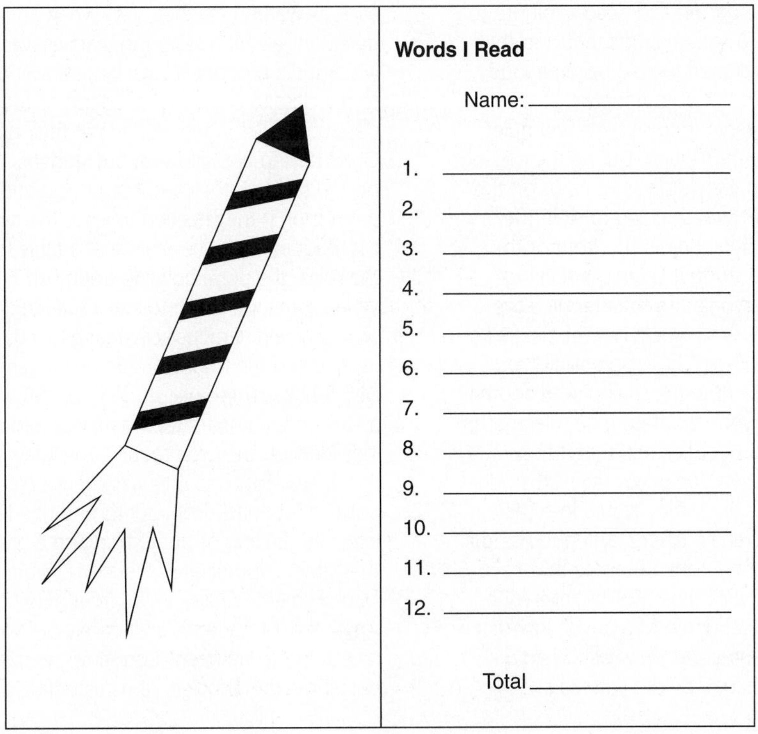

Words I Read

Name: _____

1. _____
2. _____
3. _____
4. _____
5. _____
6. _____
7. _____
8. _____
9. _____
10. _____
11. _____
12. _____

Total _____

FIGURE 3.17   Rocket Sheet

Prepare the Students

1. Tell students to bring a pencil and piece of paper when they play Word Box.
2. Teach the game to students, showing them how to put a letter in each box. Tell students to always put a marked vowel in the middle box.
3. After students put a letter into each box, ask them to say the letter sound correspondences quietly before blending them into a word.
4. Tell students to write the word they read on their paper, reading it out loud one more time after they write it.
5. Show students how to write their grand total on the page. Enthusiastically describe how, as they learn more and more words, their total numbers will get bigger and bigger.
6. Monitor students carefully as they play the game during this teaching phase to ensure that they will follow all the steps when they independently take out the word boxes.

Strategies for supporting student behaviors that are conducive to learning are described in the *In Your Classroom* feature.

In Your Classroom

Strategies to Encourage Positive Behavior

- Ms. Larson used the Teacher's Rocking Chair game to teach self-control to her kindergartners and help them learn to sit quietly for short amounts of time. Before she started playing the game with her students, when a parent, the principal, or a special education teacher would walk into the kindergarten and need a minute to talk to Ms. Larson, a few students, noticing that the teacher was occupied, would become loud or misbehave to get her attention. Ms. Larson wanted to teach everyone to sit for a few quiet moments without interrupting. During the rocking chair game, all of the children sat in rows on the carpet. One student was selected to sit in the teacher's large rocking chair in the front of the room. The selected student sat in the rocking chair surveying everyone else to determine the "quietest" student, who would get the next turn to sit in the chair. When Ms. Larson said, *"Your turn is up,"* the student in the chair picked another quiet student. Everyone wanted to be selected for the rocking chair. Students knew that if they talked during the transition when the next student was walking to the chair, they would lose their chance to sit in the chair. After starting to use the game, Ms. Larson established the rule that *"girls pick boys and boys pick girls,"* so that everyone would have a chance. Often Ms. Larson instructed students to *"pick someone who hasn't had a turn,"* or *"pick someone by the time you've*

counted to 20." Even after students had learned to quietly wait for short time periods, Ms. Larson continued to use the game because students asked for the opportunity to play it. Students learned self-control playing the game and applied these skills to other situations during the day such as waiting for their turn when answering questions about a story the teacher was reading.

- Ms. Buddin brought several large bowling trophies to her class to encourage students to follow the classroom rules when working at their tables. Quiet talking was allowed, but students were expected to finish their work or project and to ask permission if they needed to leave the table. When Ms. Buddin noticed everyone at a table following the rules, she put a bowling trophy on the surface. When someone didn't follow a rule, the trophy was removed. Gradually, working quietly became routine and the trophies were no longer needed.

- Ms. Gibbs wanted her students to become more aware of the impact their behavior had on other individuals in their community. She knew that some of her students had little experience receiving positive feedback from adults and needed to learn the feeling of pride for doing a good job that others appreciated. Thus Ms. Gibbs hung a "Compliments Chart" in the front of her classroom. Anytime the students, collectively or individually, received a compliment from anyone in the building—the principal, the custodian, another

Continued

teacher, a parent—a tally mark was put on the compliment chart. When the hundredth tally mark was put on the chart, the class earned a special surprise, which might be a pizza party or the opportunity to have a picnic lunch outside. Students who left the classroom for reading group looked forward to earning points for the class on days when their reading teacher complimented them during the lesson.

- Ms. Foley set up an "office" space where Terrance, a distractible student, could go to do his best work. By having a student desk and chair surrounded on two sides by dividers in the quietest part of the room, she could redirect him to work in the office when he could not complete independent work in a larger group. She would redirect him by saying, *"Terry, take your journal to the office where you can do your best work."* Rather than a punishment area, the "office" provided a quieter, less distracting place to complete work. Ms. Foley's goal was to get Terrance to independently go to the office when he realized that he wasn't focused on a paper or project.
- Every teacher periodically used group clapping, pats on the back, and thumbs-up to acknowledge effort, hard work, and rule following during reading class.

"Sharnicca, give yourself a thumbs-up. You wrote so much in your journal today."

"Everybody, pat yourself on the back, because you just read every word without even one mistake."

- Mr. Mixay recognized that his class liked challenges and they especially liked "fooling" the teacher and surpassing his expectations. After the students had just learned something new and still needed to use all of their concentration for success, he would often set up a challenge. Thus, when Mr. Mixay's class was supposed to spell the six irregular plural words, he said, *"This is very hard for students in your grade. Can you spell these very hard words? You will have to think very hard so I don't trick you, giving you these hard words."* Naturally the students did their best work, and Mr. Mixay shook his head and exclaimed how amazed he was that they had learned to spell such hard words. During review sessions, Mr. Mixay told his students that he was going to try to trick them by giving them difficult words to read. He smiled as he said that he was sure that they could not remember all those difficult words. Consequently, his students always rose to the challenge and read every word.

APPLIED ACTIVITIES

1. Four fact-or-fiction questions about teaching beginning word reading to students who are at risk are included below. Pair up with a partner and take turns defending your position for one of them using research sources cited in the chapter, journal articles, or information from the website resources listed in the sidebars.
   a. Beginning reading programs should stress using the context to figure out words because that is what skilled readers do. Is this fact or fiction? Explain why.
   b. An effective reading program for students who are at risk should include a high proportion of high-frequency exception words, since these are the kinds of words they are most likely to find in print. Is this fact or fiction? Explain why.
   c. Drill on word-reading skills reduces student motivation to read. Is this fact or fiction? Explain why.
   d. Decodable books are boring for children and reduce their motivation to read. Is this fact or fiction? Explain why.

2. A sample sequence of letter–sound introduction for a beginning reading program is shown below. Critique the sequence using guidelines proposed by Carnine and colleagues (2010) described in Table 3.1. Include in your critique any changes you would make.

   h t b o a d p j x e q n s f k i c y m z w u l g r v

3. In the list of words below, circle the consonant blends.

sand	clap	look	tramp	strap	stand	spat
clunk	ship	skin	think	slam	swap	grin

4. Following is a list of CVC variants. Label each as to the type of CVC word it exemplifies. For example, sat would be labeled CVC; trip would be labeled CCVC.

pen ____	mask ____	brand ____	must ____
drag ____	scrap ____	pest ____	smell ____
spank ____	mist ____	tip ____	plan ____

5. Say the following consonant blends in unison as a group without adding schwas:

   gl br st pr str cl sn fr

6. Mr. Hayes introduced the letter sound /h/ yesterday. In the past few weeks he has taught his students to identify /m/, /a/, /s/, /f/, /t/, and /b/. Demonstrate how you would instruct Mr. Hayes's class today using the format in Table 3.4: Part B to teach the new and review sounds.

7. How would you enhance the following lesson designed to introduce the /t/ sound? Show students a piece of poster board on which is displayed the letter *t* along with a picture of a tent. Explain that the letter *t* stands for the /t/ sound as in *tent*. Write the words *tiger* and *fast* on the board. Ask the students to read the two words. Distribute the *t* letter card. Have the children put the letter in their mini pocket charts and say the *t* sound.

8. Shown below are the results for three students on the DIBELS NWF measure given in January. Identify the student who is performing at benchmark levels (see Figure 3.7 on page 93 and Appendix B). How would you characterize the particular skill level for the two students not at benchmark levels? Identify specific teaching formats from the chapter that would help these two students attain benchmark levels.

DIBELS Nonsense Word Fluency Assessment and Score Sheet

Name: Shelby   Date: Dec. 5

w a b	p e v	y̶i̶l	b u̶ f	h̶u̶z	9/15
l e n	y o c	z o v̶ ⌉	t o c	a b	6/14
l e b	o m	m i s	z i v	h u v	___/14
m a j	n e p	i v	n o c	k i g	___/14
				Total:	15/57

DIBELS Nonsense Word Fluency Assessment and Score Sheet

Name: Tyrone   Date: Dec. 5

W̲a̲b̲	p̲e̲v̲	y̲i̲l̲	b̲u̲f̲	h̲u̲z̲	15/15
l̲e̲n̲	y̲o̲c̲	z̲o̲v̲	t̲o̲c̲	a̲b̲	14/14
l̲e̲b̲	o̲m̲ ⌉	m i s	z i v	h u v	5/14
m a j	n e p	i v	n o c	k i g	___/14
				Total:	34/57

DIBELS Nonsense Word Fluency Assessment and Score Sheet

Name: Shanique   Date: Dec. 5

w̲a̲b̲	p̲e̲v̲	y̲i̲l̲	b̲u̲f̲	h̶u̲z̲	14/15
l̲e̲n̲	y̲o̲c̲	z̲o̲v̲	t̲o̲c̲	a̲b̲	14/14
l̲e̲b̲	o̲m̲	m̲i̲s̲	z̲i̲v̲	h̶u̲v̲	13/14
m̲a̲j̲	n̲e̲p̲	i̲v̲	n̲o̲c̲⌉	k i g	11/14
				Total:	52/57

9. Shown below are the scores for Mrs. Green's first-grade class on the DIBELS NWF assessment in January. Identify which students are at benchmark, which students will need a Tier 2 intervention, and which students, pending further testing, might be eligible for an alternative, intensive program in Tier 3.

Student	Nonsense Words: January Letter Sounds Correct per Minute
Maria	28
Ladariu	42
Skylar	50
Tylar	17
Jatavia	45
Jaylin	38
Dezazh	66
Andrew	21
Delundre	72
Shanteria	40
Brant	56
Jarnecia	39
Christopher	48
Bryce	29
Erionah	66
Trae	78
Joshua	35
Marquez	29
Shaheed	77
Vantrell	47

10. Ms. Munoz wanted her students to practice reading the following words on the chalkboard. Demonstrate how she would teach these words using the format described in Table 3.4.

hop	sip	fin	tin
hot	sap	fox	can

11. The reading curriculum informs Ms. Foley that students need to learn the following exception words, which will be in the next story: *bough, buy,* and *month.* She plans to have students practice the following review words that came from last week's story: *ghost, steak.* Demonstrate how you would instruct Ms. Foley's class using Table 3.8 for teaching exception words.

12. Karisha is a beginning reader who has learned the following beginning reading skills:

Letter sounds: *a s m i t r b l w n f k h g*
Sight words: *a is his the*

Shown below are representative passages from three decodable books. Select the passage that would be most appropriate for Karisha. Indicate why.

Passage 1

Sam hit Kit in the hip. Sam is a big brat and will ram Matt.

Passage 2

Ed did run past his Dad. He ran fast and had fun.

Passage 3

Tom did help Mom. Tom went to get milk and a big box of hot nuts.

13. Passages from two hypothetical reading programs are shown below. By the end of November, Ms. Tonnato's students, whose DIBELS NWF scores range between 18 and 25, have learned all the short vowel sounds and the consonant sounds listed on the letter–sound chart at the end of Chapter 1. Ms. Tonnato wants to provide extra decodable reading for her students. Which passage would be more likely to lead to student success? Justify your answer.

Passage #1

The girl looked out the window. The sun was shining in the sky. "I think I will go outside today," she said. She left the house. She walked past a food stand. There was a big pile of donuts at the stand. She walked past the apple tree. There was a big cow under the apple tree. So she went home to get some lunch. I will get a sandwich, some juice, and an orange to eat.

Passage #2

Fran is fast. She can jump and hop and run fast. She gets to the swing first. I am mad. I can not jump and hop and run fast. But then I stop and think. I can hum and sing and skip. I sing for Gramps and hum for Mom. I skip up and down the steps. I will be pals with Fran. I can help Fran hum and sing and skip. Fran can help me jump and hop and run fast.

Companion Website

Now go to Chapter 3 in the Companion Website (www.pearsonhighered.com/bursuck2e), where you can do the following:

- Complete Activities that can help you more deeply understand the chapter content.
- Check your comprehension on the content covered in the chapter by going to the Chapter Quiz. Here you will be able to answer practice questions, receive feedback on your answers, and then access resources that will enhance your understanding of chapter content.
- Find Web Links that will extend your understanding of the content and strategies.

REFERENCES

Archer, A. L., Gleason, M. M., & Vachon, V. L. (2003). Decoding and fluency: Foundation skills. *Learning Disability Quarterly: Journal of the Division for Children with Learning Disabilities, 26*(2), 89 (28 pp.).

Armbruster, B., Lehr, F., & Osborn, J. (2001). *Put reading first: The research building blocks for teaching children to read.* Washington, DC: Partnership for Reading.

Avery, P., & Ehrlich, S. (1992). *Teaching American English pronunciation.* New York: Oxford Press.

Bursuck, B., Smith, T., Munk, D., Damer, M., Mehlig, L., & Perry, J. (2004). Evaluating the impact of a prevention-based model of reading on children who are at-risk. *Remedial and Special Education, 25,* 303–313.

Carnine, D. W., Silbert, J., Kame'enui, E. J., & Tarver, S. (2010). *Direct instruction reading* (5th ed.). Boston: Merrill.

Carroll, J., Davies, P., & Richman, B. (1971). *American Heritage Word Frequency Book.* Boston: Houghton Mifflin.

Cunningham, P. (2000). *Phonics they use: Words for reading and writing.* New York: Longman.

Durgunoğlu, A. (2002). Cross linguistic transfer in literacy development and implications for language learners. *Annals of Dyslexia, 52*(1), 189–206.

Durrell, D. (1963). *Phonograms in primary grade words.* Boston: Boston University.

Dynarski, M., Agodini, R., Heaviside, S., Novak, T., Carey, N., Campuzano, L., et al. (March, 2007). *Effectiveness of reading and mathematics software products: Findings from the first student cohort.* Report to Congress (Document No. PR07-04).

Ehri, L. C. (2005). Learning to read words: Theory, findings, and issues. *Scientific Studies of Reading, 9,* 167–188.

Ehri, L., & Snowling, M. (2004). Developmental variation in word recognition. In C. Stone, E. Silliman, B. Ehren, & K. Apel (Eds.), *Handbook of language and literacy* (pp. 433–460). New York: The Guilford Press.

Engelmann, S., & Bruner, E. (1995). *Reading Mastery I: Teacher's guide.* Columbus, OH: SRA Macmillan/McGraw-Hill.

Englemann, S., Carnine, L., Johnson, G., Meyer, L., Becker, W., & Eisele, J. (2008). *Corrective reading.* Columbus, OH: SRA/McGraw-Hill.

Francis, David J., Rivera, M., Lesaux, N., & Rivera, H. (2006). Research-based recommendations for instruction and academic interventions. *Practical guidelines for the education of English language learners.* Retrieved April 11, 2008, from http://www.centeroninstruction.org/files/ELL1-Interventions.pdf

Fuchs, L. S., Fuchs, D., & Kazdan, S. (1999). Effects of peer-assisted learning strategies on high school students with serious reading problems. *Remedial and Special Education, 20,* 309–318.

Fugate, M. (1997). Letter training and its effect on the development of beginning reading skills. *School Psychology Quarterly, 12,* 170–192.

Gersten, R. G. (1996). The double demands of teaching English language learners. *Educational Leadership, 53*(5), 18–22.

Gersten, R., Compton, D., Connor, C. M., Dimino, J., Santoro, L., Linan-Thompson, S., & Tilly, W. D. (2009). Assisting students struggling with reading: Response to intervention and multi-tier intervention for reading in the primary grades. A practice guide (NCEE 2009-4045) [Electronic version]. Washington, DC: National Center for Education Evaluation and Regional Assistance, Institute of Education Sciences, U.S. Department of Education. Retrieved August 29, 2009, from http://ies.ed.gov/ncee/wwc/pdf/practiceguides/rti_reading_pg_021809.pdf

Goldenberg, C. (2008, Summer). Teaching English language learners: What the research does and does not say. *American Educator, 32*(2), 8–23, 42–44.

Good, R. H., Kaminski, R. A., & Howe, D. (June, 2005). *What data tells us about children and how to support their success.* Presented at AZ Reading First Conference, Phoenix, AZ.

Good, R. H., Simmons, D., Kame'enui, E. A., & Wallin, J. (2002). *Summary of decision rules for intensive, strategic, and benchmark instruction recommendations in kindergarten through third grade* (Technical Report No. 11). Eugene: University of Oregon.

Gough, P. B., Alford, J. A. Jr., & Holley-Wilcox, P. (1981). Words and contexts. In O. J. L. Tzeng & H. Singer (Eds.), *Perception of print: Reading research in experimental psychology.* Hillsdale, NJ: Erlbaum.

Gough, P., & Walsh, M. (1991). Chinese, Phoenicians, and the orthographic cipher of English. In S. Brady & D. Shankweiler (Eds.), *Phonological processes in literacy* (pp. 199–209). Hillsdale, NJ: Erlbaum.

Grace, K. (2007). *Phonics and spelling through phoneme-grapheme mapping.* Longmont, CO: Sopris West.

Greene, J. (2009). *Language! The comprehensive literacy curriculum.* Longmont, CO: Sopris West Educational Services.

Gunn, B., Biglan, A., Smolkowski, K., & Ary, D. (2000). The efficacy of supplemental instruction in decoding skills for Hispanic and non-Hispanic students in early elementary school. *Journal of Special Education, 34*(2), 90–103.

Hempenstall, K. (2001). School-based reading assessment: Looking for vital signs. *Australian Journal of Learning Disabilities, 6,* 26–35.

Hiebert, E. (2008). Finding the right texts. In *The (mis)match between texts and students who depend on schools to become literate* (Chapter 1). New York: The Guilford Press.

Institute of Education Sciences of the National Center for Education Statistics. (2007). National Assessment of Educational Progress. Washington, DC: U.S. Department of Education. Retrieved from http://www.isbe.state.il.us/assessment/pdfs/naep_natl_rpt_reading_2007.pdf

Jones, M. W., Branigan, H. P., & Kelly, M. I. (2009). Dyslexic and nondyslexic reading fluency: Rapid automatized naming and the importance of continuous lists. *Psychonomic Bulletin & Review, 16*(3), 567–572.

Joshi, R. M., Treiman, R., Carreker, S., & Moats, L. (2008). How words cast their spell: Spelling instruction focused on language, not memory, improves reading and writing. *American Educator, 32*(4), 6–16, 42–43.

Larson, K. (2007). *The science of word recognition or how I learned to stop worrying and love the bouma.* Retrieved September 8, 2007, from http:// www.microsoft.com/typography/ctfonts/WordRecognition.aspx

Lee, J., Grigg, W., & Donahue, P. (2007). *The nation's report card: Reading 2007* (NCES 2007-496). National Center for Education Statistics, Institute of Education Sciences, U.S. Department of Education, Washington, DC.

Lindamood, P., & Lindamood, P. (1998). *The Lindamood phoneme sequencing program for reading, spelling, and speech.* Austin, TX: PRO-ED.

Lyon, R. (1998). *Overview of reading and literacy initiatives.* Statement to Committee on Labor and Human Resources, Bethesda, MD [Electronic version]. Retrieved April 28, 1998, from http://www.dys-add.com/ReidLyonJeffords.pdf

Maring, G. H., Boxie, P., & Wiseman, B. J. (2000). School-university partnerships through online pattern books. *Reading Online, 4*(5). Retrieved November, 2000, from http://www.readingonline.org/articles/art_index.asp?HREF=/articles/maring/index.html

Marzano, R. (2004). *Building background knowledge for academic achievement.* Alexandria, VA: ASCD.

Mathes, P., & Babyak, A. (2001). The effects of peer-assisted literacy strategies for first-grade readers with and without additional mini-skills lessons. *Learning Disabilities Research & Practice, 12*(1), 28–44.

McBride-Chang, C. (1999). The ABC's of the ABC's: The development of letter-name and letter-sound knowledge. *Merrill-Palmer Quarterly, 45,* 278–301.

McKenna, M.C., & Kear, D. J. (1990). Measuring attitude toward reading: A new tool for teachers. *The Reading Teacher, 54*(1), 10–23.

Moats, L. (2000). *Speech to print: Language essentials for teachers.* Baltimore, Paul H. Brookes.

Moats, Louisa C. (2005/2006, Winter). How spelling supports reading. *American Educator, 29*(4), 12–43.

Nation, K., Allen, R., & Hulme, C. (2001). The limitations of orthographic analogy in early reading development: Performance on the clue-word task depends on phonological priming and elementary decoding skill, not the use of orthographic analogy. *Journal of Experimental Child Psychology, 80,* 75–94.

National Reading Panel. (2000). *Teaching children to read: An evidence-based assessment of the scientific research literature on reading and its implications for reading instruction.* Washington, DC: National Institute of Child Health and Human Development.

Rathvon, N. (2004). *Early reading assessment: A practitioner's handbook.* New York: The Guilford Press.

Rayner, K., Chace, K., Slattery, T., & Ashby, J. (2006). Eye movements as reflections of comprehension processes in reading. *Scientific Studies of Reading, 10*(3), 241–256.

Rayner, K., Foorman, B., Perfetti, C. A., Pesetsky, D., & Seidenberg, M. S. (2001). How psychological science informs the teaching of reading. *Psychological Science in the Public Interest, 2,* 31–74. (A monograph from the American Psychological Society) Retrieved May 28, 2009, from http://www.psychologicalscience.org/journals/pspi/pdf/pspi22.pdf

Reitsma, P. (1983). Printed word learning in beginning readers. *Journal of Experimental Child Psychology, 36,* 321–339.

Roberts, G., Torgesen, J., Boardman, A., & Scammacca, N. (2008). Evidence-based strategies for reading instruction of older students with learning disabilities. *Learning Disabilities Research & Practice 23*(2), 63–39.

Share, D., & Stanovich, K. (1995). Cognitive processes in early reading development: Accommodating individual differences into a mode of acquisition. *Issues in Education: Contributions from Educational Psychology, 1,* 1–57.

Shaywitz, S. (2003). *Overcoming dyslexia: A new and complete science-based program for reading problems at any level.* New York: Alfred A. Knopf.

Stanovich, K. E. (1993/1994). Romance and reality. *The Reading Teacher, 47,* 280–291.

Torgesen, J., Wagner, R., & Rashotte, C. (1999). *TOWRE: Test of word reading efficiency examiner's manual.* Austin, TX: PRO-ED.

Wanzek, J., & Hagger, D. (2003). Teaching word recognition with blending and analogizing: Two strategies are better than one. *Teaching Exceptional Children, 36,* 32–38.

Wexler, J., Edmonds, M. S., & Vaughn, S. (2007). Teaching older readers with reading difficulties. In N. Mather (Ed.), *Evidence based interventions for students with learning and behavioral challenges* (pp. 193–214). Mahwah, NJ: Erlbaum.

Wilson, B. (2004). *Wilson reading system.* Millbury, MA: Wilson Language Training Corporation.

Yopp, H. K. (1995). Read-aloud books for developing phonemic awareness. *Reading Teacher 48,* 538–542.

4 Advanced Word Reading

Objectives

After reading this chapter you will be able to:

1. State a rationale for teaching advanced word-reading skills and identify a sequence of essential advanced word-reading skills.

2. Assess students' advanced word-reading and spelling skills in a multi-tier or RTI model.

3. Implement strategies for teaching letter combinations and affixes as preskills for reading multisyllable words.

4. Implement strategies for teaching advanced words and multisyllable regular words, structural analysis, and corresponding spelling skills in a multi-tier or RTI model.

5. Teach advanced word-reading skills to English language learners and older learners.

6. Implement games and activities that reinforce students' advanced reading skills.

Companion Website

To check your comprehension of the content covered in this chapter, go to the Companion Website (www.pearsonhighered.com/bursuck2e) and complete the Chapter Quiz for Chapter 4. Here you will be able to answer practice questions, receive feedback on your answers, and then access resources that will enhance your understanding of chapter content.

Teaching Multisyllable Words

Mr. Turner wanted his students to have a high level of success reading the new story, so he carefully spent time before the lesson planning how to introduce the new difficult words from the text. Dividing multisyllable words into parts is challenging when teaching advanced word reading for the first time. Mr. Turner needed to determine how to divide each word strategically so that students were more likely to read it correctly when they combined the parts. Wednesday morning before school, Mr. Turner wrote the words he planned to teach that day on the board. Let's take a look at his thought process and how he decided to teach these words from the story students read later that day.

regular words:

fleet flock glide places
hoping biking making
prob·ably ad·ven·ture pre·scrip·tion ner·vous·ly hor·i·zon

exception words:

papayas   chief

Mr. Turner wrote all words that he expected his students could read without any extra support as whole words in the first row. In the next row, Mr. Turner wrote the words containing a VCe pattern with an *-ing* suffix (*hoping, biking, making*). After his students said the rule related to these words and identified whether the vowel sound was long or short, Mr. Turner planned to ask his students to read each word as a whole word.

Since Mr. Turner's goal was to gradually increase the length of the word parts that students read, he decided to underline larger chunks in the next group of words. Although most of these chunks were also syllables, if Mr. Turner had divided all the words into syllables, he would have divided *ably* into two parts instead of one. He had already taught his students *horizon* as a vocabulary word and believed that his students could easily apply their decoding strategies to read it. Even though the second *o* in this word is represented by a schwa sound /ŭ/ instead of /ŏ/, because he had pretaught students the meaning of this word and used it in discussion, he anticipated that when students read the word by sight they would probably read *horizon*. Mr. Turner divided the word this way: hor i zon.

Finally, Mr. Turner taught *papayas* and *chief* as exception words. Since the word *papaya* was pivotal in the story, he planned to talk about the meaning when he introduced the word, providing vocabulary practice on the spot. On Friday, as a reinforcer, he planned to have some papayas cut so his students could taste them. Even if they were not brave enough to eat them, at least they would see what papayas look like, because the story had only a crude black-and-white line drawing of them.

Why do you think Mr. Turner chose the words that would require the least teacher support first?

Why might students need a rule to be able to decode words such as biking, hoping, and making?

Why did Mr. Turner go beyond teaching his students to decode papaya and clarify its meaning?

In Chapters 2 and 3, you learned about teaching strategies that help students develop beginning reading skills. By the end of first grade, students should be able to sound out CVC words in their heads, reading 50 or more letter sounds per minute on the DIBELS or AIMSweb Nonsense Word Fluency assessment with at least 15 words read as whole words (Good, Gruba, & Kaminski, 2002). Students should also be able to read first-grade passages accurately and at a rate of at least 40 to 60 words correct per minute, reading at the Consolidated Alphabetic Phase and instantly recognizing many words by sight. Instead of sounding out the word *slink* as five phonemes /s/ /l/ /i/ /n/ /k/, they are more likely to process it as two chunks /sl/ /ink/. Despite the significance of this accomplishment, if students are to become fluent enough decoders to tackle the reading comprehension demands of third grade and beyond, they still need to learn to apply their phonics skills to increasingly difficult words. Students need to learn to recognize and use larger letter patterns such as the *ous, tin, pre,* and *ly* to decode words. The purpose of this chapter is to provide you with explicit, systematic teaching strategies for advanced word reading. Chapter 5 will extend this focus on accuracy by providing explicit strategies for developing reading fluency. Because accuracy and fluency are closely connected, your instruction for students with advanced word-reading skills will emphasize both skills.

Why Teach Advanced Word-Reading Skills?

In a perfect world, written English would be completely regular; there would be one written symbol or grapheme for each sound in spoken English. In such a world, students who could sound out words in their heads and meet benchmark levels on the DIBELS Nonsense Word Fluency assessment would be ready to work almost exclusively on reading fluency and comprehension. Unfortunately, spoken English has 41 to 44 sounds and written English only has 26 written letters. Readers rarely encounter letters that have one unique sound in all words. Sometimes the sound of a letter depends on the adjacent letter. For example, when *t* comes before *h,* the two letters sound like /th/ in *thing* or *that*; the letter *a* is sometimes silent when it comes after an *e* in a word like *each.* Other times a letter's sound depends on letters appearing later in a word such as *made,* where the silent *e* at the end of the word results in the vowel sound /ā/. An additional source of confusion occurs when letters in a word are not logically connected to sounds, such as the *ai* in *said.*

Students who are ready to move beyond the beginning reading stage are likely to encounter other difficulties besides rule changes and irregularities. They must also be able to address the increasing prevalence of multisyllable words. Look at the following passage from an elementary school history textbook in which we have underlined all of the words containing three or more syllables.

> Militiamen were given little training. Occasionally regiments would meet at the town green where an officer would try to teach his men British battle formations. Training wasn't taken very seriously. Officers didn't demand discipline from their men because they were all friends. (Egger-Bovet & Smith-Baranzin, 1994)

Ask yourself, "Would I be able to understand this passage if I were unable to read all or most of the multisyllable words?"

What Advanced Word-Reading Skills Do I Need to Teach?

Clearly, readers who are at risk need to learn strategies to decode words containing more complex combinations of letters as well as words that contain multiple syllables. As with other steps in the process of learning to read, students who are at risk require more explicit teaching of these strategies. Two approaches have proven effective in teaching advanced word reading. The first approach emphasizes identifying known word parts, and the second approach emphasizes decoding syllable types. In the first approach, students are taught to identify one or more parts in the word, read the known parts first, and then read the whole word. For example, in order to read words like *production*, students first are taught the suffix *-tion*. Then in another lesson they are taught the prefix *pro-*. Finally, when learning this new word for the first time, they read the word parts /pro/ /duc/ /tion/ before reading the whole word *production*. Similarly, for the more simple word *such*, students learn to read the letter combination *ch* first, and then the whole word (Engelmann et al., 1999).

In the syllable approach, students are taught six common syllable types that occur in written English (Archer, Gleason, & Vachon, 2003; Greene, 2004; Moats, 2001; Wilson, 1996). These six syllable types, shown in Table 4.1, provide students with clues for figuring out the vowel sounds within the syllables. For example, a vowel within a syllable containing

TABLE 4.1 Six Syllable Types Used in Syllable-Type Instruction

Syllable Type	Examples	Description of Syllable Type
Closed	rabbit dependent rejection	A syllable having a short vowel and ending in a consonant (VC, CVC, CCVC, CVCC).
Open	table defame starvation	A syllable with a long vowel sound that is spelled with a single-vowel letter (CV, CCV).
Vowel Combinations	canteen proclaim unspeakable	A syllable with a vowel combination such as *ai, oa, ea,* or *oi* (CVVC, CCVVC, CVVCC).
R-controlled	vaporize surrender perfection	A syllable with a vowel combination such as *ar, or, er, ir,* or *ur.*
Vowel-consonant-e	escape obsolete windowpane	A syllable with a long vowel sound with a consonant and final *e* (VCe, CVCe, CCVCe).
Consonant-le	puddle rumble	A final syllable containing a consonant before *le.*

Source: Archer, A. L., Gleason, M. M., & Vachon, U. L. (2003). Decoding and fluency: Foundation skills for struggling older readers. *Learning Disability Quarterly, 26,* 89–101.

a consonant and final *e* would be long or say its name, as in *escape.* Once students are taught the syllable type, they learn to identify words by first identifying the syllable and then reading the whole word. For example, in *escape,* they would read /es/ then /cape/, and then the entire word, *escape.*

The approach for advanced word reading taken in this text is the part-by-part method, which is consistent with the synthetic phonics approach described in Chapter 3. While the syllable approach is also research-based (Archer et al., 2003; Bhattacharya, 2006), its use of multiple rules may be too difficult for younger children who are at risk because they are likely to have oral language difficulties. On the other hand, the syllable approach may be adequate for older students or those who have reading disabilities with no problems in oral language. Examples of evidence-based syllable-based programs include *Language!* (Greene, 2004) and *Wilson Reading System* (Wilson, 1996).

Letter Combinations and Affixes

To read advanced words, students need the ability to decode clusters of letters. **Letter combinations** are one type of cluster formed when two or more adjacent letters make one distinct sound. The *ch* in *church, ar* in *mart, oi* in *boil,* and *ee* in *meet* are all examples of letter combinations. Adjacent letters in a cluster can be vowels, consonants, or a combination of both. A list of common letter combinations, along with key words guiding their pronunciation, is shown in Table 4.2. These letter combinations occur frequently in common words. Included among these phonics patterns are digraphs and diphthongs. **Digraphs** are two successive letters articulated as a single phoneme. Examples of digraphs include *ch* as in *chop, th* as in *this,* and *oo* as in *book.* A complete list of digraphs with example words containing each one is in Appendix D. Another

> Practice saying the sounds for letter combinations at the Tampa Reads website where you can listen to them: **http://www.tampareads.com/realaudio/tests/indexrm.htm.**

TABLE 4.2 Letter Combinations

Letter Combination	Phonetic Pronunciation	Voiced or Unvoiced	Articulation	Stop or Continuous Sound ⚠ = Don't Add a Schwa	When Students Have Difficulty Saying the New Letter Sound:
ai	as in *tail*	voiced	More open smiling mouth position; tongue in middle of mouth; increased mouth tension	continuous	Same as /ā/
al/all	as in *call* and *royal*	voiced	Same as /au/ + /l/	continuous	Have students say "All Done-All," moving their hands apart as they say "all."
ar	as in *hard*	voiced	Tongue is curled back toward the /r/ position	continuous	Elongate this *r*-controlled vowel for 2 to 3 seconds so the student clearly hears both sounds pronounced and sees that the mouth begins in a smiley position. Prompt with a mirror if needed. In cued speech for individuals with a hearing loss, this sound is designated as a combination of the /ah/ vowel with a following /r/.
au	as in *fault*	voiced	Rounded lips; tongue moves back in mouth; increased mouth tension	continuous	English language learners often confuse this sound with /ŏ/. The /au/ sound is produced farther back and higher in the mouth. Ask students to pretend they are sadly saying, "/Au/, the poor kitty."
aw	as in *lawn*	voiced	Rounded lips; tongue moves back in mouth; increased mouth tension	continuous	Same as /au/
ay	as in *gray*	voiced	Same as the /ā/ sound in *trail*	continuous	Same as /ā/
ch	as in *chair, munching,* and *such*	voiceless	Tip of tongue briefly contacts roof of mouth: lips forward; burst of air expelled with sound	stop ⚠	Model how your lips come forward when you say the sound. Ask students to pretend they have a cold and make a /ch/ sneeze.
dge	as in *fudge*	voiced	Tip of tongue briefly contacts the roof of mouth; a burst of air is expelled with sound	stop ⚠	Same as /j/

TABLE 4.2 Continued

Letter Combination	Phonetic Pronunciation	Voiced or Unvoiced	Articulation	Stop or Continuous Sound ⚠ = Don't Add a Schwa	When Students Have Difficulty Saying the New Letter Sound:
ea	as in *meat** *ea* says /ē/ in 60% of words containing this combination.	voiced	Smiling mouth position with lips open wide; tongue high in mouth near front; increased mouth tension	continuous	Same as /ē/
ea	as in *bread*	voiced	Smiling mouth position; tongue centered in the mid front	continuous	Same as /ĕ/
ee	as in *keep*	voiced	Same as the /ea/ sound in *meat.*	continuous	Same as /ē/
er	as in *jerk*	voiced	Tongue is in center of mouth curled back toward the /r/ position	continuous	Mouth is slightly rounded for this *r*-controlled vowel sound. Have your students listen and then say the sound they hear for /er/ at www.thefreedictionary.com/er
ew	as in *stew*	voiced	Rounded lips; back of tongue in highest position; increased mouth tension	continuous	Same as /o͞o/
igh	as in *night*	voiced	Smiley face; tongue and jaw raise to a high position	continuous	Same as /ī/
ing	as in *dusting*	voiced	Glide from the the /ĭ/ sound to /ng/	continuous	Same as /ĭ/ + /ng/
ir	as in *bird*	voiced	Same as /er/	continuous	Same as /er/
kn	as in *knit*	voiced	Front of tongue behind upper teeth toward front of mouth: air expelled through nose	continuous	Same as /n/
le	as in *wiggle*	voiced	Tongue lifts behind upper teeth; air passes over sides of tongue	continuous	Same as /l/

Continued

TABLE 4.2 Continued

Letter Combination	Phonetic Pronunciation	Voiced or Unvoiced	Articulation	Stop or Continuous Sound ⚠ = Don't Add a Schwa	When Students Have Difficulty Saying the New Letter Sound:
ng	as in *sing, singer,* and *bring*	voiced	Back of tongue in contact with the soft palate toward the back of the mouth; air expelled through the nose	continuous, nasal	Point out that the back of the tongue makes the sound, while the front stays down. Have students make silly /ng/ singsongs varying intonation. For example, they could sing /ng/ to the tune to "BINGO."
oa	as in *soap*	voiced	Rounded mouth that shuts like a camera shutter; tongue in middle; increased mouth tension	continuous	Same as /ō/
oi	as in *join*	voiced	Tongue glides from low back to high front; jaw rises with the tongue; an oval-shaped mouth position to a smiling position; increased mouth tension	continuous	Begin with the /au/ sound (as in *awful*) and immediately slide into the /ee/ sound. Have students look at their mouths in the mirror as they form this sound.
o͝o	as in *book*	voiced	Slightly rounded parted lips; back of tongue high; relaxed facial muscles	continuous	Ask students to pretend that they are using all their energy while pushing a heavy elephant, saying this sound.
o͞o	as in *boot**; oo says /o͞o/ in 59% of words containing this combination.	voiced	Rounded lips; back of tongue in highest position; increased mouth tension	continuous	Ask your students to pretend they just received their favorite toy as a birthday present as they say this sound of delight.
or	as in *corn*	voiced	The vowel glides toward the /r/ position	continuous	Elongate this *r*-controlled vowel for 2 to 3 seconds so the student clearly hears both sounds pronounced and sees that the mouth starts in a rounded position. Prompt with a mirror if needed.
ou	as in *cloud*	voiced	The mouth movement glides from one articulation position to another; jaw and tongue rise as the sound is said; lips move from open to a rounded position; increased mouth tension	continuous	Ask students to pretend they just bumped their foot into the table and because it hurts they say, "ow."

TABLE 4.2   Continued

Letter Combination	Phonetic Pronunciation	Voiced or Unvoiced	Articulation	Stop or Continuous Sound ⚠ = Don't Add a Schwa	When Students Have Difficulty Saying the New Letter Sound:
ow	as in *grow*; ow* says /ō/ in 50% of words containing this combination.	voiced	Rounded mouth that shuts like a camera shutter; tongue in middle; increased mouth tension	continuous	Same as /ō/
ow	as in *clown*	voiced	Same as /ou/ as in *cloud*	continuous	Same as /ou/
oy	as in *joy*	voiced	Same as for /oi/	continuous	Same as /oi/
ph	as in *phone*	unvoiced	Upper front teeth on lower lip: air gust expelled	continuous	Same as /f/
qu	as in *queen*	unvoiced	/qu/ sounds like /kw/. Refer to the description of those letter sounds and say this sound, quickly blending them together into one sound.	continuous	Ask students to make the sound of a cuckoo clock: "kwoo-kwoo."
sh	as in *show, ashes,* and *dish.*	unvoiced	Air passes between rounded lips; teeth close but not touching;	continuous	Ask students to put their fingers in front of their mouths to feel the air as they say the sound. Show students how /sh/ is the typical "be quiet" sound and ask them to make the sound with their pointer finger raised in front of their mouth.
tch	as in *catch*	unvoiced	Tip of tongue briefly contacts roof of mouth: burst of air expelled with sound	stop ⚠	Same as /ch/
th	as in *thimble, nothing,* and *path*; th* says this sound in 74% of words containing this combination.	unvoiced	Tip of tongue between the upper front teeth as air expelled	continuous	Ask students to stick out their tongues and silently blow.
th	as in *then, mother,* and *bathe*	voiced	Tip of tongue between the upper front teeth as air expelled	continuous	Ask students to stick out their tongues and blow. Emphasize that this sound tickles their tongues.

Continued

TABLE 4.2 Continued

Letter Combination	Phonetic Pronunciation	Voiced or Unvoiced	Articulation	Stop or Continuous Sound ⚠ = Don't Add a Schwa	When Students Have Difficulty Saying the New Letter Sound:
ur	*hurt*	voiced	Same as /er/	continuous	Same as /er/
wh	as in *when*	voiced	Same as /w/ since now most native English speakers pronounce /w/ the same as /wh/**	continuous	Same as /w/

*Percentages for letter–sound combinations having two sounds come from Hanna, Hanna, Hodges, & Rudloff (1966) as cited in Carnine, Silbert, Kame'enui, & Tarver. (2010). *Direct instruction reading* (5th ed.). Boston: Merrill Prentice Hall; and Celce-Murcia, Brinton, Goodwin, & Goodwin. (1996). *Teaching pronunciation: A reference for teachers of English to speakers of other languages.* New York: Cambridge University Press.

**Celce-Murcia et al., 2002.

type of letter combination, **diphthongs,** are vowel blends in which the first sound seems to glide into the second sound. Examples of diphthongs include *ou* as in *mouse* and *oi* as in *boil.*

One-Syllable Words Containing a Letter Combination

After students have learned a particular letter combination, the teacher supports them as they decode words that contain the combination or affix. For example, Ms. Bland introduced the letter combination *ch* to her students. They were able to read the new sound correctly for two days in a row when it was mixed in with the previously introduced combinations of *ai, ar, th,* and *sh.* Ms. Bland then began to teach the class how to read one-syllable words with *ch,* such as *much, champ,* and *rich.* After students have learned to decode words with a specific letter combination, if that letter combination is contained in one of the most common word families, the teacher should teach students to read and spell related words in that family. The most common word families for advanced readers are: *ack, all, ank, ash, aw, ay, eat, ell, est, ick, ight, ill, ing, ink, ir, ock, or, ore, out, ow, uck, ump, unk,* and final *y* in one-syllable words such as *fry, shy,* and *try.*

Two-Syllable Words Containing Closed Syllables

Students begin to expand their knowledge of VC, CVC, and CVC variant words and learn to read two-syllable words comprised of two closed syllables. Now that they read letter chunks, words like *frantic* are more easily decoded as two chunks, such as /fran/ /tic/. Students begin to read words with double consonants represented by one sound in the middle of a word, such as *muffin* or *mitten.*

Words with Rule-Based Sounds

Once students can read the CVC variant words, they are ready to read words that have long vowels, including words having the **vowel-consonant-vowel pattern.** While the approach to phonics instruction taken in this text has been to avoid teaching too many rules to children who are at risk, some rules are simple enough and work often enough to make their teaching worthwhile (Johnston, 2001; Linan-Thompson & Vaughn, 2007). The VCV rule fits into this category. Students are taught the rule that if there is a vowel-consonant-vowel pattern, the first vowel says its name. Because this rule applies to multisyllable words as well, it is introduced from the beginning when students are learning easier VCe words. Examples of easier words having the VCV pattern are words that have the vowel-consonant-silent *e* pattern (**VCe words** also called silent *-e* syllables) such as *make* and *like*. Often teachers first teach the Vowel-Consonant-e rule for the words that end in silent *-e*, but that rule only applies to one-syllable words. Students then have to learn other strategies for making long vowel/short vowel decisions when reading longer multisyllable words. Since the VCV rule applies to both one- and multisyllable words, we recommend using it. After students are taught to apply the VCV rule to reading one-syllable VCe words, they learn to differentiate these words from CVC words, a difficult discrimination for many students who are at risk. To provide practice, teachers ask students to read words with short-vowel/long-vowel contrasts like *made* and *mad* or *glade* and *glad*. When students are able to decode CVC and CVCe words at a mastery level, they are ready to learn the most common word families with VCV patterns: *ake, ale, ame, ate, ice, ide, ine* and *oke*.

Initially students learn the most common sounds for the letters *c* and *g* in one-syllable words, but as they move into advanced word reading, they are often faced with making a decision between the two sounds that represent each of these letters. When we coached teachers, we observed that those who taught their students the following rules reduced student errors reading unknown words: "When *c* is followed by *e, i,* or *y,* it usually says /s/" and "When *g* is followed by *e, i,* or *y,* it usually says /j/." When students are consolidated alphabetic phase readers, they view the entire word or word part as a unit and are able to determine the sound of *c* or *g* based on the vowel that follows it. When teaching any rule, first have the students independently say the rule and then practice applying it to words. Later, when the student misreads the *g* or *c* in a word, prompt the student to read the word correctly by asking her what the *g* rule is before asking her to reread the whole word. By using a rule-based correction for misread words, the teacher encourages students to develop the habit of applying the rule to unknown words.

A final rule helps students determine the sound of *y* as a vowel at the end of words: "A final *y* says the /ē/ sound in two-syllable and longer words and /ī/ in short one-syllable words." Knowing this rule makes the sound of *y* more predictable in words like *funny, sandy,* and *shy.*

Applying Structural Analysis to Reading Regular Words

Structural analysis involves using prefixes, suffixes and root words to determine the meaning and pronunciation of words (Nagy, Winsor, Osborn, & O'Flahavan, 1993). Teaching students the most common affixes and their meaning before having them apply that knowledge to reading multisyllable words helps them decipher those words and their distinctive meanings more readily. Structural analysis skills are first introduced when students are reading at a mid-first-grade level, and by the time they are reading at a third-grade reading level, structural analysis skills are emphasized more than phonological ones. Instruction in structural analysis develops students' skills in reading multisyllable words by sight as well as by recognizing their part of speech and knowing their meaning. These skills are necessary for fluency and comprehension when reading increasingly difficult texts in social studies and science. When explicit instruction in structural analysis skills is paired with oral reading for second- and third-grade students with reading problems, reading accuracy and fluency can significantly increase (Vadasy, Sanders, & Peyton, 2006). Usually the first two-syllable words that students read are **compound** words such as *hatbox* in which two words combine to form one with a distinct meaning. Gradually contractions such as *aren't* and *shouldn't* are introduced as they become more frequent in text that the students are reading.

When students can automatically read new one-syllable words accurately, differentiating between long or short vowel sounds, teach them to apply the VCV rule to two- and three-syllable words to which **inflectional** endings have been added. Inflectional endings are suffixes such as *-ed, -es, -ing,* and *-s* that indicate tense, number, possession, or gender when added to the end of a base word. These words can present unique spellings or reading difficulties because an inflectional ending can have more than one sound or the ending can change the spelling of the base word.

In Chapter 2, you learned that one way to divide and analyze words is by breaking them into syllables. You can easily clap out the four syllables in the word *unbeliever* as *un•be•liev•er.* If, instead of syllables, you decide to divide a word into its smallest units of meaning, you have three **morphemes** (the smallest parts of words that have a distinctive meaning):

un•believe•er

- *un* means *not*
- *believe* means to accept as real
- *er* means a person who does something

In this example word, *believe* is the foundational morpheme that establishes the basic meaning of the word. Because *believe* is a complete word that can stand by itself, it is called a **base word.** When the foundational morpheme is not a complete word, such as *struct* in the word *construction,* it is called a ***root.*** All multisyllable words have at least one base word or root. Morphemes that precede the root or base word are called **prefixes;** morphemes that are added to the end of the root or base word are called **suffixes.** In our example, *un-* is the prefix and *-er* is the suffix. Both suffixes and prefixes are categorized as affixes. For example:

reseat, seating, reseating

- The word *reseat* contains the morphemes *re + seat.* The prefix is *re-; seat* is the base word. The prefix *re-* is also categorized as an affix.
- The word *seating* contains the morphemes *seat + ing.* The suffix is *-ing;* again, *seat* is the base word. The suffix *-ing* is also categorized as an affix.
- The word *reseating* contains the morphemes *re + seat + ing.* Both the prefix *re-* and the suffix *-ing* are categorized as affixes; again the base word is *seat.*
- The base word *seat* contains the letter combination *ea.*

desirable, undesirable

- The word *desirable* contains the morphemes *desire + able.* The suffix is *-able; desire* is the base word. The suffix *-able* is also categorized as an affix.
- The word *undesirable* contains the morphemes *un +desire + able.* Both the prefix *un-* and the suffix *-able* are categorized as affixes; again the base word is *desire.*

pendant, dependent

- The word *pendant* contains the morphemes *pend + ant. Pend* is the root word meaning "to hang." The suffix *-ant* is also categorized as an affix.
- The word *dependent* contains the morphemes *de + pend + ent.* Both the prefix *de* and the suffix *-ent* are categorized as affixes; again the root word is *pend.*

The careful teaching of affixes as preskills to multisyllable word reading is a key feature of effective advanced word-reading

For a list of the most common prefixes, suffixes, and roots along with their meanings, visit: **http://www.englishclub.com/vocabulary/prefixes.htm** and **http://www.dummies.com/WileyCDA/DummiesArticle/id-1186.html.**

programs (Archer et al., 2003). As with letter combinations, spend your limited class time teaching the affixes that most frequently are used in common words. A list of some of the more common beginning affixes and their meaning is provided in Table 4.3. You will notice that two letter combinations, *er* and *ing*, are also affixes.

> Learn how to use structural analysis circles and the word builder strategy at: **http://forpd.ucf.edu/strategies/ stratstructural_analysis.html.**

Words with Two or More Syllables and One or More Irregular Parts

As students read increasingly difficult passages, they encounter multisyllable words that have one or more irregular parts. Usually these irregular parts involve vowels that do not say their most common sounds. For example, in the word *obeyed*, students should be able

TABLE 4.3   Affixes

Affix	Meaning	Phonetic Pronunciation	Affix	Meaning	Phonetic Pronunciation
a	without/not/to	aside	**less**	without	restless
able/ible		drinkable, incredible	**ly**	characteristic of	happily
anti	against	antigravity	**ment**	action or process	movement
al/ial	having the characteristic of	personal, special	**mid**	middle	midterm
de	opposite	defrost	**mis**	wrongly	misjudge
dis	not, opposite	disarm	**ness**	state of, condition of	kindness
en,em	cause to	enable	**non**	not	nonsense
er/or	comparative, one who	helper, actor	**ous/eous/ious**	having the qualities of	joyous, courageous, conscious,
fore	before	forecast	**over**	over	overhand
ful	full of	thankful	**pre**	before	predetermine
ic	having the characteristics of	scientific	**re**	again	retake
il/ir/in/im	not	illegal, irrational, injustice, impossible	**semi**	half	semicircle
ing	verb form	helping	**sub**	under	substation
inter	between	intermix	**super**	above	superstar
ion/tion/ation	act, process	attraction, gradation, occasion	**s/es**	more than one	banks, boxes
ity/ty	state of	honesty, gravity	**un**	not	unbeatable
ative/itive/ive	adj. form of a noun	cooperative, sensitive, festive,	**under**	under	Underworld
			y	characterized by	grumpy

to read the -ed ending but are likely to have difficulty decoding the letters *ey*. Words having a single consonant between two vowels in a word can also be problematic when they don't follow the VCV rule. For example, students may read the word *panic* as having a long *a* because of the seeming presence of a VCV pattern in the word. Fortunately, students can also apply their decoding skills to learn these new longer words. Many times the exception sound is a schwa /uh/ such as the *e* in *totem* or the *a* in *important*. After students sound out the parts of the word, they naturally substitute the schwa when they read the word as a whole, especially if the word is in their speaking vocabulary.

One- and Two-Syllable Exception Words

Some words are so irregular that it makes sense to introduce them in the same way that exception words were introduced in beginning reading. Examples of these irregular words include *chaos, stomach,* and *chief*. These words can be introduced by telling students the word, having them spell the word, and then having them read the word again (see Table 3.8: Format for Reading Exception Words).

Spelling Exception Words: Rule- and Pattern-Based Spelling and Morphographic Spelling

Students reading at the consolidated alphabetic phase learn to spell irregular words more quickly. Their spelling instruction should mirror their new reading skills, with words they are learning to spell organized into patterns. For example, they learn that in words ending in *ack, eck, ick, ock,* and *uck,* the ending sound /k/ is spelled *ck*. Instruction should gradually introduce high-frequency prefixes, suffixes, and base words as well as more irregularly spelled words. Most spelling programs used in the general education curriculum are based on high-frequency words and do not have this careful design. In our project schools, we found that we could modify the beginning phonetic spelling programs to make them more effective, but that for advanced word readers, none of our modifications could compensate for the lack of a well-designed spelling program based on structural analysis skills. Reading skills do not directly transfer to spelling. But because the two skills are interdependent, explicit instruction in spelling benefits reading as well as spelling. When spelling a word correctly, students first search memory for the spelling. If unsuccessful, they segment the word's phonemes to write their corresponding graphemes. Finally, students look at the written word to check if it matches the form of the word stored in memory or if it matches the phonemes they hear in the word (Ehri, 1989).

How Do I Assess Advanced Word-Reading Skills in a Multi-Tier or RTI Model?

Older struggling readers have gaps in the letter–sound and structural analysis skills that they have learned to mastery. Sonnie, a student in Tier 2, may still have two digraphs that she continues to confuse, and when she reads a word with both a prefix and suffix, she tends to guess at the suffix. Before you can use your small-group time with her to fill in these holes, you first have to identify them. The Advanced Word Reading Diagnostic Assessment in Appendix G can be used to help you pinpoint what skills your students still have not mastered and where your reading instruction should start. In a diagnostic assessment like this one, pinpointing error patterns is critical so that you can determine whether the student has difficulty reading words with inflected endings or confuses long and short vowels in multisyllable words. The score sheet for this assessment has a column in which you mark each skill as correct or incorrect so that you have enough information to identify any error patterns. For example, if you look down the column for inflected endings and see a number of errors, you know that the student needs more practice with those structural analysis skills. If inflected endings are difficult for several Tier 2 students, your small-group practice will include teaching that skill. If another group of students is unable to read words with some of the basic prefixes, you can form another group to practice reading words with those problematic prefixes.

Once students are consolidated alphabetic phase readers, the primary way to monitor their reading progress is through assessing oral passage reading and comprehension. Strategies for using assessments in these areas are described more fully in Chapters 5, 6, and 7. However, there are students who, despite your best teaching efforts, may struggle learning letter combinations and affixes. These are students who tend to read grade-level passages slowly and with more errors. They are likely to be your students in Tier 2 or Tier 3. By assessing them directly on their advanced sounds, you can find out which sounds need more instruction. Additional instruction can then be provided during differentiated small-group instruction. You can assess your students on all of the common affixes and letter combinations using the Advanced Word Reading Diagnostic Assessment just discussed. A shorter way to assess student knowledge of combinations and affixes is to check your reading series and identify which letter combinations and affixes have been taught up to the time of the assessment. For example, by November, Ms. Mobley had taught the letter combinations *ch, sh, th, ea, ar, ur,* and *ow* and the affixes *a, -ing, be, -est,* and *-ly.* When she decided to assess her students in Tier 2 to see whether they had learned these sounds, Ms. Mobley selected a key word to assess each sound. She selected the word *chin* for *ch,* for *ar* she selected *part,* and for *ing* she selected the word *rusting.* She then developed a typed list of the keywords, asking her students individually to read each word on the chart in Figure 4.1. As her students read, Ms. Mobley marked her score sheet, shown in Figure 4.2, with a plus if a student read the word correctly and a 0 if not.

When scoring her students' answers, Ms. Mobley was careful to score a response as incorrect only if the student missed the targeted sound. For example, Deanna in Figure 4.2 read word number two as *bash,* rather than *dash.* Although Ms. Mobley wrote the incorrect word that Deanna read as a reminder for herself, she still scored Deanna's answer as correct because she read the *sh* sound correctly. After giving this assessment to all of the students in her class, Ms. Mobley developed a group score sheet to help her make instructional decisions about which skills to teach using more group instruction. Table 4.4 depicts the group score sheet she used to summarize the class results.

chin	grow
dash	amaze
math	rusting
real	become
farm	funniest
turn	hardly

FIGURE 4.1 Informal Assessment of Letter Combinations and Affixes (Student Sheet)

Student: Deanna   **Date:** Oct 23
Teacher: Ms. Mobley

1. **ch**in +   7. gr**ow** 0 grew
2. da**sh** + bash   8. **a**maze +
3. ma**th** +   9. rust**ing** +
4. r**ea**l +   10. **be**come +
5. f**ar**m 0 firm   11. funni**est** +
6. t**ur**n +   12. hard**ly** +

FIGURE 4.2 Informal Assessment of Letter Combinations and Affixes (Teacher Score Sheet)

TABLE 4.4   Class Score Sheet for Assessment of Letter Combinations and Affixes

Date: Oct 23 _____   Teacher: Mrs. Mobley _____

Sounds	Darrell	Gabriella	Deanna	Otis	Alexis
ch	+	+	+	o	+
sh	+	+	+	+	+
th	+	+	+	o	+
ea	+	+	+	+	+
ar	o	o	o	o	o
ur	+	+	+	o	+
ow	o	o	o	o	o
a_e	+	+	+	+	+
ing	+	+	+	+	+
be	+	+	+	+	+
est	+	+	+	+	+
ly	o	o	+	o	o

Use the lists available at this website to generate word lists containing specific letter combinations or specific syllable patterns: **http://www.resourceroom. net/readspell/wordlists/default.asp.**

Some of the word-reading, screening, and progress-monitoring assessments described in Chapter 3, "Beginning Word Reading," are appropriate for assessing word reading until the end of third grade. For older students, the TOWRE and Woodcock Reading Mastery word-reading assessments are recommended for evaluating word reading both with real words and more advanced nonsense words.

How Can I Assess Students' Advanced Spelling Skills?

Spelling assessments described in Chapter 3 included skills through the end of third grade with the exception of AIMSweb, which includes spelling skills through eighth grade. Using traditional norm-referenced diagnostic spelling assessments can be problematic (Rathvon, 2004). For example, the relatively few words at each level on most spelling assessments makes identifying error patterns for instruction difficult. Also, some tests simply require students to select a spelling word out of a group of words rather than have them produce the word in writing, the latter being the response mode required most often. Finally, scores can vary significantly on different diagnostic tests. Unlike other spelling tests, the Word Identification and Spelling Test (WIST) Regular Word Spelling subtest can be used to identify error patterns and plan instruction for students from the age of 7 through 18. On this assessment, students spell 100 one-syllable to four-syllable regular words, and scores include a record of errors for each of the six syllable types. Learn more about this assessment at http://www.proedinc.com/customer/ ProductView.aspx?ID = 2031. Appendix H has a diagnostic spelling assessment that provides information on students' spelling of letter combinations and application of the ten common spelling rules listed later in this chapter.

A kindergarten–fifth grade spelling assessment that records errors in terms of missed patterns (ex. digraphs, inflected endings) is available online at: **http:// www.csus.edu/indiv/s/ sellensh/319A%20materials/ Primary% 20Spelling%20Inventory. pdf.**

How Can I Teach Students to Decode Advanced Words and Words with Multiple Syllables?

In Chapters 1, 2, and 3, a multi-tiered instructional approach was described that allows teachers to accommodate a range of learners who are at risk. The enhancements described in those chapters also apply to teaching the advanced word-reading skills just described. No matter what reading program you are using, your likelihood of success with students who are at risk will increase with the use of advance organizers, unison responding, perky pace, support for new learning using My Turn–Together–Your Turn, systematic error corrections, cumulative review, integrated motivational strategies, and teaching to success. The formats for teaching advanced word reading in this chapter can be used for large-group Tier 1 instruction as well as small-group Tier 2 intervention sessions.

Identifying Letter Combinations and Affixes Introduced in the Curriculum

Teaching your students to identify common letter combinations and affixes in isolation before they read them in words greatly enhances their chance of success reading multisyllable words. The format for teaching combinations and affixes in isolation is shown in Table 4.5. This format is similar to the one used for teaching single-letter sounds (Table 3.3). Advanced readers learn letter combinations at a more rapid rate. Students who needed to practice new letter sounds like /b/ or /j/ for a week when they were younger now learn the sound for a new letter combination after only one or two days of practice. Because students now have more experience and knowledge with letter sounds, the teacher can introduce a new letter combination by telling students the sound and then asking them to say the sound by themselves. Togethers are only used as needed at this stage of skill development. The new sound is then practiced along with a number of previously introduced sounds using an alternating pattern. For example, when the new combination *ar* was first introduced, it was practiced using the following alternating pattern: *ar, ea, ar, th, ing, ar, ent, ea, sl, ar, br, ai, ea, ing,* and so on. Note that both letter combinations and affixes previously covered are reviewed in a typical daily lesson.

The Suffix *-ed*

Unlike the other affixes and letter combinations, the suffix *-ed* can't be introduced cleanly in isolation because it has three different sounds. The sound that *-ed* makes depends on the base word to which it is added. Therefore, teach *-ed* separately by using your students' oral language to help them determine which sound of *ed* to use rather than scalloping under the *-ed* suffix. Carnine and colleagues (2010) suggested writing the *-ed* ending on the board before presenting a series of examples to demonstrate the three different *ed* sounds. For example, Mrs. Gibbs pointed to the information in Table 4.6 when she gave instructions to students to do the following activity: First she asked students to read the word *jump.* After pointing to the *-ed* ending in the word *jumped,* she told students that *jump* plus *ed = jumped* (where *ed* takes on the sound of /t/). She then had the students read the word *land* before telling them that *land* plus *ed = landed* (where *ed* is a second syllable /ĕd/). Next, she had the students say the word *fill,* and told them that *fill* plus *ed = filled* (where *ed* takes on a /d/ sound with no extra syllable). Finally, Mrs. Gibbs tested the students' understanding by asking them to add *-ed* to a series of orally presented words (What's *lift* plus *ed?* What's *kill* plus *ed?* What's *skip* plus *ed?*)

TABLE 4.5   Format for New Letter Combinations and Affixes Introduced in the Curriculum

Objectives	After seeing a new letter combination or affix, students will say its sound with 100% accuracy.
Materials Needed	Board, chart paper, or overhead transparency and writing implement. Write the letter combinations and affixes that will be reviewed with the new letter sound. Use an alternating pattern to teach the new letter combination or affix by writing it on the board followed by one review letter combination/affix, followed by the new letter combination/affix, followed by two review letter combinations/affixes. This pattern is continued until five letter combinations or affixes separate the last two new ones (examples: **ar** ea **ar** th ing **ar** ent ea re ou **ar** ai ea ing oo _le **ar**).
Signaling	*Loop signal for continuous sounds:* After looping to the end of the letter combination, hold your finger for two seconds as students say the sound before looping your finger back to the starting point.

Loop signal for stop sounds: After looping to the end of the letter combination, bounce your finger out as students say the sound and return to the starting point. |
| **Time** | 3–5 minutes |

Instructions	**Teacher**	**Student**
	1. Advance Organizer	
	2. My Turn (Examples given for continuous and stop sounds.)	
	Point to the new letter combination or affix.	
	continuous sound: (finger to the left of letter) **"My turn. Here's our new sound for today."** (loop signal) **"/ar/."** (loop back to starting point)	/ar/
	stop sound: (finger to the left of letter) **"My turn. Here's our new sound for today."** (loop signal and bounce out) **"/ch/."** (back to starting point)	/ch/
	3. Your Turn	
	continuous sound: (finger to the left of letter) **"Your turn. What sound?"** (loop signal) (answer) (loop back to starting point) **"Yes, /ar/."**	/ar/
	stop sound: (finger to the left of letter) **"Your turn. What sound?"** (loop signal and bounce out) (answer) (back to starting point). **"Yes, /ch/."**	/ch/
	4. Individual Student Checkout	
	continuous sound: (finger to the left of letter) **"Individual turns. What sound? Inez."** (loop signal) (answer) (loop back to starting point) **"Yes, /ar/."**	/ar/
	stop sound: (finger to the left of letter) **"Individual turns. What sound? Shan."** (loop signal and bounce out) (answer) (back to starting point). **"Yes, /ch/."**	/ch/
Scaffolding Reduction	5. Your Turn to Read the Row (new plus previously learned letter combinations and affixes)	/ar/
	Starting at the first letter combination/affix move through the row of letters on the list, signaling for each letter combination/affix just as you did in Step 3. As you move through the list say, **"What sound?"** for each letter combination/affix.	/ea/ /ar/
	6. Individual Student Checkout	
	Point to random letters. Starting at the first letter combination/affix, move across the row of letters on the list, signaling for each letter combination/affix just as you did in Step 5. As you point to random letter combinations/affixes on the list say, **"Individual turns. What sound? Carmella."**	/ing/, /ar/, /ent/ . . .
Error Correction	If an error occurs at Step 3, immediately return to a My Turn–Your Turn pattern.	
	If an error occurs at Step 5 or 6, immediately return to a My Turn–Your Turn pattern. Then alternate between the missed letter and familiar letters until students identify the missed letter correctly three times.	

TABLE 4.5 Continued

Adaptations	▪ When teaching two sounds for the same letter combination (e.g., /ē/and /ĕ/for *ea*), ask students to say two sounds for the combination, saying the most common sound first. If you introduce the letter combination in this way from the start, students will have a higher probability of accurately reading an unknown word containing the letter combination. You can point to the letter combination and signal: **"Say the two sounds. First sound."** (student answer) **"Second sound."** (student answer)

Source: This script is based on one originally developed and field-tested by Carnine, D. W., Silbert, J., Kame'enui, E. J., & Tarver, S. (2010). *Direct instruction reading* (5th ed.). Boston: Merrill.

Many students who are at risk have difficulty doing this oral task. They may be influenced by their native language and routinely add a syllable to indicate past tense; they may use a dialect that does not routinely add past tense to verbs; or they may have articulation problems that make this task more difficult. These students need daily practice until they begin to hear and say these past-tense endings. Since -*ed* has three sounds, you should never expect students to read the separate -*ed* ending as a "stand-alone." Instead, have students read the base word and then the whole word. For students who do not routinely use -*ed* past-tense verbs in their oral communication, learning to read these words is as much a language task as a decoding one. After teaching students to read the word *gasp* and discussing its meaning, the teacher would do the following when she instructs the word *gasped:*

Written on board:

gasped

1. Teacher loops under "gasp" and says, *"Read the base word"* (Students read *gasp.*)
2. Teacher loops back to the beginning of the word and says, *"Now read the whole word."* (The teacher slashes under word from left-to-right as the students read *gasped.*)

Error Correction   If students can't read the word *gasped*, chances are that they are not familiar with the past tense of *gasp* as a vocabulary word. Thus the teacher should first say the word correctly ("*gasped*") before using it in a sentence loudly emphasizing the word ending. For example, the teacher says, *"Right now, I gasp because I'm thinking of all the work I have to do, but yesterday I gasp**ed** when I saw that spider in the room. Everyone say the word gasp**ed**."* After students say the word, the teacher asks them to read it once more. Note that sometimes the teacher needs to articulate the word with students. For example, saying /pt/ at the end of a word is difficult, and students with weaker phonemic awareness skills might not hear the two sounds.

Reading One-Syllable Words with Letter Combinations

Once students can read a letter combination in isolation, teach them to read it in words using the format shown in Table 4.7. In this approach, the teacher uses strategic underlining and a part-whole strategy to focus student attention on the new combination. The teacher begins by underlining the letter combination in the first three or four words. Students first read the underlined letter combination and then the entire word. After doing this procedure for the first three to four words, students then read the rest of the words in the list by sight at least two

TABLE 4.6 Action Words with *ed* Endings Tell Us What Happened in the Past

Base Word	Base Word: Past	Sound
jump	jumped	/t/
land	landed	/d/ + syllable
fill	filled	/d/

TABLE 4.7 Format for Reading One-Syllable Regular Words with Letter Combinations

Objectives	After seeing a one-syllable regular word that contains a letter combination, students will orally read the word the fast way.
Materials Needed	Board, chart paper, or overhead transparency and writing implement. Write the regular words that students will read in rows on the board. For example, if students are reading eight words, write two rows of four words. On the first day, underline the new letter combinations before students read words containing them.
Signaling	Two-part signal: **"What sound?"** or **"What word?"** initiates the signal for unison answers. 1. Loop signal. **"What sound?"** initiates the signal for unison answers. 2. Side-slash-signal. **"What word?"** initiates the signal for unison answers.
Time	Depends on the number of words with new letter combinations introduced in the reading curriculum.

Instructions	Teacher	Student
	1. Advance Organizer	
Scaffolding Reduction	2. Your Turn with Sound Prompting	
	a. (finger just to the left of underlined sound) **"Your turn. What sound?"** (loop signal) (answer) (loop back to starting point). **"Yes,** (loop signal) **/sh/."** (loop back to the left of the word)	/sh/
	b. (pointing to the left of the word.) **"What word?"** (side-slash-answer) (loop back to starting point). **"Yes, *ship.*"**	ship
Further Scaffolding Reduction	3. Your Turn without Sound Prompting	
	After the first three or four words on the list, omit the sound prompting. Remember to use a longer think time the first or second time students read words on the list.	
	"What word?" (side-slash-signal under the entire word–answer) (loop back to starting point) **"Yes, *shall.*"**	shall
	"What word?" (side-slash-signal under the entire word–answer) (loop back to starting point) **"Yes, *wish.*"**	wish
	Teach between 3 and 10 other words with the same letter combinations.	
	4. Individual Student Checkout	
	"What word? Bethany." (side-slash-signal under the entire word–answer) (loop back to starting point) **"Yes, *wish.*"**	wish
	Call on between one and three students to check for accuracy.	
Error Correction	If students make an error reading the new sound combination, ask them to tell you the sound and then read the word again. If students still make a mistake, move into a My Turn–Your Turn pattern. Then return to the beginning of the row and have students reread the words. If students make an error reading another sound they have previously learned, immediately have them sound out loud and then read the whole word. If they still make an error, return to a My Turn–Your Turn. Once the error is corrected, return to the beginning of the row and have students reread the words.	
Perk Up Your Drill	Some teachers send home a list of the words with their students for extra practice. On Friday afternoon, the class splits into assigned pairs. First one student reads to her partner who marks every correct word. Then the pair switches. The teacher monitors closely for any questions. Students keep track of their cumulative score from week to week by charting it on a thermometer.	
Adaptations	The first two or three times through the word list, give longer think time as students sound out the words with the new combination.	

Source: This script is based on one originally developed and field-tested by Carnine, D. W., Silbert, J., Kame'enui, E. J., & Tarver, S. (2010). *Direct instruction reading* (5th ed.). Boston: Merrill.

times. The first time through the list, the teacher provides more think time, gradually reducing the amount each time thereafter to build fluency. At least one third of the words in the list should have the new letter combination because newer skills require more practice. The remaining words should contain review letter combinations to build student retention. A loop signal is used for reading the underlined combination; a side-slash signal is used for reading the whole word. These are the same signals shown in Figure 3.10.

Reading One-Syllable Words Ending in VCe

Reading VCe words is difficult for students because it is the first time they encounter long vowels that are not part of a vowel combination. After saying the rule, the teacher guides the students by applying it to four or five VCe words as shown in Table 4.8. After the rule has been successfully applied to each word, the students read each word by sight. If the students make an error while reading words by sight, the teacher guides them as they reapply the rule, reread the word, and then go back to the beginning of the list and read the words by sight again. The goal for this activity is 100% accuracy.

Once students are able to read lists of VCe words without error, they are presented with a mixture of VCe and CVC words to ensure that they apply the VCV rule only when appropriate. A common problem among children who are at risk is that once they learn to read long vowel words, they have a tendency to make all vowels long, whether they are or not. For example, after Mr. Gagliano taught his students the VCV rule, he noticed that during passage reading they were reading the words *hop* as *hope, tap* as *tape,* and *rip* as *ripe.* Including Part B in this format is helpful for preventing this kind of vowel confusion.

In Part B of the VCV format, the teacher asks the questions that students will need to ask themselves in order to apply the rule independently to words and read them accurately. After the students have applied the rule to the list of words, they read the list of words by sight until they are 100% accurate. As with Part A, errors are corrected by having students reapply the rule and then go back to the beginning of the list. Once again the goal is 100% accuracy for a given list of words. Since this reading skill is especially difficult for students who are at risk, teachers often spend several days practicing reading a mixture of CVC and VCe words until students are successful. Eventually, once students learn to apply the rule, they automatically learn to distinguish VCe and CVC words without conscious thought.

With regard to signaling, a finger snap or hand clap is used for all rule application questions such as, *"Is there a vowel-consonant-vowel?"* The side-slash signal is used when it is time for students to read the word. When the teacher asks, *"So, do we say /ā/ or /ă/ for this letter?"* a snap or clap is used.

/Ū/ presents additional challenges because there are two sounds associated with it. In words like *duke,* the sound is represented by the ōō sound, but in words like *mule* and *cube,* the *u* says its name /yū/. Students who are at risk may have difficulty with this distinction. Fischer (1993) recommended teaching /yū/ for /ū/ and explained:

> I have found it unnecessary to teach both sounds explicitly. When sounding out words such as flute, rude, and June, a brief discussion of the use of /oo/ usually is sufficient for prompting the students to switch from long /u/ to long /oo/. (In fact, they have fun trying to use /u/ in those words!) (p. 130)

TABLE 4.8   Format for Reading One-Syllable Words That End with VCe: Part A

Objective	After seeing one-syllable words that end with VCe, students will orally read the words the fast way.
Materials Needed	Board, chart paper, or overhead transparency and writing implement. Write the regular words that students will read in rows on the board. In this beginning format, the word list should only contain VCe words. On the first day, underline the two vowels before students read words containing them.
Signaling	Two-part signal: 1. A finger snap 2. Side-slash signal: **"What word?"** initiates the signal for unison answers. In Part B, a looping signal is used after the teacher asks, **"What sound?"**

Instructions	Teacher	Student
	Note: The first few times you read VCe words, use a My Turn to show students how you apply the rule and read the words.	
Preskill 1	Teach students the rule for one-syllable words that end in VCe. **"When it's vowel–consonant–vowel, the first vowel says its name."** Don't move on to Step 2 until students can say this rule.	When it's vowel– consonant– vowel . . .
Preskill 2	Teach students to identify which letters are vowels and consonants.	
Format	1. Point to the first word and ask, **"Does this word have a vowel–consonant–vowel?"** (pause) (finger snap) (answer) (point to VCV letters as you affirm) **"Yes, this word has a vowel–consonant–vowel."**	yes
	2. Point to the first vowel and ask, **"So does this letter say its name?"** (pause) (finger snap) (answer) **"Yes, this letter says its name."**	yes
	3. Point to the first vowel: **"Say the name of this letter."** (finger snap) (answer) (point to the first vowel) **"Yes, /ā/."**	/ā/
	4. Point your finger to the left of the first letter in the word, pause and ask, **"What word?"** (side-slash signal under the entire word–answer) (loop back to starting point) **"Yes, *name.*"**	name
	5. Repeat this pattern for all of the words.	
	6. After students read all of the words on the list, start at the beginning and read all of the words the fast way. (point and pause) **"What word?"** (side-slash signal under the entire word–answer) (loop back to starting point) **"Yes, *name.*"**	name
	(point and pause) **"What word?"** (side-slash signal under the entire word–answer) (loop back to starting point) **"Yes, *gate.*"**	gate
	(point and pause) **"What word?"** (side-slash signal under the entire word–answer) (loop back to starting point) **"Yes, *sale.*"**	sale
Reduce Scaffolding	Gradually fade out your prompts. On day 2 or 3, you might begin omitting Step 3. If students are not successful, add that prompt for several more days. Once students can read the long vowel words when you omit Step 3, also omit Step 2 during the first time through the words.	
	7. Individual Student Checkout (point and pause) **"Individual turns. What word? Austin."** (side-slash signal under the entire word–answer) (loop back to starting point) **"Yes, *gate.*"**	gate
	(point and pause) **"What word? Chan."** (side-slash signal under the entire word–answer) (loop back to starting point) **"Yes, *sale.*"**	sale
	Call on between one and three students to check for accuracy.	

TABLE 4.8   Continued

Error Correction	If an error occurs at any step, immediately repeat steps 1–6. Repeat the rule as in step 1 if necessary.

Format for Reading a Mixture of One-Syllable CVC Words and Words That End with VCe: Part B

Objective	After seeing a combination of one-syllable CVC words and words that end with VCe students will orally read the words the fast way.
Materials Needed	Board, chart paper, or overhead transparency and writing implement. Write the regular words that students will read in rows on the board. The word list should contain a mixture of words that end in VCe and CVC words in random order.
Signal	Three-part signal: 1. A finger snap. 2. Loop signal. **"What sound?"** initiates the signal for unison answers. 3. Side-slash signal. **"What word?"** initiates the signal for unison answers.

Instructions	**Teacher**	**Student**
	1. **What's the vowel–consonant–vowel rule?** (signal 1)	When it's vowel–consonant–vowel . . .
	2. Point to the vowel. **"Does this say its name or sound?"**	
	3. **"What Word?"**	
	4. Gradually reduce your scaffolding until students can read a list of words with a combination of one-syllable CVC words and words that end with VCe with 100% accuracy.	

Error Correction	Repeat steps 1–3 with missed word and start at the beginning of the word list.
Perk Up Your Drill	If students read interspersed VCe and CVC words on a first read with at least 90% accuracy, you can play the "I'll try to trick you" game. When students first see the new word list, tell them that each year you like to trick your students and have put up a challenging list of words to try to trick them. Using an animated tone of voice and gestures, tell the students that they will read the word list and try not to be tricked by any of the words. Students will use all of their effort to avoid mistakes so the teacher can't trick them. You will find that your students never tire of these challenges.

Adaptations	▪ Check to see whether students who have difficulty reading the words with long vowels are confusing the terms *name* and *sound.* In the beginning exercises, you may need to overemphasize the word *name* when you ask, **"Say the NAME of this letter."**
	▪ Students who are most at risk may need to learn the following preskills:
	  ▪ to identify letters as vowels or consonants
	  ▪ to tell the difference between a letter name and a letter sound

Source: This script is based on one originally developed and field-tested by Carnine, D. W., Silbert, J., Kame'enui, E. J., & Tarver, S. (2010). *Direct instruction reading* (5th ed.). Boston: Merrill.

Reading Regular Words with Two or More Syllables

The format for reading regular words with two or more syllables, which is shown in Table 4.9, teaches students to see words as parts rather than as a collection of individual letters. Regular words with two or more syllables are words that can be broken into parts that can be

TABLE 4.9   Format for Reading Regular Words with Two or More Syllables

Instructions	Teacher	Student
Objective:	After seeing a regular word that contains two or more syllables, students will orally read the word the fast way.	
Materials Needed	Board, chart paper, or overhead transparency and writing implement. Write the regular words that students will read in rows on the board. For example, if students are reading eight words, write two rows of four words. On the first day, underline each part of the word before students read. *Reading* is written as <u>read</u> <u>ing</u>. *Portion* is written as <u>por</u> <u>tion</u>.	
Signaling	Two-part signal:	
	1. Loop signal. **"Read this part"** initiates the signal for unison answers. Repeat for each part of the word, moving from left to right.	
	2. Side-slash signal. **"What word?"** initiates the signal for unison answers.	
Time	Depends on the number of words introduced in the reading curriculum.	

Instructions	Teacher	Student
	1. Advance Organizer	
Scaffolding Reduction	2. Your Turn with prompting of word parts	
	"First you're going to read the parts of the word and then you'll read the whole word."	
	a. Place your finger to the left of the first underlined part of the first word written on the board (<u>read</u> <u>ing</u>).	
	"First part?" (loop signal under the underlined part)	read
	b. Point to the left of the second underlined part of the word. **"Next Part?"** (loop signal under the underlined part)	ing
	c. Loop your finger to the left of the word. **"What word?"** (side-slash signal under the entire word–answer) (loop back to starting point) **"Yes, *reading.*"**	reading
	Repeat this pattern for all of the multisyllable words on the list.	
	3. Your Turn without prompting of word parts	
	After reading all of the multisyllable words on the list, start again and read the words by sight without prompting the parts.	
	(point and pause) **"What word?"** (side-slash signal under the entire word–answer) (loop back to starting point) **"Yes, *reading.*"**	reading
	(point and pause) **"What word?"** (side-slash signal under the entire word–answer) (loop back to starting point) **"Yes, *shelter.*"**	shelter
	Teach between 10 and 15 words.	
	4. Repeat 3, even faster.	
	5. Individual Student Checkout	
	(point and pause) **"Individual turns. What word? Johnny."** (side-slash signal under the entire word–answer) (loop back to starting point) **"Yes, *candle.*"**	candle
	(point and pause) **"What word? Greta."** (side-slash signal under the entire word–answer) (loop back to starting point) **"Yes, *tailor.*"**	tailor
Error Correction	If students make an error reading the individual parts, immediately have them first orally sound out that part of the word and then read the entire part as a whole. Ask students to read the whole word one more time. Finally, return to the beginning of the row and have students reread all the words to that point.	
	If students make an error reading the whole word the fast way, immediately tell students the word; then ask them to read the word parts again before reading the whole word. Once the error is corrected, return to the beginning of the row and have students reread all of the words.	

TABLE 4.9 Continued

Perk Up Your Drill	Every time students read two rows of words correctly, have them raise their hands as if a fireworks display is rising into the sky. In unison, make the gentle sound of fireworks drifting back to the ground.
Adaptations	If students have had difficulty reading words with a new sound like /tion/, once they are reading the words accurately, find decodable books that emphasize that sound for more practice.
	If students have difficulty determining whether the vowel in an open syllable says its name or its sound, you can tell students that when you put a line above a letter, the letter says its name. Use this strategy when you anticipate that students will be unable to decode a new word such as *starvation* = <u>star</u> <u>vā</u> <u>tion</u>

Source: This script is based on one originally developed and field-tested by Carnine, D. W., Silbert, J., Kame'enui, E. J., & Tarver, S. (2010). *Direct instruction reading* (5th ed.). Boston: Merrill.

readily decoded as long as students have the prerequisite decoding skills. For example, the word *returning* can be broken up into the parts *re + turn + ing*. As long as students are capable of decoding all three parts, they can be taught how to attack the word. In this format, the teacher uses a loop signal under each decodable part as students read the parts, and then side-slashes as students read the whole word. Students read all of the words by sight after they have first read them in parts.

When students misread the part or the whole word, the teacher must instantly analyze their mistake in order to select the appropriate error correction. Her error correction will depend on whether they misread a word part or the entire word. If students misread a part of the word, the teacher supports the students by having them read the part phoneme-by-phoneme before reading that whole word part. Once students have read the missed part correctly, the teacher points slightly to the left of the word and has them once again begin reading the parts of the same word to give them some more immediate practice. When Mrs. Dettman came to the third word on Tuesday's list (*constrictor*), which she had underlined as <u>con</u> <u>strict</u> <u>or</u>, she asked everyone to read the first part, which they did with no problem. When she asked them to read the second part, they said, *"sicker,"* so she immediately put her finger slightly to the left of the *s* and asked them to sound out that part. As she looped from part to part, the students replied, "/str/ + /i/ +/ct/." Now when she asked them to read that part, they correctly answered *strict*. Mrs. Dettman enthusiastically told the group, *"Yes, this part is **strict**,"* before saying, *"Let's read this word one more time. Read the first part."* Her students then quickly read each part, *con + strict + or,* so she asked them to read the whole word, which they accurately did. Instead of having students move down the list and read the fourth word, Mrs. Dettman said, *"Starting over. Let's start at the top of the list and see if this time we can get every word correct the first time."* By returning to the top of the list and giving the students this slightly delayed practice reading *constrictor* again, she ensured that they would be likely to read it correctly when they opened their books and read the boa constrictor snake story. Of course, if word lists are long and students miss a word toward the bottom of the list, merely go up three or four words rather than returning to the top.

The second type of error correction is used when students read the parts correctly but blend them into a different word. If Mrs. Dettman's students had decoded the parts *con + strict + or* correctly, but then read the word as *contraction*, they would have made this second type of error. Recognizing the second type of error, Mrs. Dettman would switch to a My Turn strategy and tell students the word (*constrictor*). For immediate practice she would then ask her students to read the parts of the word (*con + strict + or*) before reading the whole word again (*constrictor*). Just as with the first error, Mrs. Dettman would say *"Starting over,"* and return to the top of the list so her students practice reading all of the words again. Students should now move quickly through the list reading these words by sight since they have had more practice decoding them.

TABLE 4.10   Is Your Phonics and Word Study Instruction Research Based?

	Research-Based	Not Research-Based
Phonics and Word Study	Explicit, systematic, cumulative teaching of phoneme-grapheme (sound-symbol) correspondences, syllable types, and meaningful word parts (prefixes, suffixes, roots, and base words); word-reading skills applied in text reading; "Sound it out" comes before "Does it make sense?"	Children directed to pay attention to the sense of a sentence before guessing at a word from context and the first letter; "sounding out" whole word is de-emphasized; no systematic presentation of sound—symbol correspondences; avoidance of decodable text; use of leveled books without phonetically controlled vocabulary.

Source: Adapted from Moats, L. (2007). *Whole-language high jinks: How to tell when "scientifically based reading instruction" isn't.* Washington, DC: Fordham Foundation.

Of course, if students failed to blend word parts into the whole word *constrictor* correctly because they hadn't heard of that word before, Mrs. Dettman would also teach the meaning of the word *constrictor* since understanding the meaning of the word would help students remember that word the next time they saw it in print. Table 4.10 compares systematic and explicit scientifically based research instruction in phonics and word study instruction described in Chapters 3 and 4 with other commonly used teaching methods that are not research-based.

Companion Website

Go to the Video Activities section of Chapter 4 in the Companion Website (www.pearsonhighered.com/bursuck2e) and complete the activity entitled *Advanced Word Reading: Multisyllable Regular Words.*

How Do I Teach Students to Apply Structural Analysis Skills to Reading Regular Words?

When teaching students how to apply structural analysis to reading regular words, your instruction should be as explicit as when teaching beginning decoding skills. When we expanded one-day structural analysis activities in the general education curriculum to five-day lessons, teachers told us that adding four days of practice still didn't provide enough support for their students when learning to apply a rule or the meaning of a suffix to a word. As a result, our teachers often doubled that amount of time. The teachers found that if they left the skill before students were at mastery, the rule or meaning of a prefix was quickly forgotten. They told us that the structural analysis part of the lesson needed more review than most other skills they taught during reading. Expecting students to answer in unison is also important, because only a small percentage of students have the opportunity to apply the rules otherwise. Procedures to teach contractions, prefixes, and dividing words into syllables are described next.

Teaching Contractions

Preskill   Teach your students to say the definition for a **_contraction._** *"A contraction is a short way of saying and writing two words."* Teaching the definition may take some "My Turn–Together–Your Turn" practice, and you might want to teach the definition by clapping it out or having students say it in rhythm. Students should also be able to say the definition independently as well as say the word *contraction* when you tell them the definition.

1. Write the following words on the board:
   a. we'll = we + will
   b. I'll = I + will
   c. isn't = is + not
   d. can't = can + not

2. MY TURN: Point to the first word and explain that *we'll* is a short way of saying *we will.* Point out the apostrophe. Another one of your goals for these structural analysis activities is to make sure that all of your students can say *apostrophe* when you point to that punctuation mark.

3. TOGETHER: First, ask students to read *we'll = we will;* Next, erase *we + will* and ask them what *we'll* means (*we will*). Finally, add meaning and say, *"We will go to the store. How can I say that sentence a different way?"* (answer: *"We'll go to the store."*)

4. YOUR TURN

   Ask: *"What does we'll mean?"*

5. Repeat for second word. Thereafter, before teaching another new contraction, always return to the top of the list and have the students read each contraction already taught and tell you what it means.

Your students have mastered the skill when they can tell you what a specific contraction means at the start of a lesson with no support, or when a student answers your question about the meaning of a contraction in the text she is reading. Students should learn to spell the contractions at the same time they are learning to read them.

Teaching Affixes

Preskill   Several preskills are needed before teaching students to apply the meaning of prefixes and suffixes. If you are teaching students about prefixes, they should be able to read the base or root word as well as the prefix you are teaching them. If you are teaching a prefix, then they need to know its definition. Teach the definition with My Turn–Together–Your Turn until students can say it independently. *"What's a **prefix**?"* (answer: *"A prefix is a word part added to the beginning of a base word that changes its meaning."*) The same preskills apply to teaching suffixes. *"What's a **suffix**?"* (answer: *"A suffix is a word part added to the end of a base word that changes its meaning."*) The following lesson teaches students word building with two prefixes. A lesson focused on suffixes or both would follow the same pattern. Teach only one or two prefixes or suffixes to mastery before introducing others. Add prefixes and suffixes you have taught to your word wall for easy review.

Many students need several days of instruction at the My Turn-Together level before you can add new words or reduce scaffolding. These activities require manipulating language and are more difficult than expected. Do not underestimate how difficult learning how to apply prefixes and suffixes to base and root words is for your students who are at risk. This lesson teaches the prefix *re-,* though you can teach up to two affixes during a given lesson using the same wording.

1. Write the following on the board:

   Definition: *Re-* means *again*

He <u>retells</u> the story.

Shavon <u>reset</u> the alarm clock.

2. Ask your students: "What's a prefix?" (answer: "*A prefix is a word part added to the <u>beginning</u> of a base word that changes its meaning.*") Reteach this definition if students have forgotten it.

3. Ask your students to read the definition "***Re-* means *again*.**" Ask students what *re-* means. Ask them to shut their eyes and tell you what *re-* means.

4. MY TURN: Ask students to read the first sentence. Circle the prefix, and remind students, "***re-* means *again*.**" Tell students that, because *re-* means *again*, *retells* means *tells again*. Explain that if Martina tells her mom what happened at school and then she tells her mom again a second time, she tells the story again or she **retells** the story. Ask if anyone knows someone who retells a lot of stories or information. Ask the students if *re-* is a prefix or a suffix and why. Ask the students one more time what *re-* means. Ask the students one more time what *retells* means. Erase the definition.

5. TOGETHER: Ask students to read the second sentence. Circle the prefix and ask students what *re* means. Ask students if *re* is a prefix or suffix. Then ask, "*If **re** means **again**, what does **reset** mean?*" If students are unable to answer, increase scaffolding and use a My Turn to explain. If students answer correctly, say, "*So we know that Shavon set the alarm clock once and then he set it again. He **reset** the clock. Do any of you have an alarm clock that you have to reset each day?*" Ask someone who answers what time he or she reset the clock to. Finish by saying, "*Tell me one more time what **reset** means.*"

If students struggle with a lesson, use the same base words the next day; otherwise, select new ones. When students read words in text that have the prefix *re-* or other prefixes and suffixes taught, ask them to apply the rule and tell you what the word means and why. Select words comprised of base words and affixes that your students can already spell and add them to the spelling list. Your goal is teaching the prefix *re-* at the **Your Turn** level by the third or fourth day. At that point, you will start the lesson by first asking students what *re-* means and then asking them what a new word like *redo* means. Their independent accurate answers will let you know that they were ready for that reduced support.

Dividing Words into Syllables

If you are teaching advanced word reading using syllables, these tips will lead to more effective instruction:

1. Explicitly teach each syllabication rule before asking students to apply it. When you start teaching syllabication, have students put a dot or *v* under every vowel sound before dividing the word into syllables. Remember that vowel combinations such as *ai* count as one vowel sound. Careful use of My Turns, Togethers, and Your Turns will result in higher accuracy as you gradually reduce the scaffolds to your instruction.

2. During word-reading instruction, scallop under syllables rather than word parts. Either before or after students read the words, ask them what kind of syllables they will be reading.

3. When you have your students do phoneme–grapheme mapping described in the following spelling section, ask students to draw scallops under each syllable.

4. Give the students syllable sorts (e.g., "Put all closed syllables in one pile."), which you monitor so that you can provide immediate feedback for errors.

5. If students misread r-controlled syllables, syllables with VCe endings, or syllables with letter–sound combinations, go back a step and teach students to read the letter combinations or learn the associated rule first.

How Can I Teach Rule- and Pattern-Based Spelling and Morphographic Spelling

While the processes are similar, spelling is more difficult than reading (Ehri, 2005). Ehri explained:

> The reason is that more bits of information must be remembered for correct spelling than for correct reading. When a student remembers how to read a familiar word, he or she accesses essentially one bit of information from memory, an amalgam consisting of the word's spelling, pronunciation, and meaning. However, when the student remembers how to spell a familiar word, he or she must access several bits of information from memory consisting of individual letters in the proper order. (p. 27)

Spelling instruction that is systematic and explicit leads to what have been described as "exceptional" gains in reading and writing (Ehri, 2005). While we know less about effective spelling instruction than reading, research shows that certain ways of teaching spelling, while frequently used, are ineffective. Studies also provide guidelines for how to teach spelling more systematically and explicitly. Both types of teaching strategies are described in Table 4.11.

Table 4.12 presents one format for teaching exception spelling words developed by Kinder (1990). Students can learn to conduct practice sessions following this format to provide additional practice and motivation in peer practice sessions. Although students need to learn high frequency exception words, morphographic spelling, which teaches the meaning and spelling of prefixes, suffixes, root and base words, provides the foundation for spelling thousands of new words.

Spelling instruction should only include high utility rules that have few exceptions. We identified the following ten spelling rules most commonly taught in spelling programs used in our project schools:

1. Because words don't usually end in v, always add an e after a final v such as in *dove*.
2. When words end in *ack, eck, ick, ock,* and *uck,* /k/ is spelled *ck*.
3. When words end in /j/ as in *adge, edge, idge, odge,* and *udge,* /j/ is spelled *dge*.
4. When words end in *atch, etch, itch, otch,* or *utch,* /ch/ is spelled tch.
5. The floss rule: After a short vowel at the end of the word, a final *f, s,* or *l* is doubled.
6. Final e Rule: When a word ends in *e* and you add a morphograph that begins with a vowel letter, drop the *e*.
7. Doubling Rule: When a short word ends in CVC and the next morphograph begins with a vowel, double the final consonant.
8. Plural Variation Rule: When a word ends in a "hissing" sound (/s/, /z/, /x/, /ch/, /sh/), add an *-es* to form the plural.
9. Changing y to i rule: When a word ends in consonant and y, to make the plural change the y to i before adding *-es*. Variation of rule: When a word ends in consonant and y, change the y to i before adding *-ed,- es,- er,* or *-est*.
10. Changing f rule: For words that end with the /f/ sound, change the letter f to *ves* when spelling the plural form. You can always hear the sound /v/ in the plural.

The following format for the y to i rule for plurals can be used to teach any of these spelling rules. As with teaching structural analysis in reading, students often need weeks of practice applying the rule to new words with frequent review of previously learned rules and words.

Teaching the Changing *y* to *i* Rule for Plurals

Preskill: Teach your students to independently say the y rule: *"When a word ends in* **consonant** *and* **y,** *to make the plural change the* **y** *to* **i** *before you add* **es.** Until students

TABLE 4.11 Systematic, Explicit Spelling Instruction

Ineffective	Why It's Not Effective	Effective
Giving weekly tests of 20–25 words at the end of each week	Most students retain spelling words in long-term memory better if they learn to spell 15 or fewer words a week. Lists of words for students who struggle the most with spelling should be limited to between 6 and 12 words per week.	Select 15 or fewer words per week and review those words frequently. Give students who struggle the most with spelling 6–12 words per week.
Writing words many times	This practice does not ensure words are in long-term memory because students often do this aversive task robotically without thinking about the words.	Use word-study procedures that involve seeing, hearing, saying, and writing the spelling words. Students need immediate corrective feedback from someone when they misspell a word.
Randomly selecting spelling words from lists of high frequency words or choosing words from mistakes in students' work	Poor spellers do not naturally develop strategic skills in recognizing common rule-based and morphographic spelling patterns. They need explicit instruction in phonetically spelling words, recognizing patterns, and learning morphographs.	Use a well-designed scope and sequence and common examples for spelling. Spelling instruction should progress from phonetic spelling to rule-/pattern-based spelling to morphographic spelling. 84% of words have basically regular spellings with no more than one exception sound-spelling.
Teaching students too many rules for spelling	Students can't remember numerous rules, and there are frequent exceptions to many of them.	Teach the 10 rules shown on page 171 that apply to a large number of words.
Giving students words with multiple spellings of the same letter sound in the same lesson	If students study words in the same week with four different ways to spell one sound, they become confused, and this absence of any patterns leads to increased errors.	Introduce sound patterns sequentially, coordinated with the reading program.
Expecting everyone in the class to learn the same words	Since students' skills in spelling vary as widely as they do in reading, giving everyone the same spelling words will not meet the needs of many students in the class.	Assess spelling frequently and differentiate instruction as needed.
Spelling is not integrated with reading, vocabulary, and writing	Students need to fluently retrieve correct letter sequences from long-term memory when writing. Spelling is not just a visual memory task. Integration of the phonological, orthographic, meaning, and context processors will help students generalize spellings to their writing.	Students learn to spell the words they are learning to read. Word study including the meaning of morphographs is stressed during spelling instruction. Writing topics are designed to provide students with the opportunity to use words they have learned to spell in their writing.
Spelling instruction is conducted infrequently	Students need enough practice so the words they learn are not easily forgotten. As Hunter (2004) writes: "Don't just cover material. If you do, use a shovel, cover the material with dirt, and lay it to rest, for it will be dead as far as memory is concerned." (p. 129)	Daily practice in spelling with new spelling words practiced for several days is more effective. Students orally spell words as well as write words with the opportunity for immediate feedback for errors.
After the end of the week, words learned that week are rarely if ever reviewed	Cumulative review is an essential teaching strategy for struggling learners.	Every day, several words from past spelling lessons are reviewed and if students misspell then they are retaught.

Source: Adapted from Allal (1997); Dixon & Englemann (2007); Graham (1999); Hunter (2004); and O'Connor (2007).

TABLE 4.12   Spelling Exception Words

The teaching procedure for exception words involves repeated practice, both oral and written. In this format typically four to six words are learned at a time. Some students may be able to learn only three words at a time; higher performing students may be able to learn up to ten words with good retention.

ORAL EXERCISE

(Write on the board:)   enough   touch
                         said   monk
                         where

(Teacher points to *enough* and asks students to read the word.)
WHAT WORD? (signal) "enough"
SPELL *ENOUGH* AS I POINT TO THE LETTERS, (signal) "e-n-o-u-g-h"
SPELL *ENOUGH,* (signal) "e-n-o-u-g-h"
ONCE MORE. SPELL <u>*ENOUGH,*</u> (signal) "e-n-o-u-g-h"
(Teacher erases <u>enough</u>.)
SPELL *ENOUGH,* (signal) Students visualize word and spell "e-n-o-u-g-h."

(Teacher points to *said*.)
WHAT WORD? (signal) "said"
SPELL *SAID* AS I POINT TO THE LETTERS, (signal) "s-a-i-d"
SPELL *SAID* (signal) "s-a-i-d" **ONCE MORE. SPELL *SAID,***
(signal) "s-a-i-d" (Teacher erases <u>said</u>.)
SPELL *SAID,* (signal) Students visualize word and spell "s-a-i-d." (After each new word taught, the teacher always returns to the first word in the list and asks students to spell it and then all the other words that have been introduced during the lesson up until the new word. This extra practice with the new words is called part firming because students are firming up that part of the lesson to mastery.)
SPELL <u>*ENOUGH,*</u> (signal) Students visualize word and spell "e-n-o-u-g-h."
SPELL <u>*SAID,*</u> (signal) Students visualize word and spell "s-a-i-d."

Teacher goes to third word when the first two words are spelled correctly.

(Teacher points to *where*.)
WHAT WORD? (signal) "where"
SPELL <u>*WHERE*</u> AS I POINT TO THE LETTERS, (signal) "w-h-e-r-e"
SPELL <u>*WHERE,*</u> (signal) "w-h-e-r-e" **ONCE MORE. SPELL <u>*WHERE*</u>.**
(Signal) "w-h-e-r-e" (Teacher erases <u>where</u>.)
SPELL <u>*WHERE,*</u> (signal) Students visualize word and spell "w-h-e-r-e." (The teacher part firms and returns to the beginning of the list.) **NOW SPELL <u>*ENOUGH,*</u>** (signal) Students visualize word and spell "e-n-o-u-g-h." **SPELL <u>SAID,</u>** (signal) Students visualize word and spell "s-a-i-d." **SPELL <u>WHERE,</u>** (signal) Students visualize word and spell "w-h-e-r-e."

The teacher repeats this sequence for the remaining words. She ends the lesson by dictating all the words to students. When dictating the words, she adds meaning by saying a clear sentence after saying the word. Two or three review words are always added to this part of the lesson. After students write the words, the teacher dictates a sentence that contains at least one of the new words.

Correction When students misspell a word, the teacher writes it on the board, and teaches it again before saying "Start over," and having students spell all the words on the list.

Source: Kinder, D. (1990). *Format for spelling irregular words*. Unpublished manuscript, Northern Illinois University.

can say the rule from memory, don't continue. Use several My Turn–Togethers until they can say the rule fluently. If students have difficulty memorizing the rule, have them clap it or say it rhythmically at first.

1. Write these words on the board. Every student should have a small whiteboard, marker, and eraser.

   cr<u>y</u> = cries

   cit<u>y</u> = cities

   candy = candies

   pry =

   try =

2. MY TURN: Explain to students that *cry* ends with a "**consonant** and **y**" (point to the letters as you talk); "*I change the **y** to **i** before adding **es** to make the plural. "Spell **cries** with me.*" (Students spell word)

   "*How do you make **cry** plural?*" (answer: "*Change the **y** to **i** before adding **es**.*") Ask students to spell *cries* orally. Ask them to write *cries* on their whiteboards without looking at the board. Walk around and monitor. (note: Depending on your group, you may need to do several My Turns the first day.)

3. MY TURN: Ask students if *city* ends in **consonant** and **y**." (Students answer "yes.") Point to the letters as you say, "*I change the **y** to **i** before adding **es** to make the plural. Spell **cities** with me.*" (Teacher and students spell *cities*.) "*What did you do to make the plural of city?*" (Students say the rule.) If students answer correctly, ask them to spell *cities* orally before writing it on their whiteboards. Correct any misspellings immediately.

4. TOGETHER: Ask students if *candy* ends in "**consonant** and **y**." (Students answer "yes.") Then ask, "*What do you do to make the plural of a word that ends in **consonant** and **y**?*" If students answer correctly and say, "*Change the **y** to **i** before adding **es**,* ask them to spell *candies* orally before writing it on their whiteboards. Correct any misspellings immediately. If students aren't accurate, increase support to the My Turn level.

5. If students are accurate with the last two words, tell them you will make it harder by listing two words, one that ends in consonant *y* and one that doesn't. (Write *horse* and *penny*. Don't move beyond the Together level at least on the first day and repeat the same steps as in #4.

6. Each day, gradually reduce scaffolding with the new words for that day until students can write the plurals for a list of words, some ending in consonant and *y* and some ending in *vowel* plus y, with 100% accuracy.

A detailed article synthesizing effective word study procedures for spelling can be found at: **http://www.thefreelibrary.com/LANGUAGE-BASED+SPELLING+INSTRUCTION:+TEACHING+CHILDREN+TO+MAKE . . . a063652399.**

Phoneme–grapheme mapping first described in beginning reading in Chapter 3 can also be used to reinforce advanced word-reading skills. A student's mapping of the words *match, knee,* and *unite* is shown in Figure 4.3. Because the /ī/ in *unite* results from the silent e at the end of the syllable (or if you are teaching word parts, because of the VCV pattern), a line is drawn to show the connection. The letter *e* is silent and thus is graphed in the same box as the /t/. As students learn to

m	a	tch			
kn	e̅e̅				
ū	n	ī	te		

FIGURE 4.3   Phoneme–Grapheme Mapping

map letter sounds, rule-based patterns, and syllables, they develop **metacognitive skills,** a term for the awareness of one's thought processes in thinking about how to spell advanced words (Grace, 2007).

Applying the Teaching Enhancements to a Commercial Reading Program

In this four-part activity from a general education curriculum, students are introduced to reading VCe words involving the vowels *a, o,* and *i.* Read it carefully and consider whether you would use it without modification—and why or why not.

1. Hold up a Big Book, displaying the text as you read the rhyme. Ask the students to listen for words that have the /ă/ sound as in *Sam,* and the /ā/ sound as in *name.* Repeat the process for words with long and short *i* and *o.*
2. Give letter cards to the students, read a series of words, and have students tape their letter cards to the board, spelling out the words.

   at-ate; tap-tape; cap-cape; dim-dime; kit-kite; hid-hide; not-note; rod-rode; hop-hope.
3. Ask students to read the following words and phrases.

dive	bat	home	big
came	bit	rim	gave
stop	can	make	hand

Rob's robe	Tim has time.
Smile and grin	Dave and Meg rode bikes.
Can of canes	Ken gave his mom a gift.

Analysis of Activity   The transition from long to short vowels is a difficult one for students who are at risk. First-grade teachers in Project PRIDE had to work extra hard each year helping students acquire this skill. Unfortunately, the instruction provided in Parts 1–3 is unlikely to prepare students to read the words, phrases, and sentences in Part 4. Even students in Tier 1 are likely to be confused by this lesson. Part of the problem is that expecting students to complete Part 4 successfully is too big of a goal, considering that this is the first day that the VCV rule is introduced. A more realistic goal would be to have the students apply the rule to word lists first. Only after they were successful on the word lists would the teacher move on to phrases and sentences. Students who are at risk may need several days of list practice before they are ready for the phrases and sentences.

Another major problem with this lesson is that the instruction isn't explicit enough. Although the teacher points out VCe and CVC patterns, she never demonstrates with a My Turn to show how the silent *e* rule is applied to reading words, nor are the students guided by the teacher as they apply the rule using a series of Togethers. This lesson could be easily adapted for your students who are at risk by using the format in Table 4.8.

The three-part lesson also is inefficient. If the purpose of Part 1 is to help students discriminate between long and short vowels, this skill could be taught more directly using the vowel-consonant-vowel teaching format shown in Table 4.8. In Part 2, the use of letter cards with individual students coming to the board to make words takes a lot of time and is difficult to manage. A more efficient approach would be to have students read word pairs on the board using a unison-response format. In addition, the word list in Part 2 is too predictable; the short vowel word in the word pairs always comes first, allowing students to guess the correct vowel sound without having to apply the rule.

Sometimes it is unclear to teachers how advanced reading fits within a daily reading lesson. The sample lesson plan in Appendix I shows how one teacher integrated advanced

In Your Classroom

Enhancers for Advanced Word Reading

1. Effective teaching of reading multisyllable words is enhanced by ongoing vocabulary instruction like Mrs. Gibbs's weekly "$100 words." Every Monday, Mrs. Gibbs selects a challenging multisyllable word related to positive character development. First she writes the word on the board and shows students how to decode it before giving them practice reading the new word. Mrs. Gibbs tells students what the word means before using it in sample sentences. Some students then have the opportunity to use the word in an original sentence they compose on the spot. At least once during the week, Mrs. Gibbs makes sure that students spell the word and use it in their writing. Each morning starts out with reading and discussing that week's $100 word. When Mrs. Gibbs has an extra 2 or 3 minutes during the day, she asks everyone to read in unison all of the $100 words taught from the beginning of the year and displayed on the blackboard.

   Students are eager to learn these words, because if they find an opportunity to use them in context during the day, Mrs. Gibbs gives them a fake $100 bill that can be used toward items in the treasure chest that she bought during summer garage sales. Latecia was delighted when her *Reading Mastery* teacher reminded the group that they needed to read the story one more time until they met their goal. This gave Latecia the opportunity to respond, "So, you want us to be *tenacious.*" When her *Reading Mastery* teacher exclaimed about her use of such a big word, Latecia smiled and told her that it was one of their $100 words. When Latecia returned to the room, her *Reading Mastery* teacher told Mrs. Gibbs about Latecia's use of *tenacious* so she could get her bill. Throughout the year, students learned to read and understand words like *cooperation, diligence,* and *compassion.*

2. In the afternoon, Mr. Szymck teaches a thematic unit, integrating science and social studies. He finds that during his unit, he has the opportunity to provide his students with extra review reading letter combinations that they have learned in reading. When he previews his lesson plans, he looks for any words that have patterns that his students have learned. At the start of the activity he has them read those new science words. During his unit on "Spring as a Time of Growth," he wrote the words *puddles* and *raindrops* on the board and asked students to read them. When the unit moved from the topic of water to trees, he selected the following words: *treetop, maple,* and *branches.*

word reading with vocabulary and comprehension. Although the lesson plan is designed for a tutoring session, the same lesson could also be used for teaching a larger class. Students who are learning advanced word reading also need fluency instruction to increase their reading speed. Chapter 5 will explain how a typical classroom day looks when advanced word reading and fluency are the critical skills. More suggestions for enhancing advanced word reading are in the feature, *In Your Classroom.*

What Can I Do for Students Who Are Not Developing Advanced Word-Reading Skills Even with Tier 2 Support?

Descriptions about how each tier can meet the needs of individual students as well as decision-making rules for any tier changes are detailed in Chapter 5. Table 4.13 depicts how advanced word-reading skills are taught in each of the five intensive, alternative Tier 3 programs described in previous chapters.

TABLE 4.13   Comparison of Five Common Tier 3 Approaches

	Direct Instruction: Reading Mastery	Lindamood® LiPS	Reading Recovery	Wilson Reading System	Language!
Does curriculum introduce advanced word-reading skills, explicitly, first presenting letter combinations, affixes, or syllables in isolation and then in words?	Yes	Yes	No	Yes. In addition Wilson has recently added a program *Wilson Just Words* for students in grades 4–12, which emphasizes word study in reading and spelling.	Yes
Does curriculum explicitly teach students to read multisyllable words by using prefixes, suffixes, and known word parts?	Yes	Emphasis is on syllables.	No	Emphasis is on syllables.	Emphasis is on syllables.
Does curriculum explicitly teach students to read multisyllable words by first teaching syllable rules and then providing practice applying them?	Emphasis is on morphemes/logical word parts.	Yes	No	Yes	Yes
Is connected text that contains advanced words students have learned part of the curriculum?	Yes	No, but it is encouraged.	No	Yes	Yes
Does curriculum incorporate spelling to reinforce word analysis? After students can read words, do they write the words?	Yes	Yes	Sometimes this occurs.	Yes, they are taught together, simultaneously.	Yes
Are decodable words that appear frequently in grade-appropriate reading text emphasized?	Yes	Both real and nonsense words/word parts are used.	No	Both real and nonsense words are used.	Yes
Are exception words pretaught before appearing in connected text?	Yes	Not a part of the LiPS program, but teachers are encouraged to do this.	No	Yes	Yes
Does daily instruction include a review of decodable and sight words recently learned?	Yes	This is up to teacher's discretion.	No	Yes	Word forms and phoneme-grapheme relationships taught are reviewed, but not the exact words previously taught.

How Can I Teach Advanced Word-Reading Skills to English Language Learners?

Since the regular past-tense ending -ed can be pronounced as a syllable (/ed/), as /t/, or as /d/, English language learners usually have difficulty determining what to say. If none of your strategies for teaching -ed has worked, try helping students learn and apply the following rules (Avery & Ehrlich, 1992, p. 48). Your students will need a chart listing all of the unvoiced sounds.

A. If a verb ends with /t/ or /d/, the past tense is pronounced /ed/. An example is *wanted*.
B. If a verb ends with a voiced sound, the past tense is pronounced /d/. An example is *bagged*.
C. If a verb ends with an unvoiced sound, the past tense is pronounced /t/. An example is *baked*.

If you have a few minutes at the end of the day, the **Yesterday game** provides extra practice using past-tense verbs. Write two sets of regular verbs on large cardboard cards: (*bake, bunt, hang, ski, arrive, ask, cross,* and *invent*). Once you have taught students irregular verbs, you can also add those words to the list. Divide your class in half and explain that everyone will be going back in time to yesterday. Assign a card holder for each team and ask that student to sit on a chair in front of her team and hold up one card for each person. You will need to monitor both teams and award points on a clipboard, so stand in the middle. Since everyone is symbolically going back in time, when you say "Start," one person from each team walks backwards to the card holder. Once that person arrives at the card holder, she has to turn around and say a sentence that begins with *"Yesterday, I..."* If the card holder is displaying the word *bake,* the student might say, *"Yesterday, I **baked** a cake."* When you hear the correct past-tense word used in a sentence, give a point to that team. The person then runs forward and taps another team member, and the game continues. The rules are that everyone gets a turn, and that running or walking backwards in a silly or dangerous manner forfeits one point for the team. Keep track of words that students miss so you can review them later.

> Internet resources for teachers working with English language learners are listed at this website. Links are provided to journal articles and Internet resources: **www.iteachilearn.com/uh/ guadarrama/sociopsycho/paper. htm#research%20journals.**

How Important Are Advanced Word-Reading Skills for Older Learners?

Most older learners who struggle with reading are challenged by multisyllable words. Only through explicit instruction will they acquire and learn to apply the word-analysis skills of recognizing and understanding morphemes, prefixes, and suffixes. Without word-analysis knowledge, reading more difficult text becomes increasingly frustrating. Struggling older readers often guess at words from the first sound, a difficult habit to break. The reading level of text becomes a critical issue for older learners who often have developed anxiety and avoidance toward all text because of a history of frustrating and embarrassing experiences. In addition to the difficulty of words, teachers should also consider simplicity of sentence structure and number of clauses, lengths of sentences and paragraphs, and whether the story or book includes subheadings that organize the information. Some teachers find that carefully selected newspaper and magazine articles with an easier reading level are useful age-appropriate reading materials. With such uncontrolled text, the burden is on the teacher to make sure that the text is not at a frustration level for the student. Other teachers

> Resources for older struggling readers are found at: **www.balancedreading. com/Feldman.pdf.**

select decodable chapter books that are written for older students. The older learner has expended hours of energy trying to hide reading difficulties from peers and teachers and most likely will reject books that are perceived as "babyish." Although the text is at an easier level, none of the decodable books designed for older learners looks like the picture books or books with large fonts that are written for younger students. Table 4.14 summarizes instructional needs for older learners in a multi-tier or RTI model depending on their reading level.

TABLE 4.14 Three-Tier Instructional Plan

Secondary Level 8–12	Tier 1: Grade Level English/Language Arts	Tier 1: Grade Level Content Courses	Tier 2: Strategic Instruction	Tier 3: Intensive Intervention
Learners	All students	All students	Students who need additional structured support and are between a 3rd and 7th grade reading level	Students, who have marked difficulties learning to read and are reading at lower than a 3rd grade level
Instructional Leader	Classroom/core teacher	Content teacher	Specialized reading teacher or specifically trained classroom teacher	Specialized reading teacher or special education teacher
Time Allocation	One instructional period	Scheduled content-area classes	60 minutes daily strategic reading and spelling instruction to support skills taught in core classes	Alternative, intensive, research-based reading and spelling intervention for 90–120 minutes daily
Instructional Components	Fluency, vocabulary (including work on word/root origins), background knowledge, and comprehension. Scaffolding for Tier 2 and Tier 3 students through use of graphic organizers, books on tape, assistive technology, etc.	Focus on content vocabulary and comprehension skills needed for reading expository text. Scaffolding for Tier 2 and Tier 3 students through use of graphic organizers, books on tape, AT, etc.	Advanced word reading skills/spelling, structural analysis, comprehension/ fluency and reading text at instructional level. Curriculum such as *REWARDS, REWARDS +Science, REWARDS + Social Studies, Morphographic Spelling,* or fluency programs like *Read Naturally.*	Intensive word recognition (sound/ symbol, decoding regular words, common irregular words), fluency building, spelling, reading text at instructional level. Curriculum recommended: *Wilson, Corrective Reading, Morphographic Spelling,* or *Language!*
Grouping Structure	Flexible: whole group, small group, partners	Flexible: whole group, small group, partners	Flexible homogeneous group of not more than 6 students.	Flexible homogeneous groups of 3 or fewer students

Source: Adapted from Feldman (1999); Geiger, Banks, Hasbrouck, & Ebbers (2005); Roberts, Torgesen, Boardman, & Scammacca (2008).

Technology

Advanced Word-Reading Skills

In his fifth-grade classroom, Mr. Benvenuti had a student, Maia, who was identified as having learning disabilities. Although Maia continued to receive daily systematic phonics instruction, she had not yet caught up to her peers. One of the recommendations on Maia's IEP indicated that with an **assistive technology** accommodation, Maia could independently read textbooks above her reading level. Mr. Benvenuti knew that assistive technology includes a wide variety of technology applications designed to help students with disabilities learn, communicate, enjoy recreation, and otherwise function more independently by bypassing their disabilities, but he was not aware of any technology other than taped readings that would help in this situation.

When the special education teacher told Mr. Benvenuti that she was going to try having Maia use a QuickLink Reading Pen in class and at home, Mr. Benvenuti decided to learn more about the device. He knew that few scientifically based research studies have been done investigating whether technology devices and applications improve reading. Maia's special education teacher had explained that the QuickLink wouldn't explicitly teach Maia to read more difficult words, but it should help her function more independently in content-area classes.

Mr. Benvenuti learned that the pen, powered by two AA batteries, is a portable assistive device that the student runs over words just like a highlighter to scan either a word or line of text. The pen then reads the text aloud or converts it to text in Windows. In addition, the pen can display the syllables of a scanned word and display the dictionary definitions of the word on its small screen. Mr. Benvenuti was relieved to hear that head-phones could be used so that only Maia would hear the speech. As he read the descriptions, Mr. Benvenuti listed the positive and negative aspects of the pen:

Positive Aspects to the Reading Pen

1. Great accuracy with little practice.
2. No need to press a button while scanning.
3. Comes with extensive software and built-in tools.
4. The pen can be adapted for either right-handed or left-handed individuals.

Negative Aspects to the Reading Pen

1. Cumbersome interface.
2. Editing text can be frustrating.
3. Reading different fonts can pose problems.

After looking at his list, Mr. Benvenuti decided that trying this assistive technology accommodation was a reasonable option when Maia was able to read material independently with 90% accuracy or better. His biggest concern was whether operating the pen would be frustrating or slow her reading down so much that comprehension was negatively affected.

Assistive-technology strategies for older students who do not yet have the advanced word-reading skills needed to read textbooks in social studies and science are highlighted in the *Technology* section.

What Games and Activities Will Reinforce Students' Advanced Word-Reading Skills?

Here are two games that can be adapted to a wide range of topics. The first game uses a science topic, but you can modify it to fit your curriculum.

Word Race

After students have learned to decode six difficult words from a reading selection describing ocean pollution and they accurately but slowly read them in the science story, use those words for a drill game so students get practice reading them at faster rates. Construct a table on your word-processing program with five rows and six columns. Type each of the six words into a box in every row, placing each one in a different column. Divide your students into pairs and give each pair a word-table sheet and an inexpensive sand timer that can be flipped for a 1-minute timing. When you say "Go," one student in each pair will flip the timer; the other student will begin reading all of the words starting in the upper left corner. If a student misreads a word, his partner will ask him to sound out the word and then he'll try again until he reads all of the words in less than a minute.

Short or Long Sort

When you are working with a small group, the Short or Long Sort provides extra practice for students who have learned a new long-vowel pattern. Make several sets of word cards with words containing short *a* and long *a* sounds and put each into an activity box. Select words similar to these:

rack	date	tank	play	grant
game	slap	pace	hail	safe

First, have students sort words into /ă/ or /ā/ piles. After students have sorted the cards, they should write each word in the correct column on the paper. Since you will not be able to monitor errors, select words that students can read with at least 95% accuracy. The *In Your Classroom* feature describes other motivational strategies that you can add to the Teacher–Class game.

In Your Classroom

Extending the Teacher–Class Game

Depending on the age and maturity level of your students, you can use your creativity to spice up the Teacher–Class Game and further increase the motivation level of your students. Your reading instruction will be more effective when paired with a system to encourage on-task behaviors. Research informs us that struggling readers in first grade are more likely in third grade to have poor self-control, off-task behaviors, and both externalizing and internalizing behavior problems (Morgan, Farkas, Tufis, & Sperling, 2008).

Younger Students

One of the simplest adaptations to the Teacher–Class Game is the use of a *Good Work Week* award sheet (see Figure 4.4). Every day that students win the game, the teacher puts a sticker or stamped mark next to that day of the week on their chart. On Friday, students who earned all five stickers receive a special reward or activity, which might be a selection of a prize box item, a special activity during the last twenty minutes of class on Friday, a note home to parents telling about the students' hard work, or the opportunity for the class

---

Good Work Week

Name: _____

Monday

Tuesday

Wednesday

Thursday

Friday

FIGURE 4.4 Good Work Week Award Sheet

Continued

FIGURE 4.5   Climb the Mountain to the Castle Game

to read a section of the latest story, which is videotaped for viewing immediately afterwards.

Another adaptation for younger students is called the *Climb the Mountain to the Castle* game (Figure 4.5). Before starting the game, the teacher needs between 15 and 20 large cutouts that can be taped to the wall along with colorful construction-paper circles with large numbers printed on them (numbers 10–20–30, etc.). Cutouts needed for this motivation game include a castle, fairy tale characters (some menacing and some friendly), and an interesting animal character for each team or row of students. The castle is taped at the top of the classroom wall just below the ceiling, and the numbered circles are taped up the side of the wall, creating a path from

the floor to the castle. The animal figures, which represent the student teams, all start on the beginning circle, 0. Fairy tale images are taped along the path to create interest: *"Team 4 is about to go past the spooky forest. I hope they earn enough points to go right past it without stopping."* As the teams earn points, their animals advance up the path toward the castle. When all of the teams reach the castle, the teacher gives everyone a reward or conducts a fun activity.

At the end of each class, the teacher subtracts the number of points she earned from the points earned by each of the teams. That number is added to the cumulative total and the team animal advances the number of points earned that day. The classroom wall should look like Figure 4.5. The teacher can use this game with any theme. Students can scuba dive past sharks and jellyfish to reach a treasure chest, or they can be mountain climbers attempting to climb the path going to the top of Mt. Everest.

Older Students

Teachers can combine reading and math by having students earn play money in a simulated banking experience. When students win the Teacher–Class Game, they earn play money that later can be exchanged for privileges or items. Students can collect the play money or keep track of their totals in a bankbook. Older students enjoy earning the privilege to omit one homework assignment, or earn a few minutes of extra chat time with friends. Other motivators include "work and eat" days, the opportunity to help younger students, and the opportunity to work to music. A variation on the Climb the Mountain to the Castle game for older students is creating a simulated *Carmen Sandiego* game. Display a world map with an adventure trail across the continents. Students can earn points to travel past geographical barriers such as the raging Amazon River or Mt. Everest. For more of a political science focus, students can move past political hotspots around the world until they reach their destination. Clues to their secret mission are taped to different countries that they pass, and intermittently spaced *hot* cards tell them to move back a few spaces. The final destination spot card should inform students of the surprise they have been working for.

APPLIED ACTIVITIES

1. Answer this fact-or-fiction question about advanced word reading using references from research sources cited in the chapter or from information on the website resources listed in the sidebars.
   - Phonics instruction is no longer necessary when students who are at risk have learned all of the single-letter sounds and can fluently decode one-syllable words. Is this fact or fiction? Explain why.

2. In the list of words below, underline all of the prefixes and circle the suffixes.

boyish	watering	displeased
prejudge	undesirable	writer
mistreatment	government	gently

3. Divide the following words into their morphemes. Circle all affixes.

government	deregulated	wonderful
disagreement	rewritten	reshaped

4. You wonder if your students are ready for a story about a little boy who goes to Atlantic City. Although they have learned all of the single-letter sounds, they still do not know all of the letter combinations. Your first step in analyzing whether they are ready to read this story is to identify all of the letter combinations and affixes. Underline all of the letter combinations in the following sentences and circle the affixes. As some letter clusters can be an affix in one word and a combination in another, be sure that all clusters identified as affixes directly affect the meaning of the word. For example, *er* in *her* is a letter combination because it doesn't affect the meaning of the word; however, *er* in *faster* does affect the meaning of the base word *fast* and thus is an affix.

   > Shawn looked up at the stars and wished he had fudge to eat. Whenever he went to the beach with his mom and dad, Shawn liked to get fudge. Shawn looked at his mom and said, "I am thinking about fudge now. You might think I want to play, but all I want is fudge. I do not want to go on the boat right now. A sailor needs fudge. Please go and bring me some fudge that will be chewy and hard to eat."

5. Two multisyllable words that your students will encounter in their next story are *carelessly* and *sodium*. Identify which of these words would be more difficult for students to learn. Explain your answer.

6. Map the phonemes in each of the following words. The first one is completed for you:

glade	g	l	ā	d				
bread								
grander								
bounty								
splashed								
gladden								
retake								
shoulder								
knight								
battle								
judged								
grassier								

7. Ms. Wilson gave her three Tier 2 students the test of affixes and letter combinations just described. Their results are as follows.

   Sounds Known:
   ed, s, dge, er, ch, oo, oa, ou, ow, ay, or

   Sounds Unknown:
   aw, ar, sh, wh, ea, th, ing, igh, ai, ee, y, ew

   Using the passage in Applied Activity 3, identify which words containing letter combinations and/or affixes that Ms. Wilson's Tier 2 students will not be able to decode.

8. The purpose of the following lesson from a commercial reading program is to teach the affixes -*ful,* -*ly,* and -*ness.* Identify how this lesson may be problematic for students who are at risk. Describe how you would enhance the lesson to increase the likelihood of student success.

   Lesson: Theme 5–Selection 4: Day 5

   - Read a big book to the class. When you come to the word *beautiful,* show students the word and explain that when they come to a larger word that looks new, they can try looking for a base word they know and see if an ending has been added to it.
   - Display a transparency that defines a suffix as "one kind of word ending that adds meaning to the base word." The transparency includes three

examples broken into parts that are listed in columns. Read each example for the students.

Base Word	+ Suffix =	New Word
joy	ful	joyful (full of joy)
neat	ly	neatly (in a way that is neat)
sad	ness	sadness (being sad)

   - Introduce a story about a boy who brings his pet mouse to school. In this story, three words are related to the examples above: *fearful, softly,* and *darkness.* When you come to these words, ask the students to identify the base word, the suffix, the new word, and its meaning.

9. New words in Tuesday's reading lesson include:

sighed	flights	brighter	frightened
salesman	watchman	amazing	admiring
topple	shoppers	mattress	button

   Demonstrate how you would teach these new words using the format in Table 4.9.

10. Ms. Carrier has just introduced to her students the *ou* letter combination in isolation. For the first day of word reading with *ou,* she selected the following words as examples: *sound, cloud, our, through, proud,* and *though.* Critique Ms. Carrier's choice of examples.

Companion Website

Now go to Chapter 4 in the Companion Website (www.pearsonhighered.com/bursuck2e) where you can do the following activities:

- Complete Activities that can help you more deeply understand the chapter content.
- Check your comprehension on the content covered in the chapter by going to the Chapter Quiz. Here you will be able to answer practice questions, receive feedback on your answers, and then access resources that will enhance your understanding of chapter content.
- Find Web Links that will extend your understanding of the content and strategies.

REFERENCES

Allal, L. (1997) Learning to spell in the classroom. In C. Perfetti, L. Rieben, & M. Fayol (Eds.), *Learning to spell: Research, theory, and practice.* Mahwah, NJ: Lawrence Erlbaum (pp. 129–150).

Archer, A. L., Gleason, M. M., & Vachon, V. L. (2003). Decoding and fluency: Foundation skills for struggling older readers. *Learning Disability Quarterly, 26,* 89–101.

Avery, P., & Ehrlich, S. (1992). *Teaching American English pronunciation.* New York: Oxford Press, p. 48.

Bhattacharya, A. (2006). Syllable-Based Reading Strategy for Mastery of Scientific Information. *Remedial Special Education, 27*(2), 116–123.

Carnine, D. W., Silbert, J., Kame'enui, E. J., & Tarver, S. (2010). *Direct instruction reading* (5th ed.). Boston: Merrill.

Celce-Murcia, M., Brinton, D., Goodwin, J. M., & Goodwin, J. (1996). *Teaching pronunciation: A reference for teachers of English to speakers of other languages.* New York: Cambridge University Press.

Dixon, R., & Engelmann, S. (2007). *Spelling mastery.* Desoto, TX: SRA/McGraw-Hill.

Egger-Bovet, H., & Smith-Baranzini, M. (1994). *USKids history: Book of the American Revolution* (p. 11). New York: Little Brown & Company.

Ehri, L. (1989). The development of spelling knowledge and its role in reading acquisition and reading disability. *Journal of Learning Disabilities, 22,* 356–365.

Ehri, L. (2005). Learning to read words: Theory, findings, and issues. *Scientific Studies of Reading, 9*(2), 167–188.

Engelmann, S., Carnine, L., Johnson, G., Meyer, L., Becker, W., & Eisele, J. (1999). *Corrective reading: Decoding.* Columbus, OH: SRA/McGraw Hill.

Feldman, K (1999) The California Reading Initiative and special education in California developed by the Special Education Reading Task Force. Retrieved on April 3, 2009, from http://www.calstat.org/publications/pdfs/ca_reading_initiative.pdf

Fischer, P. (1993). *The sounds and spelling patterns of English: Phonics for teachers and parents.* Farmington, ME: Oxton House

Geiger, S., Banks, A., Hasbrouck, J., & Ebbers, S. (2005). Washington State K-12 Reading Model Implementation Guide. Olympia, WA: Office of Superintendent of Public Instruction. Retrieved from http://www.k12.wa.us/Curriculuminstruct/reading/pubdocs/K-12ReadingModelFINAL6105.pdf

Good, R. H., Gruba, J., & Kaminski, R. A. (2002). Best practices in using dynamic indicators of basic emerging literacy skills (DIBELS) in an outcomes-driven model. In A. Thomas & J. Grimes (Eds.), *Best practices in school psychology IV* (pp. 699–720). Bethesda, MD: National Association of School Psychologists.

Grace, K. (2007). *Phonics and spelling through phoneme-grapheme mapping.* Longmont, CO: Sopris West.

Graham, S. (1999). Handwriting and spelling instruction for students with learning disabilities: A review, *Learning Disability Quarterly, 22,* 78–98.

Greene, J. F. (2004). *Language! A literacy intervention curriculum.* Longmont, CO: Sopris West Educational Services.

Hanna, P., Hanna, J., Hodges, R., & Rudloff, E. (1966). *Phoneme-grapheme correspondences as cues to spelling improvement.* Washington, DC: U.S. Government Printing Office.

Hunter, R. (2004) *Madeline Hunter's Mastery Teaching: Increasing instructional effectiveness in elementary and secondary schools.* Thousand Oaks, CA: Corwin Press.

Johnston, F. (2001) The utility of phonic generalizations: Let's take another look at Clymer's conclusions. *The Reading Teacher, 55*(2), 132–142.

Kinder, D. (1990). *Format for spelling irregular words.* Unpublished manuscript, Northern Illinois University.

Linan-Thompson, S., & Vaughn, S. (2007). *Research-based methods of reading instruction for English language learners, grades K-4.* Alexandria, VA: ASCD.

Moats, L. (2001). When older students can't read. *Educational Leadership, 58*(6), 36–40.

Moats, L. (2007). *Whole-language high jinks: How to tell when "scientifically based reading instruction" isn't.* Washington, DC: Fordham Foundation.

Morgan, P., Farkas, G., Tufis, P., & Sperling, R. (2008). Are reading and behavior problems risk factors for each other? *Journal of Learning Disabilities, 41*(5), 417–436.

Nagy, W., Winsor, P., Osborn, J., & O'Flahavan, J. (1993). Structural analysis: Guidelines for instruction. In F. Lehr & J. Osborn (Eds.), *Reading, language, and literacy: Instruction for the twenty-first century* (pp. 45–58). Hillsdale, NJ: Erlbaum.

O'Connor, R. (2007). *Teaching word recognition: Effective strategies for students with learning difficulties.* New York: The Guilford Press.

Rathvon, N. (2004). *Early reading assessment: A practitioner's handbook.* New York: The Guilford Press.

Roberts, G., Torgesen, J., Boardman, A., & Scammacca, N. (2008). Evidence-based strategies for reading instruction of older students with learning disabilities. *Learning Disabilities Research & Practice, 23*(2), 63–69.

Vadasy, P., Sanders, E., & Peyton, J. (2006). Paraeducator-supplemented instruction in structural analysis with text reading practice for second and third graders at risk for reading problems. *Remedial and Special Education, 27*(6), 365–378.

Wilson, B. (1996). *Wilson reading system.* Millbury, MA: Wilson Language Training.

Wilson, B., & Felton, R. (2004). *Word Identification and Spelling Test (WIST).* Austin, TX: PRO-ED.

CHAPTER

5 Reading Fluency

Objectives

After reading this chapter, you will be able to:

ORF

1. Use oral reading fluency assessment data in a multi-tier or RTI model to screen students at risk, diagnose their skill needs, place them into curricular materials, and monitor and chart their reading progress.

2. Implement the SAFER (Successful, Anxiety-Free, Engaged Reading) strategy for conducting group oral passage reading sessions.

3. Implement strategies for building student reading fluency using repeated readings and other research-based methods.

4. Implement strategies for working with older readers with fluency problems and teaching expressive reading skills to English language learners.

5. Describe the main components of a Tier 1 and Tier 2 reading lesson.

6. Identify and describe the approaches to teaching fluency of four commonly used Tier 3 programs.

7. Use games and activities to reinforce students' fluency skills.

Companion Website

To check your comprehension of the content covered in this chapter, go to the Companion Website (www.pearsonhighered.com/bursuck2e) and complete the Chapter Quiz for Chapter 5. Here you will be able to answer practice questions, receive feedback on your answers, and then access resources that will enhance your understanding of chapter content.

Mr. Rundall had taught third grade for ten years. Every summer when the state returned test score results, he was disappointed that more students in his class did not meet the state standards. He was teaching the advanced phonics strategies suggested by the school literacy coach, but his students' scores hadn't improved. After attending a summer inservice on teaching fluency, Mr. Rundall realized that he was not teaching this skill explicitly. The workshop leader stressed that if teachers used the suggestions from the workshop to increase fluency, students' comprehension would also improve. That made sense. How can students think about the meaning of what they are reading when they are spending so much time trying to decipher the larger words?

186

At the start of the school year Mr. Rundall was determined to use the new fluency building strategies he learned at the summer workshop. He knew finding enough time would be a problem; the school expected him to cover so much content in so many areas! His oral reading fluency screening assessments in the fall showed that almost half the scores for his class were unacceptably low, falling under the 50th percentile on the AIMSweb Oral Reading Fluency assessment. Mr. Rundall was able to set aside a 20-minute block of time after lunch three days per week for fluency building, but he realized there wouldn't be nearly enough time to get to each and every student, even in three days. He remembered a 15-minute paired-practice repeated reading strategy that the workshop leader had suggested that allowed all the students to practice at the same time. So Mr. Rundall paired his students, organized the materials needed for tutoring, and carefully trained his students to do the tutoring. He always monitored his students' tutoring so they performed their tutoring roles effectively. He noticed that the students enjoyed tutoring each other and were excited to see their reading rates increase on the charts they completed each day. Mr. Rundall also began to see a corresponding increase in his students' reading rates on their bimonthly progress monitoring. At the end of the year, he was overjoyed when the number of students meeting standards on the state test finally increased.

Why do you think Mr. Rundall hadn't done fluency building with his students before?

Why do you think Mr. Rundall's students' scores on the state test improved?

This vignette shows that as with phonemic awareness and word reading, gains in reading fluency for students who are at risk are not likely to occur naturally. According to recent results on the National Assessment of Educational Progress (NAEP), 44% of a representative sample of the nation's fourth graders were low in fluency (Lee, Grigg, & Donahue, 2007). Until Mr. Rundall started explicitly teaching his students to become more fluent readers, many did not develop this skill. In order to meet grade-level benchmarks, students must increase their fluency levels from 40 to 60 words correct per minute in Grade 1 to 90 wcpm by the end of Grade 2, and to 110 wcpm by the end of Grade 3. By the end of sixth grade students should reach the important milestone of reading 150 wcpm, described as the point when reading instruction shifts from "learning to read" to "reading to learn" (Good, Simmons, Kame'enui, & Wallin, 2002; Hasbrouck & Tindal, 2006). Students who are at risk need systematic, explicit teaching if they are to make this progress and move beyond beginning reading accuracy to become fluent, accurate readers.

What Is Reading Fluency, and Why Do I Need to Teach It?

In May, Ms. Dornbush had two of her second-grade students, Darrell and Damon, read out loud from a Grade 2 passage. When Ms. Dornbush recorded the percent accuracy for the two boys, she found that both of them read the passage with 94% accuracy. Ms. Dornbush was surprised at these results because she had thought Darrell was a better reader than Damon. Darrell read more words, and his good expression indicated that he understood what he was reading. Damon, on the other hand, read haltingly, sounding out some of the words as he read. His reading lacked appropriate phrasing, he frequently failed to stop at periods, and he read with little expression overall. Ms. Dornbush wondered, "How could two students who read so differently both score the same on a sample of their oral reading?"

The answer is that Ms. Dornbush's measures failed to take **fluency** into account. On a subsequent assessment, Ms. Dornbush recorded the number of words the boys read correctly

accuracy does not indicate fluency

per minute, a measure of their accuracy and fluency. This time the results revealed the differences between their reading levels. Darrell read the Grade 2 passage at a rate of 94 words correct per minute and made six errors. Damon read 68 wcpm and made four errors. Again, both read at 94% accuracy, but this time the results showed that there were major differences in fluency between the two boys. Darrell's rate exceeded the benchmark of 90 wcpm for the end of Grade 2. This score indicated that Darrell is likely to have fewer problems reading fluently and comprehending Grade 3 material. Damon's lower rate indicated he is likely to have problems in Grade 3 unless he builds his reading fluency. By initially failing to take fluency into account, Ms. Dornbush left out a key piece of assessment information, without which program planning and progress monitoring would have been difficult.

Reading fluency is the ability to read text accurately, quickly, and with expression. All three of these elements—accuracy, speed, and expression—are essential so that students can apply their fluency skills during silent reading and comprehend the text (Pikulski & Chard, 2005). In the example just described, Damon was reasonably accurate in his reading but had to focus so intently on decoding the words that he had little energy left to think about and understand what he was reading. Darrell, on the other hand, read with accuracy, speed, and expression. When reading, he could devote most of his attention, working memory, and cognition to making connections among the ideas in the text as well as between those ideas and his background knowledge. As a result, Darrell was much more likely than Damon to understand what he was reading. Chard, Ketterlin-Geller, Baker, Doabler, and Apichatabutra (2009) summarized the issue:

> If attention is consumed by decoding words, little or no capacity is available for the attention-demanding process of comprehending. Therefore, automaticity of decoding—a critical component of fluency—is essential for high levels of reading achievement. (p. 264)

Fluency becomes increasingly important as students move through the grades. As students get older, they are expected to read greater amounts of more difficult material in less time. Students who read slowly, regardless of accuracy, have little chance of keeping up with their peers. They are also less likely to practice their reading, choosing other ways to spend their time such as watching television and being with friends (Archer, Gleason, & Vachon, 2003). This lack of practice further widens the academic gulf between slow readers and their more fluent classmates in a "rich-get-richer" scenario (Stanovich, 1986).

Although fluency as discussed in this chapter involves reading connected text, fluency involves many more skills and processes with comprehension as the ultimate goal. Therefore, the approach to building fluency must be broad-based, encompassing activities to strengthen students' capacity to process information accurately and efficiently, not just at the orthographic and phonological levels, but at the contextual and meaning-based levels as well (Adams, 1990). While the theme of this chapter is building fluency, the teaching strategies described in all the other chapters directly relate to building fluency as well. Not until students attain levels of automaticity in these more foundational skills can they read connected text fluently and with understanding.

How Do I Assess Students' Reading Fluency in a Multi-Tier or RTI Model?

The ability to read passages accurately, fluently, and expressively requires that the reader engage in a number of complex processes at the same time. The reader must translate letters into sounds, blend sounds into meaningful words, access words without thinking, make meaningful connections within and between sentences, relate text meaning to prior knowledge, and make inferences to supply missing information (Fuchs, Fuchs, Hosp, & Jenkins, 2001). The beauty of oral reading fluency assessments is that in minutes the teacher is given a quick snapshot of the extent to which all of these processes are working in concert. It is not surprising that students who are able to read accurately and fluently are also likely to understand what they read (Fuchs et al., 2001; Fuchs, Fuchs, & Maxwell, 1988). Since oral reading fluency develops gradually over the school years, student scores on oral reading fluency assessments over time provide teachers with a measure that can be used for screening, diagnostic, and progress-monitoring purposes. The measures of oral reading fluency described here are DIBELS Oral Reading Fluency (DORF), AIMSweb, TPRI, and PALS. These oral reading fluency instruments are based on measures originally developed by Deno (1985).

Visit the official DIBELS website and view a teacher giving an oral reading fluency assessment to students. Directions to administer and score the test are available at the same website, as are copies that can be downloaded at no charge. **http://reading.uoregon.edu/video/ORFEstablishedReader.mov.**

Administering and Scoring Oral Reading Fluency Measures

Directions for administering and scoring the DIBELS Oral Reading Fluency assessment are shown in Figure 5.1. Directions for giving the AIMSweb and TPRI measures are similar. The teacher takes three 1-minute oral reading samples, using three passages at the student's grade level. The teacher places the passage in front of the student and begins timing as soon as the student reads the first word. As the student reads, the teacher puts a slash through any words that are read incorrectly or omitted. Self-corrections and the insertion of

---

Directions for Administering and Scoring the DIBELS Oral Reading Fluency Assessment

Oral Reading Fluency

Materials: Unnumbered copy of passage, numbered copy of passage, stopwatch, tape recorder[a] (optional)

Directions:

Place the unnumbered copy in front of the student.

Place the numbered copy in front of you but shielded so the student cannot see what you record.

Say these specific directions to the student for each passage: **"When I say 'begin,' start reading aloud at the top of this page. Read across the page."** (Demonstrate by pointing.) **"Try to read each word. If you come to a word you don't know, I'll tell it to you. Be sure to do your best reading. Are there any questions?"** (Pause.) **"Begin."**

Say **"Begin"** and start your stopwatch when the student says the first word. If the student fails to say the first word of the passage after *3 seconds,* tell him the word and mark it as incorrect, then start your stopwatch.[b]

Follow along on your copy. Put a slash (/) through words read incorrectly (see scoring procedures).

If a student stops or struggles with a word for *3 seconds,* tell the student the word and mark it as incorrect.

At the end of *1 minute,* place a bracket (}) after the last word. You may allow the student to complete the last sentence he was reading when time expired.

[a]Tape recorders facilitate error analysis.

[b]On rare occasions the student may speed-read (i.e., read the passage very fast and without expression). If this occurs, tell the student, "This is not a speed-reading test. Begin again, and be sure to do your best reading."

FIGURE 5.1   Directions for DIBELS Oral Reading Fluency Assessment

Source: https://dibels.uoregon.edu/measures/orf.php

Stars of the Sea

What fish looks like it belongs more in the sky than in the	12
sea? The answer is a starfish. Most starfish have five arms, but	25
some have many more. If a starfish loses an arm, it grows a new	39
one. A starfish can lose one or two arms and still be just fine.	53
A starfish can stretch its arms to as long as two feet. The	66
starfish uses its arms to move through water or along rocks. A	78
starfish has tiny tubes on the undersides of its arms. The tubes	91
are like sticky suction cups. The starfish can hold onto rocks	103
even in the waves. The tubes work like hundreds of tiny feet.	115
Starfish crawl along the ocean bottom, but they don't move very	126
fast.	127
A starfish eats tiny fish and plants. Its mouth is on the	139
bottom, in the center of the star. Their favorite food is shellfish,	151
and they can eat a lot. The starfish eats during high tide, when	164
the waves bring in lots of food. During low tide you might find	177
them holding onto the rocks and waiting for the tide to change.	189
Starfish come in many colors, including yellow, orange, red,	198
blue, purple, pink, and brown. They come in all sizes, from tiny	210
to very large. When many different ones are in the same area,	222
they look like a rainbow under water.	229

Total words: _29_

Total correct: _28_   Total incorrect: _1_

FIGURE 5.2 DORF Assessment Passage 1: Cierra

additional words are not counted as errors. The teacher stops the assessment at the end of 1 minute and puts a bracket after the last word read. The total number of words read, number of errors, and number of words read correctly per minute (WCPM) are then calculated. After the three passages are read, the student's median or middle score is noted. That **median score** of words read correctly per minute is the score used in instructional decision making.

Sample score sheets for Cierra, a second-grade student, on the fall DORF assessments are shown in Figures 5.2–5.4. Note that Cierra scored 28 words correct per minute on the first passage, 38 wcpm on the second passage, and 43 wcpm on passage three. Cierra's median score of 38 is the one that will be used in instructional decision making. Another important indicator provided by this assessment shows that Cierra's median errors per minute are two. This score shows that Cierra is reading with a high degree of accuracy.

> Create your own reading fluency score sheets by going to **http://www.interventioncentral.org** and clicking on the OKAPI Reading Probe Generator.

Using Oral Reading Fluency Assessment to Screen Students

The DORF, AIMSweb, and TPRI can be used to screen students who are at risk and, once they are identified, monitor their progress. Calculating fluency is optional on the PALS passages, but they can also be used this way if the teacher times the students' reading.

Twins

Six years ago my family grew from two people to four | 11

people in one day. That was the day my sister and I were ~~born~~. | 25

That was the ~~day~~ Mom and Dad had to start ~~buying~~ two of | 38

everything. My|mom and dad say we were much more than | 49

twice the work of one baby. They also said we gave back more | 62

than twice as much love and fun. | 69

We look just alike because we are identical twins, but we | 80

don't act just the same. My sister likes peas and beans and I hate | 94

them. I like grape juice and she likes apple juice. She likes to | 107

read. I would rather climb a tree than read a book. | 118

Mom and Dad are the only ones who can tell us apart when | 131

we dress the same. They know the secret. I have a mole on my | 145

ear and my sister doesn't. We look so much alike that we can | 158

even fool Grandma and Grandpa. | 168

It's nice to be a twin sometimes. We always have someone | 174

our own age who will share our secrets. Sometimes we don't | 185

want to share everything. Sometimes it is nice to have my mom | 197

or my toys all to myself. Dad says we aren't really that much | 210

alike because no person is exactly like anyone else. | 219

Total words: __40__

Total correct: __38__   Total incorrect: __2__

FIGURE 5.3   DORF Assessment Passage 2: Cierra

Oral Reading Fluency: Screening

When is it given?

- The AIMSweb ORF assessments are given at the beginning, middle, and end of first through eighth grade; the DIBELS ORF assessments are given midyear and end of year first grade and three times a year from second through sixth grade.
- The TPRI *screening* assessment does not have an oral reading fluency measure, but the TPRI oral reading fluency *inventory* assessment is commonly given to all students and can be used as a screening measure at the end of Grade 1 and at the beginning and end of the year in Grades 2 and 3. Screening word identification lists are used to place students in inventory passages determined by the highest level at which the student can read the word list with 90% accuracy.
- The PALS measures passage accuracy beginning in the fall of Grade 1 through Grade 3. Fluency is optional. Students first read word lists; the highest level at which they are able to read 15 or more words determines which passage they read, and those results are used. Passages are read orally and scored for accuracy using a running record.

Students who score as *low risk* on the DIBELS Oral Reading Fluency assessment have met the benchmark and are on track for reading at grade level (see Appendix B for DIBELS benchmark scores). For example, Rudy, who scored 62 wcpm, met the first-grade benchmark at the end of the year and is at low risk for failing to read at benchmark by the end of second grade. Cierra, the second-grade student shown in Figures 5.2–5.4, had a median score of 38 wcpm in

Riding the Bus to School

I ride a big yellow bus to school. I stand on the corner of our	15
street with my friends and we wait for the bus. My friend's	27
grandma waits with us. When it's raining, she holds an umbrella	38
to keep us dry. Sometimes when it's cold she brings us hot	50
chocolate.	51
I leave my house to walk to the bus stop after my parents go	65
to work. I watch the clock so I know when to leave. Sometimes	78
mom phones me from her office to remind me. Sometimes she	89
can't call, so I have to be sure to watch the time.	101
Our bus driver puts his flashing yellow lights on and then	112
stops right next to us. When he has stopped he turns the red	125
lights on so all the cars will stop. He makes sure we are all	139
sitting down before he starts to go. He watches out for us very	152
carefully.	153
My friends and I are the first ones to be picked up by the bus.	168
We like to sit right behind the bus driver and watch while he	181
picks up all the other kids. We know where everyone lives. By	193
the time we get to our school, the bus is almost full. Sometimes	206
the kids get noisy and the driver has to remind us to keep it	220
down. He says their noise makes it hard for him to concentrate	232
and drive safely. I am glad that our bus driver is so careful.	245

Total words: __45__

Total correct: __43__   Total incorrect: __2__

FIGURE 5.4 DORF Assessment Passage 3: Cierra

the fall of the year. This score indicates that Cierra is at *some risk,* and we would predict she might not reach a benchmark score of 90 words correct per minute by the end of second grade unless she receives extra support in fluency building. While the DORF benchmarks are generally comparable to TPRI and AIMSweb benchmarks as well as other published oral fluency norms such as those researched by Hasbrouck & Tindal (2006), the DORF end-of-first-grade benchmark of 40 wcpm to 50 wcpm is considerably lower than the TPRI benchmark of 60 wcpm. In our estimation, a score of 40 wcpm should be viewed as a minimum, because our data have shown that the rate of growth needed to move from 40 wcpm, and even 50 wcpm, to the end-of-second-grade benchmark of 90 wcpm is challenging for many students who are at risk. O'Connor (2007) describes scores below 40 wcpm in May of first grade as "dangerous" because they indicate that the odds are that students scoring that low will continue to struggle with reading in

Hasbrouck and Tindal's norms can be accessed online at **http://www. readnaturally.com/howto/orftable. htm.**

fourth grade. Hasbrouck and Tindal's widely used national norms for oral reading fluency are reported according to 25th, 50th, and 75th percentiles. Crawford (personal communication, 2004) has proposed a more simplified system for identifying children who are at risk. He set ranges for each grade that represent normal growth over the course of the year. These are: Grade 1, 0–50 words correct per minute; Grade 2, 50–100 wcpm; Grade 3, 100–150 wcpm.

Oral reading fluency concerns do not end at third grade. Readers face increasingly higher fluency challenges as they mature. The DORF tables in Appendix B extend up to

Grade 6, while Hasbrouck and Tindal's and AIMSweb norms extend through Grade 8. Unless the student is reading the passage for the first time during the screening assessment, the results are invalid.

Using Oral Reading Fluency Measures to Monitor Students' Progress

The key to accurate progress monitoring of oral reading fluency is that the passages given over time should be of comparable difficulty. Progress, or the lack of it, must result from student reading skill, not passage difficulty. Both DORF and AIMSweb have numerous graded passages available for use in progress monitoring. Other sources for progress-monitoring passages are listed at the end of this section. Teachers can use these passages to monitor the progress of students performing at or close to their natural grade levels within their developmental reading program or remedial students who have fallen behind their classmates.

> The Gray Oral Reading Test-4 (GORT-4) is a standardized test of oral reading fluency whose norms are appropriate for students from 6 years of age to 18 years, 11 months. In this assessment, which can take up to 20 minutes to administer, students read passages that increase in length and difficulty. The final score reflects both rate and accuracy.

By the middle of first grade, progress charts based on oral reading fluency assessments can be used to determine who needs extra support. In addition to helping monitor progress, progress charts help facilitate parent understanding and motivate students to improve. Figure 5.5 shows an example of a progress chart for a second-grade student. Misuou's chart shows that he started second grade at benchmark for reading at 60 wcpm. His teacher drew an **aimline** from his first score in September to the final benchmark score of 90 wcpm needed in May. This sloping aim line enabled her to determine when he was on track for meeting the year-end benchmark. ORF scores that were above the aim line indicated that Misuou was on track. Likewise, the teacher could see when Misuou's progress stalled. The chart showed that beginning in November, Misuou was no longer on track to meet the May benchmark. As soon as his teacher saw that by January 4 his scores were below the aim line, she switched Misuou into a Tier 2 intervention group so he could get more support. Misuou's chart shows that the extra support was beneficial, and by May he was at benchmark.

Using Excel (© Microsoft Corporation), you can make a progress-monitoring chart like the one depicted for Misuou. Students move into Tier 2 when their ORF scores are below the progress line, indicating that they are not on track for reading at grade level by the end of the year. Although students at benchmark might take the ORF assessment only two or three times a year, anyone who is in Tier 2 can take the test anywhere from once a week to once a month (Jenkins, Graff, & Miglioretti, 2009). However, if teachers monitor progress using one passage each time, as opposed to taking the median of three separate passages, monitoring progress every week or two is recommended. Frequent progress monitoring helps the teacher determine when scores are back on the growth line so Tier 2 can be discontinued.

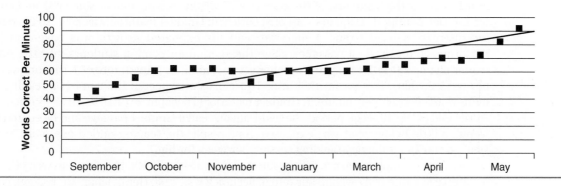

FIGURE 5.5   Grade 2 Oral Reading Fluency Progress Chart: Missuou

More resources on progress-monitoring oral reading fluency are available at the National Center for Progress Monitoring website at **http://www. studentprogress.org/weblibrary.asp.**

Once a Tier 2 student scores above the aimline four consecutive times, he is ready to move back to Tier 1 and continue without the additional support. More importantly, the teacher can also identify someone who has plateaued (scoring below the aim line for four consecutive assessments) and analyze whether difficulties with advanced word reading or fluent reading of text are contributing to the lack of progress. If a student has prepared the passage used for progress monitoring, the results are invalid.

Setting Goals and Monitoring the Progress of Students Who Are Significantly Below Grade Level

The rate at which students normally make gains in reading follows a pattern (Shaywitz, 2003), with the greatest gains occurring in the early school years, then lessening with each subsequent grade. The rate of growth also differs within each school year, with maximum growth occurring at the beginning of the year and then tapering off toward spring (Shaywitz, 2003). Shown below are expected growth rates in oral reading fluency. Rates are displayed in words correct per minute per week. Note that the *realistic* rates reflect the growth rates for typical children moving through the reading curriculum. The more *ambitious* rates apply to students who are behind in reading, as they need to make even greater gains in order to catch up. For example, Grazia is in second grade and performs at grade level. We would expect her rate of growth to be at least 1.5 words correct per minute per week. LaBron is also in second grade but is reading at a low first-grade level. In order for him to catch up, a more ambitious rate of growth of two words correct per minute per week is required.

Grade	Realistic	Ambitious
1	2.0	3.00
2	1.5	2.00
3	1.0	1.50
4	.85	1.10
5	.50	.80
6	.30	.65

Source: Fuchs, L. S., Fuchs, D., Hamlett, C. L., Walz, L., & Germann, G. (1993). Formative evaluation of academic progress: How much growth can we expect? *School Psychology Review, 22*(1), 27–48.

To demonstrate how these growth rates can help you measure the progress of your students who are lagging behind, take the case of Daquan, a fourth grader whose median DORF score at the beginning of the year was 75 wcpm, making him at some risk and eligible for Tier 2 support. Daquan's rate of accuracy in Grade 4 material was 93%, so his reading instruction used Grade 4 material, and his expected growth was based on his performance on Grade 4 passages. (See the section on placing students into the right reader on pp. 200–201.) Daquan's teacher set an ambitious growth rate of 1.10 more words per week for him. This meant that after 10 weeks she expected Daquan to be reading 11 more words correct per minute in Grade 4 material (75 wcpm + (1.10 × 10) = 86 wcpm). At the end of the 10-week period she had Daquan read a Grade 4 passage and he scored 83 wcpm, a little below what was expected. As a result, the teacher added one more extra small-group Tier 2 fluency-building session per week for him.

Another example is Carly, a fifth-grade student who is in Tier 3. In the fall, she read Grade 5 material at a rate of 47 wcpm; her rate of accuracy was 79%. Her teacher, Mr. Braden, continued to "back-test" and assess her on increasingly easier passages at lower grade levels until

In Your Classroom

Using Oral Reading Fluency to set IEP Goals and Objectives

Because oral reading fluency encompasses so many reading skills and is so closely related to reading comprehension, it is an ideal measure to use for setting annual goals and short-term objectives in reading. Here is an example of how oral reading fluency data were used to set annual goals and short-term objectives on the IEP for Ramone, a fifth-grade student with a reading disability. Ramone's instructional level at the beginning of the year was Grade 3. Instructional level is the highest grade level at which he was able to read passages with 90%–94% accuracy. Ramone's median fluency score on third-grade passages was 83 wcpm. Ramone's teacher used an ambitious rate of growth for him of 1.5 words per week to narrow the reading gap between Ramone and his peers. Ramone's goal was to read Grade 3 material at a benchmark rate of 110 words correct per minute by the end of the 18-week term. His short-term objectives were based on growth for two 9-week marking periods: 9 weeks × 1.5 words

correct per week = growth of 14 words correct per minute, per marking period.

Objective 1:

Given three passages at the Grade 3 level, Ramone will read the passages orally with a median rate of at least 97 words correct per minute by the end of the first marking period.

Objective 2:

Given three passages at the Grade 3 level, Ramone will read the passages orally with a median rate of at least 111 words correct per minute by the end of the second marking period.

Because he met benchmarks in Grade 3 passages, when Ramone's second objective was met, a new one was set based on his performance on fourth-grade material.

he determined that she could read third-grade passages with 91% accuracy (instructional level) and 81 wcpm ("some risk" for end of third grade), establishing Grade 3 as her instructional level (see pp. 200–201). Mr. Braden set Carly's growth at an ambitious 1.5 words per week in Grade 3 material. After 4 weeks, he checked her fluency on Grade 3 passages to see if she had made the expected growth of 6 wcpm (a score of 87 wcpm). When he found that she had, he felt comfortable keeping her current instructional supports in place.

For students such as Daquan and Carly who are behind their classmates in reading, short-term instructional progress can be evaluated using passages at their instructional level and the expected growth rates shown above. However, it is important to remember that only oral reading fluency scores at students' chronological grade/age levels show whether they are at benchmark. Thus, Mr. Braden also made sure that Carly was assessed three times per year using benchmark assessments for Grade 5. A way to use oral reading fluency data to set annual goals and short-term objectives on the Individualized Education Plans (IEPs) of students with disabilities is described in the *In Your Classroom* feature.

How Can I Use Oral Reading Fluency to Diagnose Student Reading Needs?

Information gathered from oral reading fluency assessments can help teachers diagnose student skill needs so that more support can be provided if needed. In this section, the collection of three types of diagnostic information is described: reading with expression, diagnosing student error patterns, and placing students in the right reader.

Other sources for graded oral reading passages are available at Edcheckup (**http://www.edcheckup.com**) and Yearly Progress Pro (**http://www. mhdigitallearning.com**). For a Web-based application that creates progress-monitoring graphs, go to Chart Dog at **http://www. interventioncentral.org.**

TABLE 5.1 Prosody Chart

	Expressive Readers	Nonexpressive Readers
Stress (loudness)	▪ Use weak stresses throughout reading. ▪ Stress increases at end of exclamatory sentences.	▪ Often stress every word. ▪ Sometimes use more than one stress per word.
Variations in pitch (intonation)	▪ Have greater variations in pitch—rise and fall in voice pitch. ▪ Use a rising pitch at the end of a sentence that asks a question or that exclaims. ▪ Use a downward pitch for a sentence making a statement.	▪ Have inappropriate pitch changes. Either sustain the same pitch for longer periods or use a rising pitch where a falling one is appropriate.
Duration (how long a word is pronounced)	▪ Lengthen the word/vowel that precedes a comma. Lengthen the last word of a sentence.	▪ Often lengthen other unexpected words in a sentence. ▪ Often do not lengthen words/vowels preceding commas or at the end of a sentence.
Chunk words into appropriate phrases	▪ Use few pauses within sentences. ▪ Use shorter pauses between sentences; shorter pauses after page turn. ▪ Pause at commas. ▪ Use punctuation to group words into natural units. ▪ Often pause at the end of clauses.	▪ Pause between words and within words more frequently; pauses can last longer; often pause after every word; awkward word groups. ▪ Are vulnerable to disruptions in text such as page turns. ▪ Chunk words with little attention to punctuation or clauses within the sentence.

Source: Based on information from Cowie, R., Douglas-Cowie, E., & Wichmann, A. (2002) and Dowhower, S. (1991).

copy above table

Reading with Expression

Although there is a strong relationship between students' oral reading fluency and reading comprehension, the extent to which students read with expression, using a level of **intonation** that reasonably approximates everyday speech, is also related to how well students comprehend what they are reading (Tindal & Marston, 1996). This ability to read text orally using appropriate phrasing, intonation, and attention to punctuation is termed **prosody.** Table 5.1 lists reading behaviors for students who read fluently and with expression compared to those who do not.

Tindal & Marston (1996) validated an assessment for expressive reading that is highly related to standardized tests of reading comprehension and that can be used along with the DIBELS Oral Reading Fluency assessment just described. After students read a passage, the teacher scores their expression using the following 5-point scale:

1 = Reads single words. No "flow." Very choppy.

2 = Some phrasing is noted (2–3 words), but still choppy.

3 = Pauses for ending punctuation. Inflection changes may not be present.

4 = Appropriate "flow" and phrasing is noted as well as attention to punctuation, with pauses and appropriate inflection most of the time.

5 = Reading generally "flows." Voice changes to reflect meaning changes. Appropriate ending inflections.

Although standard norms are not available for the scale, the student averages for fall in grades 1–8 are shown in Figure 5.6.

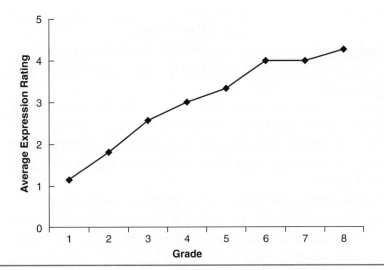

FIGURE 5.6 Average Reading Expression Ratings—Grades 1 to 8, Fall

Source: Tindal, G. & Marston, D. (1996). *Technical adequacy of alternative reading measures as perform-ance assessments.* Exceptionality, 6, 201–230.

It is recommended that you practice scoring with a colleague before you use the results to guide your instruction. During the practice session, you and a colleague should score a student's expressive reading together and compare your ratings, continuing this process until you have 90% agreement. Rating audio- or videotapes of students reading may be more convenient and easier than practicing live.

Diagnosing Student Error Patterns

Information from oral reading fluency assessments, along with the results from the expressive reading scale, helps teachers diagnose specific error patterns so that the appropriate support can be provided. The various error patterns that can be gleaned from the results of these measures are described next. Remember that when interpreting the results of your oral reading fluency and expressive reading assessments, ask yourself this important question before you intervene: Is the information I have collected consistent with the child's everyday performance? If not, you should reassess before using the interventions suggested below.

Low Accuracy, Below Benchmark for Fluency, and Low Prosody Score   Often students with low scores in all three skill areas do not have phonemic awareness and beginning decoding skills, so instruction needs to focus on developing those skills. Students who have those foundational skills but still have low accuracy and fluency typically perform well on CVC words and high-frequency sight words, but tend to make errors on words containing letter combinations and multisyllable words. Shown in Figure 5.7 is the passage-reading performance for Titus on a Grade 1 passage in May. Also in May, Titus scored 57 letter sounds correct per minute with 20 words read as whole words on DIBELS Nonsense Word Fluency.

For students such as Titus, assess knowledge of letter combinations and affixes using an assessment like the one described in Appendix G. The results let you know which letter combinations and affixes need to be taught. Titus can then be taught to decode single- or multisyllable words having these sounds. Practice should include reading the words in both lists and passages. Because of Titus's low accuracy and fluency, one would expect that he

---

Visiting Aunt Rose

My ~~Aunt~~ Rose in~~vit~~ed me to sp~~en~~d the we~~eke~~nd. ~~Aunt~~ Rose	11
doesn't have kids. She said I could be her kid for two days. She's	25
like my big ~~sister~~.	29
I like to go to visit my Aunt Rose's home. She likes to do the	44
same things I like. I like to go swimming. So does my Aunt	57
Rose. The pool where she goes also has a hot tub. I like to sit in	73
the hot tub. So does my Aunt Rose. I always bring my swimming	86
suit when I visit.	90
Our weekend was perfect. On Saturday we went out for	100
breakfast. I had strawberry pancakes with whipped cream. Then	109
we went shopping. She bought me a pink shirt. Then we went	121
swimming and sat in the hot tub.	128
On Sunday she helped me make oatmeal cookies. Then we	138
painted each other's nails. Our fingers and toes match. They are	149
bright pink. Then we went to the movies. We saw *The Lion*	161
King.	162
Aunt Rose drove me home. I handed my mother a plate of	174
the oatmeal cookies. I showed my brother my new shirt. Dad	185
admired my bright pink nails.	190
"Dad," I asked, "could I live at Aunt Rose's?"	199
"No," he said. "If you went there all the time, it wouldn't be a	213
special treat."	215

Total words: 31

Total correct: 25   Total incorrect: 6

FIGURE 5.7   DORF Progress Check: Titus

would also have low prosody. Although the teacher can use some of the fluency practice sessions as an opportunity to increase Titus's awareness of punctuation and how it alters reading, at this stage of reading the focus should center on developing accuracy and fluency.

High Accuracy, Below Benchmark for Fluency, and Low Prosody Score   These students can read grade-level material accurately but slowly. Their oral reading usually lacks expression because they are so preoccupied with identifying each word, and they are unable to think about the meaning of what they are reading. Typical ratings on the expression scale would likely be between 1 and 2. Damon, the student described at the beginning of this chapter, has this type of problem. Students like Damon benefit from a combination of fluency building and practice in developing expression.

At Fluency Benchmark but Low Prosody Score   This smallest group of students read at a rate that is at or above benchmark for their grade, but their expression ratings are below average for their grade level. They show few indications that they are thinking about what they are reading. Problems with expression can include one or more of the following indicators: does not pay attention to punctuation, fails to group words together in meaningful chunks, and intonation shows little resemblance to live speech.

Although Kassandra met the ORF benchmark and decoded all the words, she read the passage in a choppy, monotone voice:

> "Six . . . . . . year . . . . s ago my . . . . . . fam . . . ily . . . . grew from two . . . . . . people to four . . . . . people in . . . . one day. That . . . . . . was the day my sister . . . . . . and I were . . . . born. That was the . . . . . . day Mom . . . . and Dad had . . . . to start . . . ."

As she read, Kassandra did not use appropriate inflection at the end of sentences and did not adapt her reading to account for punctuation. Although she used some phrasing, she frequently paused in the middle of prepositional phrases or verbs. Kassandra would benefit from some of the expression-building activities described in the next section of this chapter. If her lack of expression is due to an oral language deficit or because English is not her primary language, Kassandra will also benefit from oral language activities that build vocabulary and grammatical structures.

Lacking Specific Skills   As you are scoring a student's oral reading performance, you may detect patterns of student errors that indicate difficulty with a particular letter combination, affix, or sight word. For example, when Dominique was reading, he missed the words *coat* and *throat*, pronouncing them as *cot* and *that*, respectively. His teacher Ms. Sanchez detected a skill pattern; Dominique could not decode the letter combination *oa*. Ms. Sanchez noticed that several other students in class were having difficulty with this letter combination as well. Therefore, Ms. Sanchez decided to reteach the *oa* combination, first reintroducing it in isolation using the format in Table 4.5, and then integrating *oa* into the daily word lists using the format in Table 4.7. Ms Sanchez also informally assessed letter combinations and affixes (see Appendix G) because she realized that there were likely to be other combinations and affixes that her students didn't know but that didn't appear in the oral reading passages. Another teacher, Mr. Utomwen, noticed that many of his students were repeatedly missing the word *chaos* in a new story they were reading. Mr. Utomwen retaught the exception word *chaos* using the format for teaching exception words in Table 3.8.

Over- or Underdependence on Context   Sometimes students reading orally make errors that point to no obvious skill deficit. For example, Trais missed 6 words out of 100, but all the words contained different sound patterns. His teacher, Mr. Nguyen, noticed that for all of the errors except one, the word Trais substituted made sense in the context of the sentence but was still incorrect. For example, he read the sentence "Leon laid the book on the table" as "Leon left the book on the table." This pattern of errors revealed that Trais was overly dependent on context. The word *left* made sense but was incorrect and didn't convey the same meaning as *laid*. Students who are overly dependent on context benefit from being rewarded for accuracy in order to break this reading habit. For example, Mr. Nguyen was able to reduce Trais's context errors by rewarding him for accurate reading. He first told Trais, "Your goal is to read these three pages making no more than one error. You'll earn two points for meeting your goal." When Trais was working toward earning points for extra time on the class computer, he was motivated to read more carefully and look at the sounds in the words rather than leaping to conclusions based on what made sense.

Another student, Evan, read the sentence "Simone ran to the *waterfall*" as "Simone ran to the *warning*." Unlike in the previous example, the word Evan substituted did not make sense in context. Evan's teacher, Ms. Williams, had noticed that Evan made this type of error at least three times for every hundred words he read. To help Evan and two other students who had a similar problem, Ms. Williams formed a small group, and for 5 minutes daily she read pairs of sentences to Evan and his classmates in the group. One sentence made sense and one didn't, as in the following examples: "The dog licked his master's hand" and "The dog licked his master's here." The students were required to identify and repeat the sentence that made sense. This simple exercise, originally suggested by Carnine, Silbert, Kame'enui, and Tarver (2010), helped Evan and his classmates begin to think about the meaning of the sentences rather than thinking about them merely as strings of words.

Assigning Students to the Right Reader

Over the course of a typical school day, students are required to read a variety of books for a number of different purposes. The classroom basal reader provides a context for teacher-directed instruction of reading skills. As they read their basals, students are typically provided with instructional support that comes in the form of instruction in word reading, vocabulary, and comprehension. Classrooms with literature-based programs may use trade books as the context for instruction rather than basals. Theoretically, in literature-based programs, students receive similar teacher support but on an individual basis. Teachers may also use these instructional readers with their students to develop fluency, or they may select books specifically for that purpose. Independent reading includes all books students select to read for pleasure or to complete assignments. As these activities are done independently, students are expected to carry them out with minimal teacher support.

Selecting reading material at a level of difficulty appropriate to the activity is important. For example, text that students read with teacher support can be somewhat more difficult than material that students are expected to read independently. In either case, the material cannot be so difficult that students become frustrated.

Armbruster, Lehr, and Osborn (2001) ascribe three levels of difficulty to classroom books or passages: independent-level text, instructional-level text, and frustration-level text. Independent-level texts can be read with at least 95% accuracy on an unrehearsed or "cold read," with no more than 1 in 20 words being difficult for the student. Material at the independent level is appropriate for fluency training as well as any reading task receiving little teacher support. Instructional-level text is unrehearsed material the student can read with at least 90% accuracy, with no more than 1 in 10 words being difficult for the student. Material at the instructional level is appropriate for basal texts or literature-based tasks as long as students get full instructional support as they navigate through the reading.

> Lexile measures can help teachers match students to the appropriate reading material. For more information, go to **http://www.Lexile.com.** You can find book-level equivalencies for PALS and six leveling systems (Basal Level, Guided Reading, Reading Recovery, DRA, Rigby PM Bench, and the Lexile framework) at **http://www.readingrockets.org/articles/21939.**

Frustration-level text is read with less than 90% accuracy. Text at this level is too difficult under any circumstance unless there is a provision for having the material read to the student. Because of their frustration, students who are reading text at this level are likely either to fidget excessively by squirming in their seats or to tune out, looking away from their reading. With leveled books, readability and word difficulty can vary considerably among books designated at one specific level, so teachers cannot assume that because one level J book is at an instructional level for a struggling reader, another level J book is (Mesmer, 2008). Partially because of this variance, caution is advised when using the results of level tests such as the DRA for determining reading level (Rathvon, 2006). Before assigning a book, scan the text to see if it appears to be at the right level. When in doubt, have the student read a representative passage and calculate the percent correct.

Occasionally you will encounter students who can read material as difficult as the third-grade level fluently and accurately, yet their DIBELS NWF scores show they are still at the beginning reading stage. For these students we suggest a careful assessment of their phonics skills along with considerable practice sounding out words and reading decodable text. An example of how to determine whether a book is appropriate for a student is shown in Figure 5.8.

If time permits, you will improve the accuracy of your findings by taking three reading samples from the text and using the median or middle score in deciding on the appropriateness of the book. Table 5.2 shows that Mr. Haas assessed Abdul on three passages from a book and found that his percentages correct were 91, 93, and 95. The median score was 93%, indicating that the book was at Abdul's instructional level. Mr. Haas knew that he would need to provide Abdul with some help if he was to successfully read and comprehend this book, and the book wouldn't be too frustrating for him.

Ms. Luden wanted to see whether a book was appropriate for her student Akayla. Here is what she did.

1. Ms. Luden selected a representative passage of about 200 words from the book and had Akayla read orally for 1 minute. She scored Akayla's performance the same way she did when giving DIBELS Oral Reading Fluency (DORF).

2. Ms. Luden calculated the number of words Akayla read, the number of errors she made, and the number of words she read correctly. The results were as follows:

   Total Words Read = 93
   Errors = 3
   Words Correct = 90

3. Ms. Luden calculated Akayla's percentage correct by dividing the number of words read correctly (90) by the total number of words read (93). Akayla's percentage was 97%, two percentage points above the 95% cutoff for the independent level. The book is appropriate for Akayla to read independently or to build Akayla's fluency.

FIGURE 5.8   Placing Students in the Right Reader

How Do I Teach My Students to Read Passages Accurately and Fluently?

Reading fluency can be viewed within the classic *good news–bad news* framework. The bad news is that reading fluency does not develop naturally for many students. If left alone, it is *not* likely to increase. The good news is that reading fluency can be increased with practice, provided that practice is guided by someone, be it a teacher, classmate, parent, or classroom aide. The two most common techniques used to provide students with reading practice are oral passage reading and strategies that encourage students to read silently, such as Sustained Silent Reading (SSR). In their report, the National Reading Panel (2000) concluded that despite its broad intuitive appeal, at the present time no evidence supports the use of silent reading of material of interest, either in or out of class. Although future studies may show otherwise, this finding seems to make sense when it comes to students who are at risk. These students may be reluctant to put much effort into their silent reading because reading is such a struggle for them. The fact that they are likely to select books that are too difficult or easy for them can further undermine their motivation to read. Finally, students who are learning to read need feedback on their performance, and teachers cannot closely monitor silent reading. For all of these reasons, the teaching strategies for building passage-reading accuracy and fluency covered in this text stress oral passage reading, a method of building fluency for which there is considerable research support. The passage-reading strategy described here includes what is referred to in this text as Successful, Anxiety-Free, Engaged Reading (SAFER).

SAFER Passage Reading

As you learned in Chapter 3, during oral passage reading conducted in the beginning stages of reading development, students read decodable books and respond in unison, sometimes

TABLE 5.2   Calculations for Abdul's Reading Samples

	Words	Errors	Words Correct	% Words Correct
Reading Sample 1	93	8	85	85/93 = 91%
Reading Sample 2	89	6	83	83/89 = 93%
Reading Sample 3	91	5	86	86/91 = 95%

sounding out each word before reading them by sight (see Table 3.9, pp. 121–122). However, once students' NWF scores are at or above 50 sounds per minute with at least 15 whole words read, they are processing sounds in chunks and able to read multisyllable words. Stories become longer, as do sentences. Traditionally at this consolidated alphabetic stage, oral passage reading in general education classes has been conducted using what is commonly called a **round-robin** approach. In this method, all students in the class read aloud from the same book, regardless of their reading levels. The teacher calls on individuals to read, following a predetermined order. Round-robin reading has been correctly criticized in a number of areas. First, when students of varying reading levels all read from the same book, it will be too difficult for some and too easy for others. The students for whom the reading is too easy are likely to become bored. Students called on to read material that is too difficult are likely to become embarrassed and frustrated. Second, when students are called on in a predetermined order, they tend to pay attention to the part they are scheduled to read and ignore the other parts of the passages. Thus, the level of practice the students actually engage in is minimal. If the goal of oral reading is to provide students with a successful experience while building their reading fluency, it is unlikely this goal will be met using round-robin reading.

This text recommends the SAFER procedure as a more effective, high-success, low-stress approach to providing students with needed reading practice. SAFER is based on procedures for instructing group oral reading originally developed by Carnine and colleagues (2010). The SAFER group oral reading procedure incorporates many of the Tier 1 enhancements described in previous chapters and is done with groups of students having similar reading levels. The text read is carefully matched to students' reading levels using an approach described earlier in this chapter. Thus, every student in the group who is asked to orally read text is capable of reading the passages successfully. Using SAFER, students are called on in random order and asked to read amounts of text that vary from one to three sentences, following along with their fingers as other students read. These SAFER components maximize student practice by encouraging students to be attentive even when it is not their turn. They also allow the teacher to monitor student performance. SAFER is also carried out at a perky pace. Teacher talk is kept simple, students are called on quickly and efficiently, comprehension questions focus on key main ideas and supporting details, and errors are corrected quickly yet systematically. Finally, increased practice is provided on an as-needed basis by requiring that students reread stories when their accuracy as a group falls below criterion levels. The teaching procedures for SAFER are shown in Table 5.3.

In Part 1 of SAFER, students read the story orally using the procedures just described. Students are expected to follow along with their fingers when other students in the group are reading, because that ensures that they are paying attention. Finger pointing also allows the teacher to monitor whether they are following along as directed. Before reading the text, the teacher announces the oral reading goal, which is to read the story as a group with at least 97% accuracy. This goal means that for every 100 words read, students are allowed to make three errors. If the accuracy of the group is below 97%, students reread the story. Staying with text until students read it at mastery is important because students should be solid on skills they have learned thus far before moving to a new story, which has even more challenging skills. Sometimes the group scores below 97%, but the errors are due to the performance of only one or two students. In that case, schedule extra passage reading for them instead of requiring the entire group to reread the story. When an error occurs, first let the student read several more words to allow for self-correction. If the student fails to self-correct, the teacher has two options: He can tell the student the word or have the student use the sounding-out strategy. When students misread exception words, the teacher tells students the word. When they misread regular words, students are encouraged to sound out the word or to apply a rule like the VCV or c-rule. The sounding-out correction has to be concise because lengthy corrections can cause the other students in the group to go off task. If a student struggles sounding out the word, the teacher immediately tells the student the word and writes it down so that later she can review the missed word. After reading the word correctly, the student returns to the beginning of the

TABLE 5.3 Format for SAFER (Successful, Anxiety-Free, Engaged Reading)

Objective	Students who have scored 50 sounds per minute or more on a Nonsense Words Fluency assessment reading at least 15 read as whole words or who are reading second-grade or higher leveled text will read a book at their instructional level with at least 97% accuracy.
Materials Needed	Use text that is at the students' instructional level.
Signaling	None
Time	Between 15 and 30 minutes

Instructions	**Teacher**
	Advance Organizers: When you tell students your behavior expectations, remind them that they must use a pointer finger to follow along with the reading. **Steps to reading stories in the curriculum and decodable books:** 1. Conduct prereading comprehension activities. 2. Tell students the error limit for the story. The error limit is based on the number of words in the story. When children exceed the error limit, discontinue reading and have them practice the words they missed before resuming the story. 3. Call on individual students randomly and have them read between 1 and 3 sentences of the story. Expect the other students to follow along with their fingers. 4. If student accuracy is high enough, include comprehension instruction. First determine whether students need questions asked after each sentence, paragraph, or page. 5. Call on students quickly and avoid unnecessary tangential teacher talk by focusing discussion on content, vocabulary, and comprehension strategy(ies) you are teaching or reviewing. (Refer to comprehension and vocabulary strategies in Chapters 6 and 7.) 6. Write missed words on the board. At the end of the story have students sound out each missed regular word and read it. If the word is an exception word, use the initial exception word teaching format to review the word, having students orally spell it. 7. Move on to the next story when students read the story with between 97% and 100% accuracy and they have completed the planned comprehension activities related to the story.
Error Correction	a. When a student makes an error, let the student read several more words, then say, **"Stop."** Do not use an abrupt or loud voice. By waiting you are giving the student a chance to self-correct. b. Point out to the student what error was made, indicating whether he misidentified a word, skipped a line, or omitted a word. c. Model the correct pronunciation of the word, or have the student sound it out. Then, ask the student to read from the beginning of the sentence. Treat omitted words as errors. d. Remember to write the missed word on the board for later practice, as described in Step 6 above. Use the list of story errors as an opportunity for extra word-reading practice.
Perk Up Your Drill	■ When students finish a story, talk briefly about the next story they will read in order to heighten their curiosity and enthusiasm. ■ Most students want the attention they get through answering a question. Instead of looking for students with hands raised to answer your questions, tell your class that you are looking for students who followed along during story reading.
Adaptations	■ Whenever possible, coordinate other activities during the day with the current story. If the story is about growing bean seeds, integrate related activities into your science period. If the story is about a historical character, try to expand on the students' knowledge by developing a related social studies lesson. ■ During story reading, if a student consistently does not follow with her finger, try having her sit next to you so you can redirect more often with a touch on the shoulder or a point to the page. If the tactic still does not work, look at her Oral Reading Fluency scores. Students who are reading text at a frustration level are usually unable to follow along after the first few sentences.

Source: This script is based on one originally developed and field-tested by Carnine, D. W., Silbert, J., Kame'enui, E. J., & Tarver, S. (2010). *Direct instruction reading* (5th ed.). Boston: Merrill Prentice Hall.

sentence and <u>rereads</u>. Making the student reread the sentence allows for immediate practice rereading the word and also enables the student to reestablish the word-reading flow necessary for comprehension. <u>Encouraging accurate reading during SAFER</u> reading sessions helps students who are at risk to develop the <u>habit of paying careful attention to text.</u>

In a study with third-grade children who had learning disabilities, Pany and McCoy (1988) found that students who previously made many oral reading errors significantly improved both on accurate word reading and on comprehension when <u>immediate corrective feedback</u> was given after every oral reading error. In contrast, feedback that was given only on errors related to the meaning of the text had no impact. A rationale for why correction procedures should stress having students look carefully at the word missed is in the *Research Note* feature.

Research Note

Correcting Errors During Oral Passage Reading

An approach commonly recommended by teachers for correcting students' oral reading errors is called the *three-cueing system*. This strategy is based on the assumption that efficient readers use three different systems to attack words: graphophonemic, syntactic, and semantic. **Graphophonemic strategies** involve looking at the letters in words by <u>breaking a word into parts</u> or matching letters and letter combinations with the sounds they make. **Syntactic strategies** involve figuring out whether the word <u>sounds right in the sentence</u>, as if someone were talking. **Semantic strategies** focus on whether or not a word <u>makes sense</u> in a sentence. Advocates of the three-cueing system assume that poor readers miss more words because they are overly dependent on graphophonemic cues or the letters and sounds in words. As explained in the following example, this is not the case.

The purpose of error corrections in the three-cueing system is to focus student attention on syntactical and semantic cues and to de-emphasize looking at the letters in words. After a student error, teachers using the three-cueing system are likely to say, "Does that word make sense?" Then they direct students' attention to the meaning of the words surrounding the missed word or the word order of the sentence. Students are told to look at the letters in the word only as a last resort. In the three-cueing system, only errors that change the meaning of the text are corrected. For example, consider these two student errors in reading the sentence:

The man rode his horse to town.

Student 1 read the word *horse* as /pony/. Student 2 read the word *horse* as /house/. In the three-cueing approach, the first error, identifying the word *horse* as /pony/ would not be corrected because the meaning of the sentence was unchanged. In contrast, the error made by student 2 indicated an overreliance on graphophonemic cues; student 2 would be corrected by being told to use semantic or syntactic cues to figure out the word (Hempenstall, 1999).

Adams (1998) has pointed out that the three-cueing system makes sense from the standpoint of reading comprehension; to get meaning from written text, readers need to use all three types of cues. However, as an approach to word identification, the three-cueing system is not consistent with the research (Adams, 1998). Research comparing the reading errors of good and poor readers has repeatedly demonstrated that proficient readers rely primarily on the letters in words when trying to identify them. The errors of proficient readers show that they most frequently attempt to decipher unknown words by using graphophonemic strategies, in contrast to poor readers, who tend to guess by looking at pictures or using the context (Adams, 1990).

This research, when applied to classroom practice, indicates that when word identification is the objective, graphophonemic cues should be stressed. When students make an error during oral passage reading, regardless of type, the teacher should prompt them to look at the letters in the word and/or sound out the word. This correction discourages guessing by sending the message to learners that it is <u>important to carefully read every word.</u>

Once students are reading longer stories, determining a 97% accuracy level becomes more challenging. A general rule of thumb is that two or fewer errors on a longer page of text is acceptable. Once the students have made between 5 and 10 word-reading errors, stop the oral reading and immediately teach those missed words using the procedures in Table 5.3:

> Learn more about the three-cueing strategy at **http://www.sedl.org/ reading/topics/cueing.html.**

- Students sound out each missed regular word and read it.
- Teacher uses the initial exception-word teaching format to review exception words, having students spell them.

After students have practiced reading the missed words, resume reading from the beginning of the story. This time students should read with a higher level of success.

As individual students in the group read and you record their errors, you are able to detect error patterns that may require new teaching. For example, Mr. Sax's students missed the following words during passage reading: *around, sound,* and *loud.* They struggled with the /ou/ sound in each of these words. Before the students reread the story, Mr. Sax conducted a mini review, first reteaching /ou/ in isolation (see Table 4.5) and then in a word list (see Table 4.7). Just before reading the story, Mr. Sax directed the students' attention to each of the three words in context and had them read each word before starting the story.

If no obvious error patterns are present, it is still helpful to practice missed words in a list before the story is reread. Do not include missed articles or connecting words such as *a, and,* or *the* in lists. Instead point out to the students that one of them was missed and ask the student to reread the sentence. Then remind students about the importance of reading each word in the passage carefully.

A final useful feature of SAFER is that it lends itself readily to including comprehension instruction. As comprehension instruction is covered in more detail in Chapter 7, we only provide several examples here of how it can be integrated into the SAFER reading format. Before students read the passage, teachers use prereading activities related to comprehension. Then, when students can read the passage with 97% accuracy, comprehension instruction is integrated during the passage reading. In many circumstances, when teachers have instructed the more difficult words before students read the text, comprehension can be integrated on the first reading. During SAFER the teacher stops frequently to clarify vocabulary or ideas, model comprehension strategies by thinking out loud, and guide students to monitor their strategy use. Teachers also use graphic organizers and ask students questions related to them. Including comprehension in SAFER has two advantages. First, through modeling, clarifying, and questioning, the teacher is modeling what a good reader does in the active thinking needed for comprehension. Students who are at risk need carefully crafted explicit models for comprehension. In addition, the act of clarifying content as it is read, sentence by sentence, paragraph by paragraph, or page by page, ensures accurate comprehension by preventing misconceptions or correcting them as soon as they occur.

Companion Website

Go to the Video Activities section of Chapter 5 in the Companion Website (www.pearson-highered.com/bursuck2e) and complete the activity entitled *Advanced Word Reading: SAFER.*

Watch a teacher instructing a small group using the script for SAFER reading shown in Table 5.3.

TABLE 5.4   Differences Between Round-Robin and SAFER Reading

Round-Robin Reading	SAFER Reading
1. Students who read out loud are grouped heterogeneously. The text is at a frustration level for some students.	1. Students who read out loud are grouped homogeneously. Although some students who are in Tier 3 may sit in the group to participate in comprehension activities, all students who read out loud can read the text at least at an instructional level.
2. Students are called on to read in a predictable order. Students can anticipate when their turn will occur.	2. Students are called on to read in random order. On any given day, a student may read twice as many times as another student. Students never can anticipate when their turn will occur.
3. Students read large chunks of text, typically a paragraph or a page. Other students can become bored or distracted when someone else reads.	3. Students never read more than three sentences of text and the class moves at a far perkier pace.
4. The teacher corrects errors by telling students the correct word. The student then continues reading. Sometimes the teacher waits a long time for the student to struggle reading the word.	4. The teacher never waits more than 3 seconds to correct the word, so that the student doesn't unduly struggle. The teacher's precise error correction depends upon whether the word is a sight word or a decodable word (see pp. 202–203).
5. Students are not expected to follow text with their fingers and often do not pay attention when other students read.	5. The teacher expects all students to follow the text with their fingers. Students are reinforced for following along with their fingers. Students pay attention and get more practice reading the words silently as other students read out loud.

SAFER and round-robin reading are sometimes confused because in both strategies students read text out loud, and the teacher is able to work with a large group of students at one time. Yet, as we have indicated, these two methods differ significantly. The differences between SAFER and round-robin reading are summarized in Table 5.4.

How Do I Teach Oral Reading Fluency and Expressive Reading?

When the oral reading fluency scores of Tier 2 and Tier 3 students don't increase, fluency training is usually the missing ingredient. Although accuracy in reading is important, often it is not sufficient for fluency. Many students who are at risk require additional practice sessions to develop automatic reading with increasingly more difficult text. As you work to improve your students' reading fluency, remember that activities designed to increase fluency always involve reading aloud. Ideally these fluency sessions are brief activities and involve having students read or reread passages at their instructional level with feedback (O'Connor, White, & Swanson, 2007). You have learned that fluent reading is also dependent on student performance on key phonological, phonic, vocabulary, and syntactical skills (Pikulski & Chard, 2005; Wolf & Katzir-Cohen, 2001). Teachers must take great care to teach these foundational skills to automaticity using the teaching strategies described throughout this text for growth in reading fluency.

Repeated Readings

This method of building student fluency can be done individually or in small groups. It only works if the students have previously read the material at an accuracy rate of 95% or higher.

1. Select a 100–300 word passage from the story just read or from other material.
2. Set a daily goal for each student that is 40% above the students' most recent fluency figure (Carnine et al., 2010). For example: Ray scored 54 words correct per minute on his most recent DORF assessment, so 40% higher than his current rate would be 54 + (54 × .40), or 54 + 22 = 76. Ray's fluency goal is 76 words correct per minute.
3. Time the student's reading of the selected passage for 1 minute. Tell the student that his goal is to read the passage at 76 words correct per minute. If the student meets the goal on the first reading, move to another passage or another student. If the student does not meet the goal, have him continue reading until he meets the goal. It may take between three and five tries to meet the goal.
4. Let the student chart his score to provide extra motivation in the form of a visual record of his progress. See Figure 5.9 for an example of a speed chart.

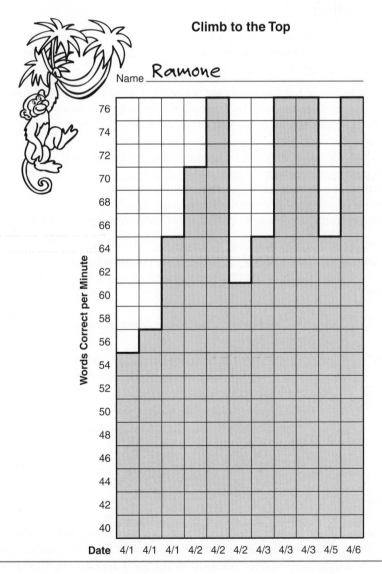

FIGURE 5.9 Chart for Speed Drills

5. Use one or more of the following strategies along with the rereadings when the goal you set is not reached on the first reading:

- Model reading the passage for the student before he rereads the passage. This model can be provided by the teacher, another student, or a taped recording.
- Allow the student to silently read the passage prior to rereading it.
- Provide drill on missed words or phrases after each reading.

Taped Readings

Ask the student to silently read a short passage that she can read with at least 95% accuracy before allowing her to read the passage into a tape recorder. Have her replay the tape so she can follow along with the text in order to listen to how her reading sounds. Encourage her to record the passage again and listen to the improvement.

Partner Reading

Since you are only one person, you cannot schedule enough one-on-one fluency sessions to meet the needs of a classroom where many students are at risk. You can overcome this problem by carefully organizing partner readings.

- Pair students whose reading levels are in the top half of your class with students whose levels are in the bottom half and adjust according to personality issues.
- Select reading material for this activity that the lower-performing student can read with at least 95% accuracy.
- Tell your students that they will be reading partners for the next three weeks.
- Designate the more advanced reader as the first-read partner and always have that student read first to model how the text should be read.
- Give both students the opportunity to read as well as to be tutors.
- Use partner reading to conduct student speed drills or other fluency activities.

An example of partner reading is a routine called Fifteen Minutes to Fluency (adapted from *The Six Minute Solution*, http://www.fcrr.org/FCRRReports/PDF/SixMinuteSolution.pdf). The steps involved in implementing Fifteen Minutes to Fluency are as follows:

Minute 1	Setup: Students get their folders and sit next to an assigned partner.
Minutes 2–6	Practice read for Student 1: Timer set for 5 minutes; Student 1 reads each sentence three times correctly with feedback from Student 2 for errors.
Minute 7	Best read: Timer is set for one minute; Student 1 is reminded to read carefully, but as quickly and smoothly as he can. Student 2 records data during the reading.
Minute 8	Student 1 finds out how many words he correctly read per minute so he can graph his score.
Minutes 9–15	Repeat process with Student 2.

Fifteen Minutes to Fluency requires careful teacher preparation and organization prior to the start of the program. In addition, partners need to be thoroughly taught to assume their role as tutor, and their performance needs to be regularly monitored. Throughout the session, the teacher walks around the room providing specific feedback to students.

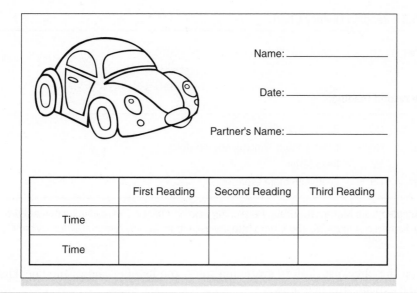

	First Reading	Second Reading	Third Reading
Time			
Time			

FIGURE 5.10   Page Races Worksheet

Page Races

This variation of student speed drills works well with partners. Give each pair of students a timer that you have taught them how to use, a grid for marking times, and a page of independent-level reading. The timer starts when the student begins reading and stops when she reaches the end of the page. The student who is timing tells the reader how fast she read the page before recording the time on the chart depicted in Figure 5.10. The reader's goal is to improve on that time for the second reading. If any words are skipped or missed, the reader starts again.

Echo Reading

Read one sentence of text aloud with appropriate intonation and phrasing. Ask the student to imitate this oral reading model. Continue this pattern of reading until the student can imitate more than one sentence at a time.

Choral Reading

Give your students a short poem or song that they can read with at least 95% accuracy. Practice reading the text in unison until everyone is reading it together as a chorus. Later you can divide the students into groups and assign various parts of the passage to each. Invite the principal to your room and give a short demonstration.

Think About Your Reading

Buy some cheap clipboards at a dollar store and put one copy of the reading fluency chart in Table 5.5 on each clipboard. After giving everyone a copy of the last book they read accurately, a clipboard, and a pencil, demonstrate how a good reader uses expression and phrasing. Then demonstrate how a choppy reader reads the same pages. Tell students that everyone will have a turn to be a listener and a reader, and explain what they will be looking for when their partners read. Divide the students into pairs and have the first reader begin reading. During the first read-through, the listener identifies any words that have been omitted or misread. The second time the story is read, the listener checks off each

TABLE 5.5   Reading Fluency Chart

My Partner_____:

After the second reading:

Yes	No	Read every word correctly.
Yes	No	Read without skipping any words.
Yes	No	Read faster.
Yes	No	Read with more expression.

Source: Adapted from Murray, B. (1999). *Developing reading fluency. The reading genie.* Auburn University. Retrieved August 28, 2009, from http://www.auburn.edu/%7Emurraba/fluency.html

quality on the checklist. Before switching roles, the listener shows the checklist to the reader and explains the markings.

Reading in Chunks

Write a sentence on the board or on student worksheets in chunks of text that match how one would read it aloud. Poems and song lyrics work well for this kind of activity. Model how you read the sentence, pausing at the end of lines, before having everyone read it in unison with you. Practice reading text like this one with the students until you are all reading with one voice:

> "Help! Help!"
> cried the Page
> when the sun got hot.
> "King Bidgood's in the bathtub,
> and he won't get out!
> Oh,
> who knows what to do?" (Wood & Wood, 1985)

Scallop the Text

Take a page of text that students can accurately read and draw scallops connecting phrases that logically are read as a unit. If doing this activity with one student, give him a copy of the page so he can follow the scallop pattern with his fingers as he reads. If doing this with the class, put the page on an overhead transparency so students can follow your finger scoops. Reread the text until the sound, the speed, and rhythm are acceptable. Then ask the student to read the same text without the scallop marks

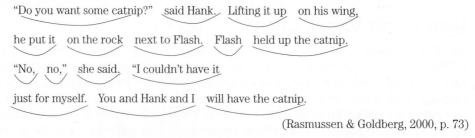

(Rasmussen & Goldberg, 2000, p. 73)

An alternative to scallops is to embed slash marks called phrase boundaries into the text at phrase junctures (Rasinski & Padak, 2008). An illustration of the use of phrase boundaries developed by Hudson, Lane, and Pullen (2005) is shown below. Note that single slashes represent shorter pauses and double slashes indicate longer pauses.

My favorite season / of the year / is summer. // I am so glad / we don't have school / in the summer. // I would rather / spend my time / playing, / and reading. //

Readers' Theatre

As long as students can read them accurately, plays work well for repeated readings with an emphasis on expression. If you are working with a large class, you can divide the students into small choral reading groups to minimize waiting time. The first one or two times through the play, whenever a group reads without expression, model how the group can make the reading sound more lively.

use for play practice

Teaching Intonation

Blevins (2001; cited in Hudson et al., 2005) described a number of ways to teach intonation explicitly. One way is to teach students to recite the alphabet by pretending that it is a conversation to show inflection (e.g., ABCD? EFG! HI? JKL. MN? OPQ. RST! UVWX. YZ!). A similar approach can be used to show the importance of punctuation to meaning by saying the same sentence using different punctuation (e.g., Dogs bark? Dogs bark! Dogs bark.). After modeling each sentence by exaggerating your intonation, ask your students to read and mirror your inflection. Do this type of activity until your students no longer need your modeling to phrase new sentences.

Duet or Shared Reading

In duet reading, the teacher and student sit next to each other and alternate reading words from the same story that has already been read (Engelmann, 2009). The teacher reads the first word, the student reads the next word, and so forth. With younger students or students new to the exercise, the teacher points to the words. Older and more experienced students can point to the words on their own. Duet reading is effective for a number of reasons. First, it is very motivating; students enjoy doing it. Duet reading also provides a built-in model for fluent reading by having the teacher read every other word. Finally, duet reading teaches students to look ahead to anticipate the next word that will be read, a key skill fluent readers possess (Rayner, 1998). Duet reading can also be done with entire groups, with the teacher reading one word and then the class reading the next in unison. Jones and Bursuck (2007) successfully used duet reading with high school students who have learning disabilities as peer partners.

The websites for the following fluency-building programs contain useful information and tips for developing fluency: Read Naturally (**http://www.readnaturally.com**); Great Leaps (**http://www.greatleaps.com**); Jamestown Timed Readings Plus (**http://www.glencoe.com/gln/jamestown/reading_rate/timed_readings_plus_science.php**); and Wilson Fluency (**http://www.wilsonlanguage.com/Fluency_description.html**).

Although related, the strategies used to develop fluency differ from the SAFER strategy used to teach passage reading accuracy described earlier in the chapter. Does teaching passage reading accuracy ultimately improve fluency? Of course. But to be effective, research-based strategies must be applied to learning activities where they are consistent with student objectives. If not, otherwise effective teaching strategies can undermine student progress. When you teach passage reading using SAFER, the immediate objectives are student accuracy and comprehension. When the objective is developing fluency, the focus becomes reading the text accurately and quickly without interruption. Problems can develop when fluency-building activities are substituted for strategies such as SAFER. In Table 5.6, the disadvantages of using

TABLE 5.6 Disadvantages of Using Fluency-Building Activities to Teach Passage Reading Accuracy

Fluency-Building Method	What Is It?	Disadvantages
Reading Text to Students Before They Read	Teacher reads the story or has students listen to it on tape.	▪ Students hear all the unusual new words before reading the story and do not have to decode them. The teacher can be fooled about the students' actual ability to read the text. ▪ This strategy provides too much support for a homogeneous group of students who can read the text at an instructional level.
Choral Reading	Teacher leads the entire class or group in reading aloud in unison.	▪ The teacher is unable to hear students' errors and thus cannot correct them systematically. ▪ The teacher can be fooled about the students' actual ability to read the text.
Echo Reading	Teacher reads a sentence and then the class rereads it aloud.	▪ Same disadvantages as with reading text to students before they read it.
Partner Reading	Pairs of readers alternate reading aloud by a set protocol.	▪ Unless one student in the pair is as accurate a reader as the teacher, and both students have been taught the protocol and follow it exactly, student errors are not corrected.
Whisper Reading or Silent Reading	Each child reads aloud (but not in unison) in a quiet voice.	▪ Teachers are unable to provide the immediate feedback for word-reading errors. ▪ The teacher can be easily fooled that students were able to read the text when they answer comprehension questions that could be answered without reading the story.
Orally Reading to Teacher in Small Groups	Students do SAFER reading in small groups.	▪ Although small-group reading instruction is effective, its use increases the amount of time in which other students in the class do independent work without a teacher's direct instruction. Behavior problems and off-task behaviors often increase when students are not directly working with the teacher for more than 15–20 minutes.

fluency-building activities as substitutes for teaching passage reading using an oral reading method such as SAFER are identified. All of these fluency-building strategies can be more appropriately used to develop fluency *after* students have read the text with 97% accuracy using SAFER.

Strategies for finding time for fluency building during a busy school day are in the *In Your Classroom* feature.

How Important Is Fluency for Older Learners?

Because significant numbers of older students do not read at grade level, many teachers in schools with large numbers of students who are at risk confront the same dilemma as this eighth-grade teacher faced each day:

> This year our district is emphasizing literacy. They gave me a two-hour reading/language arts block. I got a set of eighth-grade literature books and a set of eighth-grade grammar

In Your Classroom

Making Time for Oral Reading

Fluency will only improve if students have the opportunity to read out loud and receive feedback on their reading. You cannot afford to skip oral reading time. Squeeze more oral reading time into the day when you have a few minutes to fill before moving to a new activity.

- When students go to the computer lab, work individually with those at-risk students whose fluency has plateaued.
- If you have a morning field trip, fit reading into the afternoon. Because everyone will be tired, you will need to be especially energetic as you motivate students to do their best work. Reading should never be skipped during a scheduled school day.

- When gym class is canceled for the day, do more oral reading.
- If your students need more oral reading time, make those activities a priority rather than art projects or watching a video.
- If you play a video for your class, pull out one or two students for more oral reading practice. Most of your students would prefer having concentrated time and attention with a teacher rather than watching a video.
- If you have a sustained silent reading time for your class, use the time to work with one to three students for oral reading. If you have the students use their quiet voices and work in a corner of the room, you will not disturb the other students.

books. There are thirty-four kids in the block. Only one or two can actually read the eighth-grade literature book . . . you know, Edgar Allan Poe short stories. It's ridiculous. These kids can't read this stuff. Lots of these kids can't read at more than about third-grade level, if that. I've brought in a lot of books my own kids had when they were little, just to try to get them reading. (Greene, 1998)

One of the greatest challenges for subject-area teachers of older students with reading problems is obtaining reading material that is at students' instructional or independent reading level. Frustration-level text will only result in higher anxiety levels or tuning out. To solve this problem, some teachers scour the Internet and school libraries to find subject-area text that they can photocopy for their students and use for fluency practice.

If previous teachers have not expected older learners to orally read passages accurately in the past, students will initially complain that your high expectations are "picky." In response to the complaining, stop a student after a word-reading error that affects the meaning of the text and point out exactly how the wrong word or omission of the word changes the meaning of the text. Teachers help their students strategically think about the importance of careful reading by periodically explaining that accurate reading is essential for success on the job, for success on quizzes in classes, and for following directions. Because fluent, accurate reading requires so much concentration for the older learner who is not reading at grade level, charting progress on a graph can inject much-needed motivation. Charting progress on a predrawn graph or an Excel (© Microsoft Corporation) program helps students see their progress more concretely.

When content-area text in subjects such as social studies and science is routinely at a frustration level for older students, teachers cannot use the text to improve the students' reading skills. Only oral reading of instructional-level text benefits struggling older readers. However, there are times when students are unable to read their textbooks but need them to gain access to class content. These same students also experience problems communicating what they have learned because they can't read classroom tests. One promising software program to help with these problems is Read & Write Gold Scanning (http://www.readwritegold.com/). This program allows teachers to scan any paper-based document and convert it into an audio file. Students can then listen to their textbooks and tests. Although this method does not provide systematic instruction to increase the reading skills of older learners, the assistive technology allows students full access to the general education curriculum and a fair and equitable way to demonstrate what they have learned. More information about using assistive technology with struggling readers is in the *Technology Note*.

Technology Note

Assistive Technology in Reading

Despite years of remedial intervention aimed at improving their reading skills, reading problems experienced by children and adolescents persist into their preteen and adolescent years. At the same time, these students are spending more time in general education classes where access to content depends largely on reading texts at their frustration level. While attempts to remediate their skill deficits need to continue, **assistive technology** (AT) offers a viable supplement to alternative approaches. AT does not try to improve deficits that have shown resistance to remedial approaches, but rather provides a compensatory approach that circumvents, or "works around," deficits while capitalizing on strengths. AT can allow students to access content independently. With independence comes higher self-esteem, confidence, and the ability to navigate the road to adulthood more successfully (Patton & Polloway, 1992).

For students who are unable to read text in their content-area classes accurately and fluently but have good listening skills, a text-to-speech screen reader can be a bridge between the written text and the students' ability to process information aurally. The particular screen-reading tool required depends on how it is to be used. The various uses for screen-reader programs, along with corresponding examples of AT tools are shown below (Bisagno & Haven, 2002).

Use	AT Tool
Read aloud large volumes of straight text from the computer screen	Simple text (Apple) ReadPlease (PC)
Navigate and search the Internet	eReader (CAST.org) Home Page Reader (IBM)
Provide real-time aural feedback on written text that the student types	Co: Writer 4000 (Don Johnston) WordSmith (textHELP)
Customized visual presentation of text as well as read-aloud	Kurzweil 3000 (Kurzweil Educational Systems) WYNN (Freedom Scientific)
Ebook readers	Kindle (Amazon)Sony 505 Digital Reader

Bisagno and Haven have several additional suggestions when using AT for print access. Using a screen reader requires having an electronic version of the text to be read. E-text can be obtained from online sources such as Bookshare.org. To convert course readers and text not available electronically to e-text, a scanner, OCR software, and adequate editing time are needed. For students who prefer a human to a computerized voice, prerecorded tapes, CDs, or MP3 downloads are available from organizations such as Recording for the Blind and Dyslexic or public and college libraries. CDs have the advantage of being more navigable; a student can go directly to a page without rewinding or fast-forwarding. If a recorded version of a book is not available, an alternative is to have the book read by a volunteer or paid reader. For more technical texts such as science and math, using a human reader who has knowledge of the subject is preferable.

Finally, research suggests that repeated reading interventions to build the reading fluency of older students are less likely to result in gains in comprehension (Edmonds et al., 2009). Students who gain in comprehension are those who are taught to comprehend text directly. Therefore, along with instruction in foundational skills, be sure to provide systematic explicit instruction in comprehension strategies for your older students, always within the context of content-area material and discipline-specific literacy (National Joint Committee on Learning Disabilities, 2008).

Putting the Pieces Together: What Does a Tier 1 Classroom Look Like?

By now the major elements of word reading have been covered including phonics, advanced word reading, and fluency. Here's how all of these pieces can be put together as part of effective Tier 1 instruction.

First and Second Grade

After Christmas, most of Ms. Erdmann's first-grade students in Tiers 1 and 2 met the DIBELS Nonsense Word Fluency benchmarks. Although she encouraged them to sound out longer words, they could easily read only three- and four-letter words with short vowels. Still, adapting the general-education reading curriculum for a class of students who are at risk takes preplanning. If Ms. Erdmann was going to maintain a perky pace throughout her lessons, she needed to know exactly what sounds and words to teach and review. Our teachers have found that summary daily lesson guides help them teach the essential skills each day. Many of the large reading curriculum series include a confusing array of teacher guides, supplementary books, and workbooks. Selecting key skills to cover each day is a daunting task. The summary guides make planning easier, ensure teachers do not omit key words, and help the flow of instruction. One of Ms. Erdmann's daily lesson plans is displayed in Figure 5.11.

On this day, and every day, Ms. Erdmann started with a brief practice of the new letter combination or affix introduced in the curriculum and a review of recently learned ones. These are shown in the letter–sound correspondence section of the lesson outline. Although not shown here, Ms. Erdmann also wrote a list of CVC, VCe, and long-vowel letter combinations so that students had extra practice differentiating *make* from *mash*, *play* from *plan*, and *can* from *cane*.

About 5 minutes after the lesson started, Ms. Erdmann was ready to begin teaching the new words for the day. Before she went through the list, she taught one of the two new vocabulary words (*hatch*) that were in the lesson's story. In addition to teaching students how to decode the targeted vocabulary word, she also taught its meaning.

Then Ms. Erdmann walked to the whiteboard, where she had written the targeted words earlier in the morning. By this time of the year, the new words always included words with new letter combinations and affixes, increasingly more multisyllable words, and a few exception words. On this day, the *ou* and *ow* combinations were being practiced. All of the day's exception words were review words. Ms. Erdmann used word-reading formats from Chapters 3 and 4 to teach these words.

Word reading was followed by reading a decodable story about a hound dog, which provided more practice on the new letter combinations. Ms. Erdmann was glad when second semester came because she preferred the easier SAFER reading format to the earlier unison format. Although she focused on accuracy the first time through the story, Ms. Erdmann also integrated comprehension questions. From past years she knew that decodable stories sometimes needed a little livening up, so she hammed up the dialogue when modeling how a sentence could be read for expression. Ms. Erdmann believed that she could make any story interesting, but sometimes she had to be more theatrical and discuss more background knowledge.

Although she preferred to do more than one reading of the story, Ms. Erdmann still had to include spelling and writing in the literacy schedule. The shopkeeper story was not difficult, so she planned to have her students do partner reading right after lunch. Since her students in Tier 3 were reading different stories, she paired them up to read a story from their reading series. As she began to emphasize fluency more, she had to devise ways to fit in short rereadings. Although she could not count on all her parents, several would listen to their children read if the stories were sent home. Ms. Erdmann encouraged the other students to read to a younger sibling or grandparent so that they could get more practice.

Phonemic Awareness: (already mastered: now embedded in word-reading tasks)

Letter–Sound Correspondences (Table 4.5)

Intro: ou ow (2)

Review: oo (2) sh ew tch ing ue o_e o igh ing ang ung

Regular Words (Tables 4.7 and 4.9)

Intro: br_ow_n, f_ou_nd, h_ow_, cr_ow_n, sc_ou_t, _ou_t, c_ow_, sh_ou_t, l_ou_d, r_ou_nd, d_ow_n, cr_ow_d, n_ow_, st_ou_t, gr_ou_nd, t_ow_n, h_ou_nd

pic nic, rab bit, up set, nap kin, prin cess, bas ket, hap pen, in vent, ten nis, traf fic, down town

Review: playing, splash, moaned

Exception Words (either not decodable or students have not learned to decode letter–sound combinations in these words; Table 3.8)

Intro: no new words

Review: about, because, teacher, could, under, water, through, there

Passage Reading (Table 5.4)

Phonics Library: *The Stout Hound*

Error Limit: 2

Vocabulary (Figure 6.1)

hatch: *Hatch* means to come out of an egg. What does *hatch* mean?

- The egg started to move around because a baby dinosaur was going to come out of it. Was the baby dinosaur going to *hatch* or *not hatch*? Why?

- The green stem of a daisy plant grew out of the ground. Was the plant *hatching* or *not hatching*? Why?

- The baby alligator has a special egg tooth to cut through the egg it has been living in. Does the baby alligator have an egg tooth so he can *hatch* or *not hatch*? Why?

- Desiree slipped on a banana peel when she was running through the cafeteria and landed on the ground. Did Desiree *hatch* or *not hatch*? Why?

- Fish often come out of their eggs in open water. Do the fish *hatch* or *not hatch* in the open water? Why?

- I forgot to water my cactus plant and it died. Did the cactus plant *hatch* or *not hatch*? Why?

- What does *hatch* mean?

Spelling:

Regular Words (Figure 3.12)

Intro: grab grim trap trip

Review: (none)

Irregular Words (Table 3.8 adapted)

Intro: cow, down, now

Review: (none)

Challenge Words: crowded

Comprehension: Complete all of the comprehension and vocabulary activities listed in the book that *will extend students' understanding of the passage and mastery of comprehension strategies and vocabulary.* Many of the grammar and spelling activities contain related comprehension skills.

FIGURE 5.11   First Grade Summary, Daily Lesson Guide 8, Theme 8: Selection 2: Day 1

Beyond Second Grade

By the middle of second grade, students in Tier 1 have learned to decode a large percentage of the most common affixes and letter combinations. Word reading increasingly focuses on teaching students to decode more difficult multisyllable words. Although the classroom routine will be structured like that for first grade, the emphasis on specific activities shifts. Students know their basic phonics skills but still need to apply them to more difficult words. By the middle of second grade, teachers begin to spend a larger percentage of time on vocabulary instruction and comprehension in addition to fluency-building activities.

What Can I Do for Students Who Still Aren't Learning to Read Fluently Even with Enhancements?

By the middle of first grade, progress charts based on oral reading fluency assessments can be used to determine who needs the extra support of Tier 2 (see the earlier assessment section). In Chapter 3 we described a typical first-grade Tier 2 intervention group that meets for 30 minutes as a small group outside the classroom. In the winter semester, when daily words begin to include more long vowels and multisyllable words, first-grade students continue to practice decoding those more difficult words in their Tier 2 sessions. In addition, teachers use extra moments during the day to develop fluency by providing extra decodable reading to students in Tier 2. Any extra volunteers are assigned to provide even more oral reading time. By January, any first-grade student who scores between 30 and 49 wcpm on the DIBELS Nonsense Word Fluency assessment and/or in the "some risk" category on the DIBELS Oral Reading Fluency assessment should receive Tier 2 support. Lower scores indicate that Tier 3 intensive support is needed. Teachers using TPRI, AIMSweb, or PALS need to develop similar decision rules using norms for those measures.

Beginning in second grade when students know the majority of letter combinations, Tier 2 intervention sessions shift their focus almost exclusively to developing fluency by providing an opportunity for rereading stories in the curriculum. Classroom teachers now conduct the Tier 2 sessions by scheduling a daily small reading group at a time of day when other students are independently working or silently reading. If accuracy is high, the teacher might schedule student speed drills one day, do closely monitored partner reading the next day, and do chunk reading on the third day.

What Can I Do for Students Who Still Aren't Learning to Read Fluently Even with Tier 2 Support?

A small group of first-grade students will stay on track for grade-level reading with Tier 2 support as they learn phonemic awareness skills and begin developing alphabetic principle. However, the progress of some students stalls when their DIBELS Nonsense Word Score is in the 20s or low 30s. These students plateau at that level, and even with additional time reading decodables, they are unable to automatically read simple CVC words. Unless these students are moved into a more intensive reading program, they will continue to laboriously sound out each word before reading it. Students who have been in a differentiated instructional program since kindergarten and have not needed intensive support will rarely if ever move to Tier 3 once their decoding skills are established. With explicit teaching they should learn to apply these skills to increasingly longer words. Decision rules for placement into Tier 3 are based on norms for the DIBELS assessments shown in Appendix B. As recommended for Tier 2 decisions, teachers using TPRI, AIMSweb, or PALS need to develop similar decision rules using norms for those measures.

Table 5.7 describes how fluency is taught in several of the alternative Tier 3 programs described in previous chapters. The REWARDS program, designed to increase

TABLE 5.7 Comparison of Four Common Tier 3 Approaches

	Direct Instruction: Reading Mastery	Wilson Reading System	Language!	REWARDS
Does curriculum incorporate fluency practice into lessons after students read stories with high accuracy?	Yes, assessments are timed. In order to move to the next lesson, students must meet the specified accuracy and rate criteria set for the passage.	Emphasis is on prosody rather than on time. Students orally read text while scooping meaningful chunks.	Three "fluency builders" consisting of phonetically predictable words based on skills taught are included in each unit.	Teachers are instructed to have students read carefully selected passages from content-area text. Students record the number of correctly read words on the last timing and transfer the information to a fluency chart.
Are fluency practice sessions scheduled at least several times a week?	Yes, fluency is integrated throughout the curriculum. Performance on timed assessments is graphed.	A minimum of 2–3 lessons per substep is recommended, with the first lesson introducing the concept, the second lesson building accuracy, and the third lesson building fluency.	Yes, 1-minute timings on selected skill drills are done daily until a goal is reached. Performance on timed assessments is graphed.	Fluency practice is included in each of the twenty 40- to 50-minute lessons.
Do fluency practice sessions gradually become more challenging?	Yes, passages include more-difficult words in longer sentences as students progress through the curriculum.	Fluency is not considered to be the number of wcpm, but rather the effortless and accurate decoding of more challenging words.	Words become more challenging, but the basic format of the drill—isolated words—remains the same.	As students learn to read more multisyllable words, teachers are able to select increasingly more difficult content-area text for fluency practice.
Are specific word-per-minute goals established?	Word-per-minute goals are set for reading assessment passages. Recommendations are that first graders finish Reading Mastery 11 by the end of first grade to have grade-level fluency.	No.	Separate fluency goals are set for phonetic words and sight words. Students are expected to reach the goals for 2 out of 3 days for each drill page.	Yes. The wcpm goals are: Grades 4–5: 120–150 Grades 6–8: 150–180 Grades 9–12: 180–200
Is fluency assessed regularly?	Yes, there are assessments every few lessons on passage reading.	No.	Yes, daily through 1-minute timed drills on isolated words.	Yes, daily.
Is fluency practiced with passages and stories that students have previously read with high accuracy?	Yes.	Each sentence and story/passage is read silently, then orally while scooping with finger or pencil.	No.	Accuracy is always stressed before fluency. Students decode difficult words before reading them in passages.

the fluency of struggling older readers who can read at a fourth-grade or higher level, is included in this section for the first time.

In RTI models, Tier placement decisions are based on data, and are typically made by a team consisting of teachers, administrators, and support staff such as school psychologists and speech and language pathologists. A look at how one of our Project PRIDE teams made decisions using data from DIBELS assessments is in the *In Your Classroom* feature.

Read an evaluation of the add-on fluency program for Wilson Language (Wilson Fluency Basic Kit) at **http://www.fcrr.org/FCRRReports/PDF/WilsonFluencyBasic72707.pdf.**

In Your Classroom

A Team Uses Data-Based Decision Making

In January, the first- and second-grade teaching teams looked at the latest DORF scores to plan for Tier changes based on the assessment. Ms. Shackmann served as the recorder so she could compile a master list of changes and photocopy them for everyone. After Christmas, the team realized that a student whose assessment results indicated he should move to Tier 2 for more support had never been moved. The team recognized that improved communication was necessary to avoid such slipups. In order to prevent any other student from slipping through the cracks, the team members each had a form like the one shown in Table 5.8. They used the DIBELS Second Grade Benchmarks posted in Appendix B to determine who was in Tier 1, Tier 2, or Tier 3. During their team meeting, they filled out the last two columns once they made individual student decisions.

TABLE 5.8 Second-Grade Data

Student Name	Teacher	Sept. DIBELS ORF	Nov. DIBELS ORF	Jan. DIBELS ORF	Tier for Dec.	Tier for Jan.	Changes for Jan.
Tony	Jones	50	54	59	1	2	move to 2
Greg	Jones	65	92	106	1	1	—
Jalisha	Jones	9	12	15	3	3	move to a smaller Tier 3 group
Serabia	Jones	50	50	52	2	3	move to 3
Sonya	Jones	55	87	89	1	1	—
Taylor	Jones	43	69	79	2	1	move to 1
Justin	Jones	23	31	47	3	3	—
Simone	Jones	32	43	55	2	2	—
Lanecea	Jones	24	53	73	3	2	move to 2
John	Entwistle	60	66	91	1	1	—
Carrie	Entwistle	38	64	78	2	1	move to 1
Shantrel	Entwistle	46	48	56	1	2	move to 2
Mike	Entwistle	46	53	69	1	1	—
Tan	Entwistle	37	47	61	2	2	—

Continued

Based on the tests scores and confirmation by the teachers that further testing was not needed, the following changes were made:

Lanecea (second grade) moved from Tier 3 to Tier 2. Test results showed that her progress had dramatically increased these past few months, and she was now reading second-grade text at 73 wcpm, a level of performance warranting a move back into the general-education curriculum. However, Lanecea's Reading Mastery teacher was anxious about her moving into Tier 1, afraid that because Lanecea was shy, Tier 1 instruction within the larger class might not provide her with enough support to maintain her success. Although Lanecea's DORF score indicated that she could be placed into Tier 1, the team moved her into Tier 2 to provide her with extra support for the first few months. The team decided that if, following the next progress-monitoring period, Lanecea maintained her current progress in the general-education curriculum, they would move her into Tier 1. The general-education teacher said she thought Lanecea was ready for the move to Tier 1 because she had noticed Lanecea had begun to read the science and social studies materials used in class. The teacher suggested assigning a volunteer tutor to Lanecea for some extra support. Meanwhile, the Reading Mastery teacher would contact Lanecea once a week and ask her about stories she was reading in the new class.

Serabia (second grade), a student diagnosed with ADHD, needed to make a move in the opposite direction from Lanecea. After summer school, Serabia, who had been in Tier 3, was reading at grade level, and after much discussion was moved into Tier 2. In the early fall, she continued to make progress, so the decision seemed appropriate.

However, Serabia's DORF scores were unchanged since November, and she was rapidly falling behind. The team hypothesized that because she was so distractible, the small group had helped her pay more attention to the lessons. Whatever the reason, Serabia needed that extra support and so was moved back to the fastest-moving Tier 3 group.

The team wanted to discuss Jalisha, who was not progressing in her intensive Tier 3 group and whose DORF scores were virtually unchanged. The teaching coach agreed to watch her during reading group to determine if the teaching strategies needed fine-tuning. Following the observation, the coach felt that Jalisha would benefit from working in a smaller group, so a backup plan was worked out. One of the trained paraprofessionals who was an experienced Tier 3 teacher would begin working with Jalisha and another student in a group of two. The team agreed to check back on Jalisha in a month to see if the smaller group had triggered more progress.

Tony and Shantrel needed to move from Tier 1 to Tier 2 because they were still scoring in the 50s on the DORF, below the January cutoff for Tier 1 of 68. Taylor and Carrie no longer needed Tier 2 support. For two assessments in a row, their DORF scores were above the aimline. It was agreed that their general-education teacher would monitor them closely, giving another DORF next month to be sure that they continued making progress without Tier 2 support.

At the end of the team meeting, Ms. Shackmann summarized the changes to make sure her notes were accurate. Because it was Thursday, the team agreed that all the group changes would begin the following Monday.

How Can I Help Develop the Expressive Reading Skills of My English Language Learners?

Many English language learners first need to recognize rhythmic features in spoken English. In some other languages, changed word order indicates emphasis, in contrast to English, which often relies on intonation and stressed words (Celce-Murcia, Brinton, & Goodwin, 1996). Students can easily miss keys to comprehension when listening to a conversation, such as when a sarcastic sentence is interpreted as a statement of fact. Shades of meaning are lost when word emphasis is not interpreted. For example, the meaning of the word *okay* is affected by the way it is said. A reluctant worker who does not want to do a job may say *okay* in a resentful tone of voice, drawing out each syllable. Another person hearing about plans for a much-awaited vacation is likely to enthusiastically respond *okay!* in a thumbs-up tone of voice, signaling approval. A disgruntled teenager who knows she has no other choice but to babysit her brother on a Friday night might roll her eyes and say *okay* in a somewhat sarcastic tone of voice. Interpreting the intention of the speaker and the meaning behind what he is actually saying is a challenge for English language learners. This first step of interpretation is necessary before English language learners can reproduce these expressions in their own speech or in reading dialogue.

You can use dialogue in stories to help develop your English language learners' attention to the meaning of what they are reading. Bring the characters to life and point out expressive changes in their speech, changes that you want your students to hear in their heads as they read the text. For example, in the book *Where the Wild Things Are,* when you come to the passage

> his mother called him "WILD THING!"
> and Max said "I'll EAT YOU UP!"
> so he was sent to bed without eating anything.

you should model the rude, defiant tone that Max used when he talked back to his mother and then go an extra step by explaining that his mother sent him to bed for talking so rudely to her. Model how you overemphasize the word "anything," using hand gestures and facial expressions to convey the concept of *nothing.* Ask everyone to read the sentence using the tone of voice you did. You might want to take the lesson a step further and ask, "Did Max eat bread?" and "Did Max eat dessert?" Expecting your students to reply in full sentences provides even more directly related language practice.

In *Teaching American English Pronunciation* (1992), Avery and Ehrlich suggest these additional activities for helping students develop more expression.

Up and Down the Scale

Students whose first language is not English may need practice saying words with different pitches. When your class is reviewing vocabulary (see Chapter 6), you can use this 1-minute activity portrayed in Figure 5.12. On the board draw an upward-facing arrow alongside the numbers 1 through 5 written in a vertical column. Point to the bottom number (1) and model saying a word in a low pitch before having the student repeat. Point to number 2 and repeat at a slightly higher pitch. Go all the way up the scale until you reach number 5. Then reverse and move down pitch levels. Emphasis is on producing and hearing different levels of pitch and developing vocal muscles necessary to use in speech.

Turn Up the Volume

Show students how to say a letter sound or word, take a breath and say it louder, take a breath and say it louder, and finally take a breath and yell it out. This activity works well for everyone when the class needs a 1-minute break to release energy.

Variety Is the Spice of Life

Have your students memorize a sentence or short poem before changing how they recite it. First ask them to change one thing about their oral presentation. For example:

a. First read the poem *slowly* before reading it *quickly*.
b. First read the poem *quietly* before reading it *loudly*.
c. First read the poem in a *high pitch* before reading it in a *low pitch.*

Once students can change one dynamic, have them change two. For example, ask them to read *slowly* and *quietly* before reading *quickly* and *loudly.* Try some other combinations. Finally, ask students to change three dynamics. Ask them to read the poem *quickly, quietly,* and with a *low pitch.* Ask them to read it *quickly, loudly,* and with a *high pitch.*

5

4

3

2

1

FIGURE 5.12
Up–Down
Scale

What Games and Activities Will Reinforce Students' Fluency Skills?

Once students are fluent with a poem, story, or play, search out opportunities for your students to read the text aloud. Kindergarten teachers may appreciate it if you volunteer a pair of readers each day. Obtain a plastic microphone that plugs into a radio and let students pretend that they are recording on TV. The microphone can also serve as a motivator when students are reading a story for the third time. Poems read by your students can enliven morning announcements. Some schools allow students to read to other students in the lunchroom. Videotape your class reading and let them watch the tape to see themselves. Invite the principal or custodian into class in order to watch a choral reading. Parents always enjoy seeing their children perform. Take your students' fluent reading to the next step and encourage them to read proudly for an audience.

If younger students routinely read past final punctuation as if it is not there, spend a few days conducting punctuation walks. The first time you do this activity, you will need to show your students how you walk your fingers, starting at the beginning of the text and stopping at final punctuation. Ask students to put their two walking fingers on the first word in the sentence. When you say "sentence," tell them to walk their fingers to the end of the sentence, stopping at the punctuation mark. When you repeat the word "sentence," they should walk their fingers to the end of the next sentence. Continue in this pattern until the end of the story. Once students can easily do a basic punctuation walk, you may want to ask them to name the punctuation mark when they reach it. For added emphasis, you can have them say "period" in a matter-of-fact tone of voice; "question mark" with the rising inflection one uses at the end of a questioning sentence; and "exclamation mark" in a dramatic, exclamatory tone.

In this chapter we have covered all the elements that go into teaching reading fluency systematically and explicitly within a multi-tier/RTI system of instruction. A key assumption of RTI is that all Tiers are comprised of research-based practices. Moats (2007) provides a useful comparison between research-based and nonresearch-based strategies for building fluency in Table 5.9.

The effective implementation of RTI depends on teachers having expert classroom management skills. Strategies for making students' independent work more productive are in the *In Your Classroom* feature.

TABLE 5.9   Is Your Fluency Instruction Research-Based?

Research-Based	Not Research-Based
■ Explicit, measurable goals by grade level for oral-passage reading fluency and related subskills.	■ Reading practice in "leveled" books that provide little support for developing decoding skills.
■ Performance criteria established by research.	■ Focus on "miscue analysis" rather than words read accurately; stresses guessing rather than careful decoding.
■ Uses validated techniques such as rereading, partner reading, and reading with a model.	■ No emphasis on building fluency in subskills such as letter sounds and word reading.
	■ Avoids measurement of words correct per minute.
	■ Believes students learn to read by reading, not by instruction on specific skills.

Source: Adapted from Moats, L. (2007). *Whole language high jinks: How to tell when "scientifically-based reading instruction" isn't.* Thomas B. Fordham Institute (ERIC Document Reproduction Service No. ED 4980005).

In Your Classroom

Working Independently

When a teacher works with one group of students on fluency practice, the other students need to be engaged in productive work that will not disrupt the reading group. One key to conducting smaller reading groups is to recognize that some students have never learned to work independently. Independent work skills require specific instruction and practice, just as other classroom skills and knowledge do. Six steps used to teach independent work skills are listed, followed by more detailed descriptions for each step:

1. Identify and explain the skills and rules necessary to work independently.
2. Show students what working independently looks like.
3. Give students practice working independently in small groups with well-defined activities while you monitor closely. Use a timer to establish a clear concrete beginning and end to the independent work-time practice.
4. When working with a small reading group, sit facing students who are working independently in order to maximize monitoring. Use the timer until students no longer need it as a reminder.
5. Provide feedback and reward students for working independently.
6. Make adaptations for individual students when necessary.

Prepare for Teaching Students to Work Independently

Before you begin teaching students to work independently, determine several activities students can complete independently with at least 90% success. Students will not work quietly if they are frustrated. If Ms. Legolis introduced describing words on Monday and Tuesday and on the same days asked her students to work independently on a worksheet that required them to find describing words in sentences, many of the students would still not have the skills to do that work. The

ensuing frustration could lead to off-task behaviors. In contrast, if Mr. Dane gave his students a review sheet requiring them to circle the nouns and verbs, a skill that they learned well but still needed to review, the students would have the skills to do that work. Giving students a task to complete when they do not have the skills to complete it independently sets them up for failure.

Step 1: Identify and explain the skills and rules necessary to work independently.

Establish and enforce rules for independent work times. You might want to use the following rules:

- Respect others by keeping hands, feet, and personal objects to yourself.
- Once the timer is set, no talking is allowed until the timer rings. Don't interrupt the teacher when she is working with a group. For 15 minutes no one is allowed to talk.
- Work on your assigned activity at your assigned spot until the timer rings. If you are working at the tables and finish your work, then select one of the books in the middle of the table to silently read/scan.
- If you follow the rules after the timer is set, you'll earn 5 points when the timer rings.

Some classes require very tight rules and don't allow talking or laughing during this independent work time. Teachers who decide to set such stringent rules know that in their class a quiet giggle can turn into raucous laughter, disturbing everyone's work, or that a quiet request for help from one's neighbor can easily turn into shoving. In other classes, students can sharpen pencils when needed or quietly ask a neighbor for help. The teacher has to determine the maturity level of the class before establishing rules. Students typically will fit into one of the three categories described in Figure 5.13.

The Project PRIDE teachers found that students willingly worked quietly in order to earn a point for their

---

☺ Those students whom you encourage to **neatly complete** all work.

☺ Those students whom you encourage to complete **all** work.

☺ Those students who are still working on **following the quiet rules** while sitting with their work. You know that it is a challenge for these students to sit quietly and hope to increase the quality of their independent work gradually.

FIGURE 5.13 Expectations for Independent Work

Continued

team or table. A display chart on the wall was used for the cumulative point totals. Some teachers used a more concrete award after teams earned 20 or 30 points. Other teachers found that students were motivated by the rising point totals on the displayed chart.

Step 2: Show students what working independently looks like.

Your students who have the greatest need to learn independent work skills are those who will profit least from your verbal descriptions. Show these students what working independently looks like. Tell your students that you want to show them what quiet working looks like and sit at a desk with a pencil and paper. After quietly working for several seconds, tell students what you are doing and refer to the rules: *"This is quiet working. Mrs. Bara is quietly working until the timer rings."* Move to a computer and work quietly for a few seconds, once again telling students, *"This is quiet working. Mrs. Bara is working without interrupting the teacher."* Return to a table and read a book before telling students, *"This is quiet working. Mrs. Bara finished her work and took a book on the pile next to the table."* Your lesson will make more of an impression on students if you also include nonexamples. At this point you can add a bit of humor and theatrics for motivation. Sit next to one of the students at a table and start chatting with him. Tell your students, *"This is not quiet working. Mrs. Bara forgot and is talking."* If students are not supposed to go to the pencil sharpener during quiet work time, pretend you are a student who has left her seat to do that, and once again say, *"This is not quiet working. Mrs. Bara forgot that she isn't supposed to sharpen pencils during quiet work time."*

After showing the students examples and nonexamples, ask them more abstract questions and tell them to put their thumbs up or down depending on the answer:

- *"Should I talk to my neighbor and ask for her pencil?"* Dramatically shake your head "no" and expect that the students have their thumbs down.
- *"Should I work like this?"* As you quietly work, look to see all thumbs up.
- *"Should I get up and go to the sink?"* Another emphatic head-shaking "no."

Step 3: Give students practice working independently in small groups with well-defined activities while you monitor closely.

If simply talking about and watching the teacher model good behavior were enough, schools would have far fewer discipline problems. However, as with any skill, learning how to work independently takes practice. First, ask three or four students to come up and show everyone else how they can quietly work on a paper while everyone else watches. After 2 or

3 minutes, praise their quiet working and ask the rest of the class to clap for them.

After the small group has modeled quiet, independent working, tell the class that it is now their turn to practice. Set the timer for a predetermined number of minutes. Give the students a worksheet or project they can easily do. Before you set the timer, remind the students of the rules. For kindergarten, set the timer for only 1 minute; for second grade and above, set it for 3 or 4 minutes. You need everyone to be successful this first time. As students work, closely monitor as you walk around the room so you can redirect anyone who is not following the rules. Any time students break a rule, remind them that they are not working and must get back to work. When the timer rings, praise the students who have followed the rules and give team points to rows of students who worked diligently. In a matter-of-fact tone of voice, tell teams that haven't earned points why they didn't earn them: *"Two students at table four were talking. That team doesn't earn a point."* If students were not successful, tell the class that they need to practice again until they are successful, and repeat the process.

Practice quiet independent work using the timer at least twice a day. Gradually increase the time until students can work independently for longer periods of time.

Step 4: When working with a small reading group, sit facing students who are working independently in order to maximize monitoring. Use the timer until students no longer need it as a reminder.

Once students can independently work for 10 minutes, you can begin holding reading groups during that time. Sit facing the class with your all-seeing eye focused to catch any rule infractions. If you are successful in teaching your students to work independently, you should rarely need to say anything.

Step 5: Provide feedback and reward students for working independently.

Always provide verbal feedback at the end of the independent work time and award points. When students reach second grade, a 20-minute stretch of independent work is realistic.

Step 6: Make adaptations for individual students if necessary.

Even when you have followed all these steps in teaching students to work independently, some students may still need a little extra structure. For example, if you have an extremely impulsive student who needs more monitoring, pull up a desk near you and have that student work in closer physical proximity to your booster group. The student can still earn the point for working, as long as he can follow the rules in the period during which the timer is set.

APPLIED ACTIVITIES

1. Two fact-or-fiction questions about reading fluency are included below. Pair up with a partner and take turns defending your position for one of these questions using references from research sources cited in the chapter or from information on the website resources listed in the sidebars.
   a. Student ability to read passages accurately and fluently is highly correlated to scores on high-stakes state tests of reading comprehension. Is this fact or fiction? Explain why.
   b. It is not necessary to correct student errors in oral passage reading when those errors retain the meaning of the passage. Is this fact or fiction? Explain why.

2. Use the DIBELS tables in Appendix B to identify which of the following students' May oral reading fluency scores are at benchmark:

Marissa	Second Grade ORF	=	65 wcpm
Phil	Third Grade ORF	=	111 wcpm
Zion	First Grade ORF	=	36 wcpm
Sean	Fourth Grade ORF	=	112 wcpm
Grayson	First Grade ORF	=	61 wcpm
Mario	Second Grade ORF	=	93 wcpm
Glenn	Fourth Grade ORF	=	122 wcpm
Jaquesia	Third Grade ORF	=	101 wcpm
Jolynn	Fifth Grade ORF	=	129 wcpm
Christopher	Fourth Grade ORF	=	131 wcpm
Leroy	Third Grade ORF	=	98 wcpm
Won Chui	Second Grade ORF	=	82 wcpm
Tameka	First Grade ORF	=	33 wcpm

3. Replicate Misuou's ORF progress chart that appears on page 193.

4. A third-grade student, Juan, read 62 wcpm on the DIBELS Oral Reading Fluency assessment he took during the first week of September. When he was retested 6 weeks later, his teacher, Mr. Staley, used the *rate of expected weekly growth* chart on page 194 to determine whether Juan's score of 75 wcpm showed progress similar to a *typically successful* child in third grade. What did Mr. Staley find?

5. Because Ruben, a first grader, is behind his peers in oral reading fluency, Mrs. Wasmullen wants to make sure that his weekly gain in words read correctly per minute is at least at the *"ambitious"* level noted on the *rate of expected weekly growth* chart. If Ruben is reading 15 wcpm in January, how many words per minute should he be reading 10 weeks later to show a rate of progress at the *ambitious* level?

6. Latisha is a second-grade student in Ms. Carter's class. Latisha scored 45 words correct per minute on the January administration of the DIBELS Oral Reading Fluency assessment. This score was well below the January benchmark of 68 words correct per minute. Describe the steps Ms. Carter needs to take as she uses *repeated readings* to build Latisha's fluency.

7. In December, Sara's third-grade teacher gave her three passages to read aloud, in order to assess her fluency. On the first passage Sara made nine errors, reading a total of 83 words; on the second passage Sara made 10 errors, reading a total of 67 words; on the third passage Sara made eight errors, reading a total of 94 words. What was Sara's median words-correct-per-minute score? Identify Sara's areas of need. What other assessment that you have learned about in this book would you also give to Sara, and why?

8. Form a group with three other students from your class, select a page from this book, and take turns conducting a SAFER reading group using the format from Table 5.3. One person in the group should be designated to miss three words. After each person has a turn teaching the group, give feedback on how closely he followed the format. Was the error-correction procedure followed? Was the pace perky? Were turns between one and three sentences? Did you write missed words so you could practice them after the reading?

9. Select three sequential reading lessons from a first-grade regular-education reading curriculum and develop a guide sheet for each lesson to accompany that day's lesson. Use the adapted lesson guide in Figure 5.11 as your model to identify critical reading skills.

10. Mr. Orcutt is a second-grade teacher. In December he noticed that many of his students were below the aimline for reading at grade level by the end of the year. He decided to set aside 15 to 20 minutes every day for fluency activities. As of Friday, his students read a long story about a mountain lion with 97% accuracy. Develop a week's worth of lesson plans for the fluency portion of his reading period based on his teaching 26 pages about mountain lions. How many pages will students read for fluency development? Will they practice fluency activities with the same or different pages every day? Adjust your plans so you are prepared to account for student success or failure.

11. *First Step:* Make a progress chart for Janelle, who is a fourth grader. Include an aimline based on her September assessment. Use the following information to get started:

   You plan to give Janelle an ORF assessment in September, November, January, and May. Her first score in September is 80 wcpm. She is a relatively accurate reader, missing only two words.

Second Step: Once you have developed the progress chart that includes an aimline, fill in the following information:

Janelle's November score was 89 wcpm, her January score was 88 wcpm, and her May score was 102 wcpm. All her readings continue to show a high rate of accuracy.

Third Step: Determine whether Janelle met the fourth-grade benchmark. Was there any point during the year when you would have recommended more support for Janelle? If so, describe in detail what type of support you would have provided. What Tier placement do you think would provide appropriate support based on the ORF scores?

12. Break up into groups of three and discuss your experiences of learning a foreign language. When you read aloud in the foreign language, how did your prosody and speed compare with those in English? When you spoke the language you were learning, how did your fluency compare to your everyday language? Did any teaching techniques that the foreign-language teacher used help you become more fluent? What were some strategies that the foreign-language teacher could have used to help your prosody?

13. Identify which error pattern each of the following students display. Also describe what teaching format from the text you would use to remediate.

a. Dasia was reading Grade 2 passages and missed the following words (what Dasia said is in parentheses):

couch (cook)   round (ruined)
sound (send)   ground (grinned)

b. Esmerelda is a third-grade student who is unable to read even Grade 1– level material accurately and fluently. Her most recent score on DIBELS NWF was 37. Esmerelda still confuses long and short vowels.

c. Ramona scored at the benchmark level of 110 on Grade 3 material. However, when she reads she fails to address punctuation and reads with little intonation.

Companion Website

Now go to Chapter 5 in the Companion Website (www.pearsonhighered.com/bursuck2e) where you can:

- Complete Activities that can help you more deeply understand the chapter content.
- Check your comprehension on the content covered in the chapter by going to the Chapter Quiz. Here you will be able to answer practice questions, receive feedback on your answers, and then access resources that will enhance your understanding of chapter content.
- Find Web Links that will extend your understanding of the content and strategies.

REFERENCES

Adams, H. (1990). *Beginning to read: Thinking and learning about print.* Cambridge, MA: MIT Press.

Adams, M. J. (1998). The three-cueing system. In F. Lehr and J. Osborn (Eds.), *Literacy for all issues in teaching and learning* (pp. 73–99). New York: The Guilford Press.

Archer, A. L., Gleason, M. M., & Vachon, V. L. (2000) *REWARDS: Reading Excellence: Word Attack and Rate Development Strategies multisyllabic word reading strategies.* Frederick, CO: Sopris West–Cambrium Learning Group.

Archer, A. L., Gleason, M. M., & Vachon, V. L. (2003). Decoding and fluency: Foundation skills. *Learning Disability Quarterly, 26*(2), 89.

Armbruster, B., Lehr, F., & Osborn, J. (2001). *Put reading first: The research building blocks for teaching children to read.* Washington, DC: Partnership for Reading.

Avery, P., & Ehrlich, S. (1992). *Teaching American English pronunciation.* New York: Oxford Press, p. 48.

Bisagno, J. M., & Haven, R. M. (2002, Spring). Customizing technology solutions for college students with learning disabilities. International Dyslexia Association quarterly newsletter, *Perspectives,* 21–26. Retrieved February 10, 2010, from LDOnline: http://www.ldonline.org/ld_indepth/technology/customizing_technology.html

Blevins, W. (2001). *Building fluency: Lessons and strategies for reading success.* Scranton, PA: Scholastic.

Carnine, D. W., Silbert, J., Kame'enui, E. J., & Tarver, S. (2010). *Direct instruction reading* (5th ed.). Boston: Merrill Prentice Hall.

Celce-Murcia, M., Brinton, D., & Goodwin, J. (1996). *Teaching pronunciation: Reference for teachers of English to speakers of other languages.* Cambridge: Cambridge University Press.

Chard, D. J., Ketterlin-Geller, L. R., Baker, S. K., Doabler, C., & Apichatabutra, C. (2009). Repeated reading interventions for students with learning disabilities: Status of evidence. *Exceptional Children, 75,* 263–281.

Cowie, R., Douglas-Cowie, E., & Wichmann, A. (2002). Prosodic characteristics of skilled reading: Fluency and expressiveness in 8–10-year-old readers. *Language and Speech, 45*(1), 47–82.

Crawford, D. (2004, May). (personal communication).

Deno, S. L. (1985). Curriculum-based measurement: The emerging alternative. *Exceptional Children, 52*(3), 219–232.

Dowhower, S. (1991). Speaking of prosody: Fluency's unattended bedfellow. *Theory into Practice, 30*(3), 165–175.

Edmonds, M. S., et al. (2009). A synthesis of reading interventions and effects on reading comprehension outcomes on older struggling readers. *Review of Educational Research, 79*(1), 262–287.

Engelmann, S. (2009). Improving reading rate of low performers. Retrieved July 21, 2009, from http://www.zigsite.com/PDFs/readingrate.pdf

Engelmann, S., & Bruner, E. (1995). *Reading Mastery I: Teacher's guide.* Columbus, OH: SRA Macmillan/McGraw-Hill.

Fuchs, L. S., Fuchs, D., Hamlett, C. L., Walz, L., & Germann, G. (1993). Formative evaluation of academic progress: How much growth can we expect? *School Psychology Review, 22*(1), 27–48.

Fuchs, L. S., Fuchs, D., Hosp, M. K., & Jenkins, J. R. (2001). Oral reading fluency as an indicator of reading competence: A theoretical, empirical, and historical analysis. *Scientific Studies of Reading, 5*(3), 239–256.

Fuchs, L. S., Fuchs, D., & Maxwell, L. (1988). The validity of informal reading comprehension measures. *Remedial and Special Education, 9*(2), 20–28.

Good, R. H., Simmons, D., Kame'enui, E. A., & Wallin, J. (2002). *Summary of decision rules for intensive, strategic, and benchmark instruction—recommendations in kindergarten through third grade* (Technical Report No. 11). Eugene, OR: University of Oregon.

Greene, J. (1998). Another chance: Help for older students with limited literacy. *American Educator,* Spring/Summer, 1–6. Retrieved June 12, 2009, from http://www.aft.org/pubs-reports/american_educator/spring_sum98/greene.pdf

Greene, J. (2009). *Language! The comprehensive literacy curriculum.* Sopris West Educational Services. Longmont, CO. Available at www.sopriswest.com

Hasbrouck, J. E., & Tindal, G. (2006). Oral reading fluency norms: A valuable assessment tool for reading teachers. *The Reading Teacher, 59,* 636–644.

Hempenstall, K. (1999). Miscue analysis: A critique. *Effective School Practices, 17*(3), 85–93.

Hudson, R. F., Lane, H. B., & Pullen, P. C. (2005). Reading fluency assessment and instruction: What, why, and how? *The Reading Teacher, 58,* 702–714.

Jenkins, J. R., Graff, J. J., & Miglioretti, D. L. (2009). Estimating reading growth using intermittent CBM progress monitoring. *Exceptional Children, 75,* 151–163.

Jones, A., & Bursuck, W. (2007). Use of a variation of duet reading to increase the reading fluency of two high school students with learning disabilities. *Direct Instruction News: Effective School Practices, 7*(3), 12–15.

Lee, J., Grigg, W., and Donahue, P. (2007). *The nation's report card: Reading 2007* (NCES 2007-496). National Center for Education Statistics, Institute of Education Sciences, U.S. Department of Education, Washington, DC.

Mesmer, H. (2008). *Tools for matching readers to texts: Research-based practices solving problems in the teaching of literacy.* New York: The Guilford Press.

Moats, L. (2007). *Whole language high jinks: How to tell when "scientifically-based reading instruction" isn't.* Thomas B. Fordham Institute (ERIC Document Reproduction Service No. ED 4980005).

Murray, B. (1999). Developing reading fluency. The Reading Genie. Auburn University. Retrieved August 28, 2009, from http://www.auburn.edu/academic/education/reading_genie/fluency.html

National Joint Committee on Learning Disabilities. (2008). Adolescent literacy and older students with learning disabilities. *Learning Disability Quarterly, 31,* 211–218.

National Reading Panel. (2000). *Teaching children to read: An evidence-based assessment of the scientific research literature on reading and its implications for reading instruction.* Washington, DC: National Institute of Child Health and Human Development.

O'Connor, R. (2007). *Teaching word recognition: Effective strategies for students with learning difficulties.* New York: The Guilford Press.

O'Connor, R. E., White, A., & Swanson, H. L. (2007). Repeated reading versus continuous reading: Influences on reading comprehension. *Exceptional Children, 74,* 31–46.

Pany, D., & McCoy, K. M. (1988). Effects of corrective feedback on word accuracy and reading comprehension of readers with learning disabilities. *Journal of Learning Disabilities, 21,* 546–550.

Patton, J. R., & Polloway, E. A. (1992). Learning disabilities: The challenge of adulthood. *Journal of Learning Disabilities, 25,* 410–415, 447.

Pikulski, J. J., & Chard, D. J. (2005). Fluency: Bridge between decoding and reading comprehension. *The Reading Teacher, 58,* 510–519.

Rasinski, T. V., & Padak, N. D. (2008). *From phonics to fluency: Effective teaching of decoding and reading fluency in the elementary school.* Boston: Pearson/Allyn & Bacon.

Rasmussen, D., & Goldberg, L. (2000). *A king on a swing.* Columbus, OH: SRA, 73.

Rathvon, N. (2006). *Developmental reading assessment.* Retrieved from http://www.natalierathvon.com/images/DRA_ Review-08-25-2006.pdf

Rayner, K. (1998). Eye movements in reading and information processing: 20 years of research. *Psychological Bulletin, 124*(3), 372–422.

Shaywitz, S. (2003). *Overcoming dyslexia: A new and complete science-based program for reading problems at any level.* New York: Alfred A. Knopf.

Stanovich, K. E. (1986). Matthew effects in reading: Some consequences of individual differences in the acquisition of literacy. *Reading Research Quarterly, 21,* 360–407.

Tindal, G., & Marston, D. (1996). Technical adequacy of alternative reading measures as performance assessments. *Exceptionality, 6,* 201–230.

Wiederhold, J., & Bryant, J. (2001). *Gray Oral Reading Tests: GORT-4.* Austin, TX: Pro-Ed.

Wilson, B. (2004). *Wilson reading system.* Millbury, MA: Wilson Language Training Corporation.

Wolf, M., & Katzir-Cohen, T. (2001). Reading fluency and its intervention [Special Issue on Fluency]. *Scientific Studies of Reading, 5,* 211–238.

Wood, A., & Wood, D. (1985). *King Bidgood's in the bathtub.* New York: Harcourt Brace Jovanovich.

6 Vocabulary Instruction

Objectives

After reading this chapter, you will be able to:

1. State guidelines for deciding which vocabulary words to teach and how to assess them.

2. Implement strategies for teaching new vocabulary directly and indirectly.

3. Implement strategies to teach students to answer vocabulary questions on high-stakes tests.

4. Describe ways to provide extra vocabulary practice for students in a multi-tier or RTI program.

5. Describe strategies for teaching vocabulary to older students and English language learners.

Companion Website

To check your comprehension of the content covered in this chapter, go to the Companion Website (www.pearsonhighered.com/bursuck2e) and complete the Chapter Quiz for Chapter 6. Here you will be able to answer practice questions, receive feedback on your answers, and then access resources that will enhance your understanding of chapter content.

When Ms. Reed's students read the story *Coyote Places the Stars* (Taylor, 1993), she knew that many of them didn't know the meaning of *bounded* in the following sentence:

Bears *bounded* out of their dens.

Ms. Reed told her students, *"Bounded means jumped lightly along. When the bears bounded out of their dens, they jumped lightly along out of the dens."* She emphasized the past tense ending to the verb as she described the action. She further explained that the bears were bounding along because they were curious to see what the Coyote had done with the stars. Ms. Reed pointed to the word *bounded* that she had printed earlier on the whiteboard, asked the students to read it, and then had Delarnes, one of her students who received extra Tier 2 support, print the word on a sticky note and put it on the word wall. Before the students lined up for lunch she had Delarnes and one or two other students "walk the wall," asking them to read all the new vocabulary words for the week, including *bounded,* and explain their meanings. Ms. Reed's students in Tier 3 also participated, but they were only required to tell the meanings of the words. When her students came in from recess, Ms. Reed pointed out how she saw Josie and Raymond *bounding* over to the door from the swings. Sam, with a proud, expectant look on his face, raised his hand and asked whether *bounding* was like bouncing. Ms. Reed complimented him on recognizing such a good synonym. Later that afternoon during writing, she noticed that one of the students had used the word *bounded* in his story. Ms. Reed praised him and taped his paper to the "Good Work" board.

In a younger classroom down the hall, Ms. Falth's Tier 3 students were reading *Lad and the Fat Cat,* one of the beginning decodable *Bob* books (Maslen & Maslen, 2006). One of the pages shows a cat sitting in a box with the words *The cat is Kit. Kit sat in a box.* After students read this page, Ms. Falth engaged them in a discussion about the word *independent.* She explained that cats are very *independent* and asked the students to say the new vocabulary word. Ms. Falth then explained that the word *independent* means doing things on your own. She described ways that her cat at home showed his independence. She then asked her students to give examples from their own lives about independent cats they had known. Ms. Falth then showed students the picture of the cat in the box and asked how they thought the cat felt about being in the box, given its independent nature. She concluded the discussion by asking students about things they liked to do independently, on their own. When students answered in partial sentences, she modeled a full sentence before asking them to repeat it so that they had the opportunity to use the word *independent* as part of the answer.

How are Ms. Reed and Ms. Falth similar in their approach to teaching vocabulary?

What teaching behaviors are likely to expand the vocabularies of students who are at risk?

In Chapters 2 through 5 you learned how to teach students to read accurately and fluently. While accurate, fluent reading is necessary for reading with understanding, it is not sufficient. Students also need to know the meanings of the words they are reading. As students move into reading third- and fourth-grade-level text, a larger percentage of your instruction will shift toward teaching students to comprehend increasingly difficult text. Their success in understanding text hinges on knowing the meanings of the words they now can decode. In Chapter 6 you will learn about the key role that vocabulary instruction plays in reading.

Both decoding and comprehension are easier when students have an extensive vocabulary. If students already know the meaning of a word, they can blend words more readily after reading the individual parts, particularly for multisyllable words. For example, Alex was trying to read the word *hilarious.* He was able to read the regular parts /hil/ and /ous/. He then began to try different sounds for the irregular vowels in the middle of the word. After trying several sounds, he was able to make the connection between his oral knowledge of the word *hilarious* and the written word *hilarious* because the word was part of his oral vocabulary. Of course Alex's previous knowledge of the word *hilarious* could have also helped him decode the word using context clues. Decoding, vocabulary knowledge, and context clues enable the reader to read the new word quickly and accurately at this level of reading.

This relationship between decoding and vocabulary knowledge is reciprocal. Ehri (2000) explains that seeing a new vocabulary word activates the connections between its written letters and their sounds. As a result of making this automatic graphophonemic connection, a student is more likely to remember the word and its meaning than if he had not seen the word's spelling. The implication is that vocabulary instruction is more effective when the written word is included because of the association between the letters and sounds representing the word and their connection to memory (Ehri, 2005). Increasing the likelihood that a student will retain a new vocabulary word in long-term memory is not the only contribution that graphophonemic connections contribute to learning vocabulary. Joshi, Treiman, Carreker, & Moats (2008–2009) explain:

> Good spellers not only demonstrate a good sense of the sounds in words, they also have a good sense of the meaningful parts of words (e.g., *un-*, *desir[e]*, *-able*), the roles words play in sentences (e.g., *packed* is a past-tense verb, but *pact* is a noun), and the relationships among words' meanings that exist in spite of differences in their sounds (e.g., *image* and *imagination*).

What Is Vocabulary Instruction and Why Do I Need to Teach It?

Knowledge of vocabulary is also related to reading comprehension. As students learn to decode text of increasing difficulty, they are more likely to encounter words that are not part of their oral language, especially when reading expository text. As a result, students often need instruction in key vocabulary to make sense of what they are reading. Often a significant gap in vocabulary knowledge separates students who are at risk from their classmates. A large percentage of students who are at risk start school with considerably smaller vocabularies. Some of these differences are attributed to poverty. Before entering school, young students whose parents have jobs categorized as "professional" can be exposed to twice as many words as students whose parents are on welfare, and 50% more words than students whose parents are considered "blue collar" (Hart & Risley, 1995). Children from poverty are more likely to have less time and fewer opportunities for speaking, listening to conversation, and listening to stories read aloud. Students who come from households where English is not the first language may be just beginning to develop skills in learning and understanding English. For other students, speech and communication problems may increase the difficulty in learning more abstract words. Louisa Moats describes this gap in vocabulary knowledge as "word poverty," estimating that students who enter Grade 1 with linguistic advantages know approximately 20,000 words, while those who are linguistically disadvantaged know only about 5,000 words (Moats, 2001).

During the school day, students learn vocabulary in two ways: directly and indirectly. Because the majority of words are acquired indirectly through independent reading, when students lack the reading accuracy and fluency necessary to engage in high levels of independent reading, this source of vocabulary enrichment is closed off. Stanovich (1986) describes the rapidly widening gap between students who read independently and those who don't as the **Matthew Effect,** loosely translated as "the rich get richer and the poor get poorer." Students who read more learn more vocabulary words and acquire more background knowledge. In contrast, students who have reading problems often find reading so frustrating that they develop attitudinal problems and rarely or never choose to read independently. One research study showed that students who read independently for just 10 minutes per day experience higher rates of vocabulary growth than students who do little independent reading (Jitendra, Edwards, Sacks, & Jacobson, 2004). In addition to independent reading, listening to books and participating in daily conversation are two main sources for indirect vocabulary acquisition during the school day.

Students who are at risk are also unlikely to use context clues strategically to learn the meaning of vocabulary words on their own (Pany, Jenkins, & Schreck, 1982). In order to use context clues to figure out unknown words when reading or listening, students must understand the meaning of at least 95% of the words in the communication (Hirsch, 2003). When students with limited vocabularies do not understand basic story words such as *pal, branches, barn,* or *choose,* they are unlikely to figure out the meanings of more challenging words introduced in a new story or an explanation of a story related by the teacher. Factors that influence whether a student will learn a word from context include the following:

- The difficulty of the text and decoding skills of the reader
- Comprehension skills of the reader
- The number of times the word is encountered in the text
- The conceptual difficulty of a word
- Whether the word is important for comprehending the text
- Age of the student, with younger students having less than a 10% chance of learning the meaning of a word from context
- Prior knowledge the student has about the topic or theme of the text
- Whether the reader is an English language learner (Scott, 2005; Sousa, 2005)

While this lack of vocabulary knowledge accounts for many of the increased challenges behind teaching students who are at risk, it does not present an insurmountable obstacle. Vocabulary, like fluency, is too often ignored as part of ongoing reading instruction. If taught, vocabulary instruction often consists of "much mentioning and assigning and little actual teaching" (Beck & McKeown, 2007; p. 252) even though directly teaching new words is highly effective. Research shows that students who are at risk learn new words at the same rate as other students if they are directly taught vocabulary in school (Silverman, 2007). The challenge lies in catching them up to their peers by increasing that rate of learning. Only a teacher-directed curriculum emphasizing vocabulary has a chance of bridging the gap (Beck & McKeown, 2007; Biemiller, 2001). Students need to be taught the meanings of some words directly, and they must be taught how to figure out words on their own using the context, morphemic analysis, and the dictionary. Equally important, students must be inspired to appreciate words through word consciousness strategies such as those used by Ms. Reed and Ms. Falth in the opening vignette. Furthermore, the language interaction surrounding effective vocabulary instruction serves as a form of virtual experience, adding to student background knowledge, a critical contribution to reading comprehension (Marzano, 2004). In this chapter, strategies for assessing vocabulary knowledge and selecting and teaching essential vocabulary words are described in hopes of not just increasing the vocabulary knowledge of students, but raising their consciousness of words as well. Both strategies are necessary if we are to attain the ultimate goal of helping students read for meaning.

> Learn more about the research support behind effective vocabulary instruction at this website: **http://idea.uoregon.edu/~ncite/documents/techrep/tech13.html.**

What Vocabulary Words Do I Choose for Instruction?

Teaching vocabulary explicitly and systematically takes time and effort, both in planning and in teaching. Because of the time and effort involved in teaching vocabulary, the number of words that can be taught directly is limited. It is estimated that teachers can realistically teach 300 words per year, which translates to about 8 to 10 per week (Armbruster, Lehr, & Osborn, 2001). This limitation makes the selection of which words to teach an important responsibility of the teacher.

Armbruster and colleagues suggest that you should teach your students three kinds of words: important words, useful words, and difficult words. Important words are words that students need to know to understand the particular text they are reading. Useful words are high-frequency words that the students are likely to see repeatedly in their reading. Difficult words are words that are hard for students to understand such as words that have multiple meanings; these are words that are either spelled the same but pronounced differently, such as *invalid* (not true) and *invalid* (weak or ill), or that are spelled and pronounced the same but have different meanings, such as *fix*, as in *fix* a car, *fix* a sporting event, *fix* a cat, and so on.

Consider Mr. Halpern, who was selecting words to prepare his students to read the story "The Golden Goose" (Adams & Bereiter, 1995). The following words were underlined by the publisher as being possible vocabulary words: *Simpleton, cider, jug, feasted, inn, innkeeper, sexton, hayfields, pastor, cellar, disappeared,* and *court.* Mr. Halpern decided to spend two days preparing his students to read the story. He knew that realistically he could present no more than two words per day, so he had to decide which four words he would teach his Grade 2 students directly. He eliminated *cider* and *jug* because he felt that these were common words that his students would already know. He decided not to teach *inn* and *innkeeper* because he felt these words could be easily figured out from their context. Mr. Halpern made a mental note to make sure to include these terms in his questions after the story reading. He eliminated *pastor* and *sexton* because these words were not common and were not important for the meaning of the story. He wasn't sure whether his students, who were from the city, would know *hayfields,* but he decided not to teach it anyway because it was not important for the meaning of the story. Mr. Halpern settled on *Simpleton,* because *Simpleton* was the main character and the personal qualities that led him to be called *Simpleton* were important for the meaning of the story. Mr. Halpern also decided to teach *disappeared* and *feasted* because these were high-frequency words. *Court* was the fourth word he opted to teach because it was high frequency and, with its multiple meanings, would be difficult.

After words are selected, the question arises as to when to teach them: before, during, or after the text is read. We suggest that words essential to the meaning of the text be taught directly prior to reading but that no more than two be presented at a time. Mr. Halpern, in the example above, decided to directly teach the word *Simpleton* because of its importance to the meaning of the story. Terms in expository text that comprise needed background knowledge for comprehending the content would also qualify for teaching before reading the text.

Beck, McKeown, and Kucan (2008) point out that vocabulary should also be taught during reading. When teaching vocabulary during reading, the goal is to clarify the meaning of the word without taking students' attention away from the text. They suggest using a strategy called "Explain quickly and go on reading." For example, they clarify the word *prescription* as follows: "The doctor tore off the prescription—a prescription is a small piece of paper that a doctor writes his directions on" (Beck et al., 2008; p. 20). Vocabulary embedded in expository text may require more expansive explanations, but diverting students' attention from the story line is not an issue. Vocabulary can also be taught after reading the text, when time is less of an issue. Beck and colleagues encourage saving this time for words that are of high utility, yet robust, or full of meaning. Students who are at risk are not normally exposed to these words that are needed to provide the foundation of knowledge required for reading comprehension. Mr. Halpern selected *feasted* and *disappeared* for instruction after his students had read the story.

In the process of selecting vocabulary, recognize that a student's reading vocabulary, speaking vocabulary, and listening vocabulary are not the same and that principles that apply to one do not necessarily apply to the other. In this book, our main focus is reading vocabulary, although effective teaching of vocabulary also involves speaking vocabulary, listening vocabulary, and writing vocabulary. A teacher reading a book about volcanoes to students is enriching their listening vocabularies when emphasizing *lava* and *cinders*. Later, when students use those terms to describe the papier-mâché volcanoes they have made, they are engaging their speaking vocabularies. When those same students read a story about a child whose eyes are tearing from a *cinder* as she runs down the mountain attempting to escape the *lava* flow, the words are becoming part of their reading vocabulary. If the teacher makes *lava* one of the week's spelling words and assigns students to write a paragraph about how they would escape a lava flow in their town, that word is used in their writing vocabulary. Because research indicates that for increased comprehension students need at least 12 encounters with a new word, teachers cannot afford to miss opportunities to teach vocabulary in a variety of contexts throughout the school day (McKeown, Beck, Omanson, & Pople, 1985).

How Do I Assess My Students' Vocabulary Knowledge?

Vocabulary assessment presents more challenges than other assessments previously discussed in this book. The assumption behind vocabulary testing is that the more words on a test that students identify, the larger their vocabulary. Because only a small sample of words represent the thousands of possible vocabulary words for an assessment, the words selected have to represent a wide body of knowledge. The first question teachers should ask when assessing vocabulary is whether the test provides information on the intended vocabulary they want to test. The answer to that question depends largely on the nature and purpose of the test being considered.

Standardized norm-referenced tests of vocabulary assess general vocabulary knowledge and allow us to determine how a student's vocabulary knowledge compares to that of her peers. Using norm-referenced vocabulary assessments as screening instruments helps answer the question of whether a student's vocabulary problems are small or are large enough to warrant additional intervention (Klingner, Vaughn, & Boardman, 2007). In addition to screening, standardized measures help diagnose the specific nature of vocabulary problems such as whether the student has more difficulty with expressive or receptive language. Standardized vocabulary tests also can serve as year-end outcome measures to determine whether students have achieved grade-level performance as part of school- or district-wide accountability efforts. Because there is so much variation among vocabulary tests, when selecting one you must first examine the types of assessment tasks on the test and whether they match what you need to assess. For example, a vocabulary assessment in which students name pictures or provide oral definitions for words is assessing their speaking vocabulary, whereas a multiple-choice assessment in which students circle the correct definition of words is assessing their reading vocabulary. Teachers should always determine whether the test is assessing a skill other than vocabulary. For example, on a multiple-choice assessment, students who know the meaning of the words but cannot decode many of them are penalized for reading mistakes. Their low score may reflect a decoding deficit rather than limited vocabulary.

Teachers also need to consider whether the vocabulary assessment is testing expressive or receptive vocabulary. For example, a test requiring students to actively write or say the word or definition is measuring expressive vocabulary. Because students' receptive vocabulary is usually higher than their expressive vocabulary, they will often get higher scores on assessments in which they have to only select an answer from ones that are provided. A final concern related to standardized vocabulary assessments is the time that it can take to administer them in contrast to the other brief assessments discussed thus far in this book. Some of the tests have to be given individually and can take from 10 to 30 minutes or longer. If the teacher has no support to help assess students, classroom instructional time can be compromised. Common standardized measures of vocabulary of known reliability and validity are listed and briefly described in Appendix J.

While standardized tests are useful for screening, diagnostic, and accountability purposes, they may not capture knowledge of words taught in your classroom. As Beck et al. (2008) point out, the fact that students don't improve on standardized vocabulary tests doesn't necessarily mean they haven't learned the vocabulary words you taught them. Because general vocabulary tests usually do not include the specific words you have taught, curriculum-based assessments are more appropriate for measuring student progress because the words you assess are those you have instructed.

For young children, vocabulary knowledge can be assessed expressively by simply asking them to tell you the definition of a word (e.g., *"What does the word **feasted** mean?"*). In one recommended scoring system, first record the student's response verbatim. If the student doesn't respond after 5 seconds, or replies, *"I don't know,"* ask, *"Can you tell me anything about the word **feasted**?"* Give the student 2 points for a complete response (e.g., *"**Feasted** means to eat a very big meal."*). Score 1 point for a partial or related response (e.g., *"**Feasted** means food."*); (Coyne, Loftus, Zipoli, & Kapp, 2009).

Pictures used as prompts provide an alternative method to assess young children's knowledge of the vocabulary words you have taught (Beck & McKeown, 2007). Display a picture that represents the targeted vocabulary word you taught along with three other distraction pictures and ask students to select the correct picture (e.g., *"Which picture shows someone who is **feasting**?"*). Another option is using a verbal format such as one developed by Beck and McKeown (2007) in which children are asked to respond to pairs of *yes* or *no* questions about each word. In one type of question children are asked whether a presented meaning matches a given word (e.g., *"Is a **feast** a big special meal?" "Is a **feast** a light snack?"*). Another type of question is designed to assess the word in multiple contexts; students are asked to judge whether a brief context exemplifies a word's meaning (e.g., *"Would it be **feasting** if people were having Thanksgiving dinner?" "Would it be **feasting** if Dominic and his brother were eating a peanut butter sandwich?"*).

One method of assessing older students is using true/false and multiple-choice questions (Beck et al., 2008). These questions are most helpful if you want to know if students can recognize the meaning of a word or indicate whether a taught word fits a particular situation. True/false and multiple-choice questions are easy or difficult depending on the depth of understanding you expect from students. In our view, teachers should always aim for the greatest depth of understanding since therein lies the link to reading comprehension (Stahl & Fairbanks, 1986). Nonetheless, knowing a vocabulary word is not an "all or nothing" proposition. For example, students may know a word when it is presented in context, but still be unable to use it spontaneously (Beck, McKeown, & Kucan, 2002; Carey, 1978). Thus there may be times when using easier items is more appropriate, such as after words have first been introduced. To illustrate, here are two true/false items for the word *disappear*:

If someone disappears, it means they can no longer be seen. T or F

The word *disappear* is related to the visual sense. T or F

Note that the second example is more abstract, requiring a deeper understanding of the word. Consider the following two multiple-choice questions developed by Beck et al. for the word *diligent*.

1. Which word means *diligent*?
   fast
   hardworking
   lost
   punished

2. Which phrase means *diligent*?

   making a lot of money

   working at an interesting job

   always trying your best

   remembering everything (p. 37)

The first question is more obvious, while the latter requires deeper thought because the answer is not clearly stated. The student has to infer the answer, logically integrating information he knows about the definition with clues provided in the correct phrase. In addition to requiring deeper thinking, more challenging questions also reduce the possibility of students getting an answer correct by guessing. Although true/false and multiple-choice tests are more efficient because you can give them to the entire class at the same time, be sure that students' incorrect answers result from a lack of vocabulary knowledge, not an inability to decode the question. When in doubt about whether students are able to read the items, administer the assessment orally.

Beck et al. (2008) recommend using more challenging tests to measure students' deep knowledge of vocabulary. When students process words deeply they connect new and known learning using critical thinking (Stahl & Fairbanks, 1986). To measure the deeper processing of vocabulary, ask questions like the following ones that require students to design examples, situations, and contexts for words taught.

> What might an *ally* do for you? Why might someone need an *ally*?
>
> What is something someone might do that would be *devious*? What might give you a clue that someone was being *devious*?
>
> Why might someone say a house is *typical*?
>
> What is something you might want to be *inspired* about?
>
> Tell about a time you tried to act *nonchalantly*. (Beck et al., p. 38)

Another way to assess older students' vocabulary is determining whether they can apply morphographic rules to words making connections related to the meaning of the morphographs. Examples of morphology-based questions one teacher asked included:

> "Four of our target words this week were *pollution, population control, public transportation,* and *pesticides.* In what ways could all of these terms be connected to a larger concept?"
>
> "The concept we discussed this week was *prejudice.* How could we use the prefix and the root word for this word to help us understand its meaning?" (Allen, 1999, cited in Klingner et al., 2007, p. 50)

Espin, Busch, Shin, and Kruschwitz (2001) developed and validated a 5-minute vocabulary matching assessment to measure student knowledge of vocabulary covered in social studies. Sample items from a student-read probe are shown in Table 6.1. This assessment

TABLE 6.1 Sample Items from a Student-Read Vocabulary Probe

5. colloid	1. substance with atoms that are all alike
3. conductor	2. compounds with identical chemical formulas but different molecular structures and shapes
1. element	3. material, such as cooper wire, in which electrons can move easily
2. isomers	4. matter consisting of positively and negatively charged particles
4. plasma	5. heterogeneous mixture whose particles never settle
6. solenoid	6. a wire wrapped in a cylindrical foil

Source: Adapted from Espin, C. A., Busch, T. W., Shin, J., & Kruschwitz, R. (2001). Curriculum-based measurement in the content areas: Validity of vocabulary-matching as an indicator of performance in social studies. *Learning Disabilities Research & Practice, 16*(3), 142–151.

can be read by students or by the teacher. For the student-read assessment, the vocabulary terms are listed vertically in alphabetical order along the left side of the page, and definitions are placed in random order on the right side. Students are given 5 minutes to match the terms with their definitions. When the teacher reads the assessment, no definitions are provided on the right side. The teacher first reads the entire list of terms to the students and then reads the definitions at 15-second intervals. Students mark the term corresponding to each definition.

Because cumulative review increases student retention of new material and helps students discriminate between new and old learning, we recommend systematically including review words in all vocabulary progress monitoring assessments. In addition to providing you with valuable information about student retention, incorporating review questions into your assessments sends a signal to students that remembering what they are learning is important.

What Methods Do I Use to Teach Key Vocabulary Words?

Once you have selected the key words in a story, the next step is to decide whether to teach the word directly or indirectly. Direct teaching of vocabulary involves teaching students the meaning of vocabulary using examples, synonyms, definitions, *text talk,* graphic organizers, and key words. Indirect methods include teaching students to use strategies such as context clues, morphemic analysis, or dictionary usage so that they can determine the meaning of a word on their own. Strategies for teaching students vocabulary both directly and indirectly are described in this section.

Selecting Examples for Direct Instruction of Vocabulary

Ms. Vetrano was a kindergarten teacher in an at-risk school who was teaching her students the color red. She showed her students the following examples of red: red play dough, red car, a doll with a red dress on, and a red ball. Ms. Vetrano then pointed to her red dress and asked the children if it was an example of red. Most of the children answered, "No." Ms. Vetrano then pointed to a blue ball and asked whether it was red, and this time many students replied, "Yes." Frustrated by her students' lack of basic knowledge, Ms. Vetrano might shrug and blame the parents or preschool for not getting her students ready for kindergarten. She might also attribute the lack of learning to the students having a bad day or the moon being full. However, a close look at Ms. Vetrano's examples shows that her students were simply responding based on the examples they were given. First, Ms. Vetrano taught the concept of red using only examples that were toys. Selecting play dough, a toy car, a doll, and a ball for examples probably gave her students the false impression that only toys could be red. When she pointed to her red dress and asked the students whether it was red, the students didn't think so because her dress wasn't a toy. Logically, the students now believed that if something wasn't a toy, it couldn't be red. Ms. Vetrano could have improved her teaching of red by using a wider range of red things as examples: red clothes, red books, red crayons, etc. Unlike Ms. Vetrano, when Mr. Lopez was teaching his students the meaning of the word *cautious,* he made sure that his examples represented people who were cautious in a variety of contexts, including crossing the street, making a friend, investing in the stock market, etc.

Another problem with Ms. Vetrano's examples surfaced when students answered her second question. After her instruction, students thought that all toys were red because all the examples used were red toys. Because children tend to **overgeneralize,** or draw too general a conclusion, Ms. Vetrano needed to prevent this error by showing the students **nonexamples** that were also toys. For example, after showing the students a red ball, she could have shown them a blue ball and said that it was *not* red. Similarly, she could have shown other toys of a different color and explained that they weren't red either. When he taught the word *cautious,* Mr. Lopez used nonexamples by showing a boy running across a busy city street and a distraught investor who lost all his money in the 1929 stock market crash. Ms. Vetrano's lesson on teaching red and Mr. Lopez's examples in teaching the word *cautious* demonstrate the importance of selecting examples from multiple contexts when directly teaching the meaning of vocabulary. Unless teaching examples and nonexamples are selected carefully, students may reach the wrong conclusions about the vocabulary you are teaching. To avoid these errors, always use a range of positive examples to broaden the concept being taught, as well as at least two nonexamples to rule out overgeneralizations.

Teaching Vocabulary by Modeling

When teaching vocabulary to younger students whose limited language makes it unlikely that they will understand verbal explanations, **model** examples and nonexamples as you directly teach the word. For example, if you were teaching the meaning of *next to,* you could not verbally explain this vocabulary term without showing the position of one object next to another as you said the phrase. For one of your examples you might put a book *next to* the wall. You might choose to move a chair *next to* the desk. You might stand *next to* a student. Each time you said the new vocabulary term, you would demonstrate, so that students could physically see the placement of the object. Modeling also helps you teach concepts that are difficult to define such as *plaid,* a concept that can only be explained by presenting visual examples.

When using this technique to directly teach vocabulary, the teacher first models a series of positive examples and nonexamples of the new vocabulary word or concept. When Ms. Robertson was teaching the adverb *slowly* to her kindergarten students, she modeled the following examples and nonexamples. During her demonstration she said the key word with extra emphasis, to be certain that students' attention was on that word.

1. Mrs. Robertson walked very slowly in the front of the room and said, *"I am walking **slowly.**"*
2. She then wrote the name of a student in the class very slowly on the board and said, *"I am writing **slowly.**"*
3. She also waved good-bye very slowly and said, *"I am waving good-bye **slowly.**"*
4. Next, she ran quickly in place and said, *"I am **not** walking **slowly.**"*
5. Finally, she quickly wrote a student's name on the board using exaggerated speed and said, *"I am **not** writing **slowly.**"*

After presenting examples and nonexamples, Mrs. Robertson then tested how well students knew the examples just presented. For this phase of the teaching process, Mrs. Robertson walked slowly in front of the room and asked, *"Am I walking **slowly** or **not slowly**?"* After students answered correctly, she wrote a name slowly on the board and asked, *"Am I writing **slowly** or **not slowly**?"* Once students can accurately answer the structured testing questions, the teacher asks the students to decide whether to say the new word or other review vocabulary words in response to open-ended questions. When Mrs. Robertson reached this part of the lesson, she wrote a name slowly on the board and asked, *"How am I writing?"* The students who knew to use the key vocabulary term in their responses answered, *"slowly."* Mrs. Robertson then ran fast in place and asked the students, *"How am I running?"* The students responded, *"quickly,"* using a review word covered the previous week. If they had not already learned that term, they probably would have answered, *"not slowly."* Each time students answered the question, they had the opportunity to practice saying the new vocabulary term and to apply its meaning to a new situation.

Some teachers who want to emphasize oral language in their classroom expect their students to answer vocabulary questions in complete sentences. In these cases, students would answer, *"No, you are **not walking slowly,**"* or *"Yes, you are walking **slowly.**"* The more opportunities students have to say the word, the greater the likelihood that it will become a permanent part of their vocabulary. A format for teaching vocabulary through modeling is shown in Table 6.2.

When students answer in unison, a teacher substantially increases their active practice opportunities for saying the new word at least five times in one quick session. Follow these guidelines when developing your questions for modeling as well as for the synonym and definition formats that follow.

Guidelines for Developing Vocabulary Questions

Use the Names of Your Students in Your Examples Whenever Possible   Using the names of real students in your class can be very motivating. Also, integrating students' names into examples that are specifically tied to their lives in some way is a good way of tapping into your students' background knowledge.

> When she taught the vocabulary word *sniffing,* Ms. Carlstrom used the name of Titus, a student in her class who liked apple pie. *"Titus loves apple pie. When he walked in the door of his house the other day, he did this* (teacher makes a sniffing noise), *thinking that his grandmother had made an apple pie. Was Titus **sniffing** or **not sniffing?**"*
> *"Tell me again what **sniffing** means."*

End by Providing a Practice Opportunity   Even if the answer is "not (vocabulary word)," give your students the opportunity to respond. Ms. Carlstrom used the following nonexample when she presented the word *sniffing.*

> *"If a lion sounds like this* (teacher makes a lion's roar) *while he's chasing an elephant, is the lion **sniffing** or **not sniffing?**"* Her students laughed as they answered, *"**not sniffing.**"*

Reflect the Students' Lives with Relevant Questions   Construct your questions so they reflect experiences in the students' lives, material they are learning at school, or popular media they have seen or heard. One question Ms. Carlstrom asked connected her example of sniffing to a unit she was doing about sources of energy.

> *"When Renauld went into his house, he did this* (teacher makes a sniffing sound), *because he thought he smelled natural gas, which has a smell when it is leaking. Was Renauld **sniffing** or **not sniffing?**"*

Use the Exact Vocabulary from the Story in Your Questions and as the "Correct" Responses   Always write your questions so that students will listen to and use the exact vocabulary word used in the story. If a word in the text is written in the past tense, ask your questions so that the students have to answer in the past tense. Many students who are at risk routinely do not use the past tense form of words in their conversations. Because the meaning of text is often affected by the tense of a verb, providing extra practice using past-tense verbs should also improve students' accuracy in comprehending text and writing about events that happened in the past. Sometimes the phrase "Tell me…" can help with the phrasing of these questions.

> In all of the examples for the word *sniffing* just described, the students were required to answer with the word *sniffing,* as opposed to *sniff* or *sniffed.* If the word had instead been *sniffed,* Ms. Carlstrom would have stated her question like this: *"Tell me whether I **sniffed,** or whether I did **not sniff.**"*

TABLE 6.2   Teaching Vocabulary Through Modeling

Objective	Given 3 examples and 3 nonexamples of the new word, the students will say whether each is an example or nonexample, telling how they knew the answer, with 100% accuracy.
Materials Needed	Preparation for this activity includes selection of words. If objects are used for modeling, they should be readily available so instruction does not lag. Either prewrite the questions you will ask or jot notes about the questions on a sheet you can use for reference.
Signaling	Depending on the word, use one of these signals: Signal 1: Use finger snaps/hand claps to signal a unison response for your questions. Signal 2: Use a loop signal if asking a question about a picture.
Time	Between 2 and 5 minutes per word.
Rationale	Knowledge of vocabulary is important for reading comprehension.
Tips	■ Although you will ask for unison answers during this activity, often you will want to ask individual students to answer *why* and *how do you know* questions, which have longer answers. ■ Animate your questions with gestures and emotion related to the scenario. ■ Always phrase questions so students have the opportunity to say the vocabulary word. Rather than answering with a simple "no," expect students to answer, "not (*vocabulary word*)."

Instructions	**Teacher**	**Student**
	1. Advance Organizer	
	2. My Turn	
	■ If modeling a word, show students three positive examples and three nonexamples of the word. If teaching the word *eyebrow,* point to your eyebrow and say, "This is an eyebrow." For a nonexample, you might point to Jason's foot and say, "This is not an eyebrow."	
	3. Your Turn	
	Ask students direct questions about the vocabulary word related to positive and negative examples. Intermix your type of questions. Students should answer six questions correctly before moving on to the next step.	
	■ If modeling the word *eyebrow,* you might point to Shondra's chin and ask this nonexample question: **"Is this an eyebrow or not an eyebrow?"** You might point to Kendra's eyebrow and ask this example question: **"Is this an eyebrow or not an eyebrow?"**	not an eyebrow an eyebrow
	4. Review of previously learned words (example- and nonexample-based questions) interspersed with questions about the new word.	
	5. Individual Student Checkout	
	Ask two or three students to answer questions about the new word and/or review words.	

Error Correction	If students make an error, immediately return to a My Turn–Your Turn pattern. Later in the lesson ask students about the word they missed to provide more practice. Only use a Together if students have difficulty pronouncing the vocabulary word and could use the practice saying it with you.
Perk Up Your Drill	■ The use of students' names and the names of other staff in the building is motivating to students. ■ Students are motivated by humorous questions and examples. They especially like absurd questions. ■ Relate questions to events that have occurred in school life.

TABLE 6.2 Continued

Adaptations	▪ If you expect students to answer in complete sentences, get them into the habit of consistently answering in this way. In the beginning, some classes will answer in a complete sentence if after they answer in one or two words, you simply say to them, "Tell me in a complete sentence." In other classes where students have fewer language skills, in the beginning you will need to model the complete sentence before they repeat it. If you are consistent in expecting a complete sentence, the students will soon learn the patterns so they can do that.
	▪ You will want to use more Togethers with ESL students who could use practice articulating words.
	▪ Make sure when you use your students' names that your questions do not reflect discriminatory stereotypes. For example, when asking questions about words related to feats of strength, use girls' names as well as boys' names.

Source: This script is based on one originally developed and field-tested by Carnine, D. W., Silbert, J., Kame'enui, E. J., & Tarver, S. (2010). *Direct instruction reading* (5th ed.). Boston: Merrill Prentice Hall.

Mix in *Why* Questions After Example and Nonexample Questions   Students' answers to *why* questions give you a good idea about whether they understand the meaning of the word. After Ms. Carlstrom was sure that her students knew the definition of *sniffing,* she asked a *why* question to gauge her students' understanding of the word:

> *"This word is **sniffing**. What's the word?"*
>
> *"**Sniffing** means smelling with short breaths. What does **sniffing** mean?"*
>
> *"Watch me."* (Make a **sniffing** noise.) *"Was I **sniffing** or **not sniffing**?"*
>
> *"Why do you say that?"*

Using Synonyms to Teach New Vocabulary Directly

In this teaching strategy, teachers use a known word to teach students an unknown word having the same meaning. For example, if students don't know the meaning of the word *residence,* but know the meaning of *home, home* can be used to teach *residence.* Let's look at how a teacher uses synonyms to teach the meaning of a new word:

> Mr. Gilman first told his students, *"A residence is a home."* He then proceeded to present a series of examples and nonexamples of residence. For example, he held up a photo of a house and asked, *"This is a picture of Condy's home. Is it her **residence** or **not** her **residence**?"* After his students answered, he asked, *"Aquanetta went to the mall. Is the mall her **residence**, or **not** her **residence**? How do you know?"* After six or seven examples and nonexamples, he moved into the next phases of his teaching and reviewed the new word *residence* with other vocabulary words that students had learned in the past few weeks. Mr. Gillman pointed to a picture of a hotel and asked, *"Is this a **residence**? How do you know?"*

A sample series of teaching examples for the word *timid* is shown in Figure 6.1.

Using Definitions to Teach New Vocabulary Directly

The first step in teaching vocabulary using definitions is to have a clear, understandable definition. In most cases you cannot select definitions straight from the dictionary without adapting them. Beck et al. (2002) point out that dictionary definitions are constructed primarily to meet space limitations. Because of this constraint, dictionary definitions can be

---

Synonyms: Examples and nonexamples for teaching the word *timid*:

1. Before presenting examples and nonexamples, have students look at the word and repeat the synonym after you until they can easily say it:

   timid *"Timid* means easily frightened or shy. What does *timid* mean?"

2. Ask students questions based on examples and nonexamples of *timid.*

   ■ The new student was shy on the first day of school. Was the new student timid or not timid? How do you know?

   ■ Gabriel enjoys making everyone laugh. Is Gabriel timid or not timid? Why?

   ■ Sara is not afraid to talk in front of the class. Is Sara timid or not timid?

   ■ Marissa became easily frightened during the play and forgot her lines when she saw all the people in the audience. Did Marissa become timid or not timid? Why?

   ■ William is very friendly and outgoing. He can make friends with anyone. Is William timid or not timid?

   ■ A deer is a shy animal. Is a deer timid or not timid?

   ■ (Teacher makes a scared face with matching body posture.) Do I look timid or not timid?

   ■ On the first day of camp, Jorie was so afraid that she could hardly talk. Was Jorie timid or not timid? How do you know?

   ■ Lionel always raises his hand in class because he likes to explain the answer. Is Lionel timid or not timid? Why?

   ■ (Teacher swaggers around the room with an "I am cool look" on his face.) Do I look timid or not timid?

   ■ A robin will fly away as soon as a person comes close to it. Is a robin timid or not timid? Why?

   ■ A grizzly bear will growl and run after a human who is trying to escape from him. Is a grizzly bear timid or not timid? Why?

3. Ask students to tell you the definition for the word *timid* one more time. Ask review questions about previously learned words.

   ■ What does *timid* mean? What does *nonsense* mean? Kendra moved from Swan Hillman School to Lewis Lemon School when she was in first grade. Would you say that Kendra *transferred* or *did not transfer* to another school?

FIGURE 6.1   Direct Teaching: Synonyms

Source: Adapted from Carnine, D. W., Silbert, J., Kame'enui, E. J., & Tarver, S. (2010). *Direct instruction reading* (5th ed.). Boston: Merrill Prentice Hall.

vague and misleading. Consider the problems with these dictionary definitions as described by these authors.

> *Conspicuous:* easily seen
>
> *Typical:* being a type
>
> *Exotic:* foreign; strange; not native
>
> *Devious:* straying from the right course; not straightforward

The definition for *conspicuous* fails to communicate that something can be easily seen, yet not be conspicuous. *Conspicuous* is something that pops out at you and that is not conveyed by the definition presented here. The definition for *typical* is so vague that it sheds little light on what the word means. The definition for *exotic* includes three possible meanings, but it is unclear whether all, some, or one have to be present for something to be exotic. The definition for *devious* could be easily misinterpreted. A young learner may conclude that *devious* has to do with crooked walking or getting lost. (Beck et al., 2002, p. 34)

Dictionary definitions may also contain difficult words that students may be unable to decode or may not know the meaning of. Take, for example, the definition of *illusion:* a mistaken perception of reality. This definition includes a number of words that may be unfamiliar to students, including *perception* and *reality.* The definition "to believe something is true when it is not" would be much easier to understand.

Sometimes the definitions provided in students' reading series are clearer than dictionary definitions, but there are no guarantees. Therefore, when using definitions to teach words, it is recommended that you write your own definitions or modify dictionary or basal definitions to make them clearer. Carnine, Silbert, Kame'enui, and Tarver (2010) suggest a helpful strategy for writing a clear, comprehensive definition. They describe definitions as having two key elements: a small class to which the word belongs, and a statement of how the word differs from other members of the class. For example, take the word *sniffing.* Its class is *smelling,* and it differs from other ways of smelling because it is smelling using short breaths. Another example would be the word *south.* South is a direction (class) and it differs from other directions in that it is the direction opposite north. Beck et al. (2002) suggest using student-friendly definitions that define words using everyday language. For example, taking the word *sniffing* that was just defined, a student-friendly definition might read: when someone is smelling something using short breaths. Another example of a student-friendly definition is this definition for the word *chores:* small jobs that have to be done every day or every week. Finally, consider this student-friendly definition for the word *recipe:* a set of directions for how to cook something.

Once your definition is developed, begin teaching your students the new vocabulary word. As you point to the word on the board, assess its readability and determine whether to ask students to read the word or tell them what it says. Next say the definition, having them repeat it after you. Then, present a series of examples and nonexamples in the form of questions. As suggested earlier, use at least two positive examples of the word, making sure these examples have enough range to prevent misconceptions, as well as two nonexamples to help students rule out inappropriate generalizations. Figure 6.2 lists examples and nonexamples for the word *permanent.* Your examples should be presented in an unpredictable order.

Companion Website

Go to the Video Activities section of Chapter 6 in the Companion Website (www.pearson-highered.com/bursuck2e) and complete the activities entitled *Direct Teaching Definitions 1 and 2.*

Using *Text Talk* to Teach New Vocabulary Directly

Text Talk is a research-based direct teaching strategy and curriculum that teaches vocabulary in context using definitions (Beck & McKeown, 2007). Students actively process the meaning of each designated vocabulary word including its connection to other words, an approach shown to be superior to traditional read-alouds in which specific words are either not called out at all or merely clarified briefly while reading (Coyne et al., 2009). Use these steps when using *Text Talk* with your students.

1. Describe the word in the context of the text (e.g., *"In this story, the ogre is opposed to everything that the people want to do; he's opposed to their wanting a holiday; he's opposed to their wanting more rest from work; and he's opposed to letting the kids play."*)
2. Explain the meaning of the word.
3. Ask the children to repeat the word so that they create a phonological representation of it.
4. Provide examples of the word in contexts other than the one used in the story.

Teaching Definitions: Examples and nonexamples for teaching the word *permanent*

1. Before presenting examples and nonexamples, have students look at the word and repeat the definition after you. Say the definition slowly and with emphasis so students can easily repeat it. With more difficult definitions, you may need to inject some "Togethers" when teaching the definition. You and the students will repeat the definition together until they are able to say it by themselves.

   "Permanent means 'meant to last for a long time.' What does *permanent* mean?"

2. Ask students questions based on examples and nonexamples of *permanent.*

   - Molly bought an ice cream cone on a hot day. Is an ice cream cone permanent or not permanent? Why?

   - The mayor of Chicago paid the artist Pablo Picasso to build a large concrete sculpture that sits in the plaza. Is the sculpture permanent or not permanent? Why?

   - Patrick put his old plastic action figures into a box when he left for college. The action figures are made out of strong plastic and will probably last until his grandchildren are old enough to play with them. Are these action figure toys permanent or not permanent? Why?

   - Stuart wrote a secret spy note to his friend on paper and told his friend to destroy it after reading the message. Is the note permanent or not permanent? Why?

   - After Maria's baby teeth fell out, new, larger teeth grew in her mouth. Maria's mother told her that if she brushed these new teeth every day, she would have them for the rest of her life. Were the new teeth permanent or not permanent? Why?

3. Ask students to tell you the definitions for the word one more time. Ask review questions. "Tell me one more time what *permanent* means."

FIGURE 6.2   Direct Teaching: Definitions

Source: Adapted from Carnine, D. W., Silbert, J., Kame'enui, E. J., & Tarver, S. (2010). *Direct instruction reading* (5th ed.). Boston: Merrill Prentice Hall.

5. Have the children make judgments about examples.
6. Ask the children to construct their own examples.
7. Reinforce the word's phonological and meaning representations by asking students to say it again. Have the students read the word if they have the skills to do that.
8. Reinforce the words on subsequent days by (a) keeping charts of the words from several stories posted on the wall; (b) placing a tally mark next to the word if children hear or use one of the words; (c) attempting to use the words in regular classroom activities that occur each day such as the morning message: *"Today is Monday. Jamal wants a **feast** for his birthday."* (p. 256)

Read how an example of *Text Talk* can be applied to a children's story at **http://bit.ly/g7WWu.**

An example of how to use these steps to teach vocabulary directly is shown in Figure 6.3.

Using Semantic Maps to Teach New Vocabulary Directly

Semantic maps are visual representations of vocabulary that help students organize subject matter by having them categorize, label the categories, and discuss concepts related to a target word. The parts of the map are used to teach the class of words to which it belongs (*"What is it?"*), its characteristics (*"What is it like?"*), and some examples. A sample semantic map for *spider* is shown in Figure 6.4. When teaching the word *spider,* the teacher first presents the word to the students and places the word *spiders* into the center of the

Feast

Explain

In the story, it said that the animals found the robbers' tale full of good things to eat, and so they had a *feast*.

A *feast* is a big special meal with lots of delicious food.

Say the word with me: *"feast"*

People usually have a *feast* on a holiday or to celebrate something special. We all have a *feast* on Thanksgiving Day.

Discuss and Summarize

- Let's think about some examples of feasts. I will name some things and if they are examples of a feast, say yum! If they are not, don't say anything.

    - Eating an ice cream cone. no response

    - Eating at a big table full of all kinds of food. yum!

- If you wanted to eat a feast, what kind of food would you want?

- What's the word that means a big special meal?

FIGURE 6.3   Text Talk

Source: Adapted from Beck, I. L, & McKeown, M. G. (2007). Increasing young low-income children's oral vocabulary repertoires through rich and focused instruction. *The Elementary School Journal, 107*(3), 251–271.

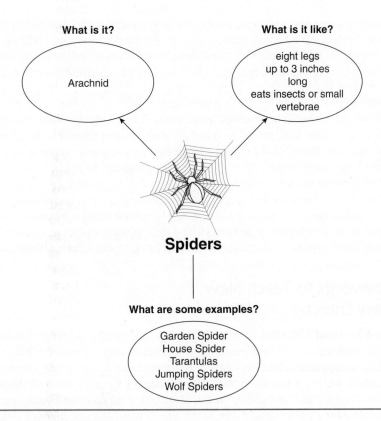

FIGURE 6.4   Semantic Map

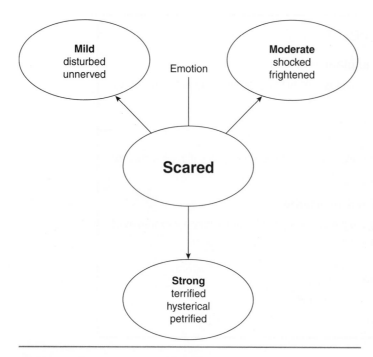

FIGURE 6.5 Emotional Word Web

Source: From Barton, J. (1996). Cited in H. W. Catts & A. G. Kamhi (2005), *Language and reading disabilities* (2nd ed.). Boston: Allyn & Bacon, p. 191.

FIGURE 6.6 Vertical and Horizontal Semantic Maps

Source: Foil, C. R., & Alber, S. R. (2002). Fun and effective ways to build your students' vocabulary. *Intervention in School and Clinic, 37*(3), 134.

map. The teacher then presents some information about spiders by describing them to students, having students read from their texts, or showing a video or DVD on spiders. If *spider* is a review word, the teacher skips the presentation of information and proceeds directly to constructing the map, asking students to supply the information, and providing support when they have forgotten details. Under the "What is it?" category, the teacher writes the larger class of living things to which spiders belong as *arachnid.* When she asks students, *"What is it like?"* the teacher helps students identify the characteristics of spiders: that they have eight legs, are up to 3 inches long, and eat insects or small vertebrates. Examples of different types of spiders are identified and written on the map. If the prior discussion went into more detail, she might lead the students to list the individual spiders as being either *ground spiders* or *web spiders.* For a follow-up activity, students complete blank semantic maps of spiders as independent work in class or as homework.

Semantic maps can also be used to show the relationships between words. Note the "emotional map" developed by Barton (1996) for the word shown in Figure 6.5, and the horizontal map developed by Foil and Alber (2002) for the word *music* shown in Figure 6.6.

Using Keywords to Teach New Vocabulary Directly

The **keyword method** (Jitendra et al., 2004) uses mnemonics to make vocabulary more meaningful to students and hence easier to understand and remember. This method involves two key components, the keyword and a visual depiction of the vocabulary word. First the teacher selects a keyword that sounds similar to some part of the vocabulary word. The keyword should be familiar to the students, concrete, and easily pictured. For example, Mastropieri (1988) taught the word *apex,* meaning the highest point, by first associating it with the keyword *ape.* For the visual that ties together the keyword, *ape,* with the definition of *apex,* Mastropieri and colleagues showed students a picture of an ape sitting on the highest point of a rock. Students were more apt to readily recall the definition of *apex* by thinking of the keyword (*ape*) and picturing that ape sitting on the highest point of a rock. An example of the keyword image for *apex* is shown below in Figure 6.7. The keyword method is most effective for students who are at risk when the keywords and corresponding visual images are generated by the teacher rather than the students (Bos & Vaughn, 2008).

FIGURE 6.7   Keyword for Apex

What Methods Do I Use to Teach Students to Learn New Vocabulary Independently?

Using Context to Teach Independent Word-Learning Strategies

While the direct instruction of vocabulary is an essential part of reading instruction, students learn most new vocabulary on their own through independent reading. Students who are at risk may be cut off from this rich source of vocabulary for a number of reasons. Certainly, problems with reading accuracy and fluency are the most serious impediments to independent reading. Also, the meaning of vocabulary words is not always made accessible by authors whose primary intention is to tell a story or explain a phenomenon (Beck et al., 2002). Thus, reading to learn requires strategies that students who are at risk may lack. You need to teach these strategies systematically and explicitly, just as you teach word-reading skills.

Using context clues to figure out the meaning of new words is one important independent vocabulary strategy students need to know. Ruddell (1999) has identified five types of context clues that can help students learn the meaning of new vocabulary within natural contexts. These clues are defined in Table 6.3 and include synonyms, definitions, antonyms, examples, and general clues. Learning to identify all of the various types of context clues is likely to be overwhelming for younger students, so it may be more appropriate for older students (Baumann, Edwards, Boland, Olejnik, & Kame'enui, 2003).

Teaching students to use context clues, especially when the context clues are definitions, examples, or more general clues, is a difficult skill for beginning teachers who will need to preplan how to indirectly teach vocabulary this way. Later, when they have more experience, teachers learn how to teach these clues more naturally on the spot during the first reading of a story. Figure 6.8 provides an example format a teacher can use when teaching vocabulary words this way. In this format, the teacher presents a small section of the passage that contains the new word, as well as words before and after that word to help students figure out its meaning. In the example shown here, students are led to figure out the meaning of the word *logical.* They first read the passage and then the targeted word, which is underlined. The teacher then asks questions that lead the students to figure out

TABLE 6.3 Types of Context Clues

Context Clue	Example
1. Definition	The author gives you a definition for the word *zenith* in the sentence.
	When the sun hit its **zenith,** which means *right overhead,* I could tell it was noon by the tremendous heat.
2. Synonym	The author uses another word that means about the same as the word you are trying to understand.
	Captain Jackson's uniform was **impeccable.** In fact, it was so *perfect* that she always had the highest score during inspection.
3. Antonym	The author uses another word that means the opposite or nearly the opposite of the word you are trying to understand.
	The soldier was very **intrepid** in battle, in contrast to the person next to him, who was quite *cowardly.*
4. Example	The author gives you several words or ideas that are examples of the word you are trying to understand.
	Tigers, lions, panthers, and leopards are some of the most beautiful members of the **feline** family.
5. General	The author gives you some general clues to the meaning of a word, often spread over several sentences.
	Patriotism was a *very strong force* in the South. People *loved their part of the country* and were *very proud to be Southerners.*

Note: In Context Clue section, italicized words provide context clues for bold words.

Source: Baumann, J., Edwards, E.., Boland, E., Olejnik, S., & Kame'enui, E. (2003). Vocabulary tricks: Effects of instruction in morphology and context on fifth-grade students' ability to derive and infer word meanings. *American Educational Research Journal, 40*(2), 447–494.

the word. In the example, the teacher asks, *"How did Lincoln prove his side of an argument?"* In the final step the students read the passage with the same word, *logical,* and then read it again, substituting a synonym or definition that means the same thing.

Although the strategy of using context clues to learn new vocabulary is helpful, it also has its limitations. First, some context clues may be easier to uncover than others. As Carnine and colleagues (2010) point out, using the context is made more difficult when the defining words are separated from the target word by other words not related to its meaning, or when the definition of the word is stated negatively. Notice how *imprint* is defined in context below.

> Sometimes a fossil is only an *imprint* of a plant or animal. Millions of years ago, a leaf fell off a fernlike plant. It dropped onto the swampy forest soil, which is called peat. The leaf rotted away. But it left the mark of its shape in the peat. The peat, with the *imprint* of the leaf, hardened.

The words that explain *imprint,* "mark of its shape," come well after the first reference to it and before the second reference, thus rendering the context clues less accessible than if they had come right after *imprint.* This means that the teacher may need to provide more support if students are to learn this new word. One suggestion would be to use the following think-aloud technique.

> *"Let's see. The word **imprint** is underlined. That means it's important and probably a word I'll need to figure out. What does it mean when a word is underlined in the story? Now I need to look at the words around **imprint** to see if I can figure it out. Hmm, sometimes the meaning of the word isn't right next to it in the story."* (Reads next part starting with Millions.) *"This sentence tells how a fossil is made. I don't see the meaning*

1. Give students a short reading passage of several sentences that contain a vocabulary word you have decided to teach. Select a passage where context clues are provided in the text.

   Example: It was while he was serving in the Illinois legislature that Lincoln decided he'd like to study to become a lawyer. He had a lawyer's <u>logical</u> mind, and he had a special knack for proving his side of an argument. Step by step, he could lay out the facts in a clear and uncomplicated way until soon enough he'd have everyone convinced.

2. Ask one student to read the passage before identifying the underlined word.

   Teacher: **"Kyle, read this passage about Lincoln."**

3. Ask another student(s) to find either the synonym or the definition of the underlined word in the passage.

   Teacher: **"How did Lincoln prove his side of an argument, Cyndie?"**

   Cyndie: "Step-by-step, he laid out the facts in a clear and uncomplicated way."

   Teacher: **"Yes, Lincoln explained all of the facts of a case *step-by-step in a clear and uncomplicated way.* That is how his mind worked. Everybody, let's read that last sentence together."**

   Class: "Step-by-step, he laid out the facts in a clear and uncomplicated way until soon enough he'd have everyone convinced."

   Teacher: **"Greg, what is a logical mind?"**

   Greg: "A mind that lays out the facts step-by-step in a clear and uncomplicated way."

4. Ask students to reread the sentence and substitute the synonym or definition for the vocabulary word.

   Teacher: **"So I could read, 'He had a lawyer's *mind that laid out the facts step-by-step in a clear and uncomplicated way.*' That's how a logical mind thinks. Everyone, let's read the entire second sentence together, but instead of reading *logical,* use the definition."**

   Class and
   Teacher: "He had a lawyer's mind that lays out the facts step-by-step in a clear and uncomplicated way and he had a special knack for proving his side of an argument."

   Teacher: **"Kwame, it's your turn to read the second sentence with the definition for *logical.*"**

   Kwame: "He had a lawyer's mind that lays out the facts step-by-step in a clear and uncomplicated way and he had a special knack for proving his side of an argument."

Notes:

- Synonym context clues are easier to teach than definition context clues. You will need to provide more support through questions and Togethers for longer definitions.

- Use regular error correction strategies when students make an error. Often students who are at risk will have difficulty with verb tense and pronouns when substituting a definition for the vocabulary word. In these cases, use more Togethers, and model the way to say the revised sentence before asking students to do the same.

FIGURE 6.8   **Indirect Teaching: Context Clues**

Source: Adapted from Carnine, D. W., Silbert, J., Kame'enui, E. J., & Tarver, S. (2010). *Direct instruction reading* (5th ed.). Boston: Merrill Prentice Hall.

> *yet. Wait—now it says the leaf left the mark of its shape in the peat. That's what an imprint is—a mark of something's shape."*

In this next example, deriving the meaning of the word *swamp* is complicated by the presence of the word *not* included in a negative definition.

> *"Back when the dinosaurs lived here, my town was a big swamp. The land was not dry like it is now."*

Watch a teacher explicitly teach students to identify the meaning of a vocabulary word through context clues at: **http://www.linkslearning.org/reading_links/8_pgr/index.html.**

In this example, the teacher might ask the following questions to guide students to the meaning of *swamp:*

"Read the passage. What's the underlined word?" (swamp) *"It says the land was not dry like it is now. If land is not dry, then what is it?"* (wet) *"Yes, wet. So, what kind of land do you think a swamp is?"* (wet land) *"Don't forget, when you see a word explained using the word **not**, you have to think extra carefully about what it means. You can get tricked."*

Using Morphemic Analysis to Teach Independent Word-Learning Strategies

Unfortunately, not all words are explained by the words around them, so students need other strategies to figure out new words. Another strategy teaches students to figure out new words using morphemes. Morphemes can be whole words such as *spell,* or they may be word parts such as the prefix *re-* or the suffix *-less.* To demonstrate how morphemes can be used to figure out the meaning of new vocabulary words, let's look at the word *careless,* which consists of two morphemes: *care* and *less.* If students know that *less* means *without,* they know that *careless* means doing something without care or without being careful. Similarly, the word *misspell* can be broken into the parts of *mis* and *spell.* If they know that *mis* means *not,* then they know that *misspell* means to *not spell* or *spell incorrectly.*

For morphemes to be helpful to students in figuring out vocabulary, they must be clearly recognizable in a word and be readily translatable into a meaningful definition. Both *misspell* and *careless* fit those criteria. Unfortunately, not all words with morphemes are so clear-cut. The meanings of many words are difficult to determine using morphemes alone, as in these examples:

The word *epidermis* is composed of two morphemes: *epi,* which means *beside* or *upon,* and *dermis,* which means *skin.* The literal definition of *epidermis,* based on its morphemes, is *upon the skin.*

The word *irreducible* is composed of four morphemes: *ir,* which means *not; re,* which means *back* or *gain; ducere,* which means *to lead;* and *ible,* which means *capable of being.* The literal definition of *irreducible,* based on its morphemes, is *not capable of being led back (to the original).*

The Lexile Power Vocabulary website at **www.lexile.com/DesktopDefault.aspx?view=ed&tabindex=2&tabid=16&tabpageid=183** assists teachers in Grades 2 through 12 develop their students' vocabulary skills.

Ducere is difficult to translate into a meaningful definition. Other morphemes have multiple meanings or are not readily recognizable. Because the utility of using morphemes varies, it is suggested that you teach your students the morphemes that are most useful. A table of common morphemes, their meanings, and example words was shown in Table 4.3 (p. 155). Strategies for teaching students to use word parts to both decode words and discern their meaning were also described under "Applying Structural Analysis to Reading Regular Words" in Chapter 4 (p. 153).

Using the Dictionary to Teach Independent Word-Learning Strategies

The definitions listed in a dictionary are often vague or contain words that students can neither decode nor understand. Perhaps that is why in studies where students were handed a dictionary and asked to create sentences, 63% of the sentences were judged to be "odd," and students frequently interpreted one or two words from a definition as being the entire meaning of a word (Beck et al., 2002). We recommend that students use learner-friendly dictionaries that are often developed for English language learners and thus use language that is accessible for any student who struggles with language. The *Collins COBUILD Learner's Dictionary* (Cobuild, 2005) and the *Easy English Dictionary* (Baker & Bettino, 1988) are effective examples. The *Easy English Dictionary,* designed for younger children and those with lower vocabularies, includes a higher proportion of black-and-white line drawings to illustrate the more concrete words. Both dictionaries contain clear sentences about each key word to help students understand the word in context. Still, caution when using any dictionary is advised, since even the best dictionaries include definitions that need to be rewritten in a more reader-friendly manner.

Besides containing unclear definitions, dictionaries often present multiple word meanings. Multiple meanings are difficult to comprehend for students who are at risk. An example of teaching students multiple meanings using the dictionary is shown in Table 6.4.

TABLE 6.4   Teaching Multiple Meanings Using the Dictionary

Teacher	Students
1. The teacher reads the word in context. **"The doctor gave the sick boy a *shot* of very strong medicine."**	
2. The teacher asks students to find the word in their dictionaries. **"Let's see if we can figure out the meaning of the word *shot* using the dictionary. Everyone, find the word *shot* in your dictionaries and raise your hand when you have found it."**	Students raise hands

3. The teacher helps students think through selecting the correct definition.
"There are three definitions in the dictionary. We know that dictionaries often have more than one definition for a word. Let's see if we can figure out which one fits our sentence from the story.
I'm going to read each definition and we'll try to figure out which one fits our sentence about the sick boy.
   1. The sound of firing a gun.
   2. A kick, throw, or hit in some games to score points.
   3. Medicine placed under the skin by a needle.	

Let's talk about the first one: the sound of firing a gun. Does that fit what the doctor is doing to the boy?"	Everyone: No
"Why doesn't it fit, Simone?"	Simone: The doctor isn't shooting a gun or something at the boy.
"Let's look at the next one: a kick, throw, or hit in some games to score points. Everyone, does that fit what the doctor is doing?"	Everyone: No
"How do you know, Latrese?"	Latrese: The doctor isn't playing a game with the boy, he's trying to make him feel better.
"Let's look at the last definition: medicine placed under the skin by a needle. Everyone, does that fit what the doctor is doing?"	Everyone: Yes
"Manny, how do you know?"	Manny: He's putting medicine in him to make him feel better.
"So, everyone, what definition fits our sentence?"	Everyone: Medicine placed under the skin by a needle.
"Yes. Now, when we talk about the Old West in social studies today, we'll talk about a different definition for *shot.* Which one do you think will fit into that story, Garth?"	Garth: The sound of firing a gun.

Before students can look up words in the dictionary, they need to learn several preskills. These preskills include the following:

1. Identifying letters.
2. Saying letters in an a–z sequence.
3. Knowing the concepts of *before* and *after.*
4. Knowing alphabetic order for the first letter.
5. Determining the position of letters relative to each other: When you call out a letter, students should be able tell you which letter comes after and which letter comes before the named one. When a student opens the dictionary to the *o* page, looking for the word *dirigible,* he needs to know that *d* comes before *o,* so he needs to jump ahead to the front quarter of the dictionary.
6. Knowing alphabetic order to the second letter.
7. Knowing alphabetic order to the third letter.
8. Scanning a dictionary page to locate a given word.
9. Knowing what guide words are, and how to locate words using them.
10. Knowing how to interpret the most common abbreviations used in dictionary entries.
11. Knowing how to interpret the most common pronunciation tips.

You have learned a number of strategies for increasing student vocabulary knowledge both directly and indirectly. In its summary of the research on vocabulary instruction, the report of the National Reading Panel (2000) stated that "dependence on a single vocabulary instruction method will not result in optimal learning" (p. 427). The *In Your Classroom* feature describes a research-based strategy that combines several of the vocabulary-teaching strategies covered in this text.

In Your Classroom

Vocabulary Instruction

Baumann and colleagues (2003) combined two methods of independent word learning, context clues and morphemic analysis, to successfully teach previously unknown vocabulary words to fifth-grade students. They taught students the following three-part strategy called the "vocabulary rule" (Figure 6.9).

When you come to a word, and you don't know what it means, use:

1. **Context Clues:** Read the sentences around the word to see if there are clues to its meaning.

2. **Word-Part Clues:** See if you can break the word into a root word, prefix, or suffix to help figure out its meaning.

3. **Context Clues:** Read the sentences around the word again to see if you have figured out its meaning.

FIGURE 6.9 Vocabulary Rule

Source: Baumann, J., Edwards, E., Boland, E., Olejnik, S., & Kame'enui, E. (2003). Vocabulary tricks: Effects of instruction in morphology and context on fifth-grade students' ability to derive and infer word meanings. *American Educational Research Journal, 40*(2), 447–494.

In order to carry out Step 2 of the vocabulary rule, Baumann and colleagues taught their fifth graders this strategy for identifying word parts and using them to figure out the meaning of a new word. Figure 6.10 lists the steps to finding word-part clues.

1. Look for the **Root Word,** which is a single word that cannot be broken into smaller words or word parts. See if you know what the root word means.

2. Look for a **Prefix,** which is a word part added to the beginning of a word that changes its meaning. See if you know what the prefix means.

3. Look for a **Suffix,** which is a word part added to the end of a word that changes its meaning. See if you know what the suffix means.

4. Put the meaning of the **Root Word** and any **Prefix** or **Suffix** together and see if you can build the meaning of the word.

FIGURE 6.10   Word-Part Clues

Source: Baumann, J., Edwards, E., Boland, E., Olejnik, S., & Kame'enui, E. (2003). Vocabulary tricks: Effects of instruction in morphology and context on fifth-grade students' ability to derive and infer word meanings. *American Educational Research Journal, 40*(2), 447–494.

Before learning the "vocabulary rule" strategy, students were taught essential preskills for applying it. They learned to identify common affixes and state their meanings, as well as to identify and describe the five types of context clues: definitions, synonyms, antonyms, examples, and general context clues.

How Can I Teach My Students to Answer Vocabulary Questions on High-Stakes Tests?

Given increased accountability, your students will take high-stakes tests in the early primary grades. As mentioned in an earlier chapter, students who read accurately and fluently on grade-level material are likely to perform at or above standard on high-stakes tests. Nonetheless, being test-wise can have a favorable impact on performance. Being test-wise means that students are familiar with the test formats and are able to apply strategies that increase their chances of getting correct answers, even when they are unsure of the correct answers. Vocabulary questions are an important part of the reading portion of most high-stakes tests. This section identifies question types your students are likely to encounter on their high-stakes tests and describes strategies to help them answer vocabulary correctly. Three of the most common types of vocabulary items on high-stakes tests include using the context, synonyms, and multiple-meaning formats (Educational Resources Inc., 2004). Examples of each of these types of item follow.

Using the Context

Alonzo thinks the stars are beautiful. He likes to *gaze* at them for hours. When he is in the country, the sky is very black so he can see the stars well.

A person who *gazes* at the stars:

A. dislikes them.
B. draws them.
C. looks at them.
D. talks to them.

Synonyms

An *incredible* story is:

A. boring.
B. unbelievable.
C. unhappy.
D. long.

Multiple Meanings

When Dashika finished the 10-mile race, she was *dead*.

In which sentence does the word *dead* mean the same thing as in the sentence above?

   A. The roses in my garden are *dead*.
   B. The beach is *dead* in the wintertime.
   C. The soldier was a *dead* shot with the rifle.
   D. The camper was *dead* after climbing uphill for 2 miles.

Strategies for teaching students to answer each of these types of vocabulary question are described in Table 6.5. Note that first the steps involved in answering the questions are clearly specified. The examples described employ think-alouds to make it clear to students not only what they have to do to answer a question, but what they need to be thinking about as they do so. Think-alouds have been shown to be an effective strategy for teaching comprehension to students who are at risk (Gersten, Fuchs, Williams, & Baker, 2001).

How Can I Provide Extra Vocabulary Practice for My Students?

Thus far, a number of effective strategies for the initial teaching of vocabulary to students who are at risk have been described. While these strategies are effective in introducing vocabulary to students, by themselves they are not enough. Reading research is quite clear that "multiple encounters are required before a word is really known, that is, if it is to affect comprehension and become a useful and permanent part of the students' vocabulary repertoire" (Beck et al., 2002, p. 73). Beck stresses that these repeated exposures must be rich, meaning that students are actively involved in "using and thinking about word meanings and creating lots of associations among words" (p. 73). This extra practice must extend beyond the classroom and into community environments as well.

Practice Activities for New Words

This section describes strategies for providing students with multiple exposures to new words. Remember that you need to provide more support and return to explicit teaching if students cannot complete these activities with at least 80% success. Student errors on these assignments provide you with an opportunity to give feedback and use an error-correction strategy. If students are old enough or you can quickly scan the worksheets, correct them on the spot so that students will profit from the immediate feedback.

Preprinted Response Cards and Write-On Response Boards   These two practice activities recommended by Foil and Alber (2002) can be carried out with large groups, because both involve the use of unison response. As stated elsewhere in this text, because everyone is participating, unison-response formats help students pay attention and increase the opportunities for practice. The teacher distributes cards that have the vocabulary word printed in large letters on the front side and the definition and an example sentence printed on the back.

After every student has several cards, the teacher tells everyone a definition and students hold up the correct vocabulary word. In another adaptation of this same activity, the teacher distributes dry-erase boards to each student along with dry-erase markers. The teacher then establishes the word bank by writing a list of vocabulary words on the board. As with the preprinted word cards, the teacher tells a definition, and students answer by writing the appropriate word from the word bank on their slates. To maintain momentum,

TABLE 6.5 Strategies for Answering Vocabulary Questions on High-Stakes Tests

Question Type 1: Using Context Clues to Determine Meaning

Example	Alonzo thinks the stars are beautiful. He likes to *gaze* at them for hours. When he is in the country, the sky is very black so he can see the stars well. A person who *gazes* at the stars— A. dislikes them. B. draws them. C. looks at them. D. talks to them.
Strategy	Read only the underlined vocabulary word and try to pick out the correct definition based on what you already know. If you can't figure out the correct definition, go back and read the sentence. Underline the clue words that can help you find the definition and try again. If you still can't find the definition, substitute each of the choices into the sentence and pick the one that makes sense. If you still can't answer the question, guess one of the answers you think might be right.
Applied Strategy	**"Let's see. The underlined vocabulary word is *gaze*. Let's see if any of the choices means *gaze*. Hmm . . . Dislikes them? Draws them? Looks at them? Talks to them? I'm not sure what the answer is."** **"I'm going to read the sentence and see if I can find words that might give me a clue about the meaning of *gaze*. I think the words *see the stars well* are important, so I will underline them in the sentence. But I'm still not quite sure of what the answer is."** **"Okay. Now I'm going to substitute each choice word in the sentence and see which makes sense."** **"'He likes to dislike them for hours.' That doesn't make sense at all. 'He likes to draw them for hours.' I don't think he would be able to draw the stars at night. It couldn't be that one. 'He likes to look at them for hours.' That one seems to make sense since it talks about being able to see the stars in the dark. I'll check the last one out just to be sure, but I think the answer is *look*. 'He likes to talk to them for hours.' That doesn't make sense. So, I think the answer is C, *looks at*."**

Question Type 2: Multiple Meaning Formats

Example	**When Dashika finished the 10-mile race, she was *dead*.** In which sentence does the word *dead* mean the same thing as in the sentence above? A. The roses in my garden are *dead*. B. The beach is *dead* in the wintertime. C. The soldier was a *dead* shot with the rifle. D. The camper was *dead* after climbing uphill for 2 miles.
Strategy	Read the underlined vocabulary word. Read the **bolded** sentence containing the word and think of a simple definition or words that mean the same thing. Read each of the four possible answer sentences, substituting your definition instead of the word. After each sentence, ask yourself, "Does this make sense?" If not, cross out that choice and repeat for the other choices. If you still can't come up with the answer, take a guess by picking one of the choices you think might be right.
Applied Strategy	**"The underlined word is *dead*. *Dead* has many meanings. I need to figure out what it means in the bolded sentence. First I'll read that sentence. 'When Dashika finished the 10-mile race, she was *dead*.' Well, even though a 10-mile race is very long, I don't think Dashika is likely to die from it. I think she would be *very tired*. So I think *dead* here means very tired. Let me put *very tired* in each sentence and see which one makes sense."**

Continued

TABLE 6.5 Continued

Applied Strategy (Continued)	"The roses in my garden are very tired.' That doesn't make sense. Roses don't get tired. I'm going to move to the next one. 'The beach is very tired in the wintertime.' That doesn't make any sense either. Then how about next one? 'The soldier was a very tired shot with the rifle.' That doesn't make sense either. Let's try the last one. 'The camper was very tired after climbing uphill for 2 miles.' That makes sense. The camper would be tired after that climb. So the answer is D."

Question Type 3: Synonyms

Example	An _incredible_ story is: A. boring. B. unbelievable. C. unhappy. D. long.
Strategy	Ask yourself what the word means without looking at the definitions given below. See if your definition is one of the four choices. If your definition is not one of the four choices, try to put each choice in a sentence and ask yourself, "Is that **incredible**?" If you still can't come up with an answer that makes sense, make a guess on one of the choices you think might be right.
Applied Strategy	"What does _incredible_ mean? I think it means _funny._ Let's see if that is a choice. Hmm . . . It isn't. Now I'm going to try to put each of the choices into a sentence and see if I can figure out the meaning of _incredible_ that way." "An incredible story. A boring story? Incredible and boring don't mean the same thing." "An incredible story. An unbelievable story? That seems right. I remember my brother talking about an incredible band. He said they were so good, he couldn't believe it. I'll look quickly at the other two choices, but I think B is the right answer. Let's see—_unhappy_? No—_long_? No, that isn't right either. I'm going to answer B for this question."

the teacher must maintain a perky pace and use a clear signal throughout the lesson (e.g., _"Boards up." or "Card up."_). Foil and Alber (2002) point out that the whiteboards don't allow for as many student answers because writing on the slates takes more time than just holding up a preprinted card. However, they state that the activity may be just as worthwhile because writing the words reinforces spelling skills.

Companion Website

Go to the Video Activities section of Chapter 6 in the Companion Website (www.pearsonhighered.com/bursuck2e) and complete the activity entitled _Middle School Science: Response Cards_ to see how a teacher uses this strategy to enhance concept understanding.

Classwide Peer Tutoring   Another way to provide extra vocabulary practice is through structured peer tutoring. In this approach, used by Miller, Barbetta, and Heron (1994), the teacher provides each student with a folder that has two pockets attached on the inside. The teacher prints "go" on one pocket, and "stop" on the other pocket. The teacher also provides students with index cards on which a vocabulary word is written on one side and its definition on the other. The students work in pairs in which they take turns being the tutor. The tutor shows each vocabulary word to his partner and asks the partner to restate the definition. Praise is given for correct answers, and corrective feedback in the form of a My Turn–Your Turn is provided for incorrect answers. Words mastered (three consecutive days correct) are put in the "stop" pocket. Words that have yet to be mastered are placed in the "go" pocket. After a predetermined time, usually around 5 minutes, the students switch roles. After both students have had their turn, they chart the number of words they have mastered on a <u>graph</u> taped to the inside of the folder. Words in the "stop" pile are reviewed periodically in subsequent days. As with any peer-tutoring procedure, tutors need to be carefully trained, and their teaching tactics closely monitored.

Companion Website

Go to the Video Activities section of Chapter 6 in the Companion Website (www.pearsonhighered.com/bursuck2e) and complete the activity entitled *Classwide Peer Tutoring.*

Never Too Many Questions   After teaching a vocabulary word, teachers need to find every opportunity to ask questions about the new word. They can ask questions immediately after students know the definition, they can ask questions before lunch, they can ask questions when the word surfaces in the story. *Who, what, where, why, when,* and *which* questions like the following provide extra opportunities for students to use the new words they have learned:

- *"What would you do if your best friend let you use a **delicate** glass to drink out of and you broke it? Have you ever broken anything that was **delicate,** and what was it?"*
- *"What are some things that make you **anxious?** Why?"*
- *"When have you seen a **procession,** and what kind of **procession** was it?"*

Making Choices   This activity recommended by Beck and colleagues (2002, p. 56) forces students to think about the precise definition of the word as applied to authentic descriptions. Even better, students answer in unison, so everyone is engaged in responding to the questions:

If any of the things I mention is a *competition,* say "competition." If not, don't say anything at all.

- a relay race
- the Olympics
- lunch with a friend
- the school spelling bee
- watching a movie

If any of the things I mention is something that might make you *chuckle,* say "chuckle." If any of the things I mention might make you *sob,* say "sob."

- your mom tickling your toes
- burning your hand on a hot plate
- watching a cartoon show where a mouse fools a cat
- seeing a clown pull a quarter out of someone's ear
- losing your money for lunch

Word Associations   In another activity, Beck and colleagues (2002, p. 44) have students make a connection between a new vocabulary word and a word that they already know and then describe why they made it. If a teacher had directly taught the words *glitter,* *pessimist, rubbish, arid,* and *antonyms,* he would write the five words on the board and ask the class to answer the following questions in unison:

- *"Tell me the word that goes with gold."* (answer: *glitter*)
- *"Tell me the word that goes with opposites."* (answer: *antonyms*)
- *"Tell me the word that goes with parched."* (answer: *arid*)
- *"Tell me the word that goes with negative."* (answer: *pessimist*)
- *"Tell me the word that goes with garbage."* (answer: *rubbish*)

Thumbs Up–Thumbs Down   This adaptation of a self-reflection activity in *Bringing Words to Life* (Beck et al., 2002; p. 45) provides review for descriptive words previously taught in class. The teacher asks students to hold their thumbs up if a trait she calls out describes them and to hold their thumbs down if the trait does not describe them. Individual students are asked to tell why they selected their answer.

- *"Are you independent? Why?"*
- *"Are you mischievous? Why?"*
- *"Are you gullible? Why?"*
- *"Are you assertive? Why?"*
- *"Are you loyal? Why?"*

Narrow Reading   An adjunct to directly teaching a "big concept" vocabulary word is **narrow reading,** where the teacher can assign different texts on the same topic so that the learner encounters the word in different contexts (Schmitt & Carter, 2000). If students have just learned the meaning of *circuit* and *electrical current,* the teacher might have everyone read the book *The Magic School Bus and the Electric Field Trip,* by Joanna Cole; photocopies of pages 41–44 of *Electricity and Magnetism Fundamentals,* by Robert Wood; and a choice of either the section on circuits in *All About Electricity,* by Melvin Berger, or the section on circuits in *The First Book of Electricity,* by Sam and Beryl Epstein.

Practice Activities for Review Words: Coordinating Vocabulary with Writing Activities

When students have the opportunity to write vocabulary words they have learned, they are more apt to remember a word when they read it in text. If the word is a spelling word, design the activity so that students practice independently spelling the word. If the word is not a spelling word, provide a written model on the board, overhead projection, or paper so students write it correctly. These are some activities you can use for vocabulary review practice:

Fill-In-the-Blank Stories   Vocabulary words are listed at the top of the page unless they are also spelling words, and students fill in the blanks of a story with appropriate words.

Dictionary "Race-and-Rite"   Each student needs a dictionary, pencil, and paper for this activity. Students are divided into three teams. If students are expected to know the spelling of the word, the teacher says the word; if students do not know the spelling, the teacher points to the word and asks students to read it. When the teacher says, "Look it up," the students race to look up the word in the dictionary. As soon as they have found the word, they write it along with the dictionary page number. Then they immediately write a complete sentence using the word. When a student has completed the task, she holds up her thumb. At a set time, the teacher says, "Stop," and quickly scans the papers of whichever team has the most thumbs raised. That team gets one point for every person who wrote the correct page number as well as a complete sentence.

The Good-bye List   The teacher keeps a list of vocabulary words that have been taught on a chart that is titled the "Good-bye List." Each morning he writes between 5 and 10 vocabulary words on the board. When students enter the room, they know that they are supposed to write the word, a definition of the word, and a sentence showing correct usage of the word. They can earn three points per vocabulary word toward their language arts grade for doing this activity correctly. If 90% of students get all three points for a word two days in a row, the word is taken off the Good-bye List. Students are encouraged to shrink the list so that the teacher is "forced" to teach even more words because he cannot keep up with his hardworking class.

Vocabulary Words as Themes   When students are asked to write a paragraph, story, or descriptive paper, the assignment should be structured so that they use targeted vocabulary words. If students have just read *Cloudy with a Chance of Meatballs,* ask them to write several sentences about what would happen if they were walking outside in the *hail.* If students have been studying about the early American *colonists,* ask them to write a page about what hardships they would face as a *colonist* on the moon.

Grids   The teacher prepares a worksheet using the table function of a word processing program. Vocabulary words are listed in the first column and students are asked to write synonyms and/or antonyms in the next column(s). The teacher needs to determine whether a dictionary or textbook is necessary for student success.

Word Journals   Once your students know basic word processing, they can use their computer lab time to make personal dictionaries using the vocabulary words you have taught them.

> Activities for teaching vocabulary are found at: **www.readingfirst.virginia.edu/index.php/elibrary/C11/.**

How Do I Teach the Language of Learning?

Teachers of younger students who are at risk are often frustrated when teaching vocabulary, because many of their students come to school unable to speak using more than three- or four-word utterances, use prepositions, or answer *where, what,* and *why* questions. Given that oral language deficits are a risk factor for later reading problems (Catts, 1991; Wilson & Risucci, 1998), these teachers' concerns are well placed. Students' oral language skills, along with listening comprehension skills, affect their ability to comprehend text. Although teaching vocabulary is essential, it is often not sufficient. Louisa Moats describes what is needed to overcome the language gap that presents additional challenges for so many students from poverty:

> From the time they enter preschool, students must experience language stimulation all day long if they are to compensate for their incoming linguistic differences. Teachers must immerse them in the rich language of books. Children need to rehearse the rules of discourse, such as staying on topic, taking turns, and giving enough information so the listener understands. Children must learn how to speak in discussions, to question, paraphrase, retell and summarize, as the recently developed standards for listening and speaking now specify. Teachers must teach directly the form, meaning, and use of words, phrases, sentences, and texts. Everything from the articulatory features of /k/ and /g/ to the construction of an organized essay is grist for the instructional mill. (Moats, 2001)

Because teachers do not have the training of speech pathologists, they often feel at a loss in developing their students' oral language skills, a loss that is substantiated by research. Close examination of typical school curricula and methods reveals that classroom exposure to literature, use of an informal language experience approach, infrequent opportunities to talk, and infrequent feedback and correction of oral language have little impact on developing students' language skills (Beimiller, 2003). By the second year of Project PRIDE, we realized that all of the kindergarten students needed a more structured language curriculum providing extensive practice. An account of the program *Language for Learning* is given in the *Research Note* section. If students who are at risk are going to comprehend written text at grade level, their classroom curriculum must ensure that the following language skills essential for learning are developed at as early an age as possible. Language curricula used in preschool and kindergarten should teach these skills.

- Answers simple "wh-" questions (who, what, where, when, and why) in a full sentence.
- Understands and answers questions for sentences that include a subject + action + object (e.g., "The girl makes cookies.") and a subject + action + location (e.g., "The camel walks on the hill.").
- Uses prepositions (on, on top of, over, in front of, in between, into, inside, beside, under, beneath, behind, in back of, through, out of).
- Understands quality (alike, same, different), amount (all, more, few), size (big, little, short), opposites (hot-cold, big-little, up-down), and categories (containers, vehicles, months, food, numbers).
- Uses articles (the, a, an) in conversation.
- Answers yes/no questions in a complete sentence.
- Knows colors, shapes, and numbers.
- Uses possessives (his, hers) and personal pronouns (we, she).
- Answers more complex "wh-" questions (e.g., "What can you do with a shovel?" "Why do you go to school?").
- Follows three-part sequence of directions (e.g., "Put your crayons in your desk, put your papers in your cubbies, and get your coats.").
- Uses *and* to chain together two concepts or actions.
- Relates information about an experience that happened in the past in more than one complete sentence.
- Uses irregular-tense verbs in conversation (hit, caught, sat).
- Speaks in complex sentences of more than four words.
- Tells what happens *first, middle,* and *last* in a sequence of events.
- Tells a story about an event or experience.
- Understands and describes the difference between things that are the same and things that are different, such as the difference between children and grown-ups.
- Uses all parts of speech in conversation.
- Uses plurals, past tense verbs, and present progressive (-ing) in speech.

Learn more about *Language for Learning* at: **https://www.sraonline.com/ products_main.html.**

How Important Is Vocabulary for Older Learners?

When an older student does not derive meaning from what she is reading, the teacher needs to assess the student's benchmark skills to determine whether she has developed alphabetic principle, can decode multisyllabic words, can read fluently, and has acquired an adequate vocabulary to read grade-level text. Whether assessment shows that reading

Research Note

Language Development

The year before Project PRIDE started, we observed kindergarten classes in all three schools and took data on students to assist in our decision making the next fall when we started coaching in the classrooms. During the observations, we noticed that although teachers read to students every day and engaged in language experience activities such as cooking, growing plants, and constructing objects related to thematic units, the language poverty of students persisted. Many students' discourse when answering teachers' questions, conversing on the playground, or describing what happened the night before was more typical of a three-year-old than an end-of-year kindergartner. Simply teaching phonemic awareness, letter sounds, and beginning decoding would be inadequate unless we could also develop the students' language skills, so necessary for comprehension.

We decided to supplement the already-established classroom language experience with the *Language for Learning* direct instruction curriculum (Engelmann & Osborn, 1999). The *Language for Learning* curriculum just described was selected because it incorporates explicit and systematic instruction of listening comprehension and oral language, provides many opportunities for each child to answer questions throughout the lessons, and introduces a careful sequence of skills. When we gave the kindergartners the curriculum pretest, our observations about their low language skills were confirmed; approximately 40% of the students had such low language skills that they tested into the beginning lessons of the program. These children were not yet using prepositions; they could not repeat a six-word sentence; they did not use articles in conversation or use the word *not* in a complete sentence, such as "He is not driving a car." Some still did not know the difference between their *chin* and *cheek* and could not differentiate between their first and last name. How could we hope to get them to fully develop reading comprehension when their language was so impoverished?

The children lowest in oral language were to receive *Language for Learning* for a half hour in groups ranging between two and eight children. In order to do this, special education teachers, student teachers, paraprofessionals, and Title I teachers were trained to teach the language groups. The teachers expressed their surprise at discovering what difficulty so many of the children had with "first" and "next" and how much practice they needed to learn those concepts. Talking about "*an* elephant" in contrast to "*a* book" and selecting the right article doesn't come easily when a child hasn't picked up that convention from the environment. After Christmas, the kindergarten teachers noticed that many of the children in *Language for Learning* were beginning to surpass their peers. The children were sequentially naming the days of the week and seasons of the year, identifying more body parts, and using plurals. It looked as if the intensive half hour of talking and more talking while sustaining attention to wait for the teacher's signal was helping these children learn language concepts more efficiently.

That year we gave the *Slingerland Listening Skills Comprehension* test to all of our kindergarten students at the beginning and end of the school year. We were interested in seeing whether the children who received *Language for Learning* made progress in listening comprehension and whether they were able to catch up to their classmates who entered kindergarten with higher language skills. The results showed that the *Language for Learning* group made significant gains in listening comprehension and that the gap between them and their peers was virtually gone. The teachers told us they felt as if they were teaching language appropriately for the first time, and that until they taught the program, they had not been aware of the many critical sequential language skills needed for more expressive conversation. They also found themselves integrating the *Language for Learning* skills into other activities throughout the day.

deficits include earlier reading skills or just vocabulary deficits, instruction should always include the direct teaching of vocabulary. An older student has not had access to the indirect learning of new words through extensive reading, and thus his reading deficit results in a smaller vocabulary.

Design of Vocabulary Instruction

Vocabulary instruction will incorporate many of the same direct and indirect teaching strategies as used with younger students, but can be more directly connected to text as the teacher discusses the author's selection of words and how the choice of a word affects the author's communication with the reader. Vocabulary instruction should rely less on synonyms and more on teaching similarities and differences between words. Beck and colleagues (2002) recommend that the teaching of vocabulary at this level incorporate four design elements: frequency, richness, extension of words beyond the classroom, and choice of vocabulary words.

Frequency   Because of the content area demands for older students, the teacher should plan on directly teaching at least 10 words per week. Words taught during previous weeks should be repeatedly reviewed.

Richness   A variety of activities should actively involve students in writing, speaking, and associating each word with other words. Activities should be designed so that students use critical thinking skills in applying what they have learned about the meaning of the word. The authors recommend that rather than have students memorize definitions, the teacher should "provide opportunities for students to use the words, explore facets of word meaning, and consider relationships among words" (Beck et al., 2002, p. 74). Answering timed true/false questions also helps students clarify and refine the meaning of new words as well as develop fluency.

Extension of Words Beyond the Classroom   The use of a *Word Wizard* chart or wall area helps students use active listening to hear new vocabulary words outside the classroom. Students earn points on the *Word Wizard* chart by bringing in evidence that they heard, saw, or used one of their assigned vocabulary words outside the classroom—in other classes, at home, in the mall, watching TV, in a book, or from any other source. McEwan (2009) describes how one middle school teacher motivated her students to use new vocabulary outside the classroom:

> I have my English students for study hall, which is a perfect time to have our little "word chats." Students have to describe when they used the word, to whom they were speaking, and exactly what they said. They can only get credit for one word per day. Amazingly, with just this little motivation, my students are using words we studied weeks ago and even other teachers are noticing their vocabulary usage. One of my C students found this activity so appealing that he is on target to be the first one to reach the 30-word prize. Javier's latest example featured his mother: "I was talking to my mom, and she was getting all dressed up to go to the movies. I told her she looked luminous." (p. 100)

Choice of Vocabulary   The choice of vocabulary words taught presents additional challenges when teaching vocabulary to older learners. A larger proportion of the words selected are from expository rather than the narrative text emphasized in the primary grades. The teacher's word selections include different considerations in content area subjects. For example, in expository text, selecting words related to the content being studied is more important than selecting those appearing more frequently in print (Marzano, 2004). Marzano and Pickering (2005) suggest a systematic process for selecting terms needed to understand expository text. First, for each subject area you teach, estimate the number of new terms that you think you can reasonably cover each week. As was earlier recommended, about two terms per day, ten per week appears to be the norm for direct vocabulary teaching, though that number may be reduced for content area instruction. For example, Marzano and Pickering recommend starting with as few as four terms per week. In a 36-week school year, the teacher would then instruct 144 words for that subject area. Next, identify the terms that you believe are critically important to the content taught. These are terms necessary for understanding the big ideas of the subject, which should also match national and state standards for the content area in question. If the number of words you select is greater than the number originally estimated, remember that Marzano's suggestion of four words per week is just a recommendation, and your students may be able to learn more words each week. If not, carefully deliberate about the importance of each word before deleting some. Finally, whenever possible, work to develop school-wide efforts to select and teach key terms in content areas (Berne & Blachowicz, 2009; Marzano, 2004). Students who are at risk benefit when instructional efforts are consistent and systematic, both within and across classrooms.

> Marzano and Pickering (2005) have compiled lists of 7,923 key vocabulary words for 11 subject areas in Grades K–12 in their book *Building Academic Vocabulary*.

How Can I Teach Vocabulary to English Language Learners?

Many vocabulary words that readers encounter have **literal,** or actual, **meanings,** such as the word *creek* in a story where Laurel, a main character, says, "I'm getting my pole and going fishing in the *creek.*" The reader can picture Laurel casting for fish in a shallow creek at the bottom of the hill where she is going fly-fishing. Other words or phrases, such as **idioms,** have **figurative meanings** where the meaning is not literal, implying more than what is said on the surface. When Stephano says, "I crashed my car and am *up a creek,*" the idiom *up a creek* means *in trouble.*

Idioms that have figurative meanings present additional challenges for English language learners. Phrases such as "to smell a rat" or "hot under the collar" must be learned as a whole, because they cannot be understood from the meanings of the separate words within them. While some idioms are regarded as slang and typically heard in oral language, other idioms are regarded as formal or informal. They are liberally sprinkled through much fiction and narrative reading, and comprehension of the text depends on the reader perceiving them as a whole and knowing their meaning.

The same recommendations given for teaching vocabulary also apply to teaching idioms. Teachers should ignore the more obscure idioms and focus their teaching on ones that students are more likely to encounter in their reading. Idioms with clear meanings should be taught first. When first teaching an idiom, teachers should consider whether learning the literal meaning of the idiom will help the student remember it. For example, the idiom "roll with the punches" means to make it through times of hardship. This phrase came to be used because rolling with the punches is a technique used in boxing where the objective is to avoid receiving a direct hit. The boxer tries to move away from the punch in an attempt to avoid the blow or at least take a less painful, glancing blow. Because this example helps the reader make sense of the idiom, the teacher could explain it when she introduces the word.

Whether the teacher refers to the literal background of the phrase or not, each idiom has a figurative meaning that the student can apply to text. Irugo (1986) recommends that teachers portray the meaning of the idiom as concretely as possible. Pictures that depict the meaning of the idiom can help the student remember the phrase, as can stories in which the phrase is used in a humorous context. Unless an idiom is supported by context in the beginning, English language learners are less likely to remember it, so having students role-play the idiom or act out sentences containing the idiom are effective teaching techniques. If the

FIGURE 6.11 A Drop in the Bucket

Source: www.goenglish.com/adropinthebucket.asp.

students' first language has a similar idiom, connecting the English idiom to that one will help the students' retention of the new phrase. Mr. Swiggums displayed the picture in Figure 6.11 on the SMART Board in front of his classroom and explained that "a drop in the bucket" is something that is not very important because it is small. He asked his students to look at the picture and see how small the water drop looked in the much larger bucket. A drop in a large bucket isn't important because you would need so many drops to fill the bucket. Next Mr. Swiggums asked his students to read in unison "A drop in the bucket," which was written next to the picture. He wanted to be sure that everyone clearly heard the new idiom and could read it. Mr. Swiggums explained that when Charlotte broke her pencil she said, "It's just a drop in the bucket," because Charlotte's dog was sick, her mom had yelled at her that morning for ripping her dress, and her best friend wasn't talking to her. Compared to the bigger problems of her dog's illness, her mom's anger, and losing her best friend, breaking a pencil was not important. Breaking the pencil was a very little problem. Breaking the pencil was just "a drop in the bucket." As Mr. Swiggums said "just a drop in the bucket," he shrugged his shoulders, threw out his hands, and made a facial expression reflecting that breaking the pencil was not important. He then asked his students to mimic his body language as they said "just a drop in the bucket" together.

In order to help develop students' understanding of English idioms, Celce-Murcia, Brinton, and Goodwin (2002) recommend that teachers use idioms for controlled practice activities when students are learning to use correct rhythm patterns and word stress in connected speech phrases. The following idioms, all containing the word *talk*, are recommended for an oral speech practice session:

> all talk and no action
> talk is cheap
> talk a blue streak
> talk shop
> talk through your hat
> talk someone's head off (Celce-Murcia et al., 2002, p. 170)

ESL

For English as a Second Language resources and activities related to teaching vocabulary, visit **http://ucaeliteachers.pbworks.com/Websites+and+Online+Resources+for+Students.**

To learn the origins of some of the most common idioms used in the United States, visit **http://www.pride-unlimited.com/probono/idioms3.html#q** and **http://www.goenglish.com/Idioms.asp.**

A teacher using this strategy would go through the list, first saying each phrase before students repeated it, imitating the teacher as closely as possible. Although students would not yet know the meaning of many of these idioms, they would be gaining familiarity with hearing the key words used within the larger idioms.

A number of Internet websites have defined idioms and illustrate them with descriptive or humorous pictures. Downloading the pictures from these sites gives the teacher easy access to instant demonstration materials. In the general reference section of larger bookstores, teachers can also find worksheets and explanations about how common idioms originated.

Fortunately, preliminary research suggests that strategies that are effective for teaching vocabulary to English-only students are also effective for English language learners (Silverman, 2007). In fact, Silverman's research suggests that English language learners' progress in response to systematic, explicit vocabulary instruction may be even greater than their English-only counterparts. Ways that effective vocabulary instruction can be delivered to both English language learners and English-only learners are described in the *Technology* section.

Technology

Using Technology to Teach Vocabulary

The National Reading Panel report (2000) indicates that computer technology can benefit the development of reading vocabulary. Several research studies investigating computer-aided vocabulary instruction for students who are at risk report increased scores on vocabulary assessments given after the conclusion of the computer intervention (Horton, Lovitt, & Givens, 1988; Segers & Verhoeven, 2003). However, too few rigorous studies have been conducted to determine what type of computer instruction is most effective in teaching reading vocabulary. Because software programmers have used a number of different strategies in their reading vocabulary teaching programs, teachers can be confused by all of the options. We have identified some of the current instructional design features available in software programs for teaching vocabulary so you can be a more informed consumer when selecting a program.

The buyer must beware of spending money for a program that is little more than a standard vocabulary worksheet. In these programs the student either matches a definition to each vocabulary term or writes the word of a definition. If the answer is correct, a pleasant chime sounds or text on the screen indicates that the answer is correct. If the answer is not correct, an unpleasant beep sounds or text pops up indicating an error. Student errors do not affect the sequence of instruction, and the student is expected to begin answering the next question whether he was right or wrong. A score is displayed at the end of the activity.

Vocabulary computer programs with more sophisticated designs may include some of the following features. At this point in time, however, regardless of the feature involved, it appears that when adults are meaningfully involved in children's computer-based instruction, the effects are greater (Nir-Gal & Klein, 2004).

- **Immediate feedback for answers**—When students answer incorrectly, the program will either reteach the word or display the correct answer.
- **Effective error correction**—When students answer incorrectly, after leading the student to answer correctly, the program will ask the same question again so that the student has the opportunity to answer correctly one more time.
- **Digitized or synthesized speech**—A study by Hebert and Murdock (1994) showed that students learn more vocabulary when a computer program integrates speech with the computer instruction.

- **Pictures or animation for teaching**—Some programs teach initial vocabulary displaying pictures or animations to illustrate new words. For example, the word *locomotive* might be illustrated by a train chugging down a track. Programs for younger students who are not yet reading often require students to select pictures that match a word spoken by a story character.
- **A variety of student responses appropriate for students' age and developmental level**—Students may click a mouse or touch their finger to the screen to select a vocabulary word or picture, move an object to a picture of a vocabulary word, paint pictures of vocabulary words, type in letters of a vocabulary word, select multiple-choice options related to the vocabulary word (e.g., antonym, synonym, correct sentence with blank, definition), or select key vocabulary terms written in hypertext (see below). Students' hands are not large enough to learn word processing until third grade, so programs for younger students should utilize a mouse or point-touch screen.
- **Easy record keeping**—Some programs allow students to save their scores or the programs automatically save their scores so the teacher can monitor progress.
- **Number of new vocabulary words learned**—Some programs introduce large sets of vocabulary words; others limit the number of vocabulary words introduced and do not introduce more until students have success with the first set. In one study, Johnson, Gersten, and Carnine (1987) studied two groups of students in Grades 9 through 12. One group learned vocabulary from a computer program that introduced small sets of only seven words; the other group's program introduced a larger set of 25 words. At the end of the intervention, the researchers concluded that the students who learned from the program that introduced small sets of words learned the specified 50 vocabulary words more quickly.
- **Teacher selection of vocabulary words**—Some flexible programs allow the teacher to input up to 20 vocabulary words, definitions, and sentences. Other programs teach predetermined vocabulary words.
- **Motivation**—Software programs teaching vocabulary have a wide variety of motivational strategies. Some programs teach vocabulary words in the

Continued

context of playing games, including "Indiana Jones"–type adventures or Save the Planet mysteries; some teach vocabulary within the context of interesting stories; some attach success with the ability to earn clues to solve a mystery; some use percentage correct scores as a motivator. Always check to see that the motivator does not consume too much instructional time.

- **Hypertext**—During the past fifteen years, **hypertext** has increasingly been used as one computer software strategy to teach vocabulary. With hypertext, the software designers link designated words (which are usually indicated by a different text color) to a database. Depending on their preferences, readers can select the designated words and bring on-screen the information in the database. Clicking on a word might link the reader to a definition of the word, to a picture of the word, to a clue for figuring out the word, or to a video of someone describing the word. Students reading electronic books on screen can select a word and immediately obtain information on it. More research is still needed to determine whether hypertext is an effective vocabulary-teaching strategy and, if so, which kinds of hypertext work best with what types of students. Note the visual aspects of the hypertext. Programmers indicate that hypertext of dark letters on a light background is less tiring for the reader than the reverse.

What Games and Activities Will Reinforce Students' New Vocabulary and Language Skills?

If students who are at risk are going to learn the vocabulary they need for success in reading more difficult text, vocabulary and language instruction must be ongoing throughout the school day, during transition periods between classes, and in science, math, art, social studies, and music classes.

Link to a free talking-picture dictionary at **www.languageguide.org/english.** Pictures are arranged into categories such as insects or colors. Running the mouse over the picture triggers a hypertext box containing the spelling of the word while a voice simultaneously says the word.

In Ms. DeMarco's class, vocabulary development is integrated into almost every daily activity. During morning announcements, the principal talks about the inspirational word of the week. After introducing the definition for the word *honorable*, the principal briefly uses the word in context to describe an individual who accomplished great things because he or she had honorable traits. The principal talks about an honorable action the person did. By the end of the week, everyone in the school knows the word *honorable*. After announcements, Ms. DeMarco, the teacher, tells students to think of someone who could be described by the mystery word. As students wait in line to go to the bathroom, she holds an impromptu discussion about individuals who the children believe have honorable characteristics.

When the literacy block of time begins, Ms. DeMarco directly preteaches three words that are in the story. A vocabulary word from last week is reviewed. As students practice reading new words that will be in the story, she selects one or two that are more difficult for the students to decode, because they don't know the meaning. Ms. DeMarco quickly gives the definition of the word and tells the meaning before asking everyone to say the meaning. She then asks several questions that force the students to use the new word in their answer. During the second reading of the story, she asks several questions requiring students to use their new vocabulary words. Students are expected to answer in complete sentences so they will get practice developing their language skills. Spelling instruction provides an opportunity to talk again about one of the words on the list, *straddle*. Because everyone needs a stretch, Ms. DeMarco asks everyone to straddle their desk chairs, to touch the floor, to stand up, and to straddle their chairs again before going back to work.

The time allotted for writing brings more opportunities to use new words. Ms. DeMarco asks the students to write about what the fox saw on his morning route to work. Besides asking students to use the vocabulary word *route* in their written paragraphs, Ms. DeMarco informs the students that she wants them to use two other vocabulary words, *creatures* and *enchanted.* Ms. DeMarco always has students work on grammar at the end of the literacy time block, and today's practice exercises using irregular past-tense forms of verbs are so difficult that she decides to have the students practice in unison so she can provide modeling and error corrections until they have more success with using these words in sentences. When students line up for lunch, they have to say the name of a friend and an adjective starting with the same letter as that name. Everyone had enjoyed this grammar activity so much earlier in the week that Ms. DeMarco used variations of it during free times.

The rest of the day is as vocabulary–language intensive as the morning. Ms. DeMarco misses no opportunities in math, science, or social studies to teach related vocabulary terms. She is always informed about what students are learning in art or music class, so she can reinforce new vocabulary learned in those classes. Ms. DeMarco anchors her direct teaching of vocabulary by having students read, spell, and write new vocabulary words as well as use them in oral communication. If there are a few moments when students are waiting to go home at the end of the day, she will throw in a quick vocabulary or language game. Some of the game activities she interjects at those times follow.

Absurdity Is Fun

What would happen if a cougar startled everyone at recess? Why aren't our shoes made of concrete? What would happen if our shoes were made of concrete? What would happen if a mouse made a thundering noise? Ms. DeMarco likes to ask absurd questions because they are excellent for getting children to think and express their ideas.

Thumbs-Up–Thumbs-Down

Ms. DeMarco's students needed more practice identifying complete sentences. First she taught her students to identify complete sentences by having them select the complete sentences from a list that included both complete and incomplete sentences. Then, Ms. DeMarco started doing the following activity. She put up a large picture on the board and asked students to describe in a complete short sentence what they saw (e.g., "There is a train." "There is a bridge."). Next, she had her students create more complex sentences using connectors (e.g., "There is a train, and there is a bridge," or better still, "There is a train crossing over a covered bridge."). In order to get everyone to participate, she had the other students in the class indicate if their classmate used a complete sentence or not by giving a soundless "thumbs-up" or "thumbs-down." When students gave incomplete sentences, she immediately moved into a My Turn correction and had everyone say the complete sentence after her. During this activity, she tried to use pictures that enabled students to use some of their new vocabulary words.

Plurals, Plurals, and More

Either because of dialect or because English was their second language, many students in Ms. DeMarco's class did not correctly use plurals, especially irregular ones, in formal syntax when answering questions or writing stories. She tried to include a plural–singular discrimination activity in her classroom schedule several times a week, even if for only a short time, to provide practice. When students made errors, she used an effective error correction.

Ms. DeMarco divided the class into two teams to play the plural game. Everyone on Team 1 was given a card with *yes* written on one side and *no* written on the other. Once the card was up, it couldn't be switched or the team didn't get a point. The members of Team 2 sat in a line, ready to walk up to the front and answer questions. Ms. DeMarco used a new vocabulary word the students had been learning or a word whose plural form needed practice. The first student on Team 2 walked up to the front and Ms. DeMarco said, *"I see one* **canyon.***"* She then said, *"Say it for* **six.***"* The same student had to answer, *"I see six* **canyons.***"* After the student said the sentence, the Team 1 members held up their cards to indicate whether the correct answer was given. Students on Team 1 got a point if the correct plural was used. Students on Team 2 got a point if every card (or 9 out of 10 cards) had the correct answer. Some questions that Ms. DeMarco asked included these:

> *"I see a* **deer.** *Say it for* **eight.***"*
>
> *"A* **chime** *rang today. Say it for* **three.***"*
>
> *"Kwame fought a* **lion.** *Say it for* **two.***"*

Strategies for motivating your students to do their best during reading class are described in *In Your Classroom.*

In Your Classroom

Motivating Your Students to Do Their Best

When you are conducting a challenging reading class, you cannot afford to waste a minute of instructional time dealing with disruptive behaviors. Before the school year begins, be proactive and plan the physical classroom environment to reflect environmental strategies supported by research as effective ways to help students stay on task, focused on their work. One of your first decisions should be determining where students will sit during large and small reading groups. Studies investigating the behavior of high-risk students showed that students have more on-task behavior and decreased disruptive behavior when they have more personal space. In classrooms where students have more space between each other, teachers are even rated by their students as more sensitive and friendly (Paine, Darch, Deutchman, Radicchi, & Rosellini, 1983). If students sit at desks, teachers often can reduce behaviors that are disruptive to the class by simply moving the desks farther apart.

In younger classrooms, students often sit on the rug during group reading time. In classrooms that are not physically large enough to have a large rug area, the wigglier children will often begin jostling each other with their elbows while invading each other's personal space. In these circumstances, teachers find themselves frequently correcting students to keep their hands and feet to themselves. In these smaller classrooms, chairs might present a better alternative for getting students to do their best work. Sometimes only one or two students in the class have a difficult time when the group is reading on the rug. For those students, a carpet square, a taped-off area, or a chair often provides the structure needed to listen and participate in the group. If older students sit around tables, reducing the number of students at one table provides more space between them.

Use of frequent activity shifts and periodic physical movement to provide students with the opportunity to stretch will also help students' concentration. The younger the student, the more activity shifts are needed. For example, after students who were sitting on the rug practiced the sound for the letter *n,* one teacher inserted a 2-minute activity where every time she said the *n* sound, the students jumped up like frogs. Then, after a short practice session blending words, the teacher asked everyone to walk to their tables to write the letter *n.* The writing practice was followed by a game where everyone stood up and in unison answered *yes* or *no* to vocabulary questions the teacher asked. Although a teacher in an older classroom can stretch teaching activities out over longer periods of time, periodic 1- or 2-minute stretch breaks can still release energy before students begin the next activity.

Teachers should also be sensitive to students' need for water. If students are actively answering in unison, their throats become parched after a while, causing them to become uncomfortable. In order to avoid this distraction, some teachers allow their students to carry water bottles; others always stop for a moment at the water fountain when the class is in the hall en route to special activities.

APPLIED ACTIVITIES

1. Answer the following fact-or-fiction questions about vocabulary using references from research sources cited in the chapter or from information on the website resources listed in the sidebars.

   a. Research shows that children learn more words directly, from instruction in school, than they learn indirectly, from listening or conversing. Is this fact or fiction? Explain why.

   b. The meaning of most words can be discerned using the context. Is this fact or fiction? Explain why.

   c. It is important that students learn the meaning of all unknown words in the story before they read the story. Is this fact or fiction? Explain why.

2. The following vocabulary words have been identified in your reading series for the upcoming story about a farmer who planted a seed that grew into a large turnip: *granddaughter, planted, grew, strong, enormous,* and *turnip.* Assuming you have only enough time to teach your second-grade students the meaning of two of these words, which words would you choose to teach? Justify your selections.

3. For the next 48 hours, make a list of words that you don't know the meaning of and note where you encountered each word. For example, you may not know the meaning of a word used by a TV broadcaster, a word mentioned in a lecture, a word you read in the newspaper, or a word in the directions for your new software program.

4. Develop either a student-friendly definition or a synonym for each of the following vocabulary words: *survive, frontier, nearby, tame,* and *orchard.*

5. For two of the words above, one using a synonym and the other a definition, develop a series of student questions to teach the meaning of the word using examples and nonexamples. Model your questions after ones shown in Figures 6.1 and 6.2. For each word, include at least three positive and three negative examples.

6. Develop a keyword for one of the following words: *burly, cram, epic, enzyme,* or *powwow.* In developing the keyword, use a similar process to the one used for the word *apex* in Figure 6.7.

7. Develop a semantic map to teach students the range of words that can be used to represent the word *charismatic.* Your semantic map should help students better understand the concept of "charismatic" by categorizing its different qualities.

8. Shown below is a passage from a Grade 2 basal. Tell how you would teach students to use context clues to figure out the meaning of the word *lack.* The thick cloud of dust, rock, and smoke would swirl around the world, blocking the sunlight for months or even years. Without sunlight, the earth would grow very cold. Their idea is that the <u>*lack*</u> of sunshine caused dinosaurs and other life forms to die.

9. Identify the words below that you would teach using morphemic analysis. For one of these words, develop a mini-script telling what you would say to your students when teaching them to use morphemic analysis to figure out its meaning.

careless	bicolor	winless
confusing	demented	unspeakable
discouraged	useful	substandard
discipline	uncomfortable	revocable

10. Your students came across the following sentence in their readers: "The boys and girls made a *dash* for the playground." You had them look up the word *dash* in their dictionaries and they found the following three meanings:

    a. a rush: We made a *dash* for the bus.

    b. a small amount: Put in just a *dash* of pepper.

    c. a short race: He won the fifty-yard *dash.*

    d. Develop a mini-script that you could use to teach students to figure out which meaning of *dash* is used in the story.

11. After lunch you can squeeze in 10 more minutes of vocabulary instruction. This week you have directly taught the following vocabulary words: *slight, hull, reflected, curve, eclipse,* and *prairie.* Plan activities you could do during that time this week to provide more practice for your class.

12. Select two idioms that contain the same word and describe at least two concrete activities you could use to teach the idioms to English language learners.

13. Analyze the strengths and weaknesses of a vocabulary software program.

Companion Website

Now go to Chapter 6 in the Companion Website (www.pearsonhighered.com/bursuck2e) where you can do the following activities:

- Complete Activities that can help you more deeply understand the chapter content.
- Check your comprehension of the content covered in the chapter by going to the Chapter Quiz. Here you will be able to answer practice questions, receive feedback on your answers, and then access resources that will enhance your understanding of chapter content.
- Find Web Links that will extend your understanding of the content and strategies.

REFERENCES

Adams, M., & Bereiter, C. (1995). *Collections for young scholars.* Chicago: Open Court Publishing.

Allen, J. (1999). *Words, words, words: Teaching vocabulary in grades 4–12.* York, ME: Stenhouse.

Armbruster, B., Lehr, F., & Osborn, J. (2001). *Put reading first: The research building blocks for teaching children to read.* Washington, DC: Partnership for Reading.

Baker, D., & Bettino, C. (1988). *Easy English dictionary.* D. McCarr, J. McCarr, L. Eckert, & S. Natwick (Eds.). Austin, TX: Pro-Ed.

Barrett, J. (1978). *Cloudy with a chance of meatballs.* New York: Atheneum Books.

Barton, J. (1996). Interpreting character emotions for literature comprehension. *Journal of Adolescent & Adult Literacy, 40*(1), 22–28. Cited in H. W. Catts & A. G. Kamhi (2005), *Language and reading disabilities* (2nd ed.). Boston: Allyn & Bacon, p. 191.

Baumann, J., Edwards, E., Boland, E., Olejnik, S., & Kame'enui, E. (2003). Vocabulary tricks: Effects of instruction in morphology and context on fifth-grade students' ability to derive and infer word meanings. *American Educational Research Journal, 40*(2), 447–494.

Beck, I., McKeown, M., & Kucan, L. (2002). *Bringing words to life: Robust vocabulary instruction.* New York: The Guilford Press.

Beck, I. L., & McKeown, M. G. (2007). Increasing young low-income children's oral vocabulary repertoires through rich and focused instruction. *The Elementary School Journal, 107*(3), 251–271.

Beck, I. L., McKeown, M. G., & Kucan, L. (2008). *Creating robust vocabulary: Frequently asked questions and extended examples* (p. 35). New York: The Guilford Press.

Berger, M. (1995). *All about electricity.* New York: Scholastic.

Berne, J., & Blachowicz, C. L. (2009). What reading teachers say about vocabulary instruction: Voices from the classroom. *The Reading Teacher, 62,* 314–323.

Biemiller, A. (2001). Teaching vocabulary: Early, direct, and sequential. *American Educator, 25,* 24–28.

Biemiller, A. (2003). Oral comprehension sets the ceiling on reading comprehension. *American Educator, 27*(1), 23–25.

Bos, C. S., & Vaughn, S. (2008). *Strategies for teaching students with learning and behavior problems* (7th ed.). Boston: Allyn & Bacon.

Carey, S. (1978). The child as word learner. In M. Halle, J. Bresnan, & G. Miller (Eds.), *Linguistic theory and psychological reality* (pp. 264–293). Cambridge, MA: MIT Press.

Carnine, D. W., Silbert, J., Kame'enui, E. J., & Tarver, S. (2010). *Direct instruction reading* (5th ed.). New Jersey: Merrill Prentice Hall.

Catts, H. (1991). The relationship between speech-language impairments and reading disabilities. *Journal of Speech and Hearing Research, 36,* 948–958.

Celce-Murcia, M., Brinton, D., & Goodwin, J. (2002). *Teaching pronunciation: A reference for teachers of English to speakers of other languages.* Cambridge: Cambridge University Press.

Cobuild, C. (2005). *Collins COBUILD dictionary.* Florence, KY: Heinle ELT.

Cole, J. (1997). *The magic school bus and the electric field trip.* New York: Scholastic.

Collections for young scholars. (1995). Chicago: Open Court Publishing.

Coyne, D. M., Loftus, S., Zipoli, R., & Kapp, S. (2009). Direct vocabulary instruction in kindergarten: Teaching for breadth versus depth. *The Elementary School Journal, 110*(1), 1–18.

Educational Resources Inc. (2004). *Strategies for high-stakes tests.* Unpublished manuscript.

Ehri, L. (2000). Learning to read and learning to spell: Two sides of a coin. *Topics in Language Disorders, 20*(3), 19–49.

Ehri, L. (2005). Learning to read words: Theory, findings, and issues. *Scientific Studies of Reading, 9,* 167–188.

Engelmann, S., & Osborn, J. (1999). *Language for learning.* Columbus, OH: SRA/McGraw-Hill.

Epstein, S., & Epstein, B. (1977). *The first book of electricity.* New York: Franklin Watts.

Espin, C. A., Busch, T. W., Shin, J., & Kruschwitz, R. (2001). Curriculum-based measurement in the content areas: Validity of vocabulary-matching as an indicator of performance in social studies. *Learning Disabilities Research & Practice, 16*(3), 142–151.

Foil, C. R., & Alber, S. R. (2002). Fun and effective ways to build your students' vocabulary. *Intervention in School and Clinic, 37*(3), 131–139.

Gersten, R., Fuchs, L. S., Williams, J. P., & Baker, S. (2001). Teaching reading comprehension strategies to students with learning disabilities: A review of research. *Review of Educational Research, 71*(1), 279–320.

Hart, B., & Risley, T. R. (1995). *Meaningful differences in the everyday experiences of young American children.* Baltimore: Paul H. Brookes.

Hebert, B. M., & Murdock, J. Y. (1994). Comparing three computer-aided instruction output modes to teach vocabulary words to students with learning disabilities. *Learning Disabilities & Practice, 9*(3), 136–141.

Hirsch, E. D. (2003). Reading comprehension requires knowledge of words and the world: Scientific insights into the fourth-grade slump and the nation's stagnant reading comprehension scores. *American Education, 27,* 10–48.

Horton, S., Lovitt, T., & Givens, A. (1988). A computer-based vocabulary program for three categories of student. *British Journal of Educational Technology, 19*(2), 131–143.

Irugo, S. (1986). A piece of cake: Learning and teaching idioms. *ELT Journal, 40*(3), 236–242.

Jitendra, A. K., Edwards, L. L., Sacks, G., & Jacobson, L. A. (2004). What research says about vocabulary instruction for students with learning disabilities. *Exceptional Children, 70,* 299–322.

Johnson, G., Gersten, R., & Carnine, D. (1987). Effects of instructional design variables on vocabulary acquisition of LD students: A study of computer-assisted instruction. *Journal of Learning Disabilities, 20*(4), 206–213.

Joshi, R. M., Treiman, R., Carreker, S., & Moats, L. (2008–2009). How words cast their spell: Spelling is an integral part of learning the language, not memorization. *American Educator, winter,* 8–18, 42–43. http://www.aft.org/pubsreports/american_educator/issues/winter08_09/joshi.pdf

Klingner, J. K., Vaughn, S., & Boardman, A. (2007). *Teaching reading comprehension to students with learning difficulties.* New York: The Guilford Press, pp. 49–51.

Marzano, R. J. (2004). *Building background knowledge for academic achievement: Research on what works in schools.* Alexandria, VA: Association for Supervision and Curriculum Development.

Marzano, R. J., & Pickering, D. J. (2005). *Building academic vocabulary: Teachers manual.* Alexandria, VA: Association for Supervision and Curriculum Development.

Maslen, B., & Maslen, J. (2006). *Bob Books: Beginning readers.* New York: Scholastic.

Mastropieri, M. A. (1988). Using the keyword methods. *Teaching Exceptional Children, 20,* 4–8.

McEwan, E. (2009). *Teach them all to read: Catching kids before they fall through the cracks* (2nd ed.). Thousand Oaks, CA: Corwin.

McKeown, M., Beck, I., Omanson, R., & Pople, M. (1985). Some effects of the nature and frequency of vocabulary instruction on the knowledge and use of words. *Reading Research Quarterly, 20,* 522–535.

Miller, A. D., Barbetta, P. M., & Heron, T. E. (1994). START tutoring: Designing, training, implementing, adapting, and evaluating tutoring programs for school and home settings. In R. Gardner et al. (Eds.), *Behavior analysis in education: Focus on measurably superior instruction* (pp. 265–282). Monterey, CA: Brooks/Cole.

Moats, L. (Summer, 2001). Overcoming the language gap. *American Educator, 25*(2), 5, 8–9. http://www.aft.org/pubsreports/american_educator/summer2001/lang_gap_moats.html

National Reading Panel. (2000). *Teaching children to read: An evidence-based assessment of the scientific research literature on reading and its implications for reading instruction.* Washington, DC: National Institute of Child Health and Human Development.

Nir-Gal, O., & Klein, P. S. (2004). Computers for cognitive development in early childhood: The teacher's role in the computer learning environment. *Information in childhood education annual,* p. 97.

Paine, S., Darch, C., Deutchman, L., Radicchi, J., & Rosellini, L. (1983). *Structuring your classroom for academic success.* Champaign, IL: Research Press.

Pany, D., Jenkins, J. R., & Schreck, J. (1982). Vocabulary instruction: Effects on word knowledge and reading comprehension. *Learning Disability Quarterly, 5,* 202–215.

Ruddell, R. B. (1999). *Teaching children to read and write: Becoming an influential teacher* (2nd ed.). Boston: Allyn & Bacon.

Schmitt, N., & Carter, R. (2000). The lexical advantage of narrow reading for second language learners. *TESOL Journal, 9*(1), 4–9.

Scott, J. (2005). Opportunities to acquire new meaning from text. In E. Hiebert & M. Kamil (Eds.), *Teaching and learning vocabulary: Bringing research to practice* (pp. 45–68). Hillsdale, NJ: Erlbaum.

Segers, E., & Verhoeven, L. (2003). Effect of vocabulary training by computer in kindergarten. *Journal of Computer-Assisted Learning, 19,* 557–566.

Silverman, R. D. (2007). Vocabulary development of English-language and English-only learners in kindergarten. *The Elementary School Journal, 107*(4), 365–384.

Sousa, D. (2005). *How the brain learns to read.* Thousand Oaks, CA: Corwin.

Stahl, S. A., & Fairbanks, M. M. (1986). The effects of vocabulary instruction: A model-based meta-analysis. *Review of Educational Research, 56*(1), 72–110.

Stanovich, K. E. (1986). Matthew effects in reading: Some consequences of individual differences in the acquisition of literacy. *Reading Research Quarterly, 21,* 360–407.

Taylor, H. (1993). *Coyote places the stars.* New York: Simon & Schuster.

Wilson, B., & Risucci, D. (1998). The early identification of developmental language disorders and the prediction of the acquisition of reading skills. In R. Masland & M. Masland (Eds.), *Preschool prevention of reading failure* (pp. 187–203). Parkton, MD: York Press.

Wood, R. (1997). *Electricity and magnetism fundamentals.* New York: McGraw-Hill.

7 Comprehension

Objectives

After reading this chapter, you will be able to:

1. Describe the knowledge and skills students need to comprehend narrative and expository text and the four key factors that influence comprehension.

2. Identify effective general teaching methods and strategies for teaching students to comprehend text.

3. Implement strategies for teaching comprehension at the sentence, paragraph, and text level.

4. Describe instruction that incorporates multiple strategies to maximize student gains in reading comprehension and motivate students to read more widely.

5. Describe ways to screen, diagnose student needs, and monitor progress in reading comprehension in a multi-tier or RTI model.

6. Identify commercial reading programs that can give struggling readers in Tier 3 a more systematic, explicit approach to learning comprehension skills.

7. Prepare students for passing high-stakes tests in reading.

8. Implement strategies for teaching comprehension skills to older students and English language learners.

Companion Website

To check your comprehension of the content covered in this chapter, go to the Companion Website (www.pearsonhighered.com/bursuck2e) and complete the Chapter Quiz for Chapter 7. Here you will be able to answer practice questions, receive feedback on your answers, and then access resources that will enhance your understanding of chapter content.

What Is Reading Comprehension, and Why Teach It?

When the principal distributed the state test results, Ms. Linder was eager to see her students' reading scores. Her fantasy was that everyone would meet the state standards, but reality was far from that. Ms. Linder noticed that most of the students in her class who met or exceeded standards on the test had also met benchmark on the most recent DIBELS assessment in Oral Reading Fluency. But that still left the 40% of her students who had not passed the state test! Not content with having 40% of her students not make AYP, Ms. Linder thought about each of the students who had not passed the state test. Several of the students had poor fluency skills and read text with longer words very slowly. Two children had poor oral language skills. One puzzle was Ricardo, a student whose primary language was Spanish and who scored above benchmark on the DIBELS Oral Reading Fluency assessment but still failed to meet standards on the state test. Benjamin, a student who was diagnosed with dyslexia, struggled with reading fluency but had strong oral language and reasoning skills. Although Benjamin scored below benchmark on the DIBELS, he surprised Ms. Linder by scoring above the standard on the state test.

What different kinds of reading problems did Ms. Linder's students exhibit?

How will the presence of these problems affect the way Ms. Linder teaches comprehension?

Reading comprehension is the active process of obtaining meaning from written text. As in Ms. Linder's class, students' comprehension problems result from a variety of factors. Shankweiler, Lundquist, and Dreyer (1999) studied a group of poor comprehenders and found that most of the students who could not comprehend had decoding problems of comparable magnitude; only about 10% of the poor comprehenders had comprehension problems even though they were good decoders. Often these poor comprehenders were English language learners such as Ricardo, who moved to this country two years ago. In contrast to the first group, a few students are always able to compensate for slow decoding, as Benjamin did. Just as with phonemic awareness, alphabetic principle, fluency, advanced word reading, and vocabulary, "one size does not fit all" when it comes to reading comprehension.

In its simplest form, reading is the ability to decode and understand the meaning of written words. However, the process of deciphering the meaning of written words is exceedingly complex because it is influenced by a number of important factors including the person who is reading, the text being read, the task the reader is trying to accomplish, and the context in which the reading is being done (RAND Reading Study Group, 2002). A visual display of these four factors is shown in Figure 7.1, followed by a more in-depth description. Effective comprehension instruction takes into account all four factors.

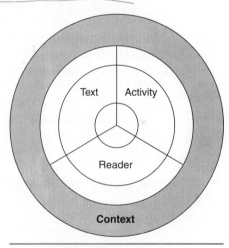

FIGURE 7.1 Factors That Affect Reading Comprehension

Text

Several characteristics of the text itself influence whether a reader comprehends text; these include text readability, text structure, and text organization. Traditionally, educators have looked to text readability as one gauge of text difficulty. Text readability formulae take into account factors such as sentence and word length as well as syntactic structure. For example, to calculate the projected grade level of a text, a teacher can use the Dale-Chall readability formula, which is based on an average sentence length and the number of unfamiliar words (Chall & Dale, 1995). The authors of this readability formula determined that readers typically find it easier to read, process, and recall a passage if the words are familiar and the sentences shorter. During the past two decades, the emphasis has shifted from classic readability formulae to other text features that also affect comprehension. The clarity of writing contributes to the ease of comprehending a text, including the presence of clear pronoun references, explicit or obvious connectives such as *because, since,* or *therefore,* and transition elements between ideas (Hiebert, 1999).

Text structure refers to the way certain types of text are organized to form a framework or pattern (Bos & Vaughn, 2008; Englert & Thomas, 1987). Students who can recognize these patterns have an easier time understanding what they read. The two broadest categories of text, **narrative text** (fiction) and **expository text** (nonfiction) are then broken down into subcategories. Science fiction, tall tales, and mystery stories are subgenres of narrative text. Examples of expository text include biographies, letters, and textbooks. Narrative text is generally much easier to comprehend than expository text, which is characterized by a greater density of technical vocabulary as well as concepts requiring considerable student background knowledge. Keep in mind that comprehension in one kind of reading matter does not automatically transfer to comprehension in others. Jahil's ease in understanding and remembering expository science text does not ensure that he will have the same facility with narrative text. If Jahil does not understand irony, he will have difficulty comprehending a narrative text that is satirical. Table 7.1 lists some differences between narrative and expository text.

It is important to teach your students what text structures are, how to recognize them in text, and how to use them to understand what they are reading. Narrative text, which has a **plot,** can be organized into meaningful parts called **story grammars** including **theme, setting,** character, problem, attempts at resolution, resolution, and reactions. Later in this chapter, visual organizers called story maps, which are used to help organize students' thinking about narrative text, will be discussed in more detail.

Expository text is also organized in specific ways, but unlike narrative text, each piece of expository text does not have the same structure. Expository text usually includes more than one text structure. Fortunately, there are key structures that occur with enough frequency to make manageable the assessing of common expository text structures and the teaching of their identification as a comprehension tool. Table 7.2 shows a list of the five common expository text structures, the ideas they communicate to the reader, and the key words that signal their presence.

Each of these expository text structures has a related graphic organizer or organizers that teachers can use to assist comprehension during or after reading. A sample of some of those organizers and how to teach them will be provided later in this chapter.

TABLE 7.1 Comparison of Narrative and Exposition

Narrative	Expository
Purpose to entertain.	Purpose to inform.
Consistent text structure; all narratives have same basic organization.	Variable text structures; different genres have different structure.
Focus on character motivations, intentions, goals.	Focus on factual information and abstract ideas.
Often require multiple perspective taking understanding points of view of different characters.	Expected to take the perspective of the writer of the text.
Can use pragmatic inferences, i.e., inference from similar experiences.	Must use logical-deductive inferences based on information in texts.
Connective words not critical—primarily *and, then, go.*	Connective words critical—wide variety of connectives, e.g., *because, before, after, when, if–then, therefore.*
Each text can stand alone.	Expected to integrate information across texts.
Comprehension is generally assessed informally in discussion.	Comprehension often assessed in formal, structured tests.

Source: Catts, H. W., & Kamhi, A. G. (1999). *Language and reading disabilities* (2nd ed.). Boston: Pearson Education, p. 159. Copyright © 1999 by Pearson Education. Reprinted by permission of the publisher.

TABLE 7.2 Expository Text Types and Characteristics

Text Type	Function	Signal Words
Descriptive	The text describes something or where something is.	**Description signals** let the reader know where: *above, over, under, outside, between, down, of, in front of, on top of, beside, to the right/left, behind, across, along, outside, inside, near, appears to be, nearby*
Sequence/procedural	The text tells how to do or make something. The text relates a sequence of events.	**Sequence** or **time signals** let the reader know information about *when* something is happening: *first . . . next . . . then, second . . . third, following this step, finally, initially, afterward, preceding, while, as, then, at last, now, ever since, in quick succession, eventually*
Cause/effect	The text gives reasons why something happens. The text tells what might happen next.	**Cause/effect signals** let the reader know when one thing is the result of something else: *because, since, reasons, then, therefore, for this reason, results, effects, consequently, so, in order, thus, as a result, thus, hence*
Problem/solution	The text states a problem and offers solutions to the problem.	**Problem/solution signals** let the reader know what the problem is or what the solution is
Comparison/contrast	The text shows how two things are the same or different.	**Compare/contrast signals** let the reader know about how things are alike or different: *different, same, alike, similar, although, however, on the other hand, but yet, still, rather than, instead of, as opposed to*
Enumerative	The text gives a list of things that are related to the topic.	**Example signals** let the reader know that this is what something means: *an example is, for instance, another, next, finally, for example, in other words, such as, in the same way as, specifically, much like, similar to*

A third text characteristic that affects comprehension is *text organization.* Text that is clearly organized around "big ideas" explicitly communicated to the reader is easier to understand than text emphasizing smaller details. Big ideas are the major concepts in a text that give meaning to all the smaller details. For example, if, in the title or an introductory list of objectives, the author of a science article highlights the big idea that the flow of energy can be controlled by conductors and insulators, and then makes an explicit connection in the text between this big idea and smaller details, the reader will be more likely to understand the text and generate insightful questions about the content.

Comprehension involves understanding various types and levels of information. The ease with which children access information from text depends on how explicitly it is written. For example, information directly stated in the text is easier to understand than information that needs to be inferred. Because texts vary in explicitness, comprehension instruction should reflect that variability by including both explicit and implicit text (Bos & Vaughn, 2008). In explicit text, information is stated directly in the text and can be learned using a minimum of background knowledge. This type of text is the easiest to comprehend. In text that is implicit, students need to use their background knowledge and reasoning skills to infer or make sense of it. For example, Ms. Chao had her students read the following paragraph:

> Susan got a pretty doll for her birthday. The doll cost her parents a lot of money. She also got a new tennis racquet and two new CDs. But Susan still didn't feel happy.

First Ms. Chao asked her students, *"What did Susan get for her birthday?"* This question required explicit information because the answer was directly stated in the text. Next, Ms. Chao asked her students, *"Why was Susan unhappy?"* This question asked for implicit information since the answer was not directly contained in the text; the students needed to use their background knowledge and reasoning skills to answer it (Bos & Vaughn, 2008).

You will find a number of articles on text elements at the TextProject website: **http://www.textproject.org/topics/text.**

Reader

Prior knowledge, or the knowledge and skills that readers bring to the reading process, also strongly influence comprehension. First and foremost is a reader's ability to decode text accurately and fluently enough to allow him to think about what he is reading. It is often claimed that large numbers of students, called "word callers," can fluently read text but do not comprehend what they are reading. In reality, research shows that only about 2.5% of all readers fall into this category, thus emphasizing the strong relationship between fluency and comprehension (Shankweiler, 1999). Students who effortlessly read the words in a text usually have the resources needed to comprehend the information in comparison to students whose energy and attention are consumed by laborious decoding. Strategies for producing fluent, accurate readers were covered in Chapters 1–5.

A student's background, language, and vocabulary knowledge also affect comprehension. If Carla has visited the Southwest, she is more apt to understand a mystery that takes place in the Arizona desert. If Connor's grandmother talks about her homeland of Vietnam, he is likely to understand clearly a well-written expository text about the Vietnam War. Strategies for building student vocabulary and other oral language skills were described in Chapter 6. Because comprehension is "an active process that requires an intentional and thoughtful interaction between the reader and the text" (National Reading Panel, 2000, p. 13), readers must actively employ various comprehension strategies as they read. Good readers make predictions based on background knowledge, focus on looking forward and backward in the text to find important information, paraphrase, explain, summarize, and construct conclusions about what they read (Smith, 1999). They employ fix-up strategies such as underlining or using a dictionary when they recognize that they are not fully understanding the text (Keene, 2002).

Activity

The nature and purpose of the reading task also affect comprehension (Moats, 2005). Motivation to continue reading can depend on whether an individual is reading for pleasure or to acquire new information. Is the text voluntary reading or part of a job or school requirement? Before the reader starts, does she have prior interest or background knowledge about the reading? All of these factors can affect students' motivation to persist and continue reading until they achieve understanding. Finally, reading may be tied to extrinsic consequences that include grades or test scores, or intrinsic consequences that involve feelings of amusement, satisfaction, or enlightenment (Moats, 2005). Consequences can affect all aspects of comprehension, including whether students stick with a task and the desire to select the correct strategies, monitor understanding, and employ fix-up strategies if needed. Gato might not have had any interest in Antarctica before reading a book on that topic that his teacher has selected, but halfway through his reading he becomes so interested in learning more about the emperor penguins and how the ice is beginning to melt that he starts rereading the book again so he understands all the information.

Context

Finally, the context in which reading occurs can have a significant effect on comprehension, especially the amount of support provided for reading by peers and teachers. McEwan (2001) explains,

> Students must experience success if they are to progress in reading proficiency. Therefore, teachers must structure learning situations that ensure success. Success increases the willingness of students to work harder and to endure some frustration. Teachers can control a student's success in three ways: (a) selection and sequencing of instructional objectives (b) grouping of students for instruction and (c) instructional procedures and activities. (p. 84)

Specific strategies for carrying out each of these ways of building success are described throughout this chapter and text. When a student is expected to read frustration-level text, feelings of inadequacy for the task can consume her attention and diminish effort. The extent to which reading is valued at home or within a student's peer group also can affect the effort that goes into reading challenging material for understanding. If several third-grade girls are reading *The Baby-Sitters Club* or Harry Potter books and then at recess discussing the hair-raising stories, other third graders are likely to pick up the same books. Many schools have strengthened their reading culture by providing incentives to students who read a certain number of books by holding book fairs and by routinely encouraging parents to read to their children. Teachers and building principals who are readers themselves and have a personal passion for reading are more likely to convey that enthusiasm to students.

What Underlying Skills Do Students Need to Comprehend Text?

Oral Reading Fluency

We have often explained that students who can read text accurately and fluently are much more likely to be able to understand what they read. Therefore, systematic, explicit instruction in phonics and oral reading fluency is at the heart of any good instructional program in reading comprehension (Pressley, 2002).

Oral Language

Chapter 6 emphasized the importance of oral language skills, including knowledge of vocabulary and figurative language. Students who come to school deficient in oral language need direct instruction in those oral language skills essential for adequate listening, speaking, and, ultimately, reading. Most instruction in reading comprehension consists of students discerning the meaning of groups of paragraphs, or passages. Yet, students' ability to understand passages depends largely on their ability to understand sentences. Moats (2005) points out that because the structure of written language is different from oral language, many children may struggle in understanding written sentences even if they are able to understand oral ones. In addition, the ability to process sentence structure efficiently aids overall reading comprehension as well as written composition (Moats, 2005). For these reasons, effective comprehension instruction often needs to include some explicit instruction at the sentence level. In this section, ways to teach sentence repetition and how to answer who, what, where, when, and why questions are discussed. Later in the chapter, strategies for teaching students to make inferences at the sentence level are described.

Sentence Repetition   Sentence repetition, or the ability to repeat verbatim a simple sentence pronounced by the teacher, is an important yet difficult skill for many young children who are at risk for reading difficulties. Both listening and reading comprehension depend on children being able to hold information in **working memory,** also called short-term memory, as they simultaneously process new information (Willingham, 2009). Carnine, Silbert, Kame'enui, and Tarver (2010) recommend providing 3 to 5 minutes of daily practice for students who cannot perform this skill. Practice can start with a simple My Turn where the teacher says the sentence, followed by a Your Turn. If students are unable to exactly repeat the sentence, the teacher can provide more support by saying the sentence and emphasizing the deleted or mispronounced part with a "pause and punch." In a pause and punch, the teacher increases her voice volume as she says the words that were

Read more about how working memory combines information from the environment and integrates it with information stored in long-term memory at **http://www.aft.org/pubs-reports/ american_educator/issues/ spring2009/index.htm.**

difficult for the students. If a pause and punch doesn't provide enough support, the teacher should move into a Together turn, saying the sentence together with students until they can say it independently (Kozloff, 2005). If students continue to struggle, the teacher should start with short three- to four-word sentences and gradually increase the length as students progress. When students are able to repeat longer sentences exactly and with normal intonation, they are ready to move to more advanced oral language skills.

Who, What, Where, When, and Why Questions   Many younger and ELL students also need to learn how to answer what Carnine and colleagues refer to as the question words: *who, what, when, where,* and *why* (Carnine et al., 2010). The authors recommend teaching *who* and *what* questions first, as these are the easiest. Instruction should follow a developmental sequence, next focusing on *when* and *where* questions before the more difficult *why* questions. To teach the question words, start instruction at the My Turn–Your Turn level as in this example of teaching *who* and *what*. As with sentence repetition, if students make errors while answering the questions, add the support of Together practice. In the beginning use a pause and punch when saying the critical question words, as in "The BIG rabbit hopped UNDER the fence."

My Turn

Teacher: **"Sarah picked up the rabbit. WHO picked up the rabbit? Sarah."** (pause) **"WHAT did Sarah do? Picked up the rabbit."**

Your Turn

Teacher: **"Tabitha ate a peach. Say that."**
Students: "Tabitha ate a peach."
Teacher: **"WHO ate a peach?"**
Students: "Tabitha."
Teacher: **"WHAT did Tabitha do?"**
Students: "Ate a peach."

Teachers should set high expectations for their students during oral language activities, requiring their students to use the correct past tense verb form of *ate* when they answer. Once students have learned to answer all five types of questions, teachers can provide cumulative review using one sentence as the basis for student answers and eliminate the pause and punch in their questions. Question words can be taught orally or using written text. As with any comprehension activity, be sure that the reading material can be read with at least 90% accuracy before using it for comprehension activities. Research-based methods for building reading-comprehension skills while reading aloud to children are explained in the *Research Note*.

Background Knowledge

The term "fourth-grade slump" describes a pattern of declining test scores that begins when many students reach fourth grade (Chall, Jacobs, & Baldwin, 1990). Students whose scores on reading tests decline do not regress in fourth grade; rather, they are expected to read increasingly difficult text that contains more specialized vocabulary and abstract ideas. Often they have no frame of reference to the topics or issues in the higher level text. Even more alarming, the gap between students unable to read increasingly difficult text and their peers only continues to widen until it becomes what has been described as the "eighth-grade cliff." In a downward spiral, these students are now cut off from the steadily increasing background knowledge or knowledge of the world that they could be learning through assigned and recreational reading.

Research Note

Using Interactive Read-Alouds to Build Comprehension Skills

A **read-aloud** is planned reading of text to students for a specific purpose. These oral-reading sessions have the potential to develop comprehension, oral language, vocabulary, core knowledge, and visualization skills, as well as to increase motivation for the subject or reading in general, but only if they are highly interactive. During highly interactive read-alouds, the teacher conducts prereading activities to prepare students to understand the context of the story. Throughout the story students have the opportunity to answer questions to clarify the meaning of the text. The teacher uses many of the comprehension strategies discussed throughout this chapter as students learn to predict, summarize what they are reading, answer critical-thinking questions, and draw conclusions. Sometimes pictures are shown to enable students to visualize the text. However, pictures are shown only after the reading to ensure that students are deriving meaning from the language. Highly interactive read-alouds have been shown to be more effective in teaching vocabulary than traditional read-alouds that follow a performance style (Beck & McKeown, 2007; Coyne, Simmons, Kame'enui, & Stoomiller, 2004). In performance-style read-alouds, teachers dramatically read the text while students passively listen to the performance. Conversation is limited to before and after the story, so students miss out on valuable opportunities to interact with the language of the text during the story. In short, simply reading aloud to children who are at risk is not enough, and caution is advised, as performance-based read-alouds take up valuable instructional time when children could be learning important reading skills (Brabham & Lynch-Brown, 2002).

Ironically, researchers have concluded that the "fourth-grade slump" results from a lack of background knowledge in the first place. Cognitive psychologists explain that adept readers connect their background knowledge to new knowledge that they read in a text. Constructing meaning from text is an active, dynamic process requiring the reader to use knowledge brought to the text. E. D. Hirsch (2000) described this process when he wrote, "It takes knowledge to gain knowledge" (p. 2). Remember a time when you read a text for which you had no background knowledge. For example, if you have little or no background in higher level European cultural history, the following paragraph makes little sense. If your background knowledge does not include the book mentioned in this text, you have few clues about the meaning of unknown vocabulary words. Hours later you will probably not remember this information you read:

> Since his death, Musil criticism has suffered from a polemical opposition between those who want to salvage Musil for a left-wing, Enlightenment tradition and those who are fundamentally apolitical and attracted primarily to his mysticism. The most basic level of this controversy concerns the philological problems of Musil's massive *Nachlass* and his intentions for the completion of *The Man Without Qualities*. The difficulty of resolving this debate lies not only in the open-endedness of Musil's work but also in his attempt to dissolve the polar style of thought which assumes the firm oppositions between romanticism and positivism, idealism and materialism. (Luft, 1980, p. 3)

Did you feel a rising tension as you tried to extract the meaning from this text? In a discussion of the relationship of prior knowledge to comprehension, the National Reading Panel report (2000) authors explain the relationship of background knowledge to reading comprehension:

> A reader must activate what he or she knows to use it during reading to comprehend a text. Without activation of what is known that is pertinent to the text, relevant knowledge may not be available during reading, and comprehension may fail; this is analogous to listening to someone speak an unknown foreign language.

If students who are at risk for reading difficulties are to move past the fourth-grade slump, they need an *information-rich* curriculum from the time they enter school. The information that students learn, whether it be the names of continents, information about the pyramids of Egypt, the origins of the early American civilization, or the properties of an alloy, are stored in long-term memory, available for use when reading books on related subjects.

The following strategies prepare students who are at risk to build their background knowledge and avoid the fourth-grade slump.

- Develop classroom libraries that have at least 50% nonfiction books. Although adults often assume that students prefer reading fiction, a study by Kletzien and Szabo (1998) indicated that when elementary students of both genders are given quality fiction and nonfiction books, they choose nonfiction at least 50% of the time.
- Use strategies described in Chapter 6 to teach vocabulary.
- Integrate gradual and cumulative teaching of information about the world we live in, starting in kindergarten. Young children enjoy learning important information about things they know nothing about, as long as it is taught well. Establish specific grade-level standards in each of the content areas that specify core factual information, and vocabulary students will learn so that teachers in upper grades can build on that foundational knowledge.
- Plan lessons so that students are reading as much expository text as narrative text during reading classes.
- Use *narrow reading* to develop students' depth of knowledge in a specific subject area. Planning an in-depth unit in science or social studies using multiple reading sources about the same subject is more effective than a less intensive approach. Lionel will know more about the Civil War if the teacher includes as part of the lesson plans a short story about Robert E. Lee, a book about Harriet Tubman and the Underground Railroad, a movie and discussion about President Lincoln, and a writing assignment about an article discussing a Yankee soldier's life.
- Weave background information into every subject area. If your third-grade students are drawing a picture of their school, teach them the meaning of *architecture* and *three-dimensional.* Everyone should be encouraged to use these same terms when they draw another building they have chosen.

> Investigate Core Knowledge lesson plans written by teachers who are developing an information-rich curriculum: **http://www.coreknowledge.org/CK/resrcs/lessons/index.htm.**

- Use strategies to activate prior knowledge and use them as a check to indicate when you need to supply missing background knowledge.

How Do I Teach Students to Comprehend Text?

Use Explicit Instruction

Research indicates that all students benefit when comprehension instruction is systematic and explicit. Lesson enhancements described in Chapter 1 are as important for teaching comprehension as they are for teaching more basic reading skills. Students need cumulative review to solidify background knowledge about the content they are reading and to continually refine their comprehension strategy skills. In order to maintain student interest, lessons need to move at a perky pace with enough reinforcement provided to bolster students' confidence. Teachers show students what reading comprehension "looks like" through **think-alouds (My Turn)** when they describe their own thought process in reading the text. This process enables students to "see" the teacher using a skill that could not otherwise be observed. Gradually teachers reduce support until students can independently vocalize their own think-alouds and are accustomed to actively thinking about what they are reading, whether for expository or narrative text (Rosenshine, 1997). McEwan (2009) refers to the process of starting instruction with strong scaffolding before gradually reducing it as "coaching" students. During the more heavily scaffolded My Turn phase, students observe their teacher applying comprehension strategies through think-alouds. Gradually the teacher carefully reduces her support by using Your Turns with feedback and close monitoring, until eventually the students independently apply those comprehension strategies.

Ask Questions

When teachers ask frequent, quality questions about text, their students retain information longer, understand the text with more clarity, integrate information from the text with their own knowledge, and become critical thinkers. We were surprised that in many classrooms we observed, teachers often waited to ask questions until after students read the text, even when student accuracy in reading the words was high. They worried that by asking questions during the story they would interrupt the students' concentration, so we reassured them that by asking frequent questions they would deepen students' understanding and thus increase attention paid to text.

Before planning what questions to ask, teachers need to determine how to divide a passage into manageable segments. Younger students who are at risk often are at the sentence-comprehension level, and unless questions are asked after every sentence, they do not integrate the information in the sentence they are reading with the preceding and forthcoming sentences. Usually older students are at the paragraph or page stage of questioning when they are learning how to pull together "big ideas" from longer text. Ankit is fortunate because his teacher asks frequent questions throughout the lesson. As the class reads a book on the Civil War, he is forced to actively think throughout the lesson because she might call on him at any time even if his hand is not raised. When Ankit answers questions supporting his answers with information from the text, he has more exposure to the content through this discussion. These exposures during discussion increase the likelihood that information about the Civil War will become a part of his long-term memory. When students were confused reading an introductory sentence about the Battle of Appomattox, the teacher's question-answer scaffolding helped Ankit understand the rest of the paragraph describing why this was such a critical battle.

Preplanning the questions that you will ask during the text reading ensures that you ask a variety of different types of questions and that the lesson moves at a perky pace. Because of design issues, packaged commercial reading programs such as those of Harcourt or Houghton Mifflin include questions that are scattered throughout the teacher manuals, often two or three pages away from where a teacher would logically ask them. In reading programs that depend on leveled texts, often the teacher has to shoulder the burden of writing out all the questions, or the recommended questions are in other source books. To help teachers remember to ask high-quality questions, we showed them how during preplanning they could write each question on a Post-it note which they then attached to the place in the book where they would ask it. Sometimes when teachers planned their lessons they put notes at the end of sentences, and sometimes they put them at the end of paragraphs, but they always asked at least one question per page.

Preplanning questions helps teachers ask quality questions that are relatively short, clear, and unambiguous. In order to plan your questions, you need to know the different types of questions teachers ask and some of the best practices related to matching questions to text. The two main categories of questions are literal and inferential questions:

1. Literal questions are questions that students can find the information for directly in the text. The questions are often facts, vocabulary, dates, times, and locations explicitly stated in the text. Some examples are: *What was the date when the war started? Who ate the beans? What city did they live in? What was the name of the first colony?*

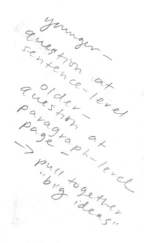
younger – question at sentence-level
older – question at paragraph – page-level
→ pull together "big ideas"

2. Inferential questions are questions for which the answers are not explicitly stated in the text. Thus, students use hints and clues in the text along with their own knowledge and experience to answer them. Some examples are: *In what season did the story take place, and what clues let you know that? How did Stuart Little's size help his family? After reading this section, do you think that Rosetta's family is poor, middle class, or rich, and what clues let you know that?*

The National Reading Panel report (2000) indicates that answering questions is probably best used as part of a multiple-strategy teaching package. The question–answer relationship (QAR) is one strategy that helps students who have difficulty answering **inference** questions. Teachers introduce the QAR strategy by explaining to students that there are four types of questions they usually answer about what they have read. "Right there" questions are literal questions with the answer stated in the reading, usually in one sentence. Answers to the next three types of questions come from thinking about what they already know or from clues in the text. Students are then introduced to the four specific kinds of questions, depicted in Figure 7.2, that they answer during or after their reading.

In the Book QARs

Right There
The answer is in the text, usually easy to find. The words used to make up the question and words used to answer the question are **Right There** in the same sentence.

In My Head QARs

Author and You
The answer is *not* in the story. You need to think about what you already know, what the author tells you in the text, and how it fits together.

**Think and Search
(Putting It Together)**
The answer is in the story, but you need to put together different story parts to find it. Words for the question and words for the answer are not found in the same sentence. They come from different parts of the text.

On My Own
The answer is *not* in the story. You can even answer the question without reading the story. You need to use your own experience.

FIGURE 7.2 Four Types of Questions

Source: T. E. Raphael. Teaching question–answer relationships revisited. *The Reading Teacher, 391*(6), p. 519. Reprinted with permission of International Reading Associatin.

TABLE 7.3   Answers to Questions

Type of Question	Question	What Mrs. Garcia Said
Right There	What type of winter was it in Boston?	The first sentence tells me that it was a cold winter in Boston. The information is **right there** in that sentence.
Think and Search	Why did Peter and Thomas look like roly-poly cubs?	The second sentence tells me that the boys looked like roly-poly cubs because they wore so much clothing, and I remember that the first sentence told me that it was cold in Boston. If they were going outside in the cold, they needed to put on all those clothes, which made them look like little cubs. By **searching** through the first two sentences and using my brain **to think,** I found the answer.
On My Own	Do you think that the boys will deliver all the wood?	The story doesn't tell me anything about this, but I can figure something out **on my own.** I know that wood is heavy. If it's cold outside maybe it is snowing and the roads are slippery. The boys might fall in the snow and not be able to deliver those heavy logs to everyone.
Author and Me	What kind of transportation do you think the boys used when they went to deliver the soap and candles?	The **author** doesn't tell me anything about the kind of transportation they used. But the author does write that the story happened a long time ago back in 1774. **I** know that cars weren't invented then and that people either rode horses, rode in carriages pulled by horses, or walked. Since these were young boys, I imagine that they walked.

After introducing the four types of questions, the teacher then asks students to read three or four sentences displayed on an overhead projection and uses a My Turn to show how and why she would answer each of the questions. For example, Mrs. Garcia completed the example grid in Table 7.3 and explained to the class how she arrived at the answer to the four questions that were based on this passage.

> It was a cold winter in Boston back in 1774, but the cut wood had to be delivered. Ethan, who was 9 years old, and Jeb, who was 10, looked like roly poly cubs when they went out, they wore so much clothing. Mom, who was sick from the fever, stayed at home close to the fire.

Teachers ask older students a higher proportion of more difficult inferential questions than they do younger ones, although both groups need a combination of the four types. When a student is unable to answer a question, the "think-aloud" strategy discussed later in this section allows the teacher to show the student how she arrives at the answer (Cotton, 1989).

Calibrate Wait-Time Before Asking Questions

Wait-time, also called think-time, is the silent pause between the last word a teacher says in a question to students and the first word a student says when answering the teacher's question. Researchers have determined that teachers' wait-time is typically less than one second (Cotton, 1989). Even though maintaining a perky pace during reading lessons is important, extending wait-time to three seconds between the end of a question and the start of the answer gives students additional time to think about their answer. This additional think-time benefits students in a number of ways:

- Students give longer, more accurate answers.
- The number of times students don't respond decreases.

- Many more students volunteer answers.
- Academic achievement in the class generally increases.
- More students who are English language learners, have speech problems, or have learning disabilities will volunteer answers.
- A few more-capable students are unable to dominate class discussion.

Since three seconds is the absolute minimum for effective wait-time, if you are unaccustomed to having a longer period of silence between your question and an answer, take three slow steps around the room or count "1-100, 2-100, 3-100" on your fingers behind your back as a reminder cue. Let your students know that you are waiting to see many students raise their hands before calling on someone to answer your question so that they will habitually start to formulate answers immediately after your questions (Cotton, 1989; Stahl, 1990).

Scaffold Incorrect Answers and "No Responses"

Often students who are at risk will not attempt to answer questions because they are worried about making errors in front of their classmates or are unsure of their speech. Even when you increase your wait-time, some of these students will not volunteer answers and when you call on them will say, *"I don't know,"* or silently shrug their shoulders. Increase your support and use the following four-step "cue-clueing procedure" so that your students who routinely do not answer questions develop the confidence and skills to begin participating. For example, if you ask, *"What is one detail in this section that led me to decide the main idea was 'Mae was fascinated by science'?"* scaffold instruction for a student whose hand was not raised, as in this example:

1. First provide a cue: *"What are some of the things that Mae was doing in this section that showed she was fascinated with learning science?"*
2. Give the student a 3-second wait-time pause to formulate an answer. If he still can't answer, then move to step 3.
3. Increase your scaffolding and provide a clue that is so overt you are certain it will lead the student to the right answer: *"Look at sentence 4 and read it."* (Student reads: "Mae spent many hours at the library reading books about science and space.") Then ask, *"So where did she go to learn more about science?"* (Student answers, "The library.")
4. Reinforce and expand the student's answer to bolster confidence: *"Yes, that's absolutely right. The information in the book describing how Mae went to the library and spent all that time reading about science and space was a clue that she must really like science."*

Asking a student to reread the key sentence providing a clue to the information is always more effective than calling on another student or simply providing the answer. When Len is unable to describe how Jo is feeling about eating the food she made, Ms. Andrist points to the key sentence and asks him to read it again. *"Think about how Jo is feeling when you read this sentence,"* urges Ms. Andrist. Len reads, *"She was on the verge of crying when she met Laurie's eyes which looked merry."* If Len then answers, *"verge of crying,"* Ms. Andrist will probe further and ask, *"So how would she **feel** if she was on the verge of crying?"* If Len still cannot answer, Ms. Andrist will explain the clues that tell her the answer. Even though this sentence looks like a basic one, it is possible that a student does not know what "met Laurie's eyes" or "verge of crying" mean. These two phrases might be particularly problematic for English language learners. A student could also be confused by the clause in the sentence describing how *merry* Laurie is. Simply asking students to reread

Learn about the different types of wait-time and think-time at **http://www.atozteacherstuff.com/pages/1884.shtml.**

the sentence and then answer doesn't provide enough support for those problems. The teacher might need to clarify vocabulary or figurative language, as was discussed in Chapter 6, or use "think-alouds," which are described in more detail in the next section.

Model Comprehension Skills Through Think-Alouds

In a classroom, you can often tell which students are not actively thinking about what they are reading or what is read to them by the glazed look in their eyes. Many struggling readers do not naturally develop an ongoing dialogue with the text and author as they read. They haven't developed metacognition, which is the conscious awareness of their thought processes while reading. Because these students do not use **metacognitive skills,** they are unable to plan, monitor, and select effective strategies when there is a problem with their comprehension. The use of think-alouds is a strategy by which a teacher models the active thinking process that skilled readers use and teaches students these skills. A teacher might choose to verbalize his thoughts about a comprehension strategy he is using, how he determines the meaning of a vocabulary word, how he determines whether he understands what he is reading, or what he predicts will come next in the text and why. Think-alouds allow teachers to develop students' metacognitive skills by making their own explicit. When a student is unable to answer inferential questions, the teacher uses a think-aloud to draw his attention to the clues in the text or the background knowledge needed to answer the question.

Struggling readers benefit from observing what skilled readers think about while reading, and teacher modeling through think-alouds provides that insight. Mr. Gramble used a think-aloud to help students understand what an *assumption* was by using the following think-aloud: *"From the text and illustration, I can tell something about Alex. She says she is unhappy because her father isn't home. I can remember a time when I was disappointed with someone and I felt sad. I can also tell that Alex does not like dressing up and her mother wants her to wear her best dress. Because she misses her father and doesn't like to dress up, I'm going to make an assumption that Alex is not going to enjoy her birthday party."* By using a think-aloud, Mr. Gramble enabled his students to see a skill that could not otherwise be observed. Although initially teachers provide all the think-alouds, gradually they reduce their support and encourage students to use think-alouds as they read the text. You will learn more about how to do this when you read the section on reciprocal teaching. Some common think-aloud starters include:

Think-aloud starters:

"I predict that this next section will be about . . . because. . . ."

"I want to learn more about. . . ."

"I wonder why. . . ."

"I have a picture in my mind of. . . ."

"I don't understand this section so I'll read ahead a few lines to see if it becomes clearer. If not, I'll reread it."

"The word _____ in the sentence gives me a clue that. . . ."

"From what I know about . . . I can tell that. . . ."

Try out one of the specific think-aloud activities at **http://bit.ly/XiEpy.**

Companion Website

Go to the Video Activities section of Chapter 7 in the Companion Website (www.pearson-highered.com/bursuck2e) and complete the activity entitled *Think Aloud Strategy* to see how a teacher employs this strategy with older students.

Use Graphic Organizers with New Text

Graphic organizers such as the semantic maps discussed in Chapter 6 are visual representations of information that depict the relationships between facts, terms, and ideas within a learning task. Other examples of graphic organizers include tables, timelines, flowcharts, or diagrams used to record, organize, analyze, synthesize, and assess information and ideas. Students with limited working memory benefit from their use as memory aids during instruction. Students with attention or listening problems also benefit from having a completed graphic before, during, or after their reading. Graphic organizers can be completed by the teacher before, during, or after reading the text. They can also be completed by students with help from the teacher or independently as practice or review after instruction. However, having students complete graphic organizers prior to instruction can be problematic. Read the following description of Mrs. Whipple's lesson and think about why her use of a graphic organizer was ineffective.

> After students independently read a story about an oafish giant, Mrs. Whipple divided her class into groups and asked each group to complete a graphic organizer listing details about six characters' attitudes toward the giant.

Mrs. Whipple didn't realize that when graphic organizers are used for independent work, those students who have the best comprehension skills usually complete the graphic organizer for the group, while other students' engagement is limited.

Note how Mrs. Palmer used My Turns to teach her students how to complete graphic organizers.

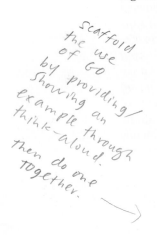

Scaffold the use of GO by providing/ showing an example through think-aloud. then do one Together.

> Mrs. Palmer discussed the graphic organizer with the entire class after they had read the story. Each student had a copy of the graphic organizer, but she also projected a large copy on the board using a think-aloud to explain, *"Today we will find out what every character thought about the Giant and write that information on our chart. Watch me answer the first one. I'm going to start looking for the first character on page one where the author introduces Rabbit. I will read everything that Rabbit says and does to find out how he feels about Giant."* (Mrs. Palmer showed the students what scanning text looks like with her eyes and finger silently moving down the page.) *"Oh, look! On page 2, Rabbit runs away from Giant and hides. I know that when someone runs away and hides they are usually scared. I will write Rabbit's name in the first box and then write in the second box that he feels scared of the giant. I'd like everyone to write that on your chart as I write it on mine."*
>
> After modeling one answer, Mrs. Palmer wanted to see if the students were ready for a Together, so she reduced her scaffolding. *"Now, I want all of you to find the place where Bear first starts talking."* Mrs. Palmer scanned the class to make sure that everyone was scanning the text. *"Now read what Bear says and does to find out how he feels about the giant."* Mrs. Palmer provided enough wait-time so that more students figured out the answer. She then called on students to explain their answers and tell where they found them in the book. If students were able to fill in the information with Togethers, Mrs. Palmer continued to provide that support throughout the class session.
>
> At the end of the lesson, Mrs. Palmer reviewed the critical content again using the graphic organizer. She asked a student to summarize the text using the graphic organizer as a guide. Later, Mrs. Palmer had students complete a blank graphic organizer for homework or independent work.

Although older students need less support, using a graphic organizer while students are reading text stimulates interest, keeps students actively thinking, and organizes information for them so that they retain it longer. Archer and Gleason (2010) suggest the following guidelines for constructing graphic organizers when using them to help students comprehend expository text (pp. 291–294).

a. **Determine the critical content (e.g., vocabulary, concepts, ideas, generalizations, events, details, facts) that you wish to teach your students.** Helping students

Attribute	Native Americans	Colonists
Land	Shared	Owned
	Lived close to it without changing it	Cleared it
	Respected it	Used it

Summary

Native Americans and colonists had different ideas about the land. Native Americans shared the land, whereas the colonists owned individual pieces of it. Native Americans lived close to the land; they respected and did not change it. Colonists used the land for their own gain.

FIGURE 7.3 Comparison–Contrast Concept Map

Source: Friend, M., & Bursuck, W. (2006). *Including students with special needs: A practical guide for classroom teachers* (5th ed). Boston: Allyn & Bacon, p. 327.

focus on the most critical information is important for several reasons. First, struggling readers may have trouble identifying the most important information in an oral lesson or textbook chapter. In most cases this information will be content stressed in your state's standards. Second, it is easier for students to remember several main ideas than many isolated details. Third, putting too much information on a graphic organizer can make it so visually complex that students may have trouble interpreting it.

b. **Organize the concepts in a visual representation.** Because the purpose of a graphic organizer is to clarify interrelationships among ideas and information, you should keep the visual display as simple as possible. Figures 7.3 and 7.4 show two examples of completed graphic organizers.

c. **Design a completed concept map.** Completing the map before you teach with it ensures that the information is clear and accurate and can be presented to your students in a timely manner.

d. **Create a partially completed concept map (to be completed by students during instruction).** Requiring students to fill out the map as you present your lesson is an excellent way to keep them on task. Also, many students with special needs benefit from a multisensory approach; seeing the information on the graphic, hearing it from the teacher, and writing it on the map helps them retain the information presented.

e. **Create a blank concept map for students to use as a postreading or review exercise.** This structure for review provides more practice for students, who are then more likely to put the information in long-term memory.

Download free graphic organizers from **http://www.eduplace.com/ graphicorganizer/index.html.**

The **story map** shown in Figure 7.4 is a graphic organizer that Ms. Barrows used to teach her students the story *The Funny Farola* (Miranda & Guerrero, 1986). This type of graphic organizer has been shown to help students with special needs read with better comprehension because it provides a visual guide to understanding and retelling stories. As the students read the story, Ms. Barrows guided their comprehension by asking the students questions about the various story elements and then recording the correct answers on the story map. As you read a description of her instruction, determine where she is using My Turns, Togethers, or Your Turns.

Ms. Barrows: Where do you think the story takes place? It's hard to tell, because the writers don't come right out and say it.

Lovell: I think it takes place in a city.

Ms. Barrows: Why do you think so, Lovell?

Lovell: Because it sounds like it's a big parade, and cities have big parades.

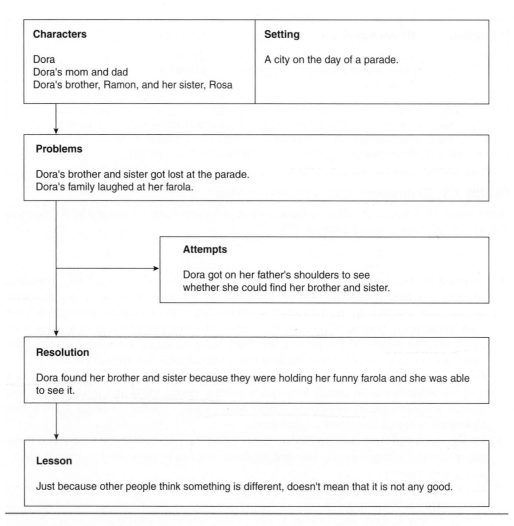

FIGURE 7.4 Story Map

Ms. Barrows: Good thinking, Lovell. When stories don't come out and say things, we have to figure it out by thinking hard, and that's what you did. Let's all fill in the setting on our maps. [They do.] Remember, we said last week that all stories have a problem that needs to be solved. Read the next four pages and find out what the problem is here. [The students read the passage.] What's the problem?

Justin: Well, Dora's little brother and sister got lost at the parade.

Ms. Barrows: Right. That's one problem. Write it on your maps. Now, does anyone see another problem?

Eliseo: I know. Dora made a farola that looked like a frog and everybody laughed at her.

Ms. Barrows: Eliseo, what's wrong with a farola that looks like a frog? I thought it looked cute.

Eliseo: I think it was because Dora's was different from everyone else's. In the pictures in the story, there were no farolas that looked like animals.

Ms. Barrows: That's right, Eliseo. Let's all put this problem on our maps. [They do.] Let's read the next page and find out what Dora and her mom and dad attempted to do to try to find her brother and sister. (Friend & Bursuck, 2008; pp. 342–343)

Companion Website

Go to the Video Activities section of Chapter 7 in the Companion Website (www.pearson-highered.com/bursuck2e) and complete the activity entitled *Mapping* to see how a teacher uses concept mapping in a lesson.

Teach Comprehension Before, During, and After Reading the Text

Comprehension strategies, content instruction, and question asking are integrated into all parts of a reading lesson occurring before, during, and after the reading. An effective way to differentiate instruction is through **frontloading** techniques used before reading to activate students' prior knowledge, discuss critical knowledge and vocabulary needed to understand the text, and provide information on text structure and comprehension strategies useful in understanding the text. English language learners benefit when pictures and objects are added to frontloading activities. Before reading a text about extreme weather, show students a two-minute video clip of a hurricane and tornado. Then discuss any related science principles necessary for understanding the text. Students from poverty who lack direct experiences that other classmates have, such as vacations at the beach or trips to Alaska, benefit from frontloading activities that fill in information they do not have (Buehl, 2008).

The most productive comprehension instruction occurs when a teacher asks a high percentage of questions requiring thought before, during, and after the reading, as shown in Table 7.4. When Mr. Hearn asks frequent questions as he is reading a biography to his students, he can readily determine whether they are accurately comprehending the information the author intends to convey. If students get lost in the text, he can help them apply strategies to fix the problem. When questions are strictly factual in nature and are left for after the reading, students fail to learn to apply comprehension strategies or use inference to answer questions.

How Do I Teach Comprehension at the Sentence Level?

Students who need sentence-level comprehension instruction the first time they read through text include younger students who are at risk, English language learners, and older, more skilled readers who are reading difficult text.

Sentences written in the **passive voice,** in which the subject of the sentence is the recipient of the action rather than the actor, are always more difficult to understand. For example, the sentence *The barking dog was chased by the yellow cat* is less clear than *The yellow cat chased the barking dog* because in the second sentence, which used the active voice, the main actor, the cat, clearly chased the barking dog. Carnine and colleagues (2010) suggest an effective strategy for teaching students to comprehend sentences written in the passive voice. The teaching format involves constructing a short sentence in the active voice and then rewriting or saying it in the passive voice. Initially the teacher begins with a My Turn, using a think-aloud, before asking questions to check for understanding. For example, in teaching passive voice, Mrs. Eckstein used the following minimally different sentences: *Allonzo screamed at Clarissa* and *Clarissa was screamed at by Allonzo.* First, she used a think-aloud and said, *"Clarissa was screamed at by Allonzo; that means Allonzo did the screaming and Clarissa was screamed at."* She then repeated each

TABLE 7.4 Before, During, and After Reading

	Teachers set purpose and use frontloading techniques to:	Students learn to:	Metacognitive questions teachers ask to activate students' thinking about the text include:
Before Reading	<ul><li>connect new text information to prior knowledge.</li><li>provide a scaffold for instruction by preteaching words students might have difficulty decoding.</li><li>increase interest in reading the text.</li><li>teach one or two vocabulary words necessary to understand the text.</li><li>introduce a graphic organizer.</li></ul>	<ul><li>read the title and headings.</li><li>look at the pictures.</li><li>predict what the passage might be about.</li><li>ask themselves what they already know about the topic.</li><li>decode and read by sight any difficult words.</li><li>consider the purpose for reading the text.</li></ul>	<ul><li>What do you think the selection might be about? Why?</li><li>What do you know about (topic/story)?</li><li>What would you be interested in learning about (topic/story)?</li><li>What do you think it would be like to_____?</li><li>What clue(s) does the title give us about the main character?</li></ul>
During Reading	<ul><li>clarify unknown vocabulary, metaphors, and concepts.</li><li>use a graphic organizer to teach a specific comprehension strategy or to provide connections between ideas, concepts, characters and other pieces of information in text.</li><li>assess students' application of comprehension strategies.</li></ul>	<ul><li>think about what they are reading and if it makes sense.</li><li>stop sometimes and summarize what they've read so far.</li><li>visualize the people, places, and events they are reading about.</li><li>imagine talking with the author while reading.</li><li>question and predict.</li><li>seek clarification when there are questions.</li><li>make inferences.</li><li>make connections between ideas, concepts, and characters in the text.</li><li>evaluate the text.</li></ul>	<ul><li>What did you think about as you read this section?</li><li>Were there any parts that were hard to understand in this section?</li><li>What did you do when you came to parts that were hard to understand?</li><li>Were there any hard words in this section?</li><li>What did you do when you didn't know a word?</li><li>What do you predict will happen next and why?</li><li>What does the author want us to know about?</li><li>Does that make sense with what the author told us before? Why?</li><li>How did the author let you know something had changed?</li></ul>
After Reading	<ul><li>help students integrate information from text with their own core knowledge.</li><li>teach students to summarize main ideas in text.</li><li>ensure that students retain core information in long-term memory.</li><li>Provide the opportunity to apply critical thinking skills.</li></ul>	<ul><li>generate questions about the text.</li><li>think about what they read and review questions/predictions.</li><li>write or speak on a specified topic related to material read.</li><li>compare what was read with something already known.</li><li>summarize a reading selection.</li><li>outline the text.</li></ul>	<ul><li>Where did you find it difficult to understand what you were reading and what fix-up strategy did you use?</li><li>What is the main idea of what you just read? How did you come to that answer?</li><li>What picture did the author paint in your head?</li><li>Do you need to reread so that you understand?</li><li>Which of your predictions was right?</li><li>How would you judge the overall quality of other students' comments? Can you give an example?</li></ul>

sentence, reduced support, and used a Your Turn, asking, *"Who was screamed at?"* and *"Who did the screaming?"* Students have mastered this skill when they can accurately answer questions about novel sentences without a My Turn.

Another aspect of written language that can make comprehension at the sentence level more difficult is the use of **pronoun referents**—the nouns to which pronouns refer. A general rule of thumb is that the closer the pronoun is to its referent, the easier it is to understand. Consider this section of text:

> Now life began to change. The Eskimo hunters could see that these tools were useful. So they became traders, too. They trapped more furs than their families needed. Then they brought the furs to the trading posts. There they could trade the furs for supplies they had never had before. Because the new tools helped Eskimo hunters get along better, they became part of the Eskimo environment. (Brandwein & Bauer, 1980; cited in Friend & Bursuck, 2008)

Many readers may have trouble figuring out who *they* refers to in this passage because the author did not clearly indicate the pronoun referent. Although the placement of most pronouns is not this problematic, they must be explicitly taught because even basic pronoun referents can be difficult for students who are at risk (Friend & Bursuck, 2008). As with other skills in this section, the teacher first must analyze the text students will be using, anticipate problems, and, through explicit instruction, prevent these problems from occurring, thus enhancing comprehension. Before students read, the teacher identifies unclear pronouns and asks students to underline those pronouns in a passage. Finally, a series of questions asked by the teacher shows students how to find out to whom or what the pronoun refers.

Chapter 6 described the problems many students have reading unfamiliar idioms (*She was dressed to kill.*) and metaphors (*He mirrors the dancer's fancy footwork and flowing arms while gyrating to the beat of the drums and guitars.*). When previewing a story or article during your lesson planning, carefully look for this figurative language and integrate the teaching suggestions in Chapter 6 into your comprehension instruction.

Moats (2005) identified four other problematic sentence structures that can impede student comprehension which are detailed in Figure 7.5. To help students with these problematic constructions, Moats suggested identifying them in advance of reading a story and then monitoring student understanding of them. Moats also suggested paraphrasing difficult sentences for students as well as engaging the students in *sentence coloring.* In sentence coloring, after several My Turns, students read the same sentence several times with different phrasing or intonation to "color" the meaning of the words (p. 23). For example, Ms. Battaglia's class came across the sentence *They will understand only this?* while reading a newspaper editorial on the street riots in France. Ms. Battaglia wanted to be sure her students understood the impact of the question mark on the meaning of the sentence. She read the sentence to her students, coloring it to emphasize the *question* by emphasizing the word *this* at the end and using intonation denoting a question: *They will understand only **this?*** To provide contrast, she colored the sentence in a different way, as it would be spoken without the question mark, emphasizing the word *they* this time: ***They will understand only this.*** Ms. Battaglia then had her students say the sentence each way, commenting on the different meaning of each, including what the original sentence meant within the context of the editorial.

Lengthy sentences like the following one from Dickens's *A Christmas Carol* pose problems because, besides taxing the reader's working memory, they typically have a compound or complex sentence structure, or both.

> *If we were not perfectly convinced that Hamlet's Father died before the play began, there would be nothing more remarkable in his taking a stroll at night, in an easterly wind, upon his own ramparts, than there would be in any other middle-aged gentleman rashly turning out after dark in a breezy spot—say Saint Paul's Churchyard for instance—literally to astonish his son's weak mind.* (Dickens, 1843)

Playing with Punctuation.

---

a. Passive Voice

Summer clothes *are to be replaced* by winter clothes.
New ideas *are often misunderstood* by those with firmly held biases.
The white minivan *was hit* head-on by the motorcycle.

b. Double Negative

We had *no* reason to think she was *un*stable.
There was *no* evidence that the suspect was *not* at home as he had claimed on the night of the robbery.
It was *not* true that he *dis*liked the gift.
I did *not* advise him *never* to reveal his intentions to her.

c. Verb Tenses and Auxiliaries

Under orders, *we were to be patient* for hours.
Would it not have been easier to say "yes"?
What would he be doing if he were here?

d. Prepositions and Articles

He put the paper *aside* to read the book.
He put the paper *beside* the book.
He put the paper *inside* the book.
This is *the* major problem.
This is *a* major problem.

e. Ambiguous Phrases, Word Order, and Placement of Phrases

Folding diapers would be expensive.
Hanging plants would require light.
They will understand only this.
Only they will understand this.
The drunken driver with the VW struck the woman.
The drunken driver struck the woman with the VW.

FIGURE 7.5   Problematic Sentence Structures

Source: From Moats, L. C. (2005). *Language essentials for teachers of reading and spelling. Module 6: Digging for meaning: Teaching text comprehension* (p. 22). Boston: Sopris West.

Strategies that can be used for teaching students to comprehend complex sentences such as this and other kinds of sentences include the following:

- Read to children and teach them to comprehend complex syntax on a regular basis, asking frequent questions at the sentence level and using graphic organizers. Through listening comprehension you directly develop students' reading comprehension skills.
- Place students into an explicit language program in preschool or kindergarten such as *Language for Learning* (Chapter 6, pp. 260–261).
- "Play mom," and when younger students or English language learners use short sentences, be a model and gently expand their sentences as feedback.
- Expect students to answer in complete sentences, and use scaffolding to help them develop that habit. If John answers your question by explaining, "went uphill to dangerous forest," reply, "You are right. The brave soldier went uphill to the dangerous forest. Now tell me your answer in a complete sentence."
- Teach formal grammar and diagramming sentences. The Language! reading program integrates diagramming into reading instruction. In one of the first lessons, students identify a sentence subject by answering the question, "What did it?" and the sentence verb by answering, "What did they do?"
- Ask quality inferential "detective" questions more frequently than "What did you think?" or "What do you predict?" questions. Teachers are surprised how difficult inferential

questions are for students. To increase motivation, always ask what specific "clue" words or background information students found in the sentence. Examples of detective questions at the sentence level include these:

Sentence: Six chicks scratch in one patch. **Detective questions:** "Are a dozen chicks scratching?" "Do the animals scratching have four legs?" "Are the chicks scratching in different places around the farm?"

Sentence: The village residents will always remember how the mysterious dragon helped them. **Detective questions:** "Do you think the village residents will remember the dragon 20 years from now?" "Did the people learn everything that could be known about the dragon?" "Was the sentence about strangers in the village helped by the dragon?"

After students answer the question, ask them to identify the word or phrase in the sentence that provided the clue. Gradually, students learn to critically think as they read and independently notice clues that give meaning to the text.

What Comprehension Strategies Do I Need to Teach?

While every reader benefits from learning and refining comprehension strategies, many students who are at risk will never move past the fourth-grade slump unless they receive explicit instruction in using them. Up until about 20 years ago, the prevailing practice for teaching reading comprehension was to provide students with practice activities consisting largely of passages followed by written comprehension questions. Very little time was spent directly teaching reading comprehension skills until ground-breaking research in the field of cognitive psychology provided evidence that, as with decoding skills, comprehension strategies also need to be taught explicitly and systematically (Duffy, 1993). Research supports the position that students can be taught to monitor their strategic behavior and performance and that this training can improve their reading.

> Learn more about how to teach reading comprehension strategies at **http://teacher.scholastic.com/reading/bestpractices/comprehension/promptsthatguide.pdf.**

Summarizing

A **summary** is a synthesis of the important ideas in a text (Armbruster, Lehr, & Osborn, 2001). Summarizing helps students identify the main ideas in expository text and recognize important story elements in narrative text. Summarizing can also help students evaluate their understanding of what they have read, tell important and unimportant information apart, and better remember what they have read. Summarizing can be done periodically after each paragraph or section or at the end of the reading. For narrative text, students can use a story map, such as the one shown in the previous section for *The Funny Farola* in Figure 7.4, to summarize the story. Younger students need structure when summarizing or they will describe one or two unrelated details from the story. If throughout the lesson you use a graphic organizer, at the end of the story it can serve as a prompt when students summarize the story. Often in kindergarten and first grade, the teacher needs to model giving a summary before asking two or three students to summarize the same story just like the teacher did.

For expository text and more difficult fiction, a summary often involves stating the main idea and supporting details of several related paragraphs. For example, Ms. Tara's students came up with the following summary based on several paragraphs from their social studies textbook about the United States economy after World War II: *"A combination of the housing boom and baby boom had a positive effect on the economy. Jobs were plentiful, and wages were high. Still, not everyone shared in the good economic times of the 1950s."* Summarizing is a difficult comprehension strategy in which students need consistent daily practice. Opportunities for practice include summarizing a section of text from the day before, summarizing sections of text during the reading, and summarizing the entire article or story at the end.

Outlines can be helpful to students as they write summaries. Two groups of outlines for summary writing are described here. The first group of outlines can be used to write easier summaries, the second to write more difficult ones.

- Outlines for easier summaries
  - Describe the beginning, middle, and end of a story and the setting.
  - Describe the main problem in the story and the outcome.
- Outlines for more difficult summaries
  - Present concrete events and facts in sequence.
  - Supply missing information through appropriate inferences.
  - Include some explanation of the causes of events.

Teachers who have students summarize the text as part of group instruction, providing feedback on their group summary before asking everyone to write their own summary, help students generalize this important skill to their writing.

Main Ideas and Details

The **main idea** is the central idea around which a piece of text is organized. The confusion that students experience when they need to identify main ideas is revealed when they write disorganized papers filled with disjointed paragraphs about random details or when their oral book reports remind you of lists of unrelated, insignificant bits of information. For example, Mary's book report, which was supposed to last three minutes, stretches on and on as she recounted every small detail. It is difficult for students to identify main ideas when they are lost in the details. Even when students are explicitly taught to identify main ideas in the primary grades, in high school they still need to refine their ability to pick out and describe the main ideas of novels and longer articles. The main idea is easier to identify when it is expressed explicitly (written in a sentence) than when it is implied (suggested without being explicitly stated). Sometimes each paragraph in text contains a main idea. When the main idea of a paragraph is explicitly described in a sentence, that sentence is called the **topic sentence.**

At first, students are taught to identify main ideas from paragraphs, but later they expand that skill to larger segments of text. Since explicit main ideas are often found in the first sentence, students often try to pull the main idea out of that sentence whether it is there or not. When they have to figure out an implied main idea by making an inference from the information in the text, sometimes they are unable to see the big picture. Teachers can prevent these problems by using a variety of teaching examples—some explicit, some not—and selecting paragraphs having topic sentences in the beginning, middle, and end. Graphic organizers such as the one in Table 7.5 used during SAFER

TABLE 7.5 Main Idea and Details Chart

Main Idea	
Detail 1	
Detail 2	
Detail 3	

reading help students differentiate between main ideas and details. Main ideas are what the reading is mostly about; details are smaller pieces of specific information that tell the reader more about the main idea, the characters, new vocabulary terms, or other elements in text.

When students notice a detail, they tell the teacher the specific detail, and the teacher writes it on the large graphic. At the end of each paragraph, through the use of think-alouds and cues as prompts, the teacher leads the students to identify the main idea. Later, she might have students read each detail and main idea listed on the chart and ask, "Is this what the whole paragraph is about?"

Dixon, Boorman, and Muti (2008) use step-by-step scaffolding to teach students to identify the main idea. Students first learn to identify who or what is talked about most, and then they learn to classify what is said about that person or thing. Combining those two pieces of information provides a main idea sentence, but two preskills are needed so that students can readily pick out this information from text. In order to determine the main idea "Suzanne is freezing in the cold," Mrs. Whitlaw's students first must know *who or what was talked about the most*. Although Suzanne's name might be mentioned once or twice in the paragraph, the word "she" or "her" might also describe her. Students need to recognize that "the red-faced girl" and "the shivering huddled form" also refer to Suzanne. These pronouns or nouns that refer to another word or name are called **anaphora.** If Mrs. Whitlaw's students are unable to recognize that these different pronouns and phrases indicate one person, she will first teach them to underline all the words in a paragraph that refer to a specified person. Students practice that skill until they can identify who is being talked about the most in a paragraph. The second preskill that Mrs. Whitlaw's students need to develop is *classification.* If text in the paragraph mentions that Suzanne's lips were blue, she was outside on a freezing day, her face was red from the cold, blowing wind, and she couldn't wait for the warm bus to arrive, in order to identify what is said about the person (Suzanne), students must classify those four details and realize that she was freezing in the cold. After learning about anaphora and developing classification skills, students are ready to identify the main idea in a variety of texts.

anaphora

> Watch a model lesson where a teacher uses think-alouds and cues to teach students how to identify the main idea in a reading passage: **http://www.linkslearning.org/reading_links/8_pgr/index.html.**

Comprehension Monitoring

For students to learn how to monitor their comprehension, teachers must teach them not only to use specific comprehension strategies, but also when to use them. If you have ever read and comprehended a nineteenth-century Russian novel by Tolstoy, you will remember that whenever you became confused about the character referred to in the text, you stopped your reading to check the character list and determine exactly who was speaking and what the relationship was to the main characters, then asked yourself whether the dialogue now made sense given the character clarification. When two characters had almost identical names, you stopped and double-checked the spelling to make sure you knew who was speaking. Proficient readers are aware when they do not know a word or when the text does not make sense, and they know how to apply the **fix-up strategies** described in Table 7.6, deciding which ones will help them with specific problems. When readers are self-monitoring, they are consistently asking themselves, "Is what I am reading making sense?" **Monitoring text** is not a natural process, but research demonstrates that it can be taught.

teach HOW & WHEN to use strategies

Armbruster and colleagues (2001) have described several comprehension-monitoring strategies that students may use.

Identify Where the Difficulty Occurs   "I don't understand the second paragraph on page 76."

TABLE 7.6   Fix-Up Strategies

Sounding out unknown words	Slowing down and rereading
Looking up a word or name (e.g., dictionary, encyclopedia, glossary, Google, Wikipedia)	Making a prediction and periodically checking whether the text corresponds to that prediction; adjusting the prediction if necessary
Reading the preface, the chapter summary, the back cover or looking for a review of the book	Taking notes during reading, making a graphic organizer, outlining the text
Reflecting on what the author is trying to say in the book	Talking to another person about a difficult section of the book
Thinking about how the book relates to background knowledge; to the reader's experiences	Creating a visual image about what the book is about
Checking the Internet for information related to a difficult section	Determining whether the information is necessary for understanding the text and ignoring it if not

Identify What the Difficulty Is   "I don't get what the author means when she says 'Arriving in America was a milestone in my grandmother's life.'"

Restate the Difficult Sentence or Passage in Their Own Words   "Oh, so the author means that coming to America was a very important event in her grandmother's life."

Look Back Through the Text   "The author talked about Mr. McBride in Chapter 2, but I don't remember much about him. Maybe if I reread that chapter, I can figure out why he's acting this way now."

Look Forward in the Text for Information That Might Help Them Resolve the Difficulty   "The text says, 'The groundwater may form a stream or pond or create a wetland. People can also bring groundwater to the surface.' Hmmm, I don't understand how people can do that . . . Oh, the next section is called 'Wells.' I'll read this section to see if it tells how they do it." (p. 50)

Self-Questioning

One way that readers become actively engaged with text is by asking themselves questions as they read. Through asking questions, students can reflect on what they are reading, asking why the author chose the words he did or let the character come to such a devastating end, why the main story character would fall in love with that rude person whose personality is so different, or whether the spurned lover has a chance of making a comeback. Kyle might notice while reading a social studies book that the authors didn't include enough information about foxholes during World War I. That observation might lead him to ask himself whether it's worth looking for another book that describes what daily life in the foxholes was like. Later, when Kyle begins reading about the Battle of Verdun, he might ask himself who it seems will be the victor of that battle. Once the information is provided in the text, he'll ask himself whether his prediction was correct. Kyle, like other competent readers, is not aware that he monitors his comprehension routinely by asking himself whether he has understood a section just read until he comes to a section where he has to answer "no." As soon as Kyle realizes he read the page or pages without complete understanding, he immediately goes back to the beginning of the section and rereads. Just as with other comprehension strategies, self-questioning can be explicitly taught and included in multiple-strategy instruction. Teachers can prompt students to ask questions at different points in the text by starting with the main question words: who, what, where, when, why, how.

Questioning the Author (QtA) is a strategy developed by Isabel Beck and colleagues that gets students started asking questions by providing them with strategy questions that they can eventually ask themselves when they read. The teacher gives the students one or more paragraphs to read and then asks them to answer these questions:

1. What is the author trying to tell you?
2. Why is the author telling you that?
3. Does the author say it clearly?
4. How could the author have said things more clearly?
5. What would you say instead? (Beck, McKeown, Hamilton, & Kucan, 1997)

Finally, strategic readers need to routinely ask additional questions as a part of self-monitoring. Questions such as "Does this make sense?" "What parts of this story are different from my reading predictions," and "Do I need to take notes to understand?" help students know when to apply fix-up strategies to increase their comprehension.

Making Inferences

Proficient readers are unaware they are inferring as they identify information in the text that is not directly provided by the author. Inferring is a difficult concept to teach to students who are at risk because it is so abstract. Since most comprehension strategies and question answering require the ability to infer, suggestions to make inferences are integrated throughout most sections of this chapter. The QAR strategy, identifying the main idea, and monitoring comprehension all require the ability to infer. An easy rule for students to remember is: *"Making an inference is using clues from the text and your own knowledge and experience to figure out what the author is trying to tell you."*

How Can I Use Multiple Strategies to Maximize Student Gains in Reading Comprehension?

You have just learned about reading comprehension strategies that are research-based. These strategies can be even more effective when used together. The National Reading Panel (2000) determined that readers benefit when multiple comprehension strategies are taught during the process of reading narrative or expository text. Multiple-strategy instruction should include teaching students when specific comprehension strategies are most effective—before, during, or after the reading, as already depicted in Table 7.4 (page 290).

One way to teach students to use multiple strategies at once is called reciprocal teaching (Palincsar & Brown, 1988). Friend and Bursuck (2008) describe reciprocal teaching as:

> [A] way to teach students to comprehend reading material by providing them with teacher and peer models of thinking behavior and then allowing them to practice these thinking behaviors with their peers. At first, the teacher leads the dialogue, demonstrating how the strategies can be used during reading. As instruction goes on, the teacher gives the students more and more responsibility for maintaining the dialogue. Eventually students are largely responsible for the dialogue, though the teacher still provides help as necessary. (p. 371)

In reciprocal teaching students are taught the skills of summarizing, self-questioning, predicting, and clarifying. In the example that follows this passage from a U.S. history text, Mr. Buerhle used reciprocal teaching with his students (Kinder, 1990).

Economic Benefits of the Colonies

The English government had many economic reasons for wanting to build colonies in the New World. One of these had to do with England's balance of trade. The balance of trade compares what a nation buys from other nations with what other nations buy from it. If other nations buy more from it than the nation buys from others the balance of trade is good.

England did not have a good balance of trade. It needed many goods that it did not make or grow. The English weather was too cold to grow sugar cane, and England did not have enough trees to supply the wood needed to build ships. As a result, England had to buy goods such as sugar and wood from other nations. In turn, other nations bought wool and other products from England. If England had colonies in the New World, they could supply raw materials to England. These products from nature, such as wood, were necessary if England were to improve its balance of trade.

The colonies could also become a new market, or place to sell products for English goods. The colonists would need many supplies, such as tools and cloth, and English merchants would provide them. This would create more business and more jobs in England.

In time, many English merchants grew rich from this trade with the colonies. The English government also grew rich by taxing the people who shipped the goods to the colonies. (Reich & Beiler, 1988)

After reading the passage, Mr. Buerhle demonstrated (My Turn) the skills of summarizing, self-questioning, predicting, and clarifying. He looked at his students and said, "I have

---

In Your Classroom

Reciprocal Teaching

The students in this class have just read a section of text that focuses on Loch Ness. They are now applying the POSSE strategy—**p**redict, **s**earch, **s**ummarize, and **e**valuate—as shown in the following example.

Teacher: What is the main topic the text is talking about?

Peg: The Loch Ness monster.

Teacher: What was this section about? What was the main idea?

Peg: Oh, the lake. I have two questions: "What is a lake?" and "What lives in it?"

Teacher: Do you mean this particular lake or any lake?

Peg: This lake. Joe?

Joe: It's foggy, it's deep, and it's long and narrow.

Peg: Don?

Don: The land beside the lake. You don't know if it is real soft and you could fall through it.

Teacher: So it could be soft and swampy.

Ann: I think the Loch Ness monster lives there.

Teacher: Is Ann answering your question, Peg?

Peg: No.

Teacher: What was your question?

Peg: I had two: "What is a lake?" and "What lives in the lake?"

Joe: But the book never answered that. I have a question about the main idea. Aren't we supposed to ask a question about the main idea?

Teacher: Just about what we read.

Joe: Yes, but Peg asked us, "What lives in the lake?" but it doesn't really mention that in the book.

Teacher: That's true. The major idea has to do with Loch Ness and what it looks like. A minor idea that we inferred rather than directly read in the article was that the Loch Ness monster lives in the lake.

Peg: Are there any clarifications?

Students: (*No response.*)

Teacher: I have a clarification. You had trouble reading some of these words and I wondered if you know what some of them mean. What does *ancestors* mean?

The teacher continues discussing vocabulary.

Source: From Englert & Mariage (1991).

Research Note

Which Should I Teach: Content or Strategies?

Educators debate whether reading comprehension instruction should emphasize teaching strategies as in this lesson or teaching content, with little evidence to support either position. Reading instruction that emphasizes content focuses students on the meaning of the text, while strategy instruction emphasizes explicit teaching of cognitive strategies. The difference between the two approaches was described by McKeown, Beck, and Blake (2009):

> For a sense of how the two approaches operate, consider a group of students who have just finished reading a short segment of text. In a strategies approach, the teacher might ask the students to summarize the text and recall what kind of information goes into a good summary. She might follow up a student's summary by asking other students if it was a good summary and why or why not. In a content approach, the teacher might ask what the portion of text had been about, and as students respond, follow up by asking how pieces of information that students contributed fit in with what is being read or why the information is important. (p. 28)

Research has shown that both types of comprehension instruction benefit learners who are at risk (Beck, McKeown, Sandora, Kucan, & Worthy, 1996; Duffy & Roehler, 1989; Palincsar & Brown, 1988), but questions remain. With regard to strategies instruction, clear guidelines for which strategies to use, and in what situations and combinations, do not exist (McKeown et al., 2009). Research-validated guidelines for how to effectively teach content are also lacking (McKeown et al., 2009). Few studies have directly compared strategies and content instruction within the same study, and for those that have (for example, McKeown et al.) the results were inconclusive. In the meantime, we recommend that comprehension instruction integrate both approaches. Students who have read expository text about a tsunami should be able to write or orally describe new knowledge they have acquired about the life-threatening waves. Activities teaching students to identify the main idea for sections of the text can be integrated within the same lesson. When a class studies *The Secret Garden* (Burnett, 2008), the teacher can emphasize content teaching so students learn to recognize and hypothesize the cause of the physical and mental changes that occurred in the characters; to identify the contrast between Mary's life, climate, and family in India and those in England; and to discuss ethical issues and their feelings about the father who abandoned his son, while also learning how to apply self-monitoring comprehension strategies.

a question. How could the colonies make England rich?" (self-questioning) "As I think about it, the British could sell their products to the colonies. They could also get raw materials from the colonies so they could manufacture goods to see and improve their balance of trade." (clarifying) "To summarize, the British want to be rich and powerful by having the colonists buy only from them, and by using the colonies' raw materials to manufacture goods for export." (summarizing) "I wonder what the colonists will think about England's trade policy. I also wonder what England will do to make the colonies trade only with them." (self-questioning) "I think that England will use its military to force the colonies to trade just with them." (predicting) The *In Your Classroom* shows another example of how to teach multiple reading comprehension strategies using reciprocal teaching. The *Research Note* discusses the issue of whether reading comprehension instruction should emphasize the teaching of strategies or content.

Table 7.7 summarizes research-based practices associated with teaching reading comprehension.

TABLE 7.7 Research-Based Comprehension Instruction

Components of Instruction	Research-Based	Not Research-Based
Comprehension	Structure of both narrative and expository text taught directly; strategies overtly modeled and practiced in a planned progression; subskills such as main idea and theme are taught and applied.	Instruction dominated by choral reading, shared reading and guided reading with undirected classroom discussion; teacher modeling (thinking aloud) the primary instructional strategy but with little scaffolding reduction; acceptance of student-constructed meanings over consensual meanings or those intended by author; student book choices emphasized often at expense of content.

Source: Adapted from Moats, L. C. (2007). *Whole language high jinks: How to tell when "scientifically-based reading instruction" isn't.* Washington, DC: Fordham Institute.

How Can I Assess and Monitor My Students' Progress in Reading Comprehension in a Multi-Tier or RTI Model?

As with any skill, you need to assess comprehension to learn which students are experiencing difficulty (screening), what specific problems they are having (diagnosis), and whether they are acquiring the reading skills you are teaching them (progress monitoring). Reading comprehension assessment should occur in the following areas: oral reading fluency, oral language, listening comprehension, basic literal and inferential comprehension, narrative comprehension, expository comprehension, and metacognitive skills.

Screening and Progress Monitoring

Maze and cloze curriculum-based assessments can be used to identify which students are having comprehension problems and to monitor their progress. Cloze or maze assessments require students to silently read a grade-level passage for three minutes. In the cloze assessment, after the initial sentence, every specified (e.g., seventh, tenth) word is deleted. Students write in the correct word that is missing. The maze is a multiple-choice variation on the cloze, but after the first sentence, every seventh word is replaced with a choice of three words inside parentheses. One of the supplied words is correct, one is the same part of speech (e.g., noun or verb), and the third does not make sense. Students circle the correct word as they silently read the test. After students complete the test, the number of words correctly circled is tallied. Teachers use a scoring template as a guide to score the assessments and put slashes through any incorrect answers before returning to the top and counting the number of correct words. The score is usually expressed as the total number of responses correct (RC) followed by the total number of errors (e.g., 37/3). As with the oral reading fluency assessments, for the benchmark assessment students read three passages and the median score is recorded as the benchmark score (Parker, Hasbrouck, & Tindal, 1992; Shinn, Deno, & Espin, 2000).

In order to accurately complete a maze or cloze assessment, students have to decode the text; apply their background knowledge; and understand basic word order (syntax), vocabulary, and sentence meaning in context (semantics). Maze assessments are preferred to cloze for English language learners because the target words are provided. Maze assessments are also the best choice for younger or at-risk students because of reduced demands

TABLE 7.8 Typical Percentile Chart for a Maze Assessment

	Percentile	Fall Benchmark RC	Winter Benchmark RC	Spring Benchmark RC
FIFTH GRADE	90	27	33	36
	75	23	26	30
	50	16	20	24
	25	10	16	16
	10	7	10	12

on fine motor skills, working memory, and spelling (Gunderson, 2008). For this reason, as well as the fact that it has established norms, the maze assessment is emphasized in the text. While both maze and cloze assessments have adequate validity for assessing comprehension, they should be given with other assessments of skills underlying comprehension, such as oral reading fluency or a word analysis assessment.

Table 7.8 depicts a benchmark table similar to one that might be used to interpret fifth-grade maze performance. Note that the data reported are the number of responses correct (RC).

The benchmark scores on a normed table like this one allow you to compare the score of a student with the scores of other students in the district or the country. This table tells you that in the fall, 75% of the students had scores of 23 RC or lower, and 25% of the students had scores of 10 RC or lower. Scores below the 50th percentile indicate that additional Tier 2 or Tier 3 support may be needed, depending on whether other reading scores reflect the same low performance. For example, Kareen is a student in Ms. Arno's class. To interpret Kareen's median RC score of 8 in August, Ms. Arno looked at the Fall Benchmark column, where she noticed that Kareen's median score of 8 was below the 25th percentile. If other reading scores mirror this one, Ms. Arno will recommend that Kareen receive Tier 3 support.

Normative growth rates similar to those you learned about in Chapter 5 for oral reading fluency are also available for maze assessments. If you are a special education teacher, these growth rates can be useful in writing meaningful IEP objectives. In Grades 1–6, the realistic weekly growth rate for maze RC is .4 per week, while an ambitious growth rate is .85 (Stecker & Lembke, 2005). When students are behind their peers, IEP projections should be based on ambitious growth rates. For example, if Kareen's teacher Ms. Arno were to set a 30-week IEP objective at the beginning of the year based on the beginning benchmark median score of 8 RC and the ambitious growth rate, she could set a 30-week objective as follows:

number of weeks _____ ×.85 RC = _____ + median score _____ = _____ RC

The computation for Kareen would look like this:

30 (number of weeks) × .85 RC (ambitious rate) = 25.5 RC + 8 RC (median score) = 33.5 RC

Before she wrote her IEP objective, Ms. Arno looked at how many responses Kareen answered incorrectly to determine her level of accuracy. Looking at accuracy can help her determine if Kareen scored below the 50th percentile because she is a slow reader or due to some other factor. Ms. Arno found that Kareen missed 4 responses, so her accuracy was 8/(8 + 4), or 8/12, equaling 67%. The percentage score indicates that Kareen is a slow and inaccurate reader. Ms. Arno decided to do further diagnostic testing to determine if poor decoding, poor fluency, or both were contributing to Kareen's comprehension deficit. She also decided to include accuracy as well as correct responses in developing this IEP objective for Kareen: "Given a grade-level maze reading passage and a 3-minute time limit, Kareen will circle the correct word choice, making 33.5 correct responses with 90% or

Norm tables for maze fluency are listed in the book *The ABC's of CBM: A practical guide to curriculum-based measurement* (Hosp, Hosp, & Howell, 2007) or can be purchased through AIMSweb and Edcheckup.

You can make your own maze sheets by visiting the Maze Passage Generator at **http://www.rti2.org/rti2/mazes.**

Primary Assessments

higher accuracy, on two out of three consecutive reading passages." Throughout the year, Ms. Arno can use the same kind of graph to monitor progress for maze as she uses for charting oral reading fluency.

You cannot conventionally assess reading comprehension for older learners or kindergarten or first-semester first-grade students who have limited decoding skills. For these students, the best option is to assess listening comprehension, which can be done in one of two ways. For younger students, use a measure specifically developed for assessing listening comprehension, such as the Texas Primary Reading Inventory (TPRI) described in Chapter 6. In this measure, students listen to a passage and then answer explicit and implicit comprehension questions about what they heard. The Early Reading Diagnostic Assessment (ERDA) is a similar listening comprehension instrument. In the ERDA, students in kindergarten listen to the teacher read passages, answer questions about the passage, and then retell the story in their own words; first-grade students look at a picture, listen to the teacher read a passage, and then answer comprehension questions about main ideas and supporting elements from the passage. For older students with limited decoding skills, use the comprehension assessment you are giving to the rest of the students and read it to them before asking the questions. While most tests haven't been standardized to account for oral administrations, giving the test orally should still provide you with an adequate basis for screening potential comprehension problems.

Diagnostic Assessment

Once you have determined that there is a comprehension problem, the next step is to identify the specific problems that contribute to poor reading comprehension. Assessing reading comprehension is difficult because of the great variance across tests as well as the multiplicity and complexity of the factors that contribute to reading comprehension performance. For example, student weaknesses in underlying skills such as decoding can have a significant effect on their comprehension scores. Sarah might have high-level comprehension skills, but if her decoding skills are weak and she has to read lengthy passages on a comprehension test, her scores will reflect low comprehension. The nature of the reading task used on a test can also limit the utility of the findings. For example, the comprehension section of the Wechsler Individual Achievement Test-II (WIAT) doesn't require students to read a large amount of text. Thus, students' scores on this test may not reflect the struggle they have reading longer expository text (Fletcher, Lyone, Ruchs, & Barnes, 2007). Researchers have revealed that a large proportion of questions on the Gray Oral Reading Test (GORT) can be answered with above-chance accuracy without reading the passage, with the final score reflecting reasoning from prior knowledge more than how accurately the student read and understood the passages (Keenan & Betjemann, 2006). For these reasons, it is recommended that teachers always validate performance on standardized tests of comprehension with curriculum-based assessments and observations of daily performance in class. When using tests of comprehension to make decisions related to eligibility for special education, we recommend synthesizing the results of two or three different reading comprehension tests (Keenan & Betjemann, 2006).

The fact that there are a variety of different comprehension problems presents another challenge for diagnostic assessment. For example, some students may lack the background, semantic, and/or syntactical knowledge needed to make inferences or glean information from the text that is not explicitly stated. Still others may be able to read accurately and fluently but don't think about what they are reading; they may need to learn how to ask themselves questions about key vocabulary and other story components as they read. Some students may have trouble monitoring their comprehension; these students cannot determine whether or not they are attaining the appropriate level of understanding, and, if not, employ fix-up strategies to improve their understanding. Finally, students may not understand how to use the organizational structures of both narrative and expository text. Described below are assessments that can be used to assess student strengths and weaknesses in the above areas.

Reading Accuracy and Fluency   As described in Chapter 5, student oral reading accuracy and fluency are strongly related to reading comprehension and can be measured using an Oral Reading Fluency measure.

Oral Language   A number of assessments used to screen and diagnose oral language problems were described in Chapter 6.

Background Knowledge   While there are some standardized tests that assess students' general level of background knowledge, background knowledge required for comprehension varies so much from text to text that it makes the most sense to assess student background knowledge at the beginning of each instructional activity. A strategy for determining how much knowledge students already have about a topic, so that you can decide how much background information to present in class prior to a reading assignment, is called the PReP (PreReading Plan) strategy (Friend & Bursuck, 2008; Langer, 1984). The PReP strategy has three major steps:

1. Preview the text or lesson and choose two to three important concepts. For example, for a science lesson, Mr. Amin, the teacher described in Step 2, chose the concept of photosynthesis and the key words *cycle* and *oxygen*.

2. Conduct a brainstorming session with students. This process involves three phases. In Phase 1 of brainstorming, students tell you what comes to mind when they hear the concept. This gives you a first glance at how much they already know about the topic. In Phase 2, students tell you what made them think of their responses in Phase 1. This information can help you judge the depth and basis for their responses and provides a springboard for students to refine their responses in Phase 3 of brainstorming. In Mr. Amin's class, two students mistakenly thought that photosynthesis had to do with photography because of the presence of *photo* in the word. This error provided an opportunity to build on students' knowledge. Mr. Amin explained that *photo* means "light" and that in photography, a camera takes in light and combines it with certain chemicals on film to make pictures. He then said that plants take in light, too, and when the light combines with chemicals in the plant, carbohydrates and oxygen are made. This process is called *photosynthesis*. In this way, Mr. Amin used what the students already knew to teach them a concept they did not know. In Phase 3, students can add to their responses based on the discussion in Phase 2.

3. Evaluate student responses to determine the depth of their prior knowledge of the topic. During this step, you can decide whether students are ready to read the text and/or listen to a lecture on photosynthesis, or they first need more information. In Mr. Amin's class, two students continued to have trouble understanding that photosynthesis was something plants did with light to make carbohydrates and oxygen. They needed more information before they were ready to read the chapter. Mr. Amin accommodated these students by showing them a video illustration of photosynthesis including concrete examples that weren't necessary to use with the rest of the class (Friend & Bursuck, 2008; p. 335).

Basic Literal and Inferential Comprehension   You can diagnose basic literal and inferential comprehension skills using the assessments listed on the next page.

Iowa Test of Basic Skills (ITBS) Form M

This assessment for Grades K and up can be given individually or in groups. Comprehension starts with Level 6, and the tasks require progressively more independence in reading as the test level increases.

Texas Primary Reading Inventory (TPRI)

In this individually given assessment for Grades 1 and 2, students read developmentally appropriate passages and answer five comprehension questions, three of which are explicit and two implicit.

Test of Reading Comprehension–Third Edition (TORC–3)

The TORC–3 measures comprehension in four ways: syntactical similarities, paragraph reading, sentence sequencing, and reading directions.

Woodcock Reading Mastery Test–Revised (WRMT–R)

In this individually administered assessment, students silently read a passage that has a word missing and then tell the examiner a word that could appropriately fill in the blank space. The passages are drawn from actual newspaper articles and textbooks.

Text Structure: Narratives   One way to assess student knowledge of narrative text structures is to turn information about **story grammars** into comprehension questions. Using story grammar questions to assess narrative comprehension skills has a number of advantages. First, focusing on story grammars ensures that the focus of the assessment is on the big ideas of stories as opposed to less important details. Second, writing clear comprehension questions that accurately measure the intended comprehension skill can be difficult. In our experience, when writing your own questions it is often difficult to discern whether students have a comprehension problem or the comprehension items simply weren't written clearly enough. For your primary readers, try these more basic story grammar questions (Carnine et al., 2010).

Who is the story about?
What is he/she trying to do?
What happens when he/she tries to do it?
What happens in the end?

For more intermediate readers, select among these possible questions for each essential story grammar (Carnine & Kinder, 1985).

Theme

What is the major point of the story?
What is the moral of the story?
What did _____ learn at the end of the story?

Setting

Where did _____ happen?
When did _____ happen?

Character

Who is the main character?
What is ____ like?

Initiating Events

What is _____'s problem?
What does _____ have to try to do?

Attempts

What did ____ do about _____?
What will _____ do now?

Resolution

How did _____ solve the problem?
How did _____ achieve the goal?
What would you do to solve _____'s problem?

Reactions

How did _____ feel about the problem?
Why did _____ do _____?
How did _____ feel at the end?
Why did _____ feel that way?
How would you feel about _____?

When assessing story grammars, first have the students read a story that they can read with at least 95% accuracy (Gunning, 2002). Older struggling readers benefit from reading the story silently, then orally. For older skilled students, the story can be read once silently. Younger students should only read the story orally (Klingner, Vaughn, & Boardman, 2004). For students with significant decoding problems, read the story as they listen. After students have heard or read the story, ask the story grammar questions and record student answers.

There are times when you might not wish to ask questions about a story. Specific questions can give students clues to the answers, and they especially help students identify the information you think is important to remember or the way you organize this information. One way to solve this problem is to have students retell stories after they read them, using a checklist during the retelling. Students then must organize the information they think is important so you can evaluate the completeness of their recall. Two requirements are necessary for effective evaluation of story retellings to occur: a standard set of criteria to evaluate the completeness of the **retelling,** and the opportunity to evaluate each student's retelling individually. Ms. Padilla used a Story Grammar Retelling Checklist to evaluate the story retelling for Chantille, a student in her class. While in this case Ms. Padilla had Chantille read the story, if Chantille had been unable to read the story with 95% accuracy, Ms. Padilla could have read it to Chantille before having her retell it.

Look at Chantille's scores shown in Table 7.9. As you can see, she had a good idea of who the main characters were and received a "+" for this component (Characters). Chantille named two problems in the story: Dora making a farola that her family laughed at, and Dora's brother and sister getting lost. Chantille identified the problem of the lost kids without being prompted, and the problem of the funny farola with prompts; thus a "+" and a "✓" were scored for Goal/Problem. It was unclear from Chantille's response exactly how the characters tried to solve their problem, so she received a minus (–) for Attempts. Chantille did say the problem was solved when Dora's brother and sister saw the frog; she received a

TABLE 7.9   Story Grammar Retelling Checklist

Student Name	Story Elements Evaluated												
	Theme		Setting		Characters		Goal/Problem		Attempts		Resolution		Reactions
Chantille	–		✓		+		+	✓	–		+	–	+

Source: Friend, M., and Bursuck, W. (2008). *Including students with special needs: A practical guide for classroom teachers* (5th ed., pp. 134–135). Boston: Pearson Education.

"+" for this element of Resolution. However, she did not say how this resolved the problem of her family laughing at the farola, so she received another minus (–). Chantille's reaction to the story was appropriate, so a "+" was scored. For Setting, Chantille received a "✓"; Ms. Padilla prompted her. Finally, Chantille received a minus (–) for Theme. This response was lacking, even after prompting.

Ms. Padilla's prompts included explicit references to the various story grammar components. For example, she asked, "You said that Dora's sister and brother got lost. What did they do to solve that problem?" as opposed to asking a more general question, such as "What happened to Dora's sister and brother?" This use of specific language makes the story grammar components more clear, a necessary structure for younger, more naïve learners.

Text Structure: Expository   Student knowledge and use of expository text structures can be assessed by having students read passages from one or more of their content-area textbooks. The passages should be at the students' independent reading level and should reflect common text structures that you want to assess. Passages from students' science or social studies books work well for this purpose. As with story grammars, students can read the passages orally, silently, or both, depending on reading skills. If students are unable to read the book with at least 95% accuracy, read the passages to them. Following reading, the student answers questions developed to assess text structure comprehension. For example, here is a brief passage from an eighth-grade social studies text (Buggey, Danzer, Mitsakos, & Risinger, 1985).

> **Striking Workers**
>
> As prices rose, labor unions demanded higher wages. Although many of these demands were met, some companies refused to give their workers adequate pay increases. The result was a number of strikes that soon threatened the stability of the American economy.

To assess overall comprehension of text, ask a main idea question based on the text structure. Here are two possible examples for this paragraph.

Why were there a number of union strikes after the war?

What happened as a result of a rise in prices after the war?

You can also use retellings to assess knowledge of text structures. Ask the student to "tell me in your own words as much information as you can remember from the selection you just read" (Gunning, 2002). If the student does not tell you enough information, ask, "Can you tell me anything more?" While the student is engaged in the retelling, note whether critical features are present in the recall. For example, you might note whether the student demonstrated knowledge of the cause-and-effect relationships among rising consumer prices, demands for higher wages, and strikes.

Metacognitive Skills   Despite their importance, most formal and informal reading assessments tend to ignore metacognitive skills, stressing pure recall or low-level inferences instead (Applegate, Quinn, & Applegate, 2002). Fortunately, you can assess metacognition by adding a metacognitive component to the assessment strategies just discussed. At first, students may engage in few or none of these metacognitive skills. However, over time, they will learn to use them as you model using think-aloud teaching strategies. One way to assess your students' metacognitive skills is to add a student think-aloud component to your comprehension assessment. In student think-alouds, students are asked occasionally to stop and voice their thoughts about the reading process while reading a text. Klingner, Vaughn, and Boardman (2004) referred to this process when they developed the Think-Along Passage (TAP) assessment method to assess the metacognitive strategies students use during reading to identify topics, predict what will happen next, monitor meaning, make inferences, and summarize. The kinds of questions that could be used in a Think-Along Passage assessment are shown in Figure 7.6.

Think Along Passage assessment (TAP) method.

Present child with book or reading passage (Example: *Too Many Tamales* by Gary Soto).

Identifying the Topic

1a. Look at this page. What do you think the story will be about?
Ex: A surprise party; lots of tamales

1b. How do you know this?
Ex: Their eyes look like this (points).

1c. If you don't know, how could you figure it out?
Ex: Turn the pages; read the book.

Possible Strategies
Scans text
Looks at title
Refers to pictures
Refers to prior knowledge
Points out words
Other

Predicting
After a significant event in the story, stop the reading (e.g., after Maria tries on her mother's ring).

2a. What do you think will happen next?
Ex: Her mom'll get mad.

2b. Why do you think that?
Ex: 'Cause she shouldn't wear her mom's ring

2c. If you don't know, how could you find out?
Ex: Read more of the story; look at the pictures.

Possible Strategies
Predicts based on prior knowledge
Predicts based on text cues
Rereads
Looks forward in the text
Uses context cues
Other

Monitoring Meaning
Choose a word that you think will be unfamiliar to the student.

3a. What do you think "masa" mean in the sentence you just read?
Ex: Dough

3b. How could you tell?
Ex: From the pictures; it's in a bowl.
Ex: They kneaded it. That's what you do with dough.

3c. If you don't know, how could you find out?

Possible Strategies
Uses context cues
Substitutes something that looks
  or sounds similar
Mentions other resources
Mentions dictionary as resource
Relates personal experience
Other

Making Inferences
Select something that is not made explicit in the story.

4a. Why do you think they put the masa on corn husks?
Ex: Cause they wanted to
Ex: To keep all the stuff together

4b. How did you decide this?
Ex: I just thought it.
Ex: I know cause I help Gramma make tamales.

4c. If you don't know, how could you figure it out?

Possible Strategies
Infers based on text cues
Infers based on prior knowledge
Relates personal experience
Gives analogy
Scans forward
Rereads
Other

Summarizing
After you or the student has finished reading the book, ask for a summary.

5a. If you wanted to tell your friends about this story, what would you tell them?

5b. How did you decide what things to tell them?

5c. If you don't know, how do you think you could decide?

Possible Strategies
Retells mostly main ideas
Retells mostly details
Organizes ideas in recall
Summaries are disorganized
Expresses opinions or reactions
Connects to personal experiences
Uses genre structure to help recall
Other

FIGURE 7.6 Think-Along Passage Protocol for Assessing Strategic Reading

Source: Based on information from Paris, S. G. (1991), cited in H. W. Catts & A. G. Kamhi (2005). *Language and reading disabilities* (2nd ed., p. 187). Boston: Pearson Education.

In Your Classroom

Motivating Your Students to Read Widely

- Provide daily opportunities for students to independently read self-selected and teacher- and peer-recommended texts. All teacher-selected material should be at the students' independent levels so they can be read with at least 95% accuracy. See pages 200–201 in Chapter 5 for guidelines on how to select the appropriate reading material for students.
- Convey enthusiasm for the books your students are reading and talk about your own reading outside of class. If students' parents aren't modeling recreational and informational reading at home, the teacher can pass along the purpose of and excitement from her reading outside of school. One week Mrs. Rice told her class about a book she was reading about magnets, since she was going to teach them that subject and wanted to learn more. Two weeks earlier she described the exciting mystery novel she was reading and the adventures the main character had in the deserts of the Sahara.
- Allow students to select books from a classroom library when they have completed their work. This minimizes behavior problems that can arise from waiting and also provides more opportunities for students to self-select books of interest.

To meet the needs of all students, classroom libraries should contain a wide range of books, from easy decodable books to challenging chapter books without pictures. As recommended in Chapter 6, 50% of the books should be nonfiction.
- Honor and encourage students' outside reading. Some schools have developed motivational plans to encourage students to read a certain number of books in order to earn awards. Be a book detective and notice what your students are reading so you can comment briefly on their selections. Students will do more reading if it leads to more attention. When Mr. Bayer was teaching the continent of Africa in social studies, he turned to Lydia and asked her to tell the most interesting thing she had learned about Africa in a book about pyramids that he had noticed her reading the previous week. When the lunch line was backed up in the hall, Mr. Bayer turned to Shelley and said that he noticed she had been reading *Little House on the Prairie*, which was always a favorite book of his students.
- Encourage a classroom reading culture by having students write blogs and tweets to comment on books they enjoyed reading.

When your students are able to read accurately and fluently, as well as understand what they read, you will have given them a powerful tool to increase their learning over a lifetime. Still, reading is only empowering insofar as students do it. That is why it is so important for teachers to motivate their students to read widely to further their own learning. Strategies for motivating your students to read widely are described in the *In Your Classroom* feature above.

How Can I Give Struggling Readers in Tier 3 a More Systematic, Explicit Approach to Learning Comprehension Skills?

A key theme of this book is that some students struggle to acquire reading skills, despite receiving Tier 1 instruction that is enhanced and reasonably well executed. For the reading components of phonemic awareness, alphabetic principle, and fluency, struggling students were provided with extra support in Tiers 2 and 3. You may find that some of your students also struggle with reading comprehension. Described below are four reading comprehension programs designed for students who can benefit from more explicit, systematic instruction delivered within a smaller instructional group.

Corrective Reading (Engelmann et al., 2008) is an intensive direct-instruction reading program for students in Grades 4–12 who are reading one or more years below grade level. The program has two tightly sequenced strands—decoding and comprehension. At specified times in the connected text activities, students are asked literal and inferential questions that are scripted in the teacher presentation books. Throughout the program, students learn key comprehension strategies to help them understand what they read, including thinking operations, information skills, reasoning skills, and sentence-writing skills, as well as strategies for organizing information, operating on information, using sources of information, using information for directions, and communicating information (Marchand-Martella, Slocum, & Martella, 2004).

Reading Success: Effective Comprehension Strategies (Dixon et al., 2008) is a reading comprehension program designed to supplement your regular reading program. It can be used with individuals from fourth grade through high school who decode at a fourth-grade level or higher, but who struggle meeting state standards in reading comprehension. Lessons take approximately 15 to 20 minutes each and can be taught daily or three times per week. The authors recommend scheduling the lessons to ensure that students finish the program before any spring testing in reading comprehension. The program teaches key comprehension skills using the scientifically based components of explicit strategy instruction, scaffolding, and review. The principal outcomes of *Reading Success* are related to inference, main idea, fact and opinion, literal comprehension, author's purpose, paraphrasing, rewriting passages, word meanings, and figurative language. The program includes placement tests as well as quizzes or tests every five lessons to test mastery of key program skills.

Text Talk, a curriculum for Grades K–3 (Beck & McKeown, 2001) focuses on comprehension and vocabulary development through the use of read-alouds and open-ended questions. The teacher reads stories that contain challenging vocabulary and enough complexity of events for children to build meaning. Throughout the read-aloud sessions, the teacher asks questions designed to encourage children to elaborate on their initial answers and draw on their background knowledge to gain understanding from the text. After students have responded to the text, pictures are discussed, and a variety of activities relating to the new vocabulary words are completed.

In the *Language!* program (Greene, 2009), comprehension is taught through the use of decodable connected text containing phonemic/graphemic concepts, vocabulary, and words that have been directly taught in the program. Reading comprehension instruction is also coordinated with instruction in expressive writing. The program stresses two key comprehension strategies within a "before, during, and after" reading instructional routine. Each story is followed by questions related to different levels of Bloom's taxonomy; the levels are introduced gradually, beginning in Unit 3. Students are directly taught the signal words for each of the six levels of the taxonomy so they can recognize what is being asked of them and can respond accordingly. They are also taught to create questions using signal words from the taxonomy. Story grammars are introduced gradually through Level 1 and into Level 2. While the Bloom questions and story grammars are stressed, *Language!* incorporates other comprehension strategies into its teaching routines, including brainstorming to build background knowledge, paraphrasing/ summarization, and the use of graphic organizers to recognize story parts.

To learn more about RTI, go to the IRIS Center website and complete modules 3, 4, and 5. Compare their recommendations for using the RTI model with recommendations that you have read about in this book. **http:// iris.peabody.vanderbilt.edu/ rti03_reading/chalcycle.htm http://iris.peabody.vanderbilt.edu/ rti04_alltogether/chalcycle.htm http://iris.peabody.vanderbilt.edu/ rti05_tier3/chalcycle.htm.**

How Do I Prepare My Students to Pass High-Stakes Tests in Reading?

While the most important job we have as teachers of reading is to teach our students to read for their own enjoyment and learning, the realities of today's culture of school accountability dictates that we must also prepare our students to perform well on high-stakes reading assessments. In our estimation, the best way to prepare students for high-stakes tests in reading is to have an effective reading program in place when children start school. Scientifically based reading programs, much like those described in this text, enable students to pass state tests by providing them with the phonemic awareness, phonics, fluency, vocabulary, and comprehension skills needed to read a wide range of text with understanding. That said, your students can still benefit from teacher-directed instruction and practice geared specifically toward your particular state test. Here are some steps to assure that the practice you provide goes beyond basic test preparation and further develops comprehension skills.

Analyze Your State Test

a. What types of passages are students required to comprehend? Most high-stakes tests in reading use narrative, expository, or functional material from everyday life such as application forms, recipes, or advertisements.
b. What levels of understanding are measured? Usually there is a mix of literal and inferential questions. Questions also test student ability to analyze and evaluate information as well as use metacognitive strategies.
c. What kinds of information are tested and how are the questions asked? Educational Resources Inc. (2004) has compiled a list of key question types as well as typical questions for each type. These are shown in Figure 7.7. Additional items and questions related to narrative prose and poetry adapted from Goudiss, Hodges, and Margulies (1999) are also included.

Teach Students to Recognize the Various Question Types   The ability to determine what a question is asking is an important first step in answering it correctly. That is why students need to be directly taught the information shown in Figure 7.7, along with other question-answering comprehension strategies like the QAR. When Travis was able to recognize that a question was asking about sequencing, he was then reminded to look for key words to help answer the question, such as *beginning, last, next,* and *before.* When Abdul recognized a vocabulary question, he automatically looked at the words around the word in the passage to figure out what it meant.

Teach Strategies for Answering Question Types Systematically and Explicitly
Just as in teaching the reading comprehension strategies described earlier in this chapter, systematic, explicit instruction works best when teaching your students to answer items on high-stakes tests. You can be systematic by working on the various question types one at a time, gradually introducing new types of questions as other types are mastered. You can be explicit by adding think-alouds to your My Turn–Together–Your Turn teaching routine. Examples of how to use think-alouds for a main idea/summarization question and a metacognitive question are shown below.

Main Idea/Summarization

I bought my car seven years ago. I haven't driven it for a year because I've been away. Yesterday I thought I'd get it ready to take out on the road again. I had a real shock when I looked at it.

Main Idea/Summarization	Author's Purpose	Moral
■ This *story* is mostly about _____. ■ What is this *story* mainly about? ■ What is another good name/title for this *story*? ■ Another title/name for the *selection* might be _____.	■ This story was written mainly to _____. ■ The writer wrote this *story* mainly to _____. ■ The *article* was written in order to _____. ■ _____ was written in order to _____.	■ The important message in the *story* is _____. ■ What lesson can be learned from this *selection*? ■ What lesson did _____ need to learn? ■ This story suggests _____.
Mood/Feeling/Emotion	**Fact and Opinion**	**Sequencing**
■ At the end of the story, _____ probably felt _____. ■ What made (character) feel _____?	■ Which of these is a fact in the story? ■ Which of these is an opinion in the story? ■ Which of the following is NOT _____? ■ All of the above are opinions except _____ _____. ■ Which of these is a fact stated in the article?	■ The boxes show _____ . ■ Which belongs in box _____? ■ What must be decided before _____? ■ In the beginning of the story _____. ■ Which of these happens last? ■ After (an event in the story), what must happen next?
Prediction	**Vocabulary**	**Sources of Information**
■ What will probably happen the next time _____? ■ What will probably happen next? ■ What probably happened after the story ended? ■ Which of these happens last? ■ What do you think will happen in the future?	■ In this story, _____ means _____. ■ In this story, a _____ is a _____. ■ What did the author mean when he said _____? ■ In this story, a _____ is like a _____. ■ In this article the phrase _____ means _____. ■ What words in the story show that _____?	■ If you wanted to find out more information, you should _____. ■ Look in a (source). ■ Look in a book called (title). ■ You would most likely find this story in a _____. ■ What is the best way to learn more about _____?
Metacognitive Questions	**Miscellaneous Stems**	**Character Analysis**
■ To skim this passage the reader would _____. ■ In order to answer question _____, the reader would _____.	■ Which question does the first paragraph answer? ■ If the author added a sentence in the story, what might he add?_____ ■ This story is a _____.	■ The most important character in the story is _____. ■ How would you describe _____? ■ How are _____ and _____ different? ■ What is the best word to describe _____?

FIGURE 7.7   Common Question Types on High-Stakes Reading Tests

Continued

Setting Analysis	Plot Analysis	Author's Point of View
■ The story takes place _____? ■ Where is the story set? ■ What time do you think _____ takes place? ■ Where is _____ at the end of the story? ■ Where do you think _____ lives? ■ How much time passes in the story?	■ What is the problem in the story? ■ How is the problem resolved?	■ What does the author think of _____? ■ What does the author think people should do if _____?

Poetry and Poetic Language
■ Which lines rhyme?   ■ What does the author mean by _____?   ■ Why do you think the author wrote that?   ■ What do the words _____ describe?   ■ What point is the author trying to make when she _____?

FIGURE 7.7   Continued

Source: Adapted from Educational Resources Inc. (2004). Strategies for taking high-stakes tests. Unpublished materials; and Goudiss, M., Hodges, V., & Margulies, S. (1999). *The ISAT coach: Grade 3 reading.* New York: Triumph Learning/Coach Books.

The back window was cracked. Two of the lights wouldn't go on. The motor needed a lot of work. The rear door wouldn't open. I don't think I can afford to fix it. It's a shame. I liked my old car.

What is this passage mainly about?

A. New cars are expensive.
B. The car lights don't work.
C. The car is in very bad shape.
D. The writer has been away. (Goudiss et al., 1999, p. 105)

Think-Aloud *Let's see. I need to figure out what this whole passage is about—not just one thing that is in the passage. Let me try the first choice, A, "New cars are expensive." That wasn't even mentioned in the story, so that can't be right. Choice B says the car lights don't work—that was in the story but it's only one thing in the story, not what the whole passage is about—so the answer can't be B. Choice C says the car is in very bad shape—that's what a lot of the sentences in the passage talked about, so it would make a good choice here. I'm going to pick C.*

How Do I Teach Comprehension to Older Learners?

Reading instruction should increasingly emphasize comprehension strategies once students are reading at a fourth- or fifth-grade level (Moats, 2001). Some students who are at risk will continue to increase their reading skills if they are in content classes with teachers who routinely weave the comprehensive strategies discussed earlier in this chapter into their instruction. A biology teacher who teaches his students to ask questions to check their understanding of the chapter on plant life, who uses think-alouds to show how to apply comprehension strategies, and who accompanies reading assignments with graphic organizers is teaching expository reading comprehension strategies along with biology. An English teacher who teaches students to answer inferential questions based on the novels they are studying, who models ways to differentiate between major events and added details, and who demonstrates how to summarize sections of the story is teaching students narrative reading comprehension strategies.

Other students who are at risk can benefit from a separate class of study skills where comprehension strategies are taught more explicitly and the teacher provides the opportunity to systematically apply those strategies to course material from their content classes. Unless they spend more time learning comprehension strategies, these students will not acquire higher reading levels. A third group of students is comprised of those who still need support in beginning or advanced word reading, some of it intensive. Because they are still advancing in their word reading skills, a smaller proportion of their instruction will include learning comprehension strategies. To help these students make the most progress, teach them to apply comprehension strategies to narrative and expository text at their independent or instructional reading level.

One of the greatest challenges for teachers of older struggling readers is finding text that is at the students' instructional level but still is interesting and content rich. In selecting text for comprehension instruction with these readers, teachers have several options. Spadorcia (2001) recommends that books be examined through many different lenses, recognizing the particular skills that less-skillful students need to learn to become better readers. If the student is past the beginning reading phase, Spadorcia recommends using balanced literacy books having a combination of many high-frequency words and some decodable words. Her analysis showed that these books had higher levels of sentence-level sophistication. *Swamp Furies* (Schraff, 1992) is an example of this type of book. Another type of book, the "high interest—low reading level decodable book," is also often appropriate for comprehension instruction. A science fiction book, *Deadly Double* (France, 1998), is a typical high–low book that falls into this category (Spadorcia, 2001). Some book series, like the *National Geographic Explorer* books, have differentiated instruction for the same topic. One set of books on the topic of lightning is written at the second- to third-grade level, while another set of books on that same topic is written at the fourth- to sixth-grade level.

Because your older readers must learn subject matter content in many of their classes, and because they are more likely to read expository text as adults, look for content books that are written at students' independent or instructional reading levels. Content books written at a lower readability or for students at a lower grade level can be used to teach comprehension strategies for expository text. If they are used for teaching content, the teacher has to be sure that all state standards for that content area are included or taught. Teaching content in social studies can be especially difficult. An explanation of why this is the case and what to do about it is in *The Reflective Teacher* feature.

The *ReadingQuest.org: Making Sense in Social Studies* website has hyperlinks to 27 reading strategies that can be integrated into social studies instruction: **http://www.readingquest.org/home.html.**

The Reflective Teacher

Why Is Social Studies Text More Difficult?

After third grade, students read a much higher proportion of nonfiction text in school. Social studies text presents greater challenges for students who are at risk. Teachers in our project noticed that students' DIBELS scores routinely dipped when they read social studies passages. Comprehending history is highly specialized reading requiring readers to critically think about evidence, the historical context of when events occurred, multiple perspectives of individuals at the time, and the significance of the events (Zarnowski, 2006). Other factors that make reading social studies, especially history, more difficult include the following:

- The text often contains vocabulary and ideas that students are not familiar with and that cannot be inferred. Students have to be skilled decoders for some of the new multisyllable words and have an adequate vocabulary for the historical and geographic terms that appear in the text. For adequate comprehension, students need to know the meaning of 95% of the words in a text, so preteaching vocabulary is critical *before* reading social studies text.
- Social studies text includes many reference words such as *this, those,* and *it*. In combination with complex sentences and difficult concepts, students can misinterpret what *this* or *those* actually refer to.
- Social studies text has a higher proportion of text written in the passive voice. Consider this sentence: "The sleds the Inuit used were made by lashing animal hides and a basket together with more animal hides." If students are unfamiliar with the word *Inuit*, they can become confused by questions such as "What was made?" and "Who rode in the sleds?"
- Unless the teacher clearly and with enthusiasm explains to students the benefits of learning the social studies information, the students may not relate to it.
- Social studies text routinely uses figurative language. If a student does not actively engage with the text or is an English language learner, visualizing the meaning of what they are reading can pose problems, as in this sentence: "In this rugged region of the country, low hills *snuggle up* to the mountains on the eastern shores."

Because social studies has its own unique challenges for struggling readers, always conduct prereading activities that clarify key vocabulary and provide students with the opportunity to read more-difficult words. After words are introduced, students need frequent, rich follow-up instruction requiring critical thinking so that they have the opportunity to use the new terms at a deeper level. Expect students to explore different facets of the new vocabulary word's meaning, use new words together, and ask questions that require them to apply meaning (e.g., teacher question: *"Which of the following situations demonstrates emancipation: 'The teenager was legally free from his parents when he turned 16' or 'The servant paid homage to the queen'?")* Finally, the use of a variety of graphic organizers to organize key information provides a blueprint students can use to study core knowledge from social studies text.

As mentioned earlier in this chapter, if the readability of a book is at an older student's instructional level, teacher read-alouds become an important instructional strategy. Using read-alouds with books or taped CDs enables older struggling readers to participate in the equivalent comprehension strategy instruction as peers. Older students will eventually need to practice using these strategies when reading text, but in this way the teacher can at least model the reasoning she uses in strategically approaching a book.

Teachers who convey their passion for reading to students and make the effort to seek out books at the students' reading levels on topics of interest to them can start to penetrate through the walls of resistance older struggling readers have developed. By the time a student reading below grade level is in middle school, one of the biggest challenges is breaking through the anxiety related to reading. The struggling reader has had years of sitting in classes hoping to avoid the humiliation of reading aloud, hearing that if she just "tried harder" she could read the book. Rekindling enthusiasm for reading as the older student gains skills is a slow process and takes careful scaffolding during instruction so the student can be successful during discussions and any oral reading. The student needs to receive twice the amount of praise and encouragement that other students need, and should have books assigned that can be read with a high degree of accuracy. When the student does not have the skills to read the assigned book in a class, taped texts should be an available accommodation whether or not the students has an IEP.

How Can I Teach Reading Comprehension to English Language Learners?

Comprehension of narrative and expository text can be challenging for English language learners who have no real-life experience with common story themes. A story that involves a typical children's birthday party in the United States, or one that takes place while family members are watching an after-Thanksgiving dinner football game, might be unduly confusing unless the teacher has explained the larger context before the reading. Eskey (2002) provides an example of five questions that might be confusing for students who have no experience with the type of party described in the following paragraph:

> It was the day of the big party. Mary wondered if Johnny would like a kite. She ran to her bedroom, picked up her piggy bank, and shook it. There was no sound. (p. 6)

Eskey explains that without discussion before reading the passage, the following questions would be difficult for students who have no cultural experience with such birthday parties:

1. What is the nature of the party in the text?
2. Are Mary and Johnny adults or children?
3. How is the kite related to the party?
4. Why did Mary shake her piggy bank?
5. What was Mary's big problem?

Expository text presents other related challenges. Even students who have developed fluent social language in English still find that academic language, the formal language of textbooks and lectures, requires different skills. Academic language has longer sentences, more complex grammar, and more technical vocabulary than social language. Also, topics in academic contexts are often more abstract, and the clues that English language learners gain from gestures and expressions are absent. A student who is proficient with social language can take up to five more years to develop academic language. That is why English language learners have to be more assertive with their teachers, because cues such as raised eyebrows or puzzled looks are usually inadequate to convey confusion in situations in which academic language is used. Of course, being assertive can raise additional problems for English language learners. Some of these students may be from cultures whose respect for teachers precludes their need to be assertive.

As you learned earlier in the chapter (see Table 7.2), signal words in text provide clues to indicate relationships among ideas and to clarify content. However, signal words provide additional challenges for English language learners. Signal words such as *for example, because, like,* and *first* link sentences and paragraphs together. They are essential for comprehension because they give the reader an indication of what will be happening. In the following sentence, the signal word *as* indicates a time relationship, letting the reader know that the makeup of the wood changed at the same time that the mud and sand of the swamps slowly turned to stone.

> As the mud and sand of the swamps slowly turned to stone, the makeup of the wood changed. (*The DK Science Encyclopedia*, 1998, p. 238)

Explicit teaching of the signal words and their function enables English language learners to use them as a strategy for increasing comprehension (Short, 1994). Teachers can use think-alouds to demonstrate how signal words provide clues for understanding, ask students to locate specific signal words in text, describe how the words provide clues to the meaning of a passage, and construct writing activities that require students to use specified signal words.

Instruction in comprehension monitoring is one of the key comprehension strategies that English language learners need. The ability to carefully monitor comprehension and apply fix-up strategies is crucial for them, because additional linguistic obstacles routinely impede their comprehension. Even though English language learners need to learn all of the comprehension strategies discussed throughout this chapter, Yu-fen Yang (2002) cautions that the focus of reading comprehension instruction first must emphasize language knowledge:

> However, the truth is that if readers do not possess sufficient language skills, then no matter how many diversified reading strategies they are equipped with, and how much training in metacognitive strategy usage they receive, the process will turn out to be fruitless if they have no basic resources to access when attempting to solve problems. They must have extensive resources to monitor whether their understanding of the text is coherent and logical. (p. 37)

Text that is directly related to the English language learner's culture or experience can reduce comprehension challenges. When texts do not have that connection, several days of prereading activities related to the topic can provide that same foundation for new vocabulary and concepts. Teaching strategies discussed in both Chapters 6 and 7 directly apply to English language learners (Francis, Rivera, Lesaux, Kieffer, & Rivera, 2006; Goldenberg, 2008). Some of the most important include the following:

- Use graphic organizers with all new text.
- Present key information about lesson content through visual cues, pictures, and gestures several times.

Learn more about the fourth-grade slump for English language learners by watching the video clip at **http:// www. readingrockets.org/webcasts/2004.**

- Model how to summarize the text, or have another student do it, before providing practice.
- Emphasize vocabulary instruction and strategies discussed in Chapter 6 whenever you teach comprehension.
- Use interactive read-alouds that provide many opportunities to participate in structured discussions of the text.

All students, including English language learners, can benefit from accessing information on the Internet. The *Technology* feature discusses ways to help students maximize their learning on the Internet.

Technology

Reading for Understanding on the Internet

The lack of valid research investigating the different skills needed to read text in books versus Internet text has fueled ongoing debate. Teachers wonder whether their students need to substantially retool and learn additional skills to derive meaning from Internet text. When MacArthur, Ferretti, Okolo, and Cavalier (2001) reviewed studies comparing reading on paper to reading unenhanced text on screen, they found no indication that reading text on screen affected students' comprehension either positively or negatively. Other studies they investigated in which students read text containing enhancements such as hyperlinks providing definitions of difficult words or main ideas showed mixed results.

Since students increasingly use the Internet in place of or in addition to a library, teachers are responsible for critically evaluating claims about the best methods to improve reading comprehension online. Unique features of Internet text may place different demands on the reader. In the course of reading, students often have to make decisions about the large volume of information instantaneously available to them. Becoming overwhelmed with these decisions, many students have been observed to "snatch and grab" the information. Rather than taking the time to evaluate critically which information is most valid and related to their research needs, students quickly hyperlink without much thought (RAND, 2002). In one large study, half of the college students lacked the skills to evaluate how valid and reputable information on nutritional supplements was (Ivanitskaya, O'Boyle, & Casey, 2006).

Social networking has gained popularity since the last edition of this book, and with its advent literacy has evolved from a solitary pursuit into a collective one. Although adults grumble about young adults' lack of spelling and writing skills, increasingly those skills influence social status on websites where a permanent record remains on Google for future employers to mine. In an article about how the Internet saved literacy, Farrell describes two academics' analysis of the increased demand for skilled reading, writing, and spelling skills:

> "You aren't just a consumer of text anymore," says Margaret Mackey, a professor at the University of Alberta's Library and Information Studies Department. "Reading now demands an almost instantaneous response, whether through commenting on a blog or writing a review on Amazon. The Internet has shortened the feedback loop on writing and has made readers more active participants," says Matt Kirschenbaum, an assistant professor of English at the University of Maryland. "Reading is more intimately associated with writing," he says. (Farrell, 2006)

Today's Internet reader must be skilled at comprehending expository text since it comprises the majority of reading on the Internet. Students who have not learned or do not apply expository strategies to paper reading cannot be expected to use them when reading on the Internet. Because estimates indicate that 90% of what students read in elementary school is narrative, students will be unable to fully utilize Internet sources unless teachers have explicitly taught and expected students to read expository text. When Schmar-Dobler (2003) compared reading strategies used in reading books to those used on the Internet, she found no differences in how readers do these things:

- Activate prior knowledge
- Determine important ideas
- Synthesize to sift important from unimportant details
- Draw inferences, reading between the lines and using background knowledge to help fill in gaps

Differences that Schmar-Dobler noted included how readers do these things:

- Rely more on skimming and scanning techniques because of the volume of text.
- Place more emphasis on using guiding questions to stay focused and to avoid getting lost in the text options
- Use Internet basic skills in order to perform tasks such as downloading appropriate text and avoiding pop-up ads that interfere with text reading

Instruction in writing skills that are so important for Internet use should start early. The *In Your Classroom* feature describes ways that Project PRIDE teachers began writing instruction in kindergarten.

In Your Classroom

Beginning Writing in Kindergarten

Beginning in kindergarten, many of the Project PRIDE teachers integrated writing activities into lesson planning to further enhance their students' reading comprehension skills. Teachers found that because students had such strong phonemic awareness skills and had learned to sound-spell, their writing was readable even when they used words that they had not yet learned to spell. Some of the writing activities that teachers planned in connection with comprehension activities were these:

- Writing summaries of stories or expository text in their own words

- Retelling a story from another character's perspective
- Writing several sentences connecting the theme of the story to something they have personally experienced
- Using a key sentence from a story as the story prompt for their writing
- Using the same graphic organizers used for reading comprehension as prewriting organizers before writing stories or informational text
- Completing charts or workbook pages requesting more information about text just read

What Games and Activities Reinforce Reading Comprehension Skills?

Some of the following games can be adapted for younger or older students. Other games are more appropriate for older groups.

Find the Hot Spots

Give students several stick-on notes to use as they read a text. Ask them to mark the described hot spots. For example, ask students to do one or a combination of the following:

- Place pink stick-on notes on pages where there is a vocabulary word they do not know or where the text is confusing.
- Place green stick-on notes on pages where they were excited about what they were reading and thought that the author's writing was exceptionally interesting.
- Place orange stick-on notes on pages where the author makes a claim that is not substantiated by facts or valid, reliable sources.
- Place blue stick-on notes on pages where the author writes about a problem.
- Place purple stick-on notes on pages where they wish they could write like that.

Provide Evidence

Divide students into small groups and give each player six cards. On three cards are adjectives used to describe the personalities of a character, and on three cards are characters from books recently read in class. Students take turns taking and discarding cards until they have a character and an adjective that match. Once a student has a match, he names the story his character is in, describes why his character has the specific personality trait, and provides evidence from the story supporting that opinion. For example, a student might explain that Mr. McGregor in *The Tale of Peter Rabbit* was mean "because he chased Peter around the garden" (Richards & Gipe, 2000).

What Would Your Character Do?

Divide students into small groups. Each student selects a card designating a character from a recently read story. The teacher then presents a situation and asks the students to think about what they know about their character from the story and describe how he or she would respond in the situation. The following is a sample situation described by the authors of this game:

> Your character is transported to a foreign land for two weeks. No one speaks your character's language. English is the only language your character speaks, reads, and writes. Your character needs food, a place to sleep, and money. What would your character do? (Richards & Gipe, 2000, p. 77)

Students should explain what their designated character would do and what evidence from the story leads them to predict that action.

Try Out Your Test-Making Skills

Divide the class into four groups. After students read expository text about social studies or science, ask them to write a specified number of questions about the main ideas of the text. Design a rubric to evaluate their test, making sure to award each team extra points if every question is about a main idea. Once students are finished writing their tests, give each group another group's test and see how well they remember the information they read. Award team points for questions answered correctly.

How Well Do I Understand?

As you read short pieces of expository text to students, ask them to raise one finger if they understand the text being read and two fingers if they do not understand it. Stop when the majority of students have two fingers raised and discuss strategies to clarify understanding of the text.

The Text Detective

Before students read an assigned text, give them short-answer worksheets with key *wh*-questions you want them to answer. Some questions might include: "In what period of time is this biography set?" "What was the main problem this character encountered growing up?" "Where did this character live most of his life?" "Who was the most influential person in this character's life?" and "Why do people say that this character is a leader?"

While games and other activities are effective in reinforcing reading comprehension skills, there is no substitute for effective, teacher-led instruction like that described in *The Reflective Teacher*.

Visit the Cultural Literacy Rocks website at **www.aft.org/pubs-reports/ american_educator/spring2004/ literacyroacks.html.**

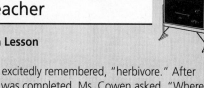

The Reflective Teacher

A Model Comprehension Lesson

Ms. Cowen's second-grade class was going to read *It's Probably Good Dinosaurs Are Extinct* by Ken Raney (1993). Before they read the book, students practiced reading the new morphemes they had recently learned and were now frequently applying to more difficult words they encountered in their reading: *age, tion, ish,* and *dis.* Next they decoded the new words that were in this story. Because students did not know the meaning of the words *extinct, roamed, existed,* and *herd,* Ms. Cowen directly taught them as vocabulary words. Three dinosaur names, *apatosaurus, protoceratops,* and *stegosaurus,* initially presented decoding challenges. Ms. Cowen knew that if students couldn't read the story with adequate accuracy, they would not understand it, so she planned her reading lessons so that students did not read the story until the second day after they had more practice with these and other new words.

On the day that students read the story, Ms. Cowen told everyone the title and, pointing to her large flip chart, asked everyone to tell her what information they already knew about dinosaurs. She wrote the students' answers on a graphic organizer (see Figure 7.8) and extended discussion through questions.

When students pointed out that some dinosaurs ate just plants, Ms. Cowen linked this story to a previous one by reminding students that several weeks ago in a different story they had learned a word that they could use for animals that ate only plants. After a hint,

someone excitedly remembered, "herbivore." After the chart was completed, Ms. Cowen asked, "Where did the dinosaurs live?" That question stumped the class, and so she drew everyone's attention to a large dinosaur picture on the wall. "Caves, they lived in caves," a girl shouted out. Ms. Cowen expanded that answer and said, "Yes, they lived everywhere on Earth. They lived in every country. They've even found dinosaur bones in ice. Some lived in water. Where did others live?" Several students chimed in and explained that some lived on land and others in the air. Ms. Cowen used the moment to expand everyone's knowledge and, pointing to the globe, told the students that scientists believe that the continents were all connected at one time.

Looking deep in thought, another child asked the teacher, "How did the scientists discover the dinosaurs?" Ms. Cowen explained how they found the bones and came up with the name "terrible lizard," which is what *dinosaur* means. "But they only found the bones—nothing else," she explained as everyone nodded their heads. At that, a student volunteered information about how her dad had bought her a computer CD about dinosaurs. One of the dinosaurs on the CD had a hard skull. Another student asked Ms. Cowen if dinosaurs were alive when she was a girl. At first Ms. Cowen joked about all the dinosaurs she would see outside the school at recess, but then she switched into a more serious mode and admitted

Continued

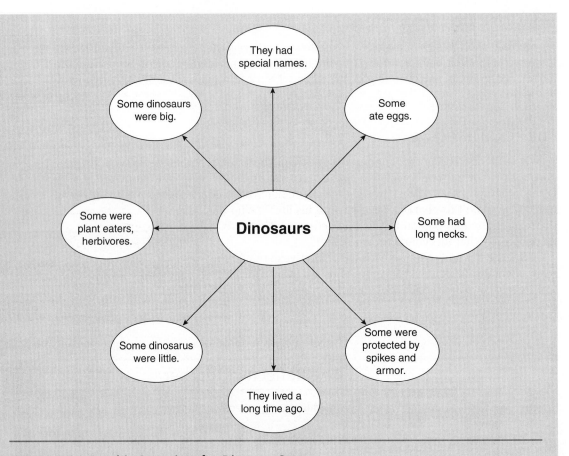

FIGURE 7.8 Graphic Organizer for Dinosaur Story

Source: Cowen, J. (2003). Unpublished materials. Rockford, IL: Rockford Public Schools.

that dinosaurs lived so long ago that there were none even when she was a baby. Most of the class seemed to enjoy the humor in this exchange.

After all the students had opened their books, Ms. Cowen explained that the new story was a fantasy story, and she asked what that meant. When one student replied, "not true," Ms. Cowen expanded the answer and explained, "Yes, the story was make-believe." Next everyone orally read the title in unison. Ms. Cowen asked students what "it's" was, since they had been studying contractions, and the class answered, "it is." One student then read two or three sentences while everyone else followed along with their fingers. At the end of that passage, Ms. Cowen asked several questions that the students enthusiastically answered:

"How does the boy feel about dinosaurs?"

"What does he wish he had?"

"How many of you wish you had a dinosaur for a pet?"

After the entire class raised their hands, one student explained why he wanted a dinosaur to help him. Then a second student read another two sentences. This

time Ms. Cowen stopped and asked, "Now the book says, 'It's probably good that dinosaurs are extinct.' What exactly does *extinct* mean?" Even though she had taught that word for two days, it took several hints for the class to remember what the difficult word meant. Wanting her students to use this word more, Ms. Cowen asked, "What would happen if dinosaurs were no longer extinct?" The students were appalled. "But they'd tear up our houses and eat our food," one answered. "They'd eat up our relatives," said another. A third girl chimed in, "They'd be very noisy at night and I couldn't sleep."

The first story reading continued with students reading passages followed by teacher questions. Information was clarified, connections drawn, understanding checked during this enjoyable story. Later, students would write and illustrate their work before it was displayed in the hallway. Two more dinosaur stories followed this one, one a narrative and the other expository. Decoding, oral-language expansion, writing, fluent reading, graphic organizers, storybook structure, and frequent questions all worked together to develop these students' reading comprehension.

APPLIED ACTIVITIES

1. Two fact-or-fiction questions about reading comprehension are included below. Pair up with a partner and take turns defending your position for one of these questions, using references from research sources cited in the chapter or from information on the website resources listed in the sidebars.

   a. While the research on developing phonemic awareness, alphabetic principle, and reading fluency is conclusive enough to guide teacher practice, we don't have a comparable knowledge base for reading comprehension. Is this fact or fiction? Explain why.

   b. Teaching reading comprehension requires that children first have a book in their hands that they are able to read. Is this fact or fiction? Explain why.

2. Shown here are the DIBELS Oral Reading Fluency and maze percentile scores for Ms. Redmond's Grade 3 class in May. Identify which children may be experiencing difficulty with reading comprehension. Using Appendix B for interpreting the DIBELS ORF scores, determine whether any of these students is also below benchmark in ORF. Why do you think students who read slowly are more likely to also have trouble with comprehension? How would you account for Roberto's performance?

Student	ORF	Maze Percentiles
Alex	115	>75
Bruno	70	<25
Celia	100	<50
Roberto	110	<50
Aquanetta	93	<50

3. In this chapter you learned that the ability to comprehend is influenced by the person reading the text, the text being read, the task the reader is trying to accomplish, and the context in which the reading is being done. For each of the following reading problems, discuss the factor(s) that are contributing to the problem.

   a. Sharif is impulsive, and when given a reading assignment tends to rush through the text and not think about what he is reading.

   b. Margaret could not understand her library book because she always selects books that are too difficult for her.

   c. The reading assignment was difficult for Darren, but by trying extra hard he was able to get through it and answer the questions. Darren needed a good score on the assignment to get a passing grade for the marking period.

   d. Rinaldo refused to read in class because his classmates are critical of anyone who does what the teacher wants.

4. Think of a recent reading assignment for one of your classes. What metacognitive skills did you exercise in completing that assignment? How helpful were these skills for the successful completion of the assignment? How could you teach these skills to students who are unable to do them?

5. Shown here is a fable relating how slow and steady wins the race. Develop a graphic organizer that could be used to guide students as they read to comprehend the passage. Write a script showing what you would say if you were using My Turn–Together–Your Turn think-alouds to teach your students the key story grammar elements.

   > One day the Rabbit made fun of the short legs and slow pace of the Turtle. The Turtle replied, laughing, "Though you may be fast as the wind, I will beat you in a race." The Rabbit, believing that to be simply impossible, agreed to the race. They agreed that their mutual friend the Fox should choose the course and fix the goal. On the day of the race the two animals started together. The Rabbit began running as fast as she could and soon got tired, lying down by the side of the trail. She fell fast asleep. The Turtle plodded along as he always did and never stopped for a moment, but went on with a slow but steady pace straight to the end of the course. Rabbit, at last waking up and moving as fast as she could, tried to catch up. Arriving at the end of the course, she saw the Turtle had reached the goal, and was comfortably resting. The Fox who had helped them laughed out loud and said, "It is true . . . slow but steady wins the race!"

6. Read the following passage taken from an eighth-grade social studies book. Identify the key text structure in the passage. Tell how you would use My Turn–Together–Your Turn think-alouds and a graphic organizer to teach students to recognize the text structure and understand the passage.

   Striking Workers

   As prices rose, labor unions demanded higher wages. Although many of these demands were met, some companies refused to give their workers pay increases. The result was a number of strikes that soon threatened the stability of the American economy.

   The rail strike was probably the most serious. The huge semitrailers and interstate highways we know today didn't exist then. Most of the nation's goods moved by rail. President Truman, who had worked feverishly to end the coal and auto strikes, was angry when the railway workers announced their strike. He said that he understood their problems, but that he couldn't allow a rail strike at the time. (Buggey et al., 1987)

7. Select a children's fiction story and generate 12 questions that you could ask students. Your questions should reflect story grammars as well as important vocabulary. Indicate which questions reflect explicit or implicit information in the text.

Companion Website

Now go to Chapter 7 in the Companion Website (www.pearsonhighered.com/bursuck2e) where you can do the following activities:

- Complete Activities that can help you more deeply understand the chapter content.
- Check your comprehension of the content covered in the chapter by going to the Chapter Quiz. Here you will be able to an-

swer practice questions, receive feedback on your answers, and then access resources that will enhance your understanding of chapter content.
- Find Web Links that will extend your understanding of the content and strategies.

REFERENCES

Applegate, M., Quinn, B., & Applegate, A. (2002). Levels of thinking required by comprehension questions in informal reading inventories. *The Reading Teacher, 56*(2), 174–180.

Archer, A., & Gleason, M. (2010). Direct instruction in content-area reading. In D. W. Carnine, J. Silbert, E. J. Kame'enui, & S. Tarver (2010), *Direct instruction reading* (5th ed.). Boston: Merrill Prentice Hall.

Armbruster, B., Lehr, F., & Osborn, J. (2001). *Put reading first: The research building blocks for teaching children to read.* Washington, DC: Partnership for Reading.

Beck, I., & McKeown, M. (2001). *Text talk.* New York: Scholastic.

Beck, I. L., & McKeown, M. G. (2007). Increasing young low income children's oral vocabulary repertoires through rich and focused instruction. *Elementary School Journal, 107*(3), 251–271.

Beck, I., McKeown, M., Hamilton, R., & Kucan, L. (1997). *Question the author: An approach for enhancing student engagement with text.* Newark, DE: International Reading Association.

Beck, I. L., McKeown, M. G., Sandora, C., Kucan, L., & Worthy, J. (1996). Questioning the author: A yearlong classroom implementation to engage students with text. *The Elementary School Journal, 96*, 385–414.

Bos, C. S., & Vaughn, S. (2008). *Strategies for teaching students with learning and behavior problems* (7th ed.). Boston: Pearson Education.

Brabham, E. G., & Lynch-Brown, C. (2002). Effects of teacher's reading-aloud styles on vocabulary acquisition and comprehension of students in the early elementary grades. *Journal of Educational Psychology, 94*(3), 465–473.

Brandwein, P. F., & Bauer, N. W. (1980). *The United States, living in our world: Research, evaluation, and writing.* Barton R. Clark et al., consulting scientists. San Francisco and New York: Center for the Study of Instruction/Harcourt Brace Jovanovich.

Buehl, D. (2008). *Classroom strategies for interactive learning.* Newark, DE: International Reading Association.

Buggey, L., Danzer, G., Mitsakos, C., & Risinger, C. (1985). *America! America!* (2nd ed.). Upper Saddle River, NJ: Prentice Hall.

Burnett, F. H. (2008). *The secret garden.* Cambridge, MA: Candlewick Press.

Carnine, D., & Kinder, D. (1985). Teaching low-performing students to apply generative and schema strategies to narrative and expository material. *Remedial and Special Education, 6*(1), 20–30.

Carnine, D. W., Silbert, J., Kame'enui, E. J., & Tarver, S. (2010). *Direct instruction reading* (5th ed.). Boston: Merrill Prentice Hall.

Chall, J., & Dale, E. (1995). *Readability revisited: The new Dale-Chall readability formula.* Brookline, MA: Brookline Books.

Chall, J., Jacobs, V., & Baldwin, L. (1990). *The reading crisis: Why poor children fall behind.* Cambridge, MA: Harvard University Press.

Cotton, K. (1989). Classroom questioning. *School Improvement Research Series.* Northwest Regional Educational Laboratory. Retrieved June 17, 2009, from http://www.nwrel.org/scpd/sirs/3/cu5.html

Coyne, M. D., Simmons, D. C., Kame'enui, E. J., & Stoomiller, M. (2004). Teaching vocabulary during shared storybook readings: An examination of differential effects. *Exceptionality, 12*, 145–162.

Dickens, C. (1843). *A Christmas carol.* Retrieved June 17, 2009, from http://www.gutenberg.org/catalog/world/readfile?fk_files=93841&pageno=2

Dixon, R., Boorman, L., & Muti, K. (2008). *Reading success: Effective comprehension strategies.* Columbus, OH: McGraw-Hill/SRA.

DK Science Encyclopedia, The. (1998). C. Beattie et al. (Eds.). New York: DK.

Duffy, G. G., & Roehler, L. R. (1989). Why strategy instruction is so difficult and what we need to do about it. In C. B. McCormick, G. E. Miller, & M. Pressley (Eds.), *Cognitive strategy research: From basic research to educational applications* (pp. 133–157). New York: Springer-Verlag.

Duffy, G. G. (1993). Rethinking strategy instruction: Four teachers' development and their low achievers' understandings. *Elementary School Journal, 93,* 231–247.

Educational Resource Inc. (2004). *Strategies for taking high-stakes tests.* Unpublished materials.

Engelmann, S., Johnson, G., Carnine, L., Meyer, L., Becker, W., & Eisele, J. (2008). *Corrective reading.* Columbus, OH: McGraw-Hill/SRA.

Englert, C., & Mariage, T. (1991). Making students partners in the comprehension process: Organizing the reading "POSSE." *Learning Disability Quarterly, 14*(2), 123–138.

Englert, C., & Thomas, C. (1987). Sensitivity to text structure in reading and writing: A comparison between learning disabled and non-learning disabled students. *Learning Disability Quarterly, 10*(2), 93–105.

Eskey, D. E. (2002). Reading and the teaching of L2 reading. *Teachers of English to Speakers of Other Languages Journal (TESOL Journal), 11*(1), 5–9.

Farrell, M. (2006, December 1). How the Internet saved literacy. *Forbes.* Retrieved July 26, 2009, from http://www.forbes.com/2006/11/30/reading-literacy-internet-tech-media_cx_mf_books06_1201literacy_print.html

Fletcher, J., Lyone, G., Ruchs, L., & Barnes, M. (2007). *Learning disabilities: From identification to intervention.* New York: The Guilford Press.

France, M. (1998). *Deadly double.* Novato, CA: High Noon Books.

Francis, D. J., Rivera, M., Lesaux, N., Kieffer, M., & Rivera, H. (2006). Practical guidelines for the education of English language learners: Research based recommendations for instruction and academic interventions. Retrieved May 3, 2005, from http://www.centeroninstruction.org/files/ELL1-Interventions.pdf

Friend, M., & Bursuck, W. D. (2008). *Including students with special needs: A practical guide for classroom teachers* (5th ed.). Boston: Pearson Education.

Goldenberg, C. (2008). Teaching English language learners: What the research does—and does not—say. *American Education* (pp. 8–44). AFT publications and reports. Retrieved May 25, 2009, from www.aft.org/pubs-reports/american_educator/issues/summer08/goldenberg.pdf

Goudiss, M., Hodges, V., & Margulies, S. (1999). *The ISAT coach: Grade 3 reading.* New York: Triumph Learning/Coach Books.

Greene, J. F. (2009). *Language! A literacy intervention curriculum.* Longmont, CO: Sopris West.

Gunderson, L. (2008). *ESL literacy instruction: A guidebook to theory and practice* (2nd ed.). New York: Routledge.

Gunning, T. (2002). *Assessing and correcting reading and writing difficulties* (2nd ed.). Boston: Allyn & Bacon.

Hiebert, E. H. (1999). Text matters in learning to read. *The Reading Teacher, 52,* 552–568.

Hirsch, E. D. (2000, Spring). You can always look it up . . . or can you? *American Educator, 24*(1), 4–9.

Hosp, M., Hosp, J., Howell, K. (2007). *The ABCs of CBM: A practical guide to curriculum-based measurement.* New York: The Guilford Press.

Ivanitskaya, L., O'Boyle, I., & Casey, A. M. (2006). Health information literacy and competencies of information age students: Results from the Interactive Online Research Readiness Self-Assessment (RRSA). *Journal of Medical Internet Research, 8*(2), e6.

Keenan J., & Betjemann, R. (2006). Comprehending the Gray Oral Reading Test without reading it: Why comprehension tests should not include passage-independent items. *Scientific Studies of Reading, 10*(4), 363–380.

Keene, E. (2002). From good to memorable: Characteristics of highly effective comprehension teaching. In C. Block, L. Gambrell, & M. Pressley (Eds.), *Improving comprehension instruction: Rethinking research, theory, and classroom practice* (pp. 80–105). San Francisco: Jossey-Bass.

Kinder, D. (1990). A reciprocal teaching example. Unpublished materials.

Kletzien, S., & Szabo, R. (1998). *Information text or narrative text? Children's preferences revisited.* Paper presented at the National Reading Conference, Austin, TX.

Klingner, J., Vaughn, S., & Boardman, A. (2004). *Teaching reading comprehension to students with learning difficulties.* New York: The Guilford Press.

Kozloff, M. (2005). Tips for effective teaching of language for learning. Retrieved July 14, 2009, from http://people.uncw.edu/kozloffm/tipsLanguageforLearning.DOC

Langer, J. (1984). Examining background knowledge and text comprehension. *Reading Research Quarterly, 19,* 468–481.

Luft, D. (1980). *Robert Musil and the crisis of European culture: 1880–1942.* Berkeley: University of California Press.

MacArthur, C., Ferretti, R., Okolo, C., & Cavalier, A. (2001, January). Technology applications for students with literacy problems: A critical review. *The Elementary School Journal, 101*(3), 73–301.

Marchand-Martella, N. E., Slocum, T. A., & Martella, R. C. (2004). *Introduction to direct instruction.* Boston: Allyn & Bacon.

McEwan, E. (2001). *Raising reading achievement in middle and high schools.* Thousand Oaks, CA: Corwin.

McEwan, E. (2009). *Teach them all to read: Catching kids before they fall through the cracks* (2nd ed.). Thousand Oaks, CA: Corwin.

McKeown, M., Beck, I., & Blake, R. (2009). Reading comprehension instruction: Focus on content or strategies. *Perspectives on Language and Literacy, 35*(2), 28–32.

Miranda, A., & Guerrero, M. (1986). The funny farola. In Adventures (pp. 42–53). Boston: Houghton Mifflin.

Moats, L. C. (March, 2001). When older students can't read. *Educational Leadership, 58*(6), 36–40.

Moats, L. C. (2005). *Language essentials for teachers of reading and spelling. Module 6: Digging for meaning: Teaching text comprehension.* Boston: Sopris West.

Moats, L. C. (2007). *Whole language high jinks: How to tell when "scientifically-based reading instruction" isn't.* Thomas B. Fordham Institute (ERIC Document Reproduction Service No. ED 4980005).

National Reading Panel. (2000). *Teaching children to read: An evidence-based assessment of the scientific research literature on reading and its implications for reading instruction.* Washington, DC: National Institute of Child Health and Human Development.

Palincsar, A. S., & Brown, A. L. (1988). Reciprocal teaching of comprehension-fostering and comprehension-monitoring activities. *Cognition and Instruction, 1,* 117–175.

Parker, R., Hasbrouck, J. E., & Tindal, G. (1992). The Maze as a classroom-based reading measure: Construction methods, reliability, and validity. *Journal of Special Education, 26,* 195–218.

Philbrick, R. (1998). *Max the mighty.* New York: Scholastic.

Pressley, M. (2002). Metacognition and self-regulated comprehension. In A. E. Farstrup & S. Samuels (Eds.), *What research has to say about reading instruction* (pp. 291–309). Newark, DE: International Reading Association.

RAND Reading Study Group. (2002). Reading for understanding: Towards an R&D program in reading comprehension. Retrieved August 10, 2009, from www.rand.org/publications/MR/MR1465

Raney, K. (1993). *It's probably good dinosaurs are extinct.* Seattle, WA: Green Tiger Press.

Reading Success Network, Southeast Comprehensive Assistance Center. (n.d.). Implications for teaching reading to English language learners: Participant materials. Retrieved August 7, 2009, from www.sedl.org/secac/rsn/ELL.pdf

Reich, J. R., & Beiler, E. L. (1988). *United States history.* Austin, TX: Holt, Rinehart & Winston.

Richards, J., & Gipe, J. (2000). Reading comprehension games for young students in mainstream settings. *Reading & Writing Quarterly, 16,* 75–80.

Rosenshine, B. (1997). Advances in research on instruction. In J. W. Lloyd, E. J. Kame'enui, & D. Chard (Eds.), *Issues in educating students with disabilities* (pp. 197–221). Mahwah, NJ: Erlbaum.

Schmar-Dobler, E. (September, 2003). Reading on the Internet: The link between literacy and technology. *Journal of Adolescent & Adult Literacy, 47*(1), 80–85.

Schraff, A. (1992). *Swamp furies.* Costa Mesa, CA: Saddleback Publishing, Inc.

Shankweiler, D. (1999). Words to meanings. *Scientific Studies of Reading, 3,* 113–127.

Shankweiler, D., Lundquist, E., & Dreyer, L. (1996). Reading and spelling difficulties in high school students: Causes and consequences. *Reading and Writing, 8*(3) 267–294.

Shinn, J., Deno, S. L., & Espin, C. (2000). Technical adequacy of the maze task for curriculum-based measurement of reading growth. *The Journal of Special Education, 34*(3), 164–172.

Short, D. (1994). Expanding middle school horizons: Integrating language, culture, and social studies. *TESOL Quarterly, 28,* 581–608.

Smith, M. (1999). Teaching comprehension from a multisensory perspective. In J. Birsh (Ed.), *Multisensory teaching of basic language skills.* Baltimore: Paul H. Brookes.

Sousa, D. (2005). *How the brain learns to read.* Thousand Oaks, CA: Corwin.

Spadorcia, S. (2001). Looking more closely at high-interest, low-level texts: Do they support comprehension? *Perspectives, 27*(2), 32–33. Retrieved March 25, 2009, from http://www.resourceroom.net/Comprehension/idahilocomp.asp

Stahl, Robert. (1990). *Using "think-time" behaviors to promote students' information processing, learning, and on-task participation: An instructional module.* Tempe: Arizona State University.

Stecker, P., & Lembke, E. (2005). Advanced applications of CBM in reading: Instructional decision-making strategies manual. Washington, DC: National Center on Student Progress Monitoring. Retrieved July 26, 2009, from http://nysrrc.monroe.edu/?q=node/43

Willingham, D. (2009). *Why don't students like school? A cognitive scientist answers questions about how the mind works and what it means for the classroom.* San Francisco: Jossey-Bass.

Yang, Y. (April, 2002). Reassessing readers' comprehension monitoring. *Reading in a Foreign Language, 14*(1). Retrieved Aug. 4, 2009, from http://nflrc.hawaii.edu/rfl/april2002/yang/yang.html

Zarnowski, M. (2006). *Making sense of history: Using high-quality literature and hands-on experiences to build content knowledge.* New York: Scholastic

APPENDIX

A Early Reading Assessment Batteries Used for Screening

	Dynamic Indicators of Basic Skills (DIBELS)	AIMSweb	Phonological Awareness Literacy Screening (PALS)	Texas Primary Reading Inventory (TPRI)
Type of Test	Curriculum-based measurement	Curriculum-based measurement	Criterion-referenced assessment	Criterion-referenced assessment
Score Reports	Benchmark goals represent minimum levels of performance for students to reach in order to be considered on track for becoming a reader. Scores are based on research indicating the predictive validity of a score related to a student meeting the next benchmark. Students' scores are reported as: 1. Benchmark or Established (student has an 80%–100% probability of reaching the next benchmark if no supplemental support is given). Usually designated as Tier 1. 2. Some Risk or Emerging (student has a 50% probability of achieving the next benchmark goal if no supplemental support is given). Usually designated as Tier 2. 3. At Risk or Deficit (student has a 0%–20% probability of achieving the next benchmark goal if no supplemental support is given). Usually designated as Tier 3.	Scores at the 90th, 75th, 50th, 20th, and 10th percentile are reported based on district and national norms. Generally, students whose scores are below the 50th percentile would need some level of additional support. Percentiles are also given for "rate of improvement," indicating expected progress for a student over the course of a year. "State prediction lines," which vary from state to state depending upon the difficulty of the state test, provide information about specific scores that students need to pass state reading tests with 70% and 80% probability. Because the difficulty level of state test scores differs quite significantly, in one state a third-grade student might need to read 95 words correct per minute to have an 80% probability of passing the state reading test, and in another state a student would need to read 120 words correct per minute to have that same probability of passing the state test.	Predetermined benchmark scores indicate that a student has met the level of minimum competency necessary to benefit from typical classroom literacy instruction. For reading text, a student's independent, instructional, and frustration reading levels are based on the percentage of words read correctly.	Students are given short screening assessments BOY and EOY. The screening test results determine which test items are given to the student from a more in-depth inventory assessment, which is given three times a year (BOY, MOY, and EOY). Test items on the inventory get progressively more difficult, and the goal is for students to eventually score "developed" on all of them by the end of the year. For reading text, a student's independent, instructional, and frustration reading levels are based on the percentage of words read correctly. Predetermined benchmark scores indicate that a student has "developed" or is "still developing" skills assessed on the screening. Students who have "still developing" scores on the TPRI at the beginning of grade 2 will be one-half year or more below grade level at the end of Grade 2 if more reading intervention is not provided.
Progress-Monitoring Forms Available	Yes, and because this is a CBM test, aimlines are used to determine whether students are on track to meet the end-of-the-year goal.	Yes, and because this is a CBM test, aimlines are used to determine whether students are on track to meet the end-of-the-year goal. The slope of student progress is also computed based on "rate of improvement" information.	Quick-checks, which are short, task-targeted assessments, are available for progress monitoring. Tasks on the quick-checks differ from tasks on screening tests, and quick-checks for the same skill get progressively more difficult.	Progress-monitoring passages are available for progress monitoring oral reading fluency every 2 to 6 weeks.

Continued

	Dynamic Indicators of Basic Skills (DIBELS)	AIMSweb	Phonological Awareness Literacy Screening (PALS)	Texas Primary Reading Inventory (TPRI)
Time Required to Give to One Child	Each assessment takes between 1 and 5 minutes. Typically between two and five assessments are given.	Each assessment takes between 1 and 5 minutes. Typically between two and five assessments are given.	Assessment battery takes between 20 and 60 minutes.	Assessment battery takes between 10 and 25 minutes.
Specific Interventions Tied to Test Scores	No, but teachers can get more information on the performance of the student by doing an informal error analysis.	No, but teachers can get more information on the performance of the student by doing an informal error analysis.	Yes; the Instructional Resources link on the PALS website provides recommended activities for each area tested.	A student's reading errors are linked to related activities in state-adopted basals and activities from an intervention activity guide.
Specific Subtests in the Screening Assessment Battery	<ul><li>Initial Sound Fluency (BOY* K–MOY* K)</li><li>Letter Naming Fluency (BOY K–BOY first)</li><li>Phoneme Segmentation Fluency (MOY K–EOY* first)</li><li>Nonsense Word Fluency (MOY K–BOY second)</li><li>Oral Reading Fluency (MOY first–EOY sixth)</li><li>Retell Fluency (first–third)</li></ul>	<ul><li>Letter Naming Fluency (BOY K–BOY first)</li><li>Letter–Sound Fluency (BOY K–BOY first)</li><li>Phoneme Segmentation Fluency (MOY K–EOY first)</li><li>Nonsense Word Fluency (MOY K–EOY first)</li><li>Oral Reading Fluency (BOY first–EOY eighth)</li><li>Spelling (BOY first–EOY eighth)</li><li>Maze (BOY first–EOY eighth)</li></ul>	Kindergarten: <ul><li>Individual rhyme awareness</li><li>Individual beginning sound awareness</li><li>Lowercase alphabet recognition</li><li>Letter–sounds ID</li><li>Spelling</li><li>Concept of word</li><li>Word recognition in isolation</li></ul> First–third grade: Level A: Entry level <ul><li>Spelling inventory</li><li>Word recognition in isolation</li><li>Letter sounds</li><li>Oral reading in context</li></ul> Level B: Alphabetics <ul><li>Alphabet recognition</li><li>Letter sounds</li><li>Concept of word</li></ul> Level C: Phonemic awareness <ul><li>Blending</li><li>Sound-to-letter</li><li>Concept of word</li></ul>	Kindergarten screening: <ul><li>Letter name–sound (sound is scored)</li><li>Blending onset-rime</li></ul> Kindergarten inventory: <ul><li>Book and print awareness</li><li>Phonemic awareness: rhyming, blending word parts, blending phonemes, deleting initial sounds, & deleting final sounds</li><li>Graphophonemic: letter name knowledge & letter-to-sound linking</li><li>Listening comprehension</li></ul> First-grade screening: <ul><li>Letter–sound task (only BOY)</li><li>Word reading</li><li>Blending phonemes</li></ul> First-grade inventory: <ul><li>Phonemic awareness: blending word parts, blending phonemes, deleting initial sounds, & deleting final sounds</li><li>Graphophonemic: initial consonant substitution, final consonant substitution, middle vowel substitution, initial blend substitution, & final blend substitution</li><li>Reading accuracy, fluency, and comprehension</li></ul> Second- & third-grade screening: <ul><li>Word list reading</li></ul> Second- & third-grade inventory: <ul><li>Graphophonemic: spelling tests</li><li>Reading accuracy, fluency, and comprehension</li></ul>

*BOY = Beginning of year   MOY = Middle of year   EOY = End of year

B DIBELS Benchmarks

	DIBELS Measure	Beginning of Year Months 1–3		Middle of Year Months 4–6		End of Year Months 7–10	
		Scores	Status	Scores	Status	Scores	Status
Kindergarten: Three Assessment Periods per Year	ISF	0–3 4–7 8 and above	At Risk Some Risk Low Risk	0–9 10–24 25 and above	Deficit Emerging Established	**Not Administered**	
	LNF	0–1 2–7 8 and above	At Risk Some Risk Low Risk	0–14 15–26 27 and above	At Risk Some Risk Low Risk	0–28 29–39 40 and above	At Risk Some Risk Low Risk
	PSF	**Not Administered**		0–6 7–17 18 and above	At Risk Some Risk Low Risk	0–9 10–34 35 and above	Deficit Emerging Established
	NWF (CLS)	**Not Administered**		0–4 5–12 13 and above	At Risk Some Risk Low Risk	0–14 15–24 25 and above	At Risk Some Risk Low Risk

	DIBELS Measure	Beginning of Year Months 1–3		Middle of Year Months 4–6		End of Year Months 7–10	
		Scores	Status	Scores	Status	Scores	Status
First Grade : Three Assessment Periods per Year	LNF	0–24 25–36 37 and above	At Risk Some Risk Low Risk	**Not Administered**		**Not Administered**	
	PSF	0–9 10–34 35 and above	Deficit Emerging Established	0–9 10–34 35 and above	Deficit Emerging Established	0–9 10–34 35 and above	Deficit Emerging Established
	NWF (CLS)	0–12 13–23 24 and above	At Risk Some Risk Low Risk	0–29 30–49 50/15 words	Deficit Emerging Established	0–29 30–49 50/15 words	Deficit Emerging Established
	ORF	**Not Administered**		0–7 8–19 20 and above	At Risk Some Risk Low Risk	0–19 20–39 40 and above	At Risk Some Risk Low Risk

Continued

Second Grade: Three Assessment Periods per Year	DIBELS Measure	Beginning of Year Months 1–3		Middle of Year Months 4–6		End of Year Months 7–10	
		Scores	Status	Scores	Status	Scores	Status
	NWF(CLS)	0–29 30–49 50 and above	Deficit Emerging Established	**Not Administered**		**Not Administered**	
	ORF	0–25 26–43 44 and above	At Risk Some Risk Low Risk	0–51 52–67 68 and above	At Risk Some Risk Low Risk	0–69 70–89 90 and above	At Risk Some Risk Low Risk

Third Grade	DIBELS Measure	Beginning of Year Months 1–3		Middle of Year Months 4–6		End of Year Months 7–10	
		Scores	Status	Scores	Status	Scores	Status
	ORF	0–52 53–76 77 and above	At Risk Some Risk Low Risk	0–66 67–91 92 and above	At Risk Some Risk Low Risk	0–79 80–109 110 and above	At Risk Some Risk Low Risk

Fourth Grade	DIBELS Measure	Beginning of Year Months 1–3		Middle of Year Months 4–6		End of Year Months 7–10	
		Scores	Status	Scores	Status	Scores	Status
	ORF	0–70 71–92 93 and above	At Risk Some Risk Low Risk	0–82 83–104 105 and above	At Risk Some Risk Low Risk	0–95 96–117 118 and above	At Risk Some Risk Low Risk

Fifth Grade	DIBELS Measure	Beginning of Year Months 1–3		Middle of Year Months 4–6		End of Year Months 7–10	
		Scores	Status	Scores	Status	Scores	Status
	ORF	0–80 81–103 104 and above	At Risk Some Risk Low Risk	0–93 94–114 115 and above	At Risk Some Risk Low Risk	0–102 103–123 124 and above	At Risk Some Risk Low Risk

Sixth Grade	DIBELS Measure	Beginning of Year Months 1–3		Middle of Year Months 4–6		End of Year Months 7–10	
		Scores	Status	Scores	Status	Scores	Status
	ORF	0–82 83–108 109 and above	At Risk Some Risk Low Risk	0–98 99–119 120 and above	At Risk Some Risk Low Risk	0–103 104–124 125 and above	At Risk Some Risk Low Risk

KEY:

ISF   **Initial Sound Fluency**
LNF   **Letter Naming Fluency**
PSF   **Phonemic Segmentation Fluency**
NWF   **Nonsense Word Fluency**
ORF   **Oral Reading Fluency**

Source: Good, R. H., & Kaminski, R. A. (Eds.). (2002). *Dynamic indicators of literacy skills* (6th ed.). Eugene, OR: Institute for the Development of Educational Achievement. Available at http://dibels.uoregon.edu/.

C Tier Decision Guidelines Used by a School District: Based on DIBELS*

Beginning of the Year

*The district increased their expectations for DIBELS NWF in kindergarten and DIBELS ORF in first grade. Those decision scores are not the same as the DIBELS benchmark guidelines.

Grade	Decision Rules
K	**Criteria for Entry into Tier 1**

All of the following:

Greater than 7 scpm	Initial Sound Fluency
Greater than 7 lcpm	Letter Naming Fluency

Criteria for Entry into Tier 2

At least one of the following **and** no criteria for entry into Tier 3:

4–7 scpm	Initial Sound Fluency
2–7 lcpm	Letter Naming Fluency

Criteria for Entry into Tier 3

One of the following:

Less than 4 scpm	Initial Sound Fluency
Less than 2 lcpm	Letter Naming Fluency

---

1   **Criteria for Entry into Tier 1**

All of the following:

35 scpm or more	Phonemic Segmentation
37 lcpm or more	Letter Naming Fluency
24 scpm or more	Nonsense Word Fluency; reading some (8 or more) whole words accurately (increased DIBELS expectations)

Criteria for Entry into Tier 2

At least one of the following and **no** criteria for entry into Tier 3:

10–34 scpm	Phonemic Segmentation Fluency
25–36 lcpm	Letter Naming Fluency
13–23 scpm	Nonsense Word Fluency; reading some (4–7) whole words accurately (increased DIBELS expectations)

Continued

Grade	Decision Rules	
	Criteria for Entry into Tier 3	
	One of the following:	
	Less than 10 scpm	Phonemic Segmentation Fluency
	Less than 25 lcpm	Letter Naming Fluency
	Less than 13 scpm	Nonsense Word Fluency, or assessment completed sound-by-sound, or fewer than 4 words read as whole words (increased DIBELS expectations)
2	**Criteria for Entry into Tier 1**	
	All of the following:	
	50 scpm or more	Nonsense Word Fluency; reading 15 words accurately as whole words
	60 wcpm or more	Oral Reading Fluency (increased DIBELS expectations)
	Criteria for Entry into Tier 2	
	At least one of the following and **no** criteria for entry into Tier 3:	
	30–49 scpm	Nonsense Word Fluency; reading most words accurately as whole words
	40–59 wcpm	Oral Reading Fluency (increased DIBELS expectations)
	Criteria for Entry into Tier 3	
	One of the following:	
	Less than 30 scpm	Nonsense Word Fluency assessment completed sound-by-sound
	Less than 40 wcpm	Oral Reading Fluency (increased DIBELS expectations)
3	**Criteria for Entry into Tier 1**	
	77 wcpm or greater	Oral Reading Fluency
	Criteria for Entry into Tier 2	
	53–76 wcpm	Oral Reading Fluency
	Criteria for Entry into Tier 3	
	Less than 53 wcpm	Oral Reading Fluency
4	**Criteria for Entry into Tier 1**	
	93 or more wcpm	Oral Reading Fluency
	Criteria for Entry into Tier 2	
	71–92 wcpm	Oral Reading Fluency
	Criteria for Entry into Tier 3	
	Less than 71 wcpm	Oral Reading Fluency
5	**Criteria for Entry into Tier 1**	
	104 or more wcpm	Oral Reading Fluency
	Criteria for Entry into Tier 2	
	81–103 wcpm	Oral Reading Fluency
	Criteria for Entry into Tier 3	
	Less than 81 wcpm	Oral Reading Fluency

Grade	Decision Rules	
6	**Criteria for Entry into Tier 1**	
	109 or more wcpm	Oral Reading Fluency
	Criteria for Entry into Tier 2	
	83–108 wcpm	Oral Reading Fluency
	Criteria for Entry into Tier 3	
	Less than 83 wcpm	Oral Reading Fluency

January Midyear

Grade	Decision Rules	
K	**Criteria for Entry into Tier 1**	
	All of the following:	
	25 scpm or more	Initial Sound Fluency†
	18 scpm or more	Phonemic Segmentation Fluency†
	27 scpm or more	Letter Naming Fluency
	13 scpm or more	Nonsense Word Fluency and reading 3 or more whole words (recommended)
	Criteria for Entry into Tier 2	
	At least one of the following and no criteria for entry into Tier 3:	
	10–24 scpm	Initial Sound Fluency
	7–17 scpm	Phonemic Segmentation Fluency
	15–26 lcpm	Letter Naming Fluency
	5–12 scpm	Nonsense Word Fluency and reading 1 or 2 whole words (recommended)
	Criteria for Entry into Tier 3	
	One of the following:	
	Less than 10 scpm	Initial Sound Fluency
	Less than 7 scpm	Phonemic Segmentation Fluency
	Less than 15 lcpm	Letter Naming Fluency
	Less than 5 scpm	Nonsense Word Fluency, or reading no whole words (tier placement considered)

†If PSF score is 18 or greater, disregard ISF score.

Grade	Decision Rules	
1	**Criteria for Entry into Tier 1**	
	All of the following:	
	35 scpm or more	Phonemic Segmentation Fluency
	50 scpm or more	Nonsense Word Fluency; reading 15 words accurately as whole words
	40 wcpm or more	Oral Reading Fluency (increased DIBELS expectations)
	Criteria for Entry into Tier 2	
	At least one of the following and **no** criteria for entry into Tier 3:	
	10–34 scpm	Phonemic Segmentation Fluency
	30–49 scpm	Nonsense Word Fluency; reading most words accurately as whole words
	20–39 wcpm	Oral Reading Fluency (increased DIBELS expectations)

Continued

Grade	Decision Rules	
	Criteria for Entry into Tier 3	
	One of the following:	
	Less than 10 scpm	Phonemic Segmentation Fluency
	Less than 30 scpm	Nonsense Word Fluency; assessment completed sound-by-sound, or fewer than 9 whole words read accurately
	Less than 20 wcpm	Oral Reading Fluency (increased DIBELS expectations)
2	**Criteria for Entry into Tier 1**	
	68 wcpm or more	Oral Reading Fluency
	Criteria for Entry into Tier 2	
	52–67 wcpm	Oral Reading Fluency
	Criteria for Entry into Tier 3	
	Less than 52 wcpm	Oral Reading Fluency
3	**Criteria for Entry into Tier 1**	
	92 wcpm or more	Oral Reading Fluency
	Criteria for Entry into Tier 2	
	67–91 wcpm	Oral Reading Fluency
	Criteria for Entry into Tier 3	
	Less than 67 wcpm	Oral Reading Fluency
4	**Criteria for Entry into Tier 1**	
	105 wcpm or more	Oral Reading Fluency
	Criteria for Entry into Tier 2	
	83–104 wcpm	Oral Reading Fluency
	Criteria for Entry into Tier 3	
	Less than 83 wcpm	Oral Reading Fluency
5	**Criteria for Entry into Tier 1**	
	115 wcpm or more	Oral Reading Fluency
	Criteria for Some Risk	
	94–114 wcpm	Oral Reading Fluency
	Criteria for At Risk	
	Less than 94 wcpm	Oral Reading Fluency
6	**Criteria for Entry into Tier 1**	
	120 wcpm or more	Oral Reading Fluency
	Criteria for Some Risk	
	99–119 wcpm	Oral Reading Fluency
	Criteria for At Risk	
	Less than 99 wcpm	Oral Reading Fluency

May

Grade	Decision Rules	
K	**Criteria for Entry into Tier 1**	
	All of the following:	
	35 scpm or more	Phonemic Segmentation Fluency
	40 lcpm or more	Letter Naming Fluency
	25 scpm or more	Nonsense Word Fluency reading 8 or more whole words accurately (increased DIBELS expectations)
	Criteria for Entry into Tier 2	
	At least one of the following and no criteria for entry into Tier 3:	
	10–34 scpm	Phonemic Segmentation Fluency
	29–39 lcpm	Letter Naming Fluency
	15–24 scpm	Nonsense Word Fluency reading some (4–7) whole words accurately (increased DIBELS expectations)
	Criteria for Entry into Tier 3	
	One of the following:	
	Less than 10 scpm	Phonemic Segmentation Fluency
	Less than 29 lcpm	Letter Naming Fluency
	Less than 15 scpm	Nonsense Word Fluency assessment completed sound-by-sound, or fewer than 4 whole words read accurately (increased DIBELS expectations)
1	**Criteria for Entry into Tier 1**	
	All of the following:	
	35 scpm or more	Phonemic Segmentation
	50 scpm or more	Nonsense Word Fluency reading 15 words accurately as whole words
	60 wcpm or more	Oral Reading Fluency (increased DIBELS expectations)
	Criteria for Entry into Tier 2	
	At least one of the following and no criteria for entry into Tier 3:	
	10–34 scpm	Phonemic Segmentation Fluency
	30–49 scpm	Nonsense Word Fluency reading most words accurately as whole words
	40–59 wcpm	Oral Reading Fluency (increased DIBELS expectations)
	Criteria for Entry into Tier 3	
	One of the following:	
	Less than 10 scpm	Phonemic Segmentation Fluency
	Less than 30 scpm	Nonsense Word Fluency assessment completed sound-by-sound, or fewer than 9 whole words read accurately
	Less than 40 wcpm	Oral Reading Fluency (increased DIBELS expectations)
2	**Criteria for Entry into Tier 1**	
	90 wcpm or more	Oral Reading Fluency
	Criteria for Entry into Tier 2	
	70–89 wcpm	Oral Reading Fluency
	Criteria for Entry into Tier 2b/3	
	Less than 70 wcpm	Oral Reading Fluency

Continued

Grade	Decision Rules	
3	**Criteria for Entry into Tier 1**	
	110 wcpm or more	Oral Reading Fluency
	Criteria for Entry into Tier 2	
	80–109 wcpm	Oral Reading Fluency
	Criteria for Entry into Tier 3	
	Less than 80 wcpm	Oral Reading Fluency
4	**Criteria for Entry into Tier 1**	
	118 wcpm or more	Oral Reading Fluency
	Criteria for Entry into Tier 2	
	96–117 wcpm	Oral Reading Fluency
	Criteria for Entry into Tier 3	
	Less than 96 wcpm	Oral Reading Fluency
5	**Criteria for Entry into Tier 1**	
	124 wcpm or more	Oral Reading Fluency
	Criteria for Entry into Tier 2	
	103–123 wcpm	Oral Reading Fluency
	Criteria for Entry into Tier 3	
	Less than 103 wcpm	Oral Reading Fluency
6	**Criteria for Entry into Tier 1**	
	125 wcpm or more	Oral Reading Fluency
	Criteria for Entry into Tier 2	
	104–124 wcpm	Oral Reading Fluency
	Criteria for Entry into Tier 3	
	Less than 104 wcpm	Oral Reading Fluency

D Consonant Blends, Consonant Digraphs, and Diphthongs

Initial Two-Phoneme Blends

l-blends	r-blends	s-blends
bl—blot	br—brig	sc—scat
cl—clam	cr—crab	sk—skin
fl—flap	dr—drum	sn—snip
gl—glad	fr—fret	sp—spot
pl—plop	gr—gram	st—stun
sl—sled	pr—prim	sw—swim
	tr—trot	

Final Two-Phoneme Blends

nk—sink	mp—camp
nd—land	lk—hulk
nt—tent	pt—slept
nk—junk	sk—disk
pt—rapt	sp—gasp
ft—gift	st—mist
lt—silt	

Initial Three-Phoneme Blends

scr—scrap
spl—split
squ—squid
spr—sprig
str—strut

Consonant Digraphs: Initial Position

ch—champ
sh—shin
th (voiceless)—thin
th (voiced)—that
ph—Phil
wh—whip

Consonant Digraphs: Final Position

ch—such
sh—dash
th (voiceless)—with
th (voiced)—bathe
ph—graph
ng—gang

Combination Consonant Digraphs and Blends

thr—thrush
shr—shrub
phr—phrase

Diphthongs

ou, ow as in found, now
oy, oi as in boy, soil

Beginning Phonics Diagnostic Assessment

Student Copy

m	B	tap
f	G	beg
l	L	cot
n	N	pin
s	R	dug
y	D	
r		flat
v	a	snip
qu	o	slim
w	u	
x	e	plum
z	i	drip
		stem
b	on	scan
c	at	
d	if	last
g	up	bent
h		gift
j	fed	
k	lip	stomp
p	sun	craft
t	man	trust
	rot	plant

Teacher's Score Sheet and Analysis Sheet for Beginning Phonics Diagnostic Assessment

Directions: Place a plus (+) by each correct answer, mark no response as NR, and place a minus (−) by each incorrect answer. Write what the child said next to incorrect answers. If the student says the name of a letter say, "That's the name of the letter, now say its sound." If it is obvious that the student cannot complete the test, discontinue it.

Student:_____ Date:_____

Consonants: Continuous Letter-Sounds	Short Vowel Letter-Sounds	CCVC words with beginning blends (just continuous sounds)
m	a	flat
f	o	snip
l	u	slim
n	e	
s	i	**CCVC words with beginning blends (least one stop sound)**
y		
r	**Vowel-Consonant Words (VC)**	plum
v		drip
qu	on	stem
w	at	scan
x	if	
z	up	**CVCC words ending with final blends**
		last
Consonants: Stop Letter-Sounds	**CVC words beginning with continuous sounds**	bent
		gift
b	fed	
c	lip	**CCVCC words with beginning and ending blends**
d	sun	
g	man	stomp
h	rot	craft
j		trust
k	**CVC words beginning with stop sounds**	plant
p		
t	tap	
	beg	
Upper Case Letter-Sounds	cot	
	pin	
B	dug	
G		
L		
N		
R		
D		

Lesson Plan for Beginning Reader

Clinical Teacher's Name: **Myra Little**   Student's Name: **Alyssa**   Date: **1/19/08**

Once-a-week progress monitoring in DIBELS Nonsense Word Fluency.   Will I progress monitor today?   Y <u>N</u>

*Remember: If students did not meet the Lesson Objective, provide an explanation. If students misread a sound or word, underline it on the lesson planning form. When students have mastered a new skill, transfer that information to your mastery list.

Materials Needed for Lesson:

Small white writing board and dry erase markers

Student copy

"Snakes" book

Prewritten letter sounds, regular words, and exception words on card stock paper

Story: *My Cat Can,* and review story before this one in case I need it

Teacher–class game template and sticker

Graphic Organizer

Phonemic Awareness:

✓ **Lesson Format used for blending:** Has mastered blending

✓ **Lesson Objective for blending:**

✓ **Five or six Words Selected for blending:**

   ☐ **Did student meet your lesson objective for blending?**   Y N*

✓ **Lesson Format used for segmenting:** Table 2.4, Segmenting Individual Phonemes

✓ **Lesson Objective for segmenting:** After hearing five words, Alyssa will independently say every sound in each of the five words with 100% accuracy when no scaffolding is provided.

✓ **Five or six Words Selected for segmenting:** <u>cup</u>, <u>run</u>, lap, <u>get</u>, wet

   ☐ **Did student meet your Lesson Objective for segmenting?**   Y <u>N</u>* Alyssa still needs My Turn–Together before segmenting words independently. When she started missing words, I went back to using that strategy.

Letter–Sound Correspondence:

✓ **Lesson Format used for teaching letter sounds:** Table 3.3 Parts A and B, New and Review Letter Sounds, and Figure 3.9, Sound Writing

✓ **Lesson Objective for teaching letter sounds:** When shown the letters *u* and *c* and eight review letters, Alyssa will independently say the corresponding 10 letter sounds with 100% accuracy.

✓ **New letter sound(s) introduced:** c, <u>u</u>

✓ **Letter sounds reviewed:** m, p, a, l, g, h, o, n

Continued

✓ **Letter sounds used for sound-writing practice:** <u>u</u>, m, a, o

- ☐ **Did student meet your Lesson Objective for letter–sound correspondence?**   **Y**   **N***
  Alyssa sometimes substituted /o/ for /u/. She was 100% on the other letter sounds, but not /u/. We'll repeat this lesson next time. I'm going to bring a mirror so she can see her mouth make the sound. She tried hard, and I know she was motivated because she wanted to earn points for herself on the teacher–student game.

Regular Words (VC, CVC, CCVC, CVCC, CCVCC words):

✓ **Lesson Format used for teaching regular words:** Tables 3.4, 3.5, and 3.6, Reading Regular Words—Parts 1, 2, and 3

✓ **Lesson Objective for teaching regular words:** When shown nine new CVC words with /u/ and five review words, after first sounding out and orally reading the words one or two times, Alyssa will read the word list by sight with 100% accuracy by the third time she reads through the list.

✓ **New regular words introduced (underline words that start with a stop sound):** <u>cup</u>, <u>run</u>, lap, nap, on, <u>top</u>, <u>can</u>, <u>cap</u>, <u>cat</u>

(Note: I didn't have her read *cup* and *run* since she still isn't accurate with the letter–sound association for *u*.)

✓ **Regular words reviewed:** pan, tin, in, not, Nat

✓ **Four or five regular words used for sound-spelling practice:** nap, top, in, not

- ☐ **Did student meet your Lesson Objective for regular words?**   **Y**   **N***
  We will need to repeat and practice CVC words with /u/ after Alyssa knows that letter sound to mastery. By the third time we read through the list, she read the other words by sight without needing to sound them out.

Exception Words: (Keep to a minimum at this reading stage. Teach only words required for reading the text.)

✓ **Lesson Format used for teaching exception words:** Table 3.8, Reading Exception Words

✓ **Lesson Objective for teaching exception words:** When shown two new and three review exception words, Alyssa will independently read the words with 100% accuracy by the second time reading the list.

✓ **New exception word(s) introduced:** from, me

✓ **Exception words reviewed:** where, my, to

- ☐ **Did student meet your Lesson Objective for exception words?**   **Y**   **N***   Alyssa has no problem learning one or two exception words and remembers the others. She still sometimes misreads "where" in text the first time, so I'm having her review it every day.

Decodable Passage Reading:

✓ **Lesson Format used for teaching passage reading:** Table 3.9, Reading Stories.

✓ **What story/series did you select for reading?** *My Cat Can*: Scholastic.

✓ **Does the student know all the letter sounds and exception words contained in the text?** If she meets prior objectives set today, she will know them. After-lesson note: When /u/ was too difficult, I didn't have her read this story.

✓ **Lesson Objective for teaching decodable passage reading:** Given a decodable book with VC and CVC words and some words with /u/ sound and letter *c* as /k/, Alyssa will orally read the book by sight with no more than one error.

✓ **Will the first reading be sound-by-sound before reading whole words, or reading words as a whole the first time?** I think that the second reading will be word-by-word, but Alyssa still makes too many mistakes without first sounding out the words the first time through the book.

□ **List the words that the student misread:** She didn't read this book—I had her go back a lesson and read the last book she had mastered to develop more fluency—100% accuracy.

□ **Did the student read text the first time with 90% accuracy?** She didn't read the planned story today because of her difficulty with the letter sound for *u*.

✓ **List two or three comprehension questions you plan to ask when the student reads the words accurately enough to interject comprehension questions.** Where did Cat run first? Where did Cat run last? What do you think Cat is dreaming about at the end of the story? Is this story about an animal that has no teeth?

□ **Did the student meet your Lesson Objective for passage reading?**   Y   **N*** If Alyssa masters the /u/ sound next session, we will read this book. Instead today we reread the book from last week, *Where Is Nat?*

Vocabulary:

✓ **Word(s) Selected for vocabulary from either the regular/exception word lists, a synonym for a word in the passage-reading story, or a word from the nonfiction comprehension read-aloud? Write out a clear definition for the word:** Both of the words I selected are from the story I will read for listening comprehension:
scales: a flat, thin, skin-like covering on the outside of a fish, snake, or lizard
harmless: not dangerous; safe

✓ **What activity will you use for teaching this word?** *Scales:* I will print two color pictures of snake scales that have fallen off different types of snakes and discuss what the scales feel like. We will talk about how these scales are different from scales that weigh things. I will ask more questions about scales later today during the science unit on reptiles. *Harmless:* After teaching Alyssa to say the definition, when I name things like "poisonous spider" or "bottle of pop," she will say either "harmless" or "dangerous."

Listening Comprehension:

✓ **What nonfiction text will you select and why?** *Green Snake* by David Schwartz. The class is studying animals, and Alyssa said she likes snakes.

✓ **List three or four questions that you will ask the student when you read the text:**

1. Before the story: "Have you ever seen a snake? Where did you see it? Was it a dangerous snake? Did you touch it?"
2. End of page 1: "Did the author say that most snakes are dangerous or harmless? What told you that was the answer? What's a question about snakes that you have right now?"
3. Middle of page 2: "Where does the female snake go to lay her eggs?"

G Advanced Word-Reading Diagnostic Assessment

Student Copy

flight	crowd	payable
dawn	shouldn't	antifreeze
roast	we're	coastal
peach	pillow	devotion
batch	subway	dismissive
stain	nephew	dreadful
pound	bother	intermix
broom	hooky	prejudge
kneel	handle	ability
shine	fried	inspire
tube	hoped	politic
wrung	traded	barely
haunt	hauling	midterm
knock	praises	goodness
boil	mocked	mistake
hawk	moaning	return
fudge	grassiest	noxious
lurks	fencing	semicircle
grown	tallest	toxic
thorn	whipping	
barges	joyless	

Teacher's Score Sheet and Analysis Sheet for Advanced Word-Reading Diagnostic Assessment

Directions: Place a plus (+) by each correct answer, mark no response as NR, and place a minus (−) by each incorrect answer. Write what the child said next to the incorrect answer.

Student: _____   Date: _____

flight _____	crowd _____	payable _____
dawn _____	shouldn't _____	antifreeze _____
roast _____	we're _____	coastal _____
peach _____	pillow _____	devotion _____
batch _____	subway _____	dismissive _____
stain _____	nephew _____	dreadful _____
pound _____	bother _____	intermix _____
broom _____	hooky _____	prejudge _____
kneel _____	handle _____	ability _____
shine _____	fried _____	inspire _____
tube _____	hoped _____	politic _____
wrung _____	traded _____	barely _____
haunt _____	hauling _____	midterm _____
knock _____	praises _____	goodness _____
boil _____	mocked _____	mistake _____
hawk _____	moaning _____	return _____
fudge _____	grassiest _____	noxious _____
lurks _____	fencing _____	semicircle _____
grown _____	tallest _____	toxic _____
thorn _____	whipping _____	
barges _____	joyless _____	

Advanced Word-Reading Diagnostic Assessment 1: Decoding Error Pattern Chart

Name: _____ **Date:** _____

After you have given the test, circle the letter combination or affix for each misread part of the word.

Analyze the Entire Word	No Try	Short Vowel	Long Vowel	-r Controlled Vowel (ar, er, ir, ur, are, ire, ere, ore, ure)	Consonant Digraph (e.g., ch, sh, th, ph, ng)	Blend (e.g., st, sl, nd, nt, lf, ld, ct, pr)	Other Letter Combination (e.g., dge, kn, al, ss)	Contraction	Inflectional Ending (plurals, -ed, -ing, -s, -er, -est)	C or g rule	Prefix	Suffix
flight	NT		igh			fl-						
dawn	NT						aw					
roast	NT		oa			-st						
peach	NT		ea		ch							
batch	NT	ă					tch					
stain	NT		ai			st-						
pound	NT					-nd	ou					
broom	NT					br-	oo					
kneel	NT		ee				kn					
shine	NT		i_e		sh							
tube	NT		u_e as oo									
wrung	NT	ŭ			ng		wr					
haunt	NT					-nt	au					
knock	NT	ŏ					kn, ck					
boil	NT						oi					

Continued

Analyze the Entire Word	No Try	Short Vowel	Long Vowel	-r Controlled Vowel (ar, er, ir, ur, are, ire, ere, ore, ure)	Consonant Digraph (e.g., sh, th, ch, ph, ng)	Blend (e.g., st, sl, nd, nt, lf, ld, ct, pr)	Other Letter Combination (e.g., dge, kn, al, ss)	Contraction	Inflectional Ending (plurals, -ed, -ing, -'s, -er, -est)	C or g rule	Prefix	Suffix
hawk	NT						aw					
fudge	NT	ŭ					dge					
lurks	NT			ur		-ks			s			s
grown	NT		ow			gr-						
thorn	NT			or	th							
barges	NT			ar					es	g(e)		es
crowd	NT					cr-	ow					
shouldn't	NT				sh	-nt		shouldn't				
we're	NT		ē					we're				
pillow	NT	ĭ	ow				ll					
subway	NT	ŭ	ay								sub	
nephew	NT	ĕ					ph, ew					
bother	NT	ŏ		er	th							
hooky	NT						oo					y
handle	NT	ă					le					
fried	NT		ī			fr-			ed			ed (d)
hoped	NT		o_e						ed			ed (t)

Continued

345

Analyze the Entire Word	No Try	Short Vowel	Long Vowel	-r Controlled Vowel (ar, er, ir, ur, are, ire, ere, ore, ure)	Consonant Digraph (e.g., sh, th, ch, ph, ng)	Blend (e.g., st, sl, nd, nt, lf, ld, ct, pr)	Other Letter Combination (e.g., dge, kn, al, ss)	Contraction	Inflectional Ending (plurals, -ed, -ing, -'s, -er, -est)	C or g rule	Prefix	Suffix
traded	NT		a_e			tr-			ed			ed
hauling	NT						au		ing			ing
praises	NT		ai						es			es
mocked	NT	ŏ					ck		ed			ed (t)
moaning	NT	oa							ing			ing
grassiest	NT	ă				gr-	ss		est (y to i)			est
fencing	NT	ĕ							ing (delete e)	c(i)		ing
tallest	NT						all		est			est
whipping	NT	ĭ			wh		pp		ing (dbl. cons.)			ing
joyless	NT						oy					less
payable	NT		ay									able
antifreeze	NT		ee			fr-					anti	
coastal	NT		oa			-st-						al
devotion	NT		ō in vo								de	tion
dismissive	NT	ĭ in miss					ss				dis	ive
dreadful	NT					dr-	ea					ful
intermix	NT	ĭ in mix		er in inter							inter	

Continued

Analyze the Entire Word	No Try	Short Vowel	Long Vowel	-r Controlled Vowel (ar, er, ir, ur, are, ire, ere, ore, ure)	Consonant Digraph (e.g., ch, sh, th, ph, ng)	Blend (e.g., st, sl, nd, nt, lf, ld, ct, pr)	Other Letter Combination (e.g., dge, kn, al, ss)	Contraction	Inflectional Ending (plurals, -ed, -ing, -'s, -er, -est)	C or g rule	Prefix	Suffix
prejudge	NT	u					dge				pre	
ability	NT	ĭ in *bil*									a	ity
inspire	NT			īre		sp					in	
politic	NT	ŏ, ĭ										ic
barely	NT			āre								ly
midterm	NT			er							mid	
goodness	NT						oo					ness
mistake	NT		a_e								mis	
return	NT			ur							re	
noxious	NT	ŏ in *nox*										ious
semicircle	NT			ir			le			c(i)	semi	
toxic	NT	ŏ										ic
Total Errors	/61	/22	/20	/10	/7	/17	/29	/2	/13	/6	/12	/26

H Diagnostic Spelling Assessment for Advanced Readers

Administration

Administer the spelling inventory the same way you would a spelling test. Use the words in a sentence to be sure students know the exact word. Sentences are provided after the word list. Assure students that this activity is not for a grade, but to help you plan for their needs. Seat students so as to minimize copying. You might want to give this test over a two-day period.

Analysis

This test assesses:

1. students' application of the 10 outlined spelling rules.
2. spelling of common word parts.

Use the Error Guide and circle each error or write in the student's spelling. Total the number of errors in a column at the bottom of the column to determine if there are distinct error patterns. Each rule number on the Error Guide corresponds to the numbered rules listed below.

Ten of the Most Helpful Spelling Rules:

1. Because words don't usually end in *v*, always add an *e* after a final *v,* such as in *dove.*
2. When words end in *ack, eck, ick, ock,* and *uck,* the /k/ is spelled *ck.*
3. When words end in *adge, edge, idge, odge,* and *udge,* the /j/ is spelled *dge.*
4. When words end in *atch, etch, itch, otch,* or *utch,* the /ch/ is spelled tch.
5. The floss rule: A final *f, s,* or *l* that appears after a short vowel is doubled.
6. Final *e* rule: When a word ends in *e* and you add a common word part that begins with a vowel, drop the *e.*
7. Doubling rule: When a short word ends CVC and the next morphograph begins with a vowel, double the final consonant.
8. Plural variation rule: When a word ends in a "hissing" sound (*-s, -z, -x, -ch, -sh*), add an *-es* to form the plural.
9. Changing *y* to *i* rule: When a word ends in a consonant and *y,* change the *y* to *i* before adding *-ed, -es, -er,* and *-est.*
10. Changing *f* rule: Some words that end in the /f/ sound change the letter *f* to *ves* in the plural form. You can always hear the sound /v/ in the plural.

Sentences to Use with Diagnostic Spelling Test

1. **Shove.** Do not **shove** anyone in the hallway.
2. **Fried.** I **fried** a fish yesterday before eating it.
3. **Enjoyment.** I get **enjoyment** from playing games.
4. **Impossible.** It's **impossible** to climb that mountain in sandals.
5. **Sharing.** The two children are **sharing** their candy.
6. **Flexible.** He is so **flexible** that he can do a backbend.
7. **Enable.** Don't **enable** his hitting by laughing at it.
8. **Tension.** After the fight, you could feel the **tension** in the air.
9. **Glorious.** What a **glorious** day it is with the sun shining.
10. **Slimy.** The worm was too **slimy.**
11. **Stormiest.** On the **stormiest** day of the year thunder roared.
12. **Portable.** I just hate to use **portable** toilets.
13. **Dustier.** The room was **dustier** than last year and I sneezed.
14. **Judging. Judging** from your frown, you are unhappy.
15. **Tireless.** The garden had no weeds because of his **tireless** work.
16. **Honesty.** Because I never lied, I was known for my **honesty.**
17. **Mocking.** They were **mocking** her for wearing a purple tie to school.
18. **Creation.** His **creation** in art class was a painting of a lizard.
19. **Grumpier.** Today I'm **grumpier** because I didn't eat breakfast.
20. **Reasonable.** Any **reasonable** kid would want 3 meals a day.
21. **Presses.** Mom **presses** our clothes with an iron.
22. **Brightly.** I smiled **brightly** after getting chocolate.
23. **Prejudge.** Don't **prejudge** my attitude until you know me better.
24. **Swelled.** His fist **swelled** after he hit the cement block.
25. **Antifreeze.** In winter I put **antifreeze** in the car.
26. **Ducking.** Sheila was **ducking** under a tree in the rain.
27. **Creative.** Juan's drawing was the most **creative** one in the class.
28. **Halves.** After I cut the orange, I gave both **halves** to Joe.
29. **Clutched.** She **clutched** her child's hand so he wouldn't get lost.
30. **Gloves.** When it gets cold, he puts on his **gloves.**
31. **Dental.** I am scared of any **dental** procedures on my teeth.
32. **Tinier.** The mouse was **tinier** than the big rat.
33. **Festive.** I made sure that the party was **festive.**
34. **Grimly.** He **grimly** walked to the principal's office.
35. **Nonsense.** I thought the eel cartoon was a lot of **nonsense.**
36. **Pledge.** Juliet will **pledge** her heart to Romeo.
37. **Quizzes.** I hope there are no **quizzes** in school the whole week.
38. **Hateful.** She's so mean that everyone thinks she's **hateful.**
39. **Helpful.** Thomas is always so **helpful** that he's very likable.
40. **Stretcher.** He went to the hospital on a **stretcher.**
41. **Snobby.** She has so much money and acts **snobby** because of it.
42. **Skinniest.** That thin boy was the **skinniest** boy I'd seen.
43. **Pennies.** I don't like **pennies** because they aren't worth anything.
44. **Novelty.** The glow worm toy that gave off sparks was a **novelty.**

Student's Score Sheet

Name: Date:

	RULES										Prefix	Suffix	Base/Root Word
	1	2	3	4	5	6	7	8	9	10			
1. shove	ve												shove
2. fried									y to i			ed	fry
3. enjoyment											en	ment	enjoy
4. impossible											im	ible	possible
5. sharing						drop e						ing	share
6. flexible												ible	flex
7. enable											en		able
8. tension						drop e						ion	tense
9. glorious									y to i			ous	glory
10. slimy						drop e						y	slime
11. stormiest									y to i			est	storm
12. portable												able	port
13. dustier									y to i			er	dusty
14. fudging		udge				drop e						ing	fudge
15. tireless												less	tire
16. honesty												y	honest
17. mocking		ock										ing	mock
18. creation						drop e						tion	create
19. grumpier									y to i			er	grumpy
20. reasonable												able	reason
21. presses					ss			es				es	press
22. brightly												ly	bright
23. prejudge		udge									pre		judge
24. swelled				ll								ed	swell
25. antifreeze											anti		freeze
26. ducking		uck										ing	duck
27. creative						drop e						ive	create
28. halves									ves			es	half
29. clutched			utch									ed	clutch
30. gloves	ve + s											s	glove
31. dental												al	dent-
32. tinier									y to i			er	tiny
33. festive												ive	fest
34. grimly												ly	grim
35. nonsense											non		sense
36. pledge		edge											pledge
37. quizzes							dbl	es				es	quiz
38. hateful												ful	hate
39. likable						drop e						able	like
40. stretcher			etch									er	stretch
41. snobby							dbl					y	snob
42. skinniest							dbl		y to i			y +est	skin
43. pennies									y to i			es	penny
44. novelty												ty	novel
Totals	/2	/2	/3	/2	/2	/7	/3	/2	/8	/1	/6	/38	/44

350

I Lesson Plan for an Advanced Word Reader*

Clinical Teacher's Name: <u>Rachel Morgan</u>   Student's Name: <u>Sean</u>   Date: <u>3/3/09</u>
Will I progress monitor today?   <u>Y</u>   N

Materials Needed for Lesson:

Small white writing board and dry erase markers for spelling

"Bad Pitches" story

Progress-monitoring folder and stories

Reading Success comprehension program: teacher copy and student copy

Prewritten letter sounds, affixes, and words on card stock paper

Teacher–class game template and sticker

Graphic organizer

Fluency materials: 5-minute reading-fluency passage and graph

---

Letter–Sound Combinations or Affixes Instruction:

✓ **Lesson Format used for teaching letter combinations/affixes/rules:** Table 4.5, New Letter Combinations and Affixes

✓ **Lesson Objective for teaching letter combinations/affixes/rules:** When (1) shown new and review written letter combinations and asked to say their corresponding sounds and (2) asked to say the "g" rule, by the end of the lesson, Sean will independently do both tasks with 100% accuracy.

✓ **New letter–sound combination(s), affix(es), or rule(s) introduced:** The *g* rule, *ea, ow, le*

✓ **Letter–sound combination(s), affix(es), or rule(s) reviewed:** *adge, ph, kn;* VCV rule

☐ **Did student meet your Lesson Objective for letter–sound combinations/affixes instruction?** Yes, he met the lesson objective. Sean said all of the letter sounds, recited the VCV rule, and remembered the *g* rule after saying it with me two times.

Regular Words That Contain Those Sounds:

✓ **Lesson Format used for teaching regular words that contain letter–sound combinations or affixes:** Tables 4.7, Teaching One-Syllable Regular Words with Letter Combinations, and 4.9, Reading Regular Words with Two or More Syllables

✓ **Lesson Objective for teaching regular words:** When shown 29 new and review words containing *ea, ow, -le,* or where he needs to apply the VCV or *g* rule, Sean will orally read the words by sight on the list with no more than one error by the second or third read-through.

✓ **New regular words introduced:** (Underlines indicate how I will scallop words the first time): <u>beat</u> en, <u>breath</u>ed, breath, <u>heaved</u>, thrown, streak, <u>leaned</u>, near, streak, mean, <u>jogged</u>, <u>be</u> <u>gan</u>, plate, home, came, zing, state, <u>um</u> <u>pire</u>, <u>mumbled</u>, gent, <u>gent</u> <u>le</u>, gem, <u>ga</u> <u>ble,</u> gave, graph

✓ **Regular words reviewed:** stuffed, nodded, whipped, grappled

Continued

Did student meet your Lesson Objective for regular words? Yes. On the first time through, reading the parts of each word before reading the whole word, Sean misread *umpire, breathed,* and *nodded.* In the second read-through reading whole words, Sean read all the words by sight with 100% accuracy.

Exception Words:

✓ **Lesson Format used for teaching exception words:** Table 3.8, Reading Exception Words
✓ **Lesson Objective for teaching exception words:** When shown one new and four review exception words, Sean will orally read the words by the second read-through with 100% accuracy.
✓ **New exception word(s) introduced:** league
✓ **Exception words reviewed:** perilous, freight, who, how

☐ **Did student meet your lesson objective for exception words?** Yes. Sean confused *who* and *how* the first time. After telling him each word and having him spell it, he returned to the top of the list and repeated the words again. Sean then read the exception words by sight with 100% accuracy by the second try. I will review these words tomorrow.

Oral Passage Reading and Comprehension:

✓ **Lesson Format used for teaching passage reading:** SAFER Reading
✓ **What story/series did you select for reading?** "Bad Pitches"
✓ **Does the student know all the letter sounds and sight words contained in the text?** I'm preteaching the words that might be difficult for him in the word-reading section of the lesson. He has learned all the relevant skills except for the *g* rule.
✓ **Lesson Objective for teaching oral passage reading:** By the second reading of the story "Some Bad Pitches," Sean will orally read the text with 97% accuracy.
✓ **List the words that the student misread and write the error number if appropriate:** Sean read "Some Bad Pitches" two times today. Sean had four errors on the first read-through. Sean read *Art* as *he, set* as *seat,* and *they* as *and,* and inserted the word *and* one time. On Sean's second read-through he had two errors. He read *what* as *that* and *for* as *from.* Most of Sean's errors were careless errors because when I used a Your Turn and asked Sean the word, he knew it every time. He hasn't had to do careful reading, where every error is corrected, and he sometimes starts skimming and skipping ahead.
✓ **Did the student read text the first time with 90% accuracy?** Yes. Sean only misread four words the first time, which was more than 90% accuracy.
✓ **Did the student meet your Lesson Objective for passage reading?** Yes, by the second read-through Sean misread only two words in the story.

☐ **Are you noticing word-reading error patterns that indicate that a new word-reading skill should be introduced?** Sean is self-correcting a lot, which is good. Sean used to have trouble locating the beginning of a sentence when he had to correct an error, but now he automatically finds the beginning of a sentence.
✓ **List some comprehension questions you plan to ask when the student reads the words accurately enough to interject comprehension questions. Be sure that the questions represent a mix of literal and inference-type questions:**
"What happened at the end of the first section?"
"What does 'It went like a streak' mean?"
"Why were the fans of the other team yelling at Art? What clues led you to think this?"
"What does 'The ball came from his hand like a shot' mean?"
"What makes Art so much better the second time he throws the ball?"
"What was the main idea in this second section of the story?"
"What makes Art throw a bad pitch again? What clues led you to think this?"
"What did the catcher say to Art? Do you think that advice helped Art, and why?"
"What do you think will happen in the next part of the story?"

During the last 15 minutes of the lesson, Sean will do the *Reading Success* comprehension program. Sean was given lesson seven today. Lesson seven is about anaphoras, classification, and inference.

Lesson Objective for teaching *Reading Success:* Given the *Reading Success* comprehension workbook and orally reading the text to the teacher, Sean will write the answers to the comprehension questions, missing no more than two questions for the lesson.

Did Sean reach his objective? Yes. Sean answered all the questions correctly for the third day in a row and enjoys doing each lesson. We should determine whether he can advance and skip some lessons in the curriculum.

Fluency:

✓ **What passage did you select, and can the student read it with at least 95% accuracy?** Yes. I selected the last reading passage he completed during the Tuesday tutoring session. Today, after ten minutes of practice, during his best read Sean read 146 words correct per minute with 100% accuracy.

✓ **What is the goal for today, and did the student meet it?** The goal is for Sean to read 122 words correct per minute. Sean went above the goal, reading 146 words correct per minute. He was disappointed that he doesn't read this fluently on the progress-monitoring passages. The progress-monitoring passage that he graphed was slightly higher than last week, but nowhere near 146 wcpm.

Vocabulary:

What word(s) did you select to teach for vocabulary from the passage-reading story or nonfiction text? Write a learner-friendly definition for the word(s): I will be choosing two vocabulary words. The words are *zing* and *mumbled.*

The definition of *zing* is "to move quickly, sometimes with a humming sound." I will tell Sean the definition of *zing* and have him repeat the definition to me. Then I will ask Sean six questions of examples and nonexamples, so I know that he understands the vocabulary word:

- "Would Sean zing a baseball to the catcher when trying to get the batter out? Why?"
- "Would a softball zing if you were softly tossing it to your partner? Why?"
- "If a ball was thrown slowly, would it make a zinging sound? Why?"
- "Would a soccer ball zing if someone were to pass it to their friend gently? Why?"
- "Would a tennis ball zing if someone hit it very hard to the other side? Why?"

The other vocabulary word is *mumble.* The definition of *mumble* is "speaking so quickly and quietly that the words are hard to hear."

- "Are the sixth graders who talk so fast that I can't hear them mumbling? Why?"
- "If you had to give a speech in your class and wanted to get an A, would you mumble? Why?"
- "If you were scared when you had to give a speech in class and no one could hear you, do you think you mumbled? Why?"
- "If the coach had something important to tell the football team, would he mumble the information to them? Why?"
- "When Sarah's teacher asked where her homework was, Sarah softly and quickly said that the dog ate it. Had Sarah mumbled?"

*This lesson plan format can also be used when planning for a class.

1. **What were your strengths?** I used a graphic organizer with Sean during the story. I have his behavior chart on the desk along with the advance organizer, so it will remind him to work hard. He crosses off the activities as we finish them. I explained the vocabulary words to Sean. Doing several Your Turns for the definitions and giving him examples and nonexamples of the vocabulary words helps Sean understand the words and remember them. Sean remembered the vocabulary words from yesterday and used them in sentences, which means the words are in his memory. During the reading, I set short-term goals for Sean because he sometimes reads so carelessly. I told him that if he could read a section without any errors he would receive a point in the

teacher–class game, and if he did get an error, I would receive a point. He seemed to enjoy this.

2. **What teaching skills do you need to work on?** I need to work on setting up opportunities in which I can earn points for myself, so Sean works his best. I have a hard time giving myself points even when it would help give him behavior feedback he needs. I'm a bit of a wimp, I think. I know all the formats fairly well, but practicing them more is something that I need to work on.

3. **What would you do differently?** Sean read above the goal for the fluency drill today. I would have raised the goal before today if I had known that he could read 146 correct words per minute with zero errors! I will raise my goal for him for Thursday. Some of the words that I chose for review words were too simple, and Sean started to act bored. I would only have chosen the more challenging words.

4. **Describe the current status of the teacher–class game you conducted today. How many points did the student need to win? Did the student win? Are you keeping a points tally, or have you constructed a motivational point tally chart? How many wins are required to earn a larger reward (larger than a sticker)? How close is the student to earning that larger reward?** Each session, Sean and I set a goal of points he needs to earn. This means that he must use his best reading finger and follow my rules. I have a weekly goal sheet and a tally sheet for myself and Sean to keep track of the points. Today Sean received a sticker, and so far he has three stickers on his weekly chart. Sean has one more sticker to earn, and he can pick something from the prize box.

APPENDIX

J Tests of Vocabulary

Name of Test	Aspect of Language Assessed	Norms	Administered	Time	Comments
Peabody Picture Vocabulary Test-4 (PPVT-4)	Receptive	2.6–adult	Individually	15 minutes	Pointing format useful for young children
Expressive Vocabulary Test (EVT-2)	Expressive	2.6–adult	Individually	3–8 minutes per subtest	Designed to be expressive companion to PPVT-4
Test of Language Development-4 (TOLD)	Receptive and expressive	Primary: 4.0–8.11 Intermediate: 8.0–17.4	Individually	Level 1: ≈30 minutes; Level 2: 65 minutes	Subtests include picture vocabulary, relational vocabulary, and multiple meanings
Test of Word Knowledge (TOWK)	Receptive and expressive	5–17	Individually	10–20 minutes	Diagnostic: multiple subtests within two levels
Wechsler Individual Achievement Test (WIAT-11)	Expressive	4–8.5	Individually	10–30 minutes	Students identify pictures that match a spoken word and provide a word that matches a picture
Woodcock Reading Mastery Test Revised (WRMT-R)	Receptive	5–7.5+ Grades K–1.6	Individually	Less than 30 minutes	Reading task involving synonyms and antonyms
Iowa Test of Basic Skill (ITBS)	Receptive	Grades K–8	Individually or group	Levels 5 and 6: 20 minutes; Levels 7 and 8: 15 minutes; Levels 9–14: 15 minutes	For Grades K & 1 (levels 5–6): picture word matching; for Grades 1 and 2 (levels 7–8): picture or stimulus word followed by set of multiple-choice definitions read orally; for Grades 3–8 (levels 9–14): multiple-choice

Continued

Name of Test	Aspect of Language Assessed	Norms	Administered	Time	Comments
					vocabulary selection presents word in context of short phrases or sentences and student chooses answer that most nearly means the same as that word.
Stanford Achievement Test–10th Edition (SAT-10)	Receptive		Individually or group		Reading subtest measures three kinds of vocabulary: synonyms, multiple meanings, and using context clues. Has listening comprehension subtest that also measures vocabulary.

Glossary

acquisition stage of learning   First stage of learning a skill when the goal is learning to perform a skill accurately.

affixes   Morphemes attached before or after a base or root word to modify its meaning.

aimline   A graph line drawn from a student's current level of performance to a fixed benchmark score. The slope of the line depicts ongoing progress scores needed to meet the final benchmark score.

alphabetic principle   The understanding that there are systematic and predictable relationships between written letters and spoken sounds.

analogy-based phonics   This approach emphasizes using known word family patterns to identify unknown words.

analytic phonics   This approach emphasizes first teaching the whole word before analyzing letter–sound relationships.

anaphora   Pronouns, nouns, or figurative phrases that refer to another word or name.

assistive technology   Any of a wide variety of technology applications designed to help students with disabilities learn, communicate, enjoy recreation, and otherwise function more independently by bypassing their disabilities. Also called *adaptive technology.*

at risk   Students who require extra support when learning to read because they are raised in poverty, have not been read to as children, were premature babies, have a primary language other than English, or have a learning disability.

automatic word recognition   To decipher words effortlessly; to read regular words without consciously blending the sounds of letters or letter clusters into words.

automatic phase   In this fifth and last phase in Ehri's model of reading development, students' accurate, fluent word reading in new text allows them to focus on comprehending the meaning of the text.

base word   The part of the word that establishes the basic meaning of the word. A base word can stand alone. In the word *undone, done* is the base word.

blending   The ability to say a spoken word when its individual phonemes are said slowly.

closed syllable   A syllable ending in a consonant as *pan* in *pancake (pan cake).*

compound word   Two separate words combined to form one word with a distinct meaning.

cloze assessment   In this curriculum-based assessment, comprehension is assessed by having students silently read a passage in which every seventh word has been removed. As they read, students supply the missing words that have been systematically deleted.

comprehension   The reason for reading; comprehension is the active process of getting meaning from written text. Comprehension is influenced by the person reading, the text being read, the task the reader is trying to accomplish, and the context in which the reading is being done (Rand Reading Study Group, 2002).

comprehension strategies   Consciously planned procedures that readers use and adapt to understand text. Examples of comprehension strategies include predicting, summarizing, and generating questions.

consolidated alphabetic phase   This fourth phase in Ehri's model of the development of word reading skills occurs when students have consolidated their phase 3 knowledge of grapheme-phoneme blends into larger units that recur in different words. Instead of processing individual letter sounds, students recognize multiletter sequences called chunks such as syllables and parts of words. The recognition of chunks leads students to identify more difficult words and remember exception words more easily.

consonant blends   Two or more successive consonants sounded out in sequence without losing their identity. Examples of consonant blends include *str* as in *street, sl* as in *sloppy,* and *nt* as in *ant.* Consonant blends are also called consonant clusters.

context   The words and sentences around an unknown word that, along with the reader's background knowledge, help identify it or explain its meaning.

context processor   Marilyn Adams's model of reading describes word recognition as an interaction between orthographic, phonological, meaning, and context processors. The context processor brings prior knowledge to bear on understanding the meaning of a word.

continuous sounds   With continuous sounds, also known as *continuants,* the airflow does not stop as the sound is pronounced, so the sound can be held as long as some air remains in the lungs. Therefore, continuous sounds can be held for several seconds.

cumulative review   The method of selecting teaching examples whereby the teacher adds previously learned material to newly learned material. Cumulative review teaches students to discriminate between new and old learning and helps students retain previously learned material.

curriculum-based measurement (CBM)   Curriculum-based measurement (CBM) is an assessment method teachers use to measure student performance in basic academic areas. CBM is characterized by an extensive research base establishing its technical adequacy as well as tasks and scoring procedures that are brief, grounded in the classroom curriculum, standardized, and fluency based. CBM is used for screening, progress monitoring, diagnostic assessment, and measurement of outcomes.

CVC variants   The first words introduced in phonics-based beginning reading programs in which all the vowels and consonants say their most common sounds. For example, the word *cat* is a CVC word; the word *mist* is a CVCC word; and the word *stump* is a CCVCC word.

decodable books   Books in which at least 70% of the words can be sounded out because the letter sounds and combinations comprising these words say their most common sounds. Decodable books also contain a relatively small proportion of previously learned, high-frequency exception words. A decodable book is readable or appropriate for instruction when on a first read the student can read the text with at least 90% accuracy.

decode   To decipher unfamiliar regular or irregular words by going from symbols (letters) to sounds.

diagnostic assessments   Longer and more in-depth assessments that provide detailed information about a student's skills and instructional needs to help the teacher plan effective instructional support. Information from diagnostic assessments can help explain why a student is not performing at an expected level.

differentiated instruction   A range of instructional options that meets the diverse needs of students.

digraphs   Two successive letters articulated as a single phoneme. Examples of digraphs include /ch/ as in *chop,* /th/ as in *this,* and /oo/ as in *book.*

diphthongs   Vowel blends in which the first sound appears to glide into the second sound. Examples of diphthongs include /ou/ as in *mouse* and /oi/ as in *boil.*

encoding   To decipher sounds into letter symbols: the opposite of decoding. Spelling requires encoding, whereas reading requires decoding.

dysteachia   When the student has the ability to learn the material or information but has not received the instruction or support needed to learn it. Inadequate instruction, poorly designed curricula, or weak delivery of instruction are root causes of dysteachia.

exception words   Also called *irregular words.* Words that cannot be conventionally sounded out and must be learned as whole words. If regular words have letter sounds that students have not yet learned in isolation, they also must be learned as whole words and are considered exception words until the student has learned those sounds.

explicit instruction   The unambiguous, clear, and direct teaching of skills and strategies. Explicit instruction includes clear instructional objectives, a clear purpose for learning, clear and understandable directions and explanations, adequate modeling, demonstration, guided and independent practice with corrective feedback, and valid assessments for instructional decision making.

expository text   Text that is written to inform, persuade, or explain; nonfiction writing. Examples of expository text include content-area textbooks, newspapers, reference books, journals, brochures, and the majority of online writing.

expressive vocabulary   Oral expressive vocabulary means using words in speaking so that other people understand you; written expressive vocabulary is communicating meaningfully through writing.

false negatives   When screening does not identify children for extra tier help who need it.

false positives   When screening identifies children for extra tier help who don't need it.

figurative meaning   A meaning that is not literal; the meaning is more picturesque, implying something other than what is said on the surface.

fix-up strategies   Comprehension strategies that readers use when they are not fully comprehending text. Rereading, underlining text, and using a dictionary are examples of fix-up strategies.

fluency   The ability to read text accurately, quickly, and with expression.

fluency-based assessments   Assessments that measure both the rate at which students perform skills as well as their accuracy. Student scores on fluency-based assessments are often reported on a per-minute basis such as words read correctly per minute or letters identified correctly per minute.

fluency stage of learning   Second stage of learning a skill when the goal is accuracy plus speed.

frontloading   A technique used before reading to activate students' prior knowledge, discuss critical knowledge and vocabulary needed to understand the text, and provide information on text structures and comprehension strategies that are useful in understanding the text.

full-alphabetic phase   This third phase in Ehri's model of the development of word reading skills occurs when students have learned the most common letter–sound associations and use this knowledge to decode unfamiliar words.

generalization stage of learning   Third stage of learning a skill when the student is accurate and fluent with the new skill or concept, but needs practice applying it to novel situations and using it for problem solving.

grapheme   A written letter or letter combination representing a single speech sound.

graphophonemic strategies   Strategies for identifying words that involve looking at the letters, breaking the word into parts, and/or matching letters and letter combinations with the sounds they make; phonics strategies.

high-frequency words   Words that appear most often in written language. They may be regular words or irregular words. Some high-frequency words are *in, of, the, that, was, when,* and *where.* Dolch and Fry have published the most common lists of high-frequency words.

hypertext   With hypertext, the software designers link designated words, usually indicated by a different text color, to a database. Readers can select the words and bring on screen the information in the database. Pressing a designated word might link the reader to a definition of the word, to a picture of the word, to a clue for figuring out the word, or to a video of someone describing the word.

idiom   A speech form or expression that cannot be understood from the meanings of the separate words comprising it, but instead must be learned as a whole. "In the same boat" is an idiom that means two or more people are in the same situation. "As fit as a fiddle" is an idiom that means "very healthy." Also called *figurative expression.*

inference   A logical conclusion or educated guess arrived at by reasoning from evidence rather than relying on direct observation. Readers make inferences by drawing on their own background knowledge or finding clues in the text when the author has not provided information directly. For example, readers make inferences to determine character motivation, analyze the behavior of the character, look for clues from the author, and think about why they or someone they know would have done the same thing.

inflectional endings   Suffixes added to the end of words such as *-ed, -es, -ing,* and *-s* that indicate tense, number, possession, or gender when added to the base word. These words can present unique spelling or reading difficulties because an inflectional ending can have more than one sound or the ending can change the spelling of the base word.

intonation   The rise and fall of the voice pitch on a scale extending from high to low. The pitch of the voice rises, falls, or remains relatively level during the pronunciation of words and sentences. Different patterns of pitch changes convey a range of meanings from the speaker's emotional state to the difference between statements, questions, and exclamations.

irregular words   Also called exception words. Words that cannot be conventionally sounded out and thus are learned as whole words.

keyword method   Method of teaching vocabulary directly that uses visual imagery to help students understand and retain word meanings.

letter combinations   A cluster in which two or more adjacent letters form one distinct sound. Examples of letter combinations include the digraphs *sh, ar,* and *ee,* and the diphthongs *oi* and *ou.*

letter–sound correspondence   Also called "letter–sound association"; the relationship between a grapheme and the phoneme(s) it represents; as /d/ representing the letter *d* in dad and /k/ representing the *c* in cat

lexical retrieval   The efficiency with which a reader can locate and apply to reading previously learned information about letters and words stored in long-term memory. Lexical retrieval is a strong predictor of reading success.

literal meaning   The primary meaning of a word. The actual meaning.

long-term memory   The unconscious memory that involves the storage and recall of information and processes over a long period of time.

main idea   The central idea around which a piece of text is organized. It may be stated explicitly (written in a sentence) or implied (suggested without being explicitly stated). Sometimes each paragraph in text contains a main idea. In a paragraph when the main idea is explicitly described in a sentence, it is called the *topic sentence.*

Matthew effect   Early success in acquiring reading skills often results in later success in reading because a good reader becomes an even more highly skilled reader, acquiring more vocabulary and background knowledge as a result of reading more; also expressed as "the rich get richer, the poor get poorer."

maze assessment   This three-minute curriculum-based measure is like the cloze comprehension test, except that it is a multiple-choice test, where students circle the correct missing word from the available choices, and it is timed.

meaning processor   Marilyn Adams's model of reading describes word recognition as an interaction between orthographic, phonological, meaning, and context processors. The meaning processor focuses on word meanings rather than the letters or sounds.

median score   The middle score. If a student reads three grade-level passages at 40 words per minute, 76 words per minute, and 50 words per minute, the median or middle score would be 50 words per minute.

metacognition   The conscious awareness of one's thought processes while reading.

metacognitive skills   The ability to consciously plan, monitor, and select effective strategies when reading for comprehension. Examples of metacognitive skills include assessing what one already knows about a given topic before reading, assessing the nature of the learning task, planning specific reading/thinking strategies, determining what needs to be learned, assessing what is comprehended or not comprehended during reading, thinking about what is important and unimportant, evaluating the effectiveness of the reading/thinking strategy, revising what is known, and revising the strategy.

metaphor   A figure of speech in which a word or phrase that ordinarily designates one thing is used to designate another, thus making an implied comparison that is not directly stated, as in "*a sea of troubles.*"

modeling   Demonstrating or directly telling; the My Turn phase of instruction.

monitoring text   Good comprehenders evaluate how well they understand while they read, and when problems arise, they are able to use "fix-up" strategies to improve their comprehension. When readers are monitoring, they are consistently asking themselves, "Is what I am reading making sense?"

morphemes   The smallest parts of words that have a distinctive meaning. In the word *unladylike,* the morphemes are *un + lady + like.*

multi-tier model   An instructional model in which students who need additional support in reading are identified through regularly scheduled research-based assessments of essential reading skills. Students who need more support receive additional research-based intervention of varying intensities called "tiers." In a typical multi-tier model, Tier 1 is the general classroom curriculum, Tier 2 provides additional small-group tutoring support, and Tier 3 is a more intensive alternative reading program.

narrative text   Text that tells a story or that relates events or dialogue; fiction.

narrow reading   When students read several different texts about the same topic.

nonexample   The opposite of an example. Vocabulary nonexamples are items or concepts that are *not* representative of the specified word. When the term *ocean* is taught, nonexamples might include *desert, sky,* or *land.*

nonsense words   Also called pseudowords, these made-up words such as vug, phlaim, or seeply follow regular spelling rules enabling the teacher to assess a student's knowledge of letter–sound correspondences as well as the ability to blend letters to form unfamiliar "nonsense" words.

norm   A statistic describing the average or typical score.

onset   The beginning sound(s) that precede(s) the vowel in a syllable.

open syllable   A syllable ending in a vowel as *pa* in *paper (pa per).*

orthographic processor   Marilyn Adams's model of reading describes word recognition as an interaction between orthographic, phonological, meaning, and context processors. The orthographic processor recognizes the visual image of words as interconnected sets of letters.

outcome assessments   End-of-the-year assessments that identify whether students achieved grade-level performance in the area tested.

overgeneralize   Draw too general a conclusion. For example, if all of the examples used to teach the concept of *red* are balls, students can draw the conclusion that something has to be a ball to be *red.*

part firming   When students make an error, the teacher reteaches immediately using a "My Turn," before having students go back to the beginning of a list, sentence, or any logical part of the learning material so that they get a chance to perform the task with 100% accuracy within a very short interval.

partial-alphabetic phase   This second phase in Ehri's model of the development of word reading skills occurs when the development of alphabetic principle allows students to begin to associate some letters with sounds and use that insight to recognize words.

passive voice sentence   The subject of the sentence is the recipient of the action rather than the actor and is always more difficult to understand. The passive sentence, *The barking dog was chased by the yellow cat,* is less clear than the active version, *The yellow cat chased the dog.*

"pause and punch"   Say with more emphasis; say louder. If Ms. Koertgen wants students to remember and say the past tense verb "worked" in a definition but knows that will be difficult for them, when she says the definition the first few times (My Turn and Together), she says the word "worked" louder than the other words.

PDA   Also called a personal digital assistant. PDAs are small handheld digital devices that store information, analyze data, and chart progress.

phoneme   The smallest unit of sound that is heard in spoken language. Phonemes are represented by back slashes; for example, /c/ + /a/ + /t/ = cat.

phonemic awareness   The ability to hear the smallest units of sounds in spoken language and to manipulate them.

phonics   The study of the relationships between letters and the sounds they represent. This term has become shorthand for describing instruction that establishes the alphabetic principle by teaching students the relationship between written letters or graphemes and the 41 to 44 sounds of spoken language or phonemes.

phonics through spelling   This approach emphasizes phonetic spelling as the foundation for word reading.

phonological processor   Marilyn Adams's model of reading describes word recognition as an interaction between orthographic, phonological, meaning, and context processors. The phonological processor processes the speech sounds of language.

plot   Fictional stories have plots composed of a sequence of events that inform the reader what happened. Typically, the plot consists of a central problem or conflict that the main character(s) has to resolve, the steps the character(s) takes to solve the problem, and the resolution of the problem.

pre-alphabetic phase   This first phase in Ehri's model of the development of word reading skills occurs when students do not yet have an understanding of the alphabetic principle and read words as memorized visual forms.

predictable books   Also called pattern books; predictable books are texts that contain repeated phrases and language patterns that allow students to read books successfully by guessing from context or pictures.

prefix   A morpheme that precedes a root or base word and modifies its meaning; also called an affix. In the word *submarine, sub* is the prefix.

prior knowledge   The sum total of what the individual knows at any given time. Prior knowledge includes knowledge of content and specific strategies.

progress-monitoring assessments   Brief assessments given during the school year that inform the teacher whether students are making adequate progress toward grade-level reading ability so support can be provided when they aren't.

pronoun referent   The noun that a pronoun refers to; the pronoun referent can be difficult to figure out for struggling readers. In general, the closer the pronoun is to its referent, the easier it is to understand.

prosody   The ability to read text orally using appropriate phrasing, intonation, and attention to punctuation.

r-controlled   An *r* after a vowel always changes the sound of the vowel. Examples are *or* as in *portrait* or *ar* as in *partial.*

rapid automatized naming (RAN)   The ability to process and identify visual information very rapidly.

read aloud   Planned reading of text to children for a specific purpose. These oral reading sessions have the potential to develop comprehension skills, oral language, vocabulary, core knowledge, ability to visualize, motivations for the subject or reading in general, and ultimately reading comprehension, but only if they are conducted in an interactional style.

reading fluency   The ability to read text accurately, quickly, and with expression.

receptive vocabulary   Oral receptive vocabulary involves understanding the meaning of words when people speak; written receptive language concerns understanding the meaning of words that are read.

regular words   Words that contain previously taught letter–sound patterns enabling the reader to sound out the words.

response to intervention (RTI)   An instructional model that uses a multi-tier system of instruction as a foundation for its process of determining eligibility for learning disability services. In RTI, a student's lack of progress in response to several high-quality research-based Tier 2 and Tier 3 interventions can be viewed as evidence of an underlying learning disability if other testing or data support that diagnosis.

retelling   The process of telling a story that one has read or heard. Teachers can use retelling to gather information about a student's reading comprehension, because when students retell a story, they must synthesize and organize information, make inferences, and draw on prior knowledge.

rime   The rest of the syllable that contains the vowel and all that follows it.

root   The part of the word that contains the basic meaning of the word. A root cannot stand alone. The words *diction, dictate, predict,* and *contradict* all have the common Latin root *dict,* which means *to say.*

round-robin reading   A method of reading in which all students in the class read aloud from the same book, regardless of their reading levels. The teacher calls on individuals to read, usually following a predetermined order.

scope and sequence   A curriculum plan, usually in chart form, in which a range of instructional objectives, skills, etc., is organized according to the successive levels at which they are taught, gradually increasing in complexity. Phonemic awareness skills, letter–sound correspondences, type of words, comprehension strategies and other skills in a systematic and explicit phonics curriculum have well-defined scope and sequence plans. Looking at a typical curricular scope and sequence chart, a teacher knows that she will teach the letter sound for *m* before *s,* CVC words before CCVC words, or summarizing before identifying main idea.

screening assessments   Brief tests conducted at the start of the school year and designed as a first step in identifying students who may be at a high risk for delayed development or academic failure in the tested skill area. Further diagnostic evaluation is needed for students who have difficulty with a screening assessment to determine whether they need extra or alternative instruction. In multi-tier models, these assessments are sometimes called "benchmark assessments" and are given three times during the year: beginning, middle, and end.

scripted lessons   Teaching formats that specify what the teacher says when presenting information or skills to students. The purpose of the scripts is to ensure that instruction is uniformly clear, efficient, and effective.

segmenting   The ability to break apart words into their individual phonemes or sounds.

semantic mapping   Visual representations of vocabulary that help students establish relationships among new and old words by having students categorize, label the categories, and discuss concepts related to a target word.

semantic strategies   Strategies for identifying words that focus on meaning. Semantic strategies focus on whether or not a word makes sense in a sentence.

setting   When and where a story takes place. The setting can be specific or indefinite and can change within the text.

sight word reading   When readers learn spelling–sound relationships so fluently that they are able to unconsciously and automatically recall the pronunciation and meaning of known words.

signal words   Signal words such as *for example, because, like,* and *first* link sentences and paragraphs together and are essential for comprehension because they give the reader clues about what is happening.

sound out   Students first say each sound in succession, moving from left to right. Students then blend the sounds together quickly to say a word. Sounding out can occur orally or subvocally.

sound–spelling relationships   The relationship between sounds and their spellings. The goal of phonics instruction is to teach students the most common sound–spelling relationships so that they can decode, or sound out, words.

stop sounds   With stop sounds, the air is completely blocked before it is expelled, either because the lips come together as with /p/, or because the tongue touches the upper mouth, as when saying /d/. Therefore, stop sounds can be held only for an instant.

story grammar   A story's grammar is the structure that the story follows. Typical story grammar elements include setting, characters, a problem or problems, plot, resolution, and theme.

story map   This type of graphic organizer portrays the story grammar of narrative text. Completing one helps students focus on the significant elements in a story as well as the relationship among these elements.

subvocal sounding-out   Deliberate sounding-out that is characterized either by lip movement unaccompanied by audible sounds or by conscious thought unaccompanied by audible sounds.

suffix   A morpheme added to the end of a root or base word; also called an *affix*. Some suffixes influence the grammar of a sentence like *-s, -ed, -ing;* other suffixes change the part of speech; for example, *-er* meaning, "one who," as in *singer.*

summarization   A monitoring strategy that helps readers evaluate their understanding of a passage they have just read. Periodically, the reader stops after having read a passage and first rephrases the main ideas before recalling key details. Summarization can be done orally or in writing. Students are often asked to summarize as one way to demonstrate their understanding of what they read.

syllable   Basic unit of speech, formed around a vowel or group of vowels that has one or more consonants preceding or following it. The word *bat* consists of one syllable; the word *spin ner* consists of two syllables.

syntactic strategies   Strategies for identifying words that focus on the conventions and rules related to sentence structure; grammatical strategies. Syntactic strategies involve figuring out whether a word sounds right in a sentence as if someone were talking.

synthetic phonics   This explicit phonics approach first teaches students individual skills (blending, segmenting, letter–sound identification, word reading) before providing practice applying these skills to carefully coordinated reading and writing activities. Student success and independence are emphasized through the use of carefully supported teaching strategies and curriculum.

systematic and explicit phonics   Phonics instruction characterized by the careful and thorough teaching of a planned, sequential set of letter–sound relationships. Systematic and explicit phonics incorporates materials that provide students with practice applying these relationships, including decodable books and other carefully coordinated reading and writing activities. Curricula that emphasize the teaching of phonics through literature or other materials, without a deliberate sequence of letter sounds and coordinated word reading activities, are not systematic or explicit phonics programs.

systematic error correction   A method of providing immediate corrective feedback to students by modeling the correct answer or skill, guiding the student to the correct answer as needed, asking students to give the answer independently, and asking students to repeat the correct answer later in the lesson.

systematic instruction   Instruction that clearly identifies a carefully selected and useful set of skills and then organizes them into a logical sequence of instruction.

theme   The subject or message that the author of narrative text wants to convey.

think-alouds   A strategy by which a teacher or a student models the active thinking process that skilled readers use. A teacher might verbalize his thoughts about a comprehension strategy he is using, how he determines the meaning of a vocabulary word, how he determines whether he understands what he is reading or what he predicts will come next in the text and why. This process enables students to see a skill that could not otherwise be observed.

think-time   The silent pause between the last word a teacher says in his question to students and the first word a student says when answering the teacher's question. This pause is also called "wait-time."

topic sentence   When the main idea in a paragraph is explicitly described in a sentence, it is called the *topic sentence*

universal design   Instructional materials and methods that are designed with built-in supports to minimize the need for differentiated instruction later on.

universal screening   Screening assessment used in multi-tier and RTI systems to identify students who, despite a research-based core reading program in Tier 1, are not making adequate progress and require extra support in Tier 2 or Tier 3.

unvoiced sounds   Sounds that are produced when the vocal cords do not vibrate.

VCe words   Words having the vowel–consonant–silent *e* pattern. Examples include *cake, mine,* and *pole.*

voiced sounds   Sounds that are produced when the vocal cords are vibrating.

wait-time   The silent pause between the last word a teacher says in his question to students and the first word a student says when answering the teacher's question. This pause is also called "think-time."

wcpm   Words correct per minute.

working memory   Also called *short-term memory.* Temporary memory that processes information in the immediate environment for a very short time. Working memory activates and integrates the knowledge retained in long-term memory with current information.

Name Index

Subject Index

VCe words. *Also see* Rules (CVC)
  explanation of, 153
  reading one-syllable, 163–165
Vocabulary. *See also* Words
  activities and games to develop, 254, 256–259, 266–269
  activities to practice, 254, 256–259
  assessment of, 234–237, 355–356
  choosing words for, 232–234
  definitions use for, 241–243
  dictionary use to develop, 250–253
  for English language learners, 263–264
  expressive, 10, 234
  for high-stakes tests, 253–256
  for independent student learning, 247–250
  for older learners, 260, 262–263
  keywords for, 246–247
  methods for instruction of, 237–238, 241–253
  modeling as, 238–242
  overview of, 10–11, 230–232
  receptive, 10, 234
  selection of important, 232–233
  semantic maps to develop, 244–246
  synonym use for, 241, 242
  technology to teach, 265–266
  Text Talk for, 243–244
Voiced sounds
  chart of, 36–40
  explanation of, 35
(Vowel-consonant-vowel patterns), 152–154

Wait-time, *See also* Think-time
Wechsler Individual Achievement Test (WIAT-11), 302, 355
Whisper reading, 212
Wilson Reading System, 64–66, 131–132, 135, 147, 177, 179, 218–219

Woodcock Reading Mastery Test Revised (WRMT-R), 94, 304, 355
Word-family instruction, 114
Word Identification and Spelling Test (WIST), 158
Word journals, 259
Word-reading skills. *See* Advanced word-reading instruction
Words. *See also* Spelling; Vocabulary; Vocabulary instruction
  base, 169–170, 153–155
  compound, 153–154
  contractions, 169
  CVC, 81–82, 85, 101–113
  CVC-variant, 81–82, 85, 92
  divided into syllables, 170
  with *-ed* endings, 159, 161, 178
  exception, 85, 93, 114–117, 156, 173
  high-frequency, 85, 93
  irregular, 85, 93, 114–117, 156, 173
  literal meanings of, 263
  multiple-meaning, 251, 254, 255–256
  multisyllable, 152–161,165–171
  one-syllable, 81–82, 85, 101–113, 145, 163–165
  pseudowords, 89–90
  regular, 80, 182, 86, 101–109, 153–155, 165–170
  root, 153–155
  signal, 274, 315–316
  VCe, 153, 163–165
Word Wall, 118
Working memory, 277
Write-on response boards, 254, 256

Yopp-Singer Test of Phoneme Segmentation (YST), 49